Illustrating Evolutionary
Computation with Mathematica

Illustrating Evolutionary Computation with Mathematica

Christian Jacob
University of Calgary

Translated from German by Christian Jacob

MORGAN KAUFMANN PUBLISHERS

AN IMPRINT OF ACADEMIC PRESS
A Harcourt Science and Technology Company
SAN FRANCISCO   SAN DIEGO   NEW YORK   BOSTON
LONDON   SYDNEY   TOKYO

Senior Editor	Denise E. M. Penrose
Publishing Services Manager	Scott Norton
Senior Production Editor	Cheri Palmer
Editorial Coordinator	Emilia Thiuri
Cover Design	Yvo Riezebos Design
Cover Image	Christian Jacob / © 2001 PhotoDisc
Copyeditor	Karen Taschek
Proofreader	Jennifer McClain
Composition	Nancy Logan
Illustration	Technology 'N Type
Indexer	Ty Koontz
Printer	Courier Corporation

Designations used by companies to distinguish their products are often claimed as trademarks or registered trademarks. In all instances where Morgan Kaufmann Publishers is aware of a claim, the product names appear in initial capital or all capital letters. Readers, however, should contact the appropriate companies for more complete information regarding trademarks and registration.

ACADEMIC PRESS
A Harcourt Science and Technology Company
525 B Street, Suite 1900, San Diego, CA 92101-4495, USA
http://www.academicpress.com

Academic Press
Harcourt Place, 32 Jamestown Road, London, NW1 7BY, United Kingdom
http://www.academicpress.com

Morgan Kaufmann Publishers
340 Pine Street, Sixth Floor, San Francisco, CA 94104-3205, USA
http://www.mkp.com

Originally published as *Principia Evolvica, Simulierte Evolution mit Mathematica*
ISBN 3-920993-48-9
© 1997 by dpunkt - Verlag fur digitale Technologie

© 2001 by Academic Press
All rights reserved
Printed in the United States of America

05   04   03   02   01   5   4   3   2   1

Library of Congress Cataloging

Jacob, Christian.
    [Principia evolvica. English]
    Illustrating evolutionary computation with Mathematica / Christian Jacob.
        p. cm.
    Includes bibliographical references and index.
    ISBN 1-55860-637-8
    1. Evolutionary programming (Computer science)   2. Evolutionary computation.
3. Mathematica (Computer program language)   I. Title.
QA76.618 .J3313 2001
006.3'1--dc21   00-048385

This book is printed on acid-free paper.

*To my parents
who taught me to explore the world.*

Contents

Preface: From Darwin to an ArtFlowers Garden

Evolution in nature, an outstanding example of natural adaptation processes at work, has resulted in a fantastic diversity of life-forms with amazing capabilities. Populations of organisms, adapting to their particular environmental conditions, form cooperating and competing teams in an evolutionary interplay of selection and variation mechanisms. The growth plans of organisms, encoded in the genomes of cells, vary from generation to generation. Finally those individuals will prevail that—largely because of their specific abilities and features —are best able to cope with their environmental conditions.

Evolution in nature

From these evolutionary principles of adaptation we can derive a number of concepts and strategies for solving learning tasks and develop optimization problems for artificially intelligent systems. Just as natural populations adapt to their environment by evolution, we can selectively modify problem-solving strategies, encode them as programs (e.g., as computer programs), and progressively adjust these programs to a predefined task representing a set of environmental constraints.

Evolutionary adaptation

Illustrating Evolutionary Computation with Mathematica consists of an introduction and three major parts. The introduction demonstrates key aspects of evolution through simple yet illustrative examples. (I) The two main streams of evolutionary algorithms, genetic algorithms, and evolution strategies are thoroughly explained and are illustrated by example experiments. (II) Focusing on evolutionary programming and genetic programming, we explain how to automatically "breed" computer programs using principles of evolution. (III) Finally, we demonstrate and explore the close connections between developmental and evolutionary processes. We illustrate these concepts by looking at developmental programs found in nature, which we model and evolve in the form of cellular automata and Lindenmayer systems.

Book overview

Introduction: The Fascination of Evolution

In the introduction we start with motivating and illustrative examples of evolution-based applications (Chapter 1): string matching by evolution, a simple optimization task; the adaptation of butterfly coloring through selection and mutation; and an example of evolutionary creativity using biomorph figures.

Part II: Evolutionary Computation

In Part I, the classic schools of evolutionary algorithms for parameter optimization—genetic algorithms and evolution strategies—are presented. In Chapter 2, we start with a general overview of why evolutionary techniques provide flexible tools for solving real-world optimization problems.

In Chapter 3, we focus on *genetic algorithms* (GA), where chromosomes are represented as strings or vectors over a discrete alphabet, analogous to nature's encoding paradigm. Various types of GA chromosomes—haploid, diploid, and polyploid—and dominance relations among alleles are explained. We continue with point mutations on various example chromosome structures. Recombinations of GA chromosomes, including meiotic recombination of double strands, are demonstrated by examples. Further operators, usually considered "secondary" operators, are discussed, including inversion, deletion, duplication, and crossing over of nonhomologous chromosomes. We show genetic algorithms in action by demonstrating the effects of recombination versus mutation. Both operators are also compared to the effects caused by other GA operators. The genetic algorithms' ability to adapt to variable environmental constraints is shown for a typical parameter optimization task. The final section on genetic algorithms illustrates a major building block of GA theory, the schema theorem, explaining its controversial mathematical background and potential in understanding the search behavior of genetic algorithms.

Evolution strategies (ES), presented in Chapter 4, draw their main application area from engineering. Individuals are represented as vectors of real numbers on which various types of mutation and recombination operators are defined. The most important of these operator variants are discussed via a number of examples. Specific selection schemes have been developed for evolution strategy, which we will explain in detail and implement as Mathematica programs. On the basis of these developed programs, we explore the capabilities of evolution strategies to solve multimodal optimization tasks, including multipopulation ES and meta-evolution schemes.

Part II: If Darwin Had Been a Programmer . . .

Whereas the two classic evolution-based algorithms—genetic algorithms and evolution strategies—primarily work with linear chromosomes, in the form of bit vectors or numbers, *evolutionary programming* (Chapter 6) and *genetic programming* (Chapter 7), introduced in Part II, are concerned with the evolution of finite-state automata and hierarchically structured computer programs, respectively. The idea of "breeding" programs through evolution is enormously fascinating and is already playing a growing role as an alternative method of computer programming. A brief history of approaches using evolutionary principles for the programming of computers is outlined in Chapter 5. *Evolutionary programming*, one of the first approaches to the application of evolutionary techniques to machine learning and to the automatic design of artificially intelligent systems, is presented in Chapter 6. *Genetic programming* in its original form, using terms (i.e., simple symbolic expressions) as the genotypic structures undergoing evolution, is described in Chapter 7. Recombination and mutation operators on these terms are presented, and a simple application example of evolving balanced mobile structures is discussed in more detail. In Chapter 8, a more extended optimization example, the "breeding" of robot control programs, further illustrates the usefulness of the genetic programming approach.

Part II

Evolutionary programming

Genetic programming

Part III: Evolution of Developmental Programs

Although the introduction and Parts I and II of this book focus on evolution at the level of populations, the spectrum of modeling evolutionary processes is extended in Part III.

In Chapter 9, we discuss simulations of pattern formation as observed for growth processes of cell configurations or plant structures. With the help of *cellular automata* (CA), we explore pattern formation in discrete spaces. Two-dimensional CAs are used to demonstrate the emergence of structures initiated by self-reproduction.

Natural morphogenesis and growth processes are modeled by parallel rewrite systems in the form of *Lindenmayer systems* (L-systems).

Part III

Cellular automata and pattern formation

L-systems and growth

Analogous to genome programs of natural cells, L-systems make possible an implicit encoding of developmental processes. A so-called turtle interpretation of L-systems allows us to simulate and visualize the morphogenesis of plantlike structures through three-dimensional computer models.

Once the fitness of L-systems, encoding developmental programs, can be evaluated, an evolutionary selection scheme can be easily applied. By using genetic programming operators to produce mutations of L-system genomes, we arrive at a system for *breeding development programs*. Consequently, evolution is simulated on two separate levels: on the level of pattern formation (controlled by an individual genome program) and on the metalevel of populations, comprising competitive sets of developmental programs.

Evolutionary L-system inference

For a simple example of pattern formation with fractal structures, in Chapter 10 we show first results of our approach to *evolutionary inference of L-systems*. Much more complex L-systems have to be designed for modeling growth, structure formation, and inflorescences of plants. In Chapter 11, examples of such developmental programs show how implicit evaluation of the pattern formation processes leads to evolution-based strategies and concepts for the breeding of virtual

Virtual plants

plants. In addition to an amazing variety of evolvable plant structures, modifications of genome programs result in a number of mutation effects on the expressed individual plants that can be observed in natural breeding experiments. Finally, we illustrate coevolutionary effects

Simulated plant ecosystems

in a plant ecosystem through interactions of multiple individual plants.

Mathematica and Evolvica

This book does not introduce Mathematica as a programming tool. Many of the evolutionary algorithm concepts, however, are illustrated using the Mathematica programming language. Evolvica[1] is used to illustrate algorithms, to visualize evolutionary concepts, and to demonstrate evolution-based solutions of optimization tasks by hands-on examples. All of the Evolvica example experiments, illustrations, animations, and movies discussed in this book can be accessed on-line under the following World Wide Web address: *http://www.cpsc .ucalgary.ca/njacob/IEC/*.

---

1. Evolvica is our Mathematica-based tutorial, programming, and experimentation environment for evolutionary computation, which has been developed over the last five years.

The Evolvica site also contains information on evolutionary computation and a short tutorial on how to use Mathematica as a scientific research tool.

Illustrating Evolutionary Computation with Mathematica is intended for your enjoyment and edification, conveying the fascination of evolutionary computation. It is the author's hope that after going through this book, you will have a better sense of the enormous potential of evolutionary computing—both in nature and in the artificial world of computers. Computer models of biological processes—in particular, evolutionary and developmental processes—can help us appreciate nature's achievements and creativity in the evolution of the design, functionality, and behavior of living organisms. For us, nature still provides an endless source of inspiration. Let us use this enormous potential and evolve novel concepts and tools to understand it. It will be especially gratifying to the author if this book provides a small building block toward this endeavor and inspires you to start your own computational explorations into the amazing world of evolution.

Acknowledgments

I would like to thank John Koza, Ingo Rechenberg, and many other colleagues and readers of *Principia Evolvica,* the German version of this book, for their encouraging feedback, without which I might not have started its revision and translation into English. Many thanks also go to my anonymous reviewers for their critical comments and helpful suggestions.

I am grateful to Camille Sinanan, who agreed to read all through the first version of my manuscript. Her appreciated remarks and editing improved my manuscript a lot.

I am particularly indebted to my editor, Denise Penrose, who kept my spirits up during the translation and rewriting of the final chapters and showed tremendous patience with me, although my manuscripts never seemed to meet the deadlines. Many thanks to the wonderful editing, production, and marketing team at Morgan Kaufmann Publishers: Cheri Palmer, Emilia Thiuri, and Courtney Garnaas. You all made me feel very comfortable working with you. For an author it is always an exciting experience to see a manuscript evolve from a set of text and graphics files into a beautifully laid out book; you know this evolutionary art exceptionally well.

1   Introduction:
The Fascination of Evolution

*Variational evolution is the concept represented by Darwin's theory
of evolution through natural selection. According to this theory, an
enormous amount of genetic variation is produced in every generation,
but only a few survivors of the vast number of offspring will themselves
reproduce. Individuals that are best adapted to the environment have the
highest probability of surviving and producing the next generation.*

Mayr 1997, p. 176

To date, between 3 and 10 million plant and animal species live on planet Earth. As human beings living in a high-tech era, we should try to keep our sense of awe and admiration for the diversity of life-forms that have evolved—and are still evolving—through natural processes. Nature provides a huge number of paradigms and solutions, which inspire us not only in our scientific quest to increase our knowledge about nature in general but in our attempts to find ever better solutions to technical, environmental, social, and cultural problems. Currently we observe a growing interest in the engineering and technical sciences in general for paradigms gleaned from nature.

Nature providing paradigms for technical systems

In a number of working examples, principles of nature have been successfully applied in the domain of technical systems. *Neural networks* are used to analyze images or to recognize handwritten text. Such networks are adaptive and, to some extent, capable of learning—that is, they can be trained through the use of examples. These computational models gleaned from nature show a remarkable flexibility. They implement algorithmic abstractions of fundamental mechanisms of information processing to be found in natural nervous systems and brains in particular. This paradigm has already opened an entirely new field of applications (Hertz, Krogh, et al. 1991; Rojas 1996; Principe, Euliano, et al. 2000).

Neural networks

The science of *bionics* focuses on how to incorporate biological principles into solutions for technical problems. The areas of interest

Bionics =
bio**logy + tech**nics

range from the development of streamlined ships and aircraft—with experiences drawn from the body shapes of sharks and penguins—to the enhancement of our understanding of organizational patterns in complex biological adaptation and regulation processes (e.g., in self-organizing ant colonies or control mechanisms of gene activities in developing organisms) (Bappert, Benner, et al. 1996; Nachtigall 1992; Nachtigall 1994; Nachtigall and Schönbeck 1994; Nachtigall and Wisser 1996; Nachtigall 1997; Nachtigall 1998).

Evolution by natural selection and mutation

What types of mechanisms have led to the remarkable diversity of adapted life-forms in nature? Living organisms are certainly among the most complex entities in our universe. But how could structures of such overwhelming complexity emerge? Is there a fundamental principle, a natural "method of experimentation," from which an exuberant and fragile interplay of organisms would result? Indeed, there is such a principle: evolution. It is somewhat remarkable, however, that complex adaptations, taking place over huge time spans—hundreds to millions of years—are in essence driven by a strikingly simple principle: iterated *selection* and *mutation,* as originally formulated by Charles Darwin more than a hundred years ago (Darwin 1859).

Chapter overview

The basic ideas of Darwin's evolution theories are still valid today. Hence, in Section 1.1, we will take a brief look at the notion of "evolution," which has many interpretations not only in biology but within the social and technical sciences. In Section 1.2, we will briefly discuss selection theory and adaptation in the context of evolution. A first example application of cumulative selection is presented in Section 1.3—we will take a detailed look at how to "evolve" a pre-defined sentence from a random sequence of characters. In Section 1.4, we give an example of how populations of butterflies adapt their wing coloring to their environment. Finally, in Section 1.5, we conclude the first part of this book with a demonstration of evolutionary creativity, which we explore through recursive line drawings, known as biomorphs.

1.1   Flavors of evolution

The term *evolution* is derived from the Latin verb *evolvere,* describing a process of unfolding or flowing. In Roman times, it referred to the unfolding of a book or piece of paper. Today the notion of evolution is used in a broader sense, denoting many types of developmental processes. The following quotes, describing the essence of evolution within a specific context, illustrate this point.

[Evolution explains the] development of life on earth, from simple   *Life on earth*
organisms to human beings.

Sebastian Vogel (Vogel 1992, p. 54)

The theory of evolution claims that all animals and plants living on earth
are modified descendants of other animals and plants which existed in
former times. Evolution is the result of inherited differences passed on   *Inheritance*
by the organisms from one generation to the next.

David Young (Young 1994, p. 11)

If evolution is like development it is not easily explained by natural   *Evolution vs. development*
selection, which is a contingent, short-term process that works with
accidental, rather than progressive, variation.

Mark Ridley (Ridley 1997)

Simulation of the evolutionary process is tantamount to a mechanization   *Evolution and artificial*
of the scientific method. . . . Here lies the chronicle of life. With this   *intelligence*
knowledge comes a new power to enhance memory, to manipulate
goals, and to make better decisions. Of even greater significance is
the possibility of creating inanimate mechanisms that possess these
same qualities.

Lawrence J. Fogel (Fogel 1999, p. 44 ff.)

Evolution is *the* characteristic feature of living beings, but it is not restricted to living organisms. Even in the context of technical systems, we talk about evolution. In social systems, we contrast evolutionary change to revolutionary change, with evolution implying a more subtle, smooth, long-term development. In its most general   *Evolution as development* translation, *evolution* denotes any type of developmental process of cell clusters, individual organisms, populations or societies, technical innovations, ideas, and so on (Fabian 1998).

In biology, developmental processes are categorized as either ontogenetic or phylogenetic. In the context of embryonic development, called *ontogeny*, evolution denotes the continuous and partly   *Ontogeny:* directed changes observable at the level of a single organism. On this   *embryonic development* level, evolution is characterized by pattern formation or growth processes (i.e., development from a simpler to a more complex state). Consider a seed as an example: from a seemingly simple seed (under the influence of light, water, and nutrients), a much more complex plant structure gradually evolves. A huge number of interacting cells are part of these developmental processes. They are partly controlled by "growth programs" encoded on the cellular genome and partly react to environmental signals and constraints. However, those morphogenetic, structure-generating processes constitute only one aspect of evolution among living organisms.

Phylogeny: populational development

Both for flora and fauna, a species' characteristic morphogenetic capabilities have a tremendous influence on its ability to evolve as a population. Of course, the success of this evolution depends on the specific constraints of an environmental niche, as well as on the population's flexibility in adapting. In this context, evolution is described as a *phylogenetic* developmental process of biological groups, formed by breeds, species, families, and so on.

In Parts I and II of this book, we focus on the phylogenetic aspects of evolutionary processes resulting from Darwinian selection theories. Structure formation processes are considered in Part III, where we integrate the ontogenetic aspects of morphogenesis into simulated phylogenetic evolution.

1.2   Adaptation and selection

Diversity of species evolved from primitives

At the beginning of the nineteenth century scientists knew that the diversity of life-forms results from a biological development: plants and animals have evolved from a few primitive species. Darwin's grandfather, Erasmus Darwin, had already developed a theory later propagated by the French zoologist Jean Baptiste de Lamarck. A question that could not be answered at that time, however, was what caused this development. What is the "driving force" of evolution?

When we look at organisms with respect to their body structures and the functionality of their organs, it is remarkable that most of them are built in a highly adapted manner, enabling them to survive and reproduce, and so to indirectly ensure the survival of their own species. The ability to adapt is a core feature of living organisms.

Adaptations of individuals and populations

Consequently, it is important to distinguish between adaptations on the level of individual organisms and adaptations on the level of populations.

Adaptations as states

Individual organisms belonging to a certain species exhibit specific features—*adaptations as states*. The abilities acquired during an individual's life span, learning and behavioral adaptation by trial and error, instruction, and experience must be distinguished from adaptations of a population over many generations. Adaptations of a species take place on the basis of inheritable traits only. Characteristics acquired through learning are not inheritable because they are not transferable through genes. The capacity to learn, however, is indeed inheritable.

The findings of geology and paleontology demonstrate that our biosphere has undergone tremendous changes over the past 3 billion years. This means that the ability to adapt to changing environmental conditions turns out to be *the* crucial factor for any species' survival and hence for the continuation of life on Earth in general. The traits observable in fossils, as well as in all living organisms to date, are the result of a huge number of primarily small adaptation processes in the course of biological evolution. Therefore, adaptations can also be considered *processes*.

Adaptations as processes

Evolution theorists are trying to find answers to the questions about the causes and fundamental mechanisms of adaptation processes in nature. Current evolution theories, though extensions of Darwin's original theories of *descendence* and *selection,* still refer to those original principles, describing evolution as an intricate interaction of cumulative selection and mutation (see Section 2.2 for a more detailed discussion).

Descendence and selection

This section demonstrates the essence of the strikingly simple selection-mutation principle. Section 1.3 discusses the cumulative adaptation effects resulting from iterated selection in combination with random mutations. In Section 1.4, we present examples of how populations of butterflies adapt their wing coloring to a specific environment through cumulative selection and mutation. Finally, in Section 1.5, interactive breeding experiments on recursive, two-dimensional figures, known as biomorphs, show the creative potential of evolutionary selection processes.

1.3 Drip by drip—cumulative selection

Gutta cavat lapidem, non vi sed saepe cadendo.
Constant dripping wears away the stone.

Latin proverb

Evolution implies the adaptation of populations of organisms to their specific environmental niches through often sophisticated methods of experimentation, developed in many cases over hundreds of millions of years. In this section, we demonstrate a simple "key experiment" to get a better idea of the core effects of nature's principles of adaptation,

Selection-mutation principle   based on iterated mutation and selection. This experiment is described in many variations in the literature in order to introduce the selection-mutation principle as a surprisingly flexible, yet simple, optimization tool (Dawkins 1986; Dawkins 1990, p. 76; Küppers 1990, p. 132 ff.; Rechenberg 1994b).

1.3.1   Task description

A simplified version of the evolutionary principle of adaptation is used to search for a predefined string, starting from an initially random sequence of characters and using iterated mutation and cumulative selection operators. We will show how the accumulation of small and random changes in conjunction with a competitive selection scheme unveils the fundamental principles of evolutionary search and adapta-

Objective string   tion. Let us define the following *objective string* that we intend to evolve:

```
EVOLUTION OF STRUCTURE, STEP BY STEP
```

We would start with a randomly generated sequence of characters that has the same length as this sentence. Through mutation, the initial string should evolve in a step-by-step manner toward the objective sentence—"drip by drip." In order to constrain the search space, we use only the 26 capital letters of the Roman alphabet. Furthermore, we need a space symbol to separate words from each other and punctuation marks such as the comma and the period. Hence we can define the alphabet Σ, from which we generate our strings, as follows:

String alphabet $\Sigma = \{A, B, C, \ldots Z, \acute{} \acute{}, \acute{}, , \acute{} .\}$

For each of the 36 positions within the predefined string, there are 29 possibilities for inserting a character or a punctuation mark. Therefore, our example sentence is *one* character sequence out of a set of

```
29^36
= 442922685423629214078250916170163198877241393
83235921
= 4.42923 · 10^52
```

possible strings of length $N = 36$. That is, any of these strings is from the set of all words of the form $\Sigma^N = \{\sigma_1 \ldots \sigma_N | \sigma_i \in \Sigma, i = 1, \ldots, N\}$. Starting from a random initial string, how can we reach a predefined sentence? How could the principles of evolution be used for an efficient exploration of this search space?

1.3.2 Single-step selection

The task of discovering a specific predefined sentence is like the legendary search for a needle in a haystack. An admittedly inefficient but simple procedure to find the objective sentence is *single-step selection*. This turns out to be nothing else but pure random search (Dawkins 1990, p. 61 ff.). We would start by generating a set of random strings of length 32; for example, the ones depicted in Figure 1.1. We would have to check whether any of these strings is (by pure chance) identical to the objective sentence.

Single-step selection

If none of the generated sentences match the predefined sentence, we would randomly generate a new set of strings, compare again, and so on. Suppose we had a 100-MHz processor that would be able to generate and check 100 million strings of length 32 per second. It would take approximately 10^{31} years to find a perfect match with the objective sentence. We might not want to wait so long. Not even evolution had such a huge time span available to develop the diversity of life-forms on our planet. Living species have been around for only about 3 to 4 billion years, which is on the order of 10^9 years.

1.3.3 Selection: "keeping the good ones . . ."

The fact that nature has been and still is tremendously successful in creating complex organisms is in essence due to a much more "intelligent" and yet simple search technique—*mutation and selection*. The single-step selection scheme described above clearly has the drawback of not relying on previously achieved results. Whenever a string does not match the objective sentence, a completely new string is generated irrespective of how close to the objective we are already. Again, looking more closely at the three random strings in Figure 1.1, we find that these strings differ in their similarity to the objective sentence. It is not

Mutation and selection

```
EVOLUTION OF STRUCTURE, STEP BY STEP        (O)
_____

,LPYJK,ZPBGXWKTEKSQ,KLVCFZSJFGVZQWG         (a)

ETTLXTKOL RF STRZGPURE CSYEPYBY SQEP        (b)

EVOLUDION OF STRUKTURE  STEP BZ,STEB        (c)
```

Figure 1.1
Random strings are compared to an objective sentence (O).

difficult to guess the first sentence (O) from the last string (c). For the
second sentence (b), only a few characters are matching (e.g., at locations 2, 3, and 5). The first string (a) seems to have little in common
with the objective sentence.

Hamming distance

We must be more precise about what we mean by similarity of
strings. A similarity measure for strings can be derived from the *Hamming distance,* used in information and coding theory. Since it is easier
to calculate with numbers than with characters, we uniquely encode
each character $\sigma \in \Sigma$ by a specific number $\tau(\sigma) \in \aleph$, where $\aleph$ denotes
the set of natural numbers $\aleph = 1, 2, 3, \ldots$ Thus we may define the
"difference" diff(s_1, s_2) of two strings $s_1, s_2 \in \Sigma^N$ of equal length N
as follows:

*Distance measure for
strings*

$$\text{diff}(s_1, s_2) = \sum_{i=1}^{N} (\tau(s_{1i}) - \tau(s_{2i}))^2.$$

Both strings s_n, $n = 1, 2$, contain N characters: $s_n = s_{n1} \ldots s_{nN}$, where
$s_{nk} \in \Sigma$, $1 \le k \le N$. The similarity between characters is calculated as
the sum of squares of the differences of their character encodings. For
a more detailed, algorithmic definition of this distance measure and
the encoding refer to the next section, where the Evolvica implementations for this "evolution of sentences" problem is described.

For the examples discussed in the following sections, we will use
this character encoding:

*Encoding characters
by numbers*

$$\tau(A) = 65, \ \tau(B) = 66, \ \tau(C) = 67, \ldots$$

$$\tau(Y) = 89, \ \tau(Z) = 90,$$

$$\tau(\acute{}) = 91, \ \tau(\acute{,}) = 92, \ \tau(\acute{.}) = 93.$$

These specific numbers are basically identical with the *ASCII* character encoding (*American Standard Code for Information Interchange*).
The only exceptions are the blank character and the punctuation
marks. The encoding sequence for letters is simply extended to these
last three elements as well. With these ingredients, we are able to calculate string differences for any string over the alphabet Σ:

$$\text{diff("STEP BY","SUEP BY")} = 0 + 1^2 + 0 + 0 + 0 + 0 = 1$$

$$\text{diff("STEP BY","UTEP BZ")} = 2^2 + 0 + 0 + 0 + 0 + 1^2 = 5$$

$$\text{diff("STEP BY","TSEQ AX")} = 1^2 + 1^2 + 1^2 + 1^2 + 1^2 = 5$$

```
EVOLUDION OF STRUKTURE   STEP BZ,STEB        (c: 519)
```
_____

```
EVOLUGION.OF,STRUKTURE   STDS BZ,STEB         (c.1: 447)

EVOLUCION OF STRUKTURE   STEP BX,STEB         (c.2: 552)

EVONUDION.OF STURKTXRE   SQEP B.ASTFB         (c.3: 1254)
```

Figure 1.2
"Mutants" of string (c) from
Figure 1.1.

Hence we can evaluate each of the three example strings from Figure 1.1 with respect to their similarity to the objective sentence. These "fitnesses" are an essential precondition for a selection scheme to work. Our chances to approach and finally match the objective sentence will obviously be increased by selecting string (c) from Figure 1.1. We can then use this string as our seed for another set of strings; that is, a set of string "mutants" with a certain degree of similarity to their "parent" string. Figure 1.2 shows string (c) from Figure 1.1 together with three mutated strings derived from seed string (c).

Selection: "keeping the good ones..."

The number in the parentheses after the colon denotes the distance of the respective mutated string from the objective string. If we were given the choice with which string to continue now, we would probably choose the first mutant. This is the closest string, with the least Hamming distance (447) to the objective string. If we continue this procedure of selecting the best string, denoting it to be the parent string, from which we generate another set of mutants, we follow a simple selection-mutation algorithm, described in more detail in the following section.

1.3.4 A simple algorithm for selection and mutation

From the previously described scheme of iteratively generating mutant strings after selecting the best, we derive the following simple selection-mutation algorithm:

1. **Initialization:** Generate an initial set $S = \{s_1, \ldots, s_n\}$ of n individuals.

2. **Initial evaluation:** Evaluate all individuals and calculate their fitnesses.

3. **Selection:** Choose the best individual $s_{best} \in S$.

Simple algorithm for cumulative selection and mutation

4. **Mutation**: From the best-selected individual generate a set of $n - 1$ mutants:

$$M = \{s_i' := \text{mut}(s_{\text{best}}) \mid i = 1, \ldots, n-1\}.$$

5. **Evaluation**: Evaluate all mutants and calculate their fitnesses.

6. **Termination check**: If at least one of the individuals has achieved the predefined maximum fitness, stop and return the best individual. Otherwise generate a new selection set:

$$S = \{s_{\text{best}}\} \cup M.$$

7. Continue with step 3.

In this algorithm, we interpret the search for an optimum as a search for a maximum fitness value. Using the Hamming distance to evaluate fitness, however, means searching for a minimum value of zero. At this point it should be noted that any maximum search can easily be turned into a minimum search and vice versa (see Section 2.3.1).

What is still missing is a suitable definition for a mutation operator. How can we generate a mutated string $\text{mut}(s)$ from a parent string s? In the last example of Figure 1.2, the three mutated strings are derived from the parent string by exchanging each character with another one. This operation is performed with a certain probability per string location. However, the new character is always in the "vicinity" (with respect to the Hamming distance) of the original character. More formally, we define string mutation as follows:

Mutation on strings
$$\text{mut}(s = s_1 \ldots s_N, r, p) = s_1' \ldots s_N',$$

where

$$s_i' = \begin{cases} s_i & \text{if } \chi > p, \\ m(s_i, r) & \text{if } \chi \leq p. \end{cases}$$

Here $\chi = \chi_{\text{real}}(0, 1)$ returns a real-value, uniformly distributed random variable from the interval $[0, 1]$. The mutation function $\text{mut}(s, r, p)$ has three parameters: a string s of length N and the mutation radius r defining the maximum distance between the mutated and the original character. Usually, for r we would choose a natural number between 0 and $\lceil |\Sigma|/2 \rceil$. Here $|\Sigma|$ denotes the number of elements in the set Σ. $\lceil x \rceil$ returns the least integer number that is larger than or equal to x. The third parameter, the character mutation probability p, determines the frequency of mutations within the string. The actual mutation operation for one character $x \in \Sigma$ is defined as

$$m(x, r) = \tau^{-1}(\tau(x) + \chi_{\text{int}}(-r, r)).$$ *Character mutation*

$\chi_{\text{int}}(y, z)$ returns a uniformly distributed, random integer number from the interval $[y, z]$. The character x is translated into its number encoding $\tau(x)$. Adding a random number $\chi_{\text{int}}(-r, r)$ results in a new encoding x' from the interval $[\tau(x) - r, \tau(x) + r]$. This number is decoded back into the character $\tau^{-1}(x')$.

Using this parametrized mutation operator, we can generate mutated strings as depicted in Figure 1.3 from the initial sentence

$s = $ EVOLUTION OF STRUCTURE, STEP BY STEP

The higher the mutation rate per character, the more locations within the string are changed. For a mutation radius of $r = 1$ the mutated character is always either one of the direct "neighbors" of the original character or remains the same: an R may mutate to a Q, an R, or an S. Figure 1.3 shows three mutated sentences and the effects of different mutation rates, $p = 0.1$, $p = 0.2$, and $p = 0.5$ for a mutation radius of $r = 1$.

Increasing the mutation radius will, of course, lead to larger mutation steps per string location, as illustrated by the examples in Figure 1.4. Here the mutation rate is kept constant at $p = 0.2$, whereas the mutants result from different mutation radii $r = 1, 2$, and 5.

The mutation rate controls how many characters are changed on average, whereas the mutation radius determines the maximum mutation step per character. What might be the most promising strategy to

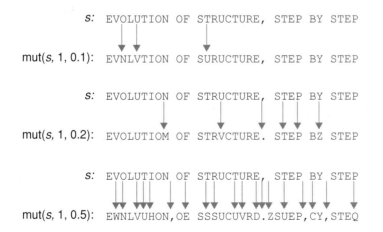

Figure 1.3
Mutation on strings with mutation radius 1 and different mutation rates.

Figure 1.4
Mutation on strings with a
constant mutation rate of 0.2
and varying mutation radii.

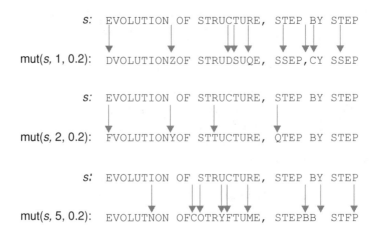

reach an arbitrary objective string, using iterated mutation and selection? Starting from an initial random string, should we apply higher or lower mutation rates? Will a large or a small mutation radius lead to a successful evolution? The experiments we will perform in Section 1.3.6 show that for constant mutation rates and radii over an evolution run, sparse and small changes are more advantageous in the long run than trying to speed up the evolution by taking larger steps. Therefore, we follow the "drop-by-drop" strategy—small, gradual steps of evolution.

1.3.5 Cumulative selection and mutation with Evolvica

In this section, we describe our Evolvica implementation of the string evolution. The Evolvica notebook is available through the *IEC* Web page (see Preface). We assign an objective string, which we want to be evolved, to the variable `objectSentence`:

In[1] := **objectSentence =
         "EVOLUTION OF STRUCTURE, STEP BY STEP"**

For encoding characters as numbers we use the built-in Mathematica function `ToCharacterCode`. The following set of numbers encodes the capital letters of the alphabet:

In[2] := **ToCharacterCode["ABCDEFGHIJKLMNOPQRSTUVWXYZ"]**

Out[2] = {65, 66, 67, 68, 69, 70, 71, 72, 73, 74, 75, 76,
           77, 78, 79, 80, 81, 82, 83, 84, 85, 86, 87, 88,
           89, 90}

For the space character, the comma, and the period we get

In[3] := **ToCharacterCode[" ,."]**

Out[3] = {32, 44, 46}

The strings we will use for the sentence evolution task are composed of these characters and punctuation marks (see Section 1.3.1). For the mutation operator, however, it is easier if all characters are encoded as a consecutive sequence of numbers. This is why we change the pre-defined number codes for the blank character and the punctuation marks to 91, 92, and 93, respectively.

```
encodeSentence[sent_String] :=
  ToCharacterCode[sent] /. {32 → 91, 44 → 92,
  46 → 93}
```

Program 1.1
Number encoding
for strings.

With the definition from Program 1.1 the objective sentence can now be encoded as a list of numbers:

In[4] := **encodeSentence[objectSentence]**

Out[4] = {69, 86, 79, 76, 85, 84, 73, 79, 78, 91, 79, 70,
         91, 83, 84, 82, 85, 67, 84, 85, 82, 69, 92, 91,
         83, 84, 69, 80, 91, 66, 89, 91, 83, 84, 69, 80}

   Of course, we also need a function to perform the reverse decoding, returning a string from a list of numbers. For this purpose we define a function that translates a vector of numbers from the set {65, 66, . . . , 93} back into a string (Program 1.2).

```
decodeSentence[sent_List] :=
  FromCharacterCode[sent /.{91 → 32, 92 → 44,
  93 → 46}]
```

Program 1.2
Decoding: from numbers to
string.

Thus we can decipher the encoded sentence again, where the % character refers to the previous output:

In[5] := **decodeSentence[%]**

Out[5] = EVOLUTION OF STRUCTURE, STEP BY STEP

We may also use a random number vector and decode it as follows:

In[6] := **t = Table[Random[Integer,{65,93}],{10}]**
          decodeSentence[t]

Out[6] = {72, 79, 83, 92, 73, 74, 86, 74, 84, 84}
          HOS,IJVJTT

To calculate the similarity of strings, we also rely on the number encoding. The "difference" between two strings of equal length was introduced as the sum of squares of the Hamming distances of the respective encoding number vectors (Program 1.1), as described in Section 1.3.3.

Program 1.3
Similarity measure for strings.

```
distanceSquared[s1_,s2_] :=
  Apply[Plus,Map[#^2&, s1 - s2]]
```

The function `distanceSquared[s1_,s2_]` calculates the componentwise difference of the two number vectors, `s1` and `s2`, maps the square function on each element of the resulting vector, and sums up the vector components by applying the `Plus` operator. Here are some examples for vectors of numbers:

In[7] := **distanceSquared[{1,2,3},{2,2,2}]**

Out[7] = 2

In[8] := **distanceSquared[{1,2,3},{2,2,1}]**

Out[8] = 5

In[9] := **distanceSquared[{1,2,3},{5,5,5}]**

Out[9] = 29

To evaluate the evolved sentences we have to calculate their distance to the objective sentence. We use the encoding vector representations of the sentences:

```
In[10] := distanceSquared[
        encodeSentence[
      "EVOLUTION OF STRUCTURE, STEP BY STEP"],
        encodeSentence[
      "EVOLUTIOM OF STRUCTURE, STEP BY STEP"]
        ]
```

Out[10] = 1

Since these two sentences differ only at position nine, the result is merely the difference between the letters N and M. There are more differences between the following sentences, resulting in a greater Hamming distance:

```
In[11] := distanceSquared[
        encodeSentence[
          "EVOLUTION OF STRUCTURE, STEP BY STEP"],
        encodeSentence[
          "EVOLUTION OF STRUCTURE, STEP,Y STEP"]
        ]
```

Out[11] = 676

The fewer differences there are at the corresponding string positions, the more similar the compared strings are. For a randomly generated string of equal length with an objective sentence, the similarities are consequently rather low. However, the sentences do have different *fitnesses*, although even approximate values are usually hard to evaluate. Who would be able to guess which of the following strings is closest to the objective sentence?

```
In[12] := distanceSquared[
        encodeSentence[
          "EVOLUTION OF STRUCTURE, STEP BY STEP"],
        t = createSentence[36]
        ]
      decodeSentence[t]
```

Out[12] = 5431
        CTLFBQGCYWVOACO,NIOPONCTDBEHHZTDVBOZ

```
In[13] := distanceSquared[
        encodeSentence[
```

```
            "EVOLUTION OF STRUCTURE, STEP BY STEP"],
        t = createSentence[36]
    ]
    decodeSentence[t]
```

Out[13] = 4902

PKHKYOILQO, B LM,GFQPBEZNMXTI.S,AQWQ

In the above examples, we have used the function create-
Sentence[n_] from Program 1.4 to generate a random string of a
specific length n. Actually, this function does not return a string but
rather its encoding number vector.

Program 1.4
Random string generation.

```
createSentence[l_:36] :=
  Table[Random[Integer, {65,93}], {l}]
```

Let us now consider how to implement an evolution scheme,
based on the selection-mutation principle. Random strings of equal
length are necessary only for the very first "generation," the set or
"population" of strings we start from (Program 1.5).

Program 1.5
Initial population.

```
initialPop[n_,l_:36] := Table[createSentence[l],{n}]
```

All further generations are created as mutated offspring from the best-
evaluated string of the current population. We define the mutation
operator for number vectors. Thus we have a general operator, independent of what is encoded by the numbers (Program 1.6). The function has to ensure that all entries remain within the interval of integers
between 65 and 93.

The function mutateSentence accepts a string in its encoded
representation (sent) as a first argument. The parameter mutDis-
tance determines the grade of change for each single number,
whereas the probability of a mutation per position is controlled by
mutRate. The actual mutation is performed as follows. First of all, a
"variation vector" is generated:

```
Table[
  If[Random[Real, {0,1}] <= mutRate,
    Random[Integer, {-mutDistance,mutDistance}],
    0
```

```
   ],
   {Length[sent]}
]
```

This vector has the same length as the vector to be mutated, and its entries are either zero, with probability 1 - mutRate, or a random integer number from the interval between -mutDistance and +mutDistance. It should be noted that this interval also includes zero; that is, the actual decision to mutate might result in a zero mutation with no change at all. Finally, the variation vector is subtracted from the vector sent. The result is a mutated number vector, encoding a mutated string that has been derived from the parent string.

Mutation operator details

You must also be careful about what might happen at the borders of the encoding interval [65, 93]. Mutations may lead to numbers that are outside the permitted number domain. This can easily be taken into account with the following replacement rules:

```
{ x_/;x < 65 :> 94 - (65 - x_);x > 93 :> 64 + (x - 93) }
```

which ensure that the encoding domain is organized as a ring structure:

```
Character: ... X, Y, Z,' ',',',',''.', A, B, C,...,
X, Y, Z,...

Code:     ... 88,89,90,91,92,93,65,66,67,...,
88,89,90,...
```

Let us look at a few example mutations of our initial objective sentence. With a mutation distance of 1 and a mutation rate of only 10% (the default settings in Program 1.6) the resulting changes are only minor.

Mutation examples

Program 1.6
Mutation.

```
mutateSentence[sent_List,mutDistance_:1,
  mutRate_:0.1] := sent -
  Table[
    If[Random[Real,{0,1}] <= mutRate,
      Random[Integer,{-mutDistance,mutDistance}],
      0
    ],
    {Length[sent]}
  ] /. {x_/;x < 65 :> 94 - (65 - x),
        x_/;x > 93 :> 64 + (x - 93)}
```

In[14] := `Table[mutateSentence[`
`        encodeSentence [objectSentence]]`
`        // decodeSentence, {5}]//ColumnForm`

Mutation radius: 1
Mutation rate: 10%

Out[14] = EVOLUTION OF RTRUCTURE, STEP BY SUEP
          EVOLUTIOO OF SSRUCTURE, STEP BY SSEP
          EVOLUTION OF STRUCTURE, STEP BY STEO
          EVNLUTION OFZTURUCSURE, RTEP BY STE
          EVOLUTION OF STRUCTURE. STEO BY STFP

In an evolutionary context this corresponds to variations in small steps. Tiny changes over many generations will, however, accumulate into astonishingly huge steps in adaptation, as we will demonstrate with the experiments described in the next section. The higher the probability for a mutation per string position, the more the whole string appears to be "twisted." Keeping the mutation radius at 1, the mutated characters never differ more than a single position (= character encoding) from the original character.

In[15] := `Table[mutateSentence[`
`        encodeSentence[objectSentence],1,0.5]`
`        // decodeSentence,{5}]//ColumnForm`

Mutation radius: 1
Mutation rate: 50%

Out[15] = EVOKUTION OG SURTCTUQE,,RTFP BYZSTEO
          FWOLUTHON OEZSTSVDTVSF, STDP BY SUDP
          EVOKTTIPN OF SSRUCUURE, STEO BY TTEQ
          EVOLTUHNO OF SURUCUURE, STEQ BY SUEP
          FUOLUSHOO,PE SURUCTUQF, STFOZAYZSTEQ

With a mutation radius of five positions, however, the similarity to the original sentence is fading.

In[16] := `Table[mutateSentence[`
`        encodeSentence[objectSentence],5,0.5]`
`        // decodeSentence,{5}]//ColumnForm`

Mutation radius: 5
Mutation rate: 50%

Out[16] = EVSMUXIOL OF PTRWCTQNHY.UTEP BX.RTER
          EVQLRTKSP MH SOTUCWQRE, UQIQ Y UTEP
          ERSJRRIONXTHCWRRUCYUNE, ZSPAPVBYCSTEQ
          BWOGUYIJN PF STRYCPUUI, STEPA.T STEP
          FYMLUYITN RFXSSRPFUTWE, OTGP BYATTCP

With the following parameter settings we are close to a totally random generation of strings:

In[17] := **Table[mutateSentence[**
           encodeSentence[objectSentence],15,1]
           // decodeSentence,{5}]//ColumnForm

Out[17] = DMBBHMUCPWJ,LCDMRRYIEROI PZAJCSVGEFM
            PXTJD BIVK,,RCV NFPAF,X,CHUEHWX,P C.
            MHZTE.YLQAQPELESNKFIJQNFYASGOPGB.FFW
            XAJGCCB,,QOQCSPWKNQLQE.DVSNLRFYRJHCC
            .JMWDBUPDD.Y,V,KGVMXTXTSUJXYBKEX FLI

Mutation radius: 15
Mutation rate: 100%

```
nextGeneration[pop_,comparedSentence_,
  mutDistance_:1,mutRate_:.1]  :=
Module[{fitnesses,minIndex,best},
  fitnesses =
    Map[distanceSquared[comparedSentence,#]&,pop];
  minIndex =
    Position[fitnesses,m = Min[fitnesses]]
    //First//First;
  best = pop[[minIndex]];

  (* include protocol functions here ... *)

  If[m == 0,
    pop,
    Join[
      Table[mutateSentence[best,mutDistance,mutRate],
        {Length[pop] - 1}],
      {best}]
  ]
]
```

Program 1.7
From one generation
to the next. . . .

Now that we can create an initial population of strings and know
how to generate a set of mutants from a single best string, we need a
function that identifies the fittest individual among a string population. This best-matching string will then be used as a mutation template for deriving offspring individuals for the next generation by
application of the mutation operator.

The function nextGeneration takes a list of number vectors
and a population of encoded strings and returns a list containing

mutated vectors of numbers as descendents from the best-evaluated string of the original list (Program 1.7). The list of vectors, `pop`, an encoded version of the objective string, `comparedSentence`, and the parameters for the mutation operator (mutation radius: `mutDistance`; mutation probability: `mutRate`) are the arguments accepted by `nextGeneration`. Each string's distance to the objective sentence is computed. In the terms of evolution theory, the resulting values are denoted as fitnesses:

Fitness by Hamming distance

```
fitnesses =
    Map[distanceSquared[comparedSentence,#]&,pop];
```

Among the list of fitness values, the minimum must be identified. Several strings might share the same fitness value. This is why we take the first of these elements in the list. This element is declared to be the *best individual*.

```
minIndex =
    Position[fitnesses,m = Min[fitnesses]]
      //First//First;
best = pop[[minIndex]];
```

If the best string turns out to be identical with the objective sentence (i.e., its Hamming distance is zero, m == 0), the original population is returned unchanged. Otherwise, a set of mutants derived from the best string constitutes the result.

```
If[m == 0,
  pop,
  Join[
    Table[mutateSentence[best,mutDistance,mutRate],
      {Length[pop] - 1}],
    {best}
  ]
]
```

For a population size of n individuals, $n - 1$ mutants (`Length[pop]` − 1) must be generated in addition to the fittest string. The hitherto best individual is appended at the end of the list. This guarantees that any individual with equal best fitness that might be found among the next generated $n - 1$ mutated strings will be selected as the new best individual for the next generation. In this way any premature convergence of the evolution process is avoided.

```
evolveSentences[comparedSentence_,popSize_:50,
  mutationDistance_:1,mutationRate_:.1]:=
Module[{},

  FixedPoint[
    nextGeneration[#,comparedSentence,
      mutationDistance,mutationRate]&,
    initialPop[popSize,Length[comparedSentence]]
  ];
]
```

Program 1.8
Evolution loop.

Now we have all the ingredients for the evolution of strings available. The evolution loop, which controls the cumulative selection-mutation over a number of generations, is defined in Program 1.8. The core evolution loop is rather simple. Starting from an initial set of randomly generated strings, all of the same length as the objective sentence (comparedSentence), subsequent generations are evolved until the population of strings no longer changes. Going by the definition of nextGeneration from Program 1.7, this termination criterion is met when the objective string has been discovered; that is, an exact copy is among the members of the current generation.

In the following section we present some typical evolution runs, discuss the results, and answer questions about which parameter settings, such as population size, maximum number of generations, mutation radius, and mutation rate, lead to effective and successful solutions to this specific optimization task.

1.3.6 Experiments with cumulated selection

Alberto: "But nothing in nature is random. Everything is due to infinitesimal changes that have taken effect over countless generations." Sophie: "Actually, it's quite fantastic to imagine."

Jostein Gaarder (Gaarder 1996, p. 416)

In this section, we discuss a few example selection-mutation experiments and investigate how the evolutionary adaptation process is

influenced by the mutation rate and by the mutation radius in particular. We will find that these experiments confirm Jostein Gaarder's
characterization of evolution as a process of tiny variations, accumu-
lating over many generations.

Our objective is to evolve the predefined sentence

EVOLUTION OF STRUCTURE, STEP BY STEP

starting from a random sequence of characters. The evolution should
be accomplished only through iterated mutation and selection. Specifically, we will answer the following questions:

❑   How many individuals per generation have to be selected so
    that the selection-mutation algorithm evolves the predefined
    sentence within at most 100 generations?

❑   What are reasonable settings for the mutation rate?

❑   How should the mutation radius be set?

Starting a string evolution

We start with a population of 60 individuals, which are varied by
a mutation rate of 10%. Each character is changed by at most two
positions (mutation radius = 2). This means that a C could mutate to
A, B, D, or E. The selection-mutation is started by the following
Evolvica commands:

In[1] := **guttaCavatLapidem=**
            ToCharacterCode[
                "EVOLUTION OF STRUCTURE, STEP BY STEP"];

In[2] := **bestSentences =**
            evolveSentences[guttaCavatLapidem,60,2,0.1];

String evolution illustrated

In each generation, the best-matching character sequence is
selected, and 59 mutants are generated from the current best
sequence. Figures 1.5 to 1.13 show the results of some typical evolution experiments with similar parameter settings. Figure 1.5 illustrates
an evolution over 95 generations, from a random initial character
sequence to the objective sentence. Each column shows the sequence
of generations from top to bottom. The listed sequences are the best
matching from each generation, the survivors of the selection process.
All characters that are not marked in gray match with the corresponding character in the objective sentence. The evolved sentences can be
generated as an animated graphics sequence as follows:

```
In[3] := Map[
          Show[
            Graphics[Text[interpretSentence[#],{0,0}],
              DefaultFont → {"Courier",24}],
            AspectRatio → .1]&,
          bestSentences
          ];
```

```
JW.H VUSZY OLLRVUEPF FSNCQGAZDSTFOBY        FXPMWTLQQ,SFZSSSTAQQUE,ZQUDL CXYPSDR
JW H VUSZY OLLRVUDPG FSNEQGAZDUTFOBY        FXPMWTLQQ,SFZSSSTARQSE,ZQUDL CXYPUDR
JWYI VUSZY OLLRVUDPG FSNGQGAZDUTFOBY        FXPLWTLOQ,QFZSSSTARQQE,ZQUDL CXYPUDR
JWYK VUSZY OLKRVUDPI ESPGQGAZDUTGOBY        FXQLUTLOQ,QFZSSSTARQQE,ZQUDN CXYPUDR
JWYK VUSZY OLKRVUDPI EUPGRGCZDUTGODY        FXQLUTLOQ,QFZSSSTARSQE,ZQUDP CWYPUDR
JWYK VUSZY OLMRVUCPK CUPGRGCZDUTIODY        FXQLUTJOQ,QFZSSSTARSQE ZQUDP CW PUDR
JWYK VUSXY OLMRVUCPK CWPGRGDZDVTGODY        FXQLUTJOO,QF,SSSTARSQE ZQUDR CW PUDP
HWWJ VSSXY,OLMRVUBPKYCWPGRGDZDVTGODY        FWOLUTJNO,OF,TSSTARSQE YQUDR.CW RUDP
HWWJ VSSXY,OMMRVUBPKYCWPGRGDZDVTGODW        DWOLUTJNO,OG,TSSTARTQE YQUDQ,CW RUDP
HWUJ VSSXY,OMMRVUBPKYCWPGSGDZDVTIODW        DWOLUTJNO,OG,TSSTARTQE YSUEO,CW RUDP
HWUJ VSSXY,OORMTUBPKYCWRGSGD DVTIODW        DWOLUTJNO,OG,TSSTBTTSE YSUEO,CW RUDP
HWUJ VSSXYZOOMRTUBPKYCWRGSED DVTIODW        DWOLUTJNO,OG,TSSTBTTRE YSUEO,AY RUDP
HWUJ VSSXYZOOMRTUAPKYCWRGSEF DVTIODW        DWOLUUJOO,OG,TSRTBTTRE YSUEO,AY RUDP
HWUJ VSTXZZOOMRTUARMYCXRGSEH DVTIODW        DWOLUUJOO,OG,TSRTBTURE YSUEP,AY RUDP


HWUJ VQTXZ OQMRTUAQMYCXRGSEH,DVTIODW        EVOLTUJON,OGZTSRTBTURE YSUEP,AY RUDP
HWUK VQTXZ OSMRTUAQMYDYRISEH,FXTIODW        EVOLTUJON,OF TSRTBTURE YSUEP,AY RSDP
HWUJ VQTXZYOSMRTUAQMYDYRISEH,FXUIODW        EVOLTTJON,OF TSRTBTURE YSUEP,AY RSDP
HWUJ VQTXZYOUMRTUASMYDYRISEH,FXUKODW        EVOLTTJON,OF TTRTBTURE ZSUEP,AY RSDP
HWSJ TQTVZYOUMRTUAQNYFYRISEH,FXUKODW        EVOLUTJON,OF TTRTBTURE ZSUEP,AY RSDP
HWSJYTQTVZYOUMRTUAQNYFYRISEH,FXUMODW        EVOLUTJON,OF TTRTBTURE ZSUEP,AY RSDP
HWQJYTQTVZYNUMRTUAQNYFYRKSEH,FXVMODX        EVOLUTIONZOF TTRTBTURE ZSSEP,BY RUDP
HWQJYTQTVZYNUMRTUAQNYFYRMSEH,EXVMODX        EVOLUTIONZOF TTRTBTURE ZSSEP,BY RUEP
HVQJYTQTVZYNUMTTUAQNYF ROSEH,EXXMODX        EVOLUTION OF TTRTBTURE ZSSEP,BY RUEP
HVQJYTQTVZYLUOTTUAQNYF ROSEH,EXYMODX        EVOLUTION OF TTRTBTURE ZSSEP BY RUEP
HVRJWTQTTZYLUOTTUAQNYF SOSEH,EWYMODX        EVOLUTION OF TTRTCTURE SSEP BY RUEP
FVRJWTQTT,YLUOTSUAQNYF UOSEH,EWYMODX        EVOLUTION OF TTRVCTURE SSEP BY RUEP
FVRJWTQTT,WJUOTSTAQNYF UOSEH,EYXMODW        EVOLUTION OF TTRVCTURE SSEP BY RUEP
FVRJWTQTT,WHUOTSTAQNYF UOSEH,EYWMODU        EVOLUTION OF TTRVCTURE SSEP BY RUEP


FVRJWTQTT,UHUOTSUAQNWF UOSEJ,EYWMODU        EVOLUTION OF STRUCTURE SSEP BY TUEP
FVRJWTQTR,UHUOTSUAQNWF UOSEJ,CYWOODU        EVOLUTION OF STRVCTURE SSEP BY RTEP
FVRJWTOTR,UHUOTSUAQNWF UOSEJ,CYWOODU        EVOLUTION OF STRVCTURE STEP BY RTEP
FVRKWTOTR,UGUOTSUAQNWF VOSEL.CXWOODU        EVOLUTION OF STRVCTURE STEP BY RTEP
FVRKWTOSR,UGUOUSUAQNWF VPSEL CXWOPDU        EVOLUTION OF STRVCTURE STEP BY RTEP
FVRKWTOSR,UGWOUSUAQNWG VPSEL CXWOPDT        EVOLUTION OF STRTCTURE STEP BY RTEP
FVRKWTOSR,UGWOUSUAQNWG XQSFL CXYOPDT        EVOLUTION OF STRTCTURE STEP BY STEP
FVPKWTOSQ,UGYQUSUAQNWG,XQSFL CXYOPDT        EVOLUTION OF STRUCTUQE STEP BY STEP
FXPKWTOSQ,UGYSSSUAQNWG,XQSFL CXYORDR        EVOLUTION OF STRUCTUQE STEP BY STEP
FXPKWTOQQ,UGYSSSUAQPWG,XQSFL CXYORDR        EVOLUTION OF STRUCTURE STEP BY STEP
FXPKWTNQQ,THYSSSTAQPWG,XQSFL CXYORDR        EVOLUTION OF STRUCTURE STEP BY STEP
FXPKWTNQQ,TFZSSSTAQQWG,ZQUFL CXYORDR        EVOLUTION OF STRUCTURE, STEP BY STEP
FXPKWTLQQ,SFZSSSTAQQWG,ZQUFL.CXYORDR
FXPMWTLQQ,SFZSSSTAQQUE,ZQUFL.CXYORDR
```

Figure 1.5
Evolution of a character sequence: 60 individuals per generation, mutation radius: 2, mutation rate: 0.1.

Within the first 50 generations (left column in Figure 1.5), the character pattern seems to stabilize rather slowly. After a while, more and more positions are switched to their correct settings. Note that these correct characters are not kept "fixed" once their desired final settings are found. Mutations may change any position at any time. However, any change from a correct to a mismatching symbol leads to a decreased fitness of the whole character sequence, and so it may not pass the selection filter.

Disadvantageous mutants can show up as the selection champions, namely, if all other individuals of the same generation are even worse. In our example, this situation occurs, for example, for the symbol U in STRUCTURE, which is correct at the beginning but is lost around generation 45. In the second column of Figure 1.5, the U reappears and is kept until the end of the evolution run.

Although at about generation 60, the best character sequence is only a few mutations off the objective sentence, the selection-mutation algorithm still requires another 20 generations to reach its goal. The more positions are set correctly, the larger is the proportion of mutants that are rated worse than the best individual so far. Therefore, the probability of generating better individuals shrinks, and the propagation speed of the evolution process decreases.

Figure 1.6 illustrates this character evolution from the perspective of the Hamming distances. Unlike Figure 1.5, here the sequential generations are arranged from bottom to top. Each row represents the Hamming distance of the character sequence evaluated as best so far. The distance at each position is illustrated by a gray square. Lighter gray values correspond to smaller distances. A white square means an exact match with the corresponding symbol in the objective sentence.

The first and second halves of the evolution sequence are depicted as zooms at the bottom of Figure 1.6. The decreasing Hamming distances are highlighted by brighter and brighter gray values. At the end, the top blank row shows the perfect match with the objective sentence. After 40 generations, the bandwidth of the Hamming distances is considerably reduced (Figure 1.6[a]). From generation 50 on (Figure 1.6[b]), the only remaining colors are white and two different gray levels, which represent the Hamming distances 0, 1, and 2. The diagrams in Figure 1.6(a) and 1.6(b) each cover half of the generations. According to these illustrations, the evolution algorithm requires about the same amount of iterations for both "coarse adjustment" and "fine tuning" of the correct symbols. During the last 20 generations, only a few traces of mismatching positions have to be eliminated. Step by step, these traces fizzle out as well.

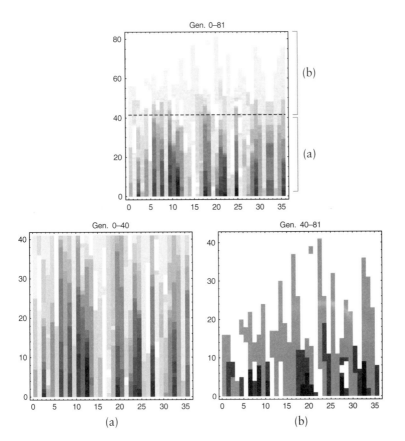

Figure 1.6
Evolution of the Hamming distances for the objective sentences from Figure 1.5: mutation radius: 2, mutation rate: 0.1.

For this example, our choice of parameter settings was rather conservative. A mutation radius of 2 changes the symbols within a Hamming distance of only 2 (for example, an F can mutate to D, E, F, G, or H). The chosen mutation rate of 10% is also relatively low. Couldn't we speed up the evolution process by increasing the mutation radius? Increasing the mutation step sizes should turn out to be advantageous, in particular during the first generations; that is, when the algorithm strives to make a coarse adaptation from the random initial character sequence to the objective string. But will we be able to reduce the total number of generations necessary to evolve toward the objective string?

Conservative parameter settings

Figures 1.7 through 1.9 suggest answers to the question of which settings for the mutation radius and mutation rate are reasonable. The mutation distance is doubled to 4, compared to the previous evolution experiment. The mutation probability is still 10%. In Figures 1.7 through 1.9, more than 160 generations are required to evolve the

Second string evolution: increased mutation distance

Fine tuning becomes more difficult

Figure 1.7
60 individuals per
generation, mutation radius:
4, mutation rate: 0.1 (Part 1).

```
PWWWRQABTHOBUGSAPLXOFLP.SJOTWE.YGJNU      EUPMUSIONZOF STQUCTUQE. STEP.BYZSTFQ
PWWWRQABTHOBUJSAPLXOFLT.SJOTWE.YGLNU      EUPMUSIONZOF STQUCTUQE. STEP.BYZSTFQ
PWWWRQABTLOAUJSCPLXOFLT.SJOTWE.YGLNU      EUPMUSIONZOF STQUCTUSE. STEP.BYZSTFQ
PWWWRQABTNOAUJSCPLXRFLT.SJOTWI.YKLNU      EUPMUSIONZOF STQUCTUSE, STEP.BYZSTFQ
PWWWRQABTNOAUJSCPLXRFLTYSJOTWE.YKPNU      EUPMUSIONZOF STQUCTUSE, STEP.BYZSTDQ
PWWWRQABTNOEUJSFPLXRFLTYSJOTWE.YKPNU      EUPMUSIONZOF STQUCTUSE, STEP.BYZSTDQ
PWWRQABTNOEUJSFPLXRJLTZSJKTWE.YKPNU       EUPMUSIONZOF STQUCTURE. STEP.BYZSTDQ
PWWRRAFTNOEUNSFPLXRLLTZSJKTWE.YKPNU       EUPMUSIONZOF STQUCTURE. STEP.BYZSTDQ
PWWSRRAFTNODUNSHPLXRLLTZSJKTWE.YKPNU      EUPMUSIONZOF STQUCTURE. STEP.BYZSTDQ
PWWRRRAFTNODURSHPLXRLLTZSNKTYEYYKPNU      EUPMUSIONZOF STQUCTURE. STEP.BYZSTDQ
PWWRRRAFPPODURSLPLXRLLTZSNKTYEYYKPNU      EUPKUSIONZOF STQUCTURE. STEP.BYZSTDQ
NWWRRRDFPPODUQSLPLXTLLTZSNKTYEYYKPNU      EUPKUSIONZOF STQUCTURE. STEP.BYZSTDQ
NWWRRRDFPTODUQSLPHXTLLTZSNKTYEVYKPNU      EUPKUTION, OF STQUCTURE. STEP.BYZSTDQ
NWWRRODFPTODYQSOPHXTLLLTZSNKTYEVYMPNU     EUPKUTION, OF STQUCTURE. STEP.BYZSTDQ
NWWRRODFPTODYQSOPHXTLLLTZSNKQYEVZMPKU     EUPKUTION, OF STQUCTURE. STEP.BYZSTDQ
NWWNRODFOVODYQSOPHXTLLLTZRNKQYEVZMPKU     EUPKUTION, OF STQUCTURE. STEP.BYZSTDQ

NWSNRRDFOVODYQSOPHXTNLXZRNNQYEVZMPKU      EUPKUTION, OF STRUCTURE. STEP.BYZSTDQ
NWSNRRDJOVODYQSOPHXTNLXZRNNQYEVZMPHU      EUPKUTION, OF STRUCTURE. STEP.BYZSTDQ
NWSNRRDMOVODYSSOPHXTPHXZRNNQWEVZMPHU      EUPKUTION, OF STRUCTURE. STEP.BYZSTDQ
NWSNRRDMOVODYSSOPHXTPHXZRQKQWEVZMPHU      EUPKUTION, OF STRUCTURE. STEP.BYZSTDQ
KWONRRDMOVODYSSOPHXTPLXZRQKQXEWZMPHU      EUPKUTION, OF STRUCTURE. STEP.BYZSTDQ
KWONURGMOVRDYSSOPHXTPLXZRKQXEWZQPHU       EUPKUTION, OF STRUCTURE, STEP.BYZSTDQ
GWONURGMOVRDYSSOPGXTPLXZRQKQXEWZQPHU      EUPKUTION, OF STRUCTURE, STEP.BYZSTDQ
GWRNURGMOVRDYSSOPGXTPIXZRQKQXCWZQPHU      EUPKUTION, OF STRUCTURE, STEP.BYZSTDQ
GWRNURGMOVRDYSSOPGXTOHXZRQIQXCWZUPHU      EUPKUTION, OF STRUCTURE, STEP.BYZSTDQ
GSRNURGMOVRDZSSOTGTTODXZRQIQXCWZUPHU      EUPKUTION, OF STRUCTURE, STEP.BYZSTDQ
GSRNURGMOVODZSVOTGTTQDXZRQIQXCWZUPHR      EUPKUTION, OF STRUCTURE, STEP.BYZSTDP
GSPNUUGOOVODZSVSTGTTQDXZUQIQXCXZUPFR      EUPKUTION, OF STRUCTURE, STEP BYZSTDP
GSPNUUGOOVODZSVSTGTTQDXZUQGQXCXZUSFR      EUPKUTION, OF STRUCTURE, STEP BYZSTDP
GSPJUUGOOVODZSVSTGTTQD ZUQGQXCXZUSFP      EUPKUTION, OF STRUCTURE, STEP BYZSTDP
GSPJUUGOOVODZSVSTGTTQD ZUQGQ.CXZUSFP      EUPKUTION, OF STRUCTURE, STEP BYZSTDP
GUPJUUGOOXODZSVSTGTTQD ZUQIQ.BXZTSFP      EUPKUTION, OF STRUCTURE, STEP BYZSTDP

GUPJUUGOOXODZSVSTCTTQD ZUSIQ.BXZSSFP      EUPKUTION, OF STRUCTURE, STEP BYZSTDP
GUPJUUGOOXODZSVSTCTTQD ZUSFQ.BXZSSFP      EUPLUTION, OF STRUCTURE, STEP BYZSTDP
GUPJUUGOOZODZSVSTCTTQD ZUSFQ.BXZSVFP      EUPLUTION, OF STRUCTURE, STEP BYZSTDP
GUPJUUGNOZODZSVSTCTTQD ZUSFQ.BXZSTFP      EUPLUTION, OF STRUCTURE, STEP BYZSTDP
GUPJUUGNOZOFZSVSTCTTQD ZUTFQ.BXZSTFP      EUPLUTION, OF STRUCTURE, STEP BYZSTDP
GUPKUUGNO OFZSVSTCTTQD ZUTFQ.BXZSTFP      EUPLUTION, OF STRUCTURE, STEP BYZSTDP
GUPKUUGNO OFZSVQTCTTQD ZUTEQ.BXZSTFP      EUPLUTION, OF STRUCTURE, STEP BYZSTFP
GUPKUUGNO OFZSVQTCTUQD ZUTEQ.BXZSTFP      EUPLUTION, OF STRUCTURE, STEP BYZSTFP
GUPKUUGNO OFZSSQTCTUQD ,UTEQ.BXZSTFP      EUPLUTION, OF STRUCTURE, STEP BYZSTFP
DUPKUUGNO OFZSSQTCTUQD ,UTEQ.BXZSTFP      EUPLUTION, OF STRUCTURE, STEP BYZSTFP
DUPKUUGNOZOFZSSQTCTUQE ,RTEQ.BXZSTFP      EUPLUTION, OF STRUCTURE, STEP BYZSTFP
DUPKUUGNOZOF SSQTCTUQE ,RTEQ.BXZSTFP      EUPLUTION, OF STRUCTURE, STEP BYZSTFP
DUPKUUGNOZOF SSQTCTUQE ,RTEP.BXZSTFP      EUPLUTION, OF STRUCTURE, STEP BYZSTFP
DUPKUUGNNZOF SSQTCTUQE  STFP.BXZSTFO      EUPLUTION OF STRUCTURE, STEP BYZSTFP
DUPKUUGNNZOF SSQTCTUQE  STFP.BXZSTFO      EUPLUTION, OF STRUCTURE, STEP BYZSTFP
DUPKUSJNNZOF SSQTCTUQE  STFP.BXZSTFO      EUPLUTION, OF STRUCTURE, STEP BYZSTFP

DUPKUSJNNZOF SSQUCTUQE. STFP.BXZSTFO      EUOLUTION OF STRUCTURE, STEP BYZSTFP
DUPKUSJNNZOF SSQUCTUQE. STFP.BXZSTFO      EUOLUTION OF STRUCTURE, STEP BYZSTFP
DUPKUSJNNZOF STQUCTUQE. STFP.BXZSTFO      EUOLUTION OF STRUCTURE, STEP BYZSTFP
DUPKUSJNNZOF STQUCTUQE. STFP.BXZSTFO      EUOLUTION OF STQUCTUQE, STEP BYZSTFP
DUPKUSJNNZOF STQUCTUQE. STFP.BXZSTFO      EUOLUTION OF STRUCTURE, STEP BYZSTFP
DUPKUSJNNZOF STQUCTUQE. STFP.BYZSTFO      EUOLUTION OF STRUCTURE, STEP BY STFP
DUPKUSJNNZOF STQUCTUQE. STFP.BYZSTFO      EUOLUTION OF STRUCTURE, STEP BY STFP
DUPKUSJNNZOF STQUCTUQE. STFP.BYZSTFO      EUOLUTION OF STRUCTURE, STEP BY STFP
DUPKUSHNNZOF STQUCTUQE. STFP.BYZSTFO      EUOLUTION OF STRUCTURE, STEP BY STFP
DUPKUSINNZOF STQUCTUQE. STFP.BYZSTFO      EUOLUTION OF STRUCTURE, STEP BY STFP
DUPKUSIONZOF STQUCTUQE. STFP.BYZSTFO      EUOLUTION OF STRUCTURE, STEP BY STFP
DUPKUSIONZOF STQUCTUQE. STFP.BYZSTFO      EUOLUTION OF STRUCTURE, STEP BY STFP
DUPKUSIONZOF STQUCTUQE. STEP.BYZSTFO      EUOLUTION OF STRUCTURE, STEP BY STFP
DUPMUSIONZOF STQUCTUQE. STEP.BYZSTFO      EUOLUTION OF STRUCTURE, STEP BY STFP
DUPMUSIONZOF STQUCTUQE. STEP.BYZSTFQ      EUOLUTION OF STRUCTURE, STEP BY STFP
EUPMUSIONZOF STQUCTUQE. STEP.BYZSTFQ      EUOLUTION OF STRUCTURE, STEP BY STFP
```

```
EUOLUTION OF STRUCTURE, STEP BY STEP
EUOLUTION OF STRUCTURE, STEP BY STEP
EUOLUTION OF STRUCTURE, STEP BY STEP
EUOLUTION OF STRUCTURE, STEP BY STEP
EUOLUTION OF STRUCTURE, STEP BY STEP
EUOLUTION OF STRUCTURE, STEP BY STEP
EUOLUTION OF STRUCTURE, STEP BY STEP
EUOLUTION OF STRUCTURE, STEP BY STEP
EUOLUTION OF STRUCTURE, STEP BY STEP
EUOLUTION OF STRUCTURE, STEP BY STEP
EVOLUTION OF STRUCTURE, STEP BY STEP
EVOLUTION OF STRUCTURE, STEP BY STEP
EVOLUTION OF STRUCTURE, STEP BY STEP
EVOLUTION OF STRUCTURE, STEP BY STEP
EVOLUTION OF STRUCTURE, STEP BY STEP
EVOLUTION OF STRUCTURE, STEP BY STEP
```

Figure 1.8
60 individuals per
generation, mutation radius:
4, mutation rate: 0.1 (Part 2).

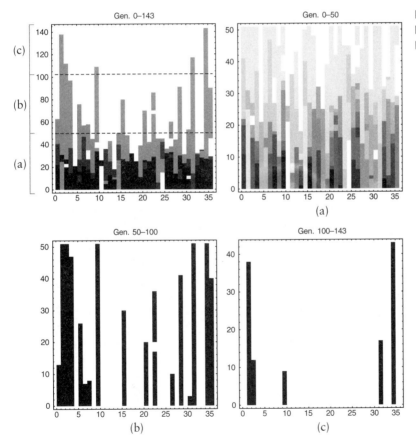

Figure 1.9
Mutation radius: 4,
Mutation rate: 0.1.

objective sentence. This evolution takes much longer than the previous experiment, which had about 90 generations. Figure 1.9 shows why this is so—it is the final phase of the evolution process, which is considerably longer. More than a hundred generations are needed for what we previously referred to as the fine-tuning phase. A mutation radius of 4 turns out to be favorable during the initial generations, but for the later phase of fine tuning, this setting is too coarse (Figure 1.9[b] and 1.9[c]). After 50 generations, only two Hamming distances remain, for which it takes about 100 generations to converge toward the objective sentence.

Third string evolution: increased mutation

In a final experiment, we briefly investigate how an increase of the mutation probability would influence the course of the character evolution. The mutation rate is now doubled to 0.2. The mutation radius is reset to a Hamming distance of 2.

Effects of increased mutation

Figures 1.10 through 1.13 illustrate a typical result from these control parameter settings. In Figure 1.11, the objective sentence seems to be within short reach after only 60 to 80 generations (compare the patterns in the right column). However, the expectation that

Figure 1.10

Evolution of the Hamming distances for the experiment of Figure 1.11, mutation radius: 2, mutation rate: 0.2.

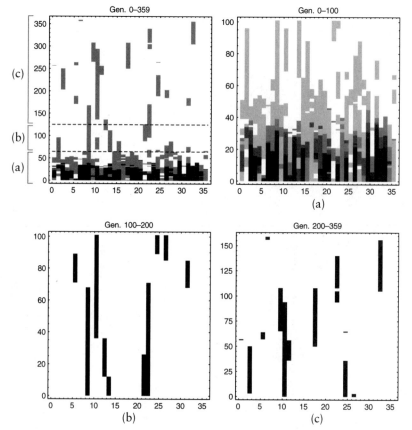

```
FVCHVNZHF,EJSP,TVDPHMFV.ZSQQYUSI,BCQ    EWOLUTIPM OF SSQUCSURE. STDOZBY STEP
FVEHVPZHF,EJSP,TVDPHNFV.ZSQQYSSI,BCQ    EWOLUTIPM OF SSQUCSURE. STDOZBY STEP
FVEHVRZHF,EJSP,TVCPHNEV.ZSQQYSUI,DCQ    EWOLUTIPM OF SSQUCSURE. STDOZBY STEP
FVGHVRZGF,EJUP,TTCPHNEV.XSOQYSUI,FCQ    EWOLUTIPM OF SSQUCSURE. STDOZBY STEP
FVGHVTZGF,GHUP,TTCOJNEV.XSOOXSUK,FCQ    EWOLUTIOM OF SSQUCTURE. TTDQ BYZSTEO
FVGHXTXGG,GHUP TTDOJPEV.XSMOXSUK,FCQ    EUOLUTIOM OF TTQUCTURE. TTDQ BYZSTEO
HVGHXTVGG,GHUP TTDOJNEV.XTMOXRWKZFCQ    EUOLUTIOM OF TTQUCTURE. TTDQ BYZSTEO
HVJHXTTGH,GHUP TTDOJMEV.YTMOXRWLZFCQ    EUOLUTIOM OF TTQUCTURE. TTDQ BYZSTEO
HVJHXTTGF.GHUR TTDOJMEW.YTKPXRWMZFCQ    EUOLUTIOM OF TTQUCTURE. RTDQ BYZSTEP
HWJHXTTGG.IHUR TTDQJMEW.YSKPXRWNZHDQ    EUOLUTIOM PF TTQUCTURE, STDQ BYZSTEP
HWJHZTTGG.IHUR TTDQLMEW.XSKNXRWNYJCQ    EUOLUTIOM PF TTQUCTURE, STDQ BYZSTEP
HWJHZTTGG,IHUR TTDQNMEY.XSKMXQWNYLAQ    EUOLUTIOM PF TTQUCTURE, STDQ BYZSTEP
HWIHZTTIG,IGUR TTEQNMEY.XTKMXPWNYLAQ    EUOLUTIOM PF TTQUCTURE, STDQ BYZSTEP
HWIHZTRIG,IGURYTTEQOMGY.XTKMXPWNYLCQ    EUOLUTIOM PF TTQUCTURE, STDQ BYZSTEP
HWIHZSQIG,IEURYTTGQOMGY.XTKMXPWPYLCQ    EUOLUTIOM PF TTQUCTURE, STDQ BYZSTEP

HVIHXSQII,JEUPYUTGQOMGY.VTKMZOWRYLCQ    EUOLUTIOM PF TTQUCTURE, STDQ BYZSTEP
HVIIXSQII,KEWPYUTGQQMG .VTKMZOYRYLCQ    EUOLUTIOM PF TTQUCTURE, STDQ BY STEP
HVIIXSQKI,LGWPYUTHQQOG .VUKMZOYRYNCQ    EUOLUTIOM PF TTQUCTURE, STDQ BY STEP
HVIIXUQKI,LGWPYUTFQSOG .VUKMZOYRXNCQ    EUOLUTIOM PF TTQUCTURE, STDQ BY STEP
GVIIXUQMI,LGWPYUTFQSOG .UUKOZNYRXNCQ    EUOLUTIOM PF TTQUCTURE, STEQ BY STEP
GUIIXUQMI,LGWPYUTFQSPG .UUKOZLYRXNCQ    EUOLUTIOM PF TTQUCTURE, STEQ BY STEP
GWJKXSPMI,LGWPWUTFQSQE.UUINZLYRVNCQ     EUOLUTIOM PF TTQUCTURE, STEQ BY STEP
GWJKVSPMI,LGWPWUTFQSOE,.UUHNZJYRVPDQ    EUOLUTIOM PF TTQUCTURE, STEQ BY STEP
FWLKVSNMI,LGWPUUTFQSOE,.UUINZJYRVPDQ    EUOLUTIOM PF TTQUCTURE, STEQ BY STEP
FWLKVSLMJ,LGWPUUTFQSOE,.VUHNZJYRVPDQ    EUOLUTIOM PF TTQUCTURE, STEQ BY STEP
GWLKVSKMJ,LGWPUSTFQSOE,.VUHNZJYTVPDQ    EUOLUTIOM PF TTQUCTURE, STEQ BY STEP
GWLKVSKMJ,LGWPUSTFQSOE,.TUHNZHYTVPDR    EUOLUTIOM PF TTQUCTURE, STEQ BY STEP
EYLKVSKMJ,LGWPUSTEQSQE,.TUHNZFYTVPDP    EUOLUTIOM PF TTQUCTURE, STEQ BY STEP
EYLKVSKMJ.LFYQUSTEQSQE,.TUHOZFYTUPDP    EUOLUTIOM PF TTRUCTURF, STEP BY STEP
FYLLVUKMJ.LF QUSTESSQE,.TUGO,FYTURDP    EUOLUTIOM PF TTRUCTURF, STEP BY STEP

FYLLVSKMJ.LH SUSTESTQE,.TTGQ,FYVURDP    EUOLUTIOM PF TTRUCTURF, STEP BY STEP
FYLLVSKMJ.MF UUSTCSTQE,,TTGQ EYVURDP    EUOLUTIOM PF TTRUCTURF, STEP BY STEP
FYMLVSKML.MF.USSTDSTQE ,TTFQ EXVURDP    EUOLUTIOM PF TTRUCTURF, STEP BY STEP
EYMLVSKML.OF USSTDQTQE,.RTFQ EXWURDP    EUOLUTIOM PF TTRUCTURF, STEP BY STEP
EWOLVSKML,OF USSRDQTQE,.RTFQ EYWSRDP    EUOLUTIOM PF TTRUCTURF, STEP BY STEP
EWQLVUINL,OF USSRDSTQE,.RTFQ EYWSRDP    EUOLUTIOM PF TTRUCTURF, STEP BY STEP
EVQKVUINL,OF UUSRDSTQE ,RTFQ EYXSREP    EVOLUTIOM OF TTRUCTURF STEP BY STEP
EVQKTUINL,OF UUSTDSTQC .RTFQ DYYSREP    EVOLUTIOM OF TTRUCTURF STEP BY STEP
EVPKTUINL,OF SUSTDSTQE .RTFQ DYYSREP    EVOLUTIOM OF TTRUCTURF STEP BY STEP
DWPKTUINM,OF SUSTDSTQE .RTFQ DYYSREP    EVOLUTIOM OF TTRUCTURF STEP BY STEP
FWPKTUINM,OF SUSTDSTQE RTFQ DYZSREP     EVOLUTIOM OF TTRUCTURF STEP BY STEP
FWPKTUINM,PF SUSTDSTQE, RTFQ DYZSTEP    EVOLUTIOM OF TTRUCTURF STEP BY STEP
FWPKTTIPM,PF SUSTDSTQE, RTFQ DYZSTEP    EVOLUTIOM OF TTRUCTURF STEP BY STEP
FWPKTTIPM,PF SURTDSTQE, RTFQ DYZSTEP    EVOLUTIOM OF TTRUCTURF STEP BY STEP
FWPKTTIPM,PF SUSUDSTQE, RTFO DYZSTEP    EVOLUTIOM OF TTRUCTURF STEP BY STEP

FWPKTTIPM,PF SUSUDSTPE, RTFP CYZSTEP    EVOLUTIOM OF TTRUCTURF STEP BY STEP
FWPKTSIPM,PF SUSVDSTRE, RTFP CYZSTEP    EVOLUTIOM OF TTRUCTURF STEP BY STEP
FWOKTSHPM,PF SUSVDSTRE, RTFP CYZSTEP    EVOLUTIOM OF TTRUCTURF STEP BY STEP
FWOKTSIPM PF SUSVDSTRE, RUFPZCYZSTEP    EVOLUTIOM OF TTRUCTURF STEP BY STEP
FWOKTSIPM OF SUSVDSTRE, RUEP,CYZSTEO    EVOLUTIOM OF TTRUCTURF STEP BY STEP
FWOKTSIOM OF SUSUDSTRE, RUDP,CYZSTEO    EVOLUTIOM OF TTRUCTURF STEP BY STEP
EWOKTSIOM OF SSSUBSTRE. RUDP,CYZSTEO    EVOLUTIOM OF TTRUCTURF STEP BY STEP
EWOLTTIOM OF SSQVBSTRE. RUDP,CYZSTEO    EVOLUTIOM OFZSTRUCTURF STEP BY STEP
EWOLTTIOM OF SSQVBSTRE. RUDP,CYZSTEO    EVOLUTIOM OFZSTRUCTURF STEP BY STEP
EWOLUTIOM OF SSQVCSVRE. SSDO CY STEO    EVOLUTIOM OFZSTRUCTURF STEP BY STEP
EWOLUTIOM OF SSQVCSVRE. SSDO CY STEO    EVOLUTIOM OFZSTRUCTURF STEP BY STEP
EWOLUTIOM OF SSQVCSVRE. SSDO CY STEO    EVOLUTIOM OFZSTRUCTURF STEP BY STEP
EWOLUTIPM OF SSQVCSURE. SSDO BY STEO    EVOLUTIOM OFZSTRUCTURF STEP BY STEP
EWOLUTIPM OF SSQUCSURE. STDOZBY STEP    EVOLUTIOM OFZSTRUCTURF STEP BY STEP
EWOLUTIPM OF SSQUCSURE. STDOZBY STEP    EVOLUTIOM OFZSTRUCTURF STEP BY STEP
```

Figure 1.11
60 individuals per generation, mutation radius: 2, mutation rate: 0.2 (Part 1).

Figure 1.12

60 individuals per generation, mutation radius: 2, mutation rate: 0.2 (Part 2).

```
EVOLUTIOM OFZSTRUCTURF   STEP BY STEP      EVOLUUION PF STRUCTURE, STEP BYZSTEP
EVOLUTIOM OFZSTRUCTURF   STEP BY STEP      EVOLUUION PF STRUCTURE, STEP BYZSTEP
EVOLUTIOM OFZSTRUCTURF   STEP BY STEP      EVOLUUION PF STRUCTURE, STEP BYZSTEP
EVOLUTIOM OFZSTRUCTURF   STEP BY STEP      EVOLUUION PF STRUCTURE, STEP BYZSTEP
EVOLUTIOM OFZSTRUCTURF   STEP BY STEP      EVOLUUION PF STRUCTURE, STEP BYZSTEP
EVOLUTIOM OFZSTRUCTURF   STEP BY STEP      EVOLUUION PF STRUCTURE, STFP BY STEP
EVOLUTIOM OFZSTRUCTURE   STEP BY STEP      EVOLUUION PF STRUCTURE, STFP BY STEP
EVOLUTIOM OFZSTRUCTURE   STEP BY STEP      EVOLUUION PF STRUCTURE, STFP BY STEP
EVOLUTIOM OFZSTRUCTURE   STEP BY STEP      EVOLUUION PF STRUCTURE, STFP BY STEP
EVOLUTIOM OFZSTRUCTURE   STEP BY STEP      EVOLUTION PF STRUCTURE, RTFP BY STEP
EVOLUTIOM OFZSTRUCTURE   STEP BY STEP      EVOLUTION PF STRUCTURE, RTFP BY STEP
EVOLUTIOM OFZSTRUCTURE   STEP BY STEP      EVOLUTION PF STRUCTURE, RTFP BY STEP
EVOLUTIOM OFZSTRUCTURE   STEP BY STEP      EVOLUTION PF STRUCTURE, RTFP BY STEP
EVOLUTIOM OFZSTRUCTURE   STEP BY STEP      EVOLUTION PF STRUCTURE, RTFP BY STEP
EVOLUTIOM OFZSTRUCTURE   STEP BY STEP      EVOLUTION PF STRUCTURE, RTFP BY STEP

EVOLUTIOM OFZSTRUCTURE   STEP BY STEP      EVOLUTION PF STRUCTURE, RTFP BY STEP
EVOLUTIOM PF STRUCTURE   STEP BY STEP      EVOLUTION PF STRUCTURE, RTFP BY STEP
EVOLUTIOM PF STRUCTURE   STEP BY STEP      EVOLUTION PF STRUCTURE, RTFP BY STEP
EVOLUTIOM PF STRUCTURE   STEP BY STEP      EVOLUTION PF STRUCTURE, RTFP BY STEP
EVOLUTIOM PF STRUCTURE   STEP BY STEP      EVOLUTION PF STRUCTURE, RTFP BY STEP
EVOLUTIOM PF STRUCTURE   STEP BY STEP      EVOLUTION PF STRUCTURE, RTFP BY STEP
EVOLUTIOM PF STRUCTURE   STEP BY STEP      EVOLUTION PF STRUCTURE, RTFP BY STEP
EVOLUTIOM PF STRUCTURE   STEP BY STEP      EVOLUTION PF STRUCTURE, RTFP BY STEP
EVOLUTIOM PF STRUCTURE   STEP BY STEP      EVNLUTION PF STRUCTURE, RTEP BY STEP
EVOLUTIOM PF STRUCTURE   STEP BY STEP      EVNLUTION PF STRUCTURE, RTEP BY STEP
EVOLUTIOM PF STRUCTURE   STEP BY STEP      EVNLUTION PF STRUCTURE, RTEP BY STEP
EVOLUTIOM PF STRUCTURE   STEP BY STEP      EVNLUTION PF STRUCTURE, RTEP BY STEP
EVOLUTIOM PF STRUCTURE   STEP BY STEP      EVNLUTION PF STRUCTURE, RTEP BY STEP
EVOLUTIOM PF STRUCTURE   STEP BY STEP      EVNLUTION PF STRUCTURE, RTEP BY STEP

EVOLUTIOM PF STRUCTURE   STEP BY STEP      EVNLUTION PF STRUCTURE, RTEP BY STEP
EVOLUTIOM PF STRUCTURE   STEP BY STEP      EVNLUTION PF STRUCTURE, RTEP BY STEP
EVOLUTIOM PF STRUCTURE   STEP BY STEP      EVNLUTION PF STRUCTURE, RTEP BY STEP
EVOLUTIOM PF STRUCTURE   STEP BY STEP      EVNLUTION NF STRUCTURE, RTEP BY STEP
EVOLUTIOM PF STRUCTURE   STEP BY STEP      EVNLUTION NF STRUCTURE, RTEP BY STEP
EVOLUTIOM PF STRUCTURE   STEP BY STEP      EVNLUTION NF STRUCTURE, RTEP BY STEP
EVOLUTIOM PF STRUCTURE   STEP BY STEP      EVNLUTION NF STRUCTURE, RTEP BY STEP
EVOLUTIOM PF STRUCTURE   STEP BY STEP      EVNLUTION NF STRUCTURE, RTEP BY STEP
EVOLUTIOM PF STRUCTURE   STEP BY STEP      EVNLUTION NF STRUCTURE, RTEP BY STEP
EVOLUTIOM PF STRUCTURE   STEP BY STEP      EVNLUTION NF STRUCTURE, RTEP BY STEP
EVOLUTIOM PF STRUCTURE   STEP BY STEP      EVNLUTION NF STRUCTURE, RTEP BY STEP
EVOLUTIOM PF STRUCTURE   STEP BY STEP      EVNLUTION NF STRUCTURE, RTEP BY STEP
EVOLUTIOM PF STRUCTURE   STEP BY STEP      EVNLUTION NF STRUCTURE, RTEP BY STEP

EVOLUTIOM PF STRUCTURE   STEP BY STEP      EVNLUTION NF STRUCTURE, TTEP BY STEP
EVOLUTIOM PF STRUCTURE   STEP BY STEP      EVNLUTION NF STRUCTURE, TTEP BY STEP
EVOLUTIOM PF STRUCTURE   STEP BY STEP      EVNLUTION NF STRUCTURE, TTEP BY STEP
EVOLUTION PF STRUCTURE   STEP BYZSTEP     EVNLUTION NF STRUCTURE, TTEP BY STEP
EVOLUTION PF STRUCTURE   STEP BYZSTEP     EVNLUTION NF STRUCTURE, TTEP BY STEP
EVOLUTION PF STRUCTURE   STEP BYZSTEP     EVNLUTION NF STRUCTURE, TTEP BY STEP
EVOLUUION PF STRUCTURE,  STEP BYZSTEP     EVNLUTION NF STRUCTURE, TTEP BY STEP
EVOLUUION PF STRUCTURE,  STEP BYZSTEP     EVNLUTION NF STRUCTURE, TTEP BY STEP
EVOLUUION PF STRUCTURE,  STEP BYZSTEP     EVNLUTION NF STRUCTURE, TTEP BY STEP
EVOLUUION PF STRUCTURE,  STEP BYZSTEP     EVNLUTION NF STRUCTURE, TTEP BY STEP
EVOLUUION PF STRUCTURE,  STEP BYZSTEP     EVNLUTION NF STRUCTURE, TTEP BY STEP
EVOLUUION PF STRUCTURE,  STEP BYZSTEP     EVNLUTION NG STRUCTURE, STEP BY STEP
EVOLUUION PF STRUCTURE,  STEP BYZSTEP     EVNLUTION NG STRUCTURE, STEP BY STEP
EVOLUUION PF STRUCTURE,  STEP BYZSTEP     EVNLUTION NG STRUCTURE, STEP BY STEP
EVOLUUION PF STRUCTURE,  STEP BYZSTEP     EVNLUTION NG STRUCTURE, STEP BY STEP
```

EVNLUTION NG STRUCTURE, STEP BY STEP   EVOLUTIONZOF STRUBTURE STEP BY STEP
EVNLUTION NG STRUCTURE, STEP BY STEP   EVOLUTIONZOF STRUBTURE STEP BY STEP
EVNLUTION NG STRUCTURE, STEP BY STEP   EVOLUTIONZOF STRUBTURE STEP BY STEP
EVNLUTION NG STRUCTURE, STEP BY STEP   EVOLUTIONZOF STRUBTURE STEP BY STEP
EVNLUTION NG STRUCTURE, STEP BY STEP   EVOLUTIONZOF STRUBTURE STEP BY STEP
EVNLUTION NG STRUCTURE, STEP BY STEP   EVOLUTIONZOF STRUBTURE, STEP BY TTEP
EVNLUTION NG STRUCTURE, STEP BY STEP   EVOLUTIONZOF STRUBTURE, STEP BY TTEP
EVNLUTION NG STRUCTURE, STEP BY STEP   EVOLUTIONZOF STRUBTURE, STEP BY TTEP
EVNLUTION NG STRUCTURE, STEP BY STEP   EVOLUTION OF STRUCTURE STEP BY TTEP
EVOLUTION NG STRUBTURE, STEP BY STEP   EVOLUTION OF STRUCTURE STEP BY TTEP
EVOLUTION NG STRUBTURE, STEP BY STEP   EVOLUTION OF STRUCTURE STEP BY TTEP
EVOLUTION NG STRUBTURE, STEP BY STEP   EVOLUTION OF STRUCTURE STEP BY TTEP
EVOLUTION NG STRUBTURE, STEP BY STEP   EVOLUTION OF STRUCTURE STEP BY TTEP
EVOLUTION NG STRUBTURE, STEP BY STEP   EVOLUTION OF STRUCTURE STEP BY TTEP

EVOLUTION NG STRUBTURE, STEP BY STEP   EVOLUTION OF STRUCTURE STEP BY TTEP
FVOLUTION NF STRUBTURE, STEP BY STEP   EVOLUTION OF STRUCTURE STEP BY TTEP
EVOLUUION NF STRUBTURE, STEP BY STEP   EVOLUTION OF STRUCTURE STEP BY TTEP
EVOLUUION NF STRUBTURE, STEP BY STEP   EVOLUTION OF STRUCTURE STEP BY TTEP
EVOLUUION NF STRUBTURE, STEP BY STEP   EVOLUTION OF STRUCTURE STEP BY TTEP
EVOLUUION NF STRUBTURE, STEP BY STEP   EVOLUTION OF STRUCTURE STEP BY TTEP
EVOLUUION NF STRUBTURE, STEP BY STEP   EVOLUTION OF STRUCTURE STEP BY TTEP
EVOLUUION NF STRUBTURE, STEP BY STEP   EVOLUTION OF STRUCTURE STEP BY TTEP
EVOLUTION NF STRUBTURE, TTEP BY STEP   EVOLUTION OF STRUCTURE STEP BY TTEP
EVOLUTIONZNF STRUBTURE, STEP BY STEP   EVOLUTION OF STRUCTURE STEP BY TTEP
EVOLUTIONZNF STRUBTURE, STEP BY STEP   EVOLUTION OF STRUCTURE STEP BY TTEP
EVOLUTIONZNF STRUBTURE, STEP BY STEP   EVOLUTION OF STRUCTURE STEP BY TTEP
EVOLUTIONZNF STRUBTURE, STEP BY STEP   EVOLUTION OF STRUCTURE STEP BY TTEP
EVOLUTIONZNF STRUBTURE, STEP BY STEP   EVOLUTION OF STRUCTURE STEP BY TTEP

EVOLUTIONZNF STRUBTURE, STEP BY STEP   EVOLUTION OF STRUCTURE STEP BY TTEP
EVOLUTIONZNF STRUBTURE, STEP BY STEP   EVOLUTION OF STRUCTURE STEP BY TTEP
EVOLUTIONZNF STRUBTURE, STEP BY STEP   EVOLUTION OF STRUCTURE STEP BY TTEP
EVOLUTIONZNF STRUBTURE, STEP BY STEP   EVOLUTION OF STRUCTURE STEP BY TTEP
EVOLUTIONZNF STRUBTURE, STEP BY STEP   EVOLUTION OF STRUCTURE STEP BY TTEP
EVOLUTIONZNF STRUBTURE, STEP BY STEP   EVOLUTION OF STRUCTURE STEP BY TTEP
EVOLUTIONZNF STRUBTURE, STEP BY STEP   EVOLUTION OF STRUCTURE STEP BY TTEP
EVOLUTIONZNF STRUBTURE, STEP BY STEP   EVOLUTION OF STRUCTURE STEP BY TTEP
EVOLUTIONZNF STRUBTURE, STEP BY STEP   EVOLUTION OF STRUCTURE STEP BY TTEP
EVOLUTIONZNF STRUBTURE, STEP BY STEP   EVOLUTION OF STRUCTURE, STEP BY TTEP
EVOLUTIONZNF STRUBTURE, STEP BY STEP   EVOLUTION OF STRUCTURE, STEP BY TTEP
EVOLUTIONZNF STRUBTURE, STEP BY STEP   EVOLUTION OF STRUCTURE, STEP BY TTEP
EVOLUTIONZNF STRUBTURE, STEP BY STEP   EVOLUTION OF STRUCTURE, STEP BY TTEP
EVOLUTIONZNF STRUBTURE, STEP BY STEP   EVOLUTION OF STRUCTURE, STEP BY TTEP

EVOLUTIONZNF STRUBTURE, STEP BY STEP   EVOLUTION OF STRUCTURE, STEP BY TTEP
EVOLUTIONZNF STRUBTURE, STEP BY STEP   EVOLUTION OF STRUCTURE, STEP BY TTEP
EVOLUTIONZNF STRUBTURE, STEP BY STEP   EVOLUTION OF STRUCTURE, STEP BY TTEP
EVOLUTIONZNF STRUBTURE, STEP BY STEP   EVOLUTION OF STRUCTURE, STEP BY TTEP
EVOLUTIONZNF STRUBTURE, STEP BY STEP   EVOLUTION OF STRUCTURE, STEP BY TTEP
EVOLUTIONZNF STRUBTURE, STEP BY STEP   EVOLUTION OF STRUCTURE, STEP BY TTEP
EVOLUTIONZNF STRUBTURE, STEP BY STEP   EVOLUTION OF STRUCTURE, STEP BY TTEP
EVOLUTIONZNF STRUBTURE, STEP BY STEP   EVOLUTION OF STRUCTURE, STEP BY TTEP
EVOLUTIONZNF STRUBTURE, STEP BY STEP   EVOLUTION OF STRUCTURE, STEP BY TTEP
EVOLUTIONZOF STRUBTURE STEP BY STEP   EVOLUTION OF STRUCTURE, STEP BY TTEP
EVOLUTIONZOF STRUBTURE STEP BY STEP   EVOLUTION OF STRUCTURE, STEP BY TTEP
EVOLUTIONZOF STRUBTURE STEP BY STEP   EVOLUTJON OF STRUCTURE, STEP BY STEP
EVOLUTIONZOF STRUBTURE STEP BY STEP   EVOLUTJON OF STRUCTURE, STEP BY STEP
EVOLUTIONZOF STRUBTURE STEP BY STEP   EVOLUTJON OF STRUCTURE, STEP BY STEP
EVOLUTIONZOF STRUBTURE STEP BY STEP   EVOLUTION OF STRUCTURE, STEP BY STEP

Figure 1.13
60 individuals per generation, mutation radius: 2, mutation rate: 0.2 (Part 3).

the evolutionary algorithm will reach its goal earlier is shattered quickly. Due to the increased mutation rate, wrong symbols are corrected faster, but correct symbols are mutated at the same increased rate as well. This lengthens the fine-tuning phase considerably. More than 250 generations are needed to eliminate the final small deviations. Figure 1.10(b) and 1.10(c) show that from generation 50 on, only Hamming distances of 0 and 1 prevail. Due to the increased mutation rate, however, new traces frequently appear, which indicate mutations to new, incorrect symbols.

Final comparison of the three-string evolutions

Finally, Figure 1.14 summarizes the evolution experiments shown in Figures 1.5, 1.7, and 1.11. Comparison of their Hamming distances shows that the coarse-tuning phase, accentuated by brackets on the left, is finished after about 40 generations and does not depend on the actual settings for the mutation radius and rate. It is the fine-tuning

Figure 1.14

Comparison of Hamming distances for the three-string evolution experiments in Figures 1.5, 1.7, and 1.11.

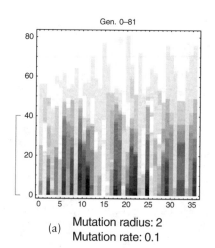

(a) Mutation radius: 2
     Mutation rate: 0.1

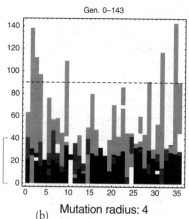

(b) Mutation radius: 4
     Mutation rate: 0.1

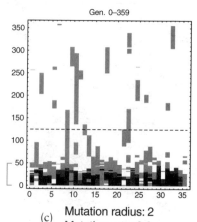

(c) Mutation radius: 2
     Mutation rate: 0.2

phase, where a small number of incorrect symbols still have to be adjusted, that has a major influence on the number of generations needed to successfully finish the evolution task. In this later phase, high mutation rates and a large variation range for mutations turn out to be disadvantageous.

1.4   Simulated mimesis of butterflies

Nature is very creative in developing mechanisms to adapt single organisms or populations of organisms to their environment. An example of evolutionary adaptation is *mimesis*, the ability of certain animals to camouflage themselves by adapting their color and shape to their surroundings. Some grasshoppers, for instance, have the shape of twigs and leaves so that they are hard to identify among their natural environment (Storch and Welsch 1973, p. 58 ff.). This way of camouflaging, which is called *phytomimesis* for mimicking of plant structures, does not result from any intended behavior of the grass- hoppers themselves, in contrast to the way chameleons can instantly adjust their body color to their surroundings. Rather, the grasshop- pers' shape and color result from an evolutionary selection process over many generations. Grasshoppers, which are almost invisible as prey, are more likely to survive and consequently produce more off- spring. Therefore, their specific shape and color traits are passed on to the following generations. Camouflaging is also observed among but- terflies, reptiles, and fishes. In particular, color adaptations to specific environments are rather common in nature. In snow-covered, arctic regions, white-colored animals prevail. Many forest inhabitants have either green or brown body colors, whereas animals living in desert regions are usually sand colored.

Mimesis

Phytomimesis

Camouflage

A classical example of mimesis is the evolution of color adapta- tion among butterflies in response to environmental changes caused by pollution in England during the time of the nineteenth-century industrial revolution (Osche 1972, p. 58; Starr and Taggart 1998, p. 286). Some butterflies, like the peppered moth (*Biston betularia*), which feed and mate at night, had specifically adapted their wing col- oring and texture to lichen-covered tree trunks, on which they pre- ferred to rest during the day. As a result of their mottled-pattern wings and body, with shades ranging from light gray to nearly black, these butterflies were almost perfectly camouflaged on the trunks.

Color adaptations of butterflies

In the middle of the nineteenth century, rising industrialization and subsequent air pollution caused most of the lichens to disappear,

Melanistic moths

and soot particles darkened the tree trunks. Consequently, the butter-flies' wing coloring, perfectly adapted to white backgrounds, didn't provide camouflage at all. Melanistic—dark-colored—moths, which were better adapted to these altered environmental conditions, now took over. Their darker wing color gave them definite selection advantage over their now clearly visible competitors. Eventually, the dark-colored mutants replaced the original light-colored moths. This adaptation of butterfly populations, a typical example of *directional*

Directional selection

selection, caused by a combination of evolutionary mutation and selection, has been observed in about 100 species of butterflies. After many efforts to reduce air pollution, nowadays a reverse adaptation effect can be observed. Since the 1970s, the number of light-colored moths is gradually increasing again (Starr and Taggart 1998, p. 286).

1.4.1 Simulating an evolving butterfly world

The simulations that we describe in the following sections will provide a model to help in understanding evolutionary adaptations of butterfly populations from mimesis effects. Our model describes a simple butter-fly world, which enables us to investigate the interactions of mutations and selections. A similar demonstration of the evolution of mimetic effects is described in Rechenberg (Rechenberg 1973, pp. 83–86).

A simple butterfly world

The butterfly world, the tree trunk, is represented by a list of vec-tors. The particular location of any butterfly on the trunk does not matter, and so we do not have to take any spatial information into account. Each vector represents either a butterfly with a particular wing color or the trunk background. In the following example, we generate 10 entries, each of which is inhabited by a butterfly with a probability of 50%.

```
In[1] := butterflies = createWorld[10,0.5];

In[2] := butterflies // ColumnForm

Out[2] = {1, 0.0730917}
         {0, BGColor}
         {1, 0.77463}
         {0, BGColor}
         {0, BGColor}
         {1, 0.981156}
         {1, 0.83795}
         {1, 0.970903}
```

```
{0, BGColor}
{0, BGColor}
```

Each vector consists of a pair of numbers. The first entry indicates whether the vector describes a butterfly (1) or background (0). The second entry contains the color encoding, either a gray level or a hue value. For all the background vectors, the second entry is BGColor, which refers to a specific value for the background color (e.g., 0.9). We visualize the butterflies by simple polygons on a colored background, where any gray value (GrayLevel) or color hues (Hue) between 0 and 1 are allowed. Here is an example:

In[3] := **Show[GraphicsArray[**
        Map[displayWorldSpot,butterflies]]];

Butterflies in a row

Depending on their wing colors, the butterflies are more or less likely to be visible to a predator, say, a bird. The black and the brighter-colored butterflies are easier to distinguish from the gray background, whereas the gray butterflies can rely more on their camouflage. The probability of being identified by a bird is proportionate to the difference between the wing (color) and background color (BGColor). Hence, a butterfly's "fitness" is the reciprocal,

$$\frac{1}{|\text{color} - \text{BGColor}|},$$

Butterfly fitness

of this color difference. The better a butterfly is camouflaged, that is, the more similar its wing color is to the background color, the greater its probability of survival. However, when we calculate the probability of a moth's being picked by a bird, the simple color difference counts.

```
butterflyMisfitness[color_,BGColor_] :=
    Abs[color - BGColor]
butterflyMisfitness[BGColor,_] := 0
```

A butterfly's "misfitness" as the probability of being picked by a bird

For a background gray level of 0.9, we calculate the following color differences for the butterfly population of the above example:

In[4] := **fits = Map[butterflyMisfitness[#//Last,0.9]&,**
        Cases[butterflies,{1,_}]]

Out[4] = {0.826908, 0.12537, 0.0811558, 0.0620496,
                0.0709028}

Given a fitness-proportionate selection scheme, these "misfitnesses" result in the following selection probabilities:

*Butterfly selection
probabilities*

In[5] := **Map[#/(Plus @@ fits)&,fits]**

Out[5] = {0.708949, 0.107486, 0.0695788, 0.0531981,
                0.0607884}

In[6] := **Plus @@ %**

Out[6] = 1.

According to these values, the first butterfly would be discovered by a bird with a probability of 70%, whereas the survival probability for the second butterfly, at almost 90%, is about three times as high. The remaining three butterflies are even more likely to survive.

To simulate the adaptation of butterfly populations over many generations, with iterated mutations and selections, we define alternate selection and reproduction phases in our butterfly world.

Selection phase

*Selection phase:
butterflies fall prey to a bird*

During the selection phase, a certain number of butterflies are selected with probabilities that are directly proportionate to their misfitness values. The selected butterflies are removed from the population. The selection phase simulates the effect that over a number of iterations (i.e., bird attacks), the better-camouflaged butterflies have a higher probability of survival.

Reproduction phase

*Reproduction phase:
mutated offspring of the
survivors*

During the reproduction phase, a certain number of individuals among the remaining butterflies are randomly chosen and allowed to reproduce one offspring butterfly each—possibly with a slightly different wing color. Only those butterflies that escaped the (bird) selection process have a chance to carry their genes into the next generation.

The following command starts an evolution simulation as described above. The exact details of the parameters that control these simulations will be discussed below.

```
In[7] := butterflyGenerations =
     evolveButterflies[
       WorldWidth → 10,
       ButterflyProbability → 0.8,
       Generations → 20,
       ReductionCreationPortion → 0.5,
       MutationProbability → 0.2,
       MutationRange → 0.5,
       BackgroundHue → 1.0,
       ColoringFunction → GrayLevel
     ];
```

This function visualizes the evolved butterfly populations over 20
iterations of the selection and reproduction phase by an animation
sequence, as illustrated in Figure 1.15. Each row of Figure 1.15 represents the butterfly population after a selection and reproduction
phase. The evolution of camouflage wing colors over 20 generations
(Generations → 20) is depicted from top to bottom. The butterfly
world, the simulated tree trunk, consists of 10 spaces for the butterflies (WorldWidth → 10), where each entry contains a butterfly with
a probability of 80% (ButterflyProbability → 0.8). The trunk
color is set to white (BackgroundHue → 1.0). Since these butterflies
operate in a noncolor world for now, the coloring function is set to
gray level (ColoringFunction → GrayLevel). Selection and
reproduction is performed on 50% of the population (Reduction-
CreationPortion → 0.5). In our example, this means that four of
the eight butterflies are selected, depending on their camouflage capability. From the remaining four butterflies, four offspring are produced, which differ from their parent with a probability of 0.2
(MutationProbability → 0.2). The mutation range determines
the actual interval within which the color can be changed. A mutation
range of 0.5 means that the color value may change by ±0.5 (Muta-
tionRange → 0.5).

Figure 1.15 shows how initially dark-colored butterflies eventually disappear from the population and are substituted for lighter-
colored mutants. Due to mutation effects, darker individuals will still
reappear after 20 generations; however, the majority of butterflies are
well adapted to the white background.

*Control options for
butterfly visualization*

Figure 1.15
Mimesis of butterflies: wing
color adaptation to a white
background. Depicted are
20 iterations of the selection
and reproduction phases.

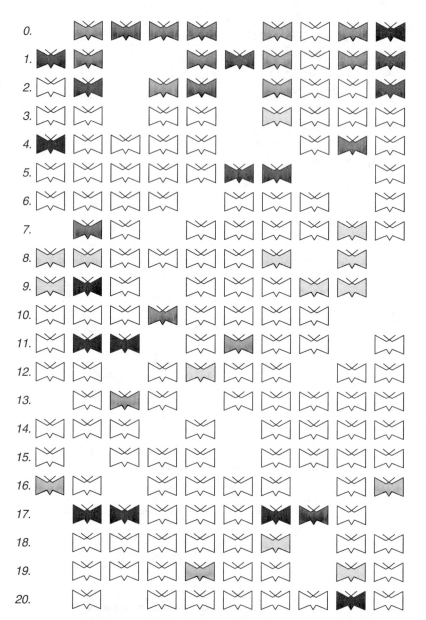

1.4.2 Camouflage on tree trunks

In the following example, we increase the number of butterflies per
population. Figure 1.16 depicts butterflies residing on a tree trunk
of size 4 by 25 "butterfly units." Here is the command to start this
simulation:

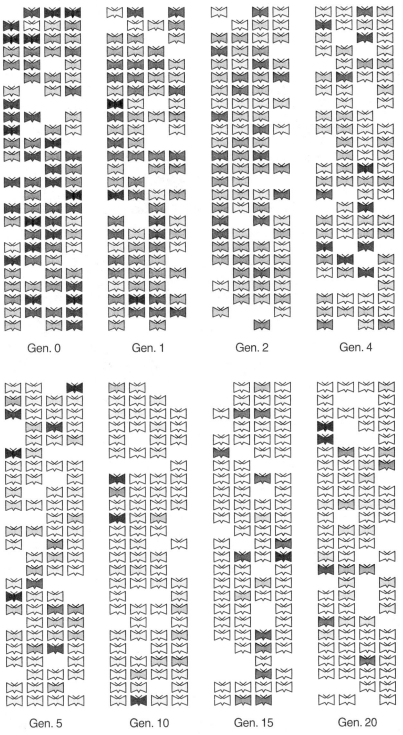

Figure 1.16
Mimesis of butterflies
(Part 1): adaptation of an
initially random-colored
population to a white
background.

Gen. 0   Gen. 1   Gen. 2   Gen. 4

Gen. 5   Gen. 10   Gen. 15   Gen. 20

From random wing colors to
white wings

```
In[8] := butterflies2D =
          evolveButterflies[
            InitialPopulation → {}, WorldWidth → 100,
            ButterflyProbability → 0.8,
            ReductionCreationPortion → 0.5,
            Generations → 20,
            MutationProbability → 0.2, MutationRange → 0.5,
            DisplayMatrixWidth → 4,
            ColoringFunction → GrayLevel,
            BackgroundHue → 1.0];
```

In this example, we simulate a world of size 100 (WorldWidth →
100), where the butterfly density is about 80% (ButterflyProbability → 0.8). We perform 20 iterations of the selection and reproduction phase (Generations → 20). The background color is again
set to white, which corresponds to a gray level of 1.0 (BackgroundHue → 1.0). The option InitialPopulation → {} starts
the simulation from a randomly generated population. The width of
the trunk in the resulting animated graphics is set by Display-
MatrixWidth. We can see from the graphics in Figure 1.16 that most
of the butterflies develop brighter color within only four generations.
This trend continues over the next generations until, in generation 20,
the vast majority of butterflies have evolved white wings.

   Now we will simulate the actual mimesis. The bright butterflies
evolved in Figure 1.16 will be used as the initial population in the following experiment, which is illustrated in Figure 1.17.

Mimesis:
from white to gray

```
In[9] := butterflies2D =
          evolveButterflies[
            InitialPopulation → Last[butterflies2D],
            WorldWidth → 100, ButterflyProbability → 0.8,
            ReductionCreationPortion → 0.5,
            Generations → 20,
            MutationProbability → 0.2, MutationRange → 0.5,
            DisplayMatrixWidth → 4,
            ColoringFunction → GrayLevel,
            BackgroundHue → 0.8
          ];
```

For this evolution run, the control parameter settings differ only in
initial population and background color. The evolution starts with the

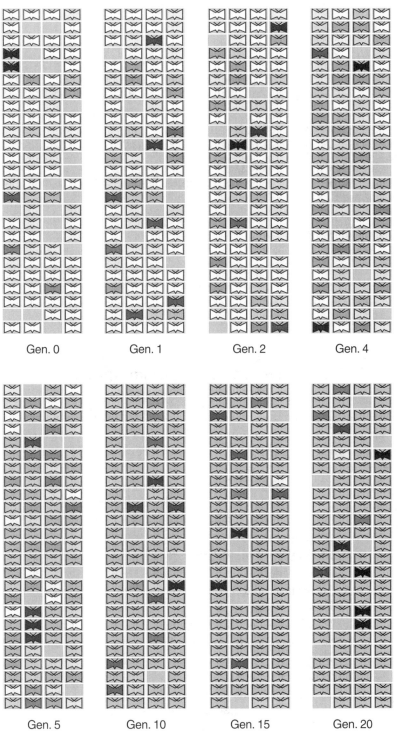

Figure 1.17
Mimesis of butterflies (Part 2): adaptation of the white population of Figure 1.16 to a gray background.

Gen. 0   Gen. 1   Gen. 2   Gen. 4

Gen. 5   Gen. 10   Gen. 15   Gen. 20

last population evolved in the previous experiment (`InitialPopu-`
`lation` → `Last[butterflies2D]`). The background color is set
to a light gray (`BackgroundHue` → `0.8`).

Figure 1.17 shows that a similar adaptation effect results. After
five iterations, the brighter butterflies constitute only a minority
within the population. After 10 generations, almost no bright individuals are represented. In generation 20, the vast majority of butterflies
are again well camouflaged.

Figure 1.18 illustrates the continued adaptation of this population
after the background is set to an even darker color (`BackgroundHue`
→ `0.4`). After 20 generations, the butterflies have adapted to this new
environment.

How many iterations might it take to readapt this population to a
plain white background? Figure 1.19 shows the results of this final
simulation, with the background color now reset to white (`Back-`
`groundHue` → `1.0`). The readaptation does not take much longer.
After 10 generations, most butterflies have white wings. Finally, at
generation 20, almost all the butterflies are perfectly adapted to a
white background.

1.5   Evolutionary creativity—biomorphs

In the previous two example projects, we have simulated evolution as
a goal-oriented process. In Section 1.3 we started with a set of randomly generated strings, hoping that iterated selection and variation
would evolve a predefined objective sentence. We showed that this is
possible, using a simple selection-mutation procedure. Whenever an
exact copy of the objective string shows up, the evolutionary algo-

The objective of evolution   rithm has reached its goal. However, this is not the way evolution
works in nature. In natural evolution there is no a priori objective that
evolution is heading to.

In the second example on butterfly mimesis in Section 1.4, the
implicit goal is to adapt wing-coloring genes so that the butterflies are
camouflaged against a particular background. In principle, this adaptation process is not much different from the character evolution
example. The distance between the wing color and a predefined (background) color must be minimized. If a large majority of butterflies are
well camouflaged, the evolutionary process is considered successful.

Natural evolution defines implicit goals by survival. Evolutionary
processes in nature are open-ended and have no explicit goal. Evolution provides the mechanisms to adapt organisms to their environment. As organisms in turn change the environment by their

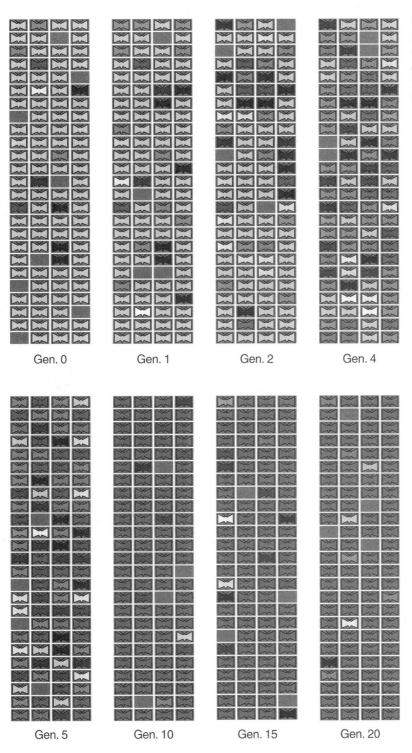

Figure 1.18
Mimesis of butterflies (Part 3): adaptation of the gray population of Figure 1.17 to a dark gray background.

Figure 1.19
Mimesis of butterflies
(Part 4): adaptation of the
dark gray population of
Figure 1.18 to a white
background (compare
Figure 1.16).

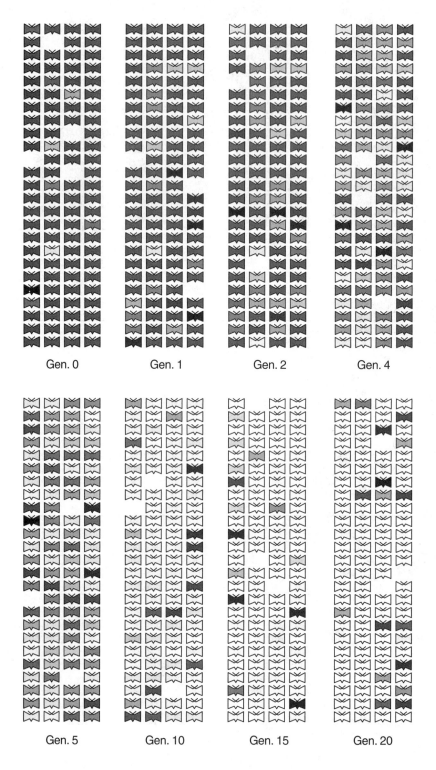

interactions, this results in open-ended feedback processes. In this section, we illustrate open-ended evolution by a simple example of how
to evolve recursive figures, known as biomorphs. We will act the part
of breeder. We use evolution to give us a range of possible paths to follow, however, without being able to tell the outcome of our evolution
experiments. The biomorph examples will also show evolution's
potential for creativity and innovation.

Interactive design by evolution

1.5.1   Biomorphs and their genes

In his book *The Blind Watchmaker* the evolutionary biologist Richard
Dawkins describes computer experiments of interactive evolution on
the basis of two-dimensional, treelike, recursive sketch figures, known
as biomorphs (Dawkins 1986; Dawkins 1989). Dawkins borrowed
this term from his colleague Desmond Morris, who coined the term
biomorphs for the animal-like figures he painted.

Interactive evolution

We refer to treelike sketch figures, as depicted in Figure 1.21, as
biomorphs. All these line drawings have a recursive structure. A certain number of branches are growing from the bottom, which fork in
a regular manner on the next-higher levels. The number of these
recursion levels is determined by a parameter, contained in the *developmental genes* of a biomorph. The biomorph structure is encoded by
a number vector (Figure 1.20). Besides the recursion depth, a number
of other morphogenetic parameters are part of the biomorph genome:
the number and the length of the branches, their thickness and
branching angle, and the color of the branches. All parameters are
variable for each recursion depth, as the actual genome representation
in Figure 1.20 explains. The maximum recursion depth is limited to 4.
Therefore, the final structure of a biomorph is described by a number
vector of length $21 = 1 + 4 \times 5$. The first gene determines the actually
used recursion depth, then five genes follow for each recursion level.

Biomorphs

Developmental genes

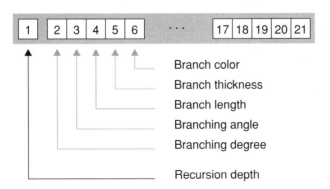

Figure 1.20
Structure of a biomorph genome.

Figure 1.21
A biomorph and a selection
of possible mutant forms.

Base genome:

3 2 3 2 4 7 2 2 2 4 7 2 2 2 4 7 2 2 2 4 7

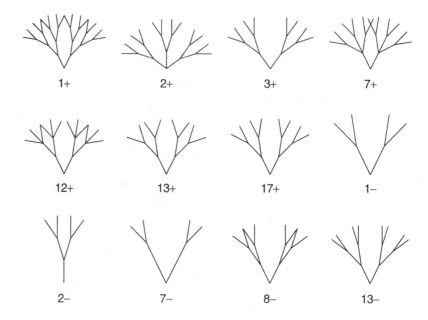

At the top of Figure 1.21, a biomorph example and its developmental genes are depicted. Let us take a closer look at this genome. The first gene, specifying the maximum recursion level, is set to 3, which means that from the following 20 genes, only the first 15 are used. The remaining genes, 17 through 21, are activated only if the first gene mutates to a 4; then these fourth-level gene settings are included as well.

1.5.2 Variations on biomorphs

Apart from the parental biomorph at the top of Figure 1.21, the other structures represent mutants (offspring), where only one gene is mutated by either a one increment or one decrement on the parent genome. The labeling 2+, for instance, means that the second gene has been mutated from 2 to 3, which leads to an additional, third branch on the first recursion level.

Figure 1.21 gives a good example of the structural effects resulting from simple point mutations. Some mutants are considerably different from the top structure (examples: 2+, 2−, 7−); others differ only marginally from their parent (examples: 3+, 13+). Even a neutral mutation is represented (example: 17+).

How many variants of biomorphs can be generated? We have to specify the parameter range for each gene. The range is not the same for all genes since we have to take into account different resolutions for the parameters. For example, the branching angles may in principle take on values between 0 and 360 degrees, whereas the recursion depth varies only between smaller numbers, such as between 1 and 4. The branching genes 2, 7, 12, and 17 can take on values from 1 to 5. All other genes may have integer values between 1 and 10. Gene 3, the branching angle, is scaled by the factor 18, resulting in angles between 18 and 180 degrees. The first gene, controlling recursion depth, is restricted to integers from 1 to 4.

Biomorph variants

In total, $4 \times 5^4 \times 10^{16} = 2.5 \times 10^{19}$ different biomorph genomes can be generated. We will be able to check and evolve only a few biomorphs from this incredibly large set of possible gene combinations.

The biomorph search space

1.5.3   Interactive evolution of biomorphs

Let us start a short exploration into the world of biomorphs and see what new and unexpected structures we discover. We start with the biomorph depicted at the upper left in Figure 1.22. Based on the genome of this biomorph, we generate 21 mutants, which are shown to its right. Each mutant is the result of a single point mutation, as described in Figure 1.21. Therefore, each mutant differs from the original genome only by ±1 in a single gene.

From this population of biomorphs, we select one that we want to act as the parental biomorph of the following generation. In Figures 1.22 through 1.24, the selected biomorphs are marked by a small cross. In this way we step from generation to generation, by interactive selection on a newly generated pool of mutants originating from the previously selected biomorph. Hence, we are breeding biomorphs by iterated mutation and selection. We are optimizing them toward traits determined by our subjective selection, with mutations providing us with a selection pool. Figures 1.23 and 1.24 illustrate how to evolve a simple biomorph into surprisingly complex and delicately built structures. Figure 1.25 compares some of the evolved biomorphs, showing a surprising increase in the complexity of their

Interactive breeding

Figure 1.22
Breeding of biomorphs
(Part 1).

Gen. 0

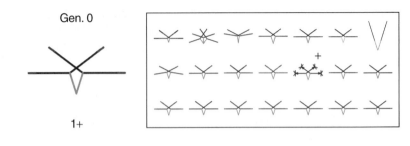

1+

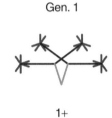

Gen. 1

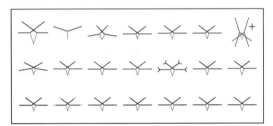

1+

Gen. 2

1+

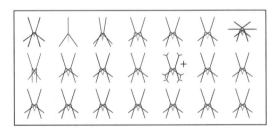

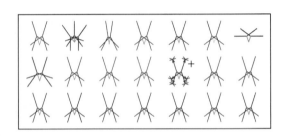

Gen. 3

1+

Gen. 4

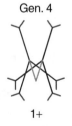

1+

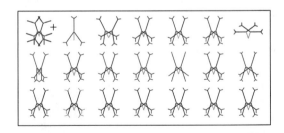

Gen. 5

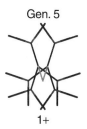

1+

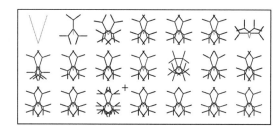

Figure 1.23
Breeding of biomorphs
(Part 2).

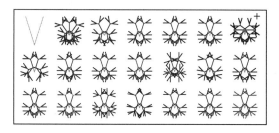

Gen. 6

1+

Gen. 7

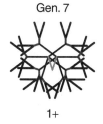

1+

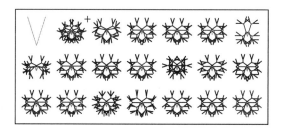

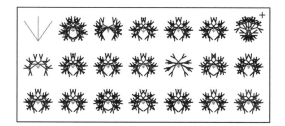

Gen. 9

1+

Gen. 10

1+

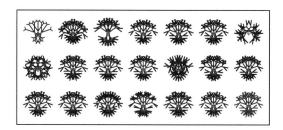

Figure 1.24
Breeding of biomorphs
(Part 3).

Gen. 12

1+

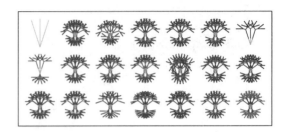

Gen. 14

1+

Gen. 16

1+

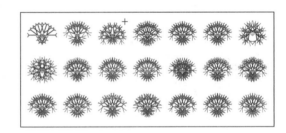

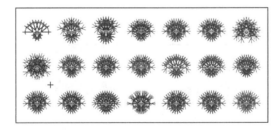

Gen. 17

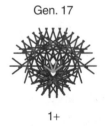

1+

Gen. 18

1+

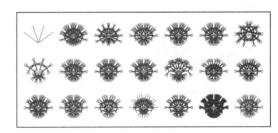

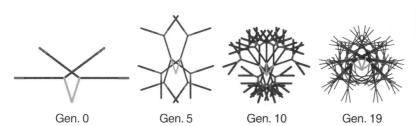

Figure 1.25
Evolved biomorphs.

| Gen. 0 | Gen. 5 | Gen. 10 | Gen. 19 |

structures in the course of the evolutionary process. The last bio-morph is a mutant of generation 18.

This breeding could continue almost forever, since there is no pre-defined goal to reach, unlike the previous evolution examples in Sections 1.3 and 1.4. Here the selection is always subjective and interactive; the selection criteria may even change from generation to generation. The incredible number of possible gene combinations provides us with an enormous variety of forms to be discovered. Color Plate 1 shows randomly generated biomorphs as well as biomorphs evolved by interactive selection and mutation. An impressive collection of colored biomorphs can also be found in *Climbing Mount Improbable* (Dawkins 1996).

1.6   Bibliographical notes

Evolution

Charles Darwin's landmark book *The Origin of Species* (1859), which describes his theory of evolution, is still worth reading. Darwin's ideas still provide the basis for today's theories of evolution. Many reprinted versions of Darwin's original work are available (e.g., Darwin 1996).

In *The Evolution of Complexity*, John Tyler Bonner discusses the role of complexity in living organisms and their evolution by means of natural selection (Bonner 1988).

Brian Goodwin suggests in *How the Leopard Changed Its Spots* that Darwinian evolution theory, that is, random mutations and natural selection, has to be replaced, or at least extended, by theories of complexity as an inherent and emergent quality of life (Goodwin 1994). In this context, Per Bak's book *How Nature Works*, explaining self-organizing complex systems and self-organized criticality, is also enlightening (Bak 1996).

The Origin of Species

The Evolution of Complexity

How the Leopard Changed Its Spots

How Nature Works

Niles Eldredge, in *The Pattern of Evolution*, takes a historical perspective on the workings between biological evolution and the physical world of "matter in motion" (Eldredge 1998).

A manifold perspective of the role of evolution not only in biology but in art, history, society, culture, and the evolution of the universe is provided in *Evolution: Society, Science and the Universe* (Fabian 1998).

Evolution theory

John Maynard Smith's *The Theory of Evolution* (1993) is a classic on this subject.

The Discovery of Evolution, by David Young, gives an illustrative overview of evolution at work (Young 1992).

A recommended textbook on evolution is Mark Ridley's *Evolution*, which also includes a very well-designed tutorial CD, including experiments, classic texts, and a glossary of evolutionary terms (Ridley 1996).

Mark Ridley edited a second book, also titled *Evolution*, which discusses a wide range of areas in evolutionary biology, including the modern synthesis of evolution theories, the role of selection, molecular evolution, adaptation to biodiversity, macroevolution, and the evolution of humans, society, culture, and philosophy (Ridley 1997).

Evolutionary design

Richard Dawkins is one of the most prominent promoters of Darwinian evolution. The string evolution experiments in Section 1.3 and the breeding of biomorphs in Section 1.5 are both adapted from *The Blind Watchmaker* (1986). Dawkins's first book, *The Selfish Gene*, which had a great influence on the understanding of evolutionary and developmental processes, is still, after almost 25 years, definitely worth reading (1976). I would also highly recommend his latest books: *Climbing Mount Improbable* (1996) and *Unweaving the Rainbow* (1998).

An up-to-date overview of computational approaches to design problems, ranging from engineering to art, computer programming, and electronic circuit synthesis, is provided in *Evolutionary Design by Computers* (Bentley 1999).

In *Evolutionary Art and Computers*, Stephen Todd and William Latham (1992) describe their artistic and algorithmic approach to the art of growing complex forms by evolutionary processes on a computer. Some parts of their work are also described in *Evolutionary Design by Computers* (Bentley 1999).

Evolutionary Art and Computers

Biomimicry

How today's innovations are more and more inspired by nature through "rediscovering life's best ideas" is reported in Janine Benyus's book *Biomimicry* (1997).

Biomimicry

Evolutionary Computation

Part I

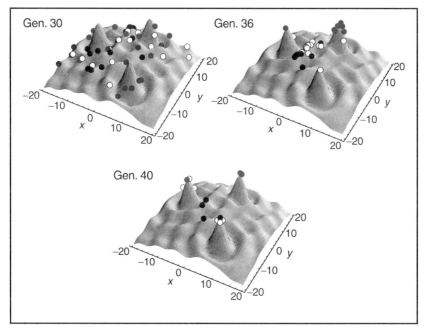

Gen. 30

Gen. 36

Gen. 40

2 Evolutionary Algorithms for Optimization

*Natural selection is the process by which the forms of organisms in a population that are best adapted to the environment increase in frequency relative to less well adapted forms over a number of generations. Charles Darwin ... was the first to see that this process can explain both **evolution** and **adaptation**.*

Ridley 1996

In this chapter, we introduce the basic principles of evolutionary algorithms, which we consider specific examples of adaptive systems. A formal representation scheme of evolving systems will provide us with the main concepts of evolutionary optimization. First, in Sections 2.1 and 2.2, we discuss a formalism to model general adaptive systems. In Section 2.3, we apply this model to Darwinian evolution, which leads us to a formulation of a general algorithmic scheme for evolutionary optimization. An example of how to use genetic algorithms, a specific class of evolutionary algorithms, for parameter optimization on a multimodal function, illustrates the basic working scheme of evolutionary optimization (Jacob 1999b).

2.1 A simplified formal model of evolution

In 1859 Charles Darwin formulated a model for explaining evolutionary processes in nature (Darwin 1859). His theory of evolution can be characterized by the following principles (Lewontin 1970; Wieser 1994):

❏ *Variability:* The genotypical population structures are heterogeneous. This means that individual phenotypes express different traits. Each individual is unique. The diversity of a

Heterogeneity of traits

population constitutes an essential precondition for the adaptability of a population to its environment.

Differential fitness

❑ *Differential fitness:* Populations evolve by the reproduction of their individuals over many generations. The reproduction rate of each phenotype, the actual organism, is determined by both the specific conditions of the environment and the organism's ability to survive and produce offspring.

Inheritance, mutation, recombination

❑ *Fitness inheritance:* The fitnesses of the phenotypes are transferred from the parents to their offspring. The copying of the genetic information (on the DNA), however, is not perfect—mutations result in slight copying errors. In addition, in sexual reproduction the father's and mother's genetic information (genotypes) merge. Hence, these variations lead to offspring with differentially different traits.

Any system that obeys these general principles will adapt to a phenotypical environment—independent of how variation occurs, which mechanisms of inheritance control the transfer of traits between generations, or what kind of selection is in effect.

The evolution of populations in nature can be modeled as a two-level process of *phenotypical selection* and *genotypical variation.* Figure 2.1 illustrates the schematic separation into an abstract phenotypical feature space E and space S of genotypical, variable structures. Each point in S represents a specific gene pool, the collection of all genetic information within a population. Any point in E is a representative of a population of individuals with specifically expressed traits. Populations may differ in their numbers of individuals and in the set of expressed features.

Phenotypical selection, genotypical variation

Figure 2.1
Evolution of populations in genotype and phenotype space.

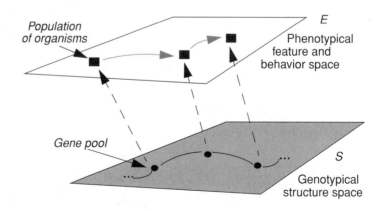

The separation of selection and variation, and the interaction between these two spaces, can be formally described as follows (Figure 2.2):

Expression: The expression of the individuals of a gene pool (1) results in a population of organisms (2).

Evaluation and selection: Depending on the fitness of the organisms, selection results in a specific, fitness-dependent distribution of the individuals (the "survivors") for the next generation (3).

Variation: New phenotypical variants are created on the level of the genotypes (4). Those individuals that are capable of reproduction pass on their genetic information to their offspring. Through mutations and recombinations the constitution of the gene pool changes (5), the phenotypical interpretation of which finally constitutes the offspring population (6).

The described scheme illustrates the feedback loop between the genotypical and phenotypical levels of evolution. In nature, the phenotypical selection of individuals occurs separate from the variation mechanisms on the genotypes. Inheritable changes of phenotypical features are only accessible via the one-way road of genotypes—going in the other direction, from phenotype to genotype, is precluded by nature. Features that an individual acquires during its lifetime (e.g., by

Phenotype and genotype

One-way road of genotype

Figure 2.2

Selection and variation: evolution of populations as a two-level process of phenotypical selection (Sel_p) and genotypical variation (Var_g).

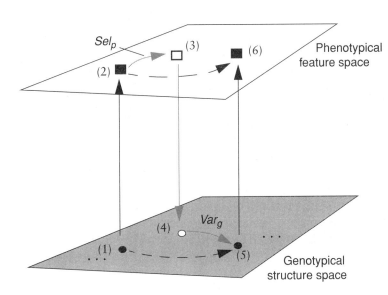

learning) have no effect on the genotype and so are not inheritable. However, the ability to learn is inheritable.

The described scheme is a first step toward a general model of evolutionary processes from the viewpoint of populations of organisms. This model will also provide the basis for evolutionary algorithms used to solve optimization processes, which we get to know as *genetic algorithms* in Chapter 3 and *evolution strategies* in Chapter 4.

Before we demonstrate specific examples of evolutionary algorithms as function optimizers, we look at evolutionary and reproductive mechanisms in the more general context of adaptive systems.

2.2 Optimization through adaptive structures

Evolution, in the form of iterated selection and variation, is nature's main mechanism to adapt individuals to specific environmental niches. Hence, evolution always coincides with *adaptation* as a process of progressive change of structures (in a general sense), which results in improved behavior when an individual interacts with an environment. Adaptive feedback processes in essence consist of the following two components (cf. Holland 1975 and Holland 1992a):

Adaptation

"Phenotype"

Environment: Constraints are set by an environment in which adaptive components are embedded, interact with one another and the environment, and are eventually evaluated in response to their behavior.

"Genotype"

Structures as adaptive components: The actual structures, which are variable and are considered to be separate from the environment, can come in many different forms. On a natural scale, the modifiable units may be chains of proteins, clusters of neurons or other cells, groups of interacting organisms, or whole ecosystems. On a mathematical scale, structures may range from simple vectors of numbers, polynomials, or analytic functions to computer programs and data structures.

Dualism of individuals

The ability to adapt, that is, the generation of sets of modifiable structures, is *the* precondition for adjustment to specific environmental constraints. In natural evolution, the separation of the environment from the variable structure set is reflected in the dualism of phenotypes and genotypes. The environment represents the expressed organisms in their ecological niches, whereas the gene pool is modeled by the structures.

2.2.1 Main components of adaptive systems

To explain the performance of an evolutionary adaptive system, we will refer to the following definitions (cf. Holland 1992a, p. 22 ff., and Figure 2.3):

Environment, *E*: The environment in which the system performs adaptation.

Components of an adaptive system

Structures, *S*: A finite set of structures, acting as the genotypes. Their phenotypes $\pi(S)$, with $\pi: S \to E$, interact with the environment.

Operators, Ω: A finite set of operators for structure modification

$$\Omega = \{\omega : S^m \to S^n\} \text{ with } m, n \in \{1, \ldots, |S|\}.$$

An operator ω maps m structures into a set of n possibly modified structures.

Evaluation function, μ_E: For each structure $s \in S$, the evaluation function returns a fitness value $\mu_E(s)$. The fitness is calculated as a reaction of the environment with the phenotypical interpretation $\pi(s)$ of the structure. The signals from the environment in response to the phenotype's performance are denoted by $\varphi(\pi(s)) \in I_E$.

Adaptation algorithm, α: An algorithm that determines how the structures in S are modified by the operators $\omega \in \Omega$ with respect to the received environmental signals I_E.

Many systems can be modeled according to these definitions. Neural networks, for example, receive their signals from an external environment. The neurons must react to these inputs, possibly adapt their connection structure (i.e., perform learning), and generate output signals in response. The neurons constitute the structures. The evaluation function is determined by the environmental feedback. Adaptations are accomplished by modifications of the connection structure or by variation of synaptic potentials. A similar scheme can be outlined for economic systems, search strategies for games, or gene regulation systems (see Holland 1992a, Chapter 3). The same general principles apply to any adaptive system.

Example: neural networks

2.2.2 Performing adaptation steps

For this simple model, we consider adaptation as a discrete, step-by-step process; that is, we assume that the system state can be observed only at times $t, t + 1, t + 2, \ldots$. A single adaptation step from a structure $s(t)$ to a modified structure $s(t + 1)$ is described as follows (Figure 2.3):

Adaptation step
$s(t) \to s(t + 1)$

Step 1. **Expression:** A structure $s(t) \in S$ is transformed into its phenotypical representation $p(t) = \pi(s(t))$, using the genotype-phenotype mapping $\pi \colon S \to E$.

Step 2. **Interaction with the environment:** In response to the performance of $p(t)$, the environment returns a set of signals $I_E(t)$. This signal set is assumed to contain specific signals referring to $p(t)$. We denote these p-related signals by $\varphi_E(p(t)) = I_{E,p}(t) \in I_E(t)$.

Step 3. **Evaluation:** The evaluation function μ_E, which is defined as $\mu_E(s(t)) = \mu_E(p(t), \varphi_E(p(t)))$, takes both the phenotype $p(t)$ and the p-specific signals into account. The structure $s(t)$ is implicitly evaluated because $p(t) = \pi(s(t))$.

Figure 2.3
Modeling adaptive systems:
a single adaptation step.

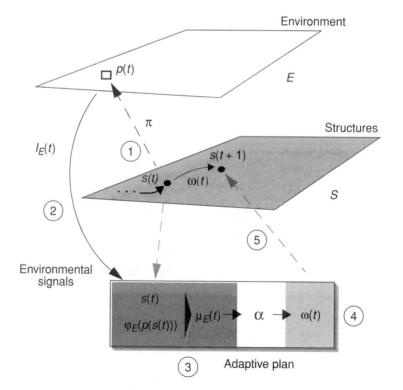

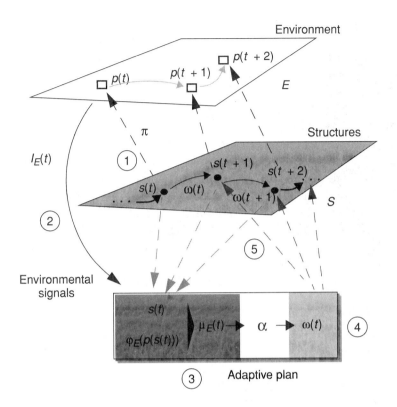

Figure 2.4
Modeling adaptive systems: steps of an adaptation sequence.

Step 4.   **Selection:** Depending on the fitness $\mu_E(s(t))$, the adaptation plan α selects an operator $\omega \in \Omega$ in order to modify the structure $s(t)$.

Step 5.   **Variation:** Applying ω to $s(t)$ usually leads to a modified structure $s(t+1) = \omega(s(t))$.

Applying this adaptation cycle iteratively results in an evolution path, both in feature and structure space, as illustrated in Figure 2.4.

In Figure 2.4, note that the distances between the points along the paths in feature (E) and structure (S) space are not necessarily equidistant. In the case of a highly nonlinear mapping between genotypical structures and phenotypical features, there is not even a close correspondence between the step sizes in both spaces. The genotype-phenotype mappings from DNA to a developed organism is an example of such a nonlinear mapping.

2.3   A general evolutionary algorithm scheme

The adaptation cycle illustrated in Figures 2.3 and 2.4 is applicable both to a single individual producing offspring and a population as a

Reproductive plan

meta-individual. The adaptive structure is either a single genotype or a gene pool as a set of evolving structures. In any case, the structural adaptations are accomplished by an interplay of selections and mutations. The adaptive plan α turns into a *reproductive plan*. The population adapts to environmental constraints by reproduction; that is, its individuals are selected for producing mutated offspring depending on their fitnesses.

The reproductive plan α relies on the gene pool as a finite set $G \in S$ of structures. Each genome $g \in G$ can be mapped into a corresponding phenotype $p \in P \subset E$. In this case, the phenotypical population P is considered to be a subset of the environment E, since for each individual all the other members of the population make up the environment (for an example, see Section 11.5, on coevolution). Consequently, we can set up the following general scheme for evolutionary algorithms, as shown in Figure 2.5. Starting from an initial pool of structures $G(t)$, for each time step t the reproductive plan α composes

Gene pool sequences

a usually modified gene pool $G(t + 1)$. Its interpreted form $P(t + 1) = \pi(G(t + 1))$ represents the offspring population. Repeating this cycle over a number of generations results in an evolving population $P(t + 1), P(t + 2), \ldots$ with an analogous gene pool sequence $G(t + 1), G(t + 2), \ldots$. New generations are produced until a termination criterion $\tau(t, G(t), P(t), \mu_E(P(t)))$ is satisfied. This termination condition takes into account the number of generations, the current structure, their phenotypical interpretations, and their fitnesses. The evolutionary optimization algorithms, which we discuss in the following chapters (*genetic algorithms* in Chapter 3 and *evolution strategies* in Chapter 4), quit the population-generating loop if a maximum number of generations is reached or an individual with a predefined optimal fitness is evolved.

2.3.1   Optimization on multimodal functions

Solving optimization problems can be considered the search for "highest points" in a multidimensional parameter space. These parameter spaces can be envisioned as more or less complex mountainous regions, as depicted in Figure 2.6 for a two-dimensional parameter space. Search spaces characterized by multiple maxima are denoted as *multimodal*.

Climbing in the fog

Now imagine a mountaineer who intends to climb the highest peak of an unexplored area. Our climber must operate under two constraints. First, there is no global information (a detailed map, for

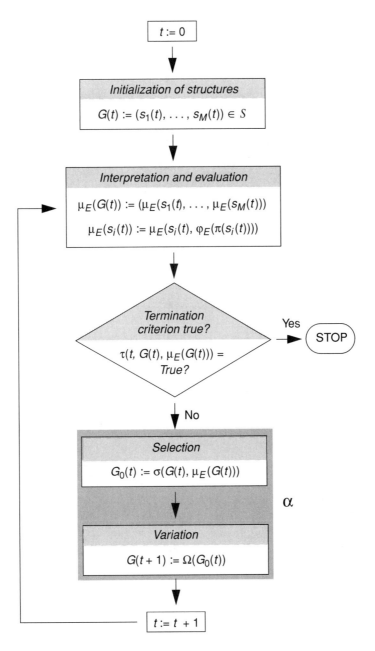

Figure 2.5
Algorithmic scheme of evolution as a reproductive plan.

instance) about the shape of the landscape. Second, fog prevents any long-distance visual information, so that the mountaineer can rely only on local information in his close vicinity. Under these conditions, what is a good strategy to discover the highest peak?

Figure 2.6
Example of a multimodal
search space.

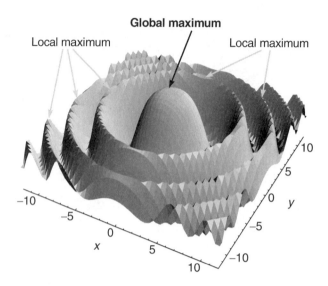

This scenario is comparable to situations when real-world optimization problems must be solved. Often it is not known whether a global maximum exists. Only seldom is any information about the structure of the search space available in advance, apart from the fact that multidimensional spaces (for more than two variables) are difficult to analyze and visualize in particular.

How should our mountaineer proceed if he wants to find the highest-possible peak starting from a randomly chosen location? A simple strategy would be to follow the direction of steepest ascent, *Gradient strategy* which corresponds to a *gradient-following strategy*. This will lead upward, step by step, until the top of a local peak is reached. Starting at location 1 in Figure 2.7, this strategy would eventually lead to location 2. Here the mountaineer takes note of the accomplished height and exact position. He does not know, however, whether he has already discovered the global maximum, so he must be willing to step down again in order to start another search from a nearby valley, for example, from location 3. With some more effort and a lot of patience, the global, highest peak will eventually be discovered. The success of this enterprise would obviously very much depend on the chosen starting position, since any point around location 3 is definitely more advantageous than positions in the vicinity of location 4, for example.

A single climber would have a hard time accomplishing this task. *A team of mountaineers* A team or several groups of mountaineers, who could communicate about their heights and positions, would have a much better chance of

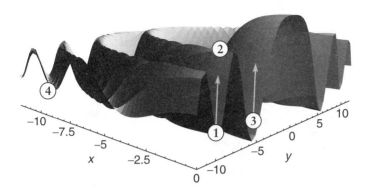

Figure 2.7
Gradient strategies in a multimodal search space.

discovering the global peak. Now the mechanisms of evolution come into play. We let a population of climbers perform the search. Each climber's height is interpreted as his fitness. Selection has to take place to focus the subsequent search on more promising regions. One selection strategy could be as follows: the higher an individual has climbed, the more likely he is to participate in the next "expedition"; that is, generation. The mountaineers' movements are determined by random variation of their current positions.

Local maxima make it difficult to find paths leading to global optima. This is especially true if the search space turns out to be a very rugged landscape, as in Figure 2.8. Using traditional search algorithms, these spaces are particularly difficult to cope with (cf. Rechenberg 1994b). For a gradient strategy, for example, the gradient for each visited search point must be computable. The search often converges toward local maxima. The following parameter optimization example illustrates why these particular problems do not necessarily occur with evolutionary algorithms.

2.3.2   Example optimization with genetic algorithms

We use genetic algorithms to demonstrate how evolution-based algorithms can solve optimization problems (Goldberg 1989; Holland 1992a). Since we explain only the basic concepts here, we will not go into too many details of the applied algorithms, as the two major classes of evolutionary algorithms—genetic algorithms and evolution strategies—are covered in depth in Chapters 3 and 4, respectively.

The optimization task is to find the global optimum of a two-dimensional, multimodal *objective function* (cf. Figure 2.6). In general, for an optimization of k parameters the objective function takes the form

Figure 2.8

Two views of a noisy
multimodal objective
function.

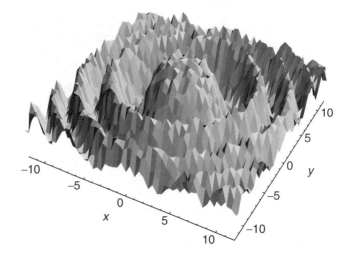

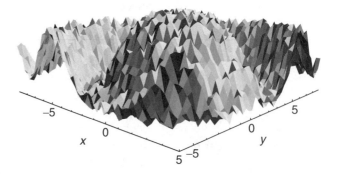

Objective function

$$f : M \to \Re, \text{ with } M = M_1 \times \ldots \times M_k.$$

$\Re$ denotes the set of real numbers. Usually the parameters are either real numbers, $M_i = \Re$, $1 \leq i \leq k$, or integers. We have to find a set of parameters $x^{\mathrm{opt}} = (x_1^{\mathrm{opt}}, \ldots, x_k^{\mathrm{opt}}) \in M$ such that the following holds:

Global maximum

$$\forall x = (x_1, \ldots, x_k) \in M : f(x) \leq f(x^{\mathrm{opt}}) = f^{\mathrm{opt}}.$$

Here f^{opt} is the global maximum at location x^{opt}. Searching for a global maximum becomes more difficult in the presence of local optima; that is, points $\hat{x}$ with

Local maxima

$$(\exists \varepsilon > 0, \forall x \in M) : \|x - \hat{x}\| < \varepsilon \Rightarrow f(\hat{x}) \geq f(x),$$

where $\|\ldots\|$ denotes the Euclidean vector norm. In particular, nonlinear, multimodal functions, as discussed in Section 2.3.1, consist of a large number of local optima. If the search space has to be constrained to specific regions, these areas can be defined by a set of q condition functions $g_j(x)$: $M_1 \times \ldots \times M_n \to \Re$ such that the actual search space M is characterized as

$$M = \{x \in M_1 \times \ldots \times M_n \mid g_j(x) \geq 0, \forall j \in \{1, \ldots, q\}\}.$$

Constrained optimization

M consists of all points x with nonnegative conditions. Any optimization can either be viewed as a *minimization* or *maximization* problem, with $\max\{f(x)\} = -\min\{-f(x)\}$. In this example, we consider parameter optimization as a maximization problem.

Minimization vs. maximization

A multimodal objective function

Let us look at the two-dimensional objective function in Figure 2.9, which has the following analytical description:

$$f(x, y) = \left(1.2 \ + \frac{\mathrm{Cos}\left(0.1 \cdot \left(x^2 + y^2\right)\right)}{1 + 0.01 \cdot \left(x^2 + y^2\right)} \right)^{-1}.$$

Objective function example

This is a typical multimodal function with a large number of local optima. The actual position of the global maximum is at coordinates $(x^{\mathrm{opt}}, y^{\mathrm{opt}}) = (0, 0)$ with a value of $f(0, 0) = 2.2 = f^{\mathrm{opt}}$. We constrain the search space to the subspace $M \subset \Re^2$ by

$$M = \{(x, y) \in \Re^2 \mid (g(x, y) \geq 0)\},$$

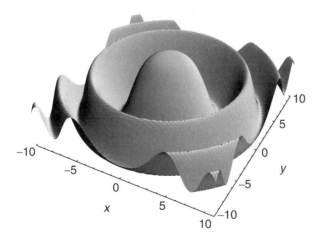

Figure 2.9
Example of a two-dimensional, multimodal objective function.

where the condition function is defined as

$$g(x, y) = \begin{cases} +1 & (\text{if } |x| \leq 10 \wedge |y| \leq 10), \\ -1 & \text{otherwise}. \end{cases}$$

This function defines the environment that, for each coordinate (x, y) within the constrained search space, returns a value $f(x, y)$, interpreted as the phenotype fitness. Thus, the phenotypical level is clearly defined. What about the genotypical level of modifiable structures? The evolvable structures have to encode two parameters, the x and y coordinates. In the following section we will discuss an example encoding and associated variation operators.

Encoding and decoding of the parameters

Genetic algorithms do not use the representation of the parameter space directly. Rather, following nature's way of encoding genetic information on the DNA double helix, genetic algorithms use an encoding scheme based on a discrete alphabet of symbols. The modifi-
Binary strings   able structures, the genotypes, are represented as *binary strings*, consisting of sequences of 0s and 1s. For our two-parameter example, a binary string with $k = k_x + k_y$ elements is partitioned into two logical segments of lengths k_x and k_y. Each segment is interpreted as the binary representation of the x and y coordinates, respectively. This means the genotypical structures have the following bit string form:

Bit-string encoding
$$s = \left(s_x, s_y\right) = \left(s_{x, 1}, \ldots, s_{x, k_x}, s_{y, 1}, \ldots, s_{y, k_y}\right).$$

For our symmetric test function we may assume identical resolutions in both x and y directions, such that $k_x = k_y$ holds. As an example, a possible genotype for $k_x = k_y = 5$ is

$$s = (0, 1, 1, 0, 0, 1, 0, 1, 1, 1),$$

where the encoding x-y coordinate segments are

$$s_x = (0, 1, 1, 0, 0) \text{ and } s_y = (1, 0, 1, 1, 1).$$

In order to interpret these strings, they must be mapped to their phenotypical representation of real numbers. The interval for each coor-
Decoding   dinate is constrained so that the *interpretation* or *decoding function* has the general form

$$\pi : \{0, 1\}^l \rightarrow \left[x_{\min}, x_{\max}\right] \times \left[y_{\min}, y_{\max}\right] \subseteq \Re^2.$$

To decode each coordinate separately, we use the pair function $\pi = \pi_x \times \pi_y$, with each function defined as

Decoding of binary strings

$$\pi_x\left(s_{x,1}, \ldots, s_{x,k_x}\right) = x_{min} + \frac{x_{max} - x_{min}}{2^{k_x} - 1}\left(\sum_{j=1}^{k_x} s_{x,k_x+1-j} \cdot 2^{j-1}\right)$$

x coordinate

$$\pi_y\left(s_{y,1}, \ldots, s_{y,k_y}\right) = y_{min} + \frac{y_{max} - y_{min}}{2^{k_y} - 1}\left(\sum_{j=1}^{k_y} s_{y,k_y+1-j} \cdot 2^{j-1}\right).$$

y coordinate

For our two example strings above, we get the following interpretations with the conditions $[x_{min}, x_{max}] = [y_{min}, y_{max}] = [-10, 10]$:

$$\pi_x\left(s_x\right) = \pi_x((0, 1, 1, 0, 0))$$

$$= -10 + \frac{10 - (-10)}{2^5 - 1}\left(0 \cdot 2^4 + 1 \cdot 2^3 + 1 \cdot 2^2 + 0 \cdot 2^1 + 0 \cdot 2^0\right)$$

Decoding the x coordinate

$$= -10 + \frac{20}{31}(8 + 4) = -10 + \frac{20 \cdot 12}{31} = -2.25$$

$$\pi_y\left(s_y\right) = \pi_y((1, 0, 1, 1, 1))$$

$$= -10 + \frac{10 - (-10)}{2^5 - 1}\left(1 \cdot 2^4 + 0 \cdot 2^3 + 1 \cdot 2^2 + 1 \cdot 2^1 + 1 \cdot 2^0\right)$$

Decoding the y coordinate

$$= -10 + \frac{20}{31}(16 + 4 + 2 + 1) = 4.83.$$

Therefore, the binary vector $s = (s_x, s_y)$ is mapped onto the coordinate

$$\pi(s) = (-2.25, 4.83).$$

We get the fitness value for this string s by evaluating the objective function at this specific coordinate:

$$\mu_{f(x,y)}(s) = f(\pi(s)) = f(-2.25, 4.83) = 0.456.$$

Algorithmic scheme of evolutionary parameter optimization

Figure 2.10 illustrates the basic reproduction scheme of a genetic algorithm working on bit strings. A set of randomly generated binary strings constitutes the initial population, from which the evolution process starts. In essence, Figure 2.10 shows only a single evolution

"Descent with modification"

Figure 2.10
Descent with modification:
parameter optimization with
genetic algorithms.

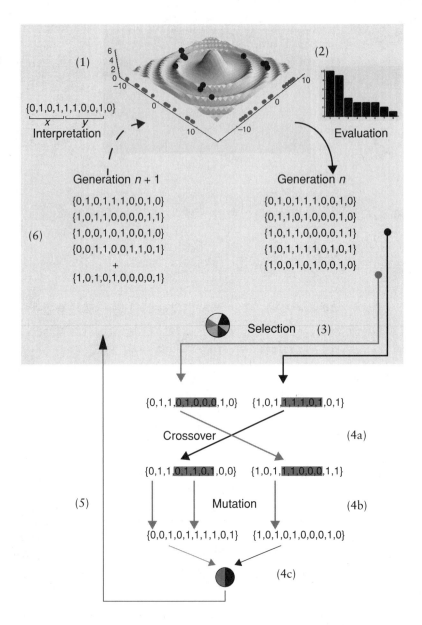

step (cf. Figure 2.3) from generation n to generation $n + 1$. This adaptation consists of the following steps:

Interpretation and evaluation: The binary strings, also denoted as chromosomes, are decoded (1) into their corresponding x-y coordinates, for which the objective function is evaluated.

Each genotypical binary string is mapped to a corresponding function value, its phenotype, which in this particular case is also identical to the string's fitness value (2).

Selection and reproduction: Now the phase of selection (3) and reproduction (5) begins, resulting in the composition of the next generation (6). Two individuals are selected from the current population. The selection is performed in a fitness-proportionate manner, illustrated by a roulette wheel (3). This selection style means that the higher an individual's fitness value, the more likely the individual's chromosome will be chosen (cf. Section 3.5.1).

Fitness-proportionate selection

Variation: The two selected bit strings are modified by two operators that are motivated from biology, a recombining *crossover* operator (4a) and a *mutation* operator (4b). The crossover operator takes two substrings of equal length from both chromosomes and interchanges them (two-point crossover). Subsequently, bits are randomly flipped from 0 to 1 and vice versa by the mutation operator. The application of these operators is associated with probabilities p_c and p_m. The crossover operator is applied with probability p_c, whereas bit mutations occur with probability p_m.

Two-point crossover

Mutation

Reproduction: Among the two modified chromosomes, one is selected (4c), which is added to the offspring population (5).

This interpretation, selection, and reproduction cycle is repeated until the offspring population (generation $n + 1$ (6)) has reached the same size as the original population in generation n.

Figure 2.11 gives an example of the population dynamics resulting from a genetic algorithm applied over 10 generations, following the reproduction scheme described. In Figure 2.11 the individuals are represented as dots at the position encoded by the corresponding chromosome. In each generation, three populations are depicted (in different gray levels), which reproduce independently from one another and refer to three different evolution runs. As the graphics show, different evolution runs lead to different results due to the stochastic components of selection and of the structure-mutating operators. In addition, the three runs start from different initial populations. The tendencies of these evolution runs, however, do not differ much. Each final population is converging toward nearly optimal regions within the fitness landscape.

Figure 2.11
A genetic algorithm in action: searching for the highest viewpoints.

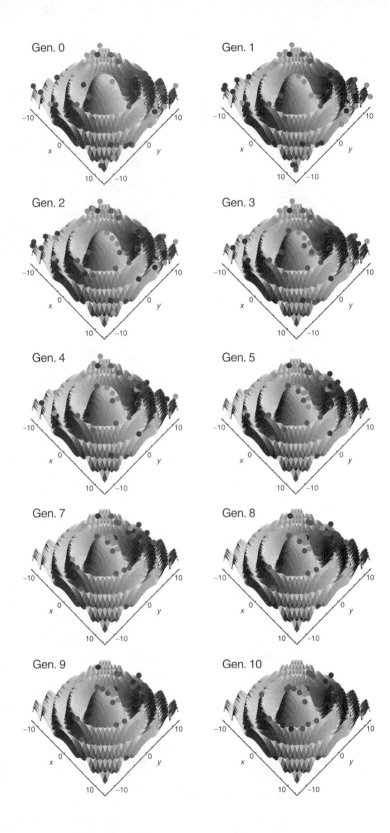

Let us take a final, detailed look at these experiments. Each population consists of 20 individuals. In generation 0, the coordinates are spread out relatively far. Many individuals end up at lower locations, most of which are hidden behind the ridges. Within the first generations, more and more individuals "climb" to higher regions. Already in generation 4, many dots appear around the highest locations on the narrow, concentric ridges and in the vicinity of the central peak. From this time on, selection can rely on a much better adapted set of individuals, which in turn speeds up the evolution process. The individuals' fitnesses have reached a higher level that the subsequent selection filter can count on. The convergence effect toward higher-level areas continues. In generation 10, the majority of individuals gather around the central hilltop and the closer concentric ridges. Each of the three populations contains individuals in the vicinity of the central peak.

Three populations looking for a peak

Whether the global optimum can be located exactly depends on the resolution of the number encodings, which is determined by the length of the bit strings. In practical applications, genetic algorithms are applied in combination with local hill-climbing procedures. The genetic algorithm then scans the global search space for "interesting" regions, whereas a traditional hill climber can easily find the last steps toward a peak.

2.4 Bibliographical notes

Books on evolutionary computation

The *Handbook of Evolutionary Computation* (Bäck, Fogel, et al. 1997) is a large collection of contributions from prominent researchers in this field. It discusses different models of evolutionary computation (EC) and hybrid approaches that combine EC with fuzzy systems, neural networks, and other optimization methods. Examples of EC implementations and a number of case studies are included that describe how to use evolutionary algorithms in computer and information sciences, engineering, physics, chemistry, biology, and medicine, as well as economics, finance, and business.

Handbook of Evolutionary Computation

A very valuable contribution from a historical perspective is *Evolutionary Computation: The Fossil Record,* edited by David Fogel (Fogel 1998). It contains original articles from researchers whose work had a major influence on the evolution of evolutionary computation. It is particularly interesting to read about the first, essential steps toward simulated evolution during the 1950s and 1960s, when

Evolutionary Computation: The Fossil Record

computer resources were too limited to demonstrate the benefits of evolutionary principles in solving optimization problems.

EC and EP

Evolutionary algorithms in the context of artificial intelligence systems are discussed in David Fogel's *Evolutionary Computation— Towards a New Philosophy of Machine Intelligence* (1995).

Evolutionary Algorithms in Theory and Practice

Thomas Bäck's *Evolutionary Algorithms in Theory and Practice* gives a detailed comparison of evolution strategies, evolutionary programming, and genetic algorithms (Bäck 1996).

Journals on evolutionary computation

EC journal

The journal *Evolutionary Computation,* published by MIT Press, had its first issue in spring 1993. The four issues per year cover all major fields of evolutionary computation, in particular genetic algorithms, genetic programming, evolution strategies, and evolutionary programming.

Transactions on EC

In April 1997 IEEE Press launched *Transactions on Evolutionary Computation* as a publication of the IEEE Neural Networks Council. This journal focuses primarily on practical applications of evolutionary algorithms and covers the major EC approaches as well.

Conferences on evolutionary computation

In addition to the growing number of specialized EC conferences, three major conferences cover most of the areas of EC:

GECCO

❑ GECCO, the Genetic and Evolutionary Computation Conference, is an annual conference that started in 1999 as an international forum for EC research (Banzhaf, Daida, et al. 1999; Whitley, Goldberg, et al. 2000). GECCO includes the former ICGA, International Conference on Genetic Algorithms, started in 1985, and GP, the Genetic Programming conference, which was first held in 1996. For more information on the ICGA and GP conferences see Section 3.9 and Section 7.6, respectively.

CEC

❑ CEC, the Congress on Evolutionary Computation (Angeline, Michalewicz, et al. 1999; Zalzala et al. 2000), is the second major conference in the field of evolutionary algorithms. CEC combines the Evolutionary Programming (EP) conference series, which started as an annual conference in 1992, and the

ICEC series, the International Conference in Evolutionary Computation, initiated in 1994 (Zurada, Marks II, et al. 1994). For more details on the EP conference see Section 6.8.

❑ The third major conference on evolutionary computation, *PPSN* which always had a wider scope on computational methods gleaned from nature, is PPSN, Parallel Problem Solving from Nature. PPSN is a biannual conference that started in 1991 as an initiative to bring together researchers from different disciplines interested in "natural" methods of computation and evolutionary algorithms in particular (Schwefel and Männer 1991; Männer and Manderick 1992; Davidor, Schwefel, et al. 1994; Voigt, Ebeling, et al. 1996; Eiben, Bäck, et al. 1998; Schoenauer, Deb, et al. 2000).

3 Genetic Algorithms

People have employed a combination of crossbreeding and selection for millennia to breed better crops, racehorses or ornamental roses. It is not as easy, however, to translate these procedures for use on computer programs. The chief problem is the construction of a "genetic code" that can represent the structure of different programs, just as DNA represents the structure of a person or a mouse.

Holland 1992b, p.66

Natural evolution implies that organisms adapt to their environment. Evolution works over many generations, covering much longer periods than those of lifetime learning. How could an individual learn to use its eyes if it hadn't been equipped with eyes through evolution? An organism without any organ of sight might not be able to react to visual stimuli, but it could be the ancestor of a species with eyelike organs. Therefore, evolution can be considered as a process of *meta-learning* on a generational level. Only evolutionary adaptations and innovations enable organisms to "optimally" react to environmental conditions. This involves an impressive potential for creativity and innovation. How else could such complex and useful organs as eyes be developed? John H. Holland, the "inventor" of genetic algorithms, talks about a *perpetual novelty* driven by evolution, which we want to use for evolution-based development of computer programs.

Adaptations by evolution, meta-learning

The first models of adaptation processes on the basis of genetic algorithms were introduced in the seminal book *Adaptation in Natural and Artificial Systems*, by John H. Holland (Holland 1975; Holland 1992a). In this book the term *adaptation*, the ability to adapt, plays a central role and is defined as a process of progressive modification of (general) structures, which leads to improved performance of the system interacting with its environment (see Section 2.2).

Adaptation through genetic algorithms

The term *genetic algorithm* (GA) describes the basic idea: algorithmic techniques, inspired by genetic principles, are used to simulate evolutionary processes. The objective is to design and implement

Genetic algorithms

robust, adaptive systems, following nature's paradigm for the evolution of genetic structures. In particular, genetic algorithms glean ideas from natural mechanisms of reproduction, especially among cells of sexually reproducing individuals. Four essential principles manifested in nature form the core ingredients of genetic algorithms: (1) the *dualism principle* of separating genetic information of the genotype from the expressed phenotype, (2) a *discrete encoding* of genotypical structures, and (3) *recombination effects* resulting from sexual reproduction. Finally, (4) *elementary building blocks,* which are combined according to specific templates, help in the composition of complex interacting systems, representing a core precondition of modular design and construction.

Genotypical and phenotypical structures

Dualism: In biological systems, the genetic information encoded in DNA is used in two ways—as genetic *information,* which is replicated, and as *instructions,* which have to be executed. This dualistic principle of information processing has already been pointed out by John von Neumann, a computer pioneer and visionary researcher, particularly in the area of self-reproducing cellular automata (Neumann and Burks 1966; see also Levy 1993a, p. 44, and Section 9.1.2). In genetic algorithms, the genotypical structures, modified by an evolutionary algorithm through recombinations and mutations, are clearly separated from the phenotypical structures, the computer programs or parameter vectors (Figure 3.1). The evolution-based variations are not performed in the space of the parameters to be optimized (as is the case, for example, with evolution strategies; see Chapter 4) but in an encoding, genotypical structure space. Hence, the principal separation of phenotype and genotype in nature is explicitly implemented by genetic algorithms.

Encoding by a discrete alphabet

Discrete encoding: In DNA strands, genetic information is encoded by a four-letter alphabet. For GA structures an analogous representation is used. Usually this is a (binary) bit string representation, but any other encoding scheme over a *discrete,* finite alphabet may be chosen as well (Section 3.1).

Reproduction and recombination

Sexual reproduction: The diploid cells of sexually reproducing individuals consist of a double set of homologous chromosomes, half each from the offspring's mother and father. During the cell division phase *meiosis,* parts of the single, paired chromosomes are mutually exchanged by crossover (Section

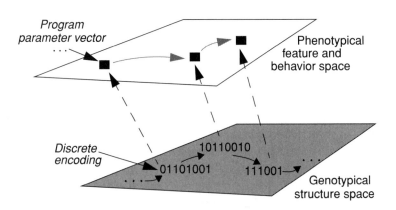

Figure 3.1
Dualism principle of genetic algorithms.

3.3.3). The resulting diploid descendant cells contain a slightly mutated chromosome set, merged from the genetic information of both parental cells (Figure 3.31).

Genetic algorithms algorithmically replicate these recombination effects and integrate them into evolutionary simulation models and optimization algorithms. Successful application of genetic algorithms in the sense of a progressive creativity in essence depends on the potential of recombination, the mixing and recomposition of elementary structural building blocks. According to Holland, by reorganizing available information one of the great advantages of evolution is utilized, namely, "its perpetual novelty in its approaches to maintaining fitness" (Levy 1993a, p. 169).

Recombinations

Unlike recombinations, point mutations do not play a prominent role in genetic algorithms, in contrast to the evolution strategic view (Chapter 4).

Point mutations

Elementary building blocks: Complex adaptive systems, such as the interactions on genome structures, are hierarchically composed of simple elementary units. Only through the interplay of genes, the building blocks of DNA, are chains of amino acids and proteins composed during the transcription and translation phases. To translate the triplets into the corresponding amino acids, building blocks of RNA, nucleotide bases are needed. The proteins produced, the proteome, constitute the "atomic units of a cell." This modular organization principle plays a decisive role in the encoding structures of genetic algorithms as well. The genotypical GA structures—an analogy to computer programs used in Turing machine tables, in assembler code, and in C, LISP, or Mathematica—are also built from

Compositon of elementary building blocks

elementary building blocks: short binary strings, command sequences, variables, constants, or symbolic expressions.

Applications

Genetic algorithms have a surprisingly broad range of application domains, from solving technical optimization problems (Goldberg 1989), mathematical function optimization (De Jong 1975), simulated evolution of social behavior of ants (Jefferson, Collins, et al. 1992), or artificial, interacting organisms (Ray 1991) to the evolutionary "breeding" of computer programs (Koza 1992; Koza 1994; Koza, Andre, et al. 1999; Banzhaf, Nordin, et al. 1997). The latter paradigm is known as *genetic programming,* which we discuss in detail in Part II of this book (Chapter 7). An extensive list of further GA application areas can be found in, among others, Goldberg 1989, p. 126 ff. or Mitchell 1996.

Binary encoding?

At the end of the 1980s, genetic algorithms received worldwide attention through promotion by David E. Goldberg (Goldberg 1989) and the development of a number of practical GA applications. Since then, the representation of adaptive GA structures seems to be mainly restricted to binary strings. Today binary encoding is still considered one of the key features of genetic algorithms. Binary alphabets are preferred because a two-value representation maximizes the number of "schemata" with respect to a given encoding (Goldberg 1986). We will examine this aspect in the context of the controversial schema theorem in Section 3.8.

Chapter overview

In the following sections we show that it is not necessary to restrict ourselves to binary GA chromosomes. Instead we introduce a number of representation schemes for GA chromosomes over arbitrary, finite, and discrete alphabets (Section 3.1). The set of variants covers haploid single-stranded chromosomes over binary strings, triplet chromosomes for simulating RNA sequences over a four-letter alphabet, and GA chromosomes with real-value alleles (Section 3.1.1). We also look at diploid chromosome strands and how to deal with dominant and recessive alleles (Section 3.1.2).

Multistranded GA chromosomes on discrete alphabets

Point mutation

Various effects of point mutations on different variants of GA chromosomes (haploid, diploid, varying discrete allele alphabets) are described in Section 3.2.

Recombination

In Section 3.3, we discuss recombination operators, developed from simple combination operators on lists into meiotic recombinations on diploid chromosomes.

Mutations on chromosome sets

Mutations on groups of chromosome subunits in the sense of biological inversions, translocations, and crossovers among nonhomologous chromosomes are introduced in Section 3.4.

The principal evolution scheme for genetic algorithms is presented in Section 3.5. For the illustrations we use a formalism originally introduced for evolution strategies (Section 4.4). Thus direct comparisons between different representatives of evolutionary algorithms are possible.

GA evolution scheme

Section 3.6 summarizes the Evolvica algorithms for implementing and experimenting with genetic algorithms.

GA with Evolvica

In Section 3.7, we demonstrate a few GA example experiments for solving parameter optimization problems. A comparison of recombination and mutation effects on the evolution of populations for a simple optimization problem illustrates the importance of recombining operators (Section 3.7.3). The following section compares the effects of further GA operators, such as inversion, duplication, and deletion, on the gene pool (Section 3.7.4). Finally, in Section 3.7.5, using a parameter optimization problem we show how genetic algorithms handle variations of the evaluation function during the evolution process.

GA in action

Chapter 3 concludes with a discussion of the controversial schema theorem, which describes characteristics of successful genotypical building blocks.

GA schema theorem

3.1 Polyploid GA chromosomes

Nature encodes the "programs" on DNA and RNA strands that implicitly describe the structure and development of organisms, based on a four-letter alphabet, the nucleotide bases—A, C, G, and T (or U). For genetic algorithms, binary strings are preferable to encode data structures to be optimized. In the following sections, however, we define general GA chromosomes as strings over discrete alphabets.

Triplet encoding vs. binary strings

3.1.1 Haploid GA chromosomes

We begin with the simplest form of a GA chromosome, a haploid single strand with alleles over a k-element alphabet $A = \{a_1, \ldots, a_k\}$. A chromosome of length n is defined as a vector s of the following form:

$$s = (s_1, \ldots, s_n) \text{ with } s_i \in A, \ 1 \leq i \leq n.$$

Single-stranded GA chromosome

A GA chromosome like this can be interpreted as a sequence of genes s_i. Each gene has a concrete representation given by its respective allele; that is, it takes a specific value from a finite domain A. In order to keep the notations simple, we do not use separate alphabets A_i for each gene locus i—all genes take their values from the same domain A.

We extend this chromosome representation by attributing each gene with its locus; that is, with its index within the gene sequence. In this way we can uniquely identify genes, even if their sequence is changed by a genetic operator (e.g., by inversion). This leads us to the following extended *GA chromosome* representation:

$$s = ((1, s_i), \ldots, (n, s_n)) \text{ with } s_i \in A, 1 \leq i \leq n.$$

In Evolvica a GA chromosome is generated by the function cre-ateChromosome[w_] from Program 3.1. The parameter w determines the width or length of the chromosome. The option Alphabet is used to set the allele alphabet. The default setting for this option is the binary alphabet {0, 1}. The second optional rule determines the polyploidy of the chromosome. We discuss this in more detail in Section 3.1.2.

We represent GA chromosomes by expressions of the form

                        chromo[q[...], p[...]],

where the first argument (q) contains the chromosome's *fitness* value (set to "undef" prior to evaluation). The p expression holds a suitable representation of the *genes*. The extended GA chromosome, including the gene indices, has the following Evolvica implementation:

          chromo[q[undef], p[{1,{s1}},..., {1,{sn}}]].

The explicit bracketing of the alleles $s_1, \ldots, s_n$ is useful for diploid and *m*-ploid GA chromosomes—whenever a gene may take one of several alternative alleles.

The option RandomLoci in Program 3.1 determines the order of sorting for the genes. For RandomLoci → False the genes are sorted according to their index numbers; for RandomLoci → True the genes are arranged randomly. The option PolyPloidy sets the number of (homologous) single strands of the chromosome (see the following sections, in particular, Section 3.1.2).

Binary chromosomes

Unlike the chromosome representation of evolution strategies (Section 4.1), where object and strategy parameters have a compact representation as real numbers, the classical form of encoding for genetic algorithms is binary strings. The reason binary strings are the preferred method of GA encoding is that information is coded as "broadly" as possible—in contrast to "compact" real numbers. The breadth, hence the resolution, of an encoding determines a genetic algorithm's capa-

```
createChromosome[width_:1,opts___] :=

Module[{alph},

   alph := Alphabet /. {opts} /.
   Options [createChromosome];

   If[RandomLoci /. {opts} /.
   Options [createChromosome],
      indices = RandomPermutation[width],
      indices = Range[width]
   ];

   chromo[q[undef],
      p @@ Map[{#,Table[randomSelect[alph],
                 {PolyPloidy /. {opts}
                  /. Options[createChromosome]}]}&,
            indices
         ]
      ]
];

Options[createChromosome] =
{
   Alphabet → {0,1},
   PolyPloidy → 1,
   RandomLoci → False
};
```

Program 3.1
Generation of polyploid GA chromosomes over a finite allele alphabet.

bility to both broadly explore and locally exploit parameter search spaces (see the schemata in Section 3.8).

Let us look at a few examples of binary GA chromosomes. With its default settings, the function createChromosome composes a random binary chromosome, as the following example shows:

In[10]:= **binaryChromo = createChromosome[15]**

Binary GA chromosome with 15 alleles

*Out[10]=*chromo[q[undef], p[{1, {1}}, {2, {0}}, {3, {1}},
        {4, {0}}, {5, {0}}, {6, {0}}, {7, {0}}, {8, {1}},
        {9, {0}}, {10, {0}}, {11, {0}}, {12, {0}}, {13,
        {1}}, {14, {1}}, {15, {1}}]]

This form of representation is quite flexible, particularly in the case of implementing more complex diploid chromosomes (Section 3.1.2). A more compact display of the GA chromosome is provided by the function compactForm in Program 3.2:

GA chromosome: compact output form without gene indices

In[11] := **% // compactForm**

Out[11] = chromo[q[undef],
             p[{1, 0, 1, 0, 0, 0, 0, 1, 0, 0, 0, 0, 1, 1, 1}]]

The gene indices are blended out, and only the alleles are extracted (Transpose[Map[Last,List @@ params]]). Setting the option SortLoci → True sorts the genes according to their indices.

Program 3.2
Compact output form for GA chromosomes.

```
compactForm[chromo[qual_q,params_p],opts___]  :=

  chromo[
    qual,
    If[SortLoci /. {opts} /. Options[compactForm],
       p @@ Transpose[Map[Last,List @@ Sort[params]]],
       p @@ Transpose[Map[Last,List @@ params]]
    ]
  ]

Options[compactForm] = {SortLoci → False};
```

For illustrating GA chromosomes in Evolvica graphically, we use the function chromosomePlot, the output of which is shown in Figure 3.2 for the example chromosome from above. The option AspectRatio sets the width-height ratio of the display.

Graphical representation of GA chromosomes

In[12] := **chromosomePlot[binaryChromo, AspectRatio → 0.2];**

Each gene is represented by a square within a "chromosome strand" bordered by a black margin. Gray and white squares represent alleles of zero and one, respectively. The gene indices are displayed along the bottom.

The following example shows how to use the option Random-Loci for sorting or randomly arranging genes. With the rule RandomLoci → True the function createChromosome creates a GA chromosome with its genes in random order:

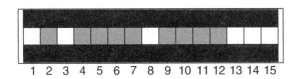

Figure 3.2
Visualization of a binary GA chromosome.

In[13] := **binaryChromoRandom =**
　　　　createChromosome[15, RandomLoci → True]

Out[13] = chromo[q[undef], p[{6, {0}}, {2, {0}}, {11, {1}},　　*GA genes in random order*
　　　　{14, {1}}, {12, {1}}, {7, {1}}, {8, {1}}, {13,
　　　　{0}}, {1, {0}}, {5, {0}}, {9, {0}}, {3, {1}},
　　　　{10, {1}}, {4, {1}}, {15, {0}}]]

Here the sequence of genes is 6, 2, 11, 14, and so on, as is also shown
in Figure 3.3(a). With its default setting the function chromosome-
Plot leaves the arrangement of the genes unchanged:

In[14] := **chromosomePlot[binaryChromoRandom,**
　　　　AspectRatio → 0.2];

　　Especially for a unified interpretation of the chromosomes, a
"normalized," sorted-gene arrangement is more suitable. Figure　　*Normalized representation*
3.3(b) shows the resulting sorted chromosome for the following func-　　*of GA chromosomes*
tion call with SortLoci → True:

In[15] := **chromosomePlot[binaryChromoRandom,**
　　　　SortLoci → True, AspectRatio → 0.2];

　　A binary form of parameter encoding is very common for genetic
algorithms and is even regarded as one of the main GA characteristics
compared to other evolution-based algorithms, as, for example, evolution strategies (Rechenberg 1994a; Rechenberg 1994b; Schwefel

(a)
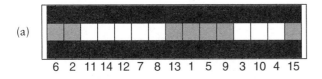

(b)

Figure 3.3
A binary GA chromosome
with genes in random
(a) and sorted (b) order.

1995, p. 105 ff. and p. 151 ff.) (cf. Chapter 4) or evolutionary programming (Fogel, Owens, et al. 1966; Fogel 1994; Fogel 1999) (cf. Chapter 6).

In the following sections we explore a little further the spectrum of information encoding over discrete alphabets. Here we follow Holland's original inspiration for his design of genetic, adaptive algorithms (Holland 1975; Holland 1992a). In the application section (Section 3.7) we return to the more traditional binary encodings.

RNA chromosomes

Triplet encoding of amino acids

Genes represent the basic units of genetic information stored in the DNA chromosomes of cells. The nucleotide bases adenine (A), cytosine (C), guanine (G), and uracil (U) form the encoding subunits, the alphabet for describing genes in the RNA. A group of three nucleotides defines a molecular code word. Each of these triplets specifies an amino acid or a genetic control command. A gene consists of a sequence of several hundred triplets, encoding a protein structure. The translation of the *codons* (triplets) into a sequence of amino acids is accomplished by *ribosomes* during the translation phase. The one-dimensional information structure in the RNA is transformed into a three-dimensional protein building block.

From codon sequences to proteins

We will attempt to simulate the translation of triplets into amino acids. To do so, we create a translation table for the triplet vocabulary of the RNA, which we implement as a set of rules (Program 3.3). Each rule has the form

$$\{x\_,\ y\_,\ z\_\} \rightarrow \texttt{Amino},$$

where the variables x, y, and z take on values from the RNA alphabet {A, C, G, U} of the four nucleotide bases and `Amino` denotes an amino acid or the control command `STOP`.

Now we can easily generate a table of all possible triplet combinations over the RNA alphabet:

```
In[16] := rnaA = {U,C,A,G};
          codons = (Outer[List,rnaA,rnaA,rnaA]
          // TableForm)
```

Triplet table over the RNA alphabet {A, C, G, U}

```
Out[16] = U U U    U C U    U A U    U G U
          U U C    U C C    U A C    U G C
          U U A    U C A    U A A    U G A
          U U G    U C G    U A G    U G G
```

```
tripletToLabel =
{
  {G,C,_}     → "Ala",  {U,G,U|C}   → "Cys",
  {G,A,U|C}   → "Asp",  {G,A,A|G}   → "Glu",
  {U,U,U|C}   → "Phe",  {G,G,_}     → "Gly",
  {C,A,U|C}   → "His",  {A,U,U|C|A} → "Ile",
  {A,A,A|G}   → "Lys",  {U,U,A|G}   → "Leu",
  {C,U,_}     → "Leu",  {A,U,G}     → "Met",
  {A,A,U|C}   → "Asn",  {C,C,_}     → "Pro",
  {C,A,A|G}   → "Gln",  {C,G,_}     → "Arg",
  {A,G,A|G}   → "Arg",  {U,C,_}     → "Ser",
  {A,G,U|C}   → "Ser",  {A,C,_}     → "Thr",
  {G,U,_}     → "Val",  {U,G,G}     → "Trp",
  {U,A,U|C}   → "Tyr",  {U,A,A|G}   → "STOP",
  {U,G,A}     → "STOP"
};
```

Program 3.3
Translation table from triplets to amino acids and stop commands.

```
C U U    C C U    C A U    C G U
C U C    C C C    C A C    C G C
C U A    C C A    C A A    C G A
C U G    C C G    C A G    C G G

A U U    A C U    A A U    A G U
A U C    A C C    A A C    A G C
A U A    A C A    A A A    A G A
A U G    A C G    A A G    A G G

G U U    G C U    G A U    G G U
G U C    G C C    G A C    G G C
G U A    G C A    G A A    G G A
G U G    G C G    G A G    G G G
```

The translation from codons into amino acids, performed in nature by the ribosomes, results from a simple application of the rules tripletToLabel in Program 3.3. The rules labelToAminoAcid, listed in Program 3.4, substitute the abbreviations for the full names of the amino acids:

In[17] := **codons /. tripletToLabel /. labelToAminoAcid**
           // TableForm

Summary of amino acids and genetic control commands encoded by RNA triplets	*Out[17]=*phenylalanine	serine	tyrosine	cysteine
	phenylalanine	serine	tyrosine	cysteine
	leucine	serine	STOP	STOP
	leucine	serine	STOP	tryptophan
	leucine	proline	histidine	arginine
	leucine	proline	histidine	arginine
	leucine	proline	glutamine	arginine
	leucine	proline	glutamine	arginine
	isoleucine	threonine	asparagine	serine
	isoleucine	threonine	asparagine	serine
	isoleucine	threonine	lysine	arginine
	methionine / START	threonine	lysine	arginine
	valine	alanine	asp. acid	glycine
	valine	alanine	asp. acid	glycine
	valine	alanine	glut. acid	glycine
	valine	alanine	glut. acid	glycine

Redundant encoding

As this summarizing table shows, nature uses a redundant encoding to specify protein building blocks. Different triplets may encode for the same amino acid, which is also a consequence of the following calculation: there are only 20 amino acids versus $4^3 = 64$ possible triplet variants.

Program 3.4
Translating into full name amino acids.

```
labelToAminoAcid =
{
  "Ala" → "alanine", "Arg" → "arginine",
  "Asn" → "asparagine", "Asp" → "asp. acid",
  "Cys" → "cysteine", "Gln" → "glutamine",
  "Glu" → "glut. acid", "Gly" → "glycine",
  "His" → "histidine", "Ile" → "isoleucine",
  "Leu" → "leucine", "Lys" → "lysine",
  "Met" → "methionine/START", "Phe" →
  "phenylalanine",
  "Pro" → "proline", "Ser" → "serine",
  "Thr" → "threonine", "Trp" → "tryptophan",
  "Tyr" → "tyrosine", "Val" → "valine"
};
```

With these preparations, we can apply the codon interpretation functions to GA chromosome structures. We generate a chromosome with 240 nucleotide bases over the allele alphabet {A, G, C, U}.

In[18] := **rnaChromo =**
      createChromosome[240, Alphabet → {A,G,C,U}];

In[19] := **rnaChromo // compactForm**

                                   RNA chromosome with 240 nucleotide bases

Out[19] = chromo[q[undef], p[{C, C, G, C, G, U, U, U, G, G,
    U, A, A, U, U, A, A, C, A, C, G, U, A, G, A, G, C,
    G, G, U, A, U, U, U, U, C, U, U, U, G, C, A, C, C,
    A, U, G, A, U, A, A, G, A, U, A, G, A, A, U, G, A,
    U, A, U, C, G, A, C, C, U, A, C, G, A, A, G, C, U,
    A, A, G, A, A, U, G, C, A, C, C, G, C, A, A, U, U,
    G, C, A, G, U, U, G, G, G, C, U, C, U, C, C, A, C,
    C, C, G, C, A, G, C, A, G, U, C, U, G, A, G, A, C,
    A, G, A, G, G, U, U, G, G, C, A, G, G, C, U, G, G,
    U, U, G, A, U, C, U, U, U, C, A, A, A, U, G, G, A,
    C, A, U, G, U, A, C, G, C, U, C, G, G, G, A, U, U,
    U, U, A, G, A, U, U, C, G, C, C, A, C, U, A, U, G,
    A, G, C, C, G, G, C, G, A, G, C, A, A, U, C, C, G,
    U, U, C, U, A, G, G, G, A, U, A, C, A, A, C, U, C,
    C, G, G, C, G, G, G, U, G}]]

With the following function call we get a graphical representation of the RNA chromosome (Figure 3.4):

In[20] := **chromosomePictogramPlot[rnaChromo,**   *Visualization of an*
      TableWidth → 15, Pictograms → {RECTANGLE}, *RNA chromosome*
      ColorFunction → GrayLevel,
      StartColor → 0.9, ColorDecrement → 0.05,
      GraphicsOptions →
        {DefaultFont → {"Helvetica-Bold",9}}]

Each of the four bases is represented by a square with a corresponding gray value. If we unite three alleles into a triplet, the nucleotide base encoding can be converted into a corresponding sequence of amino acids.

In[21] := **ribRNAChromo = ribosome[rnaChromo];**

In[22] := **ribRNAChromo // compactForm**

Figure 3.4
The "nucleotide bases" of an
RNA chromosome.

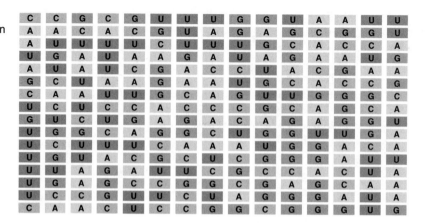

RNA chromosome
translated into a sequence
of amino acids

```
Out[22]=chromo[q[undef], p[{Pro, Arg, Leu, Val, Ile, Asn,
           Thr, STOP, Ser, Gly, Ile, Phe, Phe, Ala, Pro,
           STOP, STOP, Asp, Arg, Met, Ile, Ser, Thr, Tyr,
           Glu, Ala, Lys, Asn, Ala, Pro, Gln, Leu, Gln, Leu,
           Gly, Ser, Pro, Pro, Ala, Ala, Val, STOP, Asp,
           Arg, Gly, Trp, Gln, Ala, Gly, STOP, Ser, Phe,
           Lys, Trp, Thr, Cys, Thr, Leu, Gly, Ile, Leu, Asp,
           Ser, Pro, Leu, STOP, Ala, Gly, Glu, Gln, Ser,
           Val, Leu, Gly, Ile, Gln, Leu, Arg, Arg, Val}]]
```

Ribosomes

For this simple translation we have used the function `ribosome` in Program 3.5, which partitions the parameter list into triplets. Using the decoding function (`DecodingFunction`), the codons are translated into amino acids, according to the rules of Program 3.3.

In order to produce an analogous graphical representation of the sequence of amino acids, we must take precautions to ensure that the amino abbreviations—Ala, Arg, Asn, . . . , Tyr, Val—can be transformed into corresponding numbers or gray levels. We define an alphabet from the short notations for the amino acids in Program 3.4. The left side of each rule becomes an element of the alphabet set. Finally, the RNA punctuation mark `STOP` has to be added.

```
In[23]:= aminoAlphabet =
         Join[(First /@ labelToAminoAcid),{"STOP"}]
```

```
Out[23]={Ala, Arg, Asn, Asp, Cys, Gln, Glu, Gly, His,
          Ile, Leu, Lys, Met, Phe, Pro, Ser, Thr, Trp, Tyr,
          Val, STOP}
```

```
ribosome[chromo[qual_q,params_p],opts___] :=

Module[{paramsLists},
  paramsLists =
    Map[Partition[#,
         PartitionSize /. {opts}
         /. Options[ribosome]]&,
      Transpose[Map[Last,List @@ params]]];

  chromo[qual,
    p @@ MapIndexed[{First[#2],#1}&,
      Transpose[Map[DecodingFunction /. {opts}
        /. Options[ribosome],paramsLists]]
    ]
  ]
]

Options[ribosome] =
{
  Alphabet → {0,1}, PartitionSize → 3,
  DecodingFunction → (# /. tripletToLabel &)
};
```

Program 3.5
Decoding of GA
chromosomes analogous to
a translation by ribosomes
(Version 1).

Now the amino acid representation of the GA chromosome can
be visualized by the function chromosomePictogramPlot (Figure
3.5).

In[24] := **chromosomePictogramPlot[ribRNAChromo,**
         TableWidth → 10, ColorFunction → GrayLevel,
         StartColor → 0.9, ColorDecrement → 0.05,
         GraphicsOptions →
            {DefaultFont → {"Helvetica-Bold",9}}]

Each amino acid (and the STOP sign) is labeled with a graphical symbol and a respective gray value. We will again refer to RNA chromosomes in the context of GA mutations in Section 3.2.4.

Chromosomes with real-value alleles

To conclude this section on different forms of representation for GA
chromosomes, we show that the function createChromosome does
not necessarily restrict us to discrete, finite alphabets. Even integer or
real-value numbers from certain intervals may be specified as value
domains for the alleles.

Figure 3.5
Sequence of "amino acids"
of Figure 3.4.

In the following example the alleles are real numbers from the interval [0, 1]. The allele alphabet is not explicitly predefined as a list of values, but allele settings are defined by a rule with delayed evaluation. For each allele the function `Random[]` is called, which generates a pseudo-random number with uniform distribution from the unit interval:

GA chromosome with 10 alleles from the interval [0,1]

```
In[25] := realChromo =
             createChromosome[10, Alphabet :> {Random[]}]
```

```
Out[25] = chromo[q[undef], p[{1, {0.441805}}, {2,
          {0.393973}}, {3, {0.555884}}, {4, {0.621378}},
          {5, {0.853941}}, {6, {0.282736}}, {7,
          {0.141666}}, {8, {0.0332311}}, {9, {0.38426}},
          {10, {0.896247}}]]
```

The compact output form shows that this kind of chromosome representation is analogous to the one used for evolution strategies (Section 4.1).

```
In[26] := % // compactForm
```

Real-number GA chromosome with extracted alleles

```
Out[26] = chromo[q[undef], p[{0.441805, 0.393973,
          0.555884, 0.621378, 0.853941, 0.282736,
          0.141666, 0.0332311, 0.38426, 0.896247}]]
```

For real numbers, however, the standard graphical representation is less suitable, since it becomes difficult to visually attribute gray levels to actual numbers (Figure 3.6).

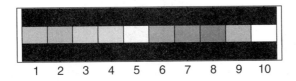

Figure 3.6
Real-number GA
chromosome with alleles
from the interval [0,1].

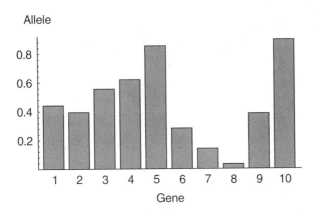

Figure 3.7
Alternative representation of
the GA chromosome in
Figure 3.6.

In[27] := **chromosomePlot[%%, AspectRatio → 0.2];**

We use the function chromosomeBarChart, which we define for
visualizing ES chromosomes (Section 4.1), for GA chromosomes, too.
The function chromosomeBarChart returns a bar plot representation of a real-value GA chromosome (Figure 3.7).

In[28] := **chromosomeBarChart[realChromo, AspectRatio → 0.5];**

After this detour to ES chromosomes, we will discuss diploid GA
chromosomes in the following sections. This means we return from
the phenotypical level of real numbers to the level of genotypical
information structures, encoded by discrete alphabets.

3.1.2 Diploidy and dominance on GA chromosomes

The term *diploidy* derives its meaning from sexual reproduction. In
the *meiotic* phase of cell division, the prestages of gametes (sperm   *Meiosis*
cells) are produced and the number of chromosomes is reduced by
half. Meiotic cell division starts with two homologous, corresponding
sets of chromosomes, originating from an egg and a sperm cell. Cells
or organisms are called *diploid* if they possess two copies of each gene,   *Diploidy of higher animals*
one from the mother and one from the father. In addition to humans   *and plants*

Haploid gametes

and animals, many plants are diploid organisms. In *haploid* ova and sperm cells (gametes), each gene is represented by only one copy on a single strand.

In the following sections, we extend the abstract haploid forms of GA chromosomes to diploid structures. We define *m*-ploid chromosomes as a collection of $m > 2$ homologous chromosomes—a mathematically justified extension for which, however, no natural counterpart has yet been observed.

Polyploid
GA chromosomes

When interpreting diploid chromosomes, the question is, Which of the alleles for each gene is actually expressed? For each gene the interpretation can choose from two alleles, namely, the allele of the "father gene" or the "mother gene." Here the topic of dominant and recessive alleles comes into play, which we will deal with at the end of this section.

Dominance

General structure of diploid and *m*-ploid chromosomes

In Section 3.1.1, we defined a single-strand chromosome of length n over a finite allele alphabet $A = \{\alpha_1, \ldots, \alpha_k\}$ as a vector s of the form

Haploid
GA chromosome

$$s = ((1, s_1), \ldots, (n, s_n)) \text{ with } s_i \in A, \ 1 \le i \le n.$$

The pair (i, s_i) uniquely identifies each gene by its index i. The exact order of these index-allele pairs is not relevant—the genes may be arranged in random order. We extend this definition of a single chromosome strand to a pair of homologous chromosomes or—in a generalized version—to a collection of $m > 2$ homologous chromosomes. We define a *diploid chromosome pair* $s^{(2)}$ as a structure with the following form:

Diploid
GA chromosome

$$s^{(2)} = ((1, (s_{11}, s_{21})), \ldots, (n, (s_{1n}, s_{2n}))).$$

For each gene locus the pair $(i, (s_{1i}, s_{2i}))$ contains the index in the first component. The second entry contains the respective alleles of the two homologous chromosome strands

$$s_1 = ((1, s_{11}), \ldots, (n, s_{1n})) \text{ and } s_2 = ((1, s_{21}), \ldots, (n, s_{2n})).$$

The $s_{ij} \in A$ with $1 \le i \le 2$ and $1 \le j \le n$ represent the alleles. In general, we can compose a collection of m chromosomes of equal lengths into a polyploid chromosome set. Hence, we define an *m-ploid chromosome* $s^{(m)}$, consisting of m homologous single chromosome strands of length n, by the following structure:

Polyploid
GA chromosome

$$s^{(m)} = ((1, (s_{11}, \ldots, s_{m1})), \ldots, (n, (s_{1n}, \ldots, s_{mn}))).$$

The polyploid chromosome $s^{(m)}$ consists of m strands

$$s_i = ((1, s_{i1}), \ldots, (n, s_{in})) \text{ with } 1 \leq i \leq m.$$

In the following sections we will look at a few examples of m-ploid chromosomes. As for each of the homologous genes, there is a set of alleles to choose from, and so the question arises, Which of the competing alleles will be actually expressed in the phenotype? Expressed alleles are called *dominant*, whereas alleles that are not interpreted by the genotype-phenotype mapping are *recessive*.

Generating and interpreting di- and *m*-ploid chromosomes

We can use the function `createChromosome` from Section 3.1.1 to generate diploid chromosomes. The GA chromosome data structure is simply extended by additional alleles for each gene. For polyploid chromosomes the symbolic expressions have the form

chromo[q[...],

p[{1, {s11, ..., sm1}}, ..., {n, {s1n, ..., smn}}]],

Data structure for polyploid GA chromosomes

where for each gene there are m competing alleles. In the function `createChromosome` the option `PolyPloidy` determines the number of homologous alleles. A binary diploid GA chromosome with 10 genes is generated as follows:

In[29] := **binaryDiploidChromo =
        createChromosome[10, PolyPloidy $\rightarrow$ 2]**

Out[29] = chromo[q[undef], p[{1, {1, 1}}, {2, {1, 1}},
        {3, {0, 0}}, {4, {1, 0}}, {5, {0, 0}},
        {6, {0, 0}}, {7, {1, 0}}, {8, {1, 1}},
        {9, {1, 0}}, {10, {1, 0}}]]

Diploid, binary GA chromosome

In[30] := **binaryDiploidChromo // compactTableForm**

Out[30] = chromo[q[undef],
        p[1 1 0 1 0 0 1 1 1 1]]
           1 1 0 0 0 0 0 1 0 0

Diploid GA chromosome in table form

We can use the function `chromosomePictogramPlot` to visualize the chromosome.

In[31] := **chromosomePictogramPlot[binaryDiploidChromo,
        ColorFunction $\rightarrow$ GrayLevel,
        GraphicsOptions $\rightarrow$ {AspectRatio $\rightarrow$ 0.1}]**

Each row in Figure 3.8 represents one of the two homologous strands. The chromosomes are arranged the same way as the output of the `compactTableForm` function.

Analogously we can generate a 3-ploid chromosome over the four-element alphabet $A = \{a, b, c, d\}$ and depict it graphically (Figure 3.9).

In[32] := **mploidChromo = createChromosome[10,**
      Alphabet → {a,b,c,d}, PolyPloidy → 3]

Triploid GA chromosome

Out[32] = chromo[q[undef], p[{1, {b, a, c}},{2, {d, b, a}},
      {3, {b, a, c}}, {4, {d, d, c}}, {5, {c, b, d}},
      {6, {d, b, d}}, {7, {d, a, d}}, {8, {d, b, d}},
      {9, {a, a, b}}, {10, {d, c, d}}]]

For each gene the compact tabular form displays the respective alleles per column. Each row is a single chromosome strand.

In[33] := **mploidChromo // compactTableForm**

Triploid GA chromosome in table form

Out[33] = chromo[q[undef],
      p[b   d   b   d   c   d   d   d   a   d]]
        a   b   a   d   b   b   a   b   a   c
        c   a   c   c   d   d   d   d   b   d

The visualization function `chromosomePictogramPlot` returns a graphical representation for the table form. Figures 3.9 and 3.10 are

Figure 3.8
Diploid GA chromosome.

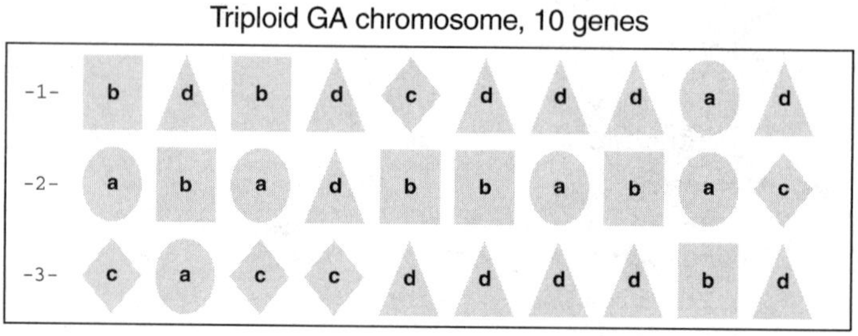

Figure 3.9
Triploid GA chromosome.

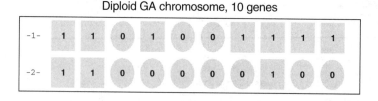

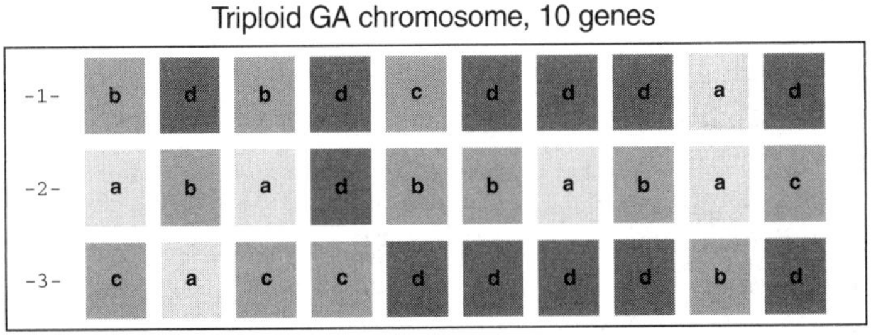

Triploid GA chromosome, 10 genes

Figure 3.10
Triploid GA chromosome.

two examples of different display settings. The letters of the alphabet are automatically converted to numbers, which correspond to gray values and/or graphical elements (triangles, squares, or disks). For Figure 3.9 we use the following command:

```
In[34] := chromosomePictogramPlot[mploidChromo,
        ColorFunction → GrayLevel,
        GraphicsOptions → {AspectRatio → 0.1}];
```

This is the function call for the graphics in Figure 3.10:

```
In[35] := chromosomePictogramPlot[mploidChromo,
        Pictograms → {RECTANGLE},
        ColorFunction → GrayLevel,
        StartColor → 0.9, ColorDecrement → 0.2,
        GraphicsOptions → {AspectRatio → 0.1}];
```

Generating and visualizing sets of chromosomes is quite easy to implement with Mathematica's function-programming capabilities. In the following section we will see that using functional-style programming also allows for easy implementation of routines for chromosome interpretation with dominant and recessive alleles.

Simulated diploidy: dominant and recessive alleles

An allele that prevails over another (*recessive*) allele is called *dominant*. The dominance or recessivity of certain alleles is often gene dependent. Whether an allele is from a sperm or an egg cell also plays an influential role. For example, in humans the allele for blood group A, inherited from the father, is dominant over a group-O gene from the mother. For each gene locus, a chromosome interpretation function for dominant and recessive alleles has to take into account (1) the set of competitive alleles (probably with an ordering on the allele alphabet), (2) the origin of each allele, and (3) the kind of gene the

Dominance and recessivity

alleles belong to (gene index). The following examples will refer to the allele alphabet {a, A, B}:

In[36] := **alleles = {a, A, B};**

The alleles are ordered according to the relation $a < A < B$. This means that allele a is recessive to A and B and allele A is dominated by B. We implement this ordering relation as a predicate RecessiveQ:

Dominance relation

In[37] := **RecessiveQ[a,A] = True;**
RecessiveQ[A,B] = True;
RecessiveQ[a,B] = True;
RecessiveQ[_,_] := False;

With these definitions we can sort an arbitrary allele sequence over the predefined alphabet:

In[38] := **Sort[{a,B,a,B,A,A},RecessiveQ]**

Out[38] = {a, a, A, A, B, B}

If we consider only diploid chromosomes, which allele combinations could occur?

All possible allele combinations

In[39] := **alleleCombinations =**
Flatten[Outer[List,alleles,alleles],1]

Out[39] = {{a, a}, {a, A}, {a, B}, {A, a}, {A, A}, {A, B}, {B, a}, {B, A}, {B, B}}

We check whether recessive and dominant alleles are correctly identified by mapping the RecessiveQ predicate on this list:

In[40] := **Map[RecessiveQ[Sequence @@ #]&,%]**

Out[40] = {False, True, True, False, False, True, False, False, False}

The predicate RecessiveQ[x_,y_] returns True if x is recessive against y. Otherwise the result is False, which means that either both alleles are identical or the first allele is dominant.

Program 3.6
Extraction of dominant alleles.

```
DominanceMap[d_List]  := Last[Sort[d,RecessiveQ]]
```

We are not interested in the relations among the competing alleles, however, but in the actual dominant allele. An extraction of
dominant alleles is implemented by the function `DominanceMap` in   *Extracting dominant alleles*
Program 3.6, which sorts each set of competing alleles according to
the dominance relation `RecessiveQ` and returns the last element.
Applying this function to the list of allele pairs returns the respective
dominant alleles:

In[41] := **Map[DominanceMap,alleleCombinations]**

Out[41] = {a, A, B, A, A, B, B, B, B}

By simple list concatenation and transposition we get a summarizing
table listing the allele pairs and their according dominant alleles:

In[42] := **{alleleCombinations,**
          Map[DominanceMap,alleleCombinations]}
       // Transpose // ColumnForm

Out[42] = {{a, a}, a}   *Table of dominant alleles*
         {{a, A}, A}
         {{a, B}, B}
         {{A, a}, A}
         {{A, A}, A}
         {{A, B}, B}
         {{B, a}, B}
         {{B, A}, B}
         {{B, B}, B}

Now that we have the basic routines for taking dominant and
recessive alleles into account, we will apply these functions to GA
chromosome structures.

Chromosome interpretation: extraction of dominant alleles

We demonstrate how to identify dominant alleles on a GA chromosome over the allele alphabet

In[43] := **alpha = {a,A,B};**

by generating a diploid chromosome of length 10:

In[44] := **diploidChromo = createChromosome[10,**
          Alphabet → alpha, PolyPloidy → 2]

Diploid
GA chromosome

Out[44] = chromo[q[undef], p[{1, {a, B}}, {2, {a, B}},
      {3, {A, A}}, {4, {a, a}}, {5, {B, a}},
      {6, {a, B}}, {7, {B, B}}, {8, {B, A}},
      {9, {a, B}}, {10, {a, A}}]]

This GA chromosome consists of two homologous single strands, as the table form shows:

In[45] := **diploidChromo // compactTableForm**

Diploid GA chromosome in
table form

Out[45] = chromo[q[undef],
      p[a   a   A   a   B   a   B   B   a   a]]
        B   B   A   a   a   B   B   A   B   A

In Figure 3.11 the two strands are depicted graphically, generated by the following function call. Darker gray values represent dominant alleles.

In[46] := **chromosomePictogramPlot[diploidChromo,**
      ColorFunction → GrayLevel,
      GraphicsOptions → {AspectRatio → 0.1}];

In order to extract dominant alleles from diploid and polyploid GA chromosomes we define the function dominance in Program 3.7. This function has basically the same structure as its diploid counterpart of Program 3.6. By the command

      MapThread[DominanceMap . . ., {paraList, indexList}]

the function defined by the DominanceMap option is mapped onto each list of homologous alleles. By using MapThread the function defined by DominanceMap has access to both the alleles (via #1) and the respective gene index (via #2).

Let us test the dominance function for our introductory example. We repeat the diploid chromosome here:

In[47] := **diploidChromo // compactTableForm**

Diploid GA chromosome
(Example 1)

Out[47] = chromo[q[undef],
      p[a   a   A   a   B   a   B   B   a   a]]
        B   B   A   a   a   B   B   A   B   A

For the dominance function Last[Sort[#]]&, where the alleles are sorted as $a < A < B$, the extraction of dominant alleles returns the following result:

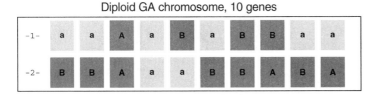

Diploid GA chromosome, 10 genes

Figure 3.11
Diploid GA chromosome
over the allele alphabet
{a, A, B}.

```
dominance[chromo[qual_q,params_p], opts___] :=

Module[{paraList,indexList},

  paraList = List @@ Map[Last,params];
  indexList = List @@ Map[First,params];

  chromo[qual,
    p @@ Transpose[
      {indexList,
       List /@ MapThread[
         DominanceMap /. {opts} /.
           Options[dominance],
         {paraList,indexList}]
      }
    ]
  ]
]

Options[dominance] =
{
  DominanceMap -> (Last[Sort[#]]&)
};
```

Program 3.7
Extraction of dominant
alleles on polyploid GA
chromosomes.

In[48] := **dominance[diploidChromo] // compactTableForm**

Out[48] = chromo[q[undef],
            p[B B A a B B B B B A]]

*GA chromosome with
dominant alleles*

Figure 3.12 depicts the graphical representation of this haploid chromosome of dominant alleles together with the initial diploid chromosome.

Figure 3.12
Diploid GA chromosome
with corresponding strand
of dominant alleles
(Example 1).

Diploid GA chromosome, 10 genes

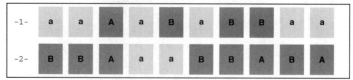

$In[49] :=$ **chromosomePictogramPlot[dominance[diploidChromo],**
        ColorFunction $\rightarrow$ GrayLevel,
        GraphicsOptions $\rightarrow$ {AspectRatio $\rightarrow$ 0.1}];

Here squares and diamonds dominate over circles. In competition to a
diamond form the square allele is recessive (gene 8). Only a single
recessive allele appears in the interpreted chromosome (gene 4), where
two identical recessive alleles (*a, a*) compete.

Let us look at a further example of defining dominance functions. Now the dominance of an allele will depend on its gene index.

Index-dependent dominance   For the chromosome in Figure 3.13(a), for genes with indices from 1
to 5 the allele of the first strand is interpreted as dominant, whereas
for all the other genes the second allele dominates.

$In[50] :=$ **diploidChromo = createChromosome[10,**
        Alphabet $\rightarrow$ alpha, PolyPloidy $\rightarrow$ 2];

$In[51] :=$ **diploidChromo // compactTableForm**

Diploid GA chromosome $Out[51]=$ chromo[q[undef],
(Example 2)
                        p[A   A   B   A   A   B   A   a   a   B]]
                           a   a   a   B   a   a   B   B   B   A

$In[52] :=$ **dominance[diploidChromo,**
        DominanceMap $\rightarrow$
        (If[#2 <=5,First[#1],Last[#1]]&)]

$In[53] :=$ **% // compactTableForm**

                        $Out[53]=$ chromo[q[undef],
Dominant alleles
                        p[A   A   B   A   A   a   B   B   B   A]]

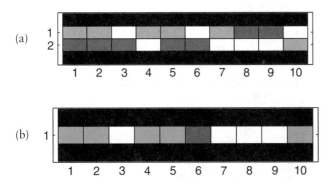

Figure 3.13
Diploid GA chromosome
with corresponding strand
of dominant alleles
(Example 2).

Figure 3.13 gives a graphical representation of the diploid chromosome and its dominant alleles.

In[54] := **chromosomePlot[%% /. letterToNumber,
        AspectRatio → 0.2];**

The first five alleles are from the first chromosome; all other alleles are copies of chromosome 2.

Using dominance relations is one way of implementing recombination effects on GA chromosomes. In Section 3.3, we demonstrate further variants of GA recombination, for example, by using recombination masks.

3.2   Point mutation on GA chromosomes

In our introductory examples on character evolution (Section 1.3) and the breeding of biomorphs (Section 1.5), we demonstrated the principal mechanisms of evolution by iterated mutation and selection. Variations of genotypical information were not achieved by merging or recombination of structural elements but by (point) mutations only. The primary effect of point mutations is to introduce new alleles into the evolution game, thereby keeping the allele bandwidth of the gene pool on a constant level. Mutations counteract one of the side effects of recombinations, which—by reorganizing already existing building blocks—tend to reduce the diversity of allele combinations. Recombinations rearrange genes, but they do not change allele settings (Section 3.3).

Mutation: perpetual novelty

With the example of binary haploid chromosomes, we first define point mutations in Section 3.2.1. A general formalization and implementation of point mutations in polyploid GA chromosomes is presented in Section 3.2.2. With additional examples we investigate

Section overview

the effects of different control parameter settings of the mutation operator on diploid GA chromosomes (Section 3.2.3) and on RNA nucleotide base sequences (Section 3.2.4). We conclude this section on GA point mutations with a mutation and visualization example of 10-dimensional parameter vectors using stylized facial expressions (Section 3.2.5).

3.2.1   Mutations on haploid GA chromosomes

We refer to Section 3.1 for the definition of a single-strand chromosome of n genes as a vector s of the following form:

Haploid GA chromosome

$$s = (s_1, \ldots, s_n) \text{ with } s_i \in A,\ 1 \le i \le n.$$

The alleles s_i take their values from the allele alphabet $A = \{a_1, \ldots, a_k\}$. To keep the formulas simple, we do not explicitly list the gene indices. For point mutations, gene loci are irrelevant. Basically, the effect of point mutation is that at randomly chosen positions the allele settings are changed. For each gene an allele is substituted by a new "value" from the allele alphabet with a certain probability p_m. The *point mutation* operator $\omega_{mut}\colon S_A \to S_A$, where S represents the set of all GA chromosomes over alphabet A, generates a new chromosome s' according to the following rules:

$$s' = (\, s_1', \ldots, s_n' \,)$$

GA point mutation

$$s_i' = \begin{cases} s \in A - \{s_i\} & \text{if } \chi \le p_m \\ s_i & \text{otherwise.} \end{cases}$$

Here χ denotes a uniformly distributed random variable from the interval $[0, 1]$, and p_m is the probability of point mutation per gene locus.

Mutation of haploid binary chromosomes

Let us examine the mutation operator with an example of a binary chromosome over allele alphabet $A = \{0, 1\}$. We generate a chromosome of length 10.

```
In[1] := binChromo = createChromosome[10]
           % // compactTableForm
```

Out[1] = chromo[q[undef], p[{1, {1}}, {2, {1}}, {3, {0}},   *Haploid binary chromosome*
     {4, {0}}, {5, {0}}, {6, {1}}, {7, {0}}, {8, {0}},
     {9, {0}}, {10, {1}}]]

    chromo[q[undef],
      p[1   1   0   0   0   1   0   0   0   1]]

This GA chromosome is depicted in Figure 3.14(a).

In[2] := **chromosomePictogramPlot[binChromo,**
      Pictograms → {RECTANGLE, DIAMOND},
      ColorFunction → GrayLevel,
      GraphicsOptions → {AspectRatio → 0.1}];

If we want to mutate all the genes, we must set the mutation probability to $p_m = 1$.

In[3] := **binChromoMut = Mutation[binChromo,**   *Mutation with $p_m = 1$*
      PointMutationProbability → 1];

In[4] := **% // compactTableForm**

Out[4] = chromo[q[undef],
      p[0   0   1   1   1   0   1   1   1   0]]

Initial chromosome

(a)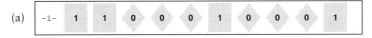

Figure 3.14
Examples of point mutations
on a haploid chromosome.

Mutant 1: *p = 1.0*

(b)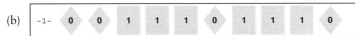

Mutant 2: *p = 0.5*

(c)

Mutant 3: *p = 0.2*

(d)

Mutant 4: *p = 0.1*

(e)

We get the "inverse" chromosome as each one is turned into a zero and vice versa (Figure 3.14[b]). The point mutation function `Muta-tion`, which we use here, will be explained in a later section (Program 3.8). The point mutation probability p_m is set by the option `Point-MutationProbability` with a value between 0 and 1.

With a setting for p_m of 50%, on average only every other gene will receive a new allele:

Mutation with $p_m = 0.5$

In[5] := **binChromoMutTwo = Mutation[binChromo,**
                   PointMutationProbability → 0.5]
              // compactTableForm

Out[5] = chromo[q[undef],
                 p[0   1   1   0   0   1   1   1   1   0]]

Here the genes 1, 3, and 7 to 10 are mutated (Figure 3.14[c]). The figure also shows results for $p_m = 0.2$ and $p_m = 0.1$, where the third and fifth gene (d) and none of the genes (e) are changed, respectively. On average we would expect one mutated gene in the last case, but since mutation is a stochastic operator, it is possible that none of the ten genes mutates at all.

3.2.2 Mutation functions for polyploid GA chromosomes

Beyond this simple introductory example, we can extend the point mutation operator to polyploid GA chromosomes. This means that for each gene location not only one allele but each of the homologous alleles might change. Whether an allele mutation is actually "visible" after the interpretation of the genetic information depends on whether mutations act on dominant or recessive alleles. The rate of mutation may also vary among genes.

A polyploid GA chromosome set $s^{(m)}$, consisting of m homologous single strands of length n

$$s_i = (s_{i1}, \ldots, s_{in}) \text{ with } 1 \leq i \leq m$$

was defined in Section 3.1.2 as follows:

Polyploid GA chromosome

$$s^{(m)} = ((s_{11}, \ldots, s_{m1}), \ldots, (s_{1n}, \ldots, s_{mn})).$$

Again, we do not explicitly list the gene indices. The alleles $s_{ij} \in A$ take their values from the alphabet $A = \{a_1, \ldots, a_k\}$. Point mutation on a polyploid GA chromosome set is defined as point mutation mapped onto the haploid allele groups. The mutated set of chromosomes

$$s'^{(m)} = ((s'_{11}, \ldots, s'_{m1}), \ldots, (s'_{1n}, \ldots, s'_{mn}))$$

is generated as follows. For each gene each according allele is substituted by a new allele entry with point mutation probability p_m.

$$s'_{ij} = \begin{cases} s \in A - \{s_{ij}\} & \text{if } \chi \leq p_m \\ s_{ij} & \text{otherwise} \end{cases} \quad \text{for } 1 \leq i \leq m,\ 1 \leq j \leq n.$$

Point mutation for polyploid GA chromosomes

Again, χ denotes a uniformly distributed random variable from the unit interval $[0, 1]$, and p_m is the probability of mutation per haploid gene entry (PointMutationProbability). The function Mutation, defined in Program 3.8, implements this point mutation on polyploid GA chromosomes.

Let us take a closer look at the optional arguments of the Mutation function. The option Alphabet sets the allele alphabet, and MutationProbability determines the probability of applying the

Program 3.8
Mutation of polyploid GA chromosomes.

```
Mutation[chromo[qual_q,params_p],opts___] :=

Module[{alph,flipProb},

   If[chi[] <= (MutationProbability /. {opts}
              /. Options[Mutation]),

     alph := Alphabet /. {opts} /. Options[Mutation];

     flipProb = PointMutationProbability /. {opts}
              /. Options[Mutation];

     chromo[q[undef],
       Map[geneMutation[#,flipProb,alph]&,params]],

     chromo[qual,params]
   ]
]

Options[Mutation] =
{
   Alphabet → {0,1},
   MutationProbability → 1.0,
   PointMutationProbability → 0.1
}
```

mutation operator to the whole chromosome set, whereas the mutation probability for each allele is defined by `PointMutationProbability`.

Program 3.9
Uniform random number.

```
chi[] := Random[Real,{0,1}]
```

The function `Mutation` first checks whether mutations should be performed on the chromosome at all. If the random number generated by `chi[]` in Program 3.9 is smaller or equal to the mutation probability `MutationProbability`, the allele alphabet (`alph`) and the point mutation probability (`flipProb`) are determined.

Program 3.10
Point mutation of
homologous alleles.

```
geneMutation[{i_,alleles_List},
   flipProb_:0.5,alphabet_:{0,1}] :=
{i,
 Map[If[chi[]<=flipProb,flip[#,alphabet],#]&,alleles
]}
```

The actual modification of the alleles is performed by the function `geneMutation` in Program 3.10, which mutates the list of alleles for each gene locus `i`. Depending on the point mutation probability, the function `flip` substitutes an allele with a new element from the allele alphabet (Program 3.11).

Program 3.11
Allele substitution.

```
flip[e_,sel_List] :=
randomSelect[Complement[sel,{e}]]
```

With this implementation of a point mutation on polyploid GA chromosomes, we can discuss mutation effects with a few more examples.

3.2.3 Mutation of diploid GA chromosomes

We start from a diploid binary chromosome of length 10 over the allele alphabet $A = \{0, 1\}$.

```
In[6] := binDiploidChromo =
         createChromosome[10, PolyPloidy → 2]
         % // compactTableForm
```

Out[6] = chromo[q[undef], p[{1, {0, 1}}, {2, {0, 0}},   *Diploid binary chromosome*
          {3, {1, 1}}, {4, {1, 1}}, {5, {1, 0}}, {6,
          {1, 1}}, {7, {0, 1}}, {8, {0, 1}}, {9, {0, 1}},
          {10, {1, 1}}]]

```
          chromo[q[undef],
              p[0   0   1   1   1   1   0   0   0   1]]
                 1   0   1   1   0   1   1   1   1   1
```

This is depicted graphically in Figure 3.15, which also shows mutants of this chromosome for point mutation probabilities $p_m = 1.0$, $p_m = 0.5$, $p_m = 0.2$, and $p_m = 0.1$. These chromosomes were generated in analogy to the following function call for a 50% point mutation:

```
In[7] := binDiploidChromoMut =                              Point mutation
         Mutation[binDiploidChromo,                         with pm = 0.5
             PointMutationProbability → 0.5 ]
         % // compactTableForm
```

Out[7] = chromo[q[undef], p[{1, {0, 0}}, {2, {1, 0}},
          {3, {0, 0}}, {4, {0, 0}}, {5, {0, 0}},
          {6, {1, 1}}, {7, {0, 0}}, {8, {0, 1}},
          {9, {1, 0}}, {10, {1, 1}}]]

```
          chromo[q[undef],
              p[0   1   0   0   0   1   0   0   1   1]]
                 0   0   0   0   0   1   0   1   0   1
```

Figure 3.15(b) shows the "inverse" variant of the initial chromosome. Each allele is replaced by its dual value. If the point mutation probability is reduced, for each gene either or both alleles may be changed (Figure 3.15[c], genes 3 and 4), or only one of the homologous alleles (Figure 3.15[c], genes 2 and 7) is mutated. A gene might also remain unchanged (Figure 3.15[c], genes 6, 8, and 10). The smaller the probability for an allele change, the fewer differences occur compared to the initial chromosome. Generally, for $p_m = 0.2$, 4 of the 20 alleles will be changed (Figure 3.15[d]), for $p_m = 0.1$ approximately 2 out of 20 will change (Figure 3.15[e]), and so on. However, for an exact calculation of the probability for a gene mutation we

Figure 3.15
Mutations of a diploid
binary chromosome.

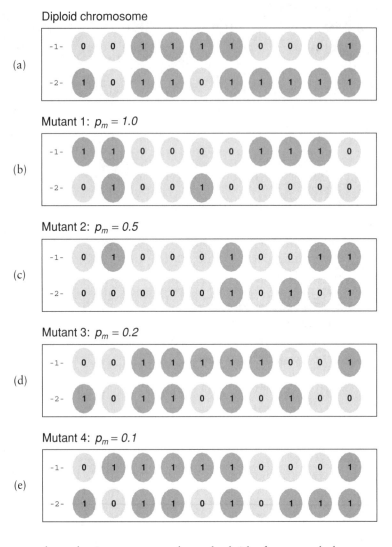

must also take into account the polyploidy factor and the average
number of dominant alleles per gene.

3.2.4 Mutations on RNA chromosomes

In this section, we return to our simple RNA translation model in Section 3.1.1, where we simulate triplet encodings of sequences of amino acids on RNA strands. Here we want to simulate point mutations on the level of nucleotide bases. Figure 3.16 gives an example of these mutation effects, where the change of a single nucleotide base can

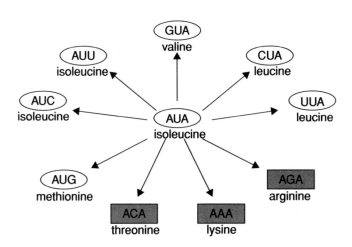

Figure 3.16
Effect of point mutations on
nucleotide bases.

result in a triplet for a different amino acid or simply a switch to an
alternative codon for the same amino acid.

We generate an RNA chromosome over allele alphabet A = {A, C,
G, U}, with 498 nucleotide bases:

In[1] := **rnaChromo = createChromosome[498,**
      Alphabet → {A,C,G,U}];

      rnaChromo // compactForm

Out[1] = chromo[q[undef], p[{A, U, G, U, A, G, C, C, C, C,   *Chromosome of nucleotide*
      U, A, A, G, C, U, C, A, G, A, U, C, C, C, C, C, G,   *bases*
      C, U, A, U, C, C, G, U, C, A, C, A, G, G, G, C, C,
      C, C, G, A, A, A, A, C, C, U, A, C, G, G, C, C, A,
      G, C, G, G, C, C, A, U, G, C, A, A, A, C, G, A, A,
      A, A, A, C, U, C, C, G, G, C, C, U, G, U, G, G, G,
      U, A, U, C, G, A, G, A, C, U, G, G, U, G, C, A, U,
      C, A, G, G, A, G, A, U, U, C, U, U, U, C, A, A, G,
      C, A, G, G, U, G, U, C, G, C, C, U, C, U, U, C, G,
      C, C, C, A, U, A, U, U, A, G, U, G, U, C, G, U, G,
      U, A, U, C, A, U, U, G, G, G, A, U, A, A, C, U, U,
      A, U, G, C, U, G, C, A, U, A, G, U, A, A, A, U, C,
      G, U, G, G, G, G, C, U, A, A, A, U, A, G, U, A, G,
      G, U, C, G, C, U, C, C, A, C, U, A, A, G, U, A, A,
      U, G, A, C, G, G, G, C, G, C, A, C, A, A, A, U, U,
      G, C, G, A, U, G, A, G, U, G, C, G, C, U, A, A, U,
      G, C, G, C, C, A, G, G, G, C, C, U, G, C, U, G, G,
      A, C, A, G, C, G, G, G, A, U, C, U, A, C, U, C, A,
      A, G, C, U, A, A, A, G, C, A, G, U, C, C, A, G, C,

```
U, U, A, C, G, A, C, C, C, C, C, U, A, U, G, G, G,
G, A, G, A, C, G, C, U, A, G, G, A, U, U, U, G, C,
A, U, G, G, C, C, G, G, G, G, U, U, U, A, A, U, C,
C, A, G, U, C, U, A, A, C, U, U, U, A, A, U, A, A,
U, U, A, U, A, C, A, G, A, U, U, A, U, C, G, C, U,
G, G, A, G, A, A, G, C, U, C, G, A, A, U, G, U, U,
C, G, C, G, A, G, A, U, U, C, C, A, C, C, C, A, A,
C, C, U, G, A, C, U, C, U, G, C, C, G, U, A, U, G,
A, G, A, C, A, G, A, G, A, G, U, G, C, C, U, G, U,
U, G, G, G, A, C, A, G, U, A, U, A, A, C, C, U, A,
G, C, G, G, U, C, A, G, C, U, A, A}]]
```

Each group of three elements (triplet) encodes for an amino acid or a genetic "punctuation mark" (such as STOP). This triplet-amino-acid translation is performed by the function `ribosome`, defined in Program 3.5 (Section 3.1.1). Applying this function to the RNA chromosome results in the following sequence of amino acids, depicted in Figure 3.17(a).

In[2] := **rnaAminos = ribosome[rnaChromo];**
          rnaAminos // compactForm

Basic RNA chromosome

Out[2] = chromo[q[undef], p[{Met, STOP, Pro, Leu, Ser,
          Ser, Asp, Pro, Pro, Leu, Ser, Val, Thr, Gly, Pro,
          Arg, Lys, Pro, Thr, Ala, Ser, Gly, His, Ala, Asn,
          Glu, Lys, Leu, Arg, Pro, Val, Gly, Ile, Glu, Thr,
          Gly, Ala, Ser, Gly, Asp, Ser, Phe, Lys, Gln, Val,
          Ser, Pro, Leu, Arg, Pro, Tyr, STOP, Cys, Arg,
          Val, Ser, Leu, Gly, STOP, Leu, Met, Leu, His,
          Ser, Lys, Ser, Trp, Gly, STOP, Ile, Val, Gly,
          Arg, Ser, Thr, Lys, STOP, STOP, Arg, Ala, His,
          Lys, Leu, Arg, STOP, Val, Arg, STOP, Cys, Ala,
          Arg, Ala, Cys, Trp, Thr, Ala, Gly, Ser, Thr, Gln,
          Ala, Lys, Ala, Val, Gln, Leu, Thr, Thr, Pro, Tyr,
          Gly, Glu, Thr, Leu, Gly, Phe, Ala, Trp, Pro, Gly,
          Phe, Asn, Pro, Val, STOP, Leu, STOP, STOP, Leu,
          Tyr, Arg, Leu, Ser, Leu, Glu, Lys, Leu, Glu, Cys,
          Ser, Arg, Asp, Ser, Thr, Gln, Pro, Asp, Ser, Ala,
          Val, STOP, Asp, Arg, Glu, Cys, Leu, Leu, Gly,
          Gln, Tyr, Asn, Leu, Ala, Val, Ser, STOP}]]

RNA mutation

Now we mutate the initial RNA chromosome such that about five out of 100 nucleotide bases will be exchanged. In nature this would

(a)

Base-RNA chromosome

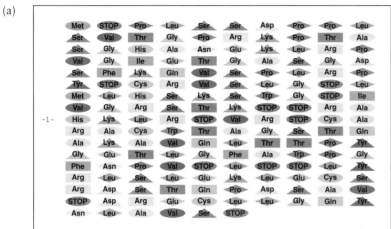

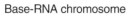

Figure 3.17
Mutation of RNA
chromosomes, sequences
of amino acids.

(b)

Mutant: *p = 0.05*

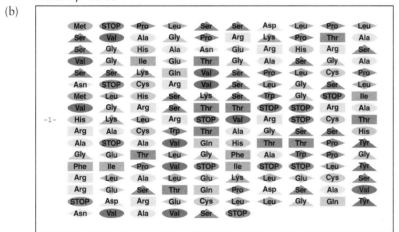

mean an extremely high rate of mutation—usually the mutation rate
in natural RNA is between 10^{-5} and 10^{-6} per nucleotide base. We use
a rate of $p_m = 0.05$ and examine the resulting sequence of amino
acids.

```
In[3] := rnaChromoMut =
    Mutation[rnaChromo,
        PointMutationProbability → 0.05,
        Alphabet → {A,C,G,U}];

In[4] := rnaAminosMut = ribosome[rnaChromoMut];
    rnaAminosMut // compactForm
```

Mutated RNA chromosome

```
Out[4] = chromo[q[undef], p[{Met, STOP, Pro, Leu, Ser,
              Ser, Asp, Leu, Pro, Leu, Ser, Val, Ala, Gly, Pro,
              Arg, Lys, Pro, Thr, Ala, Ser, Gly, His, Ala, Asn,
              Glu, Arg, His, Arg, Ser, Val, Gly, Ile, Glu, Thr,
              Gly, Ala, Ser, Gly, Ala, Ser, Ser, Lys, Gln, Val,
              Ser, Pro, Leu, Cys, Pro, Asn, STOP, Cys, Arg,
              Val, Ser, Leu, Gly, Ser, Leu, Met, Leu, His, Ser,
              Lys, Ser, Trp, Gly, STOP, Ile, Val, Gly, Arg,
              Ser, Thr, Thr, STOP, STOP, Arg, Ala, His, Lys,
              Leu, Arg, STOP, Val, Arg, STOP, Cys, Thr, Arg,
              Ala, Cys, Trp, Thr, Ala, Gly, Ser, Ser, His, Ala,
              STOP, Ala, Val, Gln, His, Thr, Thr, Pro, Tyr,
              Gly, Glu, Thr, Leu, Gly, Phe, Ala, Trp, Pro, Gly,
              Phe, Ile, Pro, Val, STOP, Ile, STOP, STOP, Leu,
              Tyr, Arg, Leu, Ala, Leu, Glu, Lys, Leu, Glu, Cys,
              Ser, Arg, Glu, Ser, Thr, Gln, Pro, Asp, Ser, Ala,
              Val, STOP, Asp, Arg, Glu, Cys, Leu, Leu, Gly,
              Gln, Tyr, Asn, Val, Ala, Val, Ser, STOP}]]
```

This new chain of amino acids is shown in Figure 3.17(b), but it is hard to see the resulting changes. The function getAlleles in Program 3.12 provides a better overview of the changes that occur. This function extracts the alleles as lists from the chromosome data structure.

Program 3.12
Extraction of alleles for RNA chromosomes.

```
getAlleles[chromo[_q,params_p]] :=
  Transpose[List @@ Map[Last,params]]
```

Now we can compute the difference between the two allele lists of the initial and the mutated chromosome:

In[5] := **getAlleles[rnaAminos] - getAlleles[rnaAminosMut]**

Identification of mutated triplets

```
Out[5] = {{0, 0, 0, 0, 0, 0, 0, -Leu + Pro, 0, 0, 0, 0,
           -Ala + Thr, 0, 0, 0, 0, 0, 0, 0, 0, 0, 0, 0, 0, 0,
           -Arg + Lys, -His + Leu, 0, Pro - Ser, 0, 0, 0, 0,
           0, 0, 0, 0, 0, -Ala + Asp, 0, Phe - Ser, 0, 0, 0,
           0, 0, 0, Arg - Cys, 0, -Asn + Tyr, 0, 0, 0, 0, 0,
           0, 0, -Ser + STOP, 0, 0, 0, 0, 0, 0, 0, 0, 0, 0,
           0, 0, 0, 0, 0, 0, Lys - Thr, 0, 0, 0, 0, 0, 0, 0,
           0, 0, 0, 0, 0, 0, Ala - Thr, 0, 0, 0, 0, 0, 0, 0,
```

```
0, -Ser + Thr, Gln - His, 0, Lys - STOP, 0, 0, 0,
-His + Leu, 0, 0, 0, 0, 0, 0, 0, 0, 0, 0, 0, 0, 0,
0, 0, Asn - Ile, 0, 0, 0, -Ile + Leu, 0, 0, 0, 0,
0, 0, -Ala + Ser, 0, 0, 0, 0, 0, 0, 0, 0, Asp -
Glu, 0, 0, 0, 0, 0, 0, 0, 0, 0, 0, 0, 0, 0, 0,
0, 0, 0, 0, Leu - Val, 0, 0, 0, 0}}
```

Indeed, a few changes occurred. The resulting list shows the entries where an amino acid is replaced by another one. The original amino acid labels are marked by a plus sign, while the new entries are marked as negative. For example, we can see from the list that the original eighth amino acid, proline (+Pro), is replaced by leucine (-Leu). Each zero entry in the list means that the amino acid entry did not change, at least not at the amino acid level. Mutations might have occurred on the nucleotide bases, but since the amino acid encoding is highly redun- *Silent mutations* dant (see Section 3.1.1) a change in a triplet does not necessarily result in a change in the corresponding amino acid. These are examples of *silent mutations*.

3.2.5 Mutations and faces

We conclude this section on GA mutations with an example of visualizing mutation effects through stylized facial expressions. Finding intuitive, quickly understandable graphical representations of multidimensional number vectors poses some difficult problems, since data plots usually have at most three spatial dimensions and a few additional dimensions available through coloring. However, a few illustrative methods have been developed for visualizing high-dimensional *Visualizing high-dimensional* data using two- or three-dimensional figures, faces, or abstract forms, *data* which are easy to grasp visually and also allow for quick comparisons of data sets.

We will show a typical example of this visualization technique for representing 10-dimensional number vectors with facial expressions (Figure 3.18). The graphics are based on the Mathematica notebook *Faces.ma*, by S. Dickson (Dickson 1995). The idea of using abstract figures for data visualization and the approach of *Chernoff figures* we *Chernoff figures* use here is described in Chernoff (Chernoff 1973). In particular, these visualizations take advantage of the human ability to recognize even slight changes in facial expressions.

We slightly modified the programs from the notebook *Faces.ma*, first of all, to make the graphical representations of the faces more appealing by adding shadows and, second, to be able to use the functions for chromosome visualization. Let us first look briefly at how

Figure 3.18
Typical Chernoff face for
visualizing multidimensional
number vectors.

number vectors are converted into facial expressions. We start with
10-dimensional vectors, the components of which are real or integer
numbers between 1 and 10. In such a vector of the form

$$(p_1, p_2, \ldots, p_{10})$$

Parametrized faces

each component parametrizes a characteristic feature of the facial
expression. The first parameter, for example, determines the width-
height ratio of the face, the second parameter sets the size of the eyes,
the third parameter influences the distance of the eyes, and so on. Figure 3.18 shows the facial expression for parameter vector

$$(6, 6, 6, 6, 6, 6, 6, 6, 6, 6).$$

Starting from this base vector, for each row in Figure 3.19, the
first, second, . . . , tenth parameter is varied between 1 and 10. The
first row, for example, from left to right, depicts the faces for the following vectors:

$$(1, 6, 6, 6, 6, 6, 6, 6, 6, 6)$$
$$(2, 6, 6, 6, 6, 6, 6, 6, 6, 6)$$
$$(3, 6, 6, 6, 6, 6, 6, 6, 6, 6)$$

$$\cdot$$
$$\cdot$$
$$\cdot$$

$$(10, 6, 6, 6, 6, 6, 6, 6, 6, 6)$$

The faces in the sixth column are identical to the reference face of
Figure 3.18. These facial expressions offer an illustrative way of representing multidimensional vectors and allow for immediate comparison of the vectors. So let us take advantage of our ability to intuitively
grasp facial expressions and use the faces to illustrate mutation effects
in GA chromosomes. For this purpose we generate a reference chromosome for which all alleles have the value 6. This will serve as the
"genome" for our referential face:

In[1] := **faceChromo =**
          createChromosome[10, Alphabet → Range[6,6]]
          % // compactTableForm

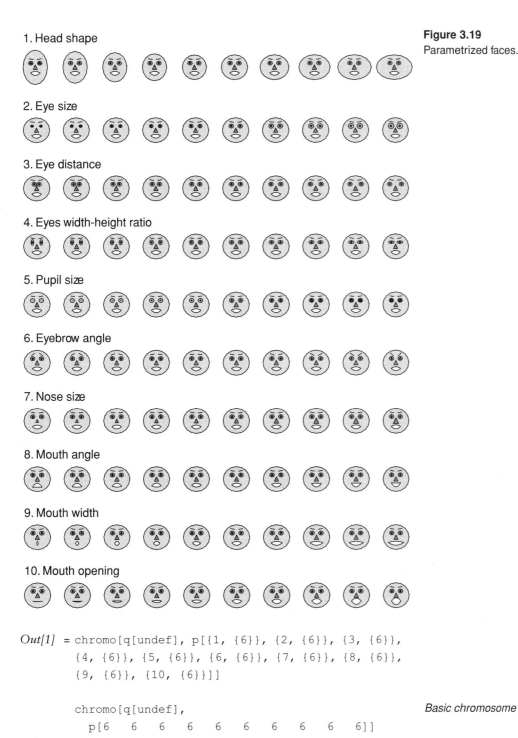

Figure 3.19
Parametrized faces.

1. Head shape

2. Eye size

3. Eye distance

4. Eyes width-height ratio

5. Pupil size

6. Eyebrow angle

7. Nose size

8. Mouth angle

9. Mouth width

10. Mouth opening

```
Out[1] = chromo[q[undef], p[{1, {6}}, {2, {6}}, {3, {6}},
         {4, {6}}, {5, {6}}, {6, {6}}, {7, {6}}, {8, {6}},
         {9, {6}}, {10, {6}}]]

         chromo[q[undef],                              Basic chromosome
            p[6   6   6   6   6   6   6   6   6   6]]
```

From GA chromosomes to
faces

The faces in Figures 3.18 and 3.19 were generated with the function chromosomeFacePlot, the definition of which we omit here for brevity. The arguments and options are analogous to the function chromosomePictogramPlot in Section 3.1. More details can be found in this section's Evolvica notebook on the *IEC* Web page (see Preface). The following command returns the reference face of Figure 3.18:

In[2] := **chromosomeFacePlot[faceChromo];**

We generate a few mutants of this reference chromosome for different mutation probabilities. To make the input a little more convenient, we define a function faceChromoMut[pm_] as listed in Program 3.13, which generates a mutant of the initial chromosome with point mutation probability p_m.

Program 3.13
Mutation of "face
chromosomes."

```
faceChromoMut[prob_] := Mutation[faceChromo,
   Alphabet → Range[1,10], MutationProbability → 1,
   PointMutationProbability → prob ];
```

The following function call returns a list of 23 mutants ($p_m = 0.1$) of the reference chromosome and displays them together with the reference face in a six-column tabular form.

Generating mutated faces

In[3] := **chromosomeFacePlot[**
              Join[{faceChromo},t = Table[faceChromoMut[0.1],
              {23}]], TableWidth → 6];

The resulting graphics are depicted in Figure 3.20. The reference face is in the top left corner. Due to a rather small mutation rate in this example, the mutated faces still bear a close resemblance to their "ancestor."

Of course, this similarity will decrease the more parameters are modified. For a mutation rate of $p_m = 0.2$ some of the faces display totally different features compared to the reference face (Figure 3.20, bottom). For a mutation rate of even 50%, totally new features appear (Figure 3.21, top). When these faces are compared with those in Figure 3.20, the effects of an increased point mutation probability are obvious. Mutations with a rate of $p_m = 1.0$ generate purely random faces. This little collection gives a taste of the large variety of facial expressions possible (Figure 3.21, bottom) but is only a small slice from the total of 10^{10} possible different faces.

Mutants 1: $p_m = 0.1$

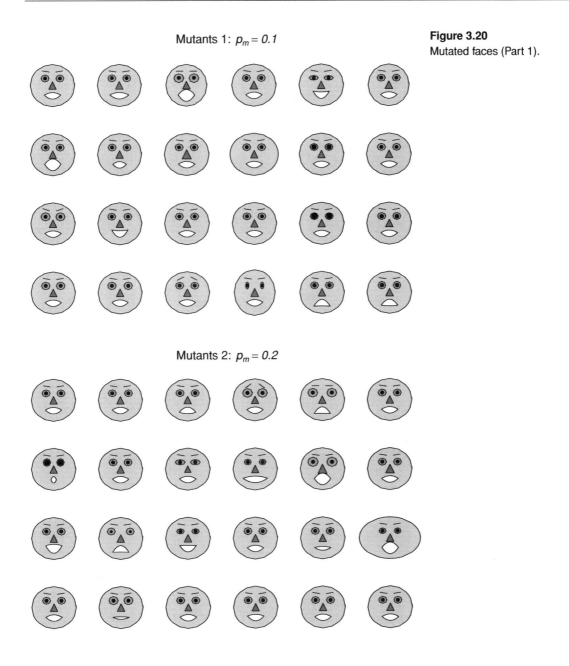

Figure 3.20
Mutated faces (Part 1).

Mutants 2: $p_m = 0.2$

3.3 GA recombination

The exchange of genetic information among different genomes plays a tremendous role in the evolution of higher living organisms. Selective point mutations may only rarely induce "innovations." The real driving force behind the evolutionary "perpetual novelty" lies in the

Figure 3.21
Mutated faces
(Part 2).

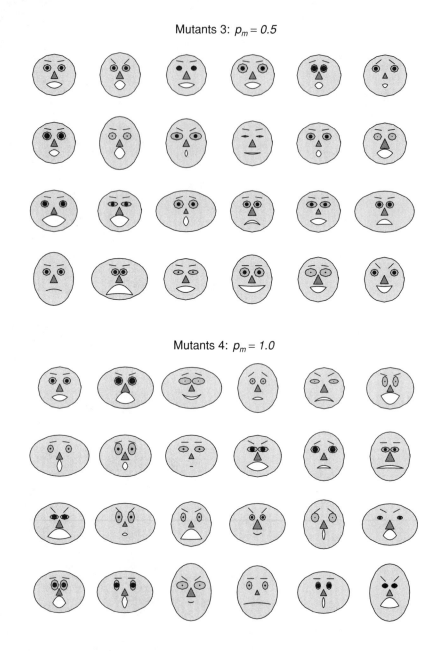

Combination of well-evaluated building blocks

combination of already tested genotypical building blocks, which are combined in new ways and expressed as improved phenotypes. The mechanisms of selection in essence ensure that well-adapted building blocks are transferred into the next generations, setting the foundation for successful further evolution of the genomes. If several of those successful building blocks meet, they might form a new and innovative team of genes, providing the basis for even better adapted and competitive phenotypes.

It is the central role of recombining genetic operators that makes genetic algorithms distinct from other evolution-based algorithmic schemes, for example, evolution strategies ((Rechenberg 1973; Rechenberg 1994b; Chapter 4) or evolutionary programming (Fogel, Owens, et al. 1966; Fogel 1999; Chapter 6). From the beginning, John Holland emphasized the significance of recombinations among several chromosomes (Holland 1975; Holland 1992a, p. 97 ff.) versus mutations, which are restricted to single chromosomes only, thereby inducing no information exchange:

Everybody thought genetic algorithms were mutations. I felt the critical thing was to convince them that something else was going on when you had recombination.

John Holland (Levy 1993a, p. 186)

Section 3.3.1 provides an introductory overview of recombinations on simple list structures, which are extended to GA chromosomes in Section 3.3.2. We then show how to simulate meiotic recombination of diploid chromosomes (Section 3.3.3). This recombination section concludes with additional illustrations of recombination effects on facial expressions (Section 3.3.4).

Section overview

3.3.1 Recombinations on lists

One of the essential effects of recombinations is that groups of neighboring genes are exchanged among several chromosomes. For evolution strategies we will get to know a variety of these operators—discrete or intermediate, global or local recombinations (Section 4.3). Since genetic algorithm alleles are always built from a discrete alphabet, intermediate GA recombinations are excluded. The basic idea of distinguishing between local and global ranges for the recombination operators is also expressed through genetic algorithms. However, the possibilities of combination among polyploid GA chromosomes are a lot more complicated, as we will see in Section 3.3.2. Right now, we discuss a few variants of recombination on simple lists or vectors. As a starting point we take m vectors or m homologous, haploid chromosomes s_1, s_2 to s_m:

Discrete recombination

$$s_1 = (s_{11}, \ldots, s_{1n}), \quad s_2 = (s_{21}, \ldots, s_{2n}), \ldots,$$
$$s_m = (s_{m1}, \ldots, s_{mn}),$$

where each $s_{ij} \in A$, $1 \le i \le m$, $1 \le j \le n$, denotes an allele from the alphabet $A = \{a_1, \ldots, a_k\}$. In general, a columnwise combination of the components can be defined by a recombining m-ary function ρ:

Componentwise
recombination

$$s_\rho = (\rho(s_{11}, \ldots, s_{m1}), \ldots, \rho(s_{1n}, \ldots, s_{mn})).$$

For the recombined vector s_ρ the respective components of vectors s_1, $s_2, \ldots, s_m$ are combined.

Binary, componentwise recombination

Let us look at the following example. Starting from two vectors s1 and s2, the function Recombine from Program 3.14 returns the scheme of a recombined vector rec_{s1s2} in the first sublist:

In[1] := {s$_1$, s$_2$} =
          {{a,b,c,d,e,f,g,h,k,l},{A,B,C,D,E,F,G,H,K,L}};

In[2] := {rec$_{s1s2}$, recMask} = Recombine[{s$_1$, s$_2$}]

Out[2] = {{r[{a, A}, 1], r[{b, B}, 2], r[{c, C}, 3],
            r[{d, D}, 4], r[{e, E}, 5], r[{f, F}, 6],
            r[{g, G}, 7], r[{h, H}, 8], r[{k, K}, 9],
            r[{l, L}, 10]}, {}}

As Program 3.14 shows, the function Recombine generates a combined list from a list of lists. It also returns another list containing a protocol of the actual combinations. In the current example this list is empty. We will explain later why this is the case. The kind of combination to be performed on the sublists is determined by the option RecombinationMode. The default setting is NORMAL, which means that the function defined by RecombinationFunction is used to recombine parameters componentwise (cf. the Recombine function of evolution strategies in Section 4.3, Program 4.8). Note that the recombining function, in addition to the corresponding parameters to be recombined, also has access to the current parameter index via the second argument. This way you can, for instance, define a recombination function oddEvenRecombination, which for even indices chooses the first and for all other indices the second vector's entry.

```
Recombine[params_List,opts___] :=

Module[{recMode, coPoints, l = Length[params//First],
        recFun},

  Switch[recMode = (RecombinationMode /. {opts}
                   /. Options[Recombine]),

    POINT[_],
      coPoints = First[recMode];
      {MapIndexed[params[[#1,First[#2]]]&,
        mask = recombinationMask[l,
           RecombinationPoints -> coPoints,
           RecombinationPartners -> Length[params]]],
       mask},

    MULTIPOINT,
      {MapIndexed[params[[#1,First[#2]]]&,
        mask =
        Table[Random[Integer,{1,Length[params]}],{l}]],
       mask},

    MASK[_],
      mask = First[recMode];
      {MapIndexed[params[[#1,First[#2]]]&,mask],mask},

    NORMAL|_,
      recFun := RecombinationFunction /. {opts}
               /. Options[Recombine];
      {MapIndexed[recFun[#1,First[#2]]&,
        Transpose[params]],{}}
  ]
]


Options[Recombine] :=
{
  RecombinationMode -> NORMAL,
  RecombinationFunction :> r
};
```

Program 3.14
Recombination on lists.

In[3] := **oddEvenRecombination[x_,i_] :=**
              If[EvenQ[i],First[x],Last[x]]

Recombination with an index-involving recombination function

    Recombine[{s1, s2},
        RecombinationFunction → oddEvenRecombination]

Out[3] = {{A, b, C, d, E, f, G, h, K, l}, {}}

This function may also be used for determining which genetic traits are taken from either the father or the mother chromosomes.

Discrete, componentwise multirecombination

Another variant of recombination, which is analogous to the discrete recombination of evolution strategies, is provided by the MULTI-POINT option.

Multirecombination

In[4] := **Recombine[{s_1, s_2},**
        RecombinationMode → MULTIPOINT]

Out[4] = {{A, b, c, D, E, f, g, h, K, L},
        {2, 1, 1, 2, 2, 1, 1, 1, 2, 2}}

For each "column" one of the two parameters is chosen at random. In fact, RecombinationMode → MULTIPOINT corresponds to the following settings:

    RecombinationMode → NORMAL,
    RecombinationFunction → (randomSelect[#1]&).

    But there is one important difference. With the MULTIPOINT setting not only the recombined vector is returned but also a recombination mask revealing detailed information about how the resulting vector was composed. The mask for the above example,

Recombination mask

$$\{2, 1, 1, 2, 2, 1, 1, 1, 2, 2\},$$

means that the first component originates from vector 2, the second and third components from the first vector, and so on.

Crossover—cross recombination of chromosomes

The kind of recombinations we have introduced up to now have very little in common with natural recombinations in genomes. In particular, exchanges of genetic material take place at the cell division phase of meiosis (see Section 3.3.3). Further natural mechanisms of recombination occur in the context of translocations. The basic recombination effect results from a crosswise interchange of chromosome segments. We can simulate this kind of recombination by setting RecombinationMode $\rightarrow$ POINT[1]:

In[5] := {recChromo, recMask} =
        Recombine[{s$_1$, s$_2$},
            RecombinationMode $\rightarrow$ POINT[1]]

Crosswise recombination

Out[5] = {{a, b, c, d, E, F, G, H, K, L},
        {1, 1, 1, 1, 2, 2, 2, 2, 2, 2}}

The two vectors are "crossed" with each other, as illustrated in Figure 3.22(a). The crossover point is between the fourth and fifth gene. In the recombined chromosome the first four parameters originate from vector s1, and the remaining parameters are taken from s2, as is also indicated by the recombination mask {1, 1, 1, 1, 2, 2, 2, 2, 2, 2}. Figure 3.22(b) shows the vector returned through Recombine. In order to get the dual crossover vector, we compute the "inverse" recombination mask

In[6] := **inverseRecombinationMask[recMask]**

Inverse recombination mask

Out[6] = {2, 2, 2, 2, 1, 1, 1, 1, 1, 1}

and derive the composition of the second vector (Figure 3.22[c]). This is exactly what the function crossoverPlot does, with which the graphics in Figure 3.22 are generated.

In[7] := **crossoverPlot[{s$_1$, s$_2$},recMask];**

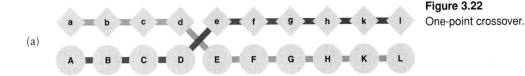

Figure 3.22
One-point crossover.

(a)

(b)

(c)

We will not delve into the implementation details of these functions, which are defined and illustrated by many examples in the Evolvica notebook of this section on the *IEC* Web page (see Preface).

The POINT[n] option is parametrized. The parameter n determines the number of crossover points, which can be between 1 and Length[s]-1, where s is one of the vectors to be recombined, which are all of equal length. Let us try multipoint recombination with four crossover points, which the operator will choose at random:

Four-point crossover

In[8] := {recChromo, recMask} =
      Recombine[{s1, s2},
        RecombinationMode → POINT[4]]

Out[8] = {{a, b, C, D, E, f, g, H, k, l},
        {1, 1, 2, 2, 2, 1, 1, 2, 1, 1}}

The resulting vectors are depicted in Figure 3.23(a). The crossover points are after the second, fifth, seventh, and eighth gene. The result is five chromosome segments that are newly combined. The two resulting recombined chromosomes are shown in Figure 3.23(b) and (c).

Masked recombination

In order to formalize generally the crossing over of chromosomes, we slightly modify the definition of recombination from that given in Section 3.3.1. When we start from m homologous, haploid chromosomes $s_1, \ldots, s_m$,

$$s_1 = (s_{11}, \ldots, s_{1n}), \; s_2 = (s_{21}, \ldots, s_{2n}), \ldots,$$
$$s_m = (s_{m1}, \ldots, s_{mn}),$$

Figure 3.23
Multipoint crossover.

(a)
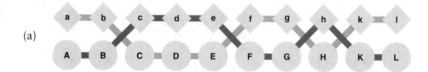

(b)

(c)

the recombined vector s_{rec} is determined by using a recombination mask μ:

$$s_{rec} = (s_{\mu_1, 1}, \ldots, s_{\mu_n, n})$$

Masked recombination

$$\mu = (\mu_1, \ldots, \mu_n \text{ with } \mu_i \in \{1, \ldots, m\}, \ 1 \leq i \leq n.$$

The *i*-th component of s_{rec} is selected from the set $\{s_{1i}, \ldots, s_{mi}\}$ of the corresponding components of the vectors to be recombined. More precisely, the selected index is defined by entry μ_i of the recombination mask μ. Hence, the chromosome composition is determined by an index mask, as the following example illustrates:

In[9] := {recChromo, recMask} =
    Recombine[{s$_1$, s$_2$},
        RecombinationMode →
            MASK[{1,1,1,1,1,2,2,2,2,2}]]

Mask recombination by example

Out[9] = {{a, b, c, d, e, F, G, H, K, L},
        {1, 1, 1, 1, 1, 2, 2, 2, 2, 2}}

By using the option RecombinationMode → MASK[μ], the Recombine function performs the composition according to mask μ. In the example, the first half of the components is taken from s1 and the second half from s2, as Figure 3.24 shows. Again, the crossed chromosomes ([a]) together with the resulting single strand ([b]) and its "inverse" strand ([c]) are depicted as well.

Comparing the formal definition of recombination with the implementation of Recombine in Program 3.14 reveals that mask recombination can be directly translated into the expression

    MapIndexed[params[[#1,First[#2]]]&, mask].

Masked recombination

Even the slightly constrained recombination scheme of crossover (POINT[_]) is actually implemented by a mask. The function

    recombinationMask[n,
        RecombinationPoints → points,
        RecombinationPartners → partners,
        RecombinationRange → range
    ]

Generation of recombination masks

is used to automatically generate recombination masks. Here n is the length of the mask vector, points determines the number of crossover points, partners sets the number of chromosomes to be

Figure 3.24
Masked crossover.

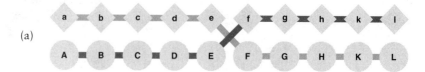

(a)

(b)

(c)

combined, and `range` is the number of chromosomes that compete for recombination. The following examples will illustrate these options.

We restrict recombination to a single crossover point so that we get a masked one-point crossover (Figure 3.25).

Masked one-point crossover

```
In[10] := {recChromo, recMask} =
            Recombine[{s1, s2},
               RecombinationMode →
               MASK[recombinationMask[Length[s1],
                  RecombinationPoints → 1]]]
```

```
Out[10] = {{A, B, C, D, E, F, g, h, k, l},
            {2, 2, 2, 2, 2, 2, 1, 1, 1, 1}}
```

The function `recombinationMask` generates an index list, where the entries change from one index to the other at exactly one position (here position seven). By default, for `recombinationMask` it is assumed that only two chromosomes are recombined; hence the index entries are restricted to either 1 or 2.

For multipoint crossovers the number of recombination points has to be increased. After each crossover point a new index, differing from the previous index entry, is selected from the set of available indices.

Masked multipoint crossover

```
In[11] := {recChromo, recMask} =
            Recombine[{s1, s2},
               RecombinationMode →
               MASK[recombinationMask[Length[s1],
                  RecombinationPoints → 6]]]
```

Figure 3.25
Masked one-point crossover.

Figure 3.26
Masked six-point crossover.

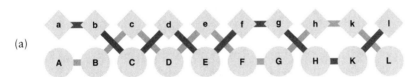

Out[11] = {{A, B, c, D, e, F, G, h, k, L},
            {2, 2, 1, 2, 1, 2, 2, 1, 1, 2}}

For this example, there are six crossover sites (Figure 3.26), where at each point the "recombination thread" changes the chromosome strand.

Multirecombination

Now let us look at multirecombination of more than two chromosomes. We generate four binary vectors,

In[12] := **fourStrands=**
          Table[Table[Random[Integer,{0,1}],{10}],{4}]

Out[12] = {{1, 0, 0, 1, 1, 0, 0, 1, 1, 0},   *Four initial chromosomes*
            {0, 0, 1, 0, 1, 0, 0, 1, 1, 0},

```
                      {1, 1, 0, 1, 1, 0, 0, 0, 0, 0},
                      {0, 0, 1, 0, 0, 1, 1, 0, 0, 0}},
```

and recombine them by three-point crossover. The fact that we now have four vectors instead of two to choose from is determined by RecombinationPartners → 4.

Binary multirecombination

```
In[13] := {recChromo, recMask} =
            Recombine[fourStrands,
              RecombinationMode → POINT[3],
              RecombinationPartners → 4 ]
```

```
Out[13] = {{1, 0, 0, 1, 1, 0, 0, 1, 1, 0},
           {3, 1, 1, 1, 3, 3, 3, 1, 1, 1}}
```

The recombination mask shows that from the four available lists only two are recombined, namely, the first and third vector, which are crossed over at three positions, as is illustrated in Figure 3.27(a). The graphics in Figure 3.27 were generated by the function chromosomePictogramMultiplePlot, which—by using the recombination mask information—can label the recombinations by corresponding "threads."

```
In[14] := chromosomePictogramMultiplePlot[
            Map[paramsToChromo,fourStrands],
            RecombinationMasks → {recMask},
            TableWidth → 10,
            Pictograms → {RECTANGLE, DIAMOND},
            LineColorFunction → GrayLevel,
            LineColor → 0.5 ];
```

If not only two but four chromosomes, for example, are to be recombined by crossover (Figure 3.27[b]), we use the RecombinationRange option accordingly. For a five-point recombination of at most four of the four strands of our initial chromosome, we would use the following function call:

Four-range multirecombination

```
In[15] := {recChromo, recMask} =
            Recombine[fourStrands,
              RecombinationMode →
              MASK[recombinationMask[10,
                    RecombinationPoints → 5,
                    RecombinationPartners → 4,
                    RecombinationRange → 4]]]
```

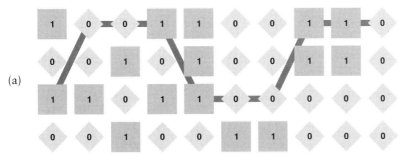

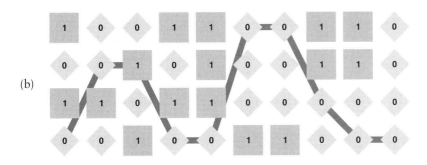

(a)

(b)

Figure 3.27
Multicrossover among several chromosomes.
(a) Three-point crossover of two out of four chromosomes.
(b) Five-point crossover among four out of four chromosomes.

Out[15] = {{0, 0, 1, 0, 0, 0, 0, 0, 0, 0},
            {4, 2, 2, 4, 4, 1, 1, 3, 4, 4}}

The resulting mask shows that all four strands are used for a recombination with five crossover points. However, usually it is not guaranteed that all indices within the `RecombinationRange` are actually selected. This option sets only the maximum possible number of different recombination partners.

3.3.2 Recombination of GA chromosomes

If we want to combine GA chromosomes, we must take a few more things into account than recombinations of simple lists. The GA chromosome data structures are not simple lists, since genes are attributed by their indices. In addition, the genes can be arranged in random order. So what should we do if we want to recombine chromosomes of equal length but with different gene arrangements? The genes must be sorted in some uniform way. Finally, we have to think about recombinations among polyploid chromosomes. Should information be interchanged among groups of genes only or among haploid single strands? Questions like these will be clarified in this section.

Gene ordering

*Polyploid
GA chromosomes*

GA recombination

For the recombination of GA chromosome structures we use the function `Recombination`, which, analogously to function `Recombine` (Program 3.14), computes a recombined chromosome from a list of chromosomes and in addition returns the recombination mask (Program 3.15). The function `Recombination` has a very simple structure. First, the parameters of all passed chromosomes from the argument list `chromos` are extracted. Generally, the genes of these chromosomes are not ordered the same way—hence, the indices of the first chromosome are computed, and all other chromosomes are sorted according to this ordering. This reordering guarantees that on

Program 3.15
Recombination of
GA chromosomes.

```
Recombination[chromos_List,opts___] :=

Module[{params, paramsSorted, indices,
        recParams, recMasks},

  (* Extract chromo parameters and indices *)
  params = Map[List @@ Last[#]&,chromos];
  indices = Map[Map[First,#]&,params];

  (* Sort parameters according to the first chromo *)
  paramsSorted = Map[Sort[#][[First[indices]]]
  &,params];

  (* Get rid of indices *)
  paramsSorted = Transpose[
    Map[Transpose[Map[Last,#]]&,paramsSorted]];

  (* Recombine parameters *)
  {recParams,recMasks} =
    Transpose[Map[Recombine[#,opts]&,paramsSorted]];

  (* Reinsert indices and return resulting chromo *)
  (* and recombination masks                      *)
  {chromo[q[undef],p @@
    MapThread[{#1,#2}&,
      {indices//First,recParams//Transpose}]],

  recMasks}
]


Options[Recombination] := Options[Recombine]
```

the one hand, genes with the same meaning are recombined. On the other hand, the genes follow the arrangement of one of the strands, where neighboring genes might have already formed a building block group. This is why genes are not merely ordered according to their indices (the normal way, from lower to higher indices), in order not to break up already constructed, possibly cooperating gene blocks.

Without any reordering, a totally random gene mixing would result, which could destroy the essential meaning of recombination— the exchange of matching gene groups. After the homologous rearrangement of genes, the function `Recombine` (Program 3.14) performs the actual new combination of the genes. Subsequently the resulting parameters are embedded in a GA chromosome structure, the gene indices following the arrangement of the first original chromosome. The resulting chromosome is returned along with its recombination mask.

Recombination of haploid chromosomes

We test the `Recombination` function for two haploid GA chromosomes over the binary alphabet $A = \{0, 1\}$. The genes are arranged at random:

```
In[16] := haploidChromos =
          Table[createChromosome[15, PolyPloidy → 1,
            RandomLoci → True],{2}]
```

```
Out[16] = {chromo[q[undef], p[{11, {0}}, {12, {1}},
            {13, {0}}, {14, {0}}, {1, {0}}, {10, {1}},
            {4, {0}}, {3, {1}}, {5, {1}}, {2, {0}},
            {8, {0}}, {6, {0}}, {9, {0}}, {7, {1}},
            {15, {1}}]],
          chromo[q[undef], p[{2, {1}}, {6, {1}},
            {14, {1}}, {3, {1}}, {8, {0}}, {11, {0}},
            {10, {1}}, {7, {1}}, {5, {0}}, {12, {0}},
            {13, {1}}, {9, {1}}, {1, {0}}, {4, {0}},
            {15, {1}}]]}
```

Two haploid binary GA chromosomes

The two chromosomes are illustrated in Figure 3.28(a). The numbers below the genes correspond to their indices. We get a recombination according to a simple one-point crossover as follows:

```
In[17] := {recChromoOne,recMasksOne} =
          Recombination[haploidChromos,
            RecombinationMode → POINT[1]]
```

One-point crossover

Out[17] = {chromo[q[undef], p[{11, {0}}, {12, {0}},
          {13, {1}}, {14, {1}}, {1, {0}}, {10, {1}},
          {4, {0}}, {3, {1}}, {5, {1}}, {2, {0}},
          {8, {0}}, {6, {0}}, {9, {0}}, {7, {1}},
          {15, {1}}]],
          {{2, 2, 2, 2, 2, 1, 1, 1, 1, 1, 1, 1, 1, 1, 1}}}

The chromosomes are crossed over after the fifth gene. Figure 3.28(b) (top) shows the chromosome resulting from this recombination (recChromoOne). The second row depicts the "dual" chromosome recChromoTwo (Figure 3.28[b] [bottom]). Note that all genes are arranged according to the first chromosome. The "crossover thread" connects the genes of the first original chromosome.

Here are the function calls that produce the graphics in Figure 3.28(b), (c), and (d):

```
In[18] := {recChromoTwo,recMasksTwo} =
      Recombination[haploidChromos,
        RecombinationMode →
        MASK[inverseRecombinationMask[recMasksOne//
      First]]
      ]
```

Out[18] = {chromo[q[undef], p[{11, {0}}, {12, {1}},
          {13, {0}}, {14, {0}}, {1, {0}}, {10, {1}},
          {4, {0}}, {3, {1}}, {5, {0}}, {2, {1}},
          {8, {0}}, {6, {1}}, {9, {1}}, {7, {1}},
          {15, {1}}]],
          {{1, 1, 1, 1, 1, 2, 2, 2, 2, 2, 2, 2, 2, 2, 2}}}

```
In[19] := chromosomePictogramMultiplePlot[
        {recChromoOne,recChromoTwo},
        Pictograms → {RECTANGLE, DIAMOND},
        GeneIndices → True,
        RecombinationMasks → {recMasksOne//First},
        LineColorFunction → GrayLevel,
        LineColor → 0.5,
        GraphicsOptions → {AspectRatio → 0.2}];
```

Analogously, the examples for a six-point crossover (Figure 3.28[c]) and random, multipoint crossover (Figure 3.28[d]) are generated. The connected genes follow the arrangement of the first chromosome (Figure 3.28[a]), whereas all the other genes, from left to right, are copies of the corresponding genes of the second partner chromosome.

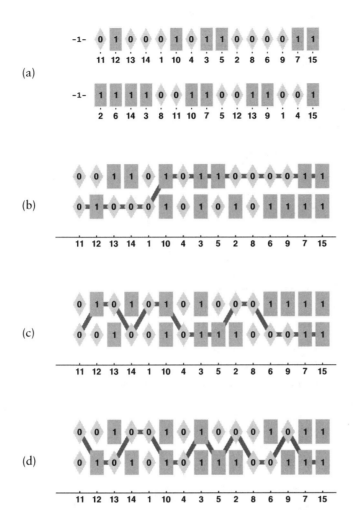

Figure 3.28

Binary crossover of haploid GA chromosomes. (a) Two haploid GA chromosomes. (b) One-point crossover. (c) Six-point crossover. (d) Multipoint crossover.

Recombination of polyploid GA chromosomes

For k GA chromosomes of length n with m-ploid genes, each chromosome $s_{(m)}^{(i)}$, $1 \leq i \leq k$, has the form

$$s_{(m)}^{(i)} = \left(\left(s_{11}^{i}, \ldots, s_{m1}^{i} \right), \ldots, \left(s_{1n}^{i}, \ldots, s_{mn}^{i} \right) \right).$$

Polyploid GA chromosome

For simplicity, we do not list the gene indices here, since these play a role only in sorting. We assume that homologous genes share the same indices. Each chromosome is labeled by its ploidy in the subscript index. The superscript index denotes the number of the chromosome:

$$s_{(m)}^{(i)}: i\text{-th } m\text{-ploid chromosome.}$$

m-ploid chromosome

Each of the m-ploid chromosomes $s_{(m)}^{(i)}$ consists of m haploid single strands, $s_{(1)}^{(i,j)}$, $1 \leq j \leq m$, which we describe as follows:

Single chromosome strand

$$s_{(1)}^{(i,j)} = \left(s_{j1}^{(i)}, \ldots, s_{jn}^{(i)} \right), \ 1 \leq i \leq k, \ 1 \leq j \leq m.$$

For each strand we extend the superscript chromosome number (i) with the strand index (j):

$s_{(1)}^{(i,j)}$: j-th haploid single strand of i-th chromosome.

From these k chromosomes the recombination operator ρ, corresponding to the `Recombination` function of Program 3.15, generates a new m-ploid chromosome $s_{(m)}^{\text{rec}}$:

Recombination of m-ploid chromosomes

$$s_{(m)}^{\text{rec}} = \rho\left(s_{(m)}^{(1)}, \ldots, s_{(m)}^{(k)} \right).$$

From the set of m-ploid chromosomes the haploid single strands $s_{(1)}^{(i,j)}$, homologous with respect to their indices, are recombined:

$$s_{(m)}^{\text{rec}} = \left(\rho'\left(s_{(1)}^{(1,1)}, \ldots, s_{(1)}^{(k,1)} \right), \ldots, \rho'\left(s_{(1)}^{(1,m)}, \ldots, s_{(1)}^{(k,m)} \right) \right)^T.$$

The recombining operator ρ' is implemented by the function `Recombine` in Program 3.14. The discrete recombination scheme on the single strands is defined by recombination masks μ_i, $1 \leq i \leq m$,

Combination of single strands

$$\rho'\left(s_{(1)}^{(1,i)}, \ldots, s_{(1)}^{(k,i)} \right) = \left(s_{(i1)}^{(\mu_{i1})}, \ldots, s_{(in)}^{(\mu_{in})} \right),$$

where the mask

Recombination masks

$$\mu_i = (\mu_{i1}, \ldots, \mu_{in}) \text{ with } \mu_{ij} \in \{1, \ldots, k\}$$

determines the indices of the selected strands (see Section 3.3.1). We can continue computing the recombined m-ploid chromosome:

Recombination of m-ploid chromosomes (continued)

$$s_{(m)}^{\text{rec}} = \left(\left(s_{11}^{(\mu_{11})}, \ldots, s_{1n}^{(\mu_{1n})} \right), \ldots, \left(s_{m1}^{(\mu_{m1})}, \ldots, s_{mn}^{(\mu_{mn})} \right) \right)^T$$

$$= \left(\left(s_{11}^{(\mu_{11})}, \ldots, s_{m1}^{(\mu_{m1})} \right), \ldots, \left(s_{1n}^{(\mu_{1n})}, \ldots, s_{mn}^{(\mu_{mn})} \right) \right).$$

We illustrate this recombination scheme by a simple example of crossing over two haploid chromosomes. We start from the two chromosomes

Two haploid chromosomes

$$s_{(1)}^{(1)} = \left(\left(s_{11}^{(1)} \right), \ldots, \left(s_{1n}^{(1)} \right) \right) \text{ and } s_{(1)}^{(2)} = \left(\left(s_{11}^{2} \right), \ldots, \left(s_{1n}^{2} \right) \right),$$

which consist of the two single strands

$$s_{(1)}^{(1,1)} = \left(s_{11}^{(1)}, \ldots, s_{1n}^{(1)} \right) \text{ and } s_{(1)}^{(2,1)} = \left(s_{11}^{(2)}, \ldots, s_{1n}^{(2)} \right).$$

We apply the recombination operators ρ and ρ' in order to compose, once again, a haploid chromosome:

$$s_{(1)}^{rec} = \rho\left(s_{(1)}^{(1)}, s_{(1)}^{(2)}\right) = \left(\rho'\left(s_{(1)}^{(1,1)}, s_{(1)}^{(2,1)}\right)\right)^T.$$

Componentwise recombination

The combination per component is performed by ρ' (Recombine) acting on the single strands. Discrete selection is determined by the recombination mask $\mu_1 = (\mu_{11}, \ldots, \mu_{1n})$. Therefore, we compute the new genes with the help of the mask μ_1 as follows:

$$s_{(1)}^{rec} = \left(s_{11}^{(\mu_{11})}, \ldots, s_{1n}^{(\mu_{1n})}\right)^T = \left(\left(s_{11}^{(\mu_{11})}\right), \ldots, \left(s_{1n}^{(\mu_{1n})}\right)\right).$$

For a crossover mask of the form $\mu_1 = (1, 1, \ldots, 2, 2)$, we would get the following recombined chromosome:

$$s_{(1)}^{rec} = \left(\left(s_{11}^{(1)}\right), \left(s_{12}^{(1)}\right), \ldots, \left(s_{1n-1}^{(2)}\right), \left(s_{1n}^{(2)}\right)\right).$$

Example

Figure 3.29 illustrates the recombination scheme for combining polyploid chromosomes. Recombining two haploid strands by crossover is depicted in Figure 3.29(a), which is the simplest but classical form of (GA or ES) recombination. If two diploid chromosomes are combined, the first and second strands of each chromosome are recombined, respectively (Figure 3.29[b]). Two strands result, which form a new diploid chromosome. Analogously, recombinations for $n > 2$ diploid chromosomes are performed (Figure 3.29[c]). For both single-strand combinations, n strands each have to be taken into account. Finally, Figure 3.29(d) shows gene mixing among two triploid chromosomes. Here three binary combinations have to be completed, resulting in a new triple-strand chromosome.

With an example, let us examine further the last case of crossing over two triploid chromosomes. We generate two triploid chromosomes of length 20 over the binary allele alphabet $A = \{0, 1\}$.

In[20] := **triploidChromos = Table[createChromosome[20,**
         PolyPloidy → 3, RandomLoci → False],{2}]

Generating triploid binary chromosomes

Out[20] = {chromo[q[undef], p[{1, {1, 0, 1}},
         {2, {0, 0, 1}}, {3, {1, 1, 1}}, {4, {0, 0, 0}},
         {5, {1, 1, 1}}, {6, {1, 0, 0}}, {7, {0, 1, 1}},
         {8, {0, 1, 0}}, {9, {0, 0, 0}},
         {10, {1, 1, 0}}, {11, {1, 0, 0}},
         {12, {0, 0, 1}}, {13, {0, 0, 0}},
         {14, {1, 1, 1}}, {15, {1, 0, 1}},
         {16, {0, 1, 1}}, {17, {0, 1, 1}},

```
                    {18, {0, 0, 1}}, {19, {1, 1, 0}},
                    {20, {0, 1, 0}}}]],
              chromo[q[undef], p[{1, {1, 1, 0}},
                 {2, {0, 0, 0}},  {3, {1, 0, 1}}, {4, {0, 1, 0}},
                 {5, {1, 0, 1}}, {6, {0, 1, 1}}, {7, {1, 1, 0}},
                 {8, {0, 1, 1}}, {9, {0, 1, 0}}, {10, {0, 0, 1}},
                 {11, {0, 1, 1}}, {12, {1, 0, 0}},
                 {13, {1, 0, 1}}, {14, {0, 0, 0}},
                 {15, {0, 0, 1}}, {16, {0, 0, 1}},
                 {17, {0, 0, 0}}, {18, {0, 0, 0}},
                 {19, {1, 1, 1}}, {20, {0, 1, 0}}}]]}
```

In Figure 3.30(a) the two triploid chromosomes are represented graphically. For each gene there is a choice among three alleles. To split the *m*-ploid chromosomes into *m* haploid single-strand chromo-

Figure 3.29
Recombination of polyploid
GA chromosomes.
(a) Two-point crossover of
two haploid chromosomes.
(b) Crossover of two diploid
chromosomes.
(c) Crossover of three
diploid chromosomes.
(d) Crossover of two triploid
chromosomes.

(a)

(b)

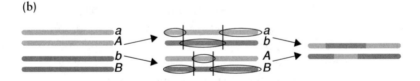

(c)

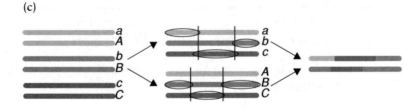

(d)

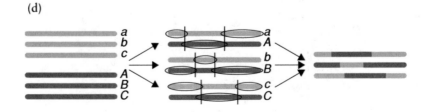

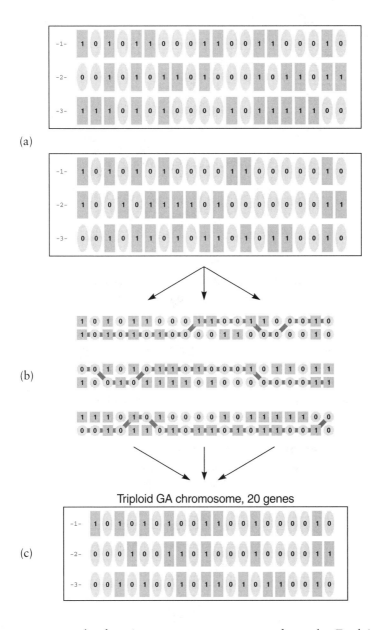

Figure 3.30
Crossover of two triploid
GA chromosomes.

(a)

(b)

(c)

Triploid GA chromosome, 20 genes

somes we use the function `splitChromosome` from the Evolvica notebook available through the *IEC* Web page (see Preface). There is also an "inverse" function `mergeChromosomes`, which combines single strands into a polyploid chromosome.

In[21]:= `splitChromos = splitChromosome /@`
           `triploidChromos`

Splitting into single strands

Out[21] = {{chromo[q[undef], p[{1, {1}}, {2, {0}},
        {3, {1}}, {4, {0}}, {5, {1}}, {6, {1}},
        {7, {0}}, {8, {0}}, {9, {0}}, {10, {1}},
        {11, {1}}, {12, {0}}, {13, {0}}, {14, {1}},
        {15, {1}}, {16, {0}},{17, {0}}, {18, {0}},
        {19, {1}}, {20, {0}}}]],
      ...},
      {...,
      chromo[q[undef], p[{1, {0}}, {2, {0}},
        {3, {1}}, {4, {0}}, {5, {1}}, {6, {1}},
        {7, {0}}, {8, {1}}, {9, {0}}, {10, {1}},
        {11, {1}}, {12, {0}}, {13, {1}}, {14, {0}},
        {15, {1}}, {16, {1}}, {17, {0}}, {18, {0}},
        {19, {1}}, {20, {0}}}]]}}

Here only the first and last haploid chromosomes are listed. When comparing the alleles, we note that the first strand contains the values of each first allele of each gene of the first chromosome (triploid-Chromos[[1]]). The last single strand contains the values of the corresponding third alleles of the genes of the second chromosome (triploidChromos[[2]]). In combining the two triploid chromosomes, we get a new three-ploid chromosome recChromo together with three recombination masks that tell which components are selected for each combination among the strands.

Recombination of triploid chromosomes

In[22] := **{recChromo,recMasks} =**
        Recombination[triploidChromos,
          RecombinationMode → POINT[3]]

Out[22] = {chromo[q[undef], p[{1, {1, 0, 0}},
        {2, {0, 0, 0}}, {3, {1, 0, 1}}, {4, {0, 1, 0}},
        {5, {1, 0, 1}}, {6, {0, 0, 0}}, {7, {1, 1, 0}},
        {8, {0, 1, 1}}, {9, {0, 0, 0}},
        {10, {1, 1, 1}}, {11, {1, 0, 1}},
        {12, {0, 0, 0}}, {13, {0, 0, 1}},
        {14, {1, 1, 0}}, {15, {0, 0, 1}},
        {16, {0, 0, 1}}, {17, {0, 0, 0}},
        {18, {0, 0, 0}}, {19, {1, 1, 1}},
        {20, {0, 1, 0}}}]],
      {{2, 2, 2, 2, 2, 2, 2, 2, 2, 1, 1, 1, 1, 1, 2, 2,
        1, 1, 1, 1}, {1, 1, 2, 2, 2, 1, 1, 1, 1, 1, 1,
        1, 1, 1, 2, 2, 2, 2, 2, 2}, {2, 2, 2, 2, 1, 1,
        2, 2, 2, 2, 2, 2, 2, 2, 2, 2, 2, 2, 2, 1}}}}

The GA chromosome `recChromo` is depicted in Figure 3.30(c). Figure 3.30(b) also shows the homologous single strands and their recombination scheme according to the recombination masks `rec-Masks`. The recombination diagrams are generated as follows:

```
In[23]:= MapThread[
          chromosomePictogramMultiplePlot[{#1,#2},
            RecombinationMasks → {#3},
            Pictograms → {RECTANGLE, DISK},
            GeneIndices → False,
            LineColorFunction → GrayLevel, LineColor → 0.5
          ]&, {splitChromos[[1]],splitChromos[[2]],recMasks}
        ];
```

The following section demonstrates a special form of recombination—the crosswise combination of chromosomes during the cell division phase of meiosis.

3.3.3 Meiotic recombination of diploid chromosomes

The recombination operators, implemented for genetic algorithms by crossover, are activated through gene exchange mechanisms during the cell division phase of meiosis (Figure 3.31), where paternal and maternal genetic information is merged by crosswise interchange of gene sequences. We will simulate the essential effects of rearranging chromosome structures and recombination of genes during the phase of so-called *reduction division* (Lewin 1983, p. 30 ff.). *Meiosis*

Meiosis starts with two haploid gametes, an egg and a sperm cell:

```
In[24]:= gametes = {egg, sperm} =
        {createChromosome[20,Alphabet → {a,b,f}],
         createChromosome[20,Alphabet → {A,B,F}]}
```
Generating two "gametes"

```
In[25]:= chromosomePictogramPlot[gametes,
          Pictograms → {RECTANGLE, DIAMOND, DISK},
          Alphabet → {a,b,f,A,B,F},
          ColorDecrement → 0.05,
          GraphicsOptions → {AspectRatio → 0.1}];
```

The chromosomes of these two gametes are depicted as single strands in Figure 3.32(a). The allele alphabet of the paternal chromosome is the set of letters {a, b, f}, whereas the alphabet for the mother chromosome consists of the capital letter set {A, B, F}. The two gametes merge into a diploid *interphase* cell (Figure 3.32[b]):

Figure 3.31
Schematic diagram of meiotic cell division with resulting pairs of recombined chromosomes. The labels (a), (b), and (c) refer to the corresponding stages in Figure 3.32.

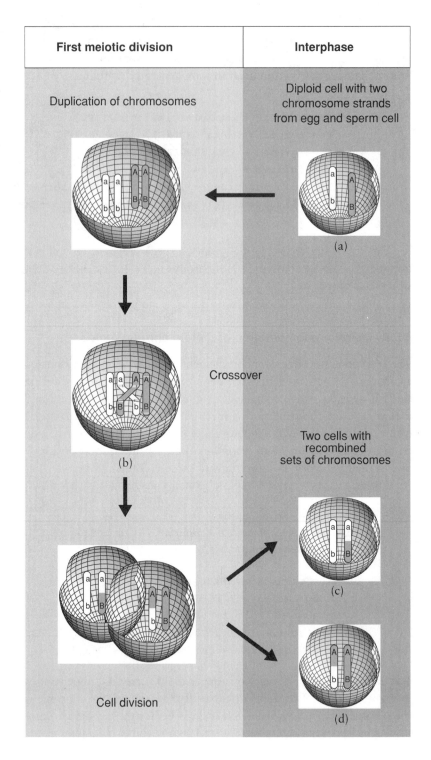

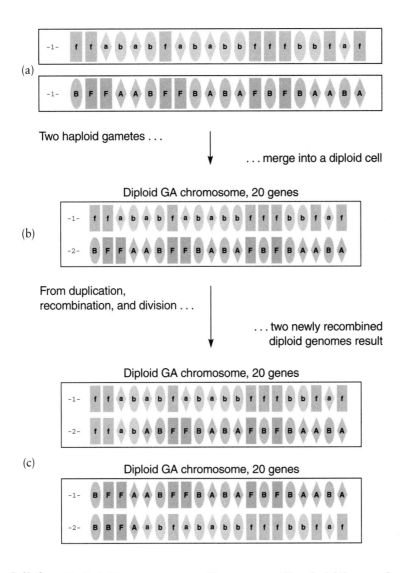

Figure 3.32
Recombination mimicking meiosis.

Two haploid gametes . . .

. . . merge into a diploid cell

From duplication, recombination, and division . . .

. . . two newly recombined diploid genomes result

In[26] := **diploidChromo = mergeChromosomes[haploidChromos];**   *Merging*

The two chromosome strands are doubled into four homologous strands. The paternal and maternal strand, arranged next to each other, break at a crossover site and recombine in a crosswise fashion (Figure 3.31[b]). In this way, gene groups from father and mother are merged. Each of the unchanged and the newly combined chromosome strands make up the diploid chromosome pair for the subsequent (first) meiotic division, from which two diploid cells result. These mechanisms are implemented by the Evolvica function meiosis,   *Meiotic recombination and division* which takes a diploid genome and transforms it into two new diploid genomes through meiotic duplication and recombination:

In[27] := **recGenomes = meiosis[genome[diploidChromo]];**

Out[27] = {genome[{chromo[q[undef], p[{1, {f, f}},
             {2, {f, f}}, {3, {a, a}}, {4, {b, b}},
             {5, {a, A}}, {6, {b, B}}, {7, {f, F}},
             {8, {a, F}}, {9, {b, B}}, {10, {a, A}},
             {11, {b, B}}, {12, {b, A}}, {13, {f, F}},
             {14, {f, B}}, {15, {f, F}}, {16, {b, B}},
             {17, {b, A}}, {18, {f, A}}, {19, {a, B}},
             {20, {f, A}}]]}],
          genome[{chromo[q[undef], p[{1, {B, B}},
             {2, {F, F}}, {3, {F, F}}, {4, {A, A}},
             {5, {A, a}}, {6, {B, b}}, {7, {F, f}},
             {8, {F, a}}, {9, {B, b}}, {10, {A, a}},
             {11, {B, b}}, {12, {A, b}}, {13, {F, f}},
             {14, {B, f}}, {15, {F, f}}, {16, {B, b}},
             {17, {A, b}}, {18, {A, f}}, {19, {B, a}},
             {20, {A, f}}]]}]}

The two resulting genomes are illustrated in Figure 3.32(c). Compare their chromosome strands with those of the initial haploid genomes. Each first strand is identical to one of the original chromosomes (gametes). The second strand is a combination of paternal and maternal genes. The first four genes originate from the father (from the mother), whereas all other genes are identical to the mother's (father's).

We do not consider the second meiotic division here, during which the two diploid cells are reduced to four haploid gametes, which again serve as starting points for further meiotic divisions.

3.3.4 Recombination with faces

In Section 3.2.5 we showed in the context of point mutations how multidimensional vectors can be visualized by simple facial expressions. Here we will illustrate a few recombination effects, again through the example of Chernoff figures. We demonstrate the effects of mixing gene groups, which encode some characteristic features. We generate random faces, which we consider as displaying parental traits, and observe how these features carry over to their offspring by recombinations. For generating random face chromosomes we use the function `randomFaceChromo` in Program 3.16, which returns a GA chromosome with 10 genes over the allele range {1, 2, . . . , 10}.

```
randomFaceChromo :=
createChromosome[10, Alphabet → Range[1,10]]
```

Program 3.16
Generation of face
chromosomes.

The creation, recombination, and visualization of the facial expressions is implemented by the function `faceRecombination` of Program 3.17. Its parameters are the number of parents and the mode of recombination.

```
faceRecombination[faces_Integer,recMode_,opts___] :=
Module[{randomFaces, recFace, recMask, r},

  randomFaces = Table[randomFaceChromo,{faces}];

  {recFace, recMask} =
  Recombination[randomFaces,
    RecombinationMode → recMode, opts];

  chromosomeFacePlot[r = Append[randomFaces, recFace]];

  {r,recMask}
]
```

Program 3.17
Recombination of face
chromosomes.

The parental faces are encoded by randomly generated chromosomes. The `Recombination` operator creates an offspring by combining gene sequences of the parent chromosome. Finally, the facial expressions of the parent and its offspring are depicted graphically by the function `chromosomeFacePlot`, which displays them in a row.

Let us look at a few examples. From two parental facial expressions we want to create a new face, which inherits head shape, eye size, distance between eyes, eye width-height ratio, and pupil size from the first parent and all other facial traits from the second parent (see Figure 3.19 for a more detailed description of the encoded facial features). We can describe this new combination of traits with a recombination mask:

Masked recombination

In[28] := `faceRecombination[2,MASK[{1,1,1,1,1,2,2,2,2,2}]]`

Three faces resulting from this recombination mask are depicted in Figure 3.33(a). Here the child's mouth, nose, and eyebrows are definitely of paternal origin. The eyes and the head shape are inherited from its mother's genes.

In the next example we use one-point crossover for gene interchange. Now which genes originate from the mother or father is no longer uniquely determined. It depends on which position is chosen as the crossover point:

One-point crossover

In[29] := `faceRecombination[2,POINT[1]]`

Can we see from Figure 3.33(b) which facial expressions are inherited from the mother's and which from the father's genome? The offspring face obviously has some familial similarity to its parents. The width and opening of the mouth are maternal traits; all other characteristics are inherited from the father. In the figure the recombination masks are also given so that you can distinguish which features originate from which face.

The examples in Figure 3.33 also show an offspring face generated by five-point crossover of two parent genomes ([c]) and the feature recombination of three parent genomes by multipoint recombination ([d], [e]). For additional examples refer to the Evolvica notebook available through the *IEC* Web page (see Preface).

3.4   Additional genetic operators

Additional genetic operators

Up to now we have introduced the two major operators used in genetic algorithm applications—recombination and mutation. In this section we discuss the operators of *inversion, deletion, duplication,* and *crossover of nonhomologous chromosomes,* a set of operators usually considered secondary in GA theory and practice. Here we would like to emphasize that genetic algorithms, in their schemes and variation of genotypical structures, show a strong analogy to mutative events actually observable in natural genomes. Or rather, genetic algorithms could profit from these analogies even more successfully if the operators discussed here were more widely integrated into current GA systems. These genetic operators are not yet part of the standard repertoire of genetic algorithms.

In natural cells chromosomes and chromosome pairs mutate in many ways. Here we will deal in particular with simulations of chro-

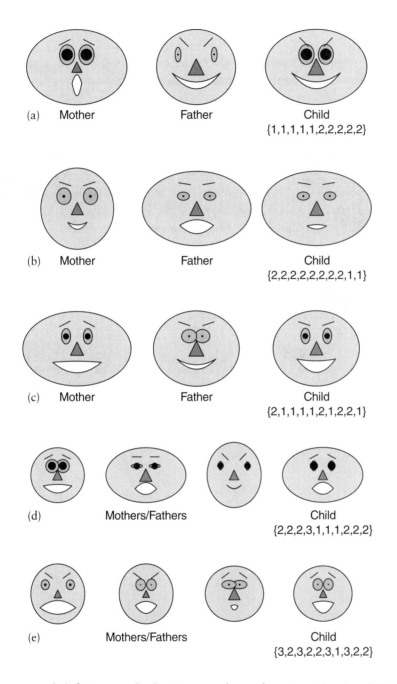

Figure 3.33
Recombined facial expressions:
(a) recombination with predefined mask,
(b) one-point crossover,
(c) five-point crossover,
(d), (e) multipoint recombination.

mosomal deficiencies, duplications, and translocations. Section 3.4.1 introduces an inversion operator that changes the ordering of genes, an effect that occurs with translocation in nonhomologous chromosomes. In Section 3.4.2, deficiency effects are explained through the

Deficiencies, duplications, translocations

example of deletion operators. Section 3.4.3 deals with gene duplications, the "dual" or "inverse" operator for deletion. Finally, in Section 3.4.4 we model crossing over between chromosomes of unequal lengths, where even the crossover points may differ.

3.4.1 Inversion

Chromosome mutations change the microscopically visible chromosome structures. During cell division, in the interphase state, break points appear at neighboring locations, which usually have a strong tendency toward restitution (i.e., they are quickly repaired) but also provide the precondition for pairwise recombination. With two break points per chromosome, deletions and inversions of complete gene groups may also occur (Figure 3.34).

Here we will first focus on inversion effects, then in Section 3.4.2 discuss gene deletions. We start from indexed, haploid GA chromosomes, as defined in Section 3.1.1. Each allele is attributed with the index of its gene:

Indexed, haploid GA chromosome

$$s = \left(\left(1, s_1\right), \ldots, \left(n, s_n\right) \right) \text{ with } s_i \in A, \ 1 \le i \le n.$$

The allele alphabet is given as $A = \{\alpha_1, \ldots, \alpha_k\}$. This form of representation corresponds to the GA chromosome structure, which we use for the Evolvica implementations. The following representation of an indexed GA chromosome is a little more compact, but contains the same information:

Compact representation

$$s = \left(s_1, \ldots, s_{i_1-1}, s_{i_1}, s_{i_1+1}, \ldots, s_{i_2-1}, s_{i_2}, s_{i_2+1}, \ldots, s_n \right).$$

We will use this representation here. For the indices we require $1 \le i_1 \le i_2 \le n$.

Figure 3.34
Inversion and deletion effects on natural chromosomes.

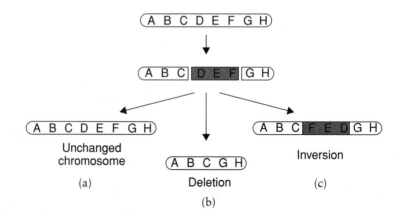

The inversion of a gene group $(s_{i_1}, s_{i_1+1}, \ldots, s_{i_2-1}, s_{i_2})$ is caused by a breaking of the chromosome at positions i_1 and i_2 and subsequent restitution of the reversed gene group $(s_{i_2}, s_{i_2-1}, \ldots, s_{i_1+1}, s_{i_1})$ back into the chromosome (Figure 3.34[c]). Hence the inverted variant s_{inv} for chromosome s is defined as

$$s_{\text{inv}} = \left(s_1, \ldots, s_{i_1-1}, s_{i_2}, s_{i_2-1}, \ldots, s_{i_1+1}, s_{i_1}, s_{i_2+1}, \ldots, s_n\right).$$

Inversion

Here the genes of the intermediate part are permuted in a specific way, namely, by sorting them from back to front. If we generalize inversion as a purely mathematical mutation operator, the rearrangement of genes can be determined by any permutation π. This leads us to a more general definition of an *inversion* operator:

$$s_{\text{inv}, \pi} = \left(s_1, \ldots, s_{i_1-1}, \pi\!\left(s_{i_1}, \ldots, s_{i_2}\right), s_{i_2+1}, \ldots, s_n\right).$$

Generalized inversion

The break points $i_1 \le i_2$ are randomly selected from the index set $\{1, \ldots, n\}$. An implementation of the inversion operator is listed in Program 3.18. When three `Take` commands are used, the initial chromosome section, the permuted fragment, and the terminal chromosome section are recomposed.

Let us try inversion on an example. We define an alphabet of letters and generate a GA chromosome structure:

$In[1]$:= `letters = {a,b,c,d,e,f,g,h,k,l,m,n,o,p,q};`

```
Inversion[chromo[qual_q,params_p], opts___] :=

Module[{l = Length[params], i1, i2, perm},

   perm = InvPermutation /. {opts} /.
   Options[Inversion];

   {i1,i2} = Sort[Table[Random[Integer,{1,l}],{2}]];

   {chromo[q[undef],
      Join[
         Take[params, Max[0,i1 - 1]],
         perm[Take[params, {i1,i2}]],
         Take[params, Min[l,i2] - l]
      ]
   ],{i1,i2}}
]

Options[Inversion] = { InvPermutation -> Reverse };
```

Program 3.18
Inversion of GA chromosomes.

In[2] := `letterChromo = paramsToChromo[letters]`

Out[2] = chromo[q[undef], p[{1, {a}}, {2, {b}}, {3, {c}},
     {4, {d}}, {5, {e}}, {6, {f}}, {7, {g}},
     {8, {h}}, {9, {k}}, {10, {1}}, {11, {m}},
     {12, {n}}, {13, {o}}, {14, {p}}, {15, {q}}]]

We get "normal" inversion without any specific setting for the permutation function (cf. the options in Program 3.18). Similar to recombining operators, the function `Inversion` returns the inverted chromosome together with the indices of the break points.

In[3] := `{invLetterChromo,cut} = Inversion[letterChromo]`

Inverted GA chromosome

Out[3] = {chromo[q[undef], p[{1, {a}}, {2, {b}}, {3, {c}},
     {4, {d}}, {12, {n}}, {11, {m}}, {10, {1}},
     {9, {k}}, {8, {h}}, {7, {g}}, {6, {f}},
     {5, {e}}, {13, {o}}, {14, {p}}, {15, {q}}]],
     {5, 12}}

Here the genes between positions 5 and 12 are reversed. Figure 3.35(a) shows the initial chromosome and 3.35(b) its inverted mutant. Figure 3.35(c) and (d) illustrate additional examples of inversion for different break points. The last chromosome ([e]) is the result of the following commands, where a random permutation is used for rearranging the gene group indices:

In[4] :=
```
RANDOM[x_] :=
    Head[x] @@ Map[x[[#]]&,RandomPermutation
    [Length[x]]]
```

"Inversion" with random permutation

In[5] :=
```
{invLetterChromo,cut} =
    Inversion[letterChromo,
    InvPermutation → RANDOM]
```

Out[5] = {chromo[q[undef], p[{1, {a}}, {2, {b}}, {3, {c}},
     {4, {d}}, {8, {h}}, {6, {f}}, {7, {g}},
     {11, {m}}, {9, {k}}, {10, {1}}, {5, {e}},
     {12, {n}}, {13, {o}}, {14, {p}}, {15, {q}}]],
     {5, 11}}

The inversion operator plays an important role in the rearrangement of relative gene positions. Recombinations (Section 3.3) modify the vicinity of genes only at break points. Inversion, however, allows

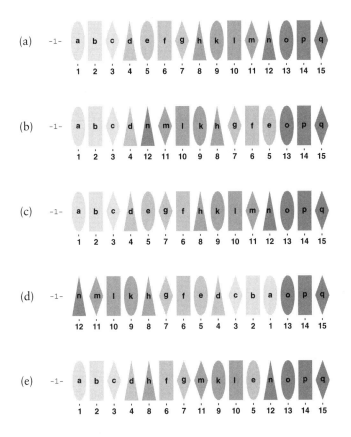

Figure 3.35
Examples of inversion.

for the repositioning of genes within a chromosome. Genes might become rearranged as neighbors, which—as a compact group—are more likely to survive further generations. The question of reproduction and stability of gene groups, identifiable by schemata, is discussed in more detail in the context of the schema theorem (Section 3.8).

Reordering of genes

3.4.2 Deletion

When a chromosome has two break points, mutation can occur in three ways: (1) the inner fragment is reinserted without any change (Figure 3.34[a]), (2) the gene group is inverted and restored (Figure 3.34[c]), or (3) the fragment gets lost (Figure 3.34[b]). The last case is known as *intercalar fragment loss* or deletion. Formally, deletion can be defined analogously to inversion. For a GA chromosome of the form

$$\left(s_1, \ldots, s_{i_1-1}, s_{i_1}, s_{i_1+1}, \ldots, s_{i_2-1}, s_{i_2}, s_{i_2+1}, \ldots, s_n\right),$$

Haploid chromosome

deletion results in a chromosome s_{del}, which loses its genes between positions i_1 and i_2:

Deletion

$$s_{del} = \left(s_1, \ldots, s_{i_1-1}, s_{i_2+1}, \ldots, s_n \right).$$

An implementation of this operator is shown in Program 3.19.

Program 3.19
Deletion on a GA
chromosome.

```
Deletion[chromo[qual_q,params_p], opts___] :=

Module[{l = Length[params], i1, i2},

  {i1,i2} = Sort[Table[Random[Integer,{1,l}],{2}]];

  {chromo[q[undef],
     Join[Take[params, Max[0,i1 - 1]],
        Take[params, Min[l,i2] - 1]]],{i1,i2}}
]
```

As for inversion (Program 3.18), the new chromosome is composed of the initial and terminal sequence. Both of these segments may be empty, namely, in the case of an initial ($i_1 = 1$) or terminal ($i_2 = n$) fragment loss. The following function call gives an example. As the initial chromosome we use the "letter chromosome" letterChromo from Section 3.4.1:

In[1] := **{delLetterChromo,cut} = Deletion[letterChromo]**

Chromosome with fragment loss

Out[1] ={chromo[q[undef], p[{1, {a}}, {2, {b}}, {3, {c}},
            {4, {d}}, {5, {e}}, {6, {f}}, {7, {g}},
            {8, {h}}, {9, {k}}, {10, {l}}, {11, {m}}]],
         {12, 15}}

The function Deletion returns the reduced chromosome and the positions for which the genes are deleted. In the above example the genes at positions 12 through 15 are lost—this is a terminal fragment loss.

Figure 3.36 depicts graphical representations of terminal fragment loss ([b]) and additional chromosomes with deletions. Example (c) is an inner fragment loss; example (d) models the deletion of an initial chromosome segment.

Deletions occur not only through breakings of a single chromosome but also as part of recombination effects resulting from crossovers of two chromosomes (see Section 3.4.4). Nature has developed

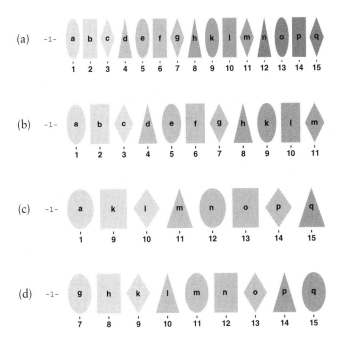

Figure 3.36
Examples of deletion effects.

a redundant form of information encoding: many genes are encoded several times on a chromosome. In addition to the regions that encode for protein structures (*exons*), there are also (large) sections on chromosomes that do not seem to be used for the encoding of any gene (*introns*). In the following section we consider a duplicating operator, which we can use to model gene copy effects.

Exons and introns

3.4.3 Duplication

The duplication of genetic information is a side effect of crosswise restitution (repair) of two homologous chromosomes; namely, if the crossover points on the strands differ in their location (Figure 3.37). A deletion on the one chromosome results in a corresponding gene duplication on the other chromosome. Formally, we define *duplication* as a gene-doubling operator on a single strand. Within a GA chromosome

$$s = \left(s_1, \ldots, s_{i_1-1}, s_{i_1}, \ldots, s_{i_2}, s_{i_2+1}, \ldots, s_n\right),$$

a randomly selected subsequence $(s_{i_1}, \ldots, s_{i_2})$ of $i_2 - i_1 + 1$ genes is copied and inserted after the original gene group:

$$s_{\text{dup}} = \left(s_1, \ldots, s_{i_1-1}, s_{i_1}, \ldots, s_{i_2}, s_{i_1}, \ldots, s_{i_2}, s_{i_2+1}, \ldots, s_n\right).$$

Duplication

Figure 3.37
Duplication effects
resulting from crossover of
homologous chromosomes.

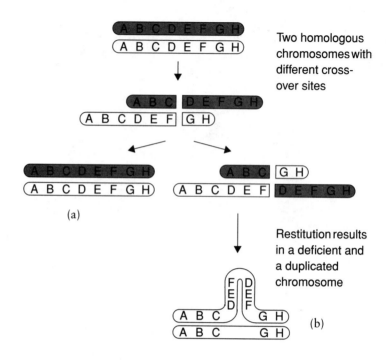

Two homologous
chromosomes with
different cross-
over sites

(a)

Restitution results
in a deficient and
a duplicated
chromosome

(b)

At least one gene is duplicated ($i_1 = i_2$). In the most extreme case, the
duplicated chromosome doubles in size ($i_1 = 1$, $i_2 = n$).

An implementation of this duplication operator is shown in Program 3.20. Analogous to the functions Inversion and Deletion,
the new chromosome is composed of the initial segment, two times
the fragment, and the terminal sequence. Besides the duplicated GA
chromosome structure, the Duplication function returns the
selected indices, from which the genes are copied.

Program 3.20
Duplication on GA
chromosomes.

```
Duplication[chromo[qual_q,params_p], opts___] :=

Module[{l = Length[params], i1, i2},

  {i1,i2} = Sort[Table[Random[Integer,{1,l}],{2}]];

  {chromo[q[undef],
    Join[
      Take[params, Max[0,i1 - 1]],
      Take[params, {i1,i2}], Take[params, {i1,i2}],
      Take[params, Min[l,i2] - 1]]],
    {i1,i2}}
]
```

Starting from the "letter chromosome" (Section 3.4.1), we can look at a small example:

```
In[1] := {dupLetterChromo, dup} =
       Duplication[letterChromo]
```

Out[1] = {chromo[q[undef], p[{1, {a}}, {2, {b}}, {3, {c}},
    {4, {d}}, {5, {e}}, {6, {f}}, {7, {g}},
    {8, {h}}, {9, {k}}, {10, {l}}, {11, {m}},
    {12, {n}}, {13, {o}}, {14, {p}}, {8, {h}},
    {9, {k}}, {10, {l}}, {11, {m}}, {12, {n}},
    {13, {o}}, {14, {p}}, {15, {q}}]],
  {8, 14}}

Chromosome with duplicated subsequence

Here the genes between positions 8 and 14 are duplicated, as Figure 3.38(a) and (b) shows. The duplication can occur for a sequence of several genes ([b] and [d]), or only for a single gene ([c]).

Whenever genes occur multiple times within a chromosome, possibly even with different alleles, generated by mutations, the question arises, Which of the duplicate genes will be expressed when the genotype is interpreted? In natural cells, duplications—mainly coupled with corresponding deficiencies (deletions)—occur with the recombination of two homologous chromosomes. Normally gametes, produced during meiotic cell division, that have deficient chromosomes are not fertilizable, whereas gametes with duplicate chromosomes are usually

Which gene is expressed?

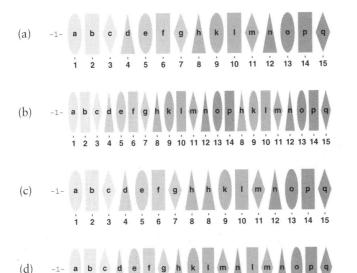

Figure 3.38
Examples of duplication.

functional. In GA chromosomes with duplicate gene information, many possibilities exist for which of the competing genes are expressed. For example, one of the competing genes might be selected at random, leading to nondeterministic interpretation functions. Or the first gene occurring from left to right might be chosen. Basically, the expression function depends very much on the actual GA application.

As we will see in Section 3.7.4 on the effects of these "secondary" GA operators, duplication and deletion operators need not be used as long as recombinations with different crossover points per chromosome or among nonhomologous chromosomes are used.

3.4.4 Crossover of nonhomologous chromosomes

Natural cell genome deficiencies and duplications occur in the context of crosswise restitution among two homologous chromosomes, where the two crossover points differ (Figure 3.39). The result of these recombinations is two chromosomes of different lengths. Up to now we have restricted recombinations to homologous chromosomes; that is, chromosomes of equal length. We also have assumed that both strands have their crossover points at exactly the same location. But what happens if the chromosomes break apart at different positions? Figure 3.39(b) and (c) illustrate this schematically. The result is two chromosomes of unequal lengths.

Figure 3.39
Translocations between nonhomologous chromosomes.

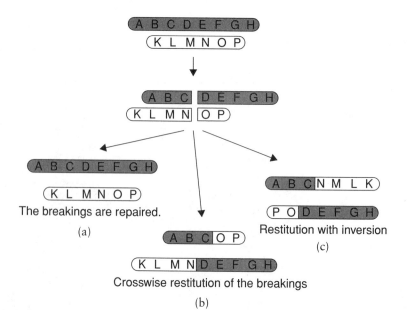

If the strands are homologous, one of the resulting chromosomes has a deficiency and the other a corresponding duplication of genes. Over and above the mere interchromosomal gene exchange, genotype modification will have new effects. These gene translocations are among the most frequent chromosome mutations (Gottschalk 1989, p. 220).

It is easy to imagine this kind of recombination for multiple crossover sites, even among nonhomologous chromosomes (Figure 3.40[b]).

We have extended the function `Recombine` from Section 3.3.1 with an additional recombination variant, `RecombinationMode` → `CROSSING[n]`, which allows for multiple crossovers between lists of unequal length for mutually different crossover points. The number of crossover sites is determined by the parameter n. Exact definitions of this extension as well as the code for the following examples can be found in the Evolvica notebook on the *IEC* Web page (see Preface). We begin with two lists of unequal length as representatives of two nonhomologous chromosomes:

In[1] := **nonHomologous =**
       {{a,b,c,d,e,f,g,h,k,l},{A,B,C,D,E,F,G,H}};

In Figure 3.41(a) both lists are depicted as chromosomes. The same letters are interpreted as alleles encoding for the same gene. We recombine the two lists with one crossover point each (CROSSING[1]):

In[2] := **{recParamsOne,recParamsTwo,coPoints} =**
       Recombine[nonHomologous,
         RecombinationMode → CROSSING[1]]

One-point crossover with different crossover points

(a)

(b)

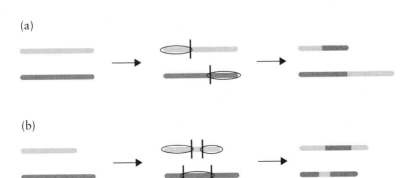

Figure 3.40
Recombination with different crossover points.
(a) One-point crossover on non-identical crossover sites. (b) Two-point crossover of nonhomologous chromosomes.

Out[2] ={{a, b, c, d, e, E, F, G, H},
        {A, B, C, D, f, g, h, k, l},
        {{6}, {5}}}

The result is two newly composed chromosomes and a list of randomly chosen crossover points. The first list has its crossover site at position 6; the second list is broken at position 5. The resulting sublists are recomposed in a crosswise fashion (Figure 3.41[b]).

The following function call gives an example of a recombination with two crossover points per chromosome (Figure 3.41[c]):

Two-point crossover with different crossover points

In[3] := **{recParamsOne,recParamsTwo,coPoints} =**
        Recombine[nonHomologous,
        RecombinationMode → CROSSING[2]]

Out[3] ={{a, b, c, F, k, l},
        {A, B, C, D, E, d, e, f, g, h, G, H},
        {{4, 9}, {6, 7}}}

Figure 3.41
Recombination effects
for nonhomologous
chromosomes with
different crossover points.

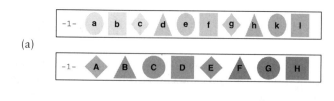
(a)

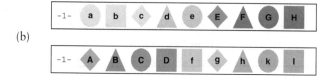
(b)

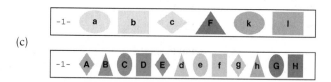
(c)

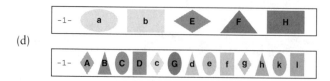
(d)

The crossover points of the first chromosome are at positions 4 and 9. Its gene sequence (d, e, f, g, h) from position 4 to 8 is transferred to the partner chromosome, where it is inserted at the first break point (position 6) (Figure 3.41[c]). On the other hand, the first chromosome receives gene F as a new entry at position 4. These are typical translocations, with a deficiency in the first chromosome and a gene duplication (double occurrence of d, D and e, E) in the second chromosome.

In[4] := {recParamsOne,recParamsTwo,coPoints} =
    Recombine[nonHomologous, RecombinationMode →
    CROSSING[3]]

Three-point crossover with different crossover points

Out[4] ={{a, b, E, F, H},
    {A, B, C, D, c, G, d, e, f, g, h, k, l},
    {{3, 4, 4}, {5, 7, 8}}}

The final example, in Figure 3.41(d), shows gene mixing for a total of six crossover points. Since two of the three break points are identical for the first chromosome and since they are locally related, we get the recombination effect of a one-point crossover for this chromosome. Duplications occur in the second chromosome; namely, for genes c, C, d, D, and g, G. Deletions as well as duplications also occur in examples (c) and (d).

3.5 Selection and GA evolution schemes

In previous sections we have discussed discrete genotypical encodings of genetic algorithms and their mutation and recombination operators. We now present the major variants of GA selection functions and the basic GA evolution scheme. We will answer questions about which individuals survive on the basis of their fitnesses and how evolution cycles of iterated selection, mutation, and recombination can be formalized and implemented into algorithmic schemes.

Section 3.5.1 provides a small collection of selection functions, which preferably are used in GA applications. In Section 3.5.2, we illustrate the GA evolution scheme in the notation originally introduced for evolution strategies (Section 4.4). An Evolvica implementation of GA evolution algorithms is introduced in detail in Section 3.6.

3.5.1 Selection functions

The criteria used for the selection of individuals, who pass their genetic information from one generation to the next, are one of the

Plus and comma strategy

key aspects that determine the success or failure of an evolutionary algorithm. In the context of evolution strategies there are a variety of selection methods, which basically work as follows. From μ parents a set of λ mutant offspring are generated and evaluated. From the selection pool of the λ mutants or the μ + λ parents and mutants, the best μ individuals for the following generation are selected (Section 4.4.2).

Genetic algorithms follow a different selection criterion, which is closely related to selection among natural organisms. In nature, an individual's survivability is determined by a range of factors. However, it is usually not the case that only the "best" individuals survive. Even a less well adapted individual may be able to generate enough offspring to pass its genetic information into the next generation.

Random survival

Fitness-proportionate selection

To model differential probabilities of survival, genetic algorithms use mechanisms of probabilistic selection. In principle, stochastic selection schemes must answer the following question: Which individuals are to be reproduced such that promising regions of the search space (or the gene pool) are discovered and further exploited? On the other hand, new paths must be taken, leading into previously unexplored regions, which might only be accessible via low fitness areas. The scheme of *fitness-proportionate selection* tries to model this balance of using both already acquired knowledge (exploitation) and investigating new territory (exploration) (Holland 1975; Holland 1992a, Chapter 5).

Differential survival probability

For a population $P = \{s_1, \ldots, s_\mu\}$ with μ individuals having fitnesses $\eta(s_i) \in \Re_0^+$, $1 \le i \le \mu$, we may calculate each individual's probability of survival $\sigma_{prop}(s_i)$ as follows:

Fitness-proportionate selection

$$\sigma_{prop}(s_i) = \frac{\eta(s_i)}{\eta_\Sigma(P)}.$$

Here $\eta_\Sigma(P)$ denotes the sum of all fitness values of the population:

$$\eta_\Sigma(P) = \sum_{s \in P} \eta(s).$$

Roulette wheel

The probability of an individual being reproduced into the next generation is proportionate to its fitness. We can imagine the fitnesses $\eta(s_i)$ arranged as segments on a roulette wheel (Figure 3.42). The size of each segment is directly proportionate to the corresponding individual's fitness.

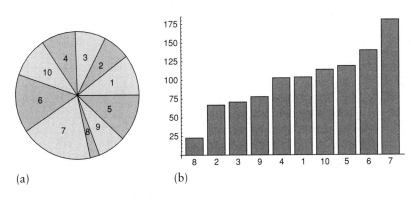

Figure 3.42
Fitness-proportionate
selection. (a) Roulette wheel
of fitness. (b) Selection
histogram for fitness-
proportionate selection.

(a)   (b)

Let us examine an example. A list of random values from the
interval [0,1] is generated, which represent the fitnesses $\eta = (P)$
$\{\eta(s_1), \ldots, \eta(s_{10})\}$ of a population of size 10.

In[1] := **randomFits = Table[Random[],{10}]**

Out[1] ={0.463469, 0.319661, 0.359034, 0.400036,   *Random fitnesses*
      0.46115, 0.663489, 0.843871, 0.109689,
      0.328695, 0.53646}

In Figure 3.42(a), these fitness values are depicted as a roulette
wheel. If we played a ball on this roulette wheel, it would be more
likely to end up in the seventh individual's segment than, say, in segment number 9.

Fitness-proportionate selection is implemented in Evolvica by the
function `selectFitProp` in Program 3.21. For the fitnesses, passed
as a list, cumulative fitness sums (`cumFits`) of segments 1, 1 to 2, 1 to
3, and so on are calculated. A random position (`r`) on the roulette
wheel is selected, and finally the index of the element is determined,
the segment of which contains the selected position.

```
SelectFitProp[fitnesses_List] :=
Module[{cumFits, r},

   cumFits = FoldList[Plus, 0, fitnesses] // Rest;
   r = Random[] Last[cumFits];

   Position[cumFits, _?(# >= r &), {1}, 1][[1,1]]

]
```

Program 3.21
Fitness-proportionate
selection.

To get an impression of the effect of fitness-proportionate selection, we perform selection a thousand times and calculate the frequency with which each individual is chosen.

Test of roulette selection

$In[2] :=$ **selections =**
      Table[selectFitProp[randomFits],{1000}];

$In[3] :=$ **freqs = Frequencies[selections];**

The individual frequencies can be illustrated by a histogram:

$In[4] :=$ **BarChart[freqs // Sort, PlotRange $\rightarrow$ All];**

The result is shown in Figure 3.42(b). As expected, individual 7 is selected most of the time, but individuals with fewer fitnesses, for example, individual 8, also have a chance of being selected for reproduction. With fitness-proportionate selection, on average any individual with fitness $\eta(s_i)$ will find

$$\mu \cdot \frac{\eta(s_i)}{\eta_\Sigma(P)}$$

of its offspring in the next generation. The essential constraint for the actual number of reproduced individuals is the predefined population size, which for genetic algorithms usually remains constant over the generations (same as for evolution strategies). The composition of the offspring generation from a population pop of μ individuals with fitnesses popFitnesses can be described by the following pseudo-code:

```
Table[pop[[selection[popFitnesses]]], {μ}].
```

The selection function determines which individuals appear in the next generation. In our previous example we have set selection = selectFitProp. The following sections present additional selection functions preferably used in GA systems.

Rank-based selection

Problem of superindividuals

Fitness-proportionate selection runs into problems if one or a few "superindividuals" occur in the population, which, compared to their competitors, have extremely high fitnesses. In such a situation it is very likely that the following generation will be dominated by these highly fit individuals. This is all right as long as these individuals are able to improve their fitness quality by additional mutations and recombinations. Unfortunately, this is seldom the case. Often it turns out that the dominating individuals represent only a local optimum in the search space. The evolutionary algorithm can escape from this local peak only if the population's diversity is kept at a fairly high level. This means that less fit individuals must also be represented. However, if the superindividuals take over, the diversity of the population and the gene pool vanishes.

Rank-based selection is used to avoid undesirable convergence effects, where differences between fitness values are normalized. The individuals are sorted according to their fitnesses. Selection is not determined by the actual fitness value but by an individual's position within a fitness rank scale. For μ individuals the best individual receives a rank of μ fitness points, the second best is assigned $\mu - 1$ points, and so on until the last individual, which gets only one point. Roulette wheel selection is then performed on the basis of these fitness points.

Rank-based selection

Program 3.22 shows the Evolvica implementation of rank-based selection by the function selectRankBased. The fitness values are attributed with indices and sorted by ascending fitness (fitsAnd-IndsSorted). Using the fitness ranks, the roulette wheel selection function selectFitProp chooses a rank position (index). The function returns the index of the individual, which is positioned at rank index. Figure 3.43(a) depicts the distribution of the selection values for the fitnesses used in the previous example (randomFits, see Figure 3.42[a]). The segment size for each individual corresponds to its rank in the fitness competition. As a test example, we perform 1000 selections and calculate the selection frequency of each individual.

Program 3.22
Rank-based selection.

```
selectRankBased[fitnesses_List] :=
Module[{fitsAndIndsSorted, index},

   fitsAndIndsSorted =
     Sort[MapIndexed[{#1,First[#2]}&,fitnesses]];

   index = selectFitProp[Range[Length[fitnesses]]];

   fitsAndIndsSorted[[index]]//Last

]
```

In[5] := **selections =**
          Table[selectRankBased[randomFits],{1000}];

Figure 3.43
Rank-based selection.
(a) Roulette wheel of
rank-based selection.
(b) Selection histogram for
rank-based selection.

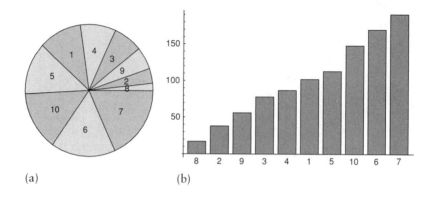

(a)   (b)

In[6] := **freqs = Frequencies[selections];**

The sorted frequencies are illustrated in Figure 3.43(b). The lineariza-
tion effect of rank-based selection in Figure 3.43(b) is clearly visible
when compared to Figure 3.42.

Elitist selection

EA versus GA

Again a comparison with ES selection functions (see Section 4.4)
seems appropriate here. Unlike genetic algorithms, ES selection of
parent individuals is not stochastic. For a (μ, λ) or $(\mu + \lambda)$ strategy,
from the set of mutants, the μ best individuals are selected as the parents of the following generation. The selection of individuals, which
are subsequently mutated, is performed at random; that is, without
taking any of the parent fitnesses into account. In genetic algorithms,

Elitist selection

this kind of selection is known as *elitist selection*. The function
selectElite in Program 3.23 implements (ES) best selection.
    The option Elite $\rightarrow \mu$ sets the portion of the individuals to be
selected, either as a percentile or as an integer value between 1 and the
population size.
    Similar to rank-based selection (Program 3.22), the fitness values
are attributed with indices and sorted by decreasing fitnesses. From
this list the μ best individuals, as determined by option Elite, are
collected, and one of them is chosen at random. Figure 3.44(a) illustrates the distribution of selection probabilities of the best five individuals. Again we use the fitness values (randomFits; compare Figure
3.42[a]) from the previous two sections.
    Among the group of these five individuals, selection is performed
at random. We almost get a uniform distribution of the selection frequencies for the best five individuals if we test for 1000 elitist selections (Figure 3.44[b]).

```
selectElite[fitnesses_List, opts___] :=
Module[{bestCount, fitsAndIndsSorted},

  bestCount = Elite /. {opts} /. Options[selectElite];

  fitsAndIndsSorted =
    Reverse[Sort[MapIndexed[{#1,First[#2]}&,
    fitnesses]]];

  selectRandom[Last /@
    If[IntegerQ[bestCount],
      Take[fitsAndIndsSorted, bestCount],
      Take[fitsAndIndsSorted,
        Max[1, Floor[bestCount Length[fitnesses]]]]]]
]

Options[selectElite] = { Elite -> 1 };
```

Program 3.23
Elitist selection.

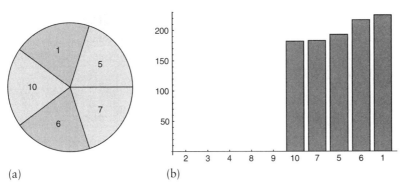

(a)   (b)

Figure 3.44
Elitist selection. (a) Roulette wheel of fitness for 50%-elitist selection.
(b) Histogram for elitist selection.

Further selection functions

Here we can present only a small collection of selection functions used in genetic algorithm systems. Additional examples can be found in, among others, Goldberg 1989, pp. 121–125, or De Jong 1975. In particular, Brindle investigated a number of deterministic and stochastic selection methods and compared them according to their suitability for exploitation and exploration of multidimensional search spaces (Brindle 1981). Detailed comparisons of GA selection schemes are reported in Blickle and Thiele 1995. They discuss tournament selection, truncation selection, linear and exponential selection, as well as proportional (fitness-proportionate) selection. In Section 6.4, we discuss tournament selection in the context of evolutionary programming.

3.5.2 GA evolution schemes

This section demonstrates the principal evolution scheme of genetic algorithms: the mutual interactions of genetic operators and selection functions. In Section 2.3.2, on parameter optimization, we already sketched the GA evolution scheme. Figure 2.5 and Figure 2.10 may serve here as illustrations again. GA evolution starts with the generation of an initial population of μ genotypical structures, usually encoded by a discrete allele alphabet. After interpretation (decoding) and evaluation of the individuals, the population enters a selection-variation cycle, which is performed until a maximum number of generations is created or until some termination criterion is fulfilled.

Figure 3.45 depicts the GA evolution scheme in graphical notation, explained in more detail in Section 4.4 on evolution strategies. The classical genetic algorithm corresponds to the evolution scheme of a $(\mu/2, \mu)$ evolution strategy. From the pool of μ parents μ pairs are selected for recombination (usually crossover) and subsequent mutation. The result is μ mutants, which are the parents for the following generation. The major difference from the ES scheme is in the selection method of the individuals to be recombined. Selection is not random but is performed according to one of the selection functions introduced in Section 3.5.1. However, usually fitness-proportionate selection is preferred.

In general, the population size μ is kept fixed over the generations. If a generation is understood as the set of λ individuals, which are newly generated by genetic operators per generation step, a few GA variants can be uniformly formalized. In Figure 3.45 the selection function σ_η, depending on the individual fitnesses $\eta(P)$, is indicated by an arrow close to the parent population P. Furthermore, the parents have to be attributed with their fitnesses; that is, they are evaluated

Comma GA strategy

GA selection

Figure 3.45

Evolution scheme of a classical genetic algorithm.

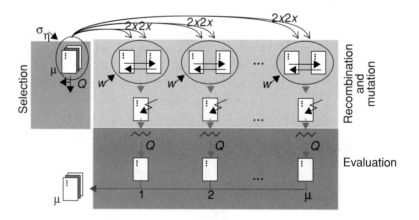

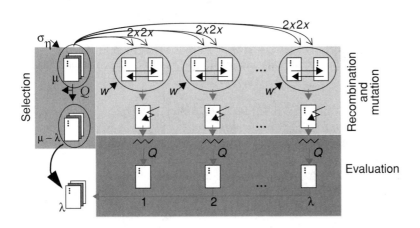

Figure 3.46
Evolution scheme of a genetic algorithm with additional elitist selection.

before any selection is performed. In evolution strategies, the fitnesses do not play any role for this selection.

Since it is rather unlikely that an individual will pass GA recombinations and mutations without any change, each individual survives at most for one generation, as the analogy to a comma evolution scheme suggests. Whenever the up-to-now best individuals should not be lost, we have to guarantee that they are passed on to the next generation. Hence, the new parent generation is composed of the $\mu - \lambda$ best individuals and the λ mutants generated from the current μ parents (Figure 3.46). Often only the single best individual of a generation is kept. Consequently, $\lambda = \mu - 1$ mutants have to be generated. In a variant of the so-called *steady state* GA the worst individual is replaced by a mutant ($\lambda = 1$) derived from the current population. That is, the $\mu - 1$ best individuals are copied into the following generation (Syswerda 1991).

Steady state GA

Many further application-specific variants of genetic algorithms are the subject of current research. For more details about GAs with more specific evolution schemes refer to Davis 1991, Goldberg 1989, Michalewicz 1992, Mitchell 1996, Mühlenbein and Schlierkamp-Voosen 1993, and Mühlenbein and Schlierkamp-Voosen 1994. These references discuss GA schemes closely related to the ones discussed here and alternative GA reproduction mechanisms.

3.6 Genetic algorithms with Evolvica

Before we demonstrate a few evolution experiments with genetic algorithms in the following section, let us first summarize the GA implementations that we have introduced so far. By combining the genetic operators of recombination, mutation, inversion, duplication, and deletion with the selection functions discussed in Section 3.5.1, we get a GA-typical evolution scheme (Figure 3.45). We will formulate genetic algorithms as a *GA strategy*, analogous to an ES scheme.

The evolution scheme for a genetic algorithm can be represented as follows:

$$\lambda_1 \left(\mu_0 / \rho_0 \overset{+}{,} \lambda_0 \| \Omega_0 \right)^{\gamma_0} \text{ GA.}$$

This corresponds to the ES notation, which is described in detail in Sections 4.4 and 4.5. This "formula" describes λ_1 independent GA experiments, each over γ_0 generations. In each generation, λ_0 mutants are generated from μ_0 parent structures. The mutated offspring are generated by the successive application of the stochastic operators of recombination, mutation, inversion, duplication, and deletion. Which of these operators are applied with which probabilities is specified by the option vector Ω_0, which might look as follows:

$$\Omega_0 = \left(p_{\text{rec}} \to 0.2, p_{\text{mut}} \to 0.1, p_{\text{inv}} \to 0, \ldots \right).$$

Here the individuals would be recombined with a probability of 0.2, mutated with a 10% probability, but none of them would be inverted.

In general, recombination can be applied among ρ_0 individuals. For the canonical genetic algorithm this means $\rho_0 = 2$. In addition, the canonical GA evolution scheme implements a comma strategy. All individuals of a generation are replaced by new individuals. Hence, a classic GA generation cycle, with crossover and mutation, is described as a

$$\left(\mu_0 / 2, \mu_0 \| \Omega_0 \right) \text{ GA.}$$

From the pool of μ_0 parents $2 \cdot \mu_0$ individuals are selected fitness proportionately and recombined in pairs by one-point crossover. The resulting μ_0 chromosomes are point mutated. They constitute the subsequent parent generation. The description of the parameters for the operators might look like this:

$$\Omega_0 = (\text{Rec} \to \text{Cross}(1), \text{Sel} \to \text{FitProp}, p_{\text{Rec}} \to 0.9, p_{\text{Mut}} \to 0.1, \ldots).$$

By integrating genetic algorithms into the ES evolution schemes notation, we have a wide range of possibilities for how to combine selection functions with genetic operators and how to compose gene pools for the next generation. The general "GA formula"

$$\lambda_1 \left(\mu_0 / \rho_0 \overset{+}{,} \lambda_0 \| \Omega_0 \right)^{\gamma_0}$$

can be slightly rewritten in Evolvica notation as a GA plus strategy:

$$\lambda_1 \ \text{GA}[\mu_0, \ \rho_0, \ \text{PLUS}, \ \lambda_0, \ \gamma_0, \ \Omega_0]$$

GA plus strategy

or GA comma strategy:

$$\lambda_1 \ \text{GA}[\mu_0, \ \rho_0, \ \text{COMMA}, \ \lambda_0, \ \gamma_0, \ \Omega_0].$$

GA comma strategy

We will also use this form of notation for the function Evolution in Program 3.24, which implements the GA evolution scheme (cf. Program 4.13) used in Evolvica.

```
Evolution[ GA[μ_?IntegerQ,  (* parents *)
              ρ_?IntegerQ,  (* recombinations *)
              σ_?AtomQ,     (* PLUS or COMMA *)
              λ_?IntegerQ,  (* children *)
              γ_?IntegerQ,  (* generations *)
              opts___]      (* options *)
           i_:1            (* independent runs *)
] :=
Module[{initialParents,evalFct,parents,children,
selPool},

  (* Generate μ initial individuals *)
  If[(initialParents = (InitialPopulation /. {opts}
      /. Options[Evolution])) === {},
    initialParents = createChromosomes[μ,
      ChromosomeWidth → (ChromosomeWidth /. {opts}
      /. Options[Evolution]),opts]];

  (* Get the evaluation function *)
  evalFct = EvaluationFunction
          /. {opts} /. Options[Evaluation];

  (* Evaluate initial individuals *)
  initialParents =
    Map[Evaluation[#,EvaluationFunction :> evalFct]&,
      initialParents];
```

Program 3.24
Algorithm for GA evolution
(Part 1).

By calling the function

$$\text{Evolution}[\lambda_1 \ \text{GA}[\mu_0, \ \rho_0, \ \text{PLUS}, \ \lambda_0, \ \gamma_0, \ \Omega_0]],$$

Starting a GA evolution experiment

λ_1 independent GA experiments are performed, each over γ_0 generations. Each population consists of μ_0 individuals, from which λ_0

Program 3.25
Algorithm for
GA evolution
(Part 2).

```
(* Iterate for i independent runs *)
Table[
  (* Iterate for γ generations *)
  NestList[
   (parents = #;
    children = Apply[pop,
      ComposeList[{
        Map[First[Recombination[#,opts]]&,#]&,
        Map[Mutation[#,opts]&,#]&,
        Map[First[Inversion[#,opts]]&,#]&,
        Map[First[Deletion[#,opts]]&,#]&,
        Map[First[Duplication[#,opts]]&,#]&,
        Map[Evaluation[#,
          EvaluationFunction :> evalFct,opts]&,#]& },

        Partition[Selection[parents,ρ*λ,
          SelectionMode → (SelectionMode
            /. {opts} /.
            Options[Evolution]),opts],ρ]
      ]//Last];

    selPool =
      Switch[s,
        PLUS, Join[parents,children],
        COMMA, children];

    Selection[selPool,μ,SelectionMode → BEST]
   ) &,
   initialParents,
   γ
  ], (* end nesting *)

 {i}] (* independent runs *)
]
```

Options to control the GA evolution function

mutant chromosomes are generated and evaluated, using the evaluation function, genetic operators, and additional control parameters described in the option list Ω_0. From the pool of μ_0 parents and λ_0 newly generated structures, the best μ_0 individuals are selected for the next generation.

The first part of Program 3.24 basically shows how the initial population is generated. At the beginning of each GA run, usually new chromosome structures are generated using the function `create-Chromosomes`. Here the chromosome width (`ChromosomeWidth`), the number of strands (`PolyPloidy`), and the allele alphabet (`Alphabet`) can be set (cf. Section 3.1). Via the option `InitialPopulation` a particular initial population may be given, as, for instance, the last generation of a previously performed GA experiment. In this case, all λ_1 (or i) independent evolution runs start with the same initial population.

The actual evolution loops are listed in Program 3.24, and independent runs are simulated by the `Table` loop command. Iterations over the generations are implemented by a nested loop (`NestList`). The `ComposeList` command turns out to be very helpful for successive applications of genetic operators and even allows for documenting the effect of each operator. The selection of individuals from the parent population is performed according to the function given by `SelectionMode`. So we might, for example, use fitness-proportionate (`FITPROP`), rank-based (`RANKBASED`), or elitist selection (`ELITE`) (cf. Section 3.5.1).

3.7   Genetic algorithms at work

In this section, we illustrate applications of different genetic algorithm schemes with the example of a typical parameter optimization problem—searching for the highest peaks of a two-dimensional multimodal function.

In the first section, we introduce visualization schemes for GA chromosome structures (Section 3.7.1). In the experiments we focus on binary strings. Section 3.7.2 deals with decoding and evaluation of genotypical GA structures. In Section 3.7.3, we compare typical effects of the two major GA operators—mutation and recombination. In Section 3.7.4, we illustrate how the major GA operators as well as a set of secondary operators (Section 3.4) influence the evolutionary dynamics of the genotypical structures. Finally, in Section 3.7.5, we demonstrate by a few example GA evolution runs that genetic algorithms are able to react quickly to changing environmental conditions; that is, to changes in the problem-specific search space. These observations confirm the flexible adaptiveness of evolutionary algorithms and of genetic algorithms in particular. We also use GA meta-strategies with subpopulations.

Section overview

3.7.1 Visualizing the genotypes

In the following experiments on GA evolution we will encode the parameters that are to be optimized as binary vectors or strings. The evolutionary dynamics can then be analyzed from two different viewpoints—on the problem-specific level of phenotypes and in genotypical structure space. Visualizing the gene pool of the evolving populations provides crucial insights into the dynamics of the adaptation processes.

Binary matrices

An interpolated contour plot is useful for this purpose (Figure 3.47). The gene pool of a population can be represented as a matrix with binary entries. The matrix width depends on the genome length; its height is determined by the number of individuals per population. The Mathematica function `ListDensityPlot` displays such a matrix as a black-and-white pattern, shown in Figure 3.47(b). Here a 0 entry of the matrix corresponds to a black square and each 1 entry is represented by a white square. A smoothed version of this representation, generated by the function `ListContourPlot`, is more convenient for observing evolution dynamics (Figure 3.47[c]). In particular, when these graphics are animated, the human eye can grasp variations or periodic patterns much more quickly. However, the exact allele settings are lost with this interpolated version. In the following examples we use both of these representations.

3.7.2 Decoding of genotypes and their evaluation

Before the information encoded on the chromosomes can be evaluated, the chromosomes must be translated into problem-specific (data) structures (cf. Section 2.3.2). In the following experiments, we represent two-dimensional coordinates as binary vectors and present decoding functions for this case. The decoding procedure is analogous if other data structures are encoded by a vector or string over discrete alphabets. A GA experiment is initiated by a function call of the form

```
In[1] := Evolution[
           GA[20,2,COMMA,20,5,
             ChromosomeWidth → 20,
             Partitions → 2,
             EvaluationFunction → evalFunc,
             ...
           ]
         ];
```

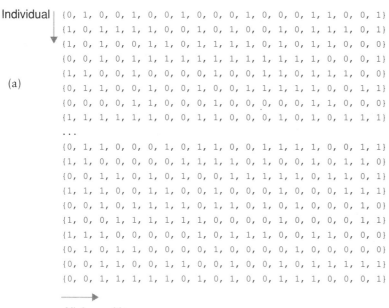

Individual
{0, 1, 0, 0, 1, 0, 0, 1, 0, 0, 0, 1, 0, 0, 0, 1, 1, 0, 0, 1}
{1, 0, 1, 1, 1, 1, 0, 0, 1, 0, 1, 0, 0, 1, 0, 1, 1, 1, 0, 1}
{1, 0, 1, 0, 0, 1, 1, 0, 1, 1, 1, 1, 0, 1, 0, 1, 1, 0, 0, 0}
{0, 0, 1, 0, 1, 1, 1, 1, 1, 1, 1, 1, 1, 1, 1, 1, 0, 0, 0, 1}
{1, 1, 0, 0, 1, 0, 0, 0, 0, 1, 0, 0, 1, 1, 0, 1, 1, 1, 0, 0}
{0, 1, 1, 0, 0, 1, 0, 0, 1, 0, 0, 1, 1, 1, 1, 1, 0, 0, 1, 1}
{0, 0, 0, 0, 1, 1, 0, 0, 0, 1, 0, 0, 0, 0, 0, 0, 1, 1, 0, 0}
{1, 1, 1, 1, 1, 1, 0, 0, 1, 1, 0, 0, 0, 1, 0, 1, 0, 1, 1, 1}
...
{0, 1, 1, 0, 0, 0, 1, 0, 1, 1, 0, 0, 1, 1, 1, 1, 0, 0, 1, 1}
{1, 1, 0, 0, 0, 0, 0, 1, 1, 1, 1, 0, 1, 0, 0, 1, 0, 1, 1, 0}
{0, 0, 1, 1, 0, 1, 0, 1, 0, 0, 1, 1, 1, 1, 1, 0, 1, 1, 0, 1}
{1, 1, 1, 0, 0, 1, 1, 0, 0, 1, 0, 0, 0, 1, 0, 0, 0, 1, 1, 1}
{0, 0, 1, 0, 1, 1, 1, 1, 0, 1, 1, 0, 1, 0, 1, 0, 0, 0, 1, 0}
{1, 0, 0, 1, 1, 1, 1, 1, 1, 0, 0, 0, 0, 1, 0, 0, 0, 0, 1, 1}
{1, 1, 1, 0, 0, 0, 0, 0, 1, 0, 1, 1, 1, 0, 0, 1, 1, 0, 0, 0}
{0, 1, 0, 1, 1, 0, 0, 0, 0, 1, 0, 0, 0, 0, 1, 0, 0, 0, 0, 0}
{0, 0, 1, 1, 0, 0, 1, 1, 0, 0, 1, 0, 0, 1, 0, 1, 1, 1, 1, 1}
{0, 0, 1, 1, 1, 1, 1, 0, 1, 0, 1, 0, 0, 1, 1, 1, 0, 0, 0, 1}

Allele position

(a)

Indiv.

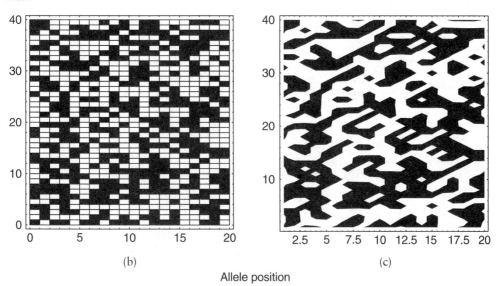

(b)   (c)

Allele position

Figure 3.47
Visualizing binary genotypes.

In this example a (20/2, 20) GA strategy over five generations is performed. Here we focus only on the options concerning decoding and evaluation. The genotypes are evaluated according to the setting of EvaluationFunction. This function also deals with the decoding of the binary strings. An example of such a decoding/evaluation

Decoding and evaluation

function is given in Program 3.26. In order to decode the strings, the function needs two input parameters: the GA chromosome width (ChromsomeWidth → M) and the number of parameters encoded on the chromosome (Partitions → m). The function Decoding partitions the string (actually it is a vector) into m segments of equal size, each of which defines a gene encoding one parameter. Finally, the DecodingFunction determines how the genes are translated into problem-specific data structures. For our example, this means that the chromosomes encode the x coordinate in the first 10 bits, and the y coordinate is represented by the remaining 10 bits. The function lettersToIntervalNumber transforms a binary string into a corresponding number from the interval given by the Interval option. For more details, see the Evolvica notebook for this section on the *IEC* Web page (see Preface).

Program 3.26
Evaluation function for binary-encoded numbers.

```
evalFunc =
(-f[List @@ Decoding[#, Partitions → 2,
  DecodingFunction →
  (lettersToIntervalNumber[#,2,Interval →
  {-1,1}]&)]]&);
```

An example of an evaluation or *objective* function, a simple parabola, is given in Program 3.27. This function is also used in the following sections in order to study the effects of genetic operators.

Program 3.27
Example of an objective function.

```
f[v_List] := Apply[Plus,Map[#^2&,v]]
```

The individuals are selected according to higher fitness values; that is, we consider the optimization task as searching for maxima. A minimum search can always be reformulated as a search for maxima by simply inverting the sign. This explains the minus sign with the objective function in Program 3.26.

3.7.3 Recombination versus mutation

In the genetic algorithm community, in practical applications as well as in theory, recombining operators have always played a more important role than simple point mutations. To shed some light on this preference for recombination, we compare the effects of binary crossover to those effects on population dynamics induced by unary mutation. We utilize the objective function in Program 3.27 as a starting point. The GA evolution system should localize the coordinates of its global minimum. In Figures 3.48 and 3.50 this lowest point is labeled by a flag.

Influence of mutation

We first consider the influence of mutation on the evolution of the population structure. We begin with five independent populations of size 10, which are evolved over 10 generations by a (10 + 10) strategy. The only genetic operator we use is mutation. The point mutation probability is set to 50%. The chromosomes of the initial population are randomly generated. Their phenotypes are widely spread over the search space (Figure 3.48, Gen. 0). After the first generation the major effect of (fitness-proportionate) selection is visible. Points initially placed near the margins are sorted out. At the same time, mutations provide a certain dispersion by introducing new allele settings. However, only those mutants that turn out to be among the top 10 of their population survive. Thus, although mutations ensure that new coordinates are explored, strict selection is performed among the mutated offspring and the parent individuals. After 10 generations, each of the

Dispersion

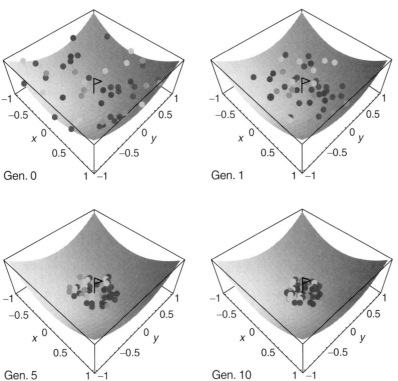

Figure 3.48
Population dynamics under the influence of mutations.

five populations, representing independent GA runs, has gathered more or less adjacent to the central global minimum.

Figure 3.49 illustrates the same evolution from the genotypical viewpoint. Each column shows the change of the gene pools of one of the five populations. The GA chromosomes in each population are sorted lexicographically from top to bottom.

Only slight convergence of the gene pool

None of the populations converges perfectly toward the global minimum point (which, of course, depends on the bit resolution used for the number encoding). This is also illustrated by the genome patterns. Only a few alleles are actually "fixed," which would be indicated by columnlike patterns.

Effects of recombinations

A much more distinct effect results from recombining operators. Recombinations can tremendously accelerate the localization of optimal points. Again we start from five independent populations, each evolved by a $(10 + 10)$ strategy over 10 generations. One-point crossover is the only genetic operator applied.

At the beginning, the points are randomly spread over the search space (Figure 3.50). After one generation the strong influence of selection is noticeable. Individuals near the margin are sorted out (Gen. 1). In comparison with generation 1 of Figure 3.48, the convergence effect of recombinations already appears to be emerging. In

Figure 3.49
Evolution of the genotypes under mutation.

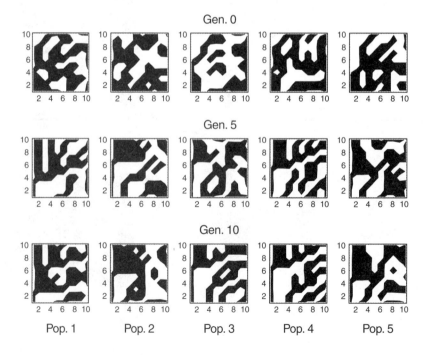

Gen. 0

Gen. 5

Gen. 10

Pop. 1   Pop. 2   Pop. 3   Pop. 4   Pop. 5

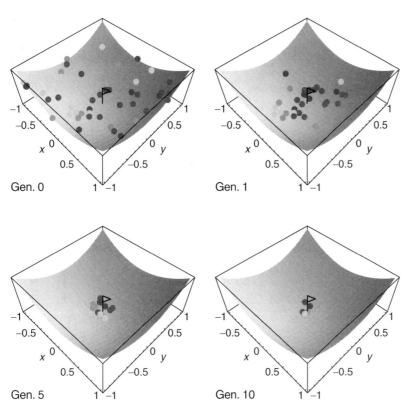

Figure 3.50
Population dynamics under the influence of recombinations.

the fifth generation convergence is clearly visible. Since crossovers only generate chromosomes with coordinates located within the smallest rectangle enclosing the current phenotypes, iterated mutual exchange of chromosome segments results in a gene pool of reduced allele diversity. Therefore, the population is gradually converging. In combination with fitness-proportionate selection this eventually leads to an accelerated convergence of the individuals around the global optimum.

Accelerated convergence

This effect is also clearly visible in the genotypical structures (Figure 3.51). In the initial gene pool the alleles are randomly distributed, illustrated by corresponding stochastic black-and-white patterns. In generation 5, most of the alleles are fixed. Large segments of the chromosomes are identical, indicated by distinct column patterns. In generation 10, the gene pool of four of the five populations consists of only a single chromosome. All individuals have identical allele settings. The inverse patterns of, for example, the first and second population result from the symmetry of the search space.

Fixing of alleles

Figure 3.51

Convergence effects of the genotypes under recombinations.

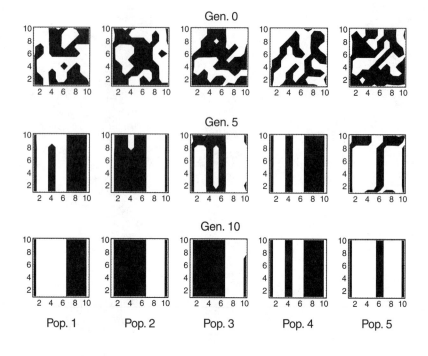

3.7.4 Effects of genetic operators

We have just illustrated the effects of mutations and recombinations on the composition of the gene pools in combination with iterated selections. Here we investigate by example the effects of the (secondary) genetic operators of inversion, deletion, and duplication. The following GA experiments are very simple; however, they provide essential insight into the mode of operation and the specific effects of each of the genetic operators.

Inversion, deletion, duplication

Again we take the objective function of Program 3.27 as a starting point. For each of the operators to be investigated, starting from the same initial population, we will perform a (20/2, 20) GA strategy over five generations. From 20 parents 20 mutants are generated, which will constitute the next-generation parents. In the case of recombinations, 2×20 individuals are crossed over.

First we examine the mutation operator. The following function call initiates a GA experiment with mutation as the only genetic operator:

Iterated mutations

```
In[1] := GApop =
         Evolution[
           GA[20,2,COMMA,20,5,
```

```
        ChromosomeWidth → 20,
        Partitions → 2,
        FitnessInterval → {0,2},
        SelectionMode → FITPROP,

        MutationProbability → 1,
          PointMutationProbability → 0.2,

        EvaluationFunction → evalFunc,
        InitialPopulation → {}
     ]
   ];
```

The bitwise probability for point mutations is set to 0.2. The function in Program 3.26 is used for evaluating the chromosomes. The genomes of the initial population are composed as random bit strings of length 20. Figure 3.52 (a) depicts the gene pool of the initial population and the distribution of individuals in the phenotypical search space of the objective function. The graphics were each generated by the following commands. The visualization of the phenotypical points results from

In[2] := `Map[subPopulationPlot[#,PointsHeight → .05]&,`   *Visualizing the phenotypes*
          `{Map[xyDecoding,{Last[GApop//First]}]}]//`
          `Transpose];`

Here it is assumed that the objective function is denoted by f and has the type structure of Program 3.27.

```
xyDecoding =
Decoding[#, Partitions → 2,
  DecodingFunction →
   (N[lettersToIntervalNumber[#,2,
   Interval → {-1,1}]]&)
]&;
```

Program 3.28
Decoding function for
binary-encoded pairs of
numbers.

The function xyDecoding translates the bit strings of the first and second half of a GA chromosome (Partitions → 2) to corresponding numbers from the interval [−1, 1], resulting in the coordinates in the search space. This is the same function used for evaluating the individuals (cf. Program 3.26).

We get the representation of the gene pool as a black-and-white matrix by the function subPopulationChromosomePlot:

Visualizing the genotypes

```
In[3] := Map[subPopulationChromosomePlot[#,
            PlotStyle → Density]&, {
            Last[GApop // Transpose]}];
```

The mesh representation of the GA chromosomes, which are sorted alphabetically from top to bottom, results from the option Plot-Style → Density. The bit string genomes are arranged along the horizontal axis. With the same function the gene pool can also be visualized as an interpolated pattern, with the PlotStyle option set to Contour:

Interpolated genotype representation

```
In[4] := Map[subPopulationChromosomePlot[#,
            PlotStyle → Contour]&,
            {Last[GApop // Transpose]}];
```

For the other genetic operators the evolution experiments are initiated according to the following template (here inversion is used as an example):

```
In[5] := GApop =
         Evolution[
           GA[20,2,COMMA,20,5,
             . . .
             InversionProbability → 1,
             . . .
             InitialPopulation → First[GApop//First]]];
```

The selection probability for the operator to be applied is set to 1. For all other operators it is set to 0. The first generation of the previous (mutation) experiment is used as the initial population. Thus, all GA runs start from the same gene pool.

Let us now take a closer look at the effects of each operator on the evolution of the populations. This time the points of the initial population are not uniformly distributed over the search space (Figure 3.52[a]). The upper-left corner remains empty.

Mutations

We had already observed the basic effect of mutation in the previous section. Here, too, it turns out that this operator sets the preconditions for explorations into new search regions (Figure 3.52[b]). After five generations even areas not considered so far are at least partly occupied. The search space is more uniformly scanned for

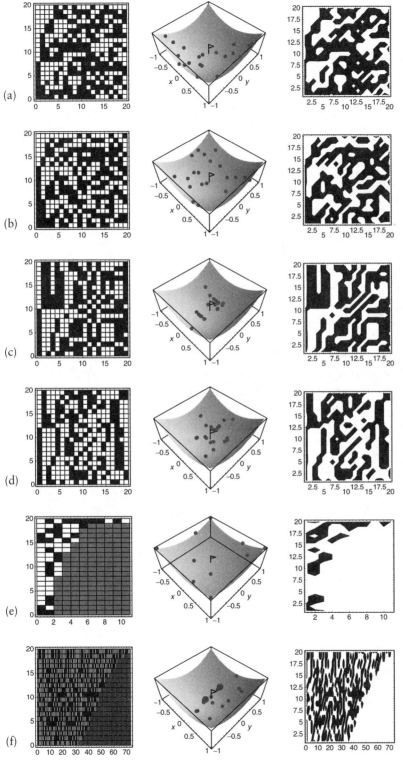

Figure 3.52
Effects of genetic operators.
(a) Initial population.
(b) Mutations.
(c) Recombinations.
(d) Inversions. (e) Deletions.
(f) Duplications.

successful areas. In the interpolated gene pool representation this effect is indicated by a rather irregular pattern.

Recombinations

The accelerated convergence effect of recombination, already observed in the previous section, is also recognizable in this comparison experiment (Figure 3.52[c]). Here we use one-point crossover between homologous GA chromosomes. A randomly chosen pair of bit strings is broken at a random position and the segments are exchanged in a crosswise fashion. Noticeably, after five generations the populations locally converge in the vicinity of the global minimum. The individuals have a tendency to gather in relatively compact groups. These groups of "related" chromosomes are also visible in the genotypical representation. In addition, clear patterns of vertical stripes have emerged, indicating an increased convergence of the chromosome segments on specific alleles.

Inversions

Interestingly, the inversion operator results in a similar concentration effect (Figure 3.52[d]). Convergence is not as intense as in the case of recombination, but compared to the initial generation, the individuals in the population have retreated to particular areas in the surroundings of the global optimum. Here we also see the forming of groups (at least in parts), which are illustrated by the gene pool graphics. The effect of allele fixing is observable, too. Basically, both recombinations and inversions leave genetic building blocks widely unchanged but rearrange their ordering or combine them anew.

Deletions

The reaction of the gene pool is totally different when deletion and duplication operators are used. In the case of deletion the chromosomes are massively shortened (Figure 3.52[e]). After five generations only a single genome has kept its original length.

Because of a diminishing number of binary digits, the resolution for the encoded coordinates is reduced. With only two remaining bits (out of eight in the original chromosomes) the points are mapped onto one of the four corners of the search space. A corresponding coarse positioning of the points results from three-, four-, and five-bit genomes. A reduced resolution of the "scan frame" by deletions can be advantageous if the search space has to be extensively combed for promising regions. However, after localization of "interesting" areas the gene pool should be able to switch back to fine-grain adaptations of its genomes. This is when duplications come into play.

Duplications

When duplication is used as the only operator, the chromosomes are tremendously enlarged—sometimes more than three times their original length (Figure 3.52[f]). In this example, the populations have been evolved over only three generations. The resolution of the coordinates grows exponentially. The points gravitate toward lower regions, even without any explicit selection (remember, we use a

[10 + 10] strategy). We can well imagine that combinations of deletion and duplication operators provide excellent secondary search methods for adaptive scanning of problem spaces. By reducing the genome lengths, deletions ensure that the search points are more widely spread, leading to a coarser but widespread scanning of the search space. The "inverse" operator of duplication can elongate the chromosomes, increase the scan resolution, and contribute to a fine adaptation of the genomes.

This short overview of GA operators and their influences on the evolution of population structures suggests that it can be advantageous to apply several genetic operators in GA evolution systems, in addition to classical recombination and mutation.

3.7.5 GA evolution under variable environmental conditions

We demonstrate with a four-stage GA experiment how genetic algorithms resolve multimodal parameter optimization problems. In addition, we illustrate the flexibility of GA populations when their individuals are adapted to changing environments. Variations of environmental conditions are modeled by first letting a population search for the highest peaks of the objective function (Figure 3.53[a]).

As soon as the three maxima are localized by the evolutionary algorithm, we switch to the second objective function (Figure 3.53([b]), the peaks of which are at different positions. We will continue the evolutionary search and observe how new optimal points are discovered. We start three independent GA evolution runs with the following settings:

Variation of the "environment"

Initiating three GA evolution runs

```
In[1] := GApops =
         Evolution[
           3 GA[20,2,PLUS,10,10,
             ChromosomeWidth → 12, Partitions → 2,
             FitnessInterval → {0,100},
             SelectionMode → FITPROP,

             MutationProbability → 0.5,
             PointMutationProbability → 0.2,
             RecombinationProbability → 0.5,
             RecombinationMode → POINT[1],
             Homologous → True,
             InversionProbability → 0.5,

             EvaluationFunction → evalFunc,
             InitialPopulation → {} ]];
```

Figure 3.53
Fitness landscapes of the
objective functions.

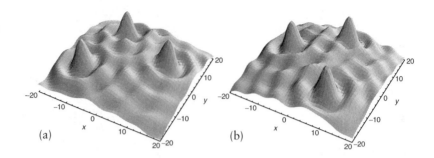

(a)   (b)

      The chromosomes have a 12-bit resolution. The x and y coordinates are encoded in the first and second halves of the binary string, respectively. Mutations, recombinations (single-point crossover), and inversions are used as genetic operators. All three operators are applied with equal probability. The initial populations are generated at random. The individuals are evaluated by the function specified as evalFunc, which we have already used in previous sections (Program 3.26).

      The objective function f, which is implicitly used by the evaluation function, is defined in Program 3.29.

Program 3.29
Multimodal objective
function.

```
g[v_List] := 50 Sin[Sqrt[Plus @@ Map[#^2&,v]]] /
                 Sqrt[Plus @@ Map[#^2&,v]] -
             Sqrt[Plus @@ Map[#^2&,v]]

f[v_List] := g[v + {11,9}] + g[v - {11,3}] +
             g[v + {6,-9}] + 100
```

Approaching the peaks

      Figure 3.54 illustrates three evolution runs (see also Color Plate 2). In generation 0, the three populations cover the search space rather uniformly. In the second generation the search effort is already concentrated to higher regions. In generation 6, each peak is occupied by at least one individual. After another four generations, all three peaks are clearly located. Individuals are still scattered far off the central peak in only one of the three populations; the two other populations converge toward the vicinity of the summit regions. These agglomerations are also visible in the convergence patterns of the respective genotypes. In the two left gene pools of generation 10 the stripes clearly stand out more than in the bit string matrix of the third population.

Figure 3.54
Searching for the highest
peaks under variable
environmental conditions.

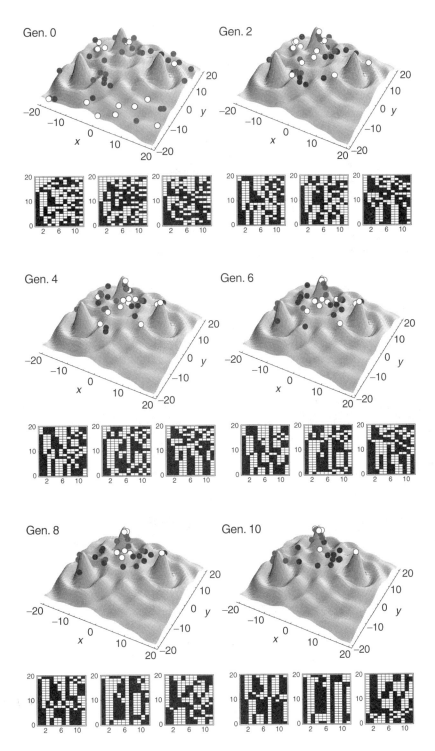

Program 3.30
Multimodal objective
function (Version 2).

```
f[v_List] := g[v - {3,12}] + g[v + {-8,12}] +
             g[v + {11,-1}] + 100
```

How will these converged populations react to changes in their evaluation environment? How long will it take before the peaks, relocated to different positions, are discovered by the search process? We switch to the objective function given in Program 3.30, the graph of which is depicted in Figure 3.53(b). Under these changed environmental conditions, we continue with a (20/2 + 10) GA strategy over 10 generations:

*Continuation of the
GA evolution*

```
In[2] := GApops = Map[First[
             Evolution[GA[20,2,PLUS,10,10,
                 ChromosomeWidth → 12, Partitions → 2,
                 FitnessInterval → {0,100},
                 SelectionMode → FITPROP,
                 MutationProbability → 0.5,
                 PointMutationProbability → 0.2,
                 RecombinationProbability → 0.5,
                 RecombinationMode → POINT[1],
                 Homologous → True,
                 InversionProbability → 0.5,

                 EvaluationFunction → evalFunc,
                 InitialPopulation → # ]]]&,
             Map[Last,GApops]];
```

We keep the same genetic operators as in the previous GA runs. To evaluate the individuals, we now use the objective function of Program 3.30.

The initial generation in Figure 3.55 shows the three final populations of the previous GA experiment (Figure 3.54, Gen. 10) in their new environment. Points with formerly high fitnesses may now have low-fitness positions, whereas other individuals with previously low fitnesses are currently evaluated much better.

*Dispersion in the search
space*

As we observe the further evolution of these three populations, it turns out that the points are again spreading over the search space. Now the third population profits from the diversity of its gene pool. Even when only a few mutations are performed, a wide range of new positions can be tested. Hence, it is this third population that locates

Relocalization of all peaks

all the new peaks in generation 10. All the highest viewpoints in the changed environment have been discovered.

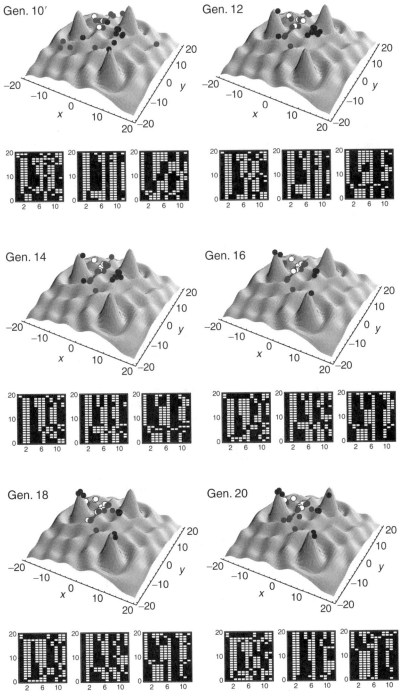

Figure 3.55
Continued evolution with the objective function of Figure 3.53(b).

Gene pool diversity

These example evolutions illustrate that adaptations to variable environmental conditions are easier for a population the larger the diversity of its gene pool is. Too strongly converged populations can also perform corresponding adaptations, by accumulated mutations; however, a much larger number of generation cycles would be necessary.

Continued evolution with comma strategy

As a final example we continue these evolution experiments with a (20/2, 20) GA strategy. The result is shown in Figure 3.56. Since continued best selection is switched off by the comma strategy, this evolution gives a general idea of the population structure dynamics solely induced by the genetic operators. The search space is, in a way, "flooded" by the individual points, and most of the fixed alleles get lost. This is recognizable by the irregular bit pattern of the tenth generation.

"Flooding" of the search space

Continuing with a plus strategy

In order to reinitiate a converging search toward the summit regions, we continue with a (20/2 + 20) strategy. The evolution of this GA run is illustrated in Figure 3.57. In combination with the genetic operators—mutation, recombination, and inversion—the now increased selection has the effect that the search effort is quickly concentrated on more exposed regions. In the end, all three peaks are pinpointed. The grade of convergence is reflected in the striped patterns of the gene pool.

Climbing of the peaks again

The short, simple experiments presented in this section should give an idea of the dynamics of genetic algorithms in solving optimization problems. In the following section, we look at some theoretical explanations of why genetic algorithms are rather successful at exploring multimodal search spaces. The so-called schema theorem, although controversial, will give some insight into GA search dynamics from a theoretical as well as a practical point of view.

3.8   Schemata—the key to GAs?

One of the essential mathematical models for understanding the search behavior of genetic algorithms is provided by the so-called *schema theorem*, originally formulated by John Holland (Holland 1975, Chapter 4; Holland 1992b, pp. 66–74). The fundamental idea is that genetic algorithms search in feature spaces, which can be characterized by similarity templates. Holland denotes these templates as *schemata*.

In Section 3.8.1, we introduce notions important for understanding the schema concepts. In Section 3.8.2, we explore schemata with a few example experiments, using Mathematica's pattern-matching

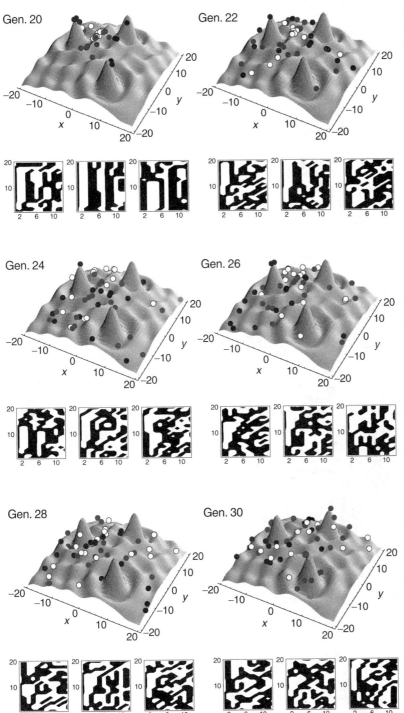

Figure 3.56
Continued GA evolution with comma strategy.

Figure 3.57
Continued GA evolution with
plus strategy.

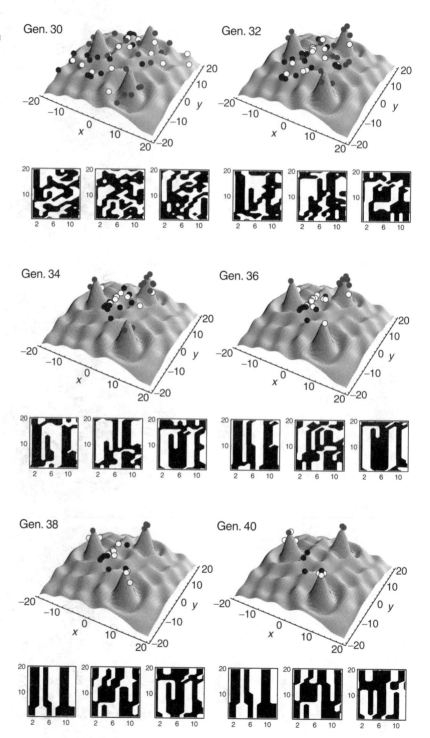

capabilities. The schema theorem in its original form is presented in Section 3.8.3. In Section 3.8.4, we outline why the original schema theorem cannot fully explain how well a genetic algorithm is performing and why, therefore, new approaches toward a better understanding of GA performance must be considered.

3.8.1 Templates for genotypical building blocks

If GA structures are considered as vectors or strings of length n over a discrete alphabet $A = \{\alpha_1, \ldots, \alpha_k\}$, schemata can be described quite easily. A *schema H_A*,

$$H_A \in A_*^n,$$ *Schema*

is a word of length n over the alphabet $A_* = A \cup \{*\}$, which is extended by the new symbol $*$. The $*$ letter represents any symbol of alphabet A. A similarity template H_A characterizes hyperplanes in n-dimensional string space A^n. For alphabet $A = \{a, b, c\}$, for example, the strings

$$\langle b, a, c, a, a, a \rangle$$
$$\langle b, b, c, a, b, c \rangle$$
$$\langle b, c, c, a, c, a \rangle$$

match the schema $H_A = \langle b, *, c, a, *, * \rangle$ since it describes strings beginning with the letter b and the letters c and a at the third and fourth position, respectively. All other positions can be substituted by any letter in the alphabet. In general, for a k-element alphabet there are $(k + 1)^n$ schemata of length n. The above schema H_A is only one from a set of $4096 = (3 + 1)^6$ possible schemata.

All strings $s = \langle s_1, \ldots, s_n \rangle \in A^n$ that match the positions filled with letters from alphabet A of a schema $H_A = \langle h_1, \ldots, h_n \rangle$ are called *instances $I(H_A)$* of H_A:

$$s_i = \begin{cases} h_i & \text{if } h_i \in A, \\ \alpha \in A & \text{otherwise.} \end{cases}$$ *Instances*

Hence, the above three strings are instances of the schema $H_A = \langle b, *, c, a, *, * \rangle$. Generally, each string of length n over an arbitrary alphabet is an instance for 2^n schemata. The string $\langle a, b \rangle$, for instance, is a representative of the four templates $\langle *, * \rangle$, $\langle *, b \rangle$, $\langle a, * \rangle$, and $\langle a, b \rangle$. In a population of p strings of length n there are at most $p \cdot 2^n$ schemata represented. To understand the schema theorem, in particular, two measures play an important role—the order and the defining length of a schema.

Order

The *order* $o(H_A)$ of a schema H_A is defined as the number of its fixed elements from the alphabet A:

$$o(H) = |\{i|h_i \in A\}|.$$

Therefore, the schema $H_{\{a, b, c\}} = \langle b, *, c, a, *, * \rangle$ is of the order $o(H_A) = 3$, whereas $H_{\{0, 1\}} = \langle 1, *, 1, *, *, 1, 0 \rangle$ has an order of $o(H_{\{0, 1\}}) = 4$. A schema H_A of length n over a k-element alphabet A and with $o(H) = x$ fixed positions represents at most $k^{(n-x)}$ instances.

Besides the number of fixed positions, their range over the string is also an important criterion for a template, at least in the context of GA chromosomes. The *defining length* $\delta(H_A)$ of a schema H_A denotes the length of the segment between the two outer positions with fixed elements:

Defining length

$$\delta(H_A) = \max\{i|h_i \in A\} - \min\{i|h_i \in A\}.$$

The schema $H_{\{0, 1\}} = \langle 0, *, 1, *, 1 \rangle$ has fixed entries at positions 1, 3, and 5. So its defining length is $\delta(H_{\{0, 1\}}) = 5 - 1 = 4$. Since the defining length δ is a measure for the probability with which fixed positions of a schema are separated by crossover (recombinations, in general), δ corresponds to the number of possible crossover points between the outer fixed positions. This is why the defining length for the schema above is not five, as you would possibly expect. Especially for schemata with only a single fixed element, for example, $H_{\{0, 1\}} = \langle *, *, 1, *, * \rangle$, we have $\delta(H_{\{0, 1\}}) = 3 - 3 = 0$.

3.8.2 Experiments with schemata

In this section we will illustrate schemata with a few example implementations. We represent strings of a fixed length over a discrete alphabet $A = \{\alpha_1, \ldots, \alpha_k\}$ as lists. A string $s = \langle 0, 1, 1 \rangle$, for example, is represented as

```
{0,1,1}.
```

This string is an instance of the schema $H_{\{0, 1\}} = \langle *, 1, * \rangle$. In Mathematica the * symbol corresponds to the (underscore) pattern _, such that a schema can be immediately represented by

Schema in Evolvica

```
{_, 1, _}.
```

The Evolvica function schemata[n] in Program 3.31 returns a list of all schemata (patterns) of a fixed length n for a particular alphabet.

Basically, the function `Outer` is used for generating the cross product of n lists over the alphabet extended by the underscore symbol (_), which stands for any expression in Mathematica's pattern notation.

```
schemata[n_Integer, opts___] :=
Module[{alph},
   alph = Alphabet /. {opts} /. Options[schemata];

   Flatten[
     Outer[List,
       Sequence @@ Table[Join[alph,{_}],{n}]],n - 1]
]

Options[schemata] = { Alphabet → {0,1} };
```

Program 3.31
Generating schemata of fixed length *n*.

The following function call returns all triple schemata over the binary alphabet $A = \{0, 1\}$:

In[3] := **schemata[3]**

Out[3] ={{0, 0, 0}, {0, 0, 1}, {0, 0, _}, {0, 1, 0},
          {0, 1, 1}, {0, 1, _}, {0, _, 0}, {0, _, 1},
          {0, _, _}, {1, 0, 0}, {1, 0, 1}, {1, 0, _},
          {1, 1, 0}, {1, 1, 1}, {1, 1, _}, {1, _, 0},
          {1, _, 1}, {1, _, _}, {_, 0, 0}, {_, 0, 1},
          {_, 0, _}, {_, 1, 0}, {_, 1, 1}, {_, 1, _},
          {_, _, 0}, {_, _, 1}, {_, _, _}}

All binary schemata of length 3

There are $27 = 3^3$ of these schemata, as we know from Section 3.8.1. For a three-element alphabet $A = \{a, b, c\}$ we get 64 different templates.

In[4] := **schemata[3, Alphabet → {a,b,c}]**

Out[4] ={{a, a, a}, {a, a, b}, {a, a, c}, {a, a, _},
          {a, b, a}, {a, b, b}, {a, b, c}, {a, b, _},
          {a, c, a}, {a, c, b}, {a, c, c}, {a, c, _},
          {a, _, a}, {a, _, b}, {a, _, c}, {a, _, _},
          {b, a, a}, {b, a, b}, {b, a, c}, {b, a, _},
          {b, b, a}, {b, b, b}, {b, b, c}, {b, b, _},
          {b, c, a}, {b, c, b}, {b, c, c}, {b, c, _},
          {b, _, a}, {b, _, b}, {b, _, c}, {b, _, _},

All triple schemata over a three-element alphabet

```
{c, a, a}, {c, a, b}, {c, a, c}, {c, a, _},
{c, b, a}, {c, b, b}, {c, b, c}, {c, b, _},
{c, c, a}, {c, c, b}, {c, c, c}, {c, c, _},
{c, _, a}, {c, _, b}, {c, _, c}, {c, _, _},
{_, a, a}, {_, a, b}, {_, a, c}, {_, a, _},
{_, b, a}, {_, b, b}, {_, b, c}, {_, b, _},
{_, c, a}, {_, c, b}, {_, c, c}, {_, c, _},
{_, _, a}, {_, _, b}, {_, _, c}, {_, _, _}}
```

What are the instances of these schemata? The function
instances[n] in Program 3.32 helps us to generate all instances of
length n over an alphabet given by the option Alphabet → alpha.

Program 3.32
Generating all instances of
length *n*.

```
instances[n_Integer, opts___] :=
Module[{alph},
   alph = Alphabet /. {opts} /. Options[instances];

   Flatten[Outer[List,Sequence @@ Table[alph,{n}]],
     n - 1]
]

Options[instances] = { Alphabet → {0,1} };
```

Again the cross-product function Outer provides a comfortable
way to generate a complete list of all possible combinations. For
binary triplets there are eight different representatives:

In[5] := **bitInstances = instances[3]**

Eight binary triple instances

Out[5] ={{0, 0, 0}, {0, 0, 1}, {0, 1, 0}, {0, 1, 1},
          {1, 0, 0}, {1, 0, 1}, {1, 1, 0}, {1, 1, 1}}

There are 27 triplets over a three-element alphabet:

In[6] := **letterInstances = instances[3,**
          Alphabet → {a,b,c}]

Instances over a three-
element alphabet

Out[6] ={{a, a, a}, {a, a, b}, {a, a, c}, {a, b, a},
          {a, b, b}, {a, b, c}, {a, c, a}, {a, c, b},
          {a, c, c}, {b, a, a}, {b, a, b}, {b, a, c},
          {b, b, a}, {b, b, b}, {b, b, c}, {b, c, a},
          {b, c, b}, {b, c, c}, {c, a, a}, {c, a, b},
```
```

{c, a, c}, {c, b, a}, {c, b, b}, {c, b, c},
{c, c, a}, {c, c, b}, {c, c, c}}

Which instances match which schemata? Checking schemata instances is easy in Mathematica and Evolvica. We only have to iteratively compare patterns. Therefore, an algorithm for generating all instances of a population pop for a particular scheme schema is as simple as the line in Program 3.33.

```
instances[schema_,pop_] := Cases[pop,schema]
```

Program 3.33
Schema instances
of a population.

For the above example we can determine all instances ending with the letter c:

In[7] := **instances[{_,_,c}, letterInstances]**

Extraction of schema instances

Out[7] ={{a, a, c}, {a, b, c}, {a, c, c}, {b, a, c},
      {b, b, c}, {b, c, c}, {c, a, c}, {c, b, c},
      {c, c, c}}

Figure 3.58 shows a collection of all "real" schemata of length 4 (the schemata consisting of only fixed positions are not listed) and their instances in population instances[4].

The smaller the order of a schema, the larger the number of its instances. Each schema with order $o(H) = x$ has $4 - x$ free positions, hence 2^{4-x} instances. For example, the template $\{0,0,1,\_\}$ has only $2 = 2^{4-3}$, whereas schema $\{\_,\_,\_,1\}$ has $8 = 2^{4-1}$ representatives.

Let us now see how to determine instances from small populations. Our example population consists of five random binary vectors.

In[8] := **pop = Table[Random[Integer], {5}, {3}];**
        pop // MatrixForm

Out[8] = 0   0   0
        1   1   1
        0   1   1
        1   1   0
        0   1   0

Population of random triples

Which schemata are represented in this population? We have to generate the set of all binary schemata of length 3 and check for each of

Figure 3.58
Instances of binary
schemata of length 4.

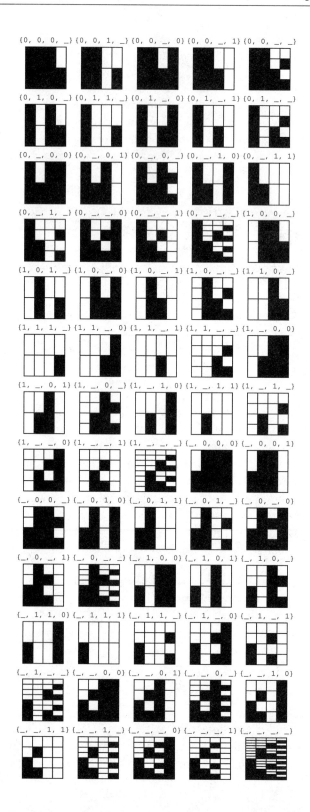

these templates whether or not the population contains a representative. This procedure is implemented by the function collect-
Instances in Program 3.34.

```
collectInstances[pop_, opts___]:=
Map[{#,instances[#,pop,opts]}&,
   schemata[Length[pop//First],opts]]
```

Program 3.34
Enumeration of all schema
instances.

The function takes a list of vectors, representing the population,
and an optional alphabet specification. The function collect-
Instances returns a collection of lists, where each list contains a
template as its first element together with a list of all corresponding
instances in population pop.

In[9] := **popInstances = collectInstances[pop]**

Out[9] = {{{0, 0, 0}, {{0, 0, 0}}},
        {{0, 0, 1}, {}},
        {{0, 0, _}, {{0, 0, 0}}},
        {{0, 1, 0}, {{0, 1, 0}}},
        {{0, 1, 1}, {{0, 1, 1}}},
        {{0, 1, _}, {{0, 1, 1}, {0, 1, 0}}},
        {{0, _, 0}, {{0, 0, 0}, {0, 1, 0}}},
        {{0, _, 1}, {{0, 1, 1}}},
        {{0, _, _}, {{0, 0, 0}, {0, 1, 1}, {0, 1, 0}}},
        {{1, 0, 0}, {}},
        {{1, 0, 1}, {}},
        {{1, 0, _}, {}},
        {{1, 1, 0}, {{1, 1, 0}}},
        {{1, 1, 1}, {{1, 1, 1}}},
        {{1, 1, _}, {{1, 1, 1}, {1, 1, 0}}},
        {{1, _, 0}, {{1, 1, 0}}},
        {{1, _, 1}, {{1, 1, 1}}},
        {{1, _, _}, {{1, 1, 1}, {1, 1, 0}}},
        {{_, 0, 0}, {{0, 0, 0}}},
        {{_, 0, 1}, {}},
        {{_, 0, _}, {{0, 0, 0}}},
        {{_, 1, 0}, {{1, 1, 0}, {0, 1, 0}}},
        {{_, 1, 1}, {{1, 1, 1}, {0, 1, 1}}},
        {{_, 1, _}, {{1, 1, 1}, {0, 1, 1}, {1, 1, 0},
         {0, 1, 0}}},

*Binary triple schemata and
their* pop *instances*

```
{{_, _, 0}, {{0, 0, 0}, {1, 1, 0}, {0, 1, 0}}},
{{_, _, 1}, {{1, 1, 1}, {0, 1, 1}}},
{{_, _, _}, {{0, 0, 0}, {1, 1, 1}, {0, 1, 1},
  {1, 1, 0}, {0, 1, 0}}}}
```

In[10] := **Length[popInstances]**

Out[10] = 27

In total we get 27 different templates, where some of them have no representatives in the population, for example, {0,0,1}, whereas others match with several instances, for example, {_,1,_}. If we are not interested in the actual schema instances but only in the number of representatives per schema, we can count the instances in the output of the collectInstances function and get a tabular summary as follows:

Counting the schema instances

In[11] := **Reverse[Sort[**
        Map[{Length[#[[2]]],#[[1]]}&,popInstances]]]
      // MatrixForm

Out[11] = 5   {_, _, _}
           4   {_, 1, _}
           3   {_, _, 0}
           . . .
           0   {1, 0, 0}
           0   {0, 0, 1}

We show only part of the actual output here—the Evolvica notebook on the *IEC* Web page (see Preface) contains all the examples in this section.

The functions for identifying schemata and their instances are particularly helpful when population sizes are too large for calculations by hand, as the following example will show. We start from a population of 20 vectors of length 10:

In[12] := **pop = Table[Random[Integer], {20}, {10}];**
         pop // MatrixForm

Population of strings of length 10

Out[12] = 0   0   1   1   1   0   0   1   1   0
            1   1   0   0   0   1   1   1   0   1
            0   0   1   1   0   0   1   0   1   1
            . . .

```
0   1   0   0   0   0   1   1   1   0
1   1   0   1   0   0   1   1   0   1
1   1   1   1   1   1   1   0   0   0
```

Only a small part of the actual output is printed. Calculating the schema instances of this population takes a little longer than in the previous short example.

In[13] := **popInstances = collectInstances[pop];**   *Determining all schema instances*

After all, 3^{10} = 59,049 schemata must be taken into account.

In[14] := **Length[popInstances]**

Out[14] = 59049

The extremely shortened table of the number of schema instances of length 10 among the population gives an insight into the computational effort necessary:

In[15] := **Take[Reverse[Sort[**
        Map[{Length[#[[2]]],#[[1]]}&,popInstances]]],
        10]
        // MatrixForm

Out[15] = {20, {_, _, _, _, _, _, _, _, _, _}}   *A selection of determined*
        {15, {_, _, _, _, _, _, 1, _, _, _}}   *schemata and their numbers*
        . . .   *of instances*
        {13, {_, _, _, _, _, 0, 1, _, _, _}}
        . . .
        {11, {_, _, _, _, _, _, _, _, _, 1}}
        . . .
        {10, {_, _, _, _, _, 0, _, _, 1, _}}
        . . .
        {9, {_, 1, 0, _, _, _, 1, _, _, _}}
        . . .
        {8, {_, _, _, _, _, _, 1, _, 1, _}}
        . . .
        {7, {_, 1, _, _, 1, _, _, _, _, _}}
        . . .
        {6, {_, _, _, _, _, _, _, 1, 1, _}}
        . . .
        {5, {_, _, _, _, _, _, _, _, 0, 0}}
        . . .

```
{4, {_, 1, 0, _, _, 0, 1, _, 0, _}}
...
{0, {0, 0, 0, 0, 0, 1, 0, 0, _, _}}
...
```

As this output shows, there are many schemata represented by a number of instances in the population pop, although many schemata are not matched by any of the strings.

Building block filters

In a way, schemata provide us with lenses through which we can observe genotypical structures. Only those "building blocks" that pass the template feature test are visible through the lens filters. But what distinguishes successful building blocks? Which schemata describe building blocks that are most likely to be passed on from generation to generation? Insights into the answers to these questions are provided by the schema theorem.

3.8.3 Schema theorem—which building blocks survive?

What is the basic reason why specific genes remain in the gene pool of natural generation sequences? Are there any features that differentiate groups of genes as more or less capable of surviving? In genetic algorithms, the notion of a schema provides an illustrative means for characterizing the structural properties of successful GA building blocks. We can also hope to draw conclusions for the dispersal of interacting, cooperating, and competing gene groups in natural populations from further extensions of the schema theorem.

Which schemata survive?

In the following section we illustrate the influences of selection and the genetic operators of mutation and crossover on the composition of a population, observed through the filter of particular schemata. We start from a population $P(t)$ in generation t. Each chromosome in this population is an instance of a single, particular scheme (with fixed positions only) or of a number of schemata. If we consider the generation sequence from the viewpoint of schemata, we want to give estimations for which of the currently represented schemata will also have corresponding instances in the following generation. So the question is not which concrete GA structures survive but which schemata do. The following considerations are taken from Holland 1975; Holland 1992a, Chapters 5 and 6; and Goldberg 1989, pp. 28–33. A clear presentation of the schema theorem, including a critical discussion, can also be found in Bäck 1996, pp. 123–130.

Surviving the selection filter

Let us first examine the influence of selection on the survivability of schemata. We calculate at which relative frequencies which schemata of a population $P(t)$ are passed on to the following generation $t + 1$. All further considerations are based on fitness-proportionate selection, since this is the preferred selection method used in GA applications.

Let $m(H(t))$ be the number of instances of schema $H(t)$ in $P(t)$. We do not explicitly mention the alphabet here, because it does not play any role in the following schemata considerations. Hence, we write $H(t)$ instead of $H_A(t)$.

The selection of individuals is determined by their fitnesses. Therefore, we also need a measure describing the fitness $\mu(H(t))$ of a schema:

$$\mu(H(t)) = \frac{1}{m(H(t))} \sum_{s \in I(H(t)) \cap P(t)} \mu(s).$$

Schema fitness

The fitness of a schema H in generation t is defined as the average fitness of the H instances $I(H(t))$ of the population $P(t)$. On average, the number of H instances of the population evolves under the influence of fitness-proportionate selection according to the following recursion equation:

$$m(H(t + 1)) = m(H(t)) \frac{\mu(H(t))}{\bar{\mu}(P(t))}$$

$$\bar{\mu}(P(t)) := \frac{1}{|P(t)|} \sum_{s \in P(t)} \mu(s).$$

Average number of H instances

Here $\bar{\mu}(P(t))$ is the average fitness of population $P(t)$. For the evolution of the population toward increased fitnesses, especially those schemata prevail that have fitnesses above the average population fitness value; that is, schemata for which the following holds:

Above-average schemata

$$\mu(H(t)) = (1 + c)\bar{\mu}(P(t)), \text{ for a constant } c > 0.$$

For these above-average schemata we derive the following relation by substituting $\mu(H(t))$ in the recursion equation with an initial value $t_0 = 0$. Thus, after t iterations we get:

$$m(H(t)) = m(H(0))(1 + c)^t.$$

Fitness-proportionate selection schemata with above-average fitnesses reproduce exponentially over a number of generations. Of course, the analog also holds for the suppression of below-average schemata from the population. These results suggest the first characteristic feature of successful templates: instances of them, represented in the population, must have *above-average fitnesses*. This claim is

Above-average fitness

hardly surprising. What is noticeable, however, is the increased rate of reproduction for successful schemata.

Surviving recombinations

Selection alone does not imply evolution. Only variations of genotypical structures by genetic operators enable a generation sequence to steadily evolve—for better or for worse. Which consequences on schemata evolution do mutations and recombinations have? For a particular schema it must be determined whether, under the influence of the genetic operators, instances of it produce again representatives of the same schema. For this purpose, we define p_{cross} to be the probability that an individual is changed by (one-point) crossover and p_{mut} to be the mutation probability per position. Thus, for each schema $H(t)$, we can calculate its probability of survival in the scope of the two genetic operators of mutation and crossover.

Crosswise recombination   We first consider crosswise recombination. Let us assume that for the following two strings s_1 and s_2 the crossover point is after the third position:

$$s_1 = \langle 0, 1, 1 | 1, 0, 0, 0 \rangle \text{ and } s_2 = \langle 1, 0, 1 | 0, 0, 1, 1 \rangle.$$

The string s_1 is an instance of the two schemata

$$H_1 = \langle *, 1, * | *, *, *, 0 \rangle,$$
$$H_2 = \langle *, *, * | 1, 0, *, * \rangle,$$

whereas s_2 is neither an H_1 nor an H_2 instance. Which of the two schemata are more likely to occur after the application of the crossover operator? We consider the two strings resulting from the recombination of s_1' and s_2':

$$s_1' = \langle 0, 1, 1, 0, 0, 1, 1 \rangle \text{ and } s_2' = \langle 1, 0, 1, 1, 0, 0, 0 \rangle.$$

Now, neither s_1' nor s_2' is an H_1 instance. For the H_2 scheme, however, we again have a representative, namely, s_2'. The loss of the H_1 *Influential factor:* instance is obviously explained by the large defining length of this *defining length* schema, which can easily be "broken" by a crossover. For the compact scheme H_2, however, this is less probable. In general, for the survival probability $p_{cross}^{survive}$ of a schema H under crossover we have:

$$p_{cross}^{survive} = 1 - \frac{\delta(H)}{n-1}.$$

Here $n-1$ corresponds to the number of possible crossover points. The larger the defining length $\delta(H)$ of a schema H is, the more probable its fixed positions will get separated from each other. Since crossover is by itself applied probabilistically, we can finally formulate the following inequality characterizing the probability for a schema $H(t)$ not to be destroyed:

$$p_{\text{cross}}^{\text{survive}} \geq 1 - p_{\text{cross}} \frac{\delta(H(t))}{(n-1)}.$$

Survival probability of a schema undergoing crossover

Resisting mutations

Mutations are another way to vary GA structures. We have defined (point) mutations as allele-varying operators. Here we assume that for each position an allele is replaced by a new entry with probability p_{mut}. How do mutations influence the evolution of schemata? If the string

$$s = \langle 0, 1, 1, 1, 0, 0, 1 \rangle,$$

as an instance of the schema $H = \langle *, 1, 1, 1, *, 0, * \rangle$, is mutated to

$$s_{\text{mut}} = \langle 0, 0, 1, 1, 0, 1, 1 \rangle,$$

then s_{mut} is no longer an H instance, since fixed schema positions have been changed, whereas the mutant

$$s = \langle 1, 1, 1, 1, 0, 0, 0 \rangle$$

is again a representative of template H. The survival probability of a schema undergoing mutation, $p_{\text{mut}}^{\text{survive}}$, is therefore directly dependent on the number of *fixed positions*, hence the order $o(H(t))$ of the chromosome:

Influential factor: fixed positions

$$p_{\text{mut}}^{\text{survive}} = (1 - p_{\text{mut}})^{o(H(t))}.$$

A mutation leaves a schema $H(t)$ if any of the fixed-position alleles are changed.

The schema theorem

In summary, we can finally derive how the number of instances of a schema H changes from one generation to the next:

$$m(H(t+1)) \geq m(H(t)) \cdot \frac{\mu(H(t))}{\overline{\mu}(P(t))} \cdot p_{\text{cross}}^{\text{survive}} \cdot p_{\text{mut}}^{\text{survive}}.$$

Schema theorem

This so-called *schema theorem* is considered the "fundamental theorem of genetic algorithms" (Goldberg 1989, p. 32 ff.). The schema theorem characterizes successful building blocks of GA structures. Those schemata with a short defining length, with only few fixed positions

Compact gene groups

and where the instances of their occurrence show above-average fitness, reproduce exponentially from generation to generation.

The vicinity of compactly arranged, highly fit gene groups is considered one of the main organizational principles derived from the schema theorem. If the genes as a functional group imply a high fitness of an individual but are widely spread over the genotype, the survival probability of these successful building blocks is rather low. Under the influence of mutations and crosswise recombinations schemata of large defining length turn out to be unstable.

Inversion

Inversion is an operator that allows for reorganization of genes without changing the genetic information. When gene groups are rearranged, it is possible that genes will be brought together that—as a compact block—can be reproduced in a more stable fashion, survive more easily, and carry essential information for an individual's fitness.

From the schema theorem, we can derive the following suggestions for practical applications of genetic algorithms in solving optimization problems. The parameter encoding has to be such that the conditions of the schema theorem are met approximately. However, the conclusions drawn from the schema theorem are valid only for the assumption of infinite population sizes. The populations in practical GA implementations are always finite, of course, so that any actually observed evolution dynamics of GA systems only coarsely follow the theoretical predictions of the schema theorem.

GA-deceptive problems

Does the schema theorem give any hints on how to select a concrete encoding in practical GA applications? Only partly. A general approach for functional, problem-specific encodings is not available, as the large number of investigations of so-called *GA-deceptive problems* suggests. The encodings and fitness landscapes of these specially designed optimization problems do not obey the schema theorem, and the GA behavior is examined for different encodings to decipher possible countermeasures (Liepins and Vose 1991; Whitley 1991; Goldberg, Deb, et al. 1992; Deb and Goldberg 1993; Forrest and Mitchell 1993; Grefenstette 1993).

3.8.4 What's wrong with the schema theorem?

The idea of using filters, the schemata, to understand the search behavior of genetic algorithms is intuitive and illustrative. But only recently it turned out that the schema theorem "does not capture the intuitive idea about what makes a GA work—that offspring with above-average fitness can be produced by recombining schemata with above-average fitness" (Altenberg 1995). In fact, the consequence of the schema theorem—that the number of schemata with above-average fitness increases over the generations—says little about the general performance of a genetic algorithm. Rather, GAs should be able to increase the upper end of the fitness distribution of their individuals in order to achieve good performance. This can be expressed in a local GA performance theorem for general representations and operators, but schemata do not seem to play any role in these evaluations (Altenberg 1995, p. 30 ff.).

Use of Price's covariance and selection theorem, in combination with appropriate measurement functions, is one way to link changes in GA properties on a macroscopic, populational scale to the microscopic dynamics of the GA chromosomes and schemata (Altenberg 1995). If the measurement function is a fitness evaluator, the evolution of the fitness distribution over one generation can be computed. Information about the evolution of the schema frequency, however, can be obtained by using a schema indicator as the measurement function. As a result the schema theorem can be expressed through Price's theorem. *Covariance and selection theorem*

In the context of explorative versus exploitative search, the two-armed bandit problem with Gaussian payoffs, which can be used as a theoretical model for optimization and also provides the basis for the GA schema theorem, is revisited in Macready and Wolpert 1998. In their article, the authors point out that genetic algorithms do not perform optimally for the Gaussian bandit problem. *Two-armed bandit revisited*

Although the role of schemata in GA performance is being revised, schemata will remain useful in understanding interrelationships between selection and mixing schemes, as is pointed out by Michael Vose's excellent theoretical analysis of a simple genetic algorithm model (Vose 1999, p. 211 ff.).

3.9 Bibliographical notes

Textbooks on genetic algorithms

The classic textbook on genetic algorithms is David Goldberg's *Genetic Algorithms in Search, Optimization, and Machine Learning* (1989). Although this book is more than 10 years old, it still serves as an excellent introduction to the field. *GAs in search, optimization, and machine learning*

A recent textbook on genetic algorithms is Melanie Mitchell's *An Introduction to Genetic Algorithms* (1996). *Introduction to GAs*

Genetic algorithms and related books

Adaptation in Natural
and Artificial Systems

For an introduction to the initial ideas about genetic algorithms, consult John Holland's original work, *Adaptation in Natural and Artificial Systems* (1975, 1992a).

Hidden order; emergence

Holland has continued his research on the adaptation and generation of complex systems from a small number of rules and laws. His recent two books are highly recommended: *Hidden Order: How Adaptation Builds Complexity* (1995) and *Emergence: From Chaos to Order* (1998).

Genetic algorithm theory

Simple GA

An excellent theoretical treatment of genetic algorithms is Michael Vose's *The Simple Genetic Algorithm: Foundations and Theory* (1999).

Uncertain Programming

Genetic algorithms in the context of stochastic, fuzzy simulation systems and uncertain programming are described in Baoding Liu's *Uncertain Programming* (1999).

Applications of genetic algorithms

Handbook of GAs

The *Handbook of Genetic Algorithms*, edited by Lawrence Davis (1991), gives an overview of early GA applications.

GA + DS = EP

In *Genetic Algorithms + Data Structures = Evolution Programs*, Zbigniew Michalewicz (1992) describes a number of GA applications for numerical optimization, constraint satisfaction, and combinatorial and machine learning problems.

Electromagnetic
optimization by GAs

How to use genetic algorithms for designing antennas, electromagnetic filters, or magnetostatic devices is described in *Electromagnetic Optimization by Genetic Algorithms* (Rahmat-Samii and Michielssen 1999).

Conference proceedings

ICGA

The first International Conference on Genetic Algorithms (ICGA), now the longest-running conference in evolutionary computation, started in 1985 (Grefenstette 1985). Since then, the ICGA was organized every other year (Grefenstette 1987; Schaffer 1989; Belew and Booker 1991; Forrest 1993; Eshelman 1995; Bäck 1997).

In 1999 the ICGA, together with the Genetic Programming Conference, was combined into GECCO, the Genetic and Evolutionary Computation Conference, one of the major conferences on evolutionary algorithms (see Section 2.4).

GECCO

The biannual workshops on Foundations of Genetic Algorithms provide a forum for current issues on GA theory (Rawlins 1991; Whitley 1993; Whitley and Vose 1995; Belew and Vose 1997; Banzhaf and Reeves 1999).

Foundations of GAs

4 Evolution Strategies

*Evolutionary algorithms are studied in many places by computer
simulations with grim determination, just as if the diversity of throwing
stones could be investigated by simulation. The only question that
remains is whether the laws of gravity could be discovered however
many stone-throwing simulations one performed. This, however, is the
objective . . .: uncovering the compact "laws of gravity" of evolution.*

Rechenberg 1994b, p.11 (translation by author)

Ideas about evolution strategies (ES), developed at the Technical University (TU) of Berlin, date to the 1960s. Ingo Rechenberg, the "father" of evolution strategies, now head of the Department of Bionics and Evolution Techniques at TU Berlin, describes his ongoing research project, initiated 30 years ago, as an attempt "to experiment *Experimenting like nature* as ingeniously as evolution does, relying on the thesis that evolution should have taught itself how to work efficiently and optimally." The objective is not to imitate biology but to gain a better understanding of evolutionary mechanisms in a "functional" and "theoretical sense."

In this chapter, we will follow a middle route between theory and practical experimentation. Of course, ES theory should get the attention it deserves, particularly since Mathematica and Evolvica superbly allow for describing and implementing the theoretical concepts of evolution strategies, as we will see. Experimentation, however, turns out to be an enormously important aid for understanding physical contexts and interactions within dynamical, stochastic systems and their outcome. In particular, computer simulations can contribute new insights into complex interacting systems. The mechanisms of evolution in conjunction with their resulting dynamical processes are certainly among the most complex systems we find in nature.

The terms "evolution" and "strategy," which strictly speaking are *Strategic evolution?* contradictory, already show that a detailed imitation of natural evolution principles is not of immediate importance in evolution strategies.

Nothing like a concerted strategy exists in biological evolution. Rather, an engineer's approach to applying fundamental mechanisms of natural evolution to technical optimization problems becomes the focus of attention in ES. Evolution strategies derive from an "evolutionary method of experimentation." An experiment performed in 1964, on the mutative evolution of flexibly connected board-shaped strips, with the objective of optimizing the configuration for minimum

Experimentum crucis

drag, is considered the *experimentum crucis* of evolution strategies (Rechenberg 1973). This unorthodox method of performing an engineering experiment caused quite a stir at the time. Some skeptics wondered whether an optimization technique, relying solely on random mutations and selection, would lead to successful results within a reasonable time limit. Usually natural evolution takes millions of years to adapt and optimize its designs. However, an impressive number of successful experiments, especially during the 1970s, performed by Rechenberg and his coworker Hans-Paul Schwefel have demonstrated that the imitation of evolution can in fact result in successful designs for technical systems (e.g., the ES design of a two-phase jet nozzle described in Rechenberg 1973; Rechenberg 1989; Rechenberg 1994a; Rechenberg 1994b, pp. 269 ff.). Later, Schwefel implemented evolution strategies on computers and used them for finding computational solutions for a huge range of parameter optimization problems (Schwefel 1977; Schwefel 1981). Today evolution strategies represent one of the three major early approaches to evolutionary computation, besides genetic algorithms (Chapter 3) and evolutionary programming (Chapter 6).

Chapter overview

In the following sections of this chapter we present "ES chromosomes," vectors of numbers, as the typical ES parameter representation scheme (Section 4.1). First and foremost, we focus on optimization problems with real numbers, because a sophisticated ES theory has been developed in this respect during the last decades. In Sections 4.2 and 4.3, we deal with mutative operators—mutation that alters an ES chromosome and different versions of recombination operators that "shuffle" the genetic information of several ES chromosomes. Section 4.4 shows the basic ES selection and reproduction scheme and its variants. In Section 4.5, we discuss meta-evolution strategies for evolving competing subpopulations. How evolution strategies are implemented in Evolvica is described in Section 4.6. In Section 4.7, some example experiments of parameter optimization problems are demonstrated, which can be used as a starting point for your own problem-specific ES experiments. We also illustrate using a meta-evolution strategy for multimodal function optimization.

4.1 Representation of individuals

Initially, evolution strategy experiments were restricted to variables with integer values, which represented parameters of an experimental setup to be optimized. Examples of these parameters are the angles of flexibly connected board-shaped strips, the radius settings of a pipe coupling, or the inner diameters of segments for a two-phase jet nozzle (Rechenberg 1989). In today's ES computer implementations *vectors of real numbers* are mainly used as the basic data structure to be optimized. For *n* parameters to be adapted, evolution strategies work with a vector **g** of the following form, which we will refer to as an *ES chromosome*:

Vectors of real numbers

$$\mathbf{g} = (p_1, p_2, \ldots, p_n) \text{ with } p_i \in \Re.$$

ES chromosome

The letter **g** for the vector symbol stands for *genotype*. To make our notation easier to read, we write vectors as row vectors. For simple ES versions only the parameters to be adjusted are taken into account for the chromosome. For more complex optimization tasks, however, it turns out to be advantageous for the evolution process to extend the set of *decision* or *object parameters*, $(p_1, \ldots, p_n)$, by a vector of *strategy parameters*, $(s_1, \ldots, s_n)$. These additional parameters serve as variances or deviations for controlling the mutation step size for each of the object variables (see Section 4.2). Hence an ES chromosome can be represented as a vector pair:

ES chromosome with object and strategy parameters

$$\mathbf{g} = (\mathbf{p}, \mathbf{s}) = ((p_1, \ldots, p_n), (s_1, \ldots, s_n)) \text{ with } p_i, s_i \in \Re.$$

The control parameters **s** are considered an *internal model* of the environmental conditions, under which the evolution process is performed (Schwefel 1981; Schwefel 1994). The adaptation of these control parameters is an integral part of the optimum search for the object parameters, as we will see in the following section, about mutation. An example of an ES chromosome is depicted in Figure 4.1.

Let us assume we want to optimize five parameters, each with a value from the interval [0, 10]. The strategy parameters may take values from [0, 1]. In Evolvica we represent such a chromosome as an expression of the following form:

```
chromo[p[objectParameters],s[strategyParameters]].
```

ES chromosome

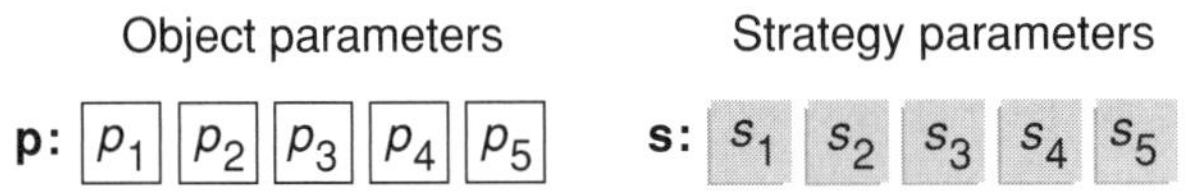

Object parameters   Strategy parameters

p: | p_1 | p_2 | p_3 | p_4 | p_5 | **s:** | s_1 | s_2 | s_3 | s_4 | s_5 |

Figure 4.1
ES chromosome with strategy parameters.

By the head symbol `chromo` we mark the data type of an ES chromosome. The example chromosome in Figure 4.2 is represented as follows:

```
chromo[p[1.6,-2.7,-3.5,-4.4,3.6],
s [0.5,0.5,0.3,0.9,0.9]].
```

Object and strategy parameters are encoded as `p[...]` and `s[...]` expressions, respectively. With the definitions of Program 4.1 we can generate a set of ES chromosomes of length 5 with the accompanying strategy parameters:

In[1] := **howMany = 2; chromoWidth = 5;**
            chromos = createChromosomes[howMany,chromoWidth,
                          ParameterRange → {-10,10},
                          StepSizeRange → {0,1}]

ES population of two
ES chromosomes

Out[1] = pop[
                chromo[q[undef],
                  p[1.60588, -2.74086, -3.45719, -4.42251, 3.55093]
                  s[0.51407, 0.540358, 0.253646, 0.88093, 0.883554]
                ],
                chromo[q[undef],
                  p[-2.99413, -1.43428, 4.80717, 3.69275, -2.14614],
                  s[0.251049, 0.39457, 0.75753, 0.673517, 0.807729]
                ]
              ]

The function `createChromosomes` will be used for generating an initial population with random parameter settings. This is why the chromosomes are not returned as a simple list but within a `pop[...]` structure. The chromosomes are given an additional parameter: the `q` expression will contain the fitness value of its respective ES chromosome. Since we did not evaluate the chromosomes, the fitness remains undefined (`undef`).

The function `showChromosome`, mapped onto each chromosome of the population, allows us to visualize the chromosomes, as the example in Figure 4.2 shows:

In[2] := **Map[showChromosome,chromos];**

Each pair of bars in Figure 4.2 shows the value of the object parameter on the left and its respective strategy parameter setting on

Program 4.1
Generating ES
chromosomes.

```
createChromosomes[
  howMany_Integer:1,width_:1,opts___] :=

Module[{paramRange,stepRange},
  paramRange = ParameterRange /. {opts}
                /.Options[createChromosomes];
  stepRange = StepSizeRange /. {opts}
                /. Options[createChromosomes];
  pop @@ Table[
    chromo[
      q @@ Table[undef,{1}],
      p @@ Table[Random[Real,paramRange],{width}],
      s @@ Table[Random[Real,stepRange],{width}]
    ],{howMany}
  ]
]

Options[createChromosomes] =
{ParameterRange → {-1,1}, StepSizeRange → {0,.1}};
```

Object and strategy parameters

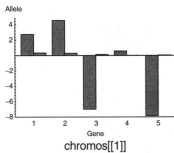

chromos[[1]]

Object and strategy parameters

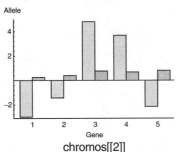

chromos[[2]]

Figure 4.2
ES chromosomes as bar
plots: each bar pair
represents an object and its
respective strategy
parameter.

the right. When we discuss mutating and recombining operators in the following sections, these graphical representations will turn out to be particularly useful.

After we have outlined how to represent ES chromosomes as two-fold vectors of numbers, the object and strategy parameters, we will discuss in the following two sections operators working on ES chromosomes. Through mutations, chromosome variants are created, whereas new compositions of vector parameters result from a *parameter blend* of several chromosomes.

4.2 Mutation

In the preceding chapters, we have shown with examples that mutations, as well as selection, are one of the driving forces of evolution. The actual definition of a mutation varies with the problem-specific context. For instance, consider the letter mutations in Section 1.3 or the mutations of the biomorph genotypes in Section 1.5. Now we will focus on a specific class of mutations on real numbers.

ES mutations

What role should mutations play in the solution of optimization tasks? Let us first consider a simple example in order to understand the fundamental idea of finding an optimum in the context of evolution strategies. Imagine that we are searching for the highest viewpoint on a hill, as depicted in Figure 4.3. Somewhere at the bottom of the hill we start with an initial (parent) individual, the coordinates of which are stored in the object parameters of its chromosome. Figure 4.4(a) gives a more detailed picture of this situation.

Figure 4.3
An ES population of six individuals climbs up to the top. The best individual of each generation is marked by an arrow.

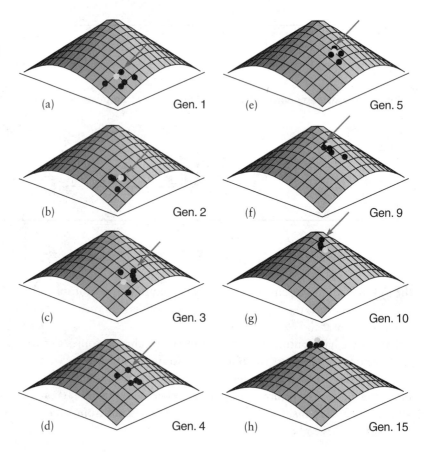

(a) Gen. 1   (e) Gen. 5

(b) Gen. 2   (f) Gen. 9

(c) Gen. 3   (g) Gen. 10

(d) Gen. 4   (h) Gen. 15

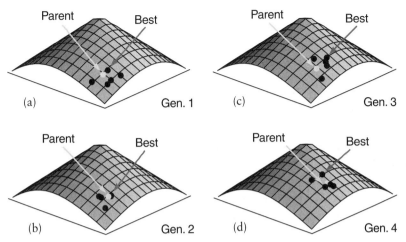

Figure 4.4
Populations of high fliers find their way to the very top by mutation and best selection.

The search for the highest point is performed as follows: from the parent individual five mutants—children or offspring—are generated, the coordinates of which are slightly different from the parent individual's. The object parameters of the mutated chromosomes often show only slight differences but sometimes larger ones compared to the original chromosome. The mutation step sizes, that is, the distances between the individuals' coordinates, is in essence determined by the strategy parameters.

Ascent by mutation

Now we have a small population of six individuals, each of which can be evaluated with respect to the posed optimization task, namely, the criterion: which of the individuals has reached the highest viewpoint up to now? If we want to reach the highest point eventually, it is certainly advantageous to choose the best individual as the new starting point, the parent individual, for the following generation. The single best individual per population is selected. Hence, the next generation can be generated in the same manner. The now best individual becomes the parent, from which another five mutants are generated, who are again evaluated for their fitness. The population winner is chosen and the next generation is set up, and so on (Figure 4.4).

With this ES selection-mutation scheme the population evolves from generation to generation, moving toward the highest point as if following an uphill gradient, and finally reaches the top viewpoint (Figure 4.3[h]). Note that for each generation the individuals stay close together; breakaways are exceptional. In evolution strategies mutation operators are preferred that result more often in only slight alterations rather than in wider variational "jumps."

For the mobility of a population, in the sense of its ability to explore the closer vicinity and farther off, it is particularly important that the survivor into the next generation not only inherit the best-so-far object parameters but also its strategy parameters. These determine the mutation step sizes, and so the mode of further exploration by the offspring population. For an ES chromosome with relatively large mutation step sizes, the offspring mutants find themselves within a wider radius around the parent individual, whereas for relatively small step sizes, the parent-offspring distances tend to be smaller. Thus, an *adaptive control of the mutation step sizes* results if even the strategy parameters are changed by mutations. As long as larger leaps of the mutants are advantageous, that is, as long as better-fit individuals are created, the strategy parameters remain more or less unchanged. However, if larger step sizes result in less-fit individuals, chromosomes with lower strategy parameters will eventually take over. For our example in Figure 4.3, this is the case when the population reaches the very top. Here wider spreading of the offspring population would lead to more individuals with lower fitness compared to their parents'. Since this self-adaptation of search control parameters is a special feature of evolution strategies, we will have a closer look at *mutative step size adaptation* in the next section.

Adaptive control of mutation step sizes

4.2.1 Mutation of object parameters

Object parameters are modified by using the strategy parameters, mimicking the biological principle that an offspring's traits are usually similar to parental traits and that, generally, erratic and large mutations are less common than slight modifications. The mutation operator ω_{mut} is defined as a componentwise addition of normally distributed random numbers. The mutated vector of object parameters $\mathbf{p}_{mut}$ is computed as

ES mutation

$$\omega_{mut}(\mathbf{p}, \mathbf{s}) = \mathbf{p}_{mut} = \mathbf{p} + N_0(\mathbf{s})$$
$$\mathbf{p}_{mut} = (p_1 + N_0(s_1), \overset{..}{\ldots}, p_n + N_0(s_n)).$$

Here $N_0(\mathbf{s}) = (N_0(s_1), \ldots, N_0(s_n))$ is a vector of Gaussian random numbers with mean zero and standard deviations s_i. The mutated ES chromosome looks as follows:

ES chromosome with mutated object parameters

$$\mathbf{g}_{mut} = (\mathbf{p}_{mut}, \mathbf{s}).$$

We restrict ourselves to the adaptation of the object parameters only. An extended variant of this mutation operator with additional mutative step size adaptation is discussed in Section 4.2.2. Here we will take a brief look at random number theory in order to better understand why normally distributed random numbers are a reasonable choice for ES mutations.

Normally distributed random numbers

A random number is called *normally* or *Gaussian distributed* if its density is of the form

$$N_\mu(\sigma) = \frac{1}{\sqrt{2\pi\sigma^2}} e^{-\frac{(x-\mu)^2}{2\sigma^2}}.$$

Gaussian density

The parameters μ and σ denote the expected value and the standard deviation, respectively. Often the variance σ^2 is given instead of the standard deviation, and the Gaussian distribution is referred to as an $N_\mu(\sigma^2)$ distribution. Mathematica provides direct access to a number of distributions defined in the package Statistics`Continuous- Distributions`:

In[1] := **Needs["Statistics`ContinuousDistributions`"]**

In[2] := **NormalDistribution[mu,sigma]**

The parameters for the function NormalDistribution are the expected value and the standard deviation. Figure 4.5 shows the Gaussian distribution $N_0(\sigma)$ for three different standard deviations $\sigma = 0.5$, 1.0, and 2.0. What is the meaning of the standard deviations for normally distributed random numbers? Using methods of random number theory, the distance of an $N_\mu(\sigma)$ distributed random variable X from the expected value can be easily explained. In Figure 4.5 the areas for $|X - \mu| \geq \sigma$ are marked in gray. On average, random numbers from the center white area appear in two out of three trials. We will justify this by the following considerations with exact numbers. For this purpose we define the density function gaussPDF[x,m,s] of an $N_\mu(\sigma)$ normal distribution:

Normal distribution

In[3] := **gaussPDF[x_,μ_:0,σ_:1] :=
        PDF[NormalDistribution[μ,σ],x]**

The integral of the density function over the intervals $[-i\sigma, i\sigma]$ for $i = 1, 2, 3$ provides the probabilities that the random variable takes values from within the white areas ($i = 1$).

Figure 4.5
Densities of normal
distributions for a constant
mean $\mu = 0$.

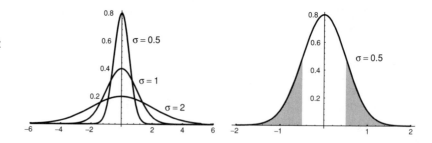
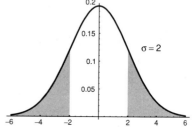
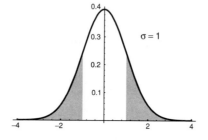

$In[4]$:= **Table[**
          Integrate[gaussPDF[x,μ,σ],
              {x,μ - i σ,μ + i σ}],
          {i,1,3}]

$Out[4]$ = $\left\{ \mathrm{Erf}\left(\frac{1}{\sqrt{2}}\right), \mathrm{Erf}(\sqrt{2}), \mathrm{Erf}\left(\frac{3}{\sqrt{2}}\right) \right\}$

Note that the values of these integrals are independent of any specific values for μ and σ. In Mathematica the integral

Error function

$$\mathrm{Erf}(x) = \frac{2}{\sqrt{\pi}} \int_0^x e^{-t^2} dt$$

of the Gaussian distribution is denoted by Erf(x). Specific values of the
error function Erf can be calculated easily:

$In[5]$:= **N[%]**

$Out[5]$ = {0.682689, 0.9545, 0.9973}

$In[6]$:= **1-%**

$Out[6]$ = {0.317311, 0.0455003, 0.0026998}

The results are summarized in the following table.

$$P(|X - \mu| \leq \sigma) \ = 0.683; \qquad P(|X - \mu| \geq \sigma) \ = 0.317$$
$$P(|X - \mu| \leq 2\sigma) = 0.954; \qquad P(|X - \mu| \geq 2\sigma) = 0.046$$
$$P(|X - \mu| \leq 3\sigma) = 0.997; \qquad P(|X - \mu| \geq 3\sigma) = 0.003$$

Error function table

Hence, the standard deviation σ of a Gaussian random variable can be illustrated as follows: the probability that its value differs more than σ from the mean value μ is about 32%. A deviation of more than 2σ from the mean occurs only with a much smaller probability of 0.046, and a deviation of more than 3σ is extremely rare.

The meaning of Gaussian random variables

Since we need a Gaussian distribution for ES mutations, we define a function gauss[μ,σ], which computes normally distributed random numbers around μ with standard deviation σ (Program 4.2).

```
Needs["Statistics`ContinuousDistributions`"]

gauss[μ_,σ_] := Random[NormalDistribution[μ,σ]]
```

Program 4.2
Generation function for normally distributed random numbers.

We examine this function by generating a list of 500 random $N_0(1)$ distributed numbers.

```
In[7] := gaussNumbers = Table[gauss[0,1],{500}];
```

In the resulting list we count how many elements lie within an interval of width 0.2, where the intervals are arranged between –5 and 5. Finally, the interval frequencies are normalized.

```
In[8] := Needs["Statistics`DataManipulation`"]
```

```
In[9] := bc = BinCounts[gaussNumbers,{-5,5,0.2}];
         bc = bc/Max[bc];
```

Plotting these frequencies as bar charts, we see that a distribution similar to the Gaussian bell shape results (Figure 4.6).

```
In[10] := Needs["Graphics`Graphics`"]
```

```
In[11] := BarChart[bc,
            PlotRange → All, Axes → True,
              BarEdges → False,
            Ticks → {Table[{i,-5 + 0.2 i}, {i,0,50,10}],
                  Automatic}];
```

Figure 4.6
The frequency histogram of
normally distributed random
numbers (a) approximates
the Gaussian density
function (b).

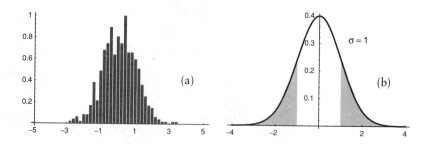

The function `gauss` returns smaller numbers (closer to mean
zero) more often than larger numbers. This is why the Gaussian distribution function provides an excellent basis for a "natural" ES mutation operator, where smaller modifications are preferred.

Mutation: small variations preferred

The parameter values of a base chromosome **p** (parent) and a mutant
chromosome $\mathbf{p}_{\text{mut}}$ (offspring) are rather similar, within a certain variational range (Figure 4.7).

The range of variation for the (object) parameters can be subtly
controlled by the set of standard deviations **s**, which is the motivation
for the definition of ES mutation as introduced previously and
depicted in Figure 4.2:

*ES mutation of the object
parameters*

$$\omega_{\text{mut}}(\mathbf{p}, \mathbf{s}) = \mathbf{p}_{\text{mut}} = \mathbf{p} + N_0(\mathbf{s}).$$

Let us now look at a few examples of how to program mutation
operators for evolution strategies. The function in Program 4.3
defines ES mutation as described above. Basically, only two lines of
code are needed:

```
p @@ MapThread[#1 + gauss[0,#2] &,
        {List @@ params, List @@ strategies}]
```

With `MapThread` the Gaussian addition is mapped on each respective
pair of object and strategy parameters. By using the `Apply` command
(short infix notation: `@@`) the head symbols p and s within the
`params` and `strategies` expressions are converted to lists, which is
necessary for `MapThread`. The resulting list gets the head symbol p,
representing the new, mutated object parameters. The strategy parameters of the mutated chromosome remain unchanged (for the
moment). The quality (fitness) is reset to "undefined" since the old fit-

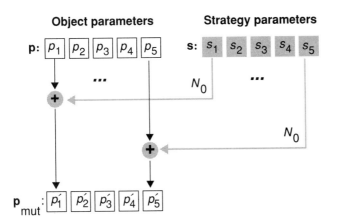

Figure 4.7
Mutation of ES
chromosomes.

Program 4.3
ES mutation (without step
size adaptation).

```
Mutation[chromo[_q,params_p,strategies_s],opts___] :=
   chromo[
      q[undef],
      p @@ MapThread[#1 + gauss[0,#2] &,
         {List @@ params, List @@ strategies}],
      strategies
   ]
```

ness value becomes obsolete and must be recalculated in the next evaluation phase.

We test this first variant of ES mutation with an example. We generate an ES chromosome with a parameter range of [–10, +10] for the
object parameters and of [1, 3] for the strategy parameters:

In[12] := **esChromo = CreateChromosome[10,**
                    ParameterRange → {-10,10},
                    StepSizeRange → {1,3}]

Out[12] = chromo[q[undef],   *ES chromosome*
         p[-4.76148, 3.25084, -4.65235, -9.77353,
           -6.8735, 9.24806, -5.52879, -5.97208,
           -4.71118, 6.93209],
         s[1.94095, 1.90875, 2.77618, 2.9601, 1.82473,
           2.8973, 1.11339, 1.60593, 1.69197, 1.70025]]

We generate a mutant offspring of this ES chromosome in the following way:

$In[13]$:= `esChromoMutated = Mutation[esChromo]`

```
Mutation values:
0.88, -3.11, -1.27, 5.59, 0.95, 0.02, -0.63, 0.47, 0.14,
-0.40
```

Mutated ES chromosome

$Out[13]$ = `chromo[q[undef],`
```
          p[-3.87947, 0.134861, -5.92226, -4.17969,
            -5.92346, 9.26824, -6.15574, -5.50551,
            -4.56813, 6.53037],
          s[1.94095, 1.90875, 2.77618, 2.9601, 1.82473,
            2.8973, 1.11339, 1.60593, 1.69197, 1.70025]]
```

Here we have extended the `gauss` function from Program 4.2 by a `Print` command so that we also get to know the random values used for each parameter mutation. These printed numbers are rounded to two decimal digits. In Figure 4.8 the resulting chromosome mutations are depicted graphically.

$In[14]$:= `showChromosomes[{esChromo,esChromoMutated}]`

Each pair of bars represents the respective parameter value of the parent (light gray) and offspring (dark gray) chromosome. The effect of "smaller mutations preferred" is clearly visible.

Up to now we have left the strategy parameters unchanged. But shouldn't the step size parameters be adapted, too? Obviously we cannot use a similar adaptation scheme for the strategy parameters since we would then need meta-strategy parameters for their mutation, and so on. We will see, however, that there are a few heuristic adaptation rules for the mutation step sizes, which we discuss in the following section.

Figure 4.8
Example of ES mutation without adaptation of the strategy parameters.

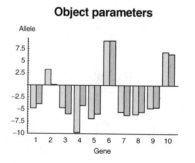
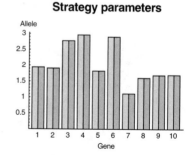

4.2.2 Mutation with step size adaptation

In this section mutation is not only restricted to object parameters but is also extended to strategy parameters. We repeat the formula for ES mutation here:

$$\mathbf{g}_{mut} = (\mathbf{p}_{mut}, \mathbf{s}_{mut})$$

$$\mathbf{p}_{mut} = \mathbf{p} + N_0(\mathbf{s}), \quad \mathbf{s}_{mut} = \alpha(\mathbf{s}).$$

ES mutation with step size adaptation

As described in the previous section, the mutated object parameters **p** are adjusted by normally distributed random numbers, the deviations of which are controlled by the strategy parameters **s**. The step sizes **s** are adapted by a function α known in the literature as the *mutative step size adaptation* (MSA) function (Rechenberg 1994b). Consequently, the mutation scheme of Figure 4.2 must be extended by the respective operation for adapting the step sizes (Figure 4.9).

MSA: mutative step size adaptation

Now the evolution algorithm must handle a much more difficult optimization task. Not only must optimal settings for the object parameters be found, but even proper step sizes have to be evolved. Implicitly, this means that we are searching for a strategy for both globally exploring the search space and, finally, locally approaching optima. But what is an "intelligent" strategy to do this? How can we tell when to switch from larger to smaller mutation steps and vice versa? In which direction should the mutants move? We will be able to answer these questions when we look at some optimization examples in Section 4.7, where this kind of meta-evolution is applied. Meta-evolution with variable strategy parameters was first proposed and further investigated by Schwefel in a number of computer experiments

In search of a proper step size adaptation strategy

Meta-evolution

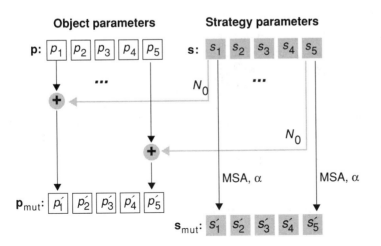

Figure 4.9
Mutation of an ES chromosome with mutative step size adaptation (MSA).

(Schwefel 1977; Schwefel 1981). Rechenberg coined the term *second-order evolution* for ES mutation strategies with step size adaptation (Rechenberg 1994b, p. 47 ff.).

Step size adaptation

We can include the step size adaptation function α very easily in our previously defined `Mutation` function without having to give a specific definition for α right now (Program 4.4).

Program 4.4
ES mutation with step size adaptation.

```
Mutation[chromo[params_x,strategies_s],opts___]] :=

Module[{alpha = StepSizeAdaptation /.
                     {opts} /.  Options[Mutation]},

   chromo[
        p @@ MapThread[#1 + gauss[0,#2] &,
           {List @@ params, List @@ strategies}],
        Map[alpha,strategies]
 ] ]

Options[Mutation] = { StepSizeAdaptation → (#&) };
```

The strategy parameters are wrapped in a `Map` expression:

```
Map[alpha, strategies].
```

Here `alpha` denotes a one-argument function, the *mutative step size adaptation function,* which modifies the respective strategy parameter values. This adaptation function is defined as an optional replacement rule (`StepSizeAdaptation → ...`), predefined as the identity function (`#&`). Hence the function defined in Program 4.4 has exactly the same effect as the simpler version of Program 4.3. Different settings for the adaptation function can now be tested easily. In the following section we will introduce a few heuristic approaches for adapting the strategy parameters.

Heuristics for step size adaptations

For implicitly controlling mutation step sizes, Rechenberg proposes adjusting the standard deviations s according to the following scheme:

$$s_{mut} = (s_1 \xi_1, \dots, s_n \xi_n)$$

MSA: Mutative step size adaptation, Example 1

$$\xi_i = \begin{cases} \beta & \chi < 0.5, \\ \dfrac{1}{\beta} & \chi \geq 0.5. \end{cases}$$

Here χ denotes a uniformly distributed random variable from the interval [0, 1], for which we can define a simple function chi (Program 4.5).

```
chi[] := Random[Real,{0,1}]
```

Program 4.5
Uniformly distributed
random variable.

We can pass this adaptation function to the mutation operator as an option:

```
StepSizeAdaptation →
     If[chi[] < 0.5,N[# 1.3],N[# 1/1.3]]& ].
```

Here we have set $\beta = 1.3$. For $n < 100$ parameters the step size adaptation factor β should take values between 1.3 and 1.5; otherwise, β should be decreased (Rechenberg 1994b, p. 48 and Chapter 14). Program 4.6 shows Rechenberg's step size adaptation function as an anonymous function in Mathematica notation.

```
If[chi[] < 0.5,N[# beta],N[# 1/beta]]&
```

Program 4.6
Rechenberg's step size
adaptation function α.

What is the general effect of this function α on the adaptation of the step sizes and on the dynamics of the evolution process? Let us look at a small example. First, we generate an ES chromosome.

In[15] := **esChromo = createChromosome[10,**
     ParameterRange → {-10,10}, StepSizeRange →
     {1,3}]

Out[15] = chromo[q[undef],
         p[-3.69453, 3.40814, 2.63204, 0.719878,
         7.9791, -9.2294, 9.74413, -3.71836, -3.7631,

ES chromosome

```
                          -3.11974],
                    s[1.52137, 2.26006, 1.88117, 1.46296, 1.29467,
                      1.3879, 1.70339, 1.39098, 2.72613, 1.92732]]
```

We mutate chromosome `esChromo` using Rechenberg's MSA function:

In[16] := **esChromoMutated = Mutation[esChromo,**
                 StepSizeAdaptation $\rightarrow$
                    If[chi[] < 0.5,N[# 1.3],N[# 1/1.3]]&]

Mutated ES chromosome with adapted step sizes

```
Out[16] = chromo[q[undef],
              p[-4.0554, 3.67028, 5.67734, 3.85623, 7.86156,
                -9.6267, 7.34684, -4.87475, 3.4449,
                -4.26694],
              s[1.17028, 1.73851, 2.44552, 1.12535, 1.68307,
                1.80426, 2.2144, 1.06999, 3.54397, 2.50552]]
```

In[17] := **showChromosomes[{esChromo,esChromoMutated}]**

In the graphical representation in Figure 4.10 the variations of the strategy parameters are more obvious. About half of the strategy parameters are increased by 30% (scaling by a factor of 1.3), whereas the others are reduced by about 23% (scaling factor 1/1.3 = 0.77).

Specific meaning of Rechenberg's step size adaptation scheme

The meaning of this specific adaptation scheme for the step sizes can probably be better understood if we look at a population evolving through mutation and (best) selection. Mutated offspring of a parent individual contain, approximately half and half, decreased as well as increased step sizes in their ES chromosomes. In the next generation, the new strategy-object parameter combinations are evaluated for their fitnesses. If the individuals of a generation are generated as mutants of the single best individual of the previous generation, the new population will test variations of the best object parameters for

Figure 4.10
ES mutation with
Rechenberg's MSA function.

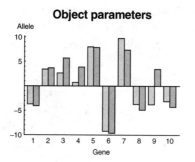
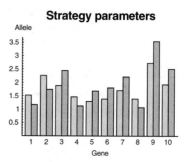

different step sizes up to now. In the long run, it is expected that the selection-mutation scheme applied to the strategy parameters will result in a dominance of those step sizes that are most advantageous; that is, they are best adapted to the specific topology of the "fitness landscape." Rechenberg refers to this process as "second-order evolution" and describes how you could envisage the expected positive effect of this mutative step size adaptation. If the optimization starts from too small strategy parameters, the step sizes will be increased "explosively." On the other hand, whenever the population approaches an optimum, the step sizes will eventually be decreased by iterated best selection and mutation (Rechenberg 1994b, p. 48).

Second order evolution

Let us look at another heuristic for step size adaptation, proposed by Hoffmeister and Bäck (1992, p. 21):

$$\mathbf{s}_{mut} = (s_1 \xi_1, \ldots, s_n \xi_n)$$

MSA: Mutative step size adaptation, Example 2

$$\xi_i = e^{N_0(\Delta\sigma)}.$$

Here the scaling parameter $\Delta\sigma$ controls the size of the step size adaptation. By using the exponential function, both negative deviations are avoided ($\xi_i > 0$) and smaller variations are preferred (multiplication by values close to 1). The step size decreases for negative values of $N_0(\Delta\sigma)$; that is, for $0 < \xi_i < 1$. For $N_0(\Delta\sigma) > 0$ the step size increases by a factor $\xi_i > 1$.

```
# E^gauss[0,deltaSigma]&
```

Program 4.7
Step size adaptation by Hoffmeister and Bäck.

We illustrate the effect of this MSA function by an example. A randomly generated ES chromosome is mutated with $\Delta\sigma = 0.5$.

```
In[18]:= esChromo = createChromosome[10,
        ParameterRange → {-10,10}, StepSizeRange →
        {1,3}]
```

```
Out[18]= chromo[q[undef],
        p[5.61013, -3.73579, 8.27, -9.271, -8.24874,
          -8.14978, 4.4291, -7.08524, -0.424771,
          -7.97561],
        s[1.20537, 2.13504, 1.17533, 1.78354, 2.97908,
          2.09498, 2.21201, 2.11341, 1.34793, 2.1807]]
```

ES chromosome

```
In[19] := deltaSigma = 0.5;
          esChromoMutated = Mutation[esChromo,
          StepSizeAdaptation →
          (# E^gauss[0,deltaSigma]&)]
```

```
Mutation values:
-1.71, 1.30, 0.37, -0.81, -1.61, 0.49, 0.92, 1.12, 0.80,
2.80
N[0, deltaSigma]:
0.34, 0.38, 0.10, -0.77, -0.72, -0.01, -0.04, 0.61,
0.72, 0.51
```

Mutated ES chromosome
with MSA of Program 4.7

```
Out[19] = chromo[q[undef],
             p[3.90357, -2.43618, 8.64377, -10.0832,
                -9.85478, -7.65646, 5.34662, -5.96546,
                0.379469, -5.17017],
             s[1.69627, 3.12521, 1.30357, 0.821559,
                1.44941, 2.07499, 2.12869, 3.90666, 2.78096,
                3.62485]]
```

Both the mutated values and the normally distributed numbers are rounded to two decimals. We get the graphical representation depicted in Figure 4.11 with the following command:

```
In[20] := showChromosomes[{esChromo,esChromoMutated}]
```

The gauss function used by the mutation operator also prints the resulting random numbers. For positive numbers the mutation step sizes are increased, whereas for negative numbers the step sizes are decreased (Figure 4.11, right diagram).

Figure 4.11
ES mutation with step size
adaptation by Hoffmeister
and Bäck.

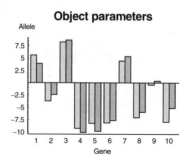
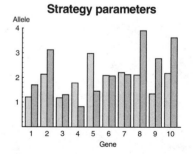

Some remarks about and further references for ES mutation

We discussed only two heuristics for mutative step size adaptation here, but there are a number of rather sophisticated MSA algorithms (e.g., *correlated mutation* [Hoffmeister and Bäck 1992]) for optimizing the progress induced by mutation, dependent on the problem-specific topological features of the fitness landscape. A more detailed discussion of MSA approaches can be found in Hoffmeister and Bäck 1992, Rechenberg 1994b, or Schwefel 1981.

4.3   Recombination

Besides mutation, evolution strategies also use recombining operators. These operators have effects similar to those of gene recombination in the genomes of natural cells, merging the genotypic information of several individual organisms. Evolution strategies apply a "blending" operator, which recombines object and strategy parameters, respectively. In this section, we first consider ES recombination among two chromosomes. A more general version for $n > 2$ recombination partners will be developed in the following sections.

For two ES chromosomes $\mathbf{a} = (\mathbf{p}_a, \mathbf{s}_a)$ and $\mathbf{b} = (\mathbf{p}_b, s_b)$ we can define a recombination operator ω_{rec} as follows:

$$\omega_{\mathrm{rec}}(\mathbf{a}, \mathbf{b}) = (\mathbf{p}', \mathbf{s}') = ((p_1', \ldots, p_n'), (s_1', \ldots, s_n'))$$

ES recombination (binary)

with

$$\begin{aligned} p_i' &= \rho_p(p_{a,i}, p_{b,i}) \\ s_i' &= \rho_s(s_{a,i}, s_{b,i}) \end{aligned} \quad \forall i \in \{1, \ldots, n\} \cdot$$

The new entries p_i' and s_i' of the recombined ES chromosome are computed by mapping the recombination functions ρ_p and ρ_s on the corresponding object and strategy parameters. For the following paragraphs we assume the same recombination function for both object and strategy parameters: $\rho = \rho_p = \rho_s$.

In Mathematica we can implement pairwise recombination as follows. We start with two parameter lists and apply the function `MapThread` in order to map `rho` onto the respective list entries:

```
In[21]:= paramsA = Array[a,5]
         paramsB = Array[b,5]
```

ES recombination in Mathematica

Out[21] = {a[1], a[2], a[3], a[4], a[5]}
          {b[1], b[2], b[3], b[4], b[5]}

In[22] := **paramsRecombined =**
          MapThread[rho,{paramsA,paramsB}]

Out[22] = {rho[a[1], b[1]], rho[a[2], b[2]], rho[a[3],
          b[3]], rho[a[4], b[4]], rho[a[5], b[5]]}

Besides the actual definition of the recombination function rho, the function MapThread plays a central role in the implementation of recombination operators.

4.3.1 Discrete and intermediate recombination

For evolution strategies, both for binary and multirecombinations, two recombination functions play a prominent role—*discrete* and *intermediate* recombination.

With *discrete* recombination one of the two respective components is randomly chosen:

Discrete ES recombination

$$\rho(x_1, x_2) = \begin{cases} x_1 & \chi \leq 0.5, \\ x_2 & \chi \leq 0.5. \end{cases}$$

Again, the function χ returns a uniformly distributed random number from the interval [0, 1]. The components x_1 or x_2 are chosen with equal probability of 50% (Figure 4.12). Discrete ES recombination is similar to the uniform crossover operator of genetic algorithms (Section 3.3).

For *intermediate* recombination the mean values of the respective components are computed (Figure 4.13):

Intermediate ES recombination

$$\rho(x_1, x_2) = \frac{x_1 + x_2}{2}.$$

This operator is used for recombinations in particular among strategy parameters. Averaging eventually results, however, in reduced diversity of the "internal model." If intermediate recombination is applied too often, the strategy entries become more and more similar. This may lead to premature convergence of the whole gene pool of the population (in case no other operator, such as mutation, is used in order to keep evolutionary step size adaptation going). We will take a closer

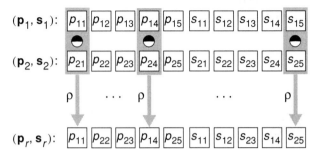

Object and strategy parameters

Figure 4.12
Discrete recombination of
two ES chromosomes
with $\rho = \rho_p = \rho_s$.

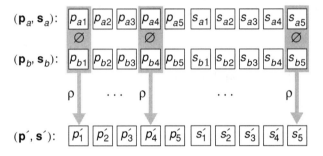

Object and strategy parameters

Figure 4.13
Intermediate recombination
of two ES chromosomes
for $\rho = \rho_p = \rho_s$.

look at the particular features of recombination operators in Section 4.7, where we present a few examples of evolution experiments.

The described recombination operators may of course be extended for the general case of $n > 2$ recombining chromosomes. An algorithmic scheme for these *multirecombinations* is given in Program 4.8. Here the function `Recombine` implements multirecombination on parameter lists.

```
Recombine[paramLists_List,opts___] :=
  MapThread[RecombinationFunction /. {opts}
     /. Options[Recombine], paramLists]

Options[Recombine] :=
{ RecombinationFunction → DISCRETE };
```

Program 4.8
Multirecombination on
parameter lists.

The recombination function ρ (see Section 4.3) is passed as an optional replacement rule for `RecombinationFunction`. In this way we can define any function, which takes a list as its argument, as the recombination function. We can predefine these functions for discrete and intermediate recombination as shown in Program 4.9.

Program 4.9
Discrete and intermediate recombination on lists.

```
DISCRETE = (randomSelect[#]&);

INTERMEDIATE = (N[Mean[#]]&);
```

Examples of how to use these operators will be discussed in the following sections. The function `Recombine` allows us to separately apply recombination functions on the object and strategy parameters, respectively. For an extended version of this recombination operator on ES chromosomes see Section 4.3.3 and Program 4.11.

4.3.2 Local and global recombinations

Up to now we have implemented recombinations only for list structures. We want to define a recombination operator that works on populations of ES chromosomes as we did for mutation operators (Section 4.2). With this extended definition of ES recombination we also want to take into account a few variants of recombination schemes, which were proposed in Schwefel 1981. In his ES implementations and experiments, Schwefel uses four recombining operators, which may either work only on a subpopulation (analogous to the version in the previous section) or may choose their recombination partners anew for each of the components. These operators can be described in detail as follows. We assume a population $P = (\mathbf{g}_1, \mathbf{g}_2, \ldots, \mathbf{g}_N)$ of N chromosomes of the form $\mathbf{g}_i = (g_{i1}, \ldots, g_{in})$ with $1 \leq i \leq N$. A multirecombination operator ω_{rec}, which combines r chromosomes, can be defined as

Local vs. global recombination

Multi–ES recombination for r chromosomes

$$\omega_{rec}(\mathbf{g}_{i_1}, \ldots, \mathbf{g}_{i_r}) = \mathbf{g}' = (g'_1, \ldots, g'_n).$$

The indices $i_1, \ldots, i_r \in \{1, \ldots, N\}$ with $i_j \neq i_k$ all must be different from each other; that is, no chromosome appears more than once as a recombination partner $(1 \leq r \leq N)$. We will take a closer look at two recombination schemes—*local* and *global* recombination. Both variants can use either discrete or intermediate recombination functions or apply any other problem-specific function for combining the respective elements.

Local recombination

In the previous section we discussed local intermediate or discrete recombination, which we will denote by $\omega_{\text{rec}}^{\text{local}}$, in detail for the binary case. For r recombination partners the entries of the recombined chromosome $\mathbf{g}'$ are computed as follows:

$$\omega_{\text{rec}}^{\text{local}}(\mathbf{g}_{i_1}, \ldots, \mathbf{g}_{i_r}) = \mathbf{g}' = (g_1', \ldots, g_n')$$

$$g_k' = \begin{cases} g_{i_1} \text{ or } \ldots \text{ or } g_{i_r} & \text{if } \rho = \rho_{\text{dis}} \\ \dfrac{1}{r} \displaystyle\sum_{m=1}^{r} g_{i_m, k} & \text{if } \rho = \rho_{\text{inter}} \end{cases}$$

Local recombination: discrete or intermediate

Figure 4.14 gives a schematic, graphical representation of local, discrete ES multirecombination for three recombination partners ($r = 3$) from a population of seven chromosomes ($N = 7$). Here the first, third, and sixth chromosomes are selected for being in the scope of recombination ($i_1 = 1$, $i_2 = 3$, $i_3 = 6$). For each column, one of the three elements is chosen at random, designated as the recombination result.

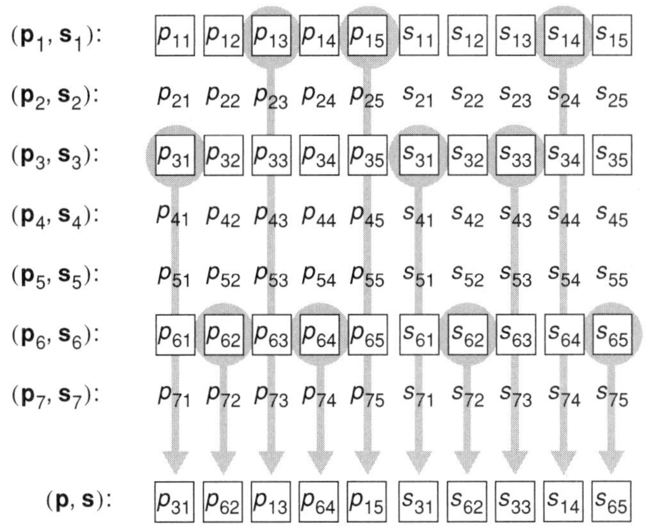

Figure 4.14
Scheme of local, discrete ES multirecombination.

This kind of recombination is termed *local* because the selection of the recombination partners—three in our example—occurs before the actual recombination. The recombination is restricted to a local group of the whole population. For an algorithmic representation of this recombination scheme in Evolvica we need only apply function Recombine of Program 4.8 on a set of r parameter lists. We define the parameters in analogy to Figure 4.14 as vectors with components p_{ik}:

In[23] := **params = Array[p,{7,5}]**

Out[23] = {{p[1, 1], p[1, 2], p[1, 3], p[1, 4], p[1, 5]},
            {p[2, 1], p[2, 2], p[2, 3], p[2, 4], p[2, 5]},
            {p[3, 1], p[3, 2], p[3, 3], p[3, 4], p[3, 5]},
            {p[4, 1], p[4, 2], p[4, 3], p[4, 4], p[4, 5]},
            {p[5, 1], p[5, 2], p[5, 3], p[5, 4], p[5, 5]},
            {p[6, 1], p[6, 2], p[6, 3], p[6, 4], p[6, 5]},
            {p[7, 1], p[7, 2], p[7, 3], p[7, 4], p[7, 5]}}

The strategy parameters are not explicitly taken into account, since their recombination works just the same way. So we can denote all parameters by p[i,k]. Moreover, the recombination function we will present at the end of this section allows us to recombine object and strategy parameters differently.

In order to select r recombination partners according to the scheme in Figure 4.14, we use the function randomSelectMultiple[params,r] of Program 4.10, which randomly selects r different elements from a list of length $N \geq r$. The r indices of the recombination partners are determined by using the function RandomPermutation from the Mathematica standard package DiscreteMath`Combinatorica`. This function implements random selection without returning, which is the selection scheme used for most lotteries (e.g., selecting 7 out of 49):

In[24] := **lottery = Range[49];**
           randomSelectMultiple[lottery,7]

Out[24] = {14, 30, 3, 6, 21, 23, 15}

Program 4.10 shows how to implement random selection without any repetition. RandomPermutation[k] generates a randomly permuted list of numbers from 1 to k. Since this is a permutation, each element from {1, . . . , k} appears exactly once. These numbers are used in `randomSelectMultiple[s_,n_]` for the indices of the list elements in `s`. For a selection of n elements only the first n entries of the index list are chosen. Hence, `randomSelectMultiple` returns a random selection of n elements of list `s`.

```
Needs["DiscreteMath`Combinatorica`"]

randomSelectMultiple[s_List,n_Integer:1] :=
  Map[s[[#]]&,Take[RandomPermutation[Length[s]],n]]
```

Program 4.10
Multiple random selection from a list.

With these preparations we can easily formulate local recombination. We choose *r* = 3 recombination partners and use a yet unspecified combination function `rho[#]&`:

In[25] := **r = 3;**
Recombine[randomSelectMultiple[params,r],
RecombinationFunction → (rho[#]&)]

Local recombination

Out[25] = {rho[{p[2, 1], p[7, 1], p[4, 1]}],
rho[{p[2, 2], p[7, 2], p[4, 2]}],
rho[{p[2, 3], p[7, 3], p[4, 3]}],
rho[{p[2, 4], p[7, 4], p[4, 4]}],
rho[{p[2, 5], p[7, 5], p[4, 5]}]}

Here the second, fourth, and seventh chromosome are selected. The `rho` function could be replaced by a specific variant of an intermediate, discrete, or other recombination mapping.

Global recombination

The selection of recombination partners for global recombination works differently from that in local recombination. Here the restriction to a group of previously defined recombination partners (a subpopulation) no longer holds. All chromosomes of a population are in the range of the recombination mapping function. Figure 4.15 illustrates this scheme of global recombination for an example of three parameters to be recombined per column.

In each column three entries are selected to which the recombination function ρ is applied (a discrete recombination in this example).

Figure 4.15
Scheme of global, ES
multirecombination
(three recombination
partners, discrete).

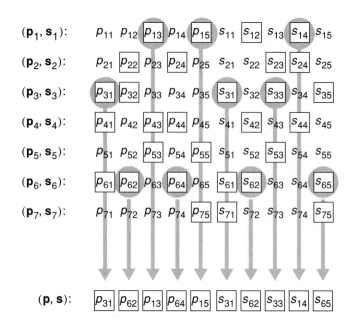

Comparing this scheme with Figure 4.14, we see that global recombinations result in an increased mixing of the genetic material. This effect helps to avoid premature convergence due to reduced diversity within the population. Premature convergence is usually one of the disadvantageous side effects of recombining operators (see Section 3.7.4 for a more detailed discussion). With global recombination this disadvantage can be alleviated without having to refrain from the positive effects of *information merging*.

Global
ES recombination

Formally, global recombination $\omega_{\text{rec},r}^{\text{global}}$ of r elements is described as follows:

$$\omega_{\text{rec},r}^{\text{global}}(\mathbf{g}_1,\dots,\mathbf{g}_N) = \mathbf{g}' = (\,g_1',\dots,g_n'\,)$$

$$g_k' = \rho\left(g_{i_1,k}^{\text{global}},\dots,g_{i_r,k}^{\text{global}}\right).$$

The whole population $P = (\mathbf{g}_1,\mathbf{g}_2,\dots,\mathbf{g}_N)$ is in the scope of the recombination operator. The indices $i_1,\dots,i_r \in \{1,\dots,N\}$ with $i_j \neq i_k$ denote the selected chromosomes that are selected anew for each column k. The resulting entries of the recombined chromosome for a discrete or intermediate recombination mapping are calculated as follows:

$$
g'_k = \begin{cases} g^{\text{global}}_{i_1,k} \text{ or } \ldots \text{ or } g^{\text{global}}_{i_r,k} & \text{if } \rho = \rho_{\text{dis}} \\[2mm] \dfrac{1}{r} \displaystyle\sum_{m=1}^{r} g^{\text{global}}_{i_m,k} & \text{if } \rho = \rho_{\text{inter}} \end{cases}
$$

Global ES recombination: discrete or intermediate

For each g'_k the elements $g^{\text{global}}_{i_m,k}$ are chosen anew from the entire set of chromosomes. The variable g'_k denotes the resulting recombination entry of column k in Figure 4.15.

Global recombination and its connection to local recombination is illustrated by a three-stage scheme in Figure 4.16. In the first step, r elements are selected at random from each column ($r = 3$), according to their sequence of selection; second, the elements are assigned to one of r temporary vectors, on which the recombination mappings can be performed locally.

In Evolvica an implementation of global recombination looks as follows. We again start with symbolic parameter lists, as we did for local recombination:

In[1] := **params = Array[p,{7,5}];**
        params // TableForm

Elements for recombination

Out[1] = p[1, 1]   p[1, 2]   p[1, 3]   p[1, 4]   p[1, 5]
        p[2, 1]   p[2, 2]   p[2, 3]   p[2, 4]   p[2, 5]
        p[3, 1]   p[3, 2]   p[3, 3]   p[3, 4]   p[3, 5]
        p[4, 1]   p[4, 2]   p[4, 3]   p[4, 4]   p[4, 5]
        p[5, 1]   p[5, 2]   p[5, 3]   p[5, 4]   p[5, 5]
        p[6, 1]   p[6, 2]   p[6, 3]   p[6, 4]   p[6, 5]
        p[7, 1]   p[7, 2]   p[7, 3]   p[7, 4]   p[7, 5]

For global recombination we are interested in the columns (see Figure 4.16), which we get by performing a row-by-row transposition of the parameter matrix:

In[2] := **Transpose[params] // TableForm**

Columns to rows ...

Out[2] = p[1,1] p[2,1] p[3,1] p[4,1] p[5,1] p[6,1] p[7,1]
        p[1,2] p[2,2] p[3,2] p[4,2] p[5,2] p[6,2] p[7,2]
        p[1,3] p[2,3] p[3,3] p[4,3] p[5,3] p[6,3] p[7,3]
        p[1,4] p[2,4] p[3,4] p[4,4] p[5,4] p[6,4] p[7,4]
        p[1,5] p[2,5] p[3,5] p[4,5] p[5,5] p[6,5] p[7,5]

Figure 4.16
Three-stage scheme of
global, multiple ES
recombination.

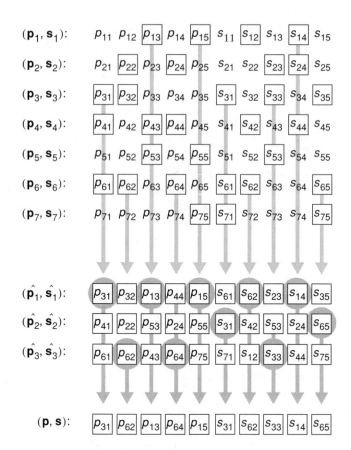

Now the selection of the elements to be recombined is performed for
each row. From each "column"—each output line above corresponds
to one of the columns in Figure 4.16—we have to select r elements:

*Selecting elements to
recombine . . .*

```
In[3] := r = 3;
         recColumnsAndIndices =
           Map[randomSelectMultiple[#,r,
           ReturnIndices → True]&, Transpose[params]]
```

```
Out[3] = {{{p[4, 1], p[1, 1], p[6, 1]}, {4, 1, 6}},
          {{p[1, 2], p[7, 2], p[6, 2]}, {1, 7, 6}},
          {{p[5, 3], p[7, 3], p[3, 3]}, {5, 7, 3}},
          {{p[4, 4], p[1, 4], p[2, 4]}, {4, 1, 2}},
          {{p[3, 5], p[1, 5], p[7, 5]}, {3, 1, 7}}}
```

Here we use an extended version of `randomSelectMultiple`, which also returns the indices of the randomly selected list elements. The output tells us that elements 4, 1, and 6 are selected in the first column; elements 1, 7, and 6 from the second column; and so on. In order to separate the list elements from their indices we transpose the output list.

In[4] := `{recColumns,recIndices} =`
       `Transpose[recColumnsAndIndices]`

Separating data structures

Out[4] =`{{{p[4, 1], p[1, 1], p[6, 1]},`
    `{p[1, 2], p[7, 2], p[6, 2]},`
    `{p[5, 3], p[7, 3], p[3, 3]},`
    `{p[4, 4], p[1, 4], p[2, 4]},`
    `{p[3, 5], p[1, 5], p[7, 5]}},`
  `{{4, 1, 6}, {1, 7, 6}, {5, 7, 3}, {4, 1, 2},`
  `{3, 1, 7}}}`

The column vectors must be transformed into ES chromosome representation (`Transpose`), on which the recombination function `Recombine` is applied. Finally the recombination function ρ is mapped onto this local set of parameter vectors:

In[5] := `Recombine[Transpose[recColumns],`
    `RecombinationFunction` → `(rho[#]&)] //`
    `TableForm`

Final recombination on a local set of elements

Out[5] = `rho[{p[4, 1], p[1, 1], p[6, 1]}]`
    `rho[{p[1, 2], p[7, 2], p[6, 2]}]`
    `rho[{p[5, 3], p[7, 3], p[3, 3]}]`
    `rho[{p[4, 4], p[1, 4], p[2, 4]}]`
    `rho[{p[3, 5], p[1, 5], p[7, 5]}]`

The result is a global mixing recombination operator. Here the first component of the recombined chromosome is composed of elements 4, 1, and 6; the second of 1, 7, and 6; the third of 5, 7, and 3, and so on.

The recombination diagram in Figure 4.17 shows the resulting chromosomes. This illustration, generated with the Evolvica function `RecombinationPlot`, is similar to the scheme in Figures 4.15 and 4.16. The selected elements are marked by shadowed disks, where the elements of each "temporary" chromosome share the same gray level. When elements with the same gray level are collected, the following chromosomes result:

Recombination diagram

$$\text{Chromosome 1: } p_{41}, p_{12}, p_{53}, p_{44}, p_{35}$$
$$\text{Chromosome 2: } p_{11}, p_{72}, p_{73}, p_{14}, p_{15}$$
$$\text{Chromosome 3: } p_{61}, p_{62}, p_{33}, p_{24}, p_{75}$$

This is a chromosome set corresponding to the set depicted in the middle of Figure 4.16, on which local recombinations are performed. We get the indices of these vectors by transposing the row numbers that are selected per column:

In[6] := **recIndices//Transpose**

Out[6] = {{4, 1, 5, 4, 3}, {1, 7, 7, 1, 1}, {6, 6, 3, 2, 7}}

We get the recombination diagram of Figure 4.17 with the following command:

Recombination diagram plot *In[7]* := **RecombinationPlot[5,7,**
              Map[MapIndexed[{#1,First[#2]}&,#]&,
                recIndices//Transpose],
              ColorFunction → GrayLevel,
              ColorIncrement → .15];

The function `RecombinationPlot[w_,h_,i_List]` generates a matrix of width `w` and height `h` with matrix elements p_{ik}, $1 \le i \le h$, $1 \le k \le w$. When the option `ParameterSymbol` is used, the symbol p can be substituted by any other string. The indices are generated automatically. In list i the column indices for the elements of each chromosome, which are marked by a colored disk, are collected. `DiskSize` sets the relative size of the disks. The option `ColorFunction` allows for switching between color or gray-level representation. Within the available color or gray scale ranges the chromosomes are attributed with different color values (`ColorIncrement`). Further-

Figure 4.17
Recombination diagram.

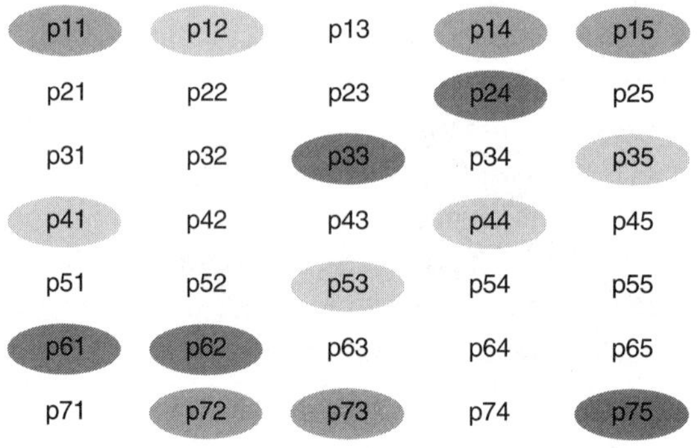

more, the column and row offsets are controlled by `Horizontal-Offset` and `VerticalOffset`, respectively. Here is a listing of the available options and their default settings:

In[8] := **Options[RecombinationPlot]**

Out[8] ={ ParameterSymbol → "p",
         DiskSize → 0.4,
         HorizontalOffset → 0, VerticalOffset → 0,
         ColorFunction → Hue, ColorIncrement → 0.1,
         DisplayFunction → $DisplayFunction
      };

The function `RecombinationPlot` is useful for identifying the actual recombined elements of a chromosome population. Further examples will be given in Section 4.3.4.

4.3.3 Multirecombination in Evolvica

Here we will summarize our experiences with local and global ES recombinations by defining a function `Recombination [chromo-Pop_pop]` as outlined in Programs 4.11 and 4.12. This recombination operator, just like the mutation operator defined in Program 4.3, works on a population of ES chromosomes; that is, expressions of the form `pop[__chromo]`. As with this function we can specify different recombination schemes and recombination mappings for the object and strategy parameters, but the resulting code becomes a little longer. The section marked by `(* Recombine object parameters *)` is simply repeated in the omitted program section on the strategy parameters, which is omitted here and marked by "...".

Treating object and strategy parameters separately implies that four options are needed in order to specify the recombination functions and the number of recombination partners (see the program section marked by `(* Collect recombination options *)`). The options control the recombination schemes in the following way:

❑ `RecombinationRange`: Global or local recombination. Accepted arguments are `LOCAL` or `GLOBAL`.

❑ `RecombinationPartners`: The number of recombination partners (for local recombination) or the number of parameters to recombine (for global recombination).

Options for the recombination function

Program 4.11
ES recombination.

```
Recombination[chromoPop_pop,opts___] :=

Module[{objects,newObjects,strategies,newStrategies,
        rpo,rps,rfo,rfs,r,io,is},

  (* Collect recombination options *)
  rpo = RecombinationPartners[OBJECTS] /. {opts}
        /. Options[Recombination];
  rps = RecombinationPartners[STRATEGIES] /. {opts}
        /. Options[Recombination];
  rfo = RecombinationFunction[OBJECTS] /. {opts}
        /. Options[Recombination];
  rfs = RecombinationFunction[STRATEGIES] /. {opts}
        /. Options[Recombination];

  (* Extract object and strategy parameters *)
  objects = Map[List @@ #[[2]]&,List @@ chromoPop];
  strategies = Map[List @@ #[[3]]&,List @@ chromoPop];

  (* Recombine object parameters *)
  Switch[RecombinationRange[OBJECTS]
        /. {opts} /. Options[Recombination],
    LOCAL,
      newObjects =
      ({r,io} = randomSelectMultiple[objects,rpo,
                  ReturnIndices → True];
       Recombine[r, Sequence @@
         Join[{opts},{RecombinationFunction → rfo}]]),
    GLOBAL,
      newObjects =
      ({r,io} = Transpose[Map[
       randomSelectMultiple[#,rpo,
         ReturnIndices → True]&,Transpose[objects]]];
       Recombine[r//Transpose, Sequence @@
         Join[{opts},{RecombinationFunction → rfo}]]);
  ];

  (* Recombine strategy parameters *)
  ...

{chromo[q[undef], p @@ newObjects, s @@ newStrategies],
 io//Sort,is//Sort}
]
```

❑ RecombinationFunction: The predefined recombination functions are DISCRETE and INTERMEDIATE (Program 4.9); however, any other recombination function can be used as well, as long as this function is able to cope with a list of parameters.

❑ RecombineTogether → True means that the indices used for the selection of recombination elements among the object parameters will also be used for the strategy parameters. This setting allows a stronger connection of the corresponding object and strategy parameters. With RecombineTogether → False the selections among the object and strategy parameters are performed independently.

Further details about the Recombination function are in the Evolvica notebook on the *IEC* Web page (see Preface). In the following section we will discuss a few examples of how to use this function for investigating ES recombination schemes.

```
Options[Recombination] =
{
 RecombinationRange[OBJECTS] → LOCAL (* or: GLOBAL *),
 RecombinationRange[STRATEGIES] → LOCAL,
 RecombinationPartners[OBJECTS] → 2,
 RecombinationPartners[STRATEGIES] → 2,
 RecombinationFunction[OBJECTS] → DISCRETE,
 RecombinationFunction[STRATEGIES] → INTERMEDIATE,
 RecombineTogether → True
};
```

Program 4.12
Options and default settings for the ES recombination function.

4.3.4 Examples of ES recombinations

The following examples demonstrate ES recombinations and their different schemes—local and global, both with object and strategy parameters combined and independent.

Local, binary ES recombination

We first generate a population of two ES chromosomes with five-element parameter vectors. Since we are not interested in any evaluation of the chromosomes here, the fitness values (q[...]) are set to *undefined*.

Two random ES
chromosomes

In[1] := **chromoPop =**
        createChromosomes[2, ChromosomeWidth → 5]

Out[1] =pop[
        chromo[q[undef],
          p[9.12204, 8.78884, 1.02017, 0.906011, 8.397],
          s[0.69252, 0.80382, 0.57489, 0.71814,
          0.66646]],
        chromo[q[undef],
          p[-7.46121, 7.52696, -3.89555, 5.49098,
          0.195431],
          s[0.79763, 0.96415, 0.61788, 0.040591, 0.31263]]
        ]

We test the option default settings of the recombination function
Recombination: local recombination for two recombination partners, where the object parameters are recombined in a discrete manner and the strategy parameter recombination mapping is set to
intermediate.

Default recombination
settings

In[2] := **Options[Recombination]**

Out[2] ={RecombinationRange[OBJECTS] → LOCAL,
        RecombinationRange[STRATEGIES] → LOCAL,
        RecombinationPartners[OBJECTS] → 2,
        RecombinationPartners[STRATEGIES] → 2,
        RecombinationFunction[OBJECTS] →
                              (randomSelect[#1] &),
        RecombinationFunction[STRATEGIES] →
                              (N[Mean[#1]] &)}

Applying the Recombination function without specifying any
options returns an ES chromosome and some additional information,
as the following example shows:

ES chromosome
recombination

In[3] := **{chromoRecomb,objIndices,strIndices} =**
        Recombination[chromoPop]

Out[3] ={chromo[q[undef],
          p[-7.46121, 8.78884, 1.02017, 5.49098,
          0.195431],
          s[0.745075, 0.883985, 0.59639, 0.379366,
          0.48955]],
        {1, 2},
        {1, 2}}

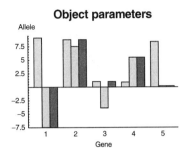
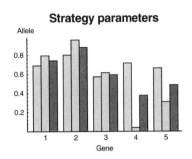

Figure 4.18
Recombination of two ES chromosomes.

The function `Recombination` also provides information about the chromosomes that have been combined; namely, the indices of the selected chromosomes for the object and strategy parameters, respectively. The symbol `chromoRecomb` is assigned the recombined chromosome, `objIndices` contains the chromosome indices for the object parameters, and `strIndices` lists the indices for the strategy parameters. These indices are needed for plotting the recombination diagram, which we omit here because we have only two chromosomes. Figure 4.18 gives a graphical illustration of the effect of this recombination. For the object parameters one of the two elements is chosen, whereas the strategy parameters are recombined by calculating their means. The diagrams of Figure 4.18 are attained with the following command:

```
In[4] := showChromosomes[{chromoPop[[1]],chromoPop[[2]],
            chromoRecomb}];
```

Within each group of bars, the first and second bars represent the respective values of the first and second chromosome. The last bar of each group is the recombination result.

Local multirecombination: discrete, intermediate, combined

Now we extend recombination to more than two ES chromosomes. We generate a population of five chromosomes, each of which contains three object and strategy parameters.

```
In[1] := chromoPop =
            createChromosomes[5, ChromosomeWidth → 3]
```

Five random ES chromosomes

```
Out[1] = pop[
            chromo[q[undef],
              p[-2.79813, 0.654928, 6.53727],
```

```
              s[0.135054, 0.123959, 0.481591]],
        chromo[q[undef],
          p[6.37728, 1.45262, -7.1102],
          s[0.413348, 0.279854, 0.206186]],
        chromo[q[undef],
          p[-4.24284, -6.27247, 2.64887],
          s[0.946638, 0.351695, 0.327861]],
        chromo[q[undef],
          p[-8.84515, 0.541711, -5.10138],
          s[0.559584, 0.564824, 0.511527]],
        chromo[q[undef],
          p[0.687754, -1.48366, 3.47803],
          s[0.859911, 0.226611, 0.487706]]]
```

This chromosome population is depicted in Figure 4.19. Bars with equal gray levels belong to the same chromosome; that is, each group of bars displays the set of corresponding chromosome (column) entries.

Among these five chromosomes three should be selected for recombination. The object parameters are recombined in a discrete manner, whereas the strategy parameters recombine intermediately.

In[2] := **{chromoRecomb, objInds, strInds} =**
          Recombination[chromoPop,
            RecombinationPartners[OBJECTS] → **3,**
            RecombinationPartners[STRATEGIES] → **3]**

Out[2] = {chromo[q[undef],
            p[6.37728, 0.541711, 3.47803],
            s[0.610947, 0.357096, 0.401806]],
          {2, 4, 5},
          {2, 4, 5}}

Figure 4.19
An ES chromosome set for recombination.

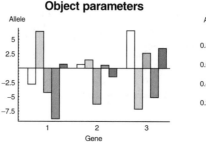

Object parameters

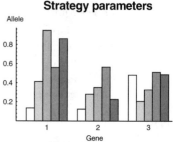

Strategy parameters

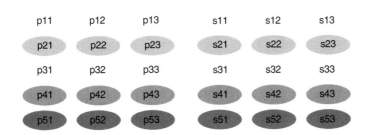

Figure 4.20
Recombination diagram for
ES recombination (*In[2]*).

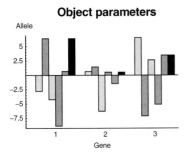 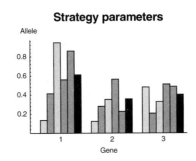

Figure 4.21
Results of local ES
recombination.

We generate a recombination diagram to get a better idea of which chromosomes are combined:

```
In[3] := showRecombination[
            Join[List @@ chromoPop,{chromoRecomb}],
            objInds, strInds];
```

The recombination diagram (Figure 4.20) shows that chromosomes 2, 4, and 5 were selected (see objInds, strInds). Compare the parameter lists with the chromosome entries and the index lists in the second output line. In addition, the graphical representation in Figure 4.21 informs us what kind of recombination was performed per element. Note that in this diagram all population members are listed, not only the recombination partners.

In the following sections we will extend the scope of the multirecombination from a local to a global context.

Global multirecombination

Again we start from the ES population in Figure 4.19. Up to now the recombination operator range was kept local; that is, the collection of recombination partners remained fixed for all parameters. In the

Figure 4.22

Recombination diagram for global ES recombination.

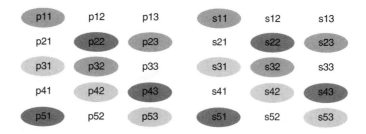

following example we let the recombination operator work globally on the whole population, both for the object and strategy parameters:

```
In[4] := {chromoRecomb, objInds, strInds} =
    Recombination[chromoPop,
        RecombinationPartners[OBJECTS] → 3,
        RecombinationPartners[STRATEGIES] → 3,
        RecombinationRange[OBJECTS] → GLOBAL,
        RecombinationRange[STRATEGIES] → GLOBAL]

Out[4] = {chromo[q[undef],
        p[-4.24284, 0.541711, -5.10138],
        s[0.647201, 0.398791, 0.401806]],
        {{3, 1, 5}, {4, 3, 2}, {5, 2, 4}},
        {{3, 1, 5}, {4, 3, 2}, {5, 2, 4}}}
```

Recombination in a global context means that the selection of recombination partners starts anew for each parameter, as Figure 4.22 illustrates. In each column different sets of elements are selected.

Since the default setting for a correlated treatment of object and strategy parameters is `RecombineTogether → True`, the selected indices for both groups of parameters are identical.

Figure 4.23 reveals the actual recombinations resulting from three out of five recombination partners. The last columns represent the resulting recombined parameter.

Multiple global and local recombination

Finally, we show an example where object and strategy parameters are not correlated in their recombination schemes; that is, they differ not only in their recombination functions but also perform on different recombination ranges with different selection schemes.

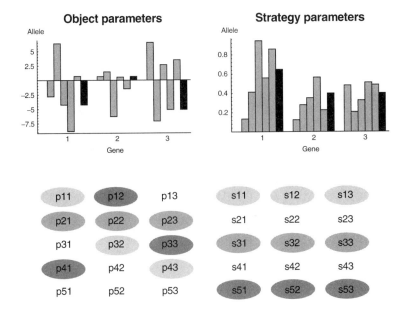

Figure 4.23
Results of global ES
recombination.

Figure 4.24
Recombination diagram:
global recombination of the
object parameters, local
recombination of the
strategy parameters.

Again we use the population in Figure 4.19 as our starting point. The object parameters will be recombined globally; the strategy parameters have a restricted local range of recombination. Whenever the recombination contexts differ, the correlation of the object and strategy recombination schemes are automatically reset to `RecombineTogether → False`.

```
In[5] := {chromoRecomb, objInds, strInds} =
         Recombination[chromoPop,
            RecombinationPartners[OBJECTS] → 3,
            RecombinationPartners[STRATEGIES] → 3,
            RecombinationRange[OBJECTS] → GLOBAL,
            RecombinationRange[STRATEGIES] → LOCAL]

Out[5] = {chromo[q[undef],
            p[-2.79813, 0.541711, -5.10138],
            s[0.647201, 0.234088, 0.432386]],
          {{1, 2, 4}, {3, 2, 1}, {4, 2, 3}},
          {1, 3, 5}}
```

Figure 4.24 schematically depicts the selected elements to be recombined. Among the object parameters the selection is performed independently for each column. For the strategy parameters elements

Figure 4.25
Local and global ES
recombination.

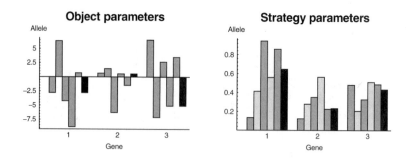

of the first, third, and fifth chromosome are locally recombined. The actual results of these recombinations are illustrated in Figure 4.25.

More examples of ES recombination variants are given in the Evolvica notebooks related to this section, which are available on the *IEC* Web page (see Preface).

4.4   Selection and reproduction schemes

In the previous sections, we presented ES operators working on vectors of numbers. We now know how to represent ES chromosomes and how to modify them by mutations and recombinations. In this section, we discuss how different evolution-based optimization algorithms can be formulated on the basis of a range of selection schemes. In order to illustrate the algorithms used for ES optimization we use a graphical notation following Rechenberg 1978 and 1994b (Figure 4.26). In Section 4.4.1, the so-called plus and comma strategies are discussed for the special case of a single parent individual. The general ES variants with several parent individuals are discussed in Section 4.4.2. Besides mutation, recombinations will be included in the ES scheme in Section 4.4.3. An extended formal notation for evolution strategies is suggested in Section 4.4.4.

4.4.1 $(1 + \lambda)$ and $(1, \lambda)$ evolution strategies

In order to illustrate different variants of evolution strategies, Rechenberg developed a graphical notation, the symbols of which resemble card games (Rechenberg 1973; Rechenberg 1978). Each ES chromosome is depicted as a card, on which the object and strategy parameters are written (Figure 4.26). An additional, zigzag-shape symbol distinguishes the phenotype, the interpreted ES chromosome, from the genotype. The card notation also contains representations for popula-

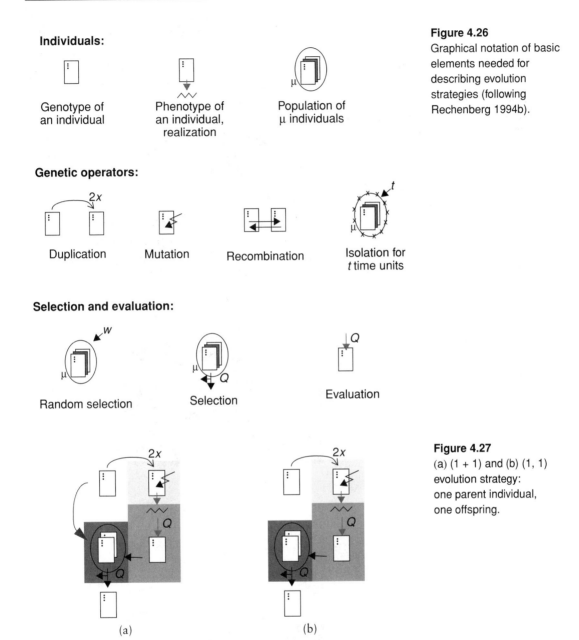

Individuals:

Genotype of an individual

Phenotype of an individual, realization

Population of μ individuals

Figure 4.26
Graphical notation of basic elements needed for describing evolution strategies (following Rechenberg 1994b).

Genetic operators:

2x

Duplication

Mutation

Recombination

Isolation for t time units

Selection and evaluation:

w

Random selection

Selection

Q

Evaluation

Figure 4.27
(a) (1 + 1) and (b) (1, 1) evolution strategy: one parent individual, one offspring.

(a)   (b)

tions and genetic operators, such as mutations and recombinations, as well as for the selection and evaluation of individuals.

The simplest and original ES scheme is known as a (1 + 1) evolution strategy. Starting from a single parent, an offspring individual is generated in the following way (Figure 4.27[a]). The evaluated parent individual, attributed with a fitness value, is duplicated. The mutation

One parent, one offspring

operator modifies the parameter settings of this copy, according to one of the mutation operators discussed in Section 4.2. The offspring's fitness is calculated. Among the parent and the newly generated individual, the best evaluated is designated the parent for the next generation.

Plus strategy: one parent individual λ offspring, selection among parents and offspring

A first generalization extends a (1 + 1) strategy to a strategy with more than a single offspring. Unlike genetic algorithms, evolution strategies work with a surplus of offspring. Therefore, the (1 + 1) strategy becomes a (1 + λ) strategy (Figure 4.28[a]). Here the parent individual is copied λ times, and again the duplicates are mutated and evaluated. Finally, the best exemplar is selected from the set of offspring and parent individuals.

Comma strategy: one parent individual, λ offspring, selection among the offspring

In the so-called (1, λ) evolution strategy the parent is excluded from the selection set for the following generation (Figure 4.28[b]). This means that any individual "lives" for only one generation. With (1 + λ) strategies it is possible for a parent individual with a relatively

Figure 4.28
(1 + λ) and (1, λ) evolution strategy: one parent individual, λ offspring.
(a) (1 + λ) ES. (b) (1, λ) ES.

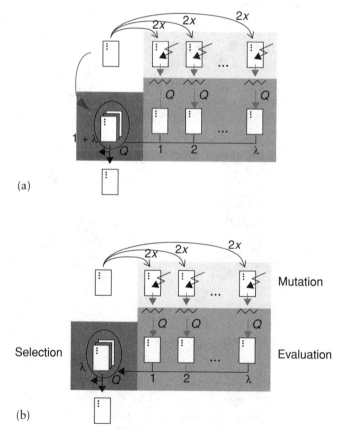

high fitness to survive for many generations. Consequently, this outstanding individual is passed on from generation to generation, and the evolution process converges. This does not occur with $(1, \lambda)$ strategies, because the parent is not part of the selection pool. The selection is performed only among the λ mutated offspring.

The variant $(1, 1)$ ES, mentioned for the sake of completeness, implements a random search rather than any optimization algorithm controlled by selection (Figure 4.27 [b]). Each individual survives for only a single generation. Regardless of possible decreased fitness, the mutated offspring determines the next point in the search space. Selection has no influence on the progress of the optimization, and so an optimization does not occur. In Section 1.3.2, we denoted a similar strategy as single-step selection.

4.4.2 $(\mu + \lambda)$ and (μ, λ) evolution strategies

Extending the parent population from a single parent to μ individuals results in $(\mu + \lambda)$ and (μ, λ) evolution strategies (Figure 4.29). In a set of μ individuals, λ exemplars are duplicated, mutated, and must pass the selection process, from which only the μ best individuals survive.

The algebraic notation of a $(\mu + \lambda)$ evolution strategy is explained as follows: μ denotes the number of parents and λ the number of offspring. The + sign means that the selection pool contains $\mu + \lambda$ individuals, both the μ parents and the λ offspring. For (μ, λ) strategies, the selection is performed exclusively on the λ descendants.

μ parents, λ offspring

It is particularly noteworthy that all individuals have the same chance of being selected for duplication and mutation. This is one of the major differences between evolution strategies and genetic algorithms, where the individuals' fitnesses determine their selection probabilities. Genetic algorithms usually perform fitness-proportionate

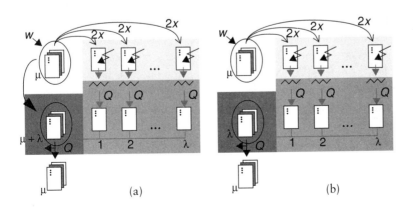

(a)   (b)

Figure 4.29
$(\mu + \lambda)$ and (μ, λ) evolution strategies.

selection, whereas evolution strategies perform best selection: from the selection pool of $\mu + \lambda$ or λ individuals, only the best μ are chosen. A precondition is that there are always enough individuals available to choose from; that is, $\lambda \geq \mu$.

Up to now the evolution schemes used only mutations for generating offspring variants, but no mixing of genes was performed. The following section shows an ES variant with recombination operators.

4.4.3 $(\mu/\rho, \lambda)$ ES: evolution strategies with recombinations

Recombination on subpopulations

Figure 4.30 shows a $(\mu/2, \lambda)$ ES extended by a binary recombination operator. The quotient notation μ/ρ denotes selection of a subpopulation of ρ individuals as recombination partners from a population of size μ. In the example in Figure 4.30, 2λ duplicates from randomly selected parent individuals are generated. Two each of these individuals are recombined, resulting in a set of λ individuals, which are subsequently mutated. In general, for a $(\mu/\rho, \lambda)$ strategy from a set of $\rho \cdot \lambda$ ES chromosomes, ρ each are combined into λ new chromosomes. Evaluation and selection are performed as usual. From the set of λ individuals the best μ are selected and constitute the initial population for the next generation.

Of course, there is also a plus strategy variant, the $(\mu/\rho + \lambda)$ ES, where the μ best individuals are selected among the μ parents and λ offspring.

4.4.4 Notes about the ES notation

The ES notation introduced in Sections 4.4.1–4.4.3 allows for a compact formulation of a range of evolution schemes. We also use this notation for genetic algorithms (Chapter 3), evolutionary programming (Chapter 6), and genetic programming (Chapter 7). Here we discuss a few extensions of this notation, which will easily lead us to meta-evolution strategies in Section 4.5. Once more we follow the "universal nomenclature for evolution strategies" (Rechenberg 1994b, pp. 92–100), with a few extensions necessary to describe evolution processes in more detail. The notation we have used up to now has the following form:

Extended ES notation

$$\left(\mu_0/\rho_0 \; {+\atop ,} \; \lambda_0 \right)^{\gamma_0} \text{ES.}$$

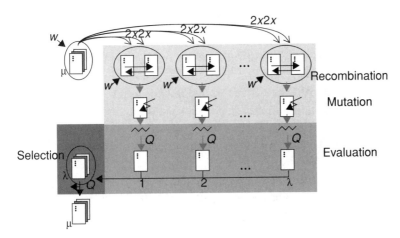

Figure 4.30
$(\mu/2, \lambda)$ evolution strategy
with recombination.

Here the following terms are used:

μ_0: number of parents;
ρ_0: size of the recombination pools;
λ_0: number of offspring;
γ_0: number of generations.

In the exponent we have added the number of generations, γ_0, for which the recombination, mutation, evaluation, and selection loop is performed.

Another disadvantage of the original ES notation is that it reveals information about operators and selection methods but does not describe which kinds of mutations and recombinations are used. This is why we will use formulas of the following form to describe ES evolution experiments, as well as evolution experiments in general:

$$\left(\mu_0/\rho_0 \ ^{+}_{,} \ \lambda_0 \ \| \ \Omega_0 \right)^{\gamma_0} \text{ES.}$$

Extended ES notation with rules list

Ω_0 denotes a list of rules for specifying operators and further parameter settings controlling an evolution run. For intermediate, global recombination (R) and mutative step size adaptation (MSA) à la Hoffmeister and Bäck (Section 4.2.2), we have the following rules:

$$\Omega_0 = \left(R \to \text{Mean}, \text{MSA} \to e^{N_0(\Delta\sigma)} \right).$$

Using replacement rules is very similar to Mathematica's way of specifying optional arguments. The evolution strategy algorithms presented in Sections 4.6 and 4.7 use exactly this idea for setting optional parameters and passing arguments to the ES functions.

4.5   Meta-evolution strategies and the island model

Evolutionary algorithms take advantage of the inherent parallelism in populations searching for optimal regions in phenotypical space. For many practical relevant optimization problems, it turns out that the generally unknown "highest viewpoint" is often not reached using only a single population. Usually this is due to an unfavorable initial location of the population. So why not send several populations on an independent search for optimal regions, each starting from different areas within the search space? Therefore, we discuss a meta-ES variant in which individuals are represented by subpopulations and evolution occurs on two levels—an individual and a populational level. We can describe parallel evolution of λ_1 populations with the following notation:

λ_1 independent ES experiments

$$\lambda_1 \left(\mu_0 / \rho_0 \ \overset{+}{,} \ \lambda_0 \parallel \Omega_0 \right)^{\gamma_0} \text{ES.}$$

Each population independently performs a $(\mu_0 / \rho_0 \ \overset{+}{,} \ \lambda_0 \parallel \Omega_0)$ evolution strategy over γ_0 generations.

In general, after γ_0 generations each of the λ_1 populations will have evolved into different regions of the search space. Some may already be farther ahead uphill, while others may have just started their climb to higher regions in their vicinity. At the end of each single meta-evolution run we find populations that can be evaluated and compared to one another with regard to their individuals' fitnesses. A population's fitness can be either the mean fitness or the evaluation of its best individual. Hence, each population can be attributed with a fitness value, and if we consider populations as meta-individuals, we can use one of the selection schemes introduced in the previous section.

Subpopulations as meta-individuals

We select the best population and continue in the following way. From this new initial (meta-parent) population we generate λ_1 mutated populations, which again evolve independently for another γ_0 generations according to a $(\mu_0 / \rho_0 \ \overset{+}{,} \ \lambda_0 \parallel \Omega_0)$ strategy. This procedure describes a meta-evolution; that is, an evolution on two levels—an inner evolution loop on the level of individuals and an outer loop on the populational level. Figure 4.31 depicts an example of such a $(\mu_1, \lambda_1 (\mu_0, \lambda_0)^{\gamma_0})$ (meta-)evolution strategy.

We may consider the ES notation as an arithmetic formula. The extended general notation for a (meta-)evolution strategy with subpopulations looks as follows:

$$\left(\mu_1/\rho_1 \overset{+}{,} \lambda_1\left(\mu_0/\rho_0 \overset{+}{,} \lambda_0 \| \Omega_0\right)^{\gamma_0} \| \Omega_1\right)^{\gamma_1} \text{ ES.}$$

Meta-evolution strategy

What kind of evolution strategy does this expression describe? We interpret from the outer to the inner brackets: initially μ_1 populations of size μ_0 are generated, where we should ensure that the "population centers" are distinct, such that each population will start its evolution in another region of the search space. A random set of $\rho_1 \cdot \lambda_1$ population duplicates is generated from the population pool, ρ_1, each of which is recombined (e.g., by interchanging individuals).

The result is λ_1 populations of size μ_0, each of which represents the initial population for a $(\mu_0/\rho_0 \overset{+}{,} \lambda_0 \| \Omega_0)$ evolution strategy. Performing the ES strategies independently over γ_0 generations is the

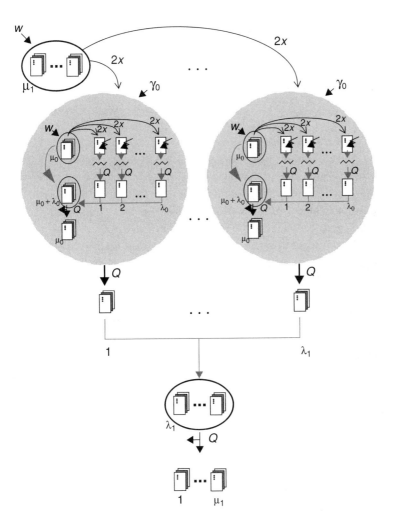

Figure 4.31
Meta-evolution strategy with subpopulations.

meta-mutation operator. Finally, the fitnesses of the resulting populations are calculated and the μ_1 best populations from the population pool of λ_1 mutated (evolved) populations or from $\mu_1 + \lambda_1$ mutant and parent populations are selected, depending on whether a comma or plus meta-strategy is performed. This meta-evolution scheme is repeated for γ_1 generations. In the end, there is a best population, which hopefully discovered a global optimum.

Population islands

Meta-evolution schemes resemble the evolution of natural populations isolated from one another for a certain period. Usually we think of separated population islands evolving independently, their populations rarely getting the chance to exchange genetic information.

Meta^n ES

Mathematically, these meta^0 and meta^1 evolution strategies can be extended to meta^n strategies, since the ES notation allows for the addition of even more evolution levels:

$$\left(\mu_n / \rho_n \overset{+}{,} \lambda_n \left(\cdots \left(\mu_1 / \rho_1 \overset{+}{,} \lambda_1 \left(\mu_0 / \rho_0 \overset{+}{,} \lambda_0 \parallel \Omega_0 \right)^{\gamma_0} \parallel \Omega_1 \right)^{\gamma_1} \cdots \right)^{\gamma_{n-1}} \cdots \right)^{\gamma_n} \text{ES}.$$

So far, no detailed investigations have been done on whether more than two levels of evolution are advantageous for practical applications in the context of optimization. Most of the time it is sufficient to keep with traditional meta^0 strategies or to use meta^1 strategies for climbing the "mountain of mountains." A few rudimentary theoreti-

Climbing meta-mountains

cal results are known about climbing up "meta-mountains" and "meta-meta-mountains" (Rechenberg 1994b, pp. 158 ff.). But the evolutionary algorithm community has yet to understand what consequences and benefits can be gained from hierarchical evolutionary optimization techniques (Mühlenbein and Schlierkamp-Voosen 1993; Mühlenbein and Schlierkamp-Voosen 1994).

4.6   Evolution strategies with Evolvica

In previous sections we have described ES operators of mutation and recombination and their Evolvica implementations. Next we will show how these operators are integrated in different ES evolution schemes through Evolvica algorithms. Section 4.7 will demonstrate with examples how to use these ES functions.

Let us first focus on traditional evolution strategies, which we denoted as meta^0 ES. Our objective is to also apply ES notation to the implemented functions. Therefore, evolution strategies of the form

$$\lambda_1 \left(\mu_0 / \rho_0 \overset{+}{,} \lambda_0 \| \Omega_0 \right)^{\gamma_0}$$

will be described in Evolvica notation as follows:

$$\lambda_1 \text{ ES}[\mu_0, \ \rho_0, \ \text{PLUS}, \ \lambda_0, \ \gamma_0, \ \Omega_0] \qquad\qquad \textit{Plus ES}$$

for a plus strategy and

$$\lambda_1 \text{ ES}[\mu_0, \ \rho_0, \ \text{COMMA}, \ \lambda_0, \ \gamma_0, \ \Omega_0] \qquad\qquad \textit{Comma ES}$$

for a comma strategy.

4.6.1 The evolution control function

Programs 4.13 and 4.14 show how to implement ES evolution schemes. Here Ω_0 (opts___) represents the set of replacement rules, which, among other parameters, specify the operators to be used or the problem-specific evaluation function. The function Evolution[...] implements λ_1 independent $(\mu_0/\rho_0 \overset{+}{,} \lambda_0 \| \Omega_0)$ ES experiments, each over γ_0 generations.

Starting a plus strategy would work as follows:

Evolution$[\lambda_1$ ES$[\mu_0, \ \rho_0, \ \text{PLUS}, \ \lambda_0, \ \gamma_0, \ \Omega_0]]$.   *Plus ES evolution*

Analogously, an evolution experiment using comma strategies is initiated by the function call

Evolution$[\lambda_1$ ES$[\mu_0, \ \rho_0, \ \text{COMMA}, \ \lambda_0, \ \gamma_0, \ \Omega_0]]$.   *Comma ES evolution*

The first part of the ES implementation in Program 4.13 shows   *Setting the initial population*
the structure of the expressions, which can be passed as arguments to the function Evolution, and lists the routines for generating the initial population. With the default settings, the initial population for each of the independent ES runs is created anew by the function createChromosomes (Program 4.1). By using the option InitialPopulation $\rightarrow$ initPop, an initial population can be explicitly set such that all λ_1 ES evolution runs start from a particular population *initPop*.

The actual evolution loop is listed in Program 4.14. The iterations   *Evolution loop*
over the generations are implemented by NestList, where the parents result from the selection of the previous generation. The offspring are generated by possible recombinations and mutations, and finally selection is performed, depending on the chosen strategy, among the pool of parents and offspring or the offspring alone.

Program 4.13
Algorithm for ($\mu/\rho + \lambda$) and
($\mu/\rho, \lambda$) evolution strategies
(Part 1).

```
Evolution[ ES[m_?IntegerQ,  (* m parents *)
                r_?IntegerQ,  (* r recombinations *)
                s_?AtomQ,     (* PLUS or COMMA *)
                l_?IntegerQ,  (* children *)
                g_?IntegerQ,  (* generations *)
                opts___]      (* options *)
           i_:1               (* independent runs *)
] :=
Module[{initialParents,evalFct,parents,children,
selPool},

  (* Generate m initial individuals *)
  If[(initialParents = (InitialPopulation /. {opts}
      /. Options[EvolutionStrategy])) === {},
    initialParents = createChromosomes[m,
      ChromosomeWidth → (ChromosomeWidth /. {opts}
        /. Options[EvolutionStrategy]),opts]];

  (* Get the evaluation function *)
  evalFct = EvaluationFunction /. {opts}
            /. Options[EvolutionStrategy];

  (* Evaluate initial individuals *)
  initialParents =
    Map[Evaluation[#,EvaluationFunction :>
      evalFct]&,
      initialParents];
```

Selection modes

For best and random selection, the function Selection of Program 4.15 is used. The option SelectionMode determines whether the howMany elements are chosen at random (RANDOM) or according to their fitnesses (BEST). For random selection an individual can be chosen more than once, which is necessary in case the number of offspring exceeds the number of parents. For selecting the best μ_0 elements, the individuals are sorted by increasing fitness and the last μ_0 elements are extracted.

Central control

The function Evolution accepts all optional arguments defined for the functions createChromosomes, Mutation, Recombination, and Selection. Hence with the arguments of the Evolution function, all the other functions for generating ES chromosomes, for mutation, for recombination, and for selection are controlled.

```
    (* Iterate for i independent runs *)
    Table[
      (* Iterate for g generations *)
    NestList[
      (parents = #;
       children =
         Map[Evaluation[#,EvaluationFunction :>
         evalFct]&,
           Map[Mutation[#,opts]&,
             Map[First[Recombination[#,
               RecombinationPartners[OBJECTS] → r,
               RecombinationPartners[STRATEGIES] → r,
               opts]]&,
               Partition[Selection[parents,r*l,
                 SelectionMode → RANDOM],r]]]];
      selPool =
        Switch[s,
          PLUS, Join[parents,children],
          COMMA, children
        ];
      Selection[selPool,m,SelectionMode → BEST]
      ) &,
      initialParents,
      g
    ], (* end nesting *)

  {i} (* independent runs *)
  ]
]
```

Program 4.14
Algorithm for $(\mu/\rho + \lambda)$ and $(\mu/\rho, \lambda)$ evolution strategies (Part 2).

4.6.2   A sample ES evolution experiment

We conclude this section with a simple example, which can also be found in the Evolvica notebooks corresponding to this chapter (see the *IEC* Web page mentioned in the Preface). In Section 4.2, we explained mutation by observing an ES population climbing uphill by iterated mutation and best selection. The evolution depicted in Figures 4.3 and 4.4 is generated as a $(1 + 5)$ evolution strategy over 15 generations. We briefly show how similar evolution experiments can be performed with the ES functions presented so far.

Program 4.15
Best and
random selection.

```
Selection[population_pop,howMany_Integer:1,opts___]
:= Module[{},
   Switch[SelectionMode /. {opts} /.
   Options[Selection],
     BEST,
       Take[population // Sort, -howMany],
     RANDOM,
       pop @@ Table[
         population[[
           Random[Integer,{1,Length[population]}]]],
         {howMany}]
   ]
]

Options[Selection] =
{
   SelectionMode → BEST (* or RANDOM *)
};
```

For this purpose we first define a function `newChromos`, which allows us to place the parent individual—and consequently also the offspring individuals—at a specific location within the parameter search space:

Placing individuals at specific locations

In[1] := **SingleParent:=**
           createChromosomes[1,ChromosomeWidth → 2,
             ParameterRange → {{8,8},{-8,-8}},
             StepSizeRange → {{0,2}}
           ]

The object parameters of the parent are set to +8 for the x coordinate and to −8 for the y coordinate. Each sublist in `ParameterRange` specifies the range for the respective parameter. The following function call initiates a $(1 + 5)$ evolution strategy over 15 generations:

Starting a (1 + 5) ES

In[2] := **gens = 15;**
           levelZeroES =
           Evolution[
             ES[1,1,PLUS,5,gens,
               ChromosomeWidth → 2,
               ParameterRange → {{-10,10}},
               StepSizeRange → {{0,1}},
               EvaluationFunction :> (f[# /. {p[x__] :>
               {x}}]&),

```
                InitialPopulation  →  SingleParent
            ]
        ];
```

The range of the object parameters is restricted to the interval [–10, 10] (option `ParameterRange`). The strategy parameter values must be in the range between 0 and 1 (option `StepSizeRange`). The initial population `newChromos` consists of a single parent individual. The evaluation function is described in Program 4.16. The replacement rule (`p[x__] :> {x}`) for the arguments of `Evaluation-Function` is necessary because the object parameters are represented as `p[...]` expressions in the ES chromosome, whereas the evaluation function `f[v_List]` of Program 4.16 is defined for vectors or lists.

```
    f[v_List] := -Sqrt[Plus @@ Map[#^2&,v]]
```

Program 4.16
Example of an evaluation function.

Graphical representations of evolution runs are generated with the function `subPopulationPlot`:

```
In[3] := parentAndMutants =
            Transpose[Map[Take[#,gens]&,levelZeroES]];

In[4] := Map[
            subPopulationPlot[#,
                PointsHeight  →  1,
                ColorFunction  →  GrayLevel,
                Colors  →  {0.9,0}]&,
            parentAndMutants
        ];
```

Normally, the function `subPopulationPlot` is used to display the individuals of independent subpopulations as points of different colors. In this example the parent individual and its mutants are considered as two separate populations, so that both classes of individuals are distinguishable by their colors. In order to make the points completely visible, their `PointsHeight` can be set to make them "float" above the fitness mountains. Whether the individuals are displayed in color or gray is set by the `ColorFunction` rule (`Hue` or `Gray-Level`). Each subpopulation may also have its own color setting (`Colors`).

Graphical output

4.7   Evolution strategies at work

This section illustrates the different variants of evolution strategies through the example of a parameter optimization problem—searching for the highest points in a two-dimensional function space. We show how a set of ES populations finds local and global maxima and how using meta-evolution strategies with subpopulations turns out to be very successful in searching for global optima. Finally, we demonstrate that independent ES populations are able to find several maxima in parallel.

4.7.1   Optimization of multimodal functions

For estimating the efficiency of optimization algorithms, so-called multimodal test functions are used. Multimodal functions are usually multidimensional functions, which, like a mountainous region in nature, show many peaks and valleys. In the context of function theory *multimodality* means that a function possesses not only one or several global maxima but also a large number of local maxima (see Section 2.3.1 and Figure 2.6).

Search strategies for multimodal functions

   It is these local maxima that pose problems for optimization algorithms if they attempt to ascend any ridge independent of its actual height. If the algorithm has climbed the global mountaintop, everything is fine, and the optimization procedure has succeeded in its job. But generally the global maximum of an optimization problem is not known in advance. If it were, a problem would not exist anymore. In most cases, it is even unknown whether *the* global optimum exists. This means that optimization techniques should be used that guarantee—at least to a certain extent—that as many high peaks as possible are discovered and that the algorithm is not distracted by searching regions of suboptimal heights. Hence, the preferred optimization method must be able to simultaneously search many locations, forget unsuccessful search paths, and discover as many ridges as possible. The examples presented in this section will show that evolutionary algorithms and evolution strategies, in particular, meet these expectations for flexible, adaptive optimization.

4.7.2   Triple sinc—a multimodal test function

To demonstrate the dynamics of evolution strategies, we use the two-dimensional triple sinc function in Figure 4.32. This function shows

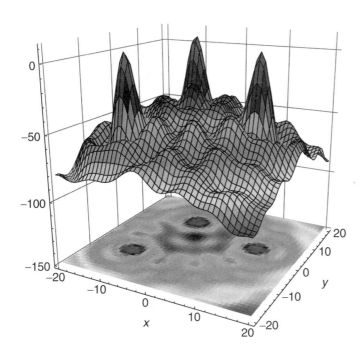

Figure 4.32
Triple sinc as a multimodal
test function.

the characteristic features of a multimodal test function. The search
space is "rugged" and has a large number of minor maxima; that is,
ridges and smaller peaks. Though three outstanding maxima are visible, namely, at coordinate locations (–11, –9), (–6, 9), and (11, 3), the
center peak at (–6, 9) is the global optimum.

This test function, which we denote as $f(x, y)$, is a combination of
three variants of the so-called sinc function, which we define as
follows:

$$g(x, y) \;=\; 50\frac{\sin\!\left(\sqrt{x^2 + y^2}\right)}{\sqrt{x^2 + y^2}} - \sqrt{x^2 + y^2}.$$ *Sinc function*

Figure 4.33(a) depicts the shape of this function, $g(x, y)$, which
has an obvious global maximum at coordinate (0, 0). An eventually
decreasing sine oscillation forms the symmetric relief of a parabolic
hill. Figure 4.32(b) shows a zoom of the central maximum.

We define the triple sinc test function as a linear combination of   *Objective function: triple sinc*
three sinc functions:

$$f(x, y) \;=\; g(x + 11, y + 9) + g(x - 11, y - 3) + g(x + 6, y - 9)$$

In the Evolvica implementation this test function is defined for more
than two dimensions, as Program 4.17 shows.

Figure 4.33
A variant of the
sinc function.

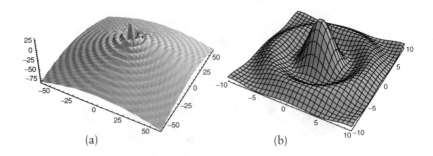

(a)   (b)

Program 4.17
Multimodal test functions *f*
and *g*.

```
g[v_List] := 50 Sin[Sqrt[Plus @@ Map[#^2&,v]]] /
                Sqrt[Plus @@ Map[#^2&,v]]
             - Sqrt[Plus @@ Map[#^2&,v]]

f[v_List] :=
  g[v + {11,9}] + g[v - {11,3}] + g[v + {6,-9}]
```

This function `f[v_List]` in its two-dimensional version will provide our test environment for different evolution strategies and meta-evolution strategies in the following sections. In discussing these examples we will try to answer the following questions:

❑ To what extent can ES populations discover local and global maxima through recombinations, mutations, and selection only?

❑ Does the application of meta-evolutions improve the search dynamics of the ES individuals?

❑ How can we climb all three peaks of the objective triple sinc function at once?

4.7.3 Three populations on their ways up

In the first example we show that ES populations are truly able to climb arbitrary hills, as we have already illustrated with ES mutation (Section 4.2). There is no guarantee, however, that the global maximum will be identified, although evolution strategies use an adaptive and inherently parallel search method.

We spread three populations with 10 individuals each within the test landscape (Figure 4.34[a]). Some of the individuals are situated on ridges or hills, while less-fit individuals find themselves in deeper valleys. Each of these populations evolves according to a $(10/2, 20)$ strategy over 10 generations. In ES nomenclature this means we perform a

$$3(10/2, 20)^{10} \text{ ES.}$$

Among the set of 10 parents, $40 = 2 \cdot 20$ randomly selected individuals are duplicated, from which two of each are recombined. After mutation and evaluation of the resulting offspring, the best 10 individuals are selected as parents for the successor generation. This evolution loop is performed over 10 generations for each of the three populations. In Evolvica the corresponding function call, initiating three independent evolution runs, is as follows:

```
In[1] := levelZeroES =
    Evolution[
      3 ES[10,2,COMMA,20,10,
        ChromosomeWidth → 2,
        ParameterRange → {-20,20},
        EvaluationFunction :>
          (f[# /. {p[x__] :> {x}}]&)]
    ]
```

Starting three ES experiments

The list `levelZeroES` consists of three sublists, one for each of the populations, each of which contains the parents of the respective generation. The graphics in Figure 4.34 are generated by applying the function `subPopulationPlot` as follows:

```
In[2] := Map[subPopulationPlot[#,
        PointsHeight → 1,
        ColorFunction → GrayLevel]&,
      levelZeroES // Transpose
    ];
```

Visualization of ES dynamics

The function `subPopulationPlot` expects a list of populations for each generation. This is why the resulting list of `levelZeroES` must be transposed. Further details on how to use this function are found in the Evolvica notebook on the *IEC* Web page (see Preface).

Let us take a closer look at the generation sequence in Figure 4.34 (see also Color Plate 3). After only one cycle of recombination, mutation, and best selection, the populations start gathering on higher regions (Gen. 1). This trend continues in the second generation (Figure 4.34[c]), shown in greater detail in Figure 4.34(d). All three populations concentrate their search efforts in the vicinity around the central peak. The effect of best selection becomes even more obvious

Three independent ES experiments

Figure 4.34
Evolution of three
independent populations
following a 3(10/2, 20)^{10} ES.

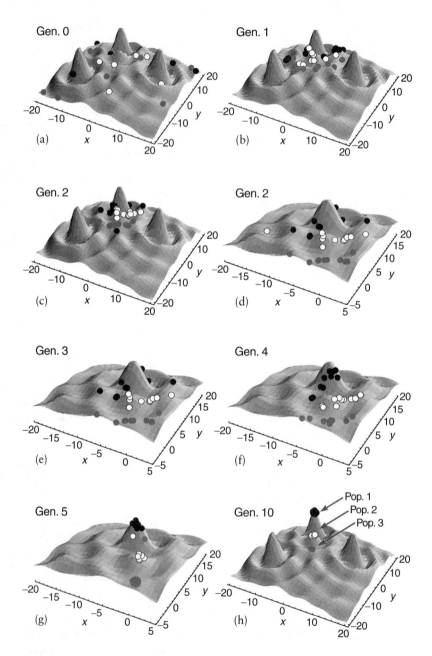

Gen. 0 (a)
Gen. 1 (b)
Gen. 2 (c)
Gen. 2 (d)
Gen. 3 (e)
Gen. 4 (f)
Gen. 5 (g)
Gen. 10 (h)
Pop. 1
Pop. 2
Pop. 3

in the course of the following generations. In generation 3, most of the individuals are located at higher regions (Figure 4.34[e]). Step by step, each population converges toward a local elevation (Figure 4.34[f], [g]), until after 10 generations, each population's individuals gather tightly together (Figure 4.34[h]), displaying local convergence.

4.7.4   Meta-evolution of three subpopulations

Three different maxima were found by the populations in Figure 4.34. One population even discovered the global optimum. But from generation 3 onward, it is obvious which path each single population will take. Population 3 (gray) would certainly be unable to climb the central peak and take the place of population 1 (black). Evaluating populations according to a meta-evolution (e.g., by calculating their mean fitnesses, selecting the best population, and generating further offspring populations), would definitely speed up and improve the optimization process. The following example shows that an acceleration effect is actually possible using a meta-evolution scheme with subpopulations. We perform a meta-evolution according to a

$$(3 + 3(10/2 + 5)^5)^5 \text{ ES.}$$

Meta-evolution experiment

As in Figure 4.34, we begin with three independent populations of 10 individuals each, which are randomly spread around the search area (Figure 4.35[a]). Three mutated copies of these three parent populations are generated. Here mutation on the level of populations simply means that the mutation operator is applied to the individuals. On each of the resulting three populations a (10/2 + 5) evolution strategy over five generations is performed, analogous to that in Figure 4.34.

After each (10/2 + 5) strategy evolution, the three most successful populations are selected from among the three evolved populations plus the three parent populations. The survivor populations are designated as the meta-parents for the next meta-generation. Population fitness is calculated as the mean fitness value of its individuals. Figure 4.35(b) depicts the new initial populations for the subsequent independent (10/2 + 5) ES runs. The described meta-evolution is initiated in Evolvica by the following function call:

```
In[1] := metaES =
    Evolution[
      ES[3,1,PLUS,
        3 ES[10,2,PLUS,5,5,
          ChromosomeWidth → 2,
          ParameterRange → {-20,20},
          EvaluationFunction :>
            (f[# /. {p[x__] :> {x}}]&)
        ],
      5
    ]
  ];
```

Starting a meta-evolution experiment

In Figure 4.35 only the best three populations are shown. Between each snapshot of a meta-population (the set of three subpopulations) three $(10/2 + 5)$ evolutions over five generations are performed. As each population gets the chance to evolve its individuals toward higher regions, promising ridges are discovered with higher probability. Already after two meta-generations, the search effort is concentrated to the two highest elevations (Figure 4.35[d]). Now competition for the highest location among the populations starts, which is finally identified in meta-generation 5 (Figure 4.35[g], [h]).

4.7.5   Ascent of all peaks

In this last optimization example, based on the test function in Figure 4.32, we demonstrate how to get evolution strategies to discover all three highest peaks. The difficulty we must cope with here lies in a partly welcome, partly obstructive ES tendency to converge toward local maxima too quickly. The area an ES population can reach obviously depends on the mutation step sizes. Large step sizes enable the population to spread its individuals within a wider radius, finding higher, better regions by selection. The population gets the chance to explore its search space more globally. Relatively small step sizes result in a more constrained local search, which means more exploitation of local search information.

ES search for all peaks

For our example, we will try the following. We start with three initial populations, the individuals of which are spread within the lower-right quadrant of the search space. For generating ES chromosomes with constrained coordinates, we use the following function:

Generating an initial population

```
In[1] := newChromos :=
            createChromosomes[10, ChromosomeWidth → 2,
              ParameterRange → {{5,20},{-20,-5}},
              StepSizeRange → {{0,10}}]
```

The x and y coordinates of the ES chromosomes are restricted to the intervals [5, 20] and [–20, –5], respectively. Furthermore, the step sizes (strategy parameters) can be adjusted within a relatively large range between 0 and 10. This gives the individuals enough mobility for a globally oriented search strategy according to a

$$3(5/2, 10)^{10} \text{ ES.}$$

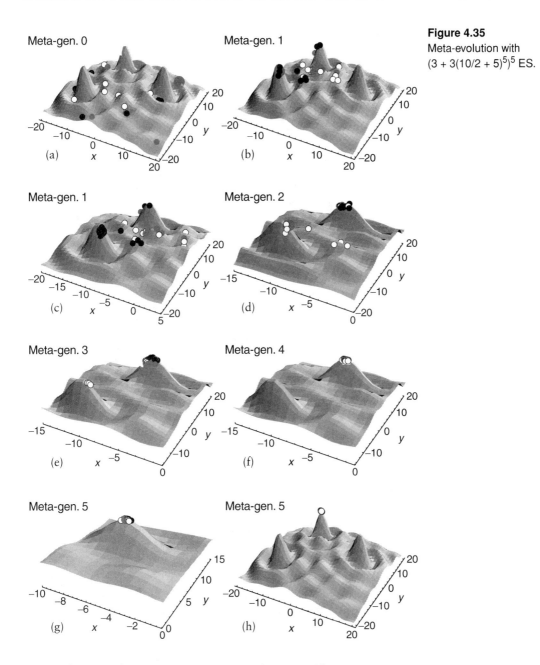

Figure 4.35
Meta-evolution with
$(3 + 3(10/2 + 5)^5)^5$ ES.

We begin with a comma strategy in order to avoid premature convergence. We initiate the first phase of the evolution with the following function call:

*Initiating an ES comma
strategy*

```
In[2] := metaES =
          Table[
            Evolution[
              ES[5,2,COMMA,10,10,
                ChromosomeWidth → 2,
                ParameterRange → {{-20,20}},
                StepSizeRange → {{0,10}},
                EvaluationFunction :>
                (f[# /. {p[x__] :> {x}}]&),
                InitialPopulation → newChromos]
            ] // First,
            {3}
          ];
```

Unlike the example in Section 4.7.3, here we realize independent evolution of three populations by explicitly starting a $(5/2, 10)^{10}$ evolution run three times. Figure 4.36 shows the distribution of the initial populations and their evolution over 10 generations. Each population succeeds in foraging ahead toward higher regions. But none of the individuals has yet discovered any of the major peaks.

We continue the $3(5/2 + 10)$ strategy for another 10 generations; that is, we start the next evolution cycle from the last populations of Figure 4.36 (cf. Figure 4.37, Gen. 10):

Continued comma strategy

```
In[3] := metaES2 =
          Map[First[
            Evolution[
              ES[5,2,COMMA,10,10,
                ChromosomeWidth → 2,
                ParameterRange → {{-20,20}},
                StepSizeRange → {{0,10}},
                EvaluationFunction :>
                  (f[# /. {p[x__] :> {x}}]&),
                InitialPopulation → #
              ]
          ]]&, metaES // Transpose // Last
          ];
```

The full evolution process up to generation 20 is depicted in Figure 4.37. Due to the relatively large variational range of the mutation step sizes, the populations can perform an extensive scan of their environment. The consequence is that the three highest peaks are actually tracked down by the evolving populations. At least one individual of

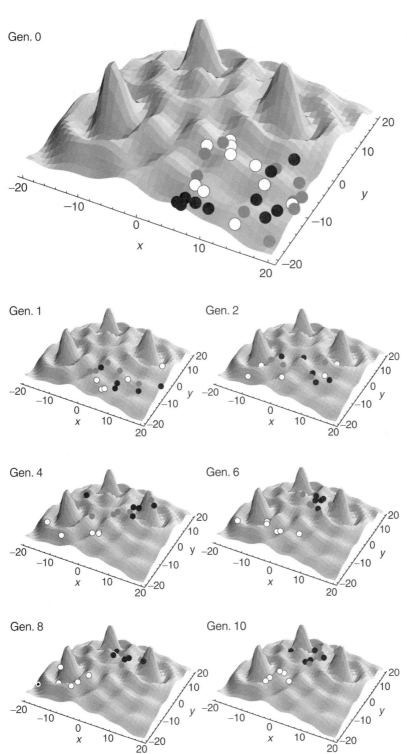

Figure 4.36
$3(5/2, 10)^{10}$ ES over 10 generations with a specific initial population.

Figure 4.37
Continued $3(5/2, 10)^{10}$
ES with the three initial
populations taken from
Figure 4.36, Gen. 10.

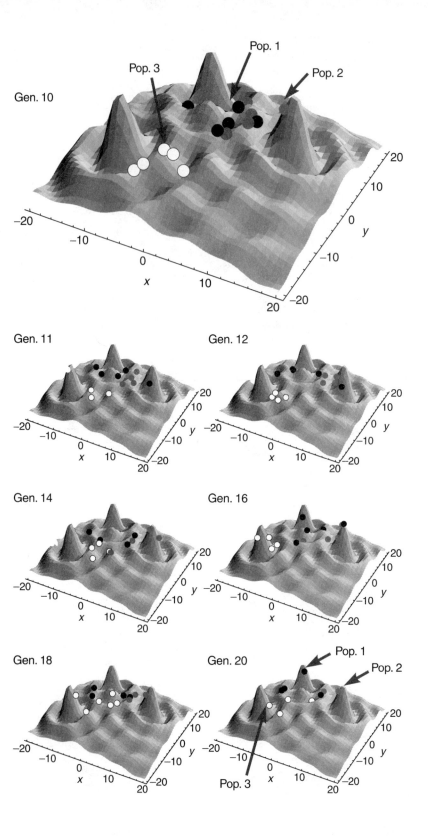

each population is on its way up to the major peaks (Figure 4.37, Gen. 20).

Now another evolution cycle should suffice to make the populations finally climb up their respective peaks. But we must be careful here. If we continue the comma strategy, we will probably lose the best individual(s). The ascent could be interrupted, even made impossible, if the only best individual gets lost on its way up to the very top. Hence, we change the evolution to a plus strategy, a

$$3(5/2 + 10)^{10} \text{ ES,}$$

Finally a plus strategy . . .

which guarantees that the current best individual is always among the best five selected survivors, at least as long as no better individual appears. So the last evolution cycle is initiated by

```
In[4] := metaES3 =
    Map[First[
      Evolution[
        ES[5,2,PLUS,10,10,
          ChromosomeWidth -> 2,
          ParameterRange -> {{-20,20}},
          StepSizeRange -> {{0,10}},
          EvaluationFunction :>
            (f[# /. {p[x__] :> {x}}]&),
          InitialPopulation -> #
        ]
      ]]&, metaES2 // Transpose // Last
    ];
```

Here the initial population is Gen. 20 from Figure 4.37. Now each population can climb its respective peak (Figure 4.38). For two populations, these climbs seem quite determined (populations 1 and 2), partly with smaller digression, as for population 3 (Figure 4.38, Gen. 21 and 22). At Gen. 30, all populations have gathered their individuals around the top peak regions. Finally, all three peaks have been ascended successfully, some of the peaks by even more than one population, as Figure 4.39 shows.

Figure 4.38

Change to a plus strategy: $3(5/2 + 10)^{10}$ ES with the three initial populations taken from Figure 4.37, Gen. 20.

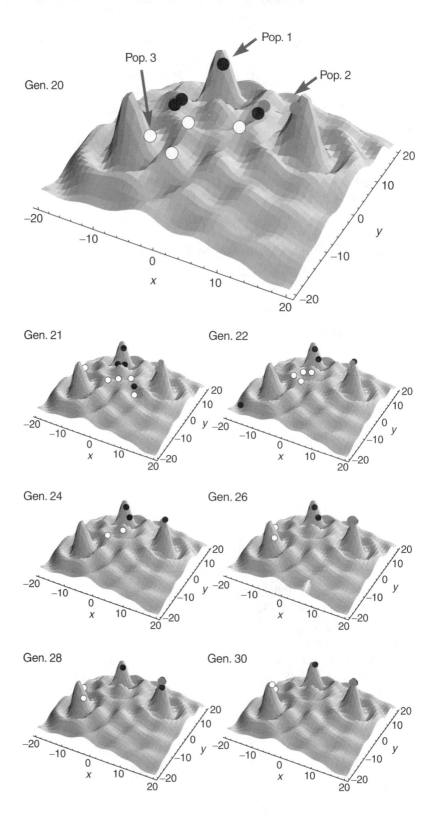

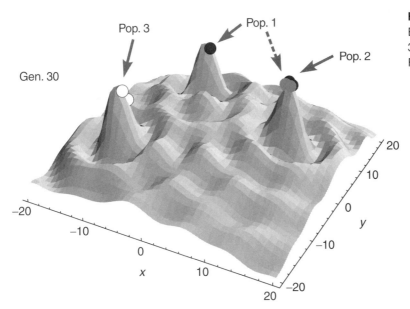

Figure 4.39
Enlarged result of the $3(5/2 + 10)^{10}$ ES of Figure 4.38, Gen. 30.

4.8 Bibliographical notes

Books on evolution strategies

Ingo Rechenberg's classic texts on evolution strategies, *Evolutionsstrategie* (1973) and *Evolutionsstrategie '94* (1994b), are still available only in German, but the latter book is currently being translated into English.

Evolutionsstrategie

An early description of evolution strategies is *Cybernetic Solution Path of an Experimental Problem* (Rechenberg 1965). This text is reproduced in Fogel 1998. Rechenberg also described the evolution strategy approach in several articles, for example, Rechenberg 1989 and Rechenberg 1994a.

Cybernetic Solution Path

Numerical Optimization of Computer Models is the English translation of Hans-Paul Schwefel's German dissertation (1977) on using evolution strategies for numerical optimization problems (Schwefel 1981). This work is one of the early, significant contributions to ES theory, also demonstrating computer implementations and applications to parameter optimization.

Numerical Optimization of Computer Models

In his 1995 book *Evolution and Optimum Seeking*, Hans-Paul Schwefel gives a thorough description of evolution strategies in the context of hill-climbing, random, and direct search strategies for parameter optimization tasks (Schwefel 1995).

Evolution and Optimum Seeking

Conferences

ICGA, GECCO, CEC, PPSN

A conference solely devoted to evolution strategies has never been initiated. Instead ES researchers have published in other conferences on evolutionary computation, such as ICGA, the International Conference on Genetic Algorithms (see Section 3.9); the Conference on Evolutionary Programming (see Section 6.8); and the major evolutionary algorithm conferences: ICEC, the International Conference on Evolutionary Computing; GECCO, the Genetic and Evolutionary Computation Conference; CEC, the Congress on Evolutionary Computation; and PPSN, the Parallel Problem Solving from Nature conference (see Section 2.4).

If Darwin Had Been a Programmer . . .   Part II

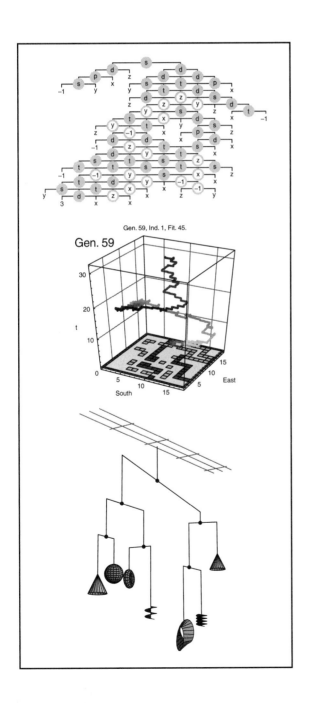

5 Programming by Evolution

Living organisms are consummate problem solvers. They exhibit a versatility that puts the best computer programs to shame. This observation is especially galling for computer scientists, who may spend months or years of intellectual effort on an algorithm, whereas organisms come by their abilities through the apparently undirected mechanism of evolution and natural selection.

Holland 1992b

The development of an embryo into an adult living being is controlled by an incredible number of complex, interacting "growth programs." Each cell "knows" exactly how it must develop in relation to neighboring cells, which proteins are to be produced, and in which way to differentiate for specific tasks. The genome of each cell serves as a reservoir of manifold *control programs,* which can be activated and switched off—depending on intra- and extracellular environmental conditions. They even interact and mutually re- and deactivate each other. Nature has not only equipped living organisms with programs for physical development but has also developed "intelligent software" for monitoring and controlling body functions, movements, and actions by brains and nervous systems. From a system and software engineering point of view, it is surprising that these "intelligent" programs and control systems are not the result of selective programming. Rather, they emerged from seemingly aimless mechanisms of evolution and adaptation. Nature's methods of programming are amazing, and they teach us that programming by evolution not only is feasible but also can lead to impressive results.

Evolution: nature's programming method

The most complex program systems ever created by human beings are dwarfed by the control programs developed by nature, which ensures the survival of living organisms. All the attempts to use evolutionary principles to develop computer programs show how constrained "programming by evolution" still is. A major problem is

Programming by evolution

finding suitable representations for program structures so that, similar to cellular chromosomes, new program variants can be evolved by simple recombinations and mutations. Another problem is the enormously high computing times required. In order to perform successful program evolution (for high-level programming tasks), very large populations are often necessary (with 10,000 or more individuals), resulting in time-consuming evaluations of the set of program individuals. At the current speed of advancement in computer technologies, however, within a few years these problems will be alleviated and future computer systems will provide a fruitful basis for evolution as an alternative programming tool.

Overview of Part II

Chapter 5 serves as the introductory section on evolution-based induction of computer programs, the main theme of the second part of this book. In Chapter 6, we look at *evolutionary programming,* an approach initiated during the 1960s, at almost the same time that evolution strategies and genetic algorithms entered the stage. Evolutionary programming (EP) constitutes one of the early, successful attempts to evolve programmable structures or, in today's terminology, *intelligent agents,* in the form of finite state machines. In Chapter 7, we introduce *genetic programming* (GP) as an extension of genetic algorithms. A comprehensive example of a classical GP application, the *AntTracker,* is discussed in Chapter 8, where we demonstrate the breeding of control programs, navigating a robot within a mazelike environment.

Chapter overview

In this chapter, we briefly discuss problem-specific programming compared to evolution-based program development (Section 5.1). A historical survey of evolutionary programming approaches documents the most important steps toward programming by evolution (Section 5.2)—from simple mutations on assembler code to evolutionary and genetic programming on symbolic expressions and more complex data structures.

5.1   Evolving versus programming

For parameter optimization through evolution-based methods of genetic algorithms and evolution strategies, the genotypes have a simple structure: vectors of numbers or strings over discrete alphabets. This results in straightforward definitions of the genetic operators as well as in relatively easy decoding functions for translating genotypical information into problem-specific parameters. The situation becomes more complex in two ways if computer programs—descriptions of algorithms—undergo evolution processes. On the one hand, the encodings of programs should reflect the hierarchical structures of command sequences, conditions, loops, subprograms, function definitions, sets of rules, and so on. On the other hand, decoding and interpretation of program structures constitute a multistep process (Figure 5.1). The program code, saved on a "genome," usually represents a problem-specific programming language or data structures, which eventually have to be translated into a concrete programming language. Only then can this program source code be interpreted or compiled into an executable program.

Hierarchically structured programs

If a program, the "phenotype" of the program genome, is executed in the context of a specific "environment," defined by the optimization or programming problem, the program individual can be evaluated depending on its performance. Many factors may be taken into account for evaluation; for example, whether the program does solve the predefined task, its required computing time, or the length of its source code. Considering a population of such program individuals, an evolutionary algorithm can perform selection for the next generation on the basis of the program fitnesses and furthermore generate new program variants through genome-modifying operators, such as recombinations and mutations.

Evaluation of program genomes

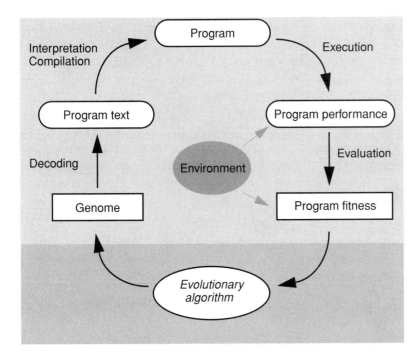

Figure 5.1
Induction of computer programs by evolutionary algorithms.

Which coding strategy should actually be used for encoding program structures and which evolutionary algorithm should be applied depend on the specific optimization or design problem to be solved. Specific examples are presented in the following chapter, which provides an overview of systems that have been implemented in evolutionary program induction and development.

5.2   Evolution and programming: a survey

Since the very beginning of computer software, programmers have tried to alleviate the tedious task of writing and generating computer code by inventing software development tools, such as editors, syntax checkers, code generators, compiler-compilers, and so on. More adventurous programmers try to avoid the drudgery of programming at all—they take program development a step further. Why shouldn't they, in the traditional sense of knowledge and rule-based programming, leave it to the computer itself to find a suitable algorithm to solve a specific problem? Given a set of building blocks, which are necessary for formulating an appropriate solution algorithm, the discovery of a suitable algorithmic solution and composition of building blocks could be left to a meta-algorithm. Moreover, if the algorithms can be evaluated by their ability to solve a posed problem, a selection procedure would provide a suitable filter among the programs. Basically, this is exactly what evolution is doing, too. New structures are composed by recombinations and mutations from given building blocks, which might be able to win in the competitive race of selection. So why shouldn't programmers take advantage of evolution's creativity?

Evolving versus programming

Unfortunately, evolution-based program induction turns out to be rather complicated in practice. This is demonstrated by the many approaches to evolutionary program development, dating to the 1950s. One major problem is to find simple, yet flexible representations for computer programs.

Problem of program representation

> The chief problem is the construction of a "genetic code" that can represent the structure of different programs, just as the DNA represents the structure of a person or a mouse.
>
> John H. Holland (Holland 1992b)

Color Plates

Gen. 0

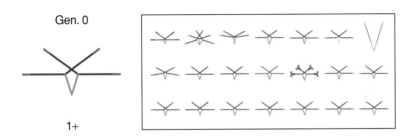

1+

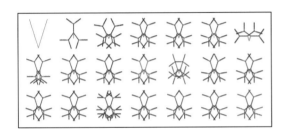

Gen. 5

1+

Gen. 10

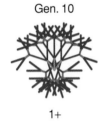

1+

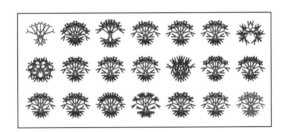

Gen. 14

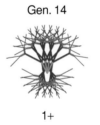

1+

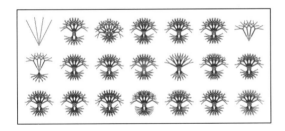

Gen. 18

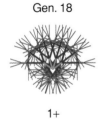

1+

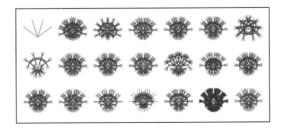

Color Plate 1
Breeding of biomorphs
(Section 1.5).

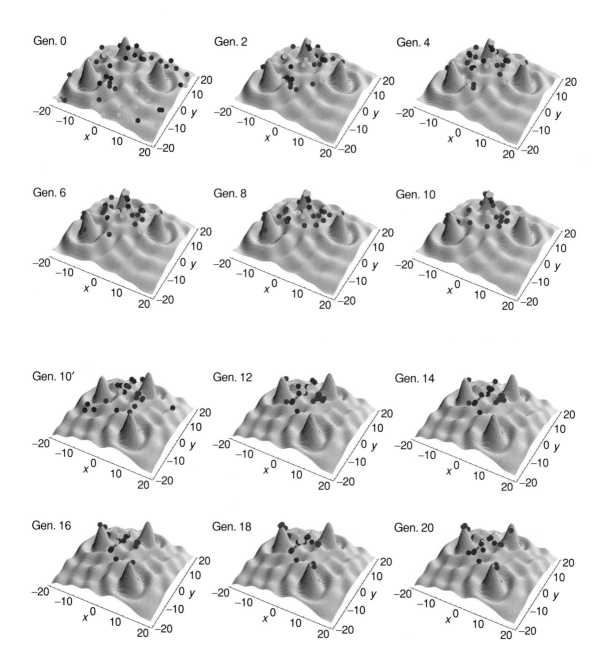

Color Plate 2
Genetic algorithms in action: Three independent populations (red, green, and blue dots) are climbing the peaks under a changing objective function (Section 3.7.5).

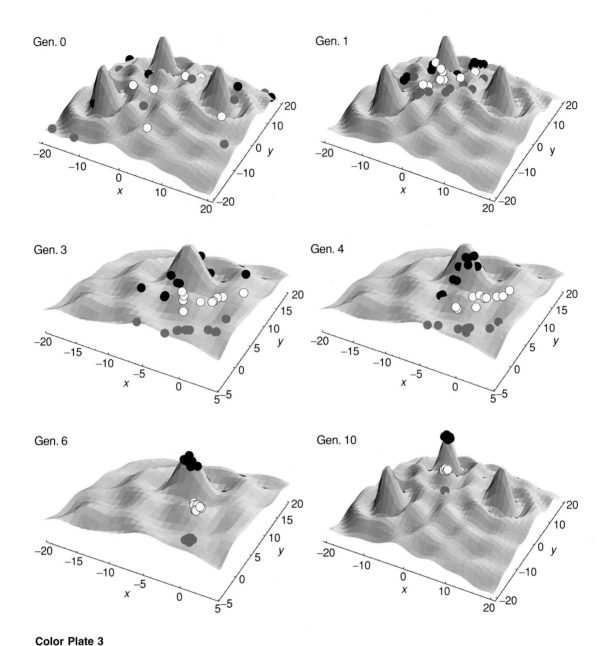

Color Plate 3
Evolution strategies in action: Three independent populations (black, white, and gray dots) climb the peaks following a 3(1/2, 20) strategy over 10 generations (Section 4.7.3).

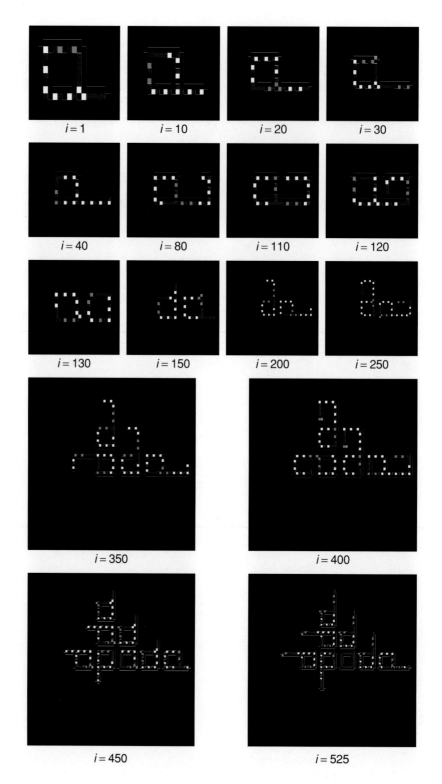

$i = 1$ $i = 10$ $i = 20$ $i = 30$

$i = 40$ $i = 80$ $i = 110$ $i = 120$

$i = 130$ $i = 150$ $i = 200$ $i = 250$

$i = 350$ $i = 400$

$i = 450$ $i = 525$

Color Plate 4
Self-reproducing loops as
cellular automata
(Section 9.1.2).

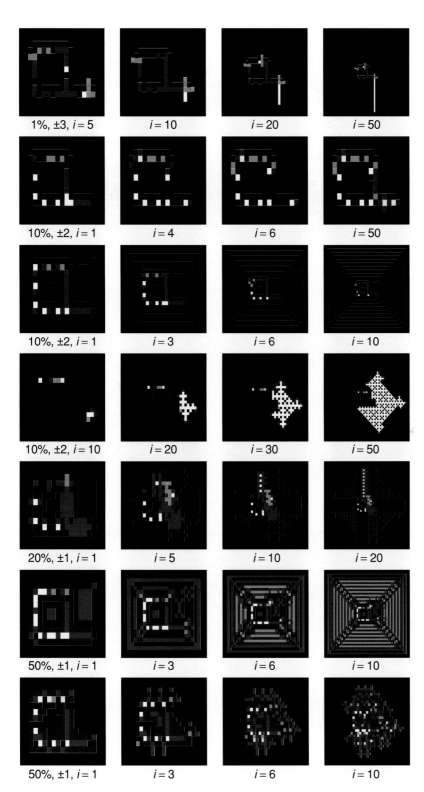

1%, ±3, $i = 5$ $i = 10$ $i = 20$ $i = 50$

10%, ±2, $i = 1$ $i = 4$ $i = 6$ $i = 50$

10%, ±2, $i = 1$ $i = 3$ $i = 6$ $i = 10$

10%, ±2, $i = 10$ $i = 20$ $i = 30$ $i = 50$

20%, ±1, $i = 1$ $i = 5$ $i = 10$ $i = 20$

50%, ±1, $i = 1$ $i = 3$ $i = 6$ $i = 10$

50%, ±1, $i = 1$ $i = 3$ $i = 6$ $i = 10$

Color Plate 5
Mutated "loops:" cellular
automata mutations
(Section 9.1.2).

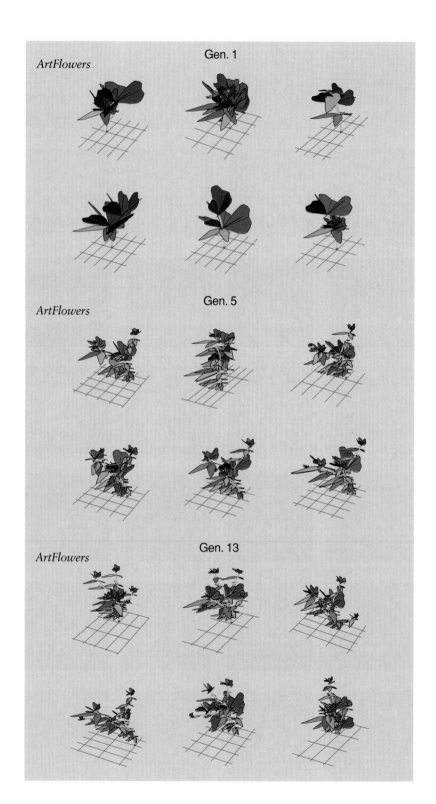

ArtFlowers   Gen. 1

ArtFlowers   Gen. 5

ArtFlowers   Gen. 13

Color Plate 6
"Breeding" of plant
structures (Section 11.3).

Gen. 1

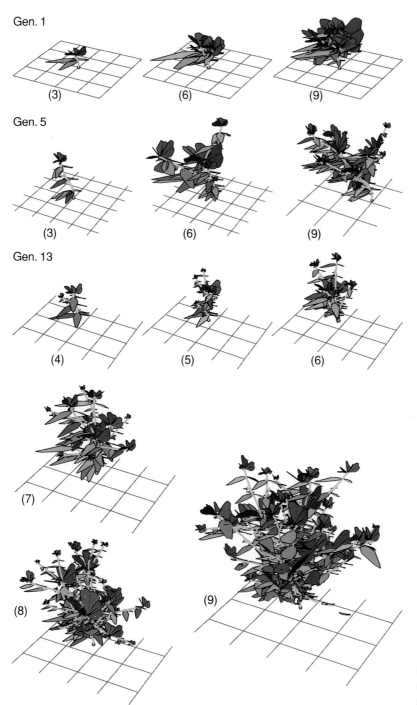

(3) (6) (9)

Gen. 5

(3) (6) (9)

Gen. 13

(4) (5) (6)

(7)

(8) (9)

Color Plate 7
Growth of selected plant
structures (Section 11.4).

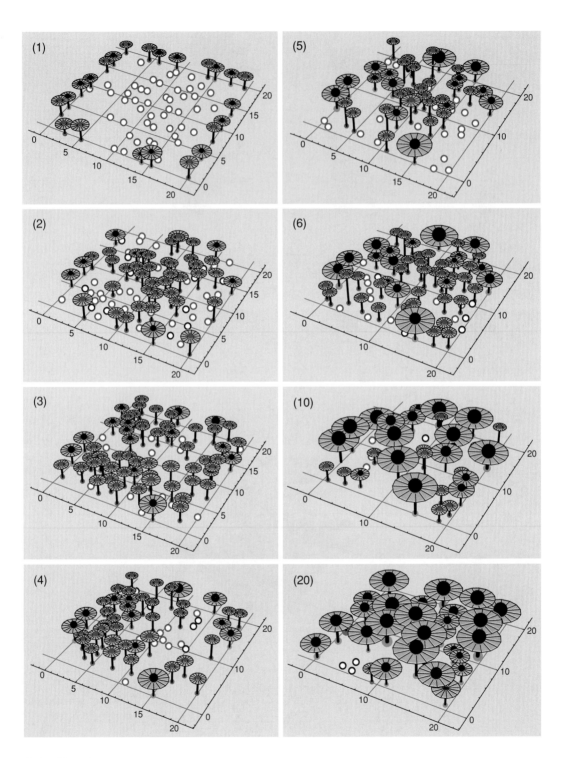

Color Plate 8
Simulation of competitive plant evolution in a succession scenario (Section 11.5).

What kinds of programs are particularly suited to evolutionary algorithms? For genetic algorithms, machine code instructions, encoded in binary chromosomes, seem to be most suited for implementing assembler languages. But are those the programming languages that we would like to write and develop by evolution? What about program evolution in higher programming languages, such as the "breeding" of programs in Pascal, C, C++, LISP, or Mathematica?

Assembler vs. higher programming languages

In the following sections we give an overview of program evolution—starting from mutative development of assembler programs to evolution of symbolic expressions, which are a universal form of representation for higher-order programming languages. A short section on so-called *classifier systems* describes evolution of rule systems inspired by interacting genome programs in natural cells.

Mutated assembler programs

In the early 1950s, Friedberg et al. investigated how to generate assembler programs by stochastic methods and how to develop new programs by purely random mutations (Friedberg 1958; Friedberg, Dunham, et al. 1959). Their assembler language is designed for a virtual computer with a single-bit register. Each program consists of 64 instructions. The generated programs are executed and then evaluated on whether they implement a particular algorithm, such as two-bit addition. Recombinations are not applied, nor are any crossover operators. Only the mutation operator exchanges instructions within a program or randomly generates new instructions.

Assembler programs for one-bit registers

The program individuals are not organized in populations and are not evolved over a number of generations. There is no reproduction scheme. When generating new program variants, the (parent) program fitnesses are not taken into account. Instead each program is attributed with a success counter, which is incremented with each successfully passed evaluation test. The success counter also determines the individual-specific mutation rate. The more successful a program performs, the fewer instructions are mutated.

Success counter and adaptive mutation

In the end, it turns out that the simulated evolution mechanisms of *automatic programming* are no better suited than pure random search. This is mainly due to the lack of any selection scheme. The program evolutions implemented by Friedberg et al. basically correspond to $(1, \lambda)$ evolution strategies (Section 4.4). From a parent program λ mutants are generated, of which the best program constitutes the starting point for the next mutation-evaluation cycle. More advanced implementations of this kind of program evolution were not possible at that time because of memory restrictions on the available IBM 704 computer hardware (Fogel 1998, pp. 143–162).

Importance of recombination

A short time later, Bremermann recognized the importance of recombination for the success of evolutionary program development (Bremermann 1962). He and his group optimized vectors of discrete and continuous object variables with applications in linear programming. He applied mutation as well as recombination (discrete and intermediate) operators, analogous in many ways to today's GA and ES operators (Bremermann, Rogson, et al. 1965). The reproduction cycle used corresponds to a $(\mu/\rho, \lambda)$ scheme with recombination. In the end, this approach to program evolution also proved not as successful as expected. The optimization problems chosen were too simple for the evolutionary methods to gain any advantage over conventional optimization techniques (Fogel 1998, pp. 314–352).

Evolution of finite automata

Evolutionary programming of finite automata

A very flexible, successful approach to program evolution based on an operational programming model is provided by Fogel, Owens, and Walsh: adapting finite automata by mutation and reproduction to problem-specific machine learning tasks (Fogel, Owens, et al. 1966; Fogel 1999). In this approach, known as *evolutionary programming* (EP), individuals represent descriptions of finite automata, encoding the number of states, the state transitions, the initial state, and the transition outputs. The input and output alphabet is predefined and fixed for all automata (Chapter 6).

EP reproduction scheme

In one of the problems investigated, for a bit sequence of input signals the next output signal must be predicted by an automaton. Initially, a population of two randomly generated automata descriptions is evaluated with regard to its output behavior. The better of the two individuals is reproduced and passed on to the next generation. Two more individuals are generated as mutants of one of the "parent" individuals (a (3 + 3) scheme). Mutations may change any of the encoded elements. States can be deleted or new states can be added. Transitions are modifiable. The input and output letters of the states can be varied. Recombining operators are not used, however.

More general evolutionary programming

This approach has been extended and developed further over many years. Although known as evolutionary programming today (Fogel, Owens, et al. 1966), programs in the sense of problem-specific, high-level programming languages have not been taken into account in this specific version of evolutionary programming. The major aspect of implementing EP systems either focuses on the manipulation of finite automata (Fogel 1992; Fogel 1994) or primarily deals with parameter optimization problems (Fogel 1992; Fogel and Atmar 1992)—the domain of evolution strategies.

More general approaches to evolutionary programming also exist, in which problem-specific data structures are adapted by specifically designed mutation operators and combined with a general selection scheme. A number of successful EP applications in the areas of neural networks, game theory, grammar induction, and robot control programs are reported in Angeline 1993 and many more in the proceedings of the annual Evolutionary Programming Conference (Fogel and Atmar 1992; Fogel and Atmar 1993; Sebald and Fogel 1994; McDonnell, Reynolds, et al. 1995; Fogel, Angeline, et al. 1996; Angeline, Reynolds, et al. 1997; Porto, Saravanan, et al. 1998; Angeline, Michalewicz, et al. 1999; Zalzala et al. 2000).

EP = data structures + problem-specific operators

Classifier systems

In the course of his investigations of adaptive systems, John Holland developed a class of programs later known as genetic algorithms (Chapter 3). Holland's objective was to design a genetic code through which the structure of any computer program could be represented (Holland 1992a, p. 45). The idea of submitting populations of programs, describing complex strategies of behavior, to an adaptation process already appears in his earlier work (Holland 1962), with parallels to Friedberg's work on automatic programming (Friedberg 1958; Friedberg, Dunham, et al. 1959).

Genetic code for computer programs

Holland's ideas about evolution-based adaptation of computer programs gave rise to the concept of *classifier systems*. Here a program consists of a set of condition-action rules of the following form:

Classifier system

If conditions *a, b, c, . . .* are fulfilled,

then perform actions *x, y, z, . . .*

The rules are encoded as two-folded strings over the alphabet {0, 1, *}. For instance, a rule of the form

$$0\ 1\ ^* \rightarrow 1\ 0\ 0\ 1$$

Classifier rule

would mean:

If condition 2 is true and condition 1 is not true,

then perform actions 1 and 4.

Classifier

*Adaptations by genetic
algorithms*

The third condition is not relevant for this rule, indicated by the *
symbol. The arrow, separating the condition and action part, is not
encoded on the string. A finite set of rules like this defines a *classifier*, a
program system responding to signals from its environment. Genetic
algorithms are used to adapt populations of classifiers to specific environmental conditions. If the actions result in changing environmental
signals or if the actions generate signals by themselves, a system of
interacting programs can be simulated, analogous to mutative gene
activations of cellular chromosomes and closely following the operon
model of gene regulation by Britten and Davidson (Britten and Davidson 1969). More detailed descriptions of classifier systems can be
found in Booker, Goldberg, et al. 1989; Goldberg 1989, Chapter 6;
and Holland 1992a, pp. 171–184.

Broadcast language

An early version of classifier rules is the *broadcast language*, a
rule language that allows for more complex interactions between subprograms (Holland 1975, Chapter 8). The broadcast language allows,
for instance, filtering of parametrized signals received from a classifier
and passing them on to the action part. The rule alphabet consists of
10 symbols for the formatting and filtering of signals and for inter-
punctuation of condition and action segments (Holland 1975, pp. 144
ff.). Specific application examples for classifier systems are reported in
Goldberg 1989, p. 219 ff., among others.

Despite their intriguing design for evolution-based adaptive and
learning systems, classifier systems have not yet played a major part in
the arena of program evolution. One of the major problems with classifier systems is the evaluation of the rules and how to measure the
contribution of a rule to the overall behavior of the classifier. How are
the actions induced by a rule to be evaluated against previous and further actions initiated by other rules? If the rule set is evolved by a
genetic algorithm, an evaluation for each rule is required.

*Bucket brigade:
a payoff scheme for rules*

One possible reinforcement scheme is called the *bucket brigade*,
where rules pass on part of their payoff to those classifiers through the
actions of which they have been activated. The indirectly paid-off
rules can again pass on part of their payoff. Thus, a cascade of payoffs
is distributed over the rule system. This results in an extremely complex and partly delayed adaptation behavior for classifier systems,
which seems to make them less attractive for practical optimization
tasks. Classifier systems certainly provide an important basis, however, for the understanding and modeling of gene interactions on cellular genomes.

Program induction with genetic algorithms

Research activities in the area of genetic algorithms initiated increased attention to the promising results achieved with evolution-based program induction. The use of genetic algorithms for breeding programs on the basis of problem-specific programming languages was widely investigated and discussed soon after genetic algorithms became more known to the broader scientific community (Cramer 1985; De Jong 1987; Fujiki and Dickinson 1987). Here are just a few examples (for more references, see Section 5.3). Cramer (1985) encodes compositions of binary operations on strings of constant length, which are optimized by genetic algorithms. But one disadvantage of genetic algorithms remains. Hierarchically composed and dynamically modifiable structures, which computer programs are, cannot easily be mapped on binary strings of constant length. As a possible solution, Wineberg and Oppacher propose a mapping scheme that converts programs, represented as tree-structured terms (with width and height restrictions), into binary strings of equal length (Wineberg and Oppacher 1994).

Program induction by genetic algorithms

Recently at least two approaches have turned out to be promising in evolutionary program development, both of which refer to GA methodologies. The first approach is genetic programming with *linear genomes,* encoding assembler programs for a virtual register machine. The second is genetic programming on *term structures,* which are particularly easy to implement as functional programs in LISP or Mathematica. For a comparison of these two forms of program representation, see also Figure 7.1.

Genetic programming with linear genomes

With the *binary genetic programming* (BGP) approach, assemblerlike program instructions are directly encoded on binary strings. As a 32-bit instruction, each single operation has the form

Linear (machine-) program genome

0111001001 | 10001001011 | 10111010101
Operation   Operand 1   Operand 2

A program consists of a set of m instructions, which are sequentially encoded on a genome of length $32 \cdot m$. For interpretation by a genotype-phenotype mapping, the virtual register machine instructions are translated into a higher programming language (C) and compiled into an executable program. Variations on the program genome are generated by normal GA mutations and crossover operations (Nordin 1995).

Compiling GP

Obviously the encodings of the machine instructions must be defined in such a way that binary strings, resulting from mutations and crossovers, can again be mapped into executable program code; that is, the encoding structures must be *closed* with respect to the genetic operators used. On the other hand, the genetic operators could be designed such that they lead only to syntactically correct bit combinations. This is taken into account by a further variant of linear genetic programming—*compiling GP* (CGP), where specific mutations and recombinations are applied. One example is the use of "protected" chromosome segments. Crossover points for recombination operators can be situated only outside these areas. After any mutations, the resulting operation code is checked for its validity or for whether the operands access only allowed register addresses (Banzhaf 1993; Nordin 1995; Keller and Banzhaf 1996).

Genetic programming on symbolic expressions

Terms of Boolean operators

The methodology of classifier systems inspired a number of additional approaches to evolution-based program induction. Bickel and Bickel developed a rule-based expert system, in which the condition part of each rule is represented by Boolean operators (Bickel and Bickel 1987). Wilson extended the bucket brigade algorithm for the evaluation of rules and proposed a hierarchical representation scheme for programs and subprograms (Wilson 1987a; Wilson 1987b). His

Hierarchical rule systems

approaches led to a hierarchy of rule systems instead of sequential representations of rules in classifier systems.

Evolution of simple LISP programs

Evolutionary program induction on structures of higher programming languages were developed by Hicklin, who investigated how to generate LISP programs by selective reproduction and mutation operators (Hicklin 1986). This approach was continued by Fujiki et al., who extended the set of genetic operators for LISP structures by recombinations and inversions (Fujiki 1986; Fujiki and Dickinson 1987). The *prisoner's dilemma,* a well-known problem in game theory, is used as a test bed. The evolved programs are restricted to simple condition operations for describing a game-playing strategy. Axelrod also used genetic algorithms to evolve strategies for the prisoner's dilemma in the context of competitive and cooperating agent-based systems (Axelrod 1997).

Game strategies for the prisoner's dilemma

Linear vs. hierarchical program structures

These approaches represent an essential advancement in evolution-based programming. The central (genome) data structures are no longer linear but rather hierarchically structured genomes on which programs (implemented in higher programming languages) can be represented in a more natural way. Currently John Koza and his coworkers are promoting and propagating their genetic programming problem solver. Initially, Koza used *hierarchical genetic algorithms* for the breeding of computer programs (Koza 1989). Further developments of this approach resulted in a sophisticated evolution system for LISP programs (Koza 1990). His book *Genetic Programming: On the Programming of Computers by Means of Natural Selection* (Koza 1992) and the following volumes (Koza 1994; Koza, Andre, et al. 1999) present an impressive number of examples of program evolution in areas as diverse as robot control, function regression, classification, analog circuit design, and software engineering. The initial book coined the term *genetic programming* for GA-based program induction on tree- or term-structured expressions.

Hierarchical genetic algorithms

Genetic programming paradigm

Using the language of LISP to represent program structures is in no way accidental. Compared to other computer languages, a number of characteristic features make LISP—like Mathematica—particularly apt for program induction based on evolutionary algorithms. LISP or Scheme (Steel and Sussman 1975) belong to the few programming languages that are defined by an extremely simple and uniform syntax. The central structuring unit, from which all LISP instructions and also all data structures are composed, is the *list* (hence its name: *LISt Programming*).

LISP and Mathematica

$$(f\ t_1 \ldots t_n)$$

is the general form of a LISP expression. The symbol f represents the operator; t_1 to t_n are the corresponding operands. Indeed, both f and $t_1, \ldots, t_n$ can be again list structures of this form; for instance,

$$(((Deriv\ 2)\ Sin)\ Pi).$$

This function would calculate the second derivative of *Sin(x)* at position π. The Mathematica programming language also has an analogous structure. Each instruction or data structure is composed of a *symbolic expression*. In Mathematica the above function would be written as

Symbolic expressions

```
Derivative[2][Sin][Pi].
```

A uniform program structure like this offers essential advantages for use in genetic programming. With regard to genetic operators, there is no difference between program and data structures. Consequently, their uniformity allows for relatively easy manipulation, and the programs are immediately interpretable and executable.

GP = GA + symbolic
expressions

The homogeneous construction principle of programs encoded by symbolic expressions, analogous to the homogeneity of binary GA strings, further contributes to problem-independent and uniform definitions of the genetic operators, also a major advantage of genetic algorithms.

Overview of Part II

Evolutionary programming of finite state automata and genetic programming of symbolic expressions are discussed in detail in the following chapters. In Chapter 6, we demonstrate the evolutionary programming approach and illustrate it with an evolutionary breeding experiment of predictor finite state machines. In Chapter 7, we introduce the "classical" GP approach proposed by Koza, namely, program evolution on term structures, which are a special subclass of symbolic expressions. The evolution of mobile structures illustrates this paradigm. A more detailed example of GP program evolution is discussed in Chapter 8, where control programs for navigating a simple robot in a mazelike environment are evolved.

5.3   Bibliographical notes

History of evolution-based programming

Evolutionary Computation:
Fossil Record

An excellent collection of major contributions to the area of evolution-based programming since the 1950s is *Evolutionary Computation: The Fossil Record*, edited by David Fogel (1998).

Alternative approaches to evolution-based programming

TIERRA

Thomas Ray's evolutionary *TIERRA* system attracted a lot of interest (Ray 1991; Levy 1993a, pp. 219–230). *TIERRA* simulates a population of self-reproducing assembler programs competing for memory and computing time. The TIERRA system is currently being extended to a distributed worldwide network "ecosystem."

Conferences

EP conference

Another in-depth source for approaches to programming by evolution is the annual Evolutionary Programming Conference series, started in 1992 (Fogel and Atmar 1992; Fogel and Atmar 1993; Sebald and Fogel 1994; McDonnell, Reynolds, et al. 1995; Fogel, Angeline, et al. 1996; Angeline, Reynolds, et al. 1997; Porto, Saravanan, et al. 1998),

which finally evolved into the Congress on Evolutionary Computation   *CEC, GP, and GECCO*
(Angeline, Michalewicz, et al. 1999; Zalzala et al. 2000).

The annual Genetic Programming Conference was initiated in
1996 (Koza, Goldberg, et al. 1996; Koza, Deb, et al. 1997; Koza, Banzhaf, et al. 1998) and finally led to GECCO, the annual Genetic and
Evolutionary Computation Conference (Banzhaf, Daida, et al. 1999;
Whitley, Goldberg, et al. 2000).

6　Evolutionary Programming

Intelligent behavior is a composite ability to predict one's environment coupled with a translation of each prediction into a suitable response in light of some objective. Success in predicting an environment is a prerequisite to intelligent behavior.

Fogel 1999, p. 3

In the early days of artificial intelligence (AI), during the 1950s and 1960s, research in understanding intelligence through the construction of computational systems followed two distinctly different schools of thought: what might be called the "bottom-up" and "top-down" approaches to modeling intelligent behavior. From the bottom-up, or *bionics,* viewpoint, implementations of intelligence start at the level of neurons in order to build artificial brains. Once the construction and operation of these neural networks is understood, mechanisms such as learning, memorization, pattern association, planning, and control—all intelligent tasks, carried out by natural brains—can be built on top of these adaptive "machines." A vast number of neural network architectures and learning algorithms developed since then have proved this subsymbolic approach to be rather successful but still limited within the larger picture of how to create intelligent systems. The second, top-down, approach takes a psychological perspective. Artificial intelligence is achieved by analyzing and modeling thought processes through a structured set of rules (if-then rules) as is reflected, for example, in today's expert systems or mathematical theorem provers. This symbolic approach, known as *heuristic programming*, relies mainly on generally useful rules, which eventually turned out to be difficult to apply and adjust to noisy and nonstationary environments.

Bottom-up AI: neural networks

Top-down AI: heuristic programming

　　There is another approach to building intelligent systems. Nature has invented many ways of coping with noisy and dynamic environments—through evolutionary "design" processes that, over the last

Evolutionary programming

3.5 billion years, created organisms of increasing intellect. In 1961 Lawrence Fogel, an electrical engineer then working for the National Science Foundation, proposed applying the concepts of natural evolution, selection, and stochastic mutation to design artificially intelligent agents (Fogel 1999). Fogel termed his approach *evolutionary programming* (EP), in contrast to heuristic programming. Although this alternative approach to artificial intelligence raised many objections within the scientific community at the time, Fogel continued his research on evolutionary programming, finally finding two EP enthusiasts and coworkers in Alvin Owens and Michael Walsh. Their experiments, conducted over the years into the 1970s, dealt mainly with the

Evolution of finite state machines

question of how to evolve computer programs—implemented as finite state machines—for prediction, control, and pattern classification tasks. The evolutionary programming approach and the results of these experiments were summarized in *Artificial Intelligence Through Simulated Evolution* (Fogel, Owens, et al. 1966), the first book in the field of evolutionary computation. Since then, evolutionary programming has developed into one of the major streams of evolutionary computation—alongside evolution strategies (Chapter 4), genetic algorithms (Chapter 3), and genetic programming (Chapter 7).

Chapter overview

In this chapter, we focus on the original concepts and experiments of evolutionary programming, namely, the evolution of finite state machines. Section 6.1 describes how to encode computer programs as finite state automata (FSA). In Section 6.2, we discuss mutation operators on these finite state machines and how to randomly generate FSA in Section 6.3. The general EP selection and reproduction scheme is presented in Section 6.4, where the analogies to evolution strategies will become clear. Section 6.5 explains how we implement evolutionary programming of finite state machines in Evolvica. An example of an EP evolution experiment will be discussed in Section 6.6. Finally, in Section 6.7, we discuss recent developments in evolutionary programming. These EP approaches use any evolvable representation of data structures and programs as suggested from the problem domain.

6.1   Computer programs as finite state machines

Deriving models of the environment

One important element of intelligent behavior of organisms is their ability to derive models of their environment from external input signals. Based on these observations, an organism is then capable of making predictions about its environment. Each day we rely heavily on our mental models of the world and on our ability to derive predictions about future events. For example, if you see a car driving straight toward you, your world model, that is, your experience, tells you that the car will soon arrive where you are right now and hit you. So you step aside and let the car pass, and your prediction ability may have saved your life.

Suppose we want to design "intelligent agents" that are able to make such predictions about their environment. The agents would experience a sequence of input signals, derive a model of their environment, and finally predict the next input signal that is supposed to come from the environment. A flexible computational means to implement simple input-output prediction mappings of environmental signals is provided by finite state (Mealy) machines, which are discussed in the following section. Most of the ideas and experiments presented here follow the "classic" evolutionary programming approach described in Fogel, Owens, et al. 1966, and more recently in Fogel 1999.

Intelligent agents as predictors

6.1.1   How finite state machines work

Figure 6.1 shows an example of a finite state Mealy machine. This machine can be in either of the four *states* 1, 2, 3, or 4, represented by circles. The machine can react to input signals 0, 1, or 2, which are denoted by the numbers associated with each arc, by switching to (possibly) another state while outputting a response signal. In the diagram, an arc from state *A* to *B* denotes a *transition* between these states, where the corresponding label *x/y* refers to the input signal *x* and its output signal *y*, respectively. The *initial* state, the state in which the machine would start to listen for input signals after a reset, is

States

Transitions

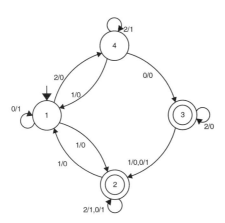

Figure 6.1
Example of a finite state (Mealy) automaton.

marked by a black vertical arrow. The states with double circles are designated as *final* states, which may be used for special purposes, such as halting the automaton. However, for our prediction tasks, we will treat final states no differently from any other state.

Automata package

For implementing the core functionality of finite state automata (FSA), we use a modified version of Alon Levy's `Automata` package. This Mathematica package provides a large set of functions to construct, modify, execute, and visualize deterministic as well as nondeterministic finite state machines, including Mealy and Moore automata (Levy 1991). The example automaton in Figure 6.1 can be described as follows:

```
In[1] := << Automata.m
```

A handcrafted Mealy automaton

```
In[2] := myMealy = MakeAutomaton[Mealy,{1, 2, 3, 4},
         {{1, 0, 1, 1},{1, 1, 2, 0},{1, 2, 4, 0},
          {2, 0, 2, 1},{2, 1, 1, 0},{2, 2, 2, 1},
          {3, 0, 2, 1},{3, 1, 2, 0},{3, 2, 3, 0},
          {4, 0, 3, 0},{4, 1, 1, 0},{4, 2, 4, 1}},
         1,
         {2, 3},{0, 1, 2}];
```

In the `MakeAutomaton` command we first specify the type of automaton, which is `Mealy` in our case and means that the automaton is able to produce output signals. The second input is a list of the automaton's states ({1, 2, 3, 4}), followed by a list of the transitions, where each entry {s_1, i, s_2, o} denotes a transition from state s_1 to state s_2 for an input signal i and an output signal o. The next parameters are the initial state (1), the set of final states ({2, 3}), and the input-output alphabet ({0, 1, 2}). This automaton can be visualized as shown in Figure 6.1 by using the command `ShowAutomaton[myMealy]`.

FSA response to input signals

Now we can test this automaton's response to a periodic sequence of input signals. We define a subsequence of length 10 consisting of symbols 0, 1, or 2. This subsequence is repeated five times and presented to the `myMealy` automaton:

```
In[3] := subSequence = Table[Random[Integer,
         {0, 2}], {10}]; periodic = Table[subSequence {5}]
         automatonResponse[myMealy, periodic // Flatten]
```

```
Out[3] = {{0, 0, 0, 2, 1, 2, 0, 1, 2, 2}, {0, 0, 0, 2, 1,
          2, 0, 1, 2, 2}, {0, 0, 0, 2, 1, 2, 0, 1, 2, 2},
          {0, 0, 0, 2, 1, 2, 0, 1, 2, 2}, {0, 0, 0, 2, 1, 2,
          0, 1, 2, 2}}
```

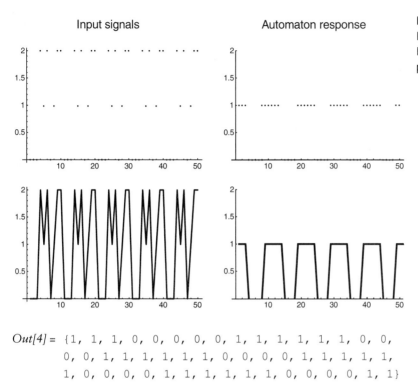

Figure 6.2
Response of the example
FSA in Figure 6.1 to a
periodic input signal.

Out[4] = {1, 1, 1, 0, 0, 0, 0, 0, 1, 1, 1, 1, 1, 1, 0, 0,
         0, 0, 1, 1, 1, 1, 1, 1, 0, 0, 0, 0, 1, 1, 1, 1, 1,
         1, 0, 0, 0, 0, 1, 1, 1, 1, 1, 1, 0, 0, 0, 0, 1, 1}

The outputs show the periodic input signals and the automaton response, respectively. Figure 6.2 depicts both of these lists graphically. It can be clearly seen that the automaton returns a periodic signal, too. The two graphs at the top of Figure 6.2 show the signals as discrete dots, whereas in the plots at the bottom, the signal points are connected, giving a better impression of the input-output patterns.

As this example shows, finite state automata are well capable of modeling complex input-output mappings. The behavior of this machine could be interpreted as recognizing particular patterns in an input signal; in this case, specific arrangements of sequences of peaks.

6.1.2   Predicting the environment with FSAs

How can we implement a finite state automaton to predict its environment? In the example in Figure 6.2, the automaton would predict its input signal if its output reproduced the input, but the response would be at least one symbol ahead of the—then predicted—input. To understand the key concept of this prediction task, let us look at a simpler example. Figure 6.3(a) shows a two-state automaton with binary   *A wishful predictor*

Figure 6.3
A wishful predictor (a) and
its performance (b) for a
particular input sequence.

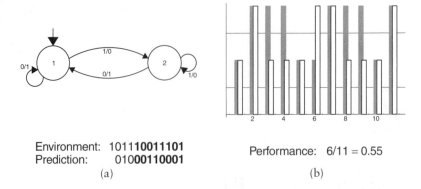

Environment: 1011**10011101**
Prediction: 01000**110001**

(a)

Performance: 6/11 = 0.55

(b)

input and output. The automaton has to respond to the environmental input as depicted at the bottom of Figure 6.3(a). The responses of
the automaton to this input sequence are interpreted as a prediction of
the next input signal from the environment. So, after the first input
signal of 1, the automaton outputs a zero, hence predicting a 0 to be
the next input signal, which is in fact the case. The automaton also
correctly predicts the next input but fails on the following, where the
predicted 0 does not match the 1 coming from the environment. We
can perform the prediction-input comparison for all the input signals
and finally evaluate the performance of the automaton with respect to
this particular environment. It predicts 6 out of 11 signals correctly, as
the bar chart in Figure 6.3(b) illustrates, which shows the input and
predicted signals as gray and white bars, respectively.

A perfect predictor

A perfect predictor machine and its performance for the example
environment is shown in Figure 6.4. This eight-state machine has been
constructed by hand, but we will see in Section 6.6, when we demonstrate FSA evolution, that smaller automata can predict just as well.

Accommodation phase

This handcrafted machine predicts all of the inputs perfectly well
right after the first input signal, which is not a very realistic scenario.
Usually organisms must get more input in order to come up with reasonable predictions. This is why we will grant the machines an initial
phase where they simply "observe" but do not have to predict correctly. After this accommodation phase, the machines are expected to
start their prediction tasks. In Figures 6.3 and 6.4, we have marked
the input-output signals relevant for prediction in bold. In both cases,
the machines have to make their predictions after they have seen the
first four input signals.

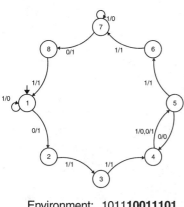

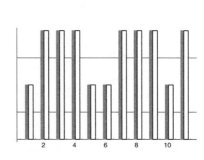

Figure 6.4
A perfect predictor (a) and its performance (b) for a particular input sequence.

Environment: 101110011101
Prediction: 01110011101
(a)

Performance: 11/11 = 1.0
(b)

6.2   Mutation operators on FSA

In order to use evolutionary mechanisms to design finite state automata that predict specific environments, we need to think about two things: (1) how to generate random machines that will serve as an initial population to start the evolution from and (2) how to generate slightly modified machines from already existing automata by mutation operators. We will discuss FSA mutations now and postpone the generation of random machines until the next section.

Given a description of a finite state automaton with its input-output alphabet, its set of states, with a designated initial state, and its transitions, what would be reasonable operators to alter such an automaton? Here is a list of possible mutation operators (some of them suggested in Fogel, Owens, et al. 1966):

Mutations on finite state machines

❑ Changing the initial state;

❑ Modifying the set of states by adding or deleting states;

❑ Modifying the set of transitions by adding or deleting transitions;

❑ Modifying transitions by changing a transition's input or output symbol, changing its source, or altering its target.

Unlike the bit-oriented mutation operators used in genetic algorithms, these mutation operations are specifically tailored to the FSA problem domain. Using problem-specific operators to search for new variants within a solution space is a key characteristic of evolutionary

EP: problem-specific data
structures and mutation
operators

programming. Instead of mapping problem-specific data structures onto more generally applicable binary strings—hence, with the advantage of more generally defined genetic operators—evolutionary programming systems usually try to use data structures that are "naturally" derived from the problem domain involved. Mutations are then defined for these data structures directly, which has the advantage that modification operators that are already established in a particular problem domain can be integrated in a straightforward fashion. In this respect, evolutionary programming is similar to evolution strategies—both of them represent engineering approaches to evolutionary computation.

In the following sections, we discuss the FSA mutation operators listed above, explaining in detail how they work and showing examples of how they affect FSA input-output behavior.

6.2.1 Changing the initial state

An automaton's performance may be changed by altering its initial state. In Figure 6.5, we show the same four-state automaton configuration with different initial states. For the given input signal, three of the four automata respond with the same output pattern, whereas the fourth machine reacts differently for the initial four signals. Obviously, the effect of an initial state mutation depends on an automaton's degree of symmetry and its redundancy.

Evolvica function for
changing the initial state

For randomly switching to another initial state, we use the Evolvica mutation function MutationFSA[ChangeInitial-State][-Automaton-], which is listed in Program 6.1. This function first determines all the states available for becoming the new initial state, altInitialStates; that is, the current initial state is excluded. If the current initial state is the only state of the automaton,

Program 6.1
Changing the initial state.

```
FSAMut[ChangeInitialState][aut_] :=
   Module[{tmpAut = aut, altInitialStates},

      altInitialStates =
      Complement[States[tmpAut],{InitialState[tmpAut]}];

      If[altInitialStates === {},
         tmpAut,
         ReplacePart[tmpAut,
            randomSelect[altInitialStates], 4]]]
```

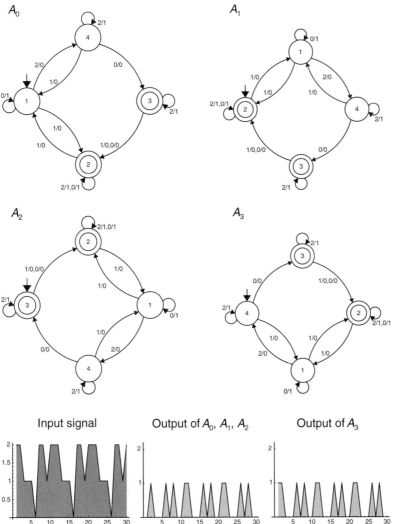

Figure 6.5
FSA mutation: changing the initial state.

no mutation is performed. Otherwise a randomly selected state from `altInitialStates` replaces the current initial state entry at position 4 (compare the input form for an automaton in Section 6.1.1).

6.2.2 Modifying the set of states

Changing the number of states of an automaton can greatly influence its overall performance. We will look at two complementary operations for altering the number of states: adding and deleting a single state.

Adding a state

Adding a single state

Adding a single state to an automaton without connecting this state to any of the existing states does not alter the machine's behavior. Therefore, changes can result only from integrating a new state into the network of transitions. These additional interconnections can be made in several ways. Figure 6.6 shows an example of a four-state automaton, A_0, which, for the given input signal, does not respond with any output, depicted as an output value of -1. This automaton simply cannot deal with inputs starting with more than a single 2 signal, because neither state 3 nor state 4 has a transition for input signal 2.

Network of new transitions

In each of the automata A_1, A_2, and A_3 a state s_{new} has been added to the set of states $\text{States}[A_i] := \text{States}[A_i] + \{s_{new}\}$. Connections from and to the new state are established as follows. For each symbol in the input alphabet $in(A_i)$ a transition is established from the new state s_{new} to any of the states $s \in \text{States}[A_i]$ (including the added state

Figure 6.6
FSA mutation: adding a state.

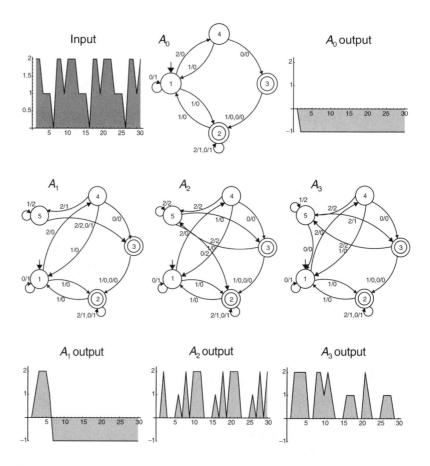

itself). The output symbol associated with each of these transitions is chosen randomly from the set of output symbols.

For possible connections going into s_{new}, we have to be a little more careful to keep the automaton deterministic; that is, no state should have more than one transition for any of the symbols from the input alphabet. Therefore, for any state $s \in$ States$[A_i] - \{s_{new}\}$, the set of input symbols in(s) that are not already covered by outgoing connections has to be determined. Whenever this set is not empty, in$(s) \neq \{\}$, a transition from s to s_{new} can be established with an input signal taken randomly from the set in(s). The output signal for this connection can be defined at random from the set of output symbols.

Keeping the FSA deterministic

Figure 6.6 shows three examples of automata with newly added and interconnected states. Note that whereas outgoing connections are established for all input symbols, incoming connections are only set up for a subset of all possible connections. For example, in automaton A_1 there is no transition from state 3 to state 5. However, this connection for input signal 2 has been added in automaton A_2 and A_3.

Example automata with additional states

As the output signal diagrams show, the overall behavior of the new five-state automata depends on the number of established connections and their input and output symbols. The addition of a new state is clearly a mutation operator with a wide range of effects on the overall behavior of an automaton. As we will see in the evolution experiments in Section 6.6, this mutation operator is one of the main creative sources in the evolutionary design of finite state automata.

The Evolvica function `FSAMut[AddState][-Automaton-]` for the adding-a-state mutation is shown in Program 6.2. First the `AddState` function from the `automaton` package extends the set of states by one (`newState`). The next two commands add random connections to (`randomConnectionsTo`) and from (`randomConnectionsFrom`) `newState`. Finally, the updated automaton `tmpAut` is returned.

Evolvica function for adding a new state

Deleting a state

The complementary operator to adding a state is deletion of a state. This operator works in a straightforward manner. A state from the set of states, excluding the initial state, is selected at random and deleted from the state set. This means, of course, that all connections to and from the deleted state disappear as well. Figure 6.7 gives three examples where states 2, 3, and 4 are deleted in automata A_1, A_2, and A_3, respectively.

Deleting a single state and all its related connections

Program 6.2
FSA mutation: adding a
state.

```
FSAMut[AddState][aut_] :=
  Module[{tmpaut = aut, newState},

  (* Add a new state *)
  AddState[tmpAut, newState = Last[States[tmpAut]] + 1];

  (* Add connections to this new state *)
  tmpAut = randomConnectionsTo[newState, tmpAut];

  (* Add connections from this new state *)
  tmpAut = randomConnectionsFrom[newState, tmpAut];

  (* Return new automaton *)
  tmpAut
]
```

Figure 6.7
FSA mutation: deleting a
state.

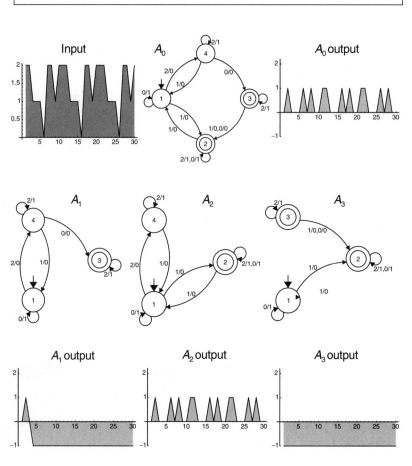

Since automaton A_0 does not enter state 3 for the given input sequence, the deletion of state 3 has no effect on the output behavior of automaton A_2. States 2 and 4, however, are crucial for the processing of the input sequence. Therefore, the deletion of any of these states brings the performance almost to a halt (A_1 and A_3).

The Evolvica function FSAMut[DeleteState][-Automaton-] is listed in Program 6.3. The variable deleteableStates contains all states of the current automaton tmpAut that can be deleted, excluding the initial state. If the automaton consists of only one state, which also is the initial state, the automaton is not changed. Otherwise the DeleteState function from the Automata package is used to erase a randomly selected state.

Evolvica function for deleting a state

```
FSAMut[DeleteState][aut_] :=
  Module[{tmpAut = aut,
    deleteableStates =
      Complement[States[aut], {InitialState[aut]}]},

    If[deleteableStates === {},
      tmpAut,
      DeleteState[tmpAut, randomSelect
      [deleteableStates]]
  ] ]
```

Program 6.3
FSA mutation: deleting a state.

6.2.3 Modifying the set of transitions

As we did for the states, we can change the set of transitions by adding or deleting connections. Here are the details on these two mutations.

Changing the number of transitions

Adding a transition

Since we want to keep our automata deterministic, a transition $t(s_1, i, s_2, o)$, from state s_1 to s_2 for input symbol i, can be added only if i is not already covered by another transition $t(s_1, i, s, o')$, for any state s. That is, we establish a new transition $t(s_1, i, s_2, o)$ only if $i \notin \text{in}(s_1)$.

The mutation operator randomly selects a state $s \in \text{States}[A]$ for which $\text{in}(s) \neq \{\}$, then a connection $t(s, i, s', o)$ is established, with i randomly selected from $\text{in}(s)$, where $s' \in \text{States}[A]$ and o is any output symbol.

Adding a single transition— caveat: determinism

In Figure 6.8, starting from automaton A_0, automaton A_1 has an additional transition $t(5, 2, 1, 1)$ between states 5 and 1 for input symbol 2. The automata A_2 and A_3 are extended by connections from state 5 to 2 and state 5 to 3, respectively. Each of these additional transitions changes the automaton behavior in a significant way.

Evolvica function for adding a transition

The function `FSAMut[AddTransition][-Automaton-]` in Program 6.4 implements the mutation of adding a transition. This function first determines for each state which input symbols are not yet covered by outgoing transitions. The list `in` contains the set of available input symbols for each state. From this list, the states (`availStates`) and their corresponding input symbols (`availInputs`) can be extracted. Putting these two lists together and transposing them merges each state with a list of its available input symbols, from which one entry is selected at random (`randStateAndInputs`). If the automaton is complete, no new transitions can be added to any state, so that `randStateAndInputs` is empty. Otherwise a new transition

Figure 6.8
FSA mutation: adding a transition.

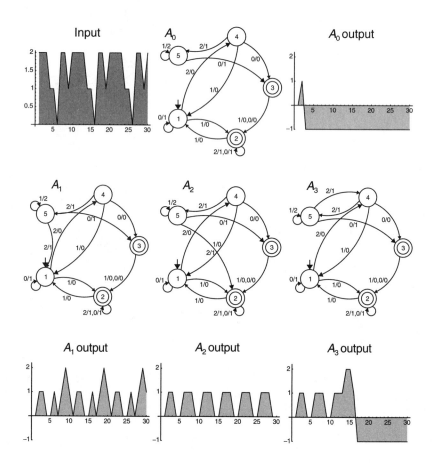

is added (`AddTransition`) with the following properties: (1) it starts from the selected state, which is the first entry of the `randStateAnd-Inputs` list; (2) it covers one of the input symbols available for this state, which is the second entry of the `randStateAndInputs` list; (3) the target of this transition is a state randomly selected from the set of states of `tmpAut`; and (4) its output symbol is a random selection from the automaton's alphabet. Finally the resulting mutated automaton, with a new additional transition, is returned.

```
FSAMut[AddTransition][aut_] :=
  Module[{tmpAut = aut, in, availStates, availInputs,
    randStateAndInputs},

    in = Map[Complement[Alphabet[tmpAut],
      Map[First, #]] &, tmpAut[[3]]];

    availStates = Flatten[Position[in, x_ /; x ≠ {}]];
    availInputs = Cases[in, x_ /; x ≠ {}];

    randStateAndInputs =
      randomSelect[
        Transpose[{availStates, availInputs}]];


    If[randStateAndInputs === {},
      tmpAut,
      tmpAut = AddTransition[tmpAut,
        {randStateAndInputs[[1]],
        randomSelect[randStateAndInputs[[2]]],
        randomSelect[States[tmpAut]],
        randomSelect[Alphabet[tmpAut]]}]]]]
```

Program 6.4
FSA mutation: adding a transition.

Deleting a transition

The inverse mutation to adding a transition is deletion of a transition. Its implementation is straightforward. A transition is randomly chosen from the set of all transitions of an automaton, and the transition is deleted.

Deleting a single transition

Depending on which connection is erased, this mutation may have dramatic effects on the input-output mapping of an automaton, as the three examples in Figure 6.9 show. The connections in the A_0

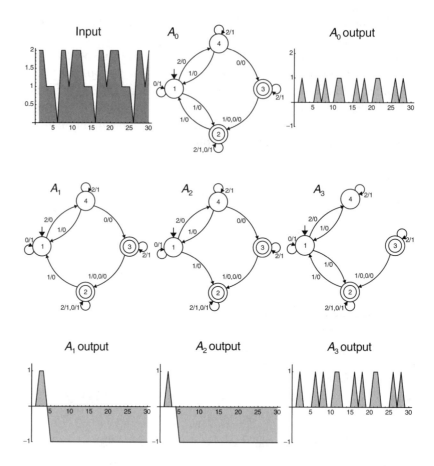

states 1 and 2 seem to be crucial for the performance of this automaton. A deletion of any of these two connections results in an error response for the given input signal (A_1, A_2). The connection between states 4 and 3, however, is not used for the given input sequence by the automaton and can therefore be deleted without any effect on the input-output mapping (A_3).

Evolvica function for deleting a transition

The function FSAMut[DeleteTransition][-*Automaton*-], listed in Program 6.5, randomly selects a transition from the set of all transitions of automaton tmpAut. The selected transition is deleted,

Program 6.5
FSA mutation: deleting a transition.

```
FSAMut[DeleteTransition][aut_] :=
  Module[{tmpAut = aut, randTrans},
    randTrans = randomSelect[Transitions[tmpAut]];
    tmpAut = DeleteTransition[tmpAut, randTrans]]
```

using the `DeleteTransition` function of the `Automata` package, and the modified automaton is returned.

6.2.4 Modifying transitions

Instead of adding and deleting transitions, we may also want to change the current transition settings by

Mutation operators for modifying transitions

- ❑ Changing a transition's input symbol,

- ❑ Changing a transition's output symbol,

- ❑ Changing a transition's source state, or

- ❑ Changing a transition's target state.

The following sections describe these mutations in detail.

Changing a transition's input symbol

We assume that a transition $t(s_1, i, s_2, o)$ has been selected from the set of all transitions of an automaton A_0. For changing the input symbol of a particular transition, we again have to deal with the problem of keeping the automaton deterministic.

In order to keep A_0 deterministic, the new input symbol $i_{new} \neq i$ for the selected transition must be an element of Inputs$[A_0]$ – in(s_1). That is, i_{new} is not yet used by any of the transitions leaving state s_1. In Figure 6.10, for the recurrent transition at state 5 and the connection from state 5 to state 1, the input symbol is changed from 0 and 1 to the new symbol 2, respectively, resulting in automata A_1 and A_2. For the given input signal, the single-peak response of automaton A_0 has changed to a periodic answer (A_1) and a three-peak output pattern (A_2).

Changing the input symbol—caveat: determinism

The function FSAMut[ChangeTransitionInputSymbol] [-Automaton-] listed in Program 6.6 is similar to the function for adding a transition (Program 6.4). First, for each state the set of still available input symbols must be determined. The list in contains the set of available input symbols for each state. From this list, both the states (availStates), for which input symbols of their outgoing transitions could be changed, and the corresponding set of alternative input symbols (availInputs) for these transitions are extracted. A state and its corresponding yet available input symbols are randomly chosen from the transposition of these two lists (randStateAndInputs). A transition is chosen randomly from the set of outgoing

Evolvica function to change an input symbol

Figure 6.10

FSA mutation: changing a transition's input signal.

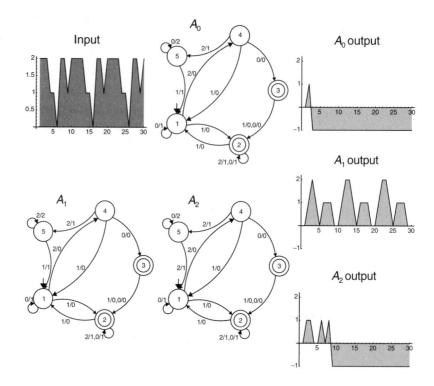

transitions of this selected state. If there are no transitions that could change their input symbols, the automaton is returned unchanged. Otherwise first the selected transition is deleted (`DeleteTransition`) and the new transition, with a new input symbol from the available input symbol set (encoded as the second entry of `randStateAndInputs`), is added (`AddTransition`). The automaton with an alternative input symbol for one of its transitions is returned.

Changing a transition's output symbol

Randomly changing an output symbol

Changing the output symbol of any transition is easy, because no constraints have to be taken into account other than selecting a different output symbol. The mutated automaton will keep its general output pattern, though, with some additional modulations.

The example automata A_1, A_2, and A_3 in Figure 6.11 illustrate this effect. All four automata, including A_0, display the same periodic response but with slight differences in the output modulation. For automaton A_1 the recurrent transition at state 4 has changed its out-

```
FSAMut[ChangeTransitionInputSymbol][aut_] :=
  Module[{tmpAut = aut, in, availStates, availInputs,
    randStateAndInputs, randTrans},

    in = Map[Complement[Alphabet[tmpAut],
        Map[First, #]] &, tmpAut[[3]]];

    availStates = Flatten[Position[in, x_ /; x ≠ {}]];
    availInputs = Cases[in, x_ /; x ≠ {}];

    randStateAndInputs = randomSelect[
        Transpose[{availStates, availInputs}]];

    randTrans = randomSelect[Cases[Transitions
        [tmpAut], {randStateAndInputs[[1]], __}]];

    If[randStateAndInputs === {},
        tmpAut,
        tmpAut = DeleteTransition[tmpAut, randTrans];
        tmpAut = AddTransition[tmpAut,
          ReplacePart[randTrans,
            randomSelect[randStateAndInputs[[2]]],
            2]]]]
```

Program 6.6
FSA mutation: changing a transition's input signal.

put from 1 to 2. Automaton A_2 differs in the output of the transition from state 4 to state 1—the output is changed from 0 to 2. Finally, the transition from state 1 to 2 has a new output symbol of 2 in automaton A_3. This mutation seems to be a candidate for matching input signals with specific output, as is required for the prediction task. Once an automaton has evolved a periodic response pattern, a few changes in the output signals might result in a perfect predictor.

The function FSAMut[ChangeTransitionOutputSymbol] [-Automaton-] first selects a random transition from the set of all transitions in automaton tmpaut (Program 6.7). If the automaton has no transition at all, the automaton is returned unchanged. Otherwise the ChangeTransition function replaces the output symbol, at position 4 of the transition data structure, with a new output symbol. The new output symbol is a random selection from the automaton's alphabet symbols excluding the current output symbol (Complement[Alphabet [...],...]).

Evolvica function for randomly changing an output symbol

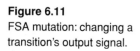

Figure 6.11
FSA mutation: changing a
transition's output signal.

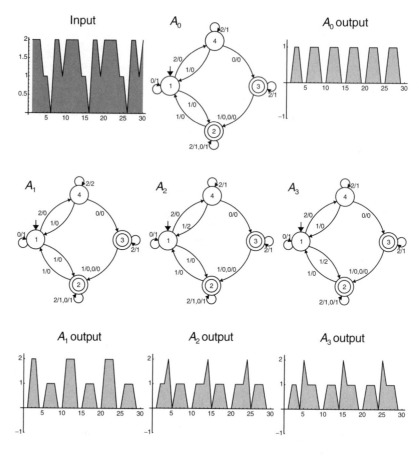

Program 6.7
FSA mutation: changing a
transition's output signal.

```
FSAMut [ChangeTransitionOutputSymbol] [aut_] :=
    Module[{tmpAut = aut, randTrans},
      randTrans = randomSelect[Transitions[tmpAut]];

      If[randTrans === {},
        tmpAut,
        tmpAut = ChangeTransition[tmpAut,
          ReplacePart[randTrans,
            randomSelect[Complement[Alphabet[tmpAut],
              {randTrans[[4]]}]], 4]]]]
```

Changing a transition's source

*Changing the source of a
transition—caveat:
determinism*

In order to change the state from which a transition originates, we
have to make sure that the determinism of the new source state is pre-
served. Let us look at the examples in Figure 6.12. The transition from

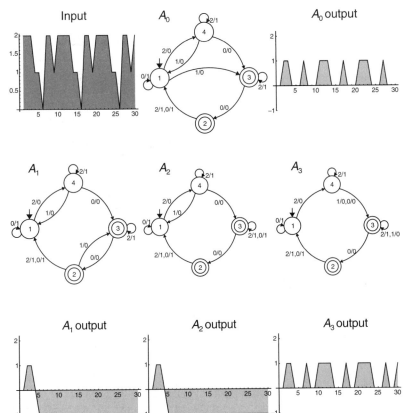

Figure 6.12
FSA mutation: changing a transition's source.

state 1 to state 3 in automaton A_0 is the one we are going to change. In automaton A_1 we redirect the source of this transition to state 2, which reduces the response to only a single peak.

In automaton A_2 the transition source is set to state 3, which results in an additional recurrent connection at state 3. Again the output signal is reduced to a single peak. Trying to let the 1-to-3 connection in A_0 originate from state 4 creates a conflict with the already existing connection from state 4 to 1, which reacts on the same input symbol 1. Here we simply assume that this conflict is resolved by keeping either of the conflicting transitions. In the case of automaton A_3, the previous connection emanating from state 4 is replaced by the redirected transition.

The function FSAMut[ChangeTransitionSource][-Automaton-] in Program 6.8 is similar to the functions for adding a transition (Program 6.4) or for changing an input symbol (Program 6.6). The list in contains the set of available input symbols for each state. From this list, both the states (availStates), for which alternative input symbols of their outgoing transitions are still available, and the

Evolvica function for changing a transition source

Program 6.8
FSA mutation: changing a
transition's source.

```
FSAMut[ChangeTransitionSource][aut_] :=
  Module[{tmpAut = aut, in, availStates, availInputs,
    randStateAndInputs, randTrans},

    in = Map[Complement[Alphabet[tmpAut],
        Map[First, #]] &, tmpAut[[3]]];

    availStates = Flatten[Position[in, x_ /; x ≠ {}]];
    availInputs = Cases[in, x_ /; x ≠ {}];

    randStateAndInputs = randomSelect[
      Transpose[{availStates, availInputs}]];

    randTrans = randomSelect[Cases[Transitions[tmpAut],
      {_,
       Apply[Alternatives, randStateAndInputs[[2]]],
       _, _}]];

    If[(randStateAndInputs === {}) || (randTrans==={}),
      tmpAut,
      tmpAut = DeleteTransition[tmpAut, randTrans];
      tmpaut = AddTransition[tmpAut,
        ReplacePart[
          randTrans, randStateAndInputs[[1]], 1]]]]
```

corresponding set of alternative input symbols (availInputs) are extracted. A state and an input symbol are chosen randomly from the transposition of these two lists (randStateAndInputs). The next step is to choose a transition (randTrans) from the automaton's transition set, which uses any of the input symbols in randState-AndInputs. If no transition with this property can be found or if all states already cover all of the symbols of the alphabet, the automaton is returned unchanged. Otherwise the transition randTrans is deleted from the automaton and a new transition is inserted. This new transition differs from randTrans only in the modified source state (ReplacePart[randTrans,...]). Finally, the mutated automaton with a redirected transition source is returned.

Changing a transition's target

Redirecting a transition target

The target of any transition can be redirected to another state in a straightforward manner. The example automata in Figure 6.13 illus-

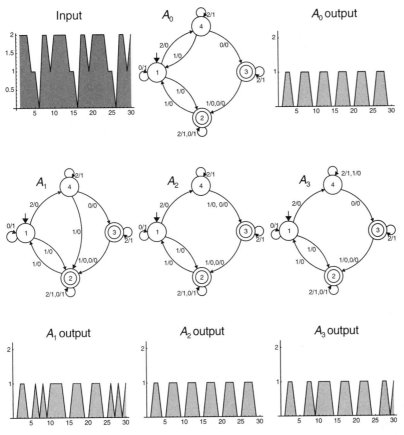

Figure 6.13
FSA mutation: changing a transition's target.

trate the effect of redirecting the transition from state 4 to state 1 to states 2, 3, and 4, respectively. With state 3 as the new target of this connection (A_2), the output signal does not change, whereas for the other two redirections the output keeps its periodic pattern but is frequency modulated (A_1, A_3).

The `FSAMut[ChangeTransition][-Automaton-]` in Program 6.9 selects a random transition, `randTrans`, and tests whether new target states for this transition are available (`newTargets`). If either the automaton does not possess any transition or there are no alternative target states (i.e., it is a single-state automaton), the automaton is returned unchanged. Otherwise the `ChangeTransition` function replaces the target state in transition `randTrans` and inserts this transition into the automaton, where the original `randTrans` transition is deleted.

Now that we have explored some possible mutations on finite state machines, it should be clear that there are many different ways to

Evolvica function for transition redirection

Program 6.9

FSA mutation: changing a
transition's target.

```
FSAMut[ChangeTransitionTarget][aut_] :=
  Module[{tmpAut = aut, randTrans, newTargets},

    randTrans = randomSelect[Transitions[tmpAut]];
    newTargets =
      Complement[States[tmpAut], {randTrans[[3]]}]

    If[(randTrans === {}) || (newTargets === {}),
      tmpAut,
      tmpAut = ChangeTransition[tmpAut,
        ReplacePart[randTrans,
          randomSelect[newTargets], 3]]]]
```

modify them. In the evolution experiments described in Section 6.6,
we will use all of these mutation operators. The experiments will
show that some of these mutations are more effective than others during specific phases of the evolutionary search process.

6.3   Automatic generation of finite state machines

We must now think about how to automatically generate populations
of finite state automata, from which to start an evolution process. The
mutation operators described in the previous sections will be used on
these populations to create new automata configurations with, hopefully, increased prediction performance.

For creating a random finite state automaton, we use the Evolvica
function makeRandomMealy[*states, alphabet, transDen-
sity*] listed in Program 6.10. This function needs a list of states, an
alphabet for the input and output symbols, and a connection density
value between 0.0 and 1.0. The function creates a list of random transitions between the given states and for the given alphabet (trans).
The initial state (initial) is randomly selected among the set of
states. Since we do not need to refer to final states for our prediction
tasks, our automata have no final states (finals = {}). Finally, the
function MakeAutomaton from the Automata package (Section
6.1.1) is used to create an automaton with the specified entries.

For generating a random (Mealy) machine, we usually do not
want to provide all of these input parameters. In particular, these
parameters should vary within a specific range. Therefore, we define
the function makeRandomAutomaton[*maxNumberOfStates*] from

```
makeRandomMealy[
  states_List, alphabet_List, transDensity_Real] :=
  Module[{trans, initial, finals},

    trans = Table[randomTransition[states, alphabet],
      {transDensity*Length[states]*Length[alphabet]}];

    initial = randomSelect[states];
    finals = {};

    MakeAutomaton[Mealy, states, trans, initial,
      finals, alphabet]]
```

Program 6.10
Creating a random finite state automaton.

Program 6.11, where the only input parameter is the maximum number of states for an automaton to be generated. This function automatically chooses a specific number of states (but at least two), sets a binary input-output alphabet ({0, 1}), and randomly selects the connection density to a value between 0.5 and 1.0.

```
makeRandomAutomaton[maxNumberOfStates_Integer] :=
  makeRandomMealy[
    Range[Random[Integer, {2, maxNumberOfStates}]],
    {0, 1},
    Random[Real, {0.5, 1.}]]
```

Program 6.11
Creating a random finite state automaton (simplified version).

The function makeRandomAutomata[*howMany, maxStates*] in Program 6.12 is used to generate a population of randomly generated finite state machines, which possess at most *maxStates* states.

```
makeRandomAutomata[
  howMany_Integer, maxStates_Integer] :=
    Table[makeRandomAutomaton[maxStates], {howMany}]
```

Program 6.12
Generating a population of finite state automata.

Figure 6.14 gives an example of a population of 20 randomly generated automata using the makeRandomAutomata function. Some of the automata are sparsely connected or have isolated states with no connections to other states or only outgoing connections.

Figure 6.14

An example population of 20 randomly generated finite state automata.

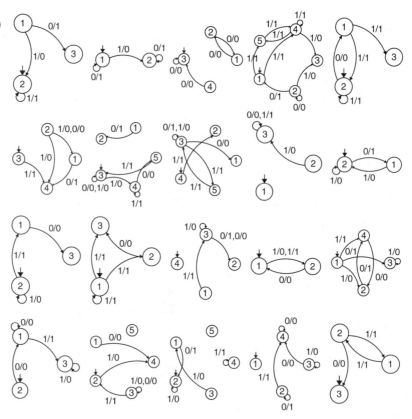

Most of these randomly generated automata are not performing well on any input signal, to say nothing of their ability to serve as predictor machines. But as we will see in the evolution experiments discussed in Section 6.6, even if we start with a crude set of initial automata, the mutation operators from Section 6.2 in conjunction with selection mechanisms discussed in Section 6.4 will gradually evolve better and better predictors.

6.4 EP selection and evolution scheme

The basic selection scheme for evolutionary programming is a probabilistic variant of $(\mu + \lambda)$ selection in evolution strategies (Section 4.4.2). The EP reproduction scheme is outlined in Figure 6.15. From a population of μ parents, λ individuals are selected at random (denoted by the arrow labeled r) and copied into the offspring population. For each offspring, a mutation operator from the operator pool is selected

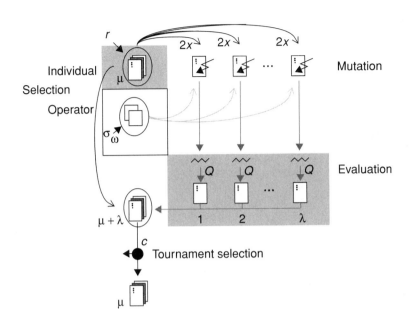

Figure 6.15
Basic evolution scheme of
evolutionary programming
on term structures (plus-EP
scheme).

and applied. σ_ω is the function for selecting the weight-attributed
mutation operators (see Section 8.2 for details).

Each mutant is evaluated based on the problem-specific evaluation function Q. The parents and the newly generated offspring constitute a selection pool of $\mu + \lambda$ individuals. Up to now, every step has
followed the plus selection scheme of evolution strategies (cf. Figure
4.30). Here comes the difference. Instead of selecting the best μ individuals from the selection pool, evolutionary programming uses a
tournament selection among the $\mu + \lambda$ individuals, which is performed
as follows.

Each individual $i \in \{1, \ldots, \mu + \lambda\}$ has to compete against   *Tournament selection*
$c < \mu + \lambda$ competitors, which are all chosen at random. The parameter
c is often referred to as the *tournament size*. Each of the c competitor's
fitness values Q_n are compared to Q_i, the fitness of individual i. The
number of the c individuals that are worse than individual i are
counted. This number is denoted as the individual's *score*. After these
tournaments, all $\mu + \lambda$ individuals are ranked in descending order of
their score values. The μ individuals with the highest scores are
selected to form the next parent population.

The function `selectTournament[`*fitnesses*`]` in Program 6.13   *Evolvica function for*
implements the tournament selection scheme. First the number of com-   *tournament selection*
petitors, `howManyCompetitors`, is determined by evaluating the
`TournamentCompetitors` option (Program 6.14). The `fits-`
`AndInds` data structure is a list of pairs—an individual's fitness value

Program 6.13
Tournament selection.

```
selectTournament[fitnesses_, opts___] :=
  Module[{howManyCompetitors, fitsAndInds,
    competitors, wins, fit, scoresAndIndsSorted},

    howManyCompetitors = (TournamentCompetitors
      /. {opts} /. Options[selectTournament]);

    fitsAndInds =
      MapIndexed[{#1, First[#2]} &, fitnesses];

    competitors = Map[randomSubset[fitsAndInds,
      howManyCompetitors, {#}] &, fitsAndInds];

    wins = MapThread[(fit = First[#1];
      Count[Map[(fit > First[#]) &, #2], True]) &,
        {fitsAndInds, competitors}];

    scoresAndIndsSorted = Map[Last,
      Sort[MapIndexed[{#1, First[#2]} &, wins]]];
    Sort[Take[scoresAndIndsSorted,
      -Best /. {opts} /. Options[selectTournament]]]]]
```

combined with its index. The competitors for each element are determined by generating random subsets of length howManyCompetitors from the fitsAndInds list. Finally, each individual's number of wins is calculated by checking whether the individual's fitness is higher than its competitors'. The resulting winning scores are indexed and sorted (scoresAndIndsSorted) and the best individuals are extracted, the number of which is determined by the Best option.

Program 6.14
Options for the
selectTournament
function.

```
Options[selectTournament] =
{ TournamentCompetitors → 1, Best → 1 };
```

For example, for a tournament selection among 11 fitness values, with a tournament size of five and a final selection size of the best five individuals, you would call the function as follows:

In[5] := **testFits = {3.1, 4.3, 5.2, 2.0, 1.7, 7.8, 9.9, 10.2, 3.5, 5.2, 6.1};**

In[6] := `selectTournament[testFits,`
         `TournamentCompetitors → 5, Best → 5]`

Out[6] = `{6, 7, 8, 10, 11}`

The outputs are the indices of the individuals that scored as the best five in the tournaments.

6.5 Evolutionary programming with Evolvica

Following the formal notation, which we already used to describe the reproduction and selection schemes of genetic algorithms (Section 3.5) and evolution strategies (Section 4.4), a general evolutionary programming experiment can be characterized as an

$$\lambda_1 \left(\mu_0 \; \overset{+}{,} \; \lambda_0 \parallel \Omega_0 \right)^{\gamma_0} \text{EP scheme.}$$

EP scheme

This "formula" denotes λ_1 independently performed EP experiments, each performed over γ_0 generations. From μ_0 parent individuals, the mutation operators generate λ_0 offspring. Depending on whether a plus-EP strategy or a comma-EP strategy is used, the μ_0 best individuals that survive the tournament selection process are designated to be the parents for the next generation. The selection pool consists either of the λ_0 offspring individuals alone (comma-EP) or of the λ_0 offspring together with the μ_0 parent individuals (plus-EP). The classic EP strategy selects from a pool of the parents together with their offspring (plus-EP strategy).

The set of mutation operators that are available to generate variations in the offspring population are defined in the options vector Ω_0, which may also contain settings for further control parameters, such as the tournament size:

$$\Omega_0 = (\text{OpPool} \rightarrow \{ \text{AddState}_{0.25}, \text{DeleteState}_{0.25}, \ldots \},$$

EP scheme options

$$\text{Tournament} \rightarrow 10, \ldots)$$

In this example, the mutation operators for changing the initial state, adding or deleting a state, and so on, are attributed with weights that translate into relative selection probabilities for these operators. The tournament size is denoted by the parameter Tournament. Using this notation to characterize EP evolution experiments, we can translate the plus-EP and comma-EP strategies into Evolvica expressions as follows:

*Comma- and plus-EP
strategies in Evolvica*

$$\lambda_1 \ \text{EP}[\mu_0, \ \text{PLUS}, \ \lambda_0, \ \gamma_0, \Omega_0]$$

and

$$\lambda_1 \ \text{EP}[\mu_0, \ \text{COMMA}, \ \lambda_0, \ \gamma_0, \Omega_0].$$

This notation is also used in the Evolution function listed in Program 6.15, which implements the EP selection and reproduction scheme as illustrated in Figure 6.15. A command of the form

*Starting EP evolution
experiments . . .*

$$\text{Evolution}[\lambda_1 \ \text{EP}[\mu_0, \ \text{PLUS}, \ \lambda_0, \ \gamma_0, \Omega_0]]$$

initiates λ_1 independent EP experiments over γ_0 generations. Each population consists of μ_0 individuals, from which λ_0 offspring are derived using the mutation operators specified in Ω_0. After evaluating the mutated offspring, a pool of the μ_0 parent and the λ_0 offspring is formed from which the best μ_0 individuals are determined using a tournament selection scheme.

*Evolvica EP evolution
function*

For the Evolution function in Program 6.15, only those sections are listed that refer directly to the EP reproduction scheme. The function starts with setting up a list of available (mutation) operators and their selection weights (opsAndProbs). The selectOperator function, which performs fitness-proportionate selection on the selection weights, refers to this list whenever an operator has to be chosen. The EvaluationFunction option defines the function to be used for calculating the individuals' fitnesses. The Table command collects the results of *i* independent evolution experiments. The Nest-List function is used to iterate over *g* generations, always using the previous result as the starting point (initial generation) for the following iteration. The While loop generates l (λ_0) offspring individuals, children, which are subsequently evaluated. Depending on whether a plus- or comma-EP strategy is used, the selection pool either comprises the parents and their offspring or only the offspring individuals.

Finally, the Selection function extracts the best *m* (μ_0) individuals by a tournament selection scheme.

*Options for the EP evolution
function*

The default option settings for the Evolution function (Program 6.16) specify an empty initial population and a fitness-proportionate offspring selection scheme (FITPROP). The classic EP scheme would use a random selection (RANDOM) instead (cf. Figure 6.15). The Max-States option defines the maximum number of states the randomly generated automata of the initial population will have. The Opera-tors list specifies all the available mutation operators on finite state machines. Each operator is associated with a relative selection weight. By default, all these weights are set to the same value. If an automatic adaptation scheme for the operator ranks (cf. Section 8.2) is used, these

```
Evolution[
  EP[m_?IntegerQ,    (* parents          *)
     s_?AtomQ,       (* PLUS or COMMA     *)
     l_?IntegerQ,    (* children          *)
     g_?IntegerQ,    (* generations       *)
     opts___]              (* options *)
   i_:1               (* independent runs *)
] :=

Module[{...},
  ...
  opsAndProbs = Operators /.{opts}
  /. Options[Evolution];
  selectOperator := First[Transpose[opsAndProbs]][[
    selectFitProp[Last[Transpose[opsAndProbs]]]]];
  ...

  (* Get the evaluation function *)
  evalFct = EvaluationFunction
            /. {opts} /. Options[Evaluation];
  ...
  (* Iterate for i independent runs *)
  Table[
    (* Iterate for g generations *)
    NestList[

      ( parents = #; children = pop[];

        While[Length[children] < l,
          children = children ~Join~
            selectOperator[parents, opts]];

        children = Map[Evaluation[#,
          EvaluationFunction :> evalFct,opts]&,
          Take[children,l]];

        selPool = Switch[s,
          PLUS, Join[parents,children], COMMA,
          children];

        Selection[selPool, m,
          SelectionMode -> TOURNAMENT, opts]];) &,
        initialParents, g ], (* end nesting *)

    {i} (* independent runs *) ]]
```

Program 6.15
Evolution scheme of
evolutionary programming.

weights will change during the evolution process, depending on the positive and negative contributions of each operator to improve the overall fitness value of the population.

Program 6.16

Options for the *Evolution* function.

```
Options[Evolution] =
{
   InitialPopulation → {},
   SelectionMode → FITPROP,

   MaxStates → 10,

   Operators → {
     {ChangeInitialState, 1},

     {AddState, 1},
     {DeleteState, 1},

     {AddTransition, 1},
     {DeleteTransition, 1},

     {ChangeTransitionInputSymbol, 1},
     {ChangeTransitionOutputSymbol, 1},
     {ChangeTransitionSource, 1},
     {ChangeTransitionTarget, 1}
   }};
```

6.6   Evolutionary programming at work

Now that we have looked at how to use finite state machines as predictors of environmental signals, how to encode FSA in an Evolvica data structure, how to modify the state machines in order to let the FSA agents behave differently, and finally how an EP reproduction and selection scheme works, we will explore the evolution of finite state automata using evolutionary programming. Let us assume we want to evolve automata that predict the following sequence of binary signals:

In[1] := **environ = {1, 0, 1, 1, 1, 0, 0, 1, 1, 1, 0, 1};**

An automaton is presented the first four signals, without having to do any prediction. After this accommodation phase, the FSA is evaluated on how well it predicts the following eight signals. For calculating an automaton's prediction quality, we use the function listed in Program 6.17. The function automatonResponse[*aut, environ*] returns the sequence of output signals by which the automaton *aut* would respond given the input signals *environ*. As a second output, the last state reached by the automaton is returned.

```
predictionQuality[aut_Automaton, environ_List,
   initial_Integer:1] :=
  Module[{response, toPredict, hits, lastPredict,
    lastState, fit},

    {response, lastState} =
     automatonResponse[aut, environ];

    response = Drop[response, initial - 1];
    lastPredict = Last[response];

    response = Drop[response, -1];
    toPredict = Drop[environ, initial];

    hits = response - toPredict;

    fit = N[Count[hits, 0]/Length[hits]];

    {fit,
      lastPredict === First[environ],
      lastState === InitialState[aut]}
  ]
```

Program 6.17
Evaluating the prediction
quality of a finite state
automaton.

Evaluating automaton
prediciton

The actual response, which is relevant for the prediction task, results from dropping the initial signals and the last signal, which is the prediction for a 13th input signal of the 12-signal environment. For the signals to predict (toPredict), the initial input sequence is ignored. The hits list contains the element-by-element differences of the automaton's response and the actual input. Counting the number of zeros occurring in this hits list gives the number of exact predictions by the automaton. Dividing this number by the length of the signals to be predicted results in a normalized prediction quality value (fit). The second and third returned values, respectively, indicate whether the very last symbol predicted is equal to the first input signal and whether the automaton has also reached its initial state again. With these two additional predicates we can determine whether an automaton is also capable of predicting a *periodic sequence* of the given input signals.

This predictionQuality function is used in Program 6.18 to calculate a fitness value, evalAutomaton[*aut, environ*], of an automaton *aut* for a specific environment *environ*.

Program 6.18
FSA evaluation.

```
evalAutomaton[aut_Automaton, environ_] :=
  Module[{p, l, lastEqFirstQ, initialQ, fit},

    {p, lastEqFirstQ, initialQ} =
      predictionQuality[aut, environ, 4];

    If[ p < 1., Return[p],

        fit = 1 + 1/
        Length[States[pruneAutomaton[aut]]];

        If[initialQ, fit = fit + 1];
        If[lastEqFirstQ, fit = fit + 1];

        fit
    ]];
```

This evaluation function, however, takes another aspect of FSA evolution into account. As long as an automaton has not yet reached the quality of a perfect predictor for a given input sequence, its fitness value is calculated as described above, using the predictionQuality function (Return[p]). Once perfect predictor FSA are evolved, selection changes its focus: the machines should get as small as possible; that is, reduce their number of states. This means that best-predictor machines with fewer states have an evolutionary advantage over automata that use a larger number of states for achieving the same prediction quality. With too many states allowed, an FSA could easily try to memorize a specific input sequence. But our objective is to evolve more compact machines that can then also be used as predictors for more general signal patterns. Therefore, the fitness evaluation in evalAutomaton changes for perfect predictors. Their fitness is calculated as $1 + 1/n$, where n is the number of states. Consequently, the fewer states an automaton possesses, the higher its fitness will be. Furthermore, the fitness is increased by 1 if at the end of the prediction, the automaton has reached its initial state again (initialQ) and if the automaton would also correctly predict the first input signal (lastEqFirstQ). With these two additional criteria, we can check whether an automaton not only perfectly predicts a given input sequence e (except for the initial signals) but also would predict a periodic iteration of this sequence ($e^+ = eeeee \ldots$). Fogel's original experiments also included a penalty for complexity based on the number of

In search of minimum automata

Compact, perfect predictors for periodic sequences

states but used a different evaluation function compared to Program 6.18 (Fogel, Owens, et al. 1966, p. 37).

Now we have all the ingredients to start an FSA evolution experiment. We use the `Evolution` function, as implemented in Program 6.15, and perform a $(50, 100)^{200}$ EP strategy:

An FSA evolution experiment

```
In[2] := Evolution[
            EP[50, COMMA, 100, 200,
                Operators → { {Mutation, 1} },
                EvaluationFunction →
                    (evalAutomaton[#, environ]&),
                TournamentCompetitors → 10,
                PruneProbability → 0.5,
                InitialPopulation → {} ,
                MaxStates → 20,
            ]
        ];
```

Instead of using a traditional plus-EP strategy, we show this experiment with a comma-EP strategy because in our experiments the comma strategy seemed to be slightly superior. From a population of 50 parent FSA, an offspring population of 100 mutated machines is generated, from which the best 50 automata are selected by tournament to be the parents for the following generation. The tournament size of 10 is determined by the option `TournamentCompetitors`. Whenever an FSA mutation has to be performed, the mutation operator (`Mutation`) chooses an element from the list of weight-attributed FSA mutations in Program 6.16 by fitness-proportionate selection. For this experiment we do not use any automatic weight adaptation scheme (Section 8.2). Therefore, the weights remain fixed during the evolution runs. The evaluation function uses `evalAutomaton` from Program 6.18 for the specific signal sequence `environ` defined above. The initial population is set to an empty list so that the 50 machines to start from are generated automatically at random. These automata will have at most 20 states (`MaxStates`).

Comma-EP strategy

In order to reduce the growth in size of the automata, about 50% of the population are pruned (`PruneProbability`). Pruning removes singleton states that have no transitions going to and from them. If no pruning is performed, the evolution tends to generate automata with an increasing number of states. These automata tend to be more robust against mutations. If pruning is applied to all automata, it is harder for the mutation operators to generate "innovative" variations, because many mutations tend to have deleterious

Automata pruning

Evolution results:
initial generation

effects on the automata's behaviors. A 50% chance of pruning keeps enough robust automata in the gene pool, while at the same time smaller automata have the chance to compete against them.

Figures 6.16 through 6.23 show the results of a typical FSA evolution experiment. The figures display only the coarse structures of the automata to illustrate the great initial variety and their gradually evolving structural connection patterns. In generation 0, a diversity of structures is displayed by the randomly generated initial population of 50 FSA. The first number above each automaton denotes its fitness, whereas the second number refers to the number of states of the unpruned automaton. The prediction quality of the best randomly constructed five-state machine is 0.625.

Generation 30:
reduced diversity

For the following generations, only the best 25 machines are depicted. In generation 30, the diversity of structures is reduced to automata with about 10 to 13 states, with several patterns of connectivity. Automata that do predict the given input sequence perfectly appear in generation 60. For these machines the prediction quality is exactly 1, which means that they now have to compete for a smaller number of states while sustaining their prediction quality. Their fitness is composed of the $1 + 1/n$ value, where n is the number of states, plus an increment of 1 for either having reached the initial state or correctly predicting the first input signal (cf. Program 6.18). In generation 70, perfect predictors for the periodic input sequence are evolved. Most of the machines have between 10 and 12 states. During the subsequent generations, more and more compact automata appear on the scene, with six states in generation 100 and five states in generation 110. Over the following 90 generations, the automaton structures vary only slightly. However, the number of transitions is finally reduced from eight (in generation 110) to seven (in generation 200).

Generation 60:
perfect predictors

Generation 70:
perfect periodic predictors

Compacting the predictors

A detailed look at selected
automata

Figures 6.24 through 6.26 show a selection of the best-evolved finite state automata predictors. Each automaton is labeled with two values: its fitness value and the number of states of the pruned automaton. To the right of the FSA in Figures 6.24 and 6.26, a prediction diagram illustrates the input-output performance of each machine. The input sequence is drawn as the smaller, light gray pattern in the foreground. The automaton's corresponding prediction signals are plotted double the size as a darker signal pattern in the background. The prediction diagrams are plotted with the input sequence repeated three times so that the total predicted signal length is 24. The initial four signals, which are not part of the prediction evaluation, have been removed from these plots.

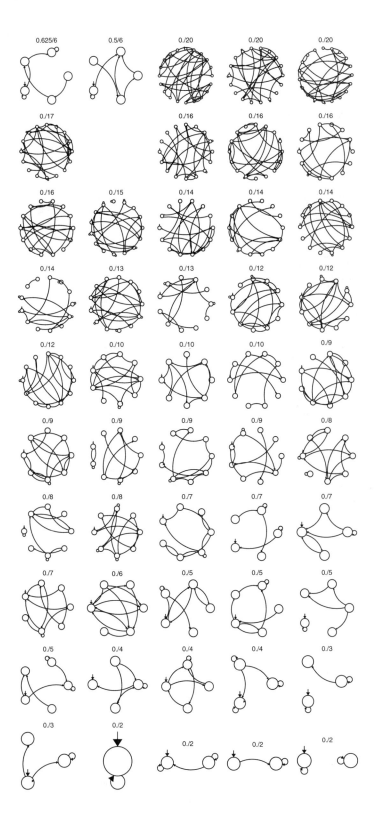

Figure 6.16
Evolved finite state automata—generation 0: diversity of structures.

Figure 6.17
Evolved finite state
automata—generation 30:
reduced structural diversity.

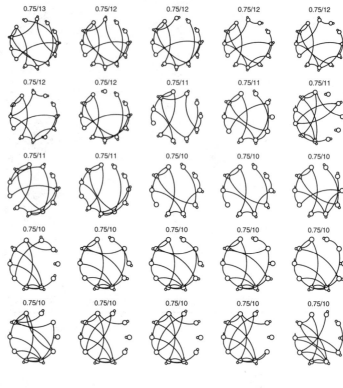

Figure 6.18
Evolved finite state
automata—generation 60:
perfect predictors.

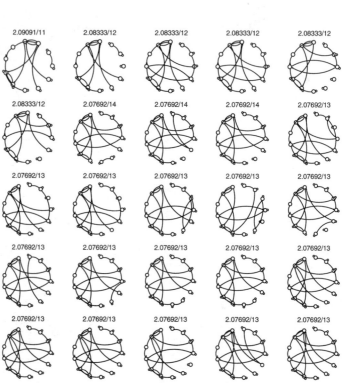

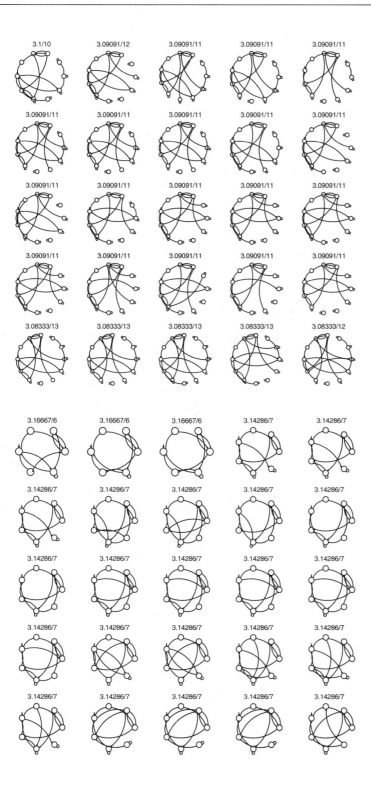

Figure 6.19
Evolved finite state automata—generation 70: perfect periodic predictors.

Figure 6.20
Evolved finite state automata—generation 100: reduction of complexity.

Figure 6.21
Evolved finite state
automata—generation 110:
simpler periodic predictors.

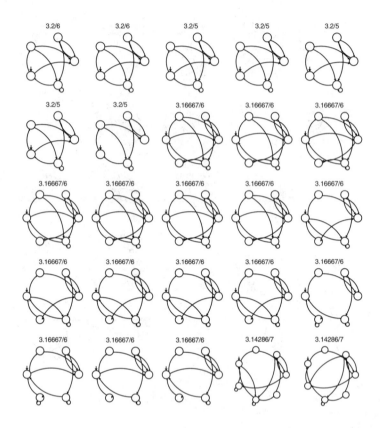

In generation 0, the best machine simply predicts a constant 1. The machine in generation 10 is much closer to a good predictor and follows the oscillation of the input signals. The best automata of generations 20 and 30 seem to achieve the same fitness with a slightly delayed constant-1 prediction and with a larger number of states. Here the evolution process has to pay the price for not including the parents in the selection pool, which in later generations, however, leads to an increased diversity of the FSA structures.

Generations 40 and 50 in Figure 6.25 show a definite improvement: the prediction quality is raised to 0.875, using 13 states. A major evolution step occurs in generation 60. A perfect predictor for the first input sequence is evolved. However, this machine (with fitness 2.09) does not end its prediction at the initial state, so that the following two iterations of the input sequence are not predicted accurately. It is only
Perfect periodic predictor   generation 70 that evolves the perfect predictor for a periodic repetition of the input sequence. This machine returns to the initial state at the end of each input segment and continues its correct prediction.

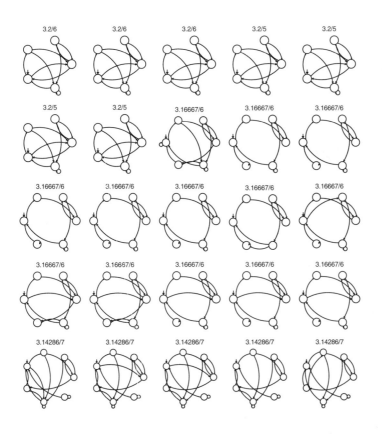

Figure 6.22
Evolved finite state
automata—generation 120:
simpler periodic predictors.

Over the following 130 generations, this automaton structure is
pruned by evolution to seven states in generation 90, to six states in
generation 100, and finally to a five-state machine in generation 180.
Over the next 20 generations, this structure is further evolved toward
another five-state automaton with the number of transitions finally
reduced from nine to seven.

Subsequent pruning

This evolution experiment is in fact slightly different from the
original FSA evolutions performed by Fogel et al. (1966). Right from
the start, we are evaluating the performance of the machine prediction
based on all symbols after the fourth, whereas Fogel and his coworkers used the first four symbols as a basis for predicting the fifth, then
the first five symbols for predicting the sixth, and so on. Here we followed Fogel's comment that "the goal need not be restricted to the
prediction of each next symbol. In fact, this same evolutionary procedure is suitable for seeking any well-defined goal within the constraints imposed by the allowable expenditure" (1999, p. 44). This
places evolutionary programming with finite state automata in the
context of general artificial intelligence search techniques.

*Differences to the "original"
EP experiments*

Figure 6.23
Evolved finite state
automata—generation 200:
five-state perfect, periodic
predictors.

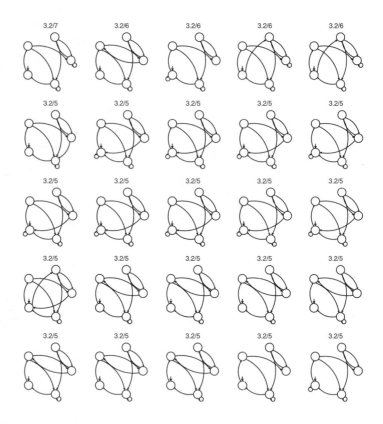

6.7   Diversification of evolutionary programming

In this section we discuss two further aspects of evolutionary programming. In Section 6.7.1, we describe extensions of the original FSA evolutions over the last 40 years. Section 6.7.2 outlines some of the recent diversifications of evolutionary programming into other problem domains, such as numerical parameter optimization.

6.7.1   Extensions of FSA evolution

The available computer speeds and memory configurations in the 1960s considerably constrained the evolution experiments of finite state automata. Consequently, many ideas for improving the overall performance of FSA evolution could only be proposed at those times. A few of these ideas are mentioned in Fogel, Owens, et al. 1966, pp. 21–25, and summarized in Fogel 1999, p. 31. The introduction of variable *mutation step sizes* was proposed to increase the efficiency of

Variable mutation step sizes

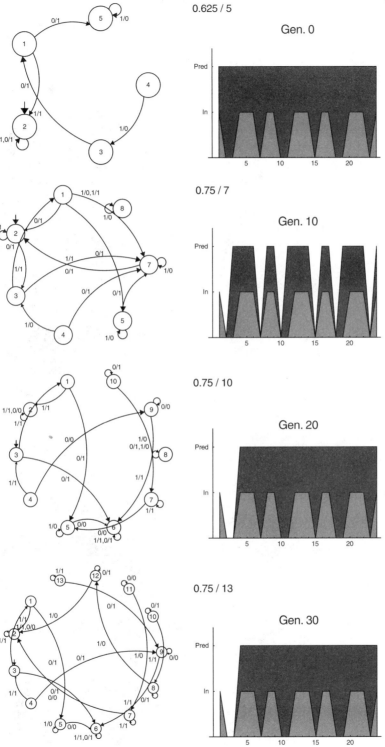

0.625 / 5

Gen. 0

0.75 / 7

Gen. 10

0.75 / 10

Gen. 20

0.75 / 13

Gen. 30

Figure 6.24
Toward perfect predictors: a selection of the best-evolved finite state machines (generations 0 to 30).

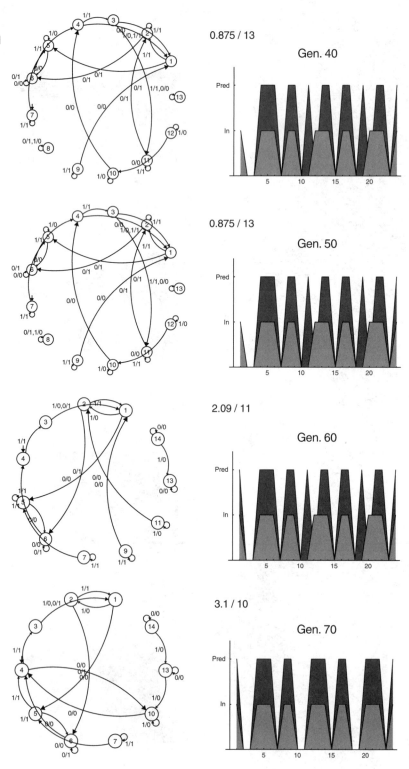

Figure 6.25
Toward perfect predictors: a selection of the best-evolved finite state machines (generations 40 to 70).

0.875 / 13

Gen. 40

0.875 / 13

Gen. 50

2.09 / 11

Gen. 60

3.1 / 10

Gen. 70

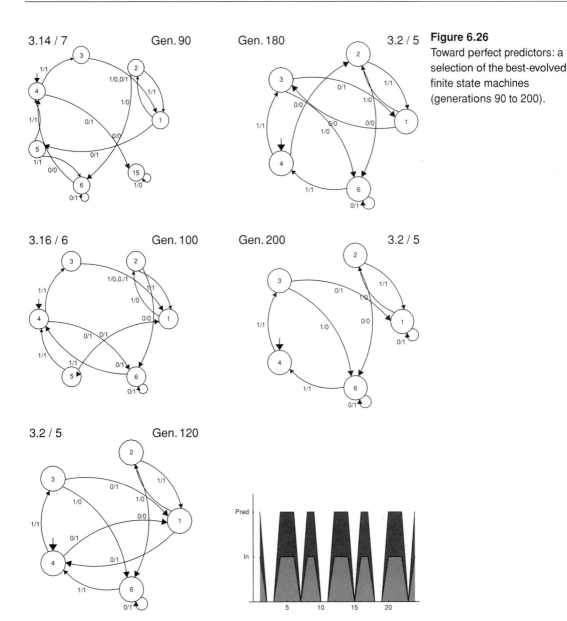

Figure 6.26
Toward perfect predictors: a selection of the best-evolved finite state machines (generations 90 to 200).

evolution. Adapting mutation rates was considered only later by Dearholt and his group (Dearholt 1976). Keeping lower-ranked parents and performing mutations in *proportion to normalized evaluation scores* was another suggestion. However, more than two decades passed before a proportional selection scheme, similar to the fitness-proportionate selection used in genetic algorithms (Section 3.5.1), was seriously taken into consideration to solve the traveling salesman

Fitness-dependent mutation

Majority logic recombination problem (Fogel 1988). An analogy of *recombination* based on major-ity logic (ML) was proposed, where an ML machine is combined from several FSA as a composite of the states from each FSA (Fogel, Owens, et al. 1966, pp. 21–25).

Between 1976 and 1985, only "limited work in evolutionary pro-gramming was performed," as David Fogel (1995, p. 84) admits. In 1985 some of the ideas and experiments for evolving finite state machines were extended by Lawrence and David Fogel, father and

FSA experiments revisited son. They revisited their prediction experiments with a population size of 12 (instead of three, as in the original experiment) on cyclic, possibly noisy input signals of varying lengths, on sequences gener-ated by Markov transitions or Fibonacci series and with different evaluation functions, mutation rates, and a varying number of muta-tions per automaton (Fogel 1999, pp. 68–72).

Benefits of recombination? The strong belief of the genetic algorithm community in the advantageous effect of recombination operators on evolution pro-cesses—papers on the importance of crossover at the First Interna-tional Conference on Genetic Algorithms provide much evidence of this belief (Grefenstette 1985)—initiated a comparison of one-parent mutation operators to two-parent recombination for EP applications with finite state automata predictors. The results of these experiments showed no advantage of using the crossover operator that even slightly reduced predictive performance of the FSA in these particular experiments (Fogel 1986).

The next chapter provides a more detailed discussion on the importance of different genetic operators for parameter and program optimization (see Section 3.7.4 for a comparison of GA operators on binary strings and Section 8.2, where we analyze the varying stages of influence of GP operators on symbolic expression evolution).

6.7.2   Recent diversification and evolution of EP

Combinatorial and parameter optimization More recently, since the beginning of the 1990s, the evolution of finite state automata has taken a backseat in the evolutionary programming community. Instead within the last decade, EP applications and research have focused on combinatorial and parameter optimization problems. Representations for data, programs, or systems to be opti-mized are chosen directly from the problem domain. The same applies to the mutation operators, which are designed in such a way that they

Strong causality obey the principle of *strong causality*. This was noticed earlier by Rechenberg (1973) and is now a generally accepted principle in the evolution strategy community (Section 4.2.1). Basically, the principle of strong causality demands a tight connection between mutation step sizes and their (phenotypical) effects on the evolved object; that is, small mutations on the representation level should also, preferably, result in minor changes on the level of the encoded objects, behaviors, systems, or whatever the chosen domain of optimization is. Strong causality ensures a strong linkage between the traits of each parent and its offspring.

The much wider diversity of EP applications in the 1990s has occurred in conjunction with the increased applicability of other evolutionary computation approaches during the last decade, due to the availability of fast and inexpensive computers and a growing need to tackle difficult real-world optimization problems. This diversity can be seen in the variety of problems that have been tackled with evolutionary programming since then. Evolutionary programming has been applied to

EP application domains

❑ Path planning,

❑ The design and training of neural networks,

❑ Fuzzy systems,

❑ Hierarchical systems,

❑ Automatic control,

❑ Game playing and the evolution of game strategies,

❑ General function optimization,

❑ Combinatorial optimization, and

❑ The evolution of art.

These problem domains are also being investigated with all the other major players in evolutionary computation today—genetic algorithms (GA, Chapter 3), evolution strategies (ES, Chapter 4), and genetic programming (GP, Chapter 7). They are also reflected in the diverse evolutionary algorithm approaches documented in the proceedings of the Annual Conference on Evolutionary Programming (Fogel and Atmar 1992; Fogel and Atmar 1993; Sebald and Fogel 1994; McDonnell, Reynolds, et al. 1995; Fogel, Angeline, et al. 1996; Angeline, Reynolds, et al. 1997; Porto, Saravanan, et al. 1998).

Toward unified evolutionary computation

In general, it seems that the "ES-EP-GA-GP ecosystem" is evolving toward a more unified notion of *evolutionary algorithms* as general adaptable concepts for problem solving, "which are particularly well suited for solving difficult optimization problems, rather than a collection of related and ready-to-use algorithms" (Bäck, Hammel, et al. 1997).

6.8   Bibliographical notes

Books on evolutionary programming

Artificial Intelligence Through Simulated Evolution

The classic book on evolutionary programming, describing the first experiments using finite state automata to evolve "intelligent agents," is *Artificial Intelligence Through Simulated Evolution,* by Lawrence Fogel, Alvin Owens, and Michael Walsh (1966).

One of the original research papers on early evolutionary programming (Fogel, Owens, et al. 1965) is reproduced in Fogel 1998.

Intelligence Through Simulated Evolution

From today's perspective, Lawrence Fogel gives in his book *Intelligence Through Simulated Evolution* a detailed overview of evolutionary programming during the last forty years, with shifts from finite state automata evolution to parameter optimization and many other optimization domains (Fogel 1999).

Conferences on evolutionary programming

EP conference

The series of the annual Conference on Evolutionary Programming started in 1992. The very first EP conferences focused strongly on evolutionary programming theory and applications (Fogel and Atmar 1992; Fogel and Atmar 1993). Over the years, this conference evolved into a major general forum for researchers in evolutionary computation (EC), including genetic algorithms, evolution strategies, genetic programming, and other EC approaches (Sebald and Fogel 1994; McDonnell, Reynolds, et al. 1995; Fogel, Angeline, et al. 1996; Angeline, Reynolds, et al. 1997; Porto, Saravanan, et al. 1998). Since 1999, to reflect this wider scope, the EP conference has been continued annually under the new name Congress on Evolutionary Computation (Angeline, Michalewicz, et al. 1999).

CEC

7 Genetic Programming

The individual structures that undergo adaptation in genetic programming are hierarchically structured computer programs. The size, the shape, and the contents of these computer programs can dynamically change during the [evolution] process.

Koza 1992, p. 80

Many computer programmers are skeptical about the idea of developing programs by applying the "blind watchmaker" principle of evolution. Some of us may remember programming as a tedious job—at least at the beginning, when programs do not run because a simple semicolon is missing or a comma has been misplaced. How can an evolutionary system, generating program code more or less randomly, succeed in developing syntactically correct and executable programs?

The solution lies in an adequate form of representation for the program structures to be evolved. Just as we do not interpret texts as a sequence of separate characters but as words, sentences, paragraphs, and so on, so are computer programs composed in modular units. They consist of functions, subprograms, variable declarations, instruction sequences, loops, conditionals, and so on. Hence if a representation of programs on the level of such modules can be found, then the idea of "breeding" programs by evolution is no longer unrealistic. Examples in the previous chapter have shown this, and we will again demonstrate this by "breedings" of computer programs in this and the following chapters.

Adequate representation of computer programs

On the basis of genetic algorithms, John Koza and his research group developed a programming system for genetically generating and optimizing LISP computer programs for specific problem domains (Koza 1989; Koza 1990; Koza 1992; Koza 1994; Koza, Andre, et al. 1999). The reproduction scheme is analogous to the one used for genetic algorithms, hence the term *genetic programming*. Fitness-proportionate selection performs filtering on a set of program genomes.

GAs and GP

Those programs representing a better solution algorithm are preferably selected for the following generation. Variations on the program-encoding genomes are generated by recombinations and mutations.

The major difference between genetic algorithms and genetic programming is that program structures are not encoded as linear genomes (Figure 7.1[b], [c]) but as terms or simple symbolic expressions. The units being mutated and recombined do not consist of characters or command sequences but of functional (LISP) modules, which can be represented as tree-structured chromosomes (Figure 7.1[a]).

Using tree-structured chromosomes also implies a reinterpretation of recombining and mutating genetic operators. The elementary building blocks now correspond to subtrees (subterms) or leaves (end nodes), which can either be exchanged between tree-structured chromosomes or replaced by new term structures. In comparison to linear program genomes, this gives totally new possibilities for program modification by genetic operators. The terms directly correspond to hierarchical program structures. In principle, the chromosome sizes

Tree-structured chromosomes

Figure 7.1
Tree-structured versus linear program genomes.
(a) Tree-structured term.
(b) Rule set of a classifier system (linear binary encoding). (c) Instruction sequences in assembler (linear binary encoding).

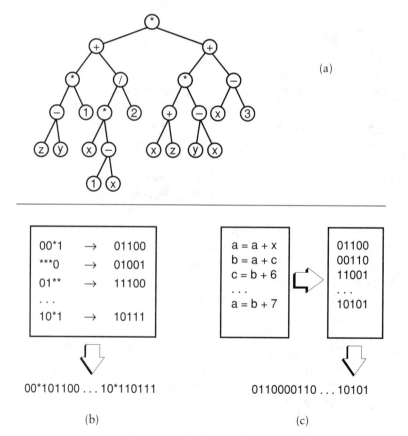

are not restricted either in depth or in width. This means that the encoded programs are adaptive in almost any way, both in size or shape and in their semantic, algorithmic contents.

Even some biologists consider the introduction of tree-structured chromosomes an essential research advancement in the context of *artificial life*, stated by evolutionary biologist William Hamilton:

> *I think tree-shaped chromosomes are the coming wave. It may also be good for biologists to understand the limitations which may be forced on life by the fact that it always has to work with linear chromosomes.*

> W. Hamilton (Levy 1993a, p. 177)

In the following sections, we will first introduce in more detail terms as genotypic expressions (Section 7.1) and show in particular how to generate random term structures. These structures serve as initial populations for program evolutions from a set of problem-specific functions. In Section 7.2, we discuss a GP recombination operator as the analog to the crossover used in genetic algorithms. A mutation operator on terms is defined in Section 7.3. The basic GP evolution scheme, which is in essence derived from GA schemes, is discussed in Section 7.4. Finally, a first GP example on the evolution of mobiles is the topic of Section 7.5.

Chapter overview

7.1 Symbolic expressions as genotypical program structures

> *The set of possible structures in genetic programming is the set of all possible combinations of functions that can be composed recursively from the set of . . . functions . . . and the set of . . . terminals.*

> Koza 1992, p. 80

Terms can be described as tree-structured compositions of functions and terminals. An exact definition of GP terms is given in Section 7.1.1. The set of functions and terminals is determined by the problem to be solved by genetic programming. This raises the question of which functions and terminals are "sufficient" for a specific problem domain. How can the reservoir of combinable elements be defined such that on the one hand, an algorithmic solution (an evolved program) can in principle be found but on the other, the creative potential

Terms as tree structures

of evolution is not constrained in such a way that only certain combinations of building blocks can be reasonably interpreted as computer programs? These completeness and closure properties of problem domains and program search spaces with respect to the reservoir of functions and terminals are discussed in Section 7.1.3. Evolvica implementations of GP term generation are presented in Section 7.1.2.

7.1.1 Term-structured GP expressions

Let us suppose we want to generate expressions as depicted in Figure 7.1(a). The inner nodes of the tree structures carry labels from the set $\{+, -, *, /\}$, and the leaves are attributed with variables or numbers from the set $\{x, y, z, 1, 2, 3\}$. In general, the elementary building blocks are prespecified by two sets—problem-specific functions and terminals. A reservoir of composable basic elements is provided by the *function symbols* from the set

Problem-specific functions

$$F = \{f_1, f_2, \ldots, f_N\}.$$

Each of these function symbols $f \in F$ is attributed with an arity $\sigma(f)$, defining the number of arguments of f:

$$\sigma(F) = \{\sigma(f_1), \sigma(f_2), \ldots, \sigma(f_N)\}.$$

Furthermore, the set

Problem-specific terminals

$$T = \{t_1, t_2, \ldots, t_M\}$$

defines the *terminals*. However, these elements can also be considered as function symbols with arity zero, so that both sets can be merged into a reservoir S of basic building blocks:

$$S = F \cup T.$$

Since the terminals frequently play a specific role in generating GP structures, they are often kept separate from the function symbols. *Problem-specific building blocks* The set of problem-specific elementary components must be specifically designed for each problem domain. This is one of the main difficulties in genetic programming. As for genetic algorithms, the coding of parameters in essence determines whether the evolution procedure will succeed or fail. It is the collection of functions and terminals on which the GP algorithm has to rely while trying to evolve innovative and optimized program structures by recombination and mutation. In general, the set of GP terms, GP-term$_{F \cup T}$ over a function set F and a terminal set T, is defined as follows:

❏ Each terminal $t \in T$ is a GP term.

❏ For $f \in F$, $\sigma(f) = n$ and $g_1, \ldots, g_n \in$ GP-term$_{F \cup T}$ the expression $f[g_1, \ldots, g_n]$ is also a GP term.

In genetic programming, terminals from T typically represent program variables or constants (numbers, truth values, etc.), whereas function symbols from F stand for problem-specific operations. The sets of functions and terminals must be defined for each problem domain, as the following selection of functional/terminal building blocks shows (Koza 1992, p. 80):

❏ Arithmetic operations: PLUS, MINUS, MULT, DIV, . . .

❏ Relations: LESS, EQUAL, GREATER, . . .
❏ Mathematical functions: SIN, COS, EXP, LOG, . . .
❏ Boolean operations: AND, OR, NOT, . . .
❏ Command sequences: PROGN
❏ Conditionals: IF-THEN-ELSE, COND, . . .
❏ Iterations and loops: DO-UNTIL, WHILE-DO, FOR-DO, . . .
❏ Domain-specific functions: MOVE-RANDOM, IF-FOOD-HERE, PICK-UP, . . . (Koza 1992, p. 331).

The term-structured programs, which can be generated from these elementary building blocks, usually represent a pseudo-code for commands and data structures of a concrete programming language. In order to encode computer programs in term structures, all programming constructs must be transformed into a functional form. This transformation is relatively easy if the programming language is already based on a functional syntax or provides inherent functional structures.

Terms and functional expressions provide an almost universal form for representing hierarchical structures. This is known not only from mathematical formulas but also from both LISP and Mathematica. Most of the programs and data structures written in these languages are constructed as simple functional symbolic expressions. However, the set of terms is only a subset of general *symbolic expressions,* which provide the actual building blocks in LISP and Mathematica (see Section 5.2). More precisely, in symbolic expressions even the function symbols may be proper terms. To give a Mathematica example, the expression

```
Derivative[2][Sin][π]
```

describes an executable program; namely, the computation of the second derivative of the sine function evaluated at position π, which is finally evaluated to zero. Symbolic expressions like this one are not in the set of GP terms and therefore cannot be described as term expressions. In the subsequent chapters, we will use more advanced GP evolution schemes working on proper symbolic expressions, but in this chapter, we focus on traditional GP term structures.

7.1.2 Generating GP terms

Given two finite sets of functions F and terminals T, tree or term structures can be composed recursively. For the building blocks

Example building blocks

$$S = \{ \text{Mult}_2, \text{Add}_2, \text{If-Then-Else}_3, \text{Equal}_2, A_0, B_0, C_0, D_0 \}$$

the step-by-step construction of a term from GP-term$_s$ is illustrated in Figure 7.2. The indices of the symbols in S correspond to their arity. All constants have arity zero.

Recursive construction of GP terms

A symbol is randomly selected from the function set; for example, the 3-ary function If-Then-Else. Each of the branches can be extended by further subtrees. Again elements are selected at random from the function set S. This recursive procedure is repeated until all leaf nodes are marked with terminals. In principle, the depth and width of these terms are not constrained. For practical purposes (storage space and computation time for term evaluation), however, it is better not to exceed a predefined tree depth.

Mathematica makes implementing a term generator function easy, as shown in Program 7.1. In Evolvica, we define a function `randomExpr`, which takes the maximal term depth as its first argument. The terms are generated from the sets of `functions` and `terminals`. The second argument (`pat`) specifies an initial pattern, which is

Figure 7.2
Step-by-step composition of a GP term.

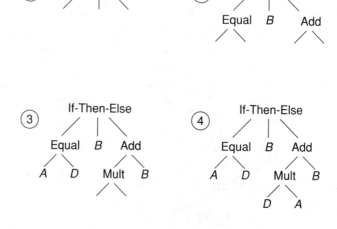

used as the "tree root" and has to comply with the function and terminal sets. The function `randomSelect` is used to select an expression, matching `pat`, from the list of functions (Program 7.2).

```
randomExpr[depth_?Positive, pat_Blank,
          functions_List, terminals_List] :=
Module[{p},
  p = randomSelect[Cases[functions,pat]];
  If[AtomQ[p], p,
    Map[randomExpr[depth - 1,#,
      functions,terminals]&,p]]
]

randomExpr[0, pat_Blank, functions_, terminals_] :=
  randomSelect[Cases[terminals,pat]]
```

Program 7.1
Term composition on a set of functions and terminals.

```
randomSelect[s_List] :=
  s[[Random[Integer,{1,Length[s]}]]]
```

Program 7.2
Random selection on lists.

The function `randomExpr` is recursively applied to the arguments of the selected expression, with the maximum term depth decreased by 1. The recursion ends if either an atomic expression is selected or depth 0 is reached. In the latter case, the leaf node is substituted by a randomly selected terminal.

Let us look at a few examples. We represent the function symbols by *patterns*, which allow us to define the function heads as well as their arities in a straightforward manner. Four 2-ary function symbols and 10 terminals are given:

Patterns

In[1] := **functions = {p[_,_], s[_,_], t[_,_], d[_,_]};**
          terminals := {x, y, z, Random[Integer,{-3,3}]};

Here x, y, and z represent variables. Integer constants are in the range between −3 and 3. According to the set $S = F \cup T$, we define

In[2] := **functionsAndTerminals = functions ~Join~**
          terminals;

Now we generate a list of random GP terms with a maximum depth of 1:

Depth-1 terms

```
In[3] := Table[randomExpr[1, _,
              functionsAndTerminals, terminals], {8}]
```

```
Out[3] ={z, d[y, y], z, t[z, 0], d[z, z], x, x, p[y, -3]}
```

As the output shows, the expressions have either depth 0 or 1. Only terminals or functional expressions with variables or constants in their arguments can be generated in this way. For terms with head p a maximum depth of 2, we enter the following command:

Depth-2 terms

```
In[4] := Table[randomExpr[2, _p,
              functionsAndTerminals, terminals], {5}]
```

```
Out[4] ={p[s[x, z], y], p[p[x, y], y], p[p[y, y],
           t[x, z]], p[z, d[z, y]], p[z, d[-3, y]]}
```

The initial pattern is _p, and we pass as the function set both the function and terminal expressions. Hence, not only complete binary trees, such as p[p[y, y], t[x, z]], are generated but also "incomplete" terms, such as p[s[x, z], y] or p[z, d[-3, y]] can be found. However, simple terms like these are not of interest for genetic programming. The following expressions with a maximum depth of 20 give a more realistic picture of the typical complexity of GP terms used for program evolution.

```
In[5] := Table[
             randomExpr[20, _, patternsAndAtoms, atoms],
           {10}] // TableForm
```

Typical GP terms

```
Out[5] =d[d[s[t[x, d[s[s[d[-1, z], d[s[-1, y],
           t[t[d[p[z, d[-1, -1]], -1], z], p[z, t[s[d[s[-1,
           d[p[x, x], z]], -1], z], x]]]]], z], p[p[z,
           p[t[t[y, s[t[x, s[p[y, d[s[d[x, s[y, p[z, z]]],
           d[s[p[s[z, y], t[x, x]], d[t[-3, 0], p[x, x]]],
           x]], y]], t[-1, t[t[-1, s[-1, s[t[y, d[y, 0]],
           t[p[1, y], y]]]], t[d[-1, y], d[t[x, p[z, z]],
           p[z, x]]]]]]]], z]], p[z, y]], x]], -1]]], y],
           d[y, -1]], x]
         y
         s[p[p[x, -1], x], t[d[d[-1, d[x, -1]], -1], -1]]
         s[d[p[s[-1, y], x], z], d[d[s[y, p[z,
           p[t[s[d[s[z, t[d[-1, d[d[s[t[-1, y], s[d[t[s[y,
           s[-1, y]], y], x], x]], y], t[t[t[-1, x],
```

```
        d[d[d[t[d[3, y], t[x, x]], s[z, x]], p[x, y]],
        p[x, t[y, t[z, y]]]]], -1]]], d[z, t[y, p[-1,
        p[t[-1, -1], s[s[s[x, -1], x], z]]]]]]]], z], x],
        s[z, d[-1, y]]], t[s[x, -1], -1]]]], p[p[s[z,
        d[d[t[y, y], p[t[-1, x], -1]], x]], z], d[s[s[y,
        s[x, d[y, s[p[x, d[s[t[s[s[y, -1],
        t[s[y, -1], x]], z], x], x]], z]]]], x], -1]]],
        d[t[t[d[z, z], y], x], p[d[z, s[y, d[z,
        t[x, -1]]]], x]]]]
      t[d[t[z, -1], d[y, t[s[z, p[y, z]], x]]],
        d[x, y]]
      p[z, z]
      d[x, d[y, y]]
      y
      -1
      y
```

Figure 7.3 depicts some of the generated terms as tree structures. These graphics are produced with the function TermPlot, which is part of the Evolvica GP notebook available on the *IEC* Web site (see Preface). Program 7.3 gives a list of the options for TermPlot. By using TreeWidth and TreeHeight, the width and height of a tree can be adjusted. LineColor sets the coloring of the lines, and Text-Color and LabelColor determine the color of the text as well as the background shading of the function symbols. Whether to use Hue or GrayLevel to interpret the color values is set by the ColorFunc-tion option. TextFont should be used for setting the text font and size.

Program 7.3
Options for the TermPlot function.

```
Options[TermPlot] =
{ TreeWidth → 1, TreeHeight → 0.2,
  ColorFunction → GrayLevel, LineColor → 0,
  TextColor → 0, TextFont → {"Courier-Bold",10},
  LabelColor → 0.9
};
```

The TermPlot function is typically used as follows:

In[1] := **TermPlot[f[g[x,h[y,p[t,k,k,l,m],d,e]],f[i,j]]];**

Figure 7.3
Tree representation of
terms.

The graphical output for this function call is depicted in Figure
7.4(a). The term structures can also be composed from bottom to top
(Figure 7.4[b]) if a negative value is chosen for TreeHeight.

In[2] := **TermPlot[f[g[x,h[y,p[t,k,k,l,m],d,e]],f[i,j]],**
         TreeHeight → -.5, TextFont → {"Times", 10}];

Defining building blocks
through patterns

Let us look at a few more examples of term generation that make
even better use of Mathematica's pattern-matching capabilities. In the
following example we assume that the number of arguments is fixed
for only two function symbols, whereas for the other functions the

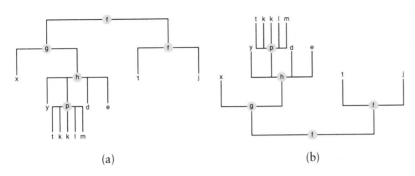

(a)   (b)

Figure 7.4
Two ways of term
visualization by `TermPlot`.

number of arguments may range between 1 and `maxArgs`. Here we leave the numbers of arguments for the functions `p[__]` and `t[__]` variable.

In[3] := `functions = {p[__], t[__], s[_,_], d[_,_]};`
          `terminals := {x, y, z, Random[Integer,{-3,3}]};`

In[4] := `functionsAndTerminals = functions ~Join~`
          `terminals;`

In[5] := `maxArgs = 5;`

With the last command we set the maximum number of arguments per subexpression to 5. We generate 10 expressions with root symbol p:

In[6] := `Table[randomExpr[1, —p,`
          `functionsAndTerminals, terminals], {10}]`

Terms with variable numbers of arguments

Out[6] = `{p[z], p[x, z, y, y, x], p[z, x], p[z, z, x, 2],`
        `p[y, 3, z, x], p[y, z], p[-1, -3, -1],`
        `p[-1, y, z, x], p[z, z, x], p[z, z, z, z, y]}`

The number of arguments ranges between 1 and 5. In order to cope with a variable number of arguments, the function `randomExpr` has to be extended by two definitions, taking `BlankSequence` patterns (`__`) into account (Program 7.4).

     The Evolvica notebook contains additional definitions including zero-arity functions, the arguments of which match the Mathematica pattern `___` (`BlankNullSequence`). The notebook is available on the *IEC* Web site (see Preface).

Program 7.4
Generating GP terms
with variable numbers of
arguments.

```
randomExpr[depth_?Positive, pat_BlankSequence,
           functions_, terminals_] :=
  Sequence @@ Table[
    randomExpr[depth - 1,_,functions,terminals],
    {Random[Integer,{1,maxArgs}]}]

randomExpr[0, pat_BlankSequence,
           functions_, terminals_] :=
  Sequence @@ Table[randomSelect[Cases
  [terminals,_]],
    {Random[Integer,{1,maxArgs}]}]
```

7.1.3 Requirements for program building blocks

Arithmetic expressions

In our first examples of GP term generation, we chose arithmetic expressions for a particular reason. Mathematical expressions, such as t = Times, p = Plus, s = Subtract, and d = Divide, obey the convenient property of being *closed* under composition. This means that the composition of any arithmetic expressions always results in a syntactically correct and reasonably interpretable expression. For general program structures, however, this is not necessarily the case, as we will show in the following example.

Let us reconsider the program building blocks we used at the beginning of Section 7.1.2. In Figure 7.2, we illustrated the step-by-step construction of GP terms over the function set

$$S = \{\text{Mult}_2, \text{Add}_2, \text{If-Then-Else}_3, \text{Equal}_2, A, B, C, D\}.$$

Using the same recursive procedure, it is also possible to compose a term as depicted in Figure 7.5.

Closure property of GP terms

This example highlights the problem of this approach to generating randomly structured GP terms. If the functions and terminals to be composed are selected in a context-free fashion, no type restrictions are taken into account. Hence, the semantics of the terms must be extended such that there are reasonable interpretations for all possible compositions of terms. If the symbols *A*, *B*, and *D* in Figure 7.5 represent numbers and if Boolean values *True* and *False* are interpreted as numbers 1 and 0, respectively, then the type inconsistencies in the returned values of the first and third arguments of the If-Then-Else function are removed. Furthermore, the definition of If-Then-Else must be extended such that the conditional section works not only for Boolean values but also for numbers that are implicitly treated as

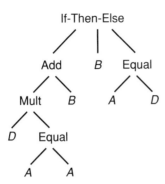

Figure 7.5
Problematic GP term.

truth values. This property demanded of the GP terms is called *closure*, which must be checked for any set of problem-specific building blocks. The functions and terminals made available to a term generation system must be closed with regard to composition, since in their simplest form, GP terms are defined only for a single data type.

Another important requirement for problem-specific building blocks is their *completeness*—that is, the functions and terminals used to describe solutions for a problem-specific task must be chosen in such a way that the evolution system actually has access to all the elementary building blocks required for a solution. For many simple program inductions (for instance, the approximation of trigonometric functions or the evolution of Boolean or arithmetic expressions), the setup of functions and terminals is a standard task (Koza 1992, pp. 238 ff.). For many practical relevant program inductions, however, it is usually not obvious at all which building blocks are indispensable for a problem solution. What constitutes a problem-specific, reasonable reservoir of building blocks often only becomes visible during the evolution experiments. There is one rule of thumb, however: it is usually advantageous to provide the evolution system with a wider range of functions than are actually necessary to solve a specific problem. It is one of the implicit characteristics of evolutionary systems that building blocks that turn out to be unsuitable or redundant will eventually either be excluded from or integrated into the program structures, respectively.

Completeness of GP building blocks

Problem-specific building blocks

Further problems arising from closure and completeness requirements are discussed in Koza 1992, pp. 79 ff. The examples discussed in detail in this volume give a number of hints and suggestions for promising functions and terminal sets for function regression or the evolution of physical formulas, control programs for broom balancing, and navigation of robots. The two subsequent volumes, which demonstrate an even wider spectrum of GP applications, are also recommended (Koza 1994; Koza, Andre, et al. 1999).

7.2   GP recombination of program structures

The central GP operator for generating new term structures is a modified variant of one-point crossover used in genetic algorithms (Section 3.3.2). Substrings are exchanged by crossing two linear GA chromosomes. The analogy for tree-structured GP chromosomes works as follows: randomly selected subtrees are interchanged among two terms, as is illustrated in Figure 7.6.

In detail, GP crossover among two terms s_1 and s_2 is performed as follows. A node for identifying a subterm is chosen at random in each of the term trees. Both inner nodes (including the root node) as well as leaf nodes can be chosen. In Figure 7.6, the selected subtrees are marked by triangular shapes. The two recombined terms t_1 and t_2 result from a crosswise exchange of the selected subtrees.

GP vs. GA and ES recombination

When we compare term crossover to crossover operators used in genetic algorithms (Section 3.3) or recombinations for evolution strategies (Section 4.3), an interesting aspect of GP crossover arises: recombinations performed on two identical terms, GP crossover, usually result in a pair of new structures whenever the selected crossover nodes and the exchanged subterms are different (Figure 7.7).

Figure 7.6
Crossover among term structures.

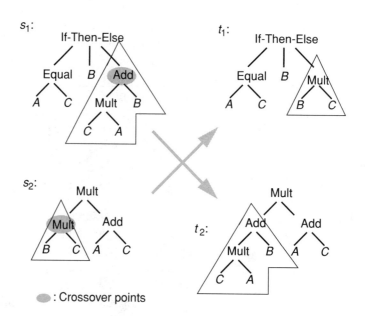

● : Crossover points

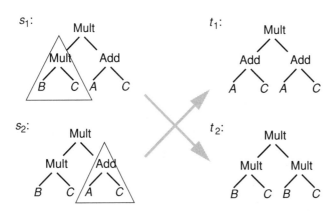

Figure 7.7
Crossover among identical
term structures.

It is this property of GP crossover that makes GP evolution systems (based on symbolic expressions) much less prone to premature convergence than, say, genetic algorithms working on binary string encodings. For identical recombination partners, GA crossover is nothing but a reproduction operator, which passes on identical copies of the chromosomes into the next generation. Since crossover on binary strings enhances the similarity among the genotypical structures (cf. the GA experiments in Sections 3.7.3 and 3.7.4), the mutation operator is in essence needed to replenish the gene pool with new gene settings. In the traditional form of genetic programming, propagated by Koza and his group, almost no mutation operators are used (Koza 1992; Koza 1994). Four so-called secondary operators—mutation, permutation, encapsulation, and decimation—are described but are not used in the evolution experiments (with only a few exceptions) (Koza 1992, pp. 105–112). Therefore, GP crossover on term structures is considered the only essential operator for structure modifications in canonical genetic programming.

Term crossover: the primary GP operator

Applying this GP crossover operator to any symbolic expression, not only restricted to terms, turns out to be problematic. The unconstrained interchange of substructures ad lib may result in syntactically incorrect expressions. In Section 7.2.2 we discuss this problem in more detail.

7.2.1   Term recombination in Evolvica

The functions provided by Evolvica for the manipulation of term structures allows for an easy implementation of GP recombination. We introduce term recombination in two steps—first as a function `exprRecombination` for multicrossover on a list of expressions

Program 7.5

Recombination of terms.

```
exprRecombination[exprs_List] :=
Module[{randPos, randSubs},

  randPos = Map[
    randomSelect[Position[#, _, Heads → False]]&,
    exprs];

  randSubs =
  MapThread[Part[#1, Sequence @@ #2]&,
  {exprs,randPos}];

  {MapThread[ReplacePart,
    {exprs, RotateRight[randSubs], randPos}],
    randPos}
]
```

GP recombination function

and finally as a function Recombination for GP chromosomes, performing crossover on a population of GP structures.

The Evolvica function exprRecombination defined in Program 7.5 is an extended version of the GP crossover (Figure 7.6), introduced in the previous section. For each of the expressions (exprs) in the list, a random node position (randPos) is selected. The option Heads → False ensures that no head positions are chosen in order to always select complete subtrees. For the selected positions the respective subexpressions (randSubs) are extracted, which are finally exchanged among the expressions using ReplacePart. For two expression trees the application of RotateRight results in a crosswise interchange of GP terms. For recombination on more than two expressions, each subterm is inserted at the selected crossover position of the following expression in the list.

We must be careful in the case where the root position ({}) is selected in one expression. The standard definition of the built-in Mathematica function ReplacePart does not give the desired result. Entering a command of the form

```
ReplacePart[term, newTerm, {}]
```

returns the expression term as the result. In this situation, however, the GP crossover operator should replace the original term with the new term, newTerm. We take this into account by extending the definition of ReplacePart as listed in Program 7.6.

```
Unprotect[ReplacePart];

ReplacePart[expr_, new_, {}] := new

Protect[ReplacePart];
```

Program 7.6
Extending the definition of
ReplacePart.

Let us look at a few term recombination examples. First we define
a set of function and terminal building blocks:

```
In[7] := functions = {p[__], s[_,_], t[__], d[_,_]};
         terminals := {x, y, z, Random[Integer,{-3,3}]};
         functionsAndTerminals =
         functions ~Join~ terminals;
```

*Function and terminal
building blocks*

The following two expressions are used as recombination partners:

```
In[8] := exprs = Table[randomExpr[5, _,
                 functionsAndTerminals, terminals],{2}]
            // TableForm
```

```
Out[8] = d[x, y]
         s[-2, t[z, d[t[1], -2], y, p[x, z, z, y, -2]]]
```

Since both terms are very different in their structures, recombination of
the two expressions also results in noticeable structure modifications:

```
In[9] := {recExprs, recPos} = exprRecombination[exprs]
```

Recombination of two terms

```
Out[9] = {{d[p[x, z, z, y, -2], y],
           s[-2, t[z, d[t[1], -2], y, x]]}, {{1}, {2, 4}}}
```

Besides the recombined terms, the function `exprRecombination`
returns a list of the selected crossover points. From these we can learn
that the first argument of the d expression is interchanged with the
fourth argument of the second subexpression of the s partner term
(Figure 7.8).

The following example demonstrates the case when the root position of the first expression is selected (Figure 7.9). The first expression
is inserted into the second tree at position {2, 4}, while the original
subterm completely substitutes the first expression.

*Recombination at root
position*

Figure 7.8
GP recombination among
two terms.

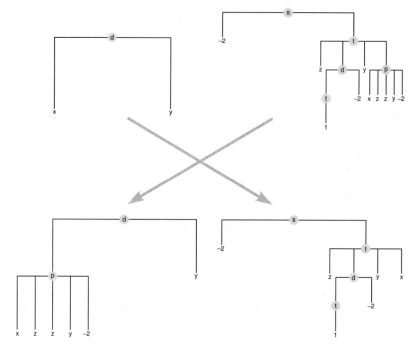

Figure 7.9
Effect of recombination
when a root node is selected
as crossover point.

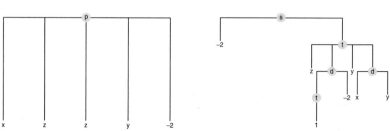

In[10] := **{recExprs, recPos} = exprRecombination[exprs];**

Out[10] = {{p[x, z, z, y, -2],
            s[-2, t[z, d[t[1], -2], y, d[x, y]]]},
            {{}, {2, 4}}}

We demonstrate term recombinations on a list of expressions with
a final example. We generate five term structures:

In[11] := **exprs = Table[randomExpr[5, _,**
                functionsAndTerminals, terminals],{5}]
            // TableForm

Out[11]= s[y, t[z, d[-2, -2], -2, y, t[z, x, y, y, x]]]
        d[x, p[x, -2, z]]
        p[p[x, s[x, x], x, s[z, z]]]
        y
        x

These expressions are now recombined in turn:

In[12]:= **{recExprs, recPos} = exprRecombination[exprs];**   *GP term recombination*
        recPos

Out[12]= {{2, 2}, {2, 1}, {1}, {}, {}}

For the last two terms the root is selected as the crossover point so
that they are completely replaced by new expressions:

In[13]:= **recExprs // TableForm**

Out[13]= s[y, t[z, x, -2, y, t[z, x, y, y, x]]]
        d[x, p[d[-2, -2], -2, z]]
        p[x]
        p[x, s[x, x], x, s[z, z]]
        y

Each expression "inherits" the selected substructures of its left neighbor term in the list. The first expression is the neighbor of the last term
in the list. Hence, the second expression gets the subtree at position
{2, 2} from its left neighbor and inserts it at position {2, 1}. The original subexpression at this position is passed on to the third term in the
list, and so on.

     In Figure 7.10 these recombinations are depicted in graphical
form. Each tree on the right is constructed from two structures in the
left column. The tree structure representations are generated with the
function `TermPlot`, which is included in the Evolvica notebook
available on the *IEC* Web site (see Preface).

     For the GP evolution system, which we will describe in Section   *GP chromosomes*
7.4, the program terms are encoded as GP chromosomes. Analogous
to the ES and GA chromosomes already introduced, GP chromosomes
have a structure of the form

                `chromo[q[fitness], p[programTerm]].`

The `q` expression contains the fitness value of the program structure
embedded in a `p` term. The Evolvica function `Recombination` for
recombining two GP chromosomes is defined in Program 7.7.

Figure 7.10
GP recombination on a list
of terms.

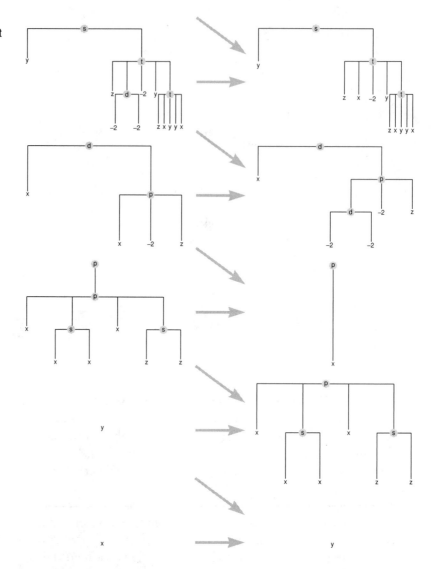

The function Recombination works on a population of GP
chromosomes, from which two program individuals to be recombined
(exprOne, exprTwo) are selected. Fitness-proportionate selection is
normally used for the selection function. However, the selection procedure can be redefined by the SelectionMode option. For the two
selected GP chromosomes, the function exprRecombination performs normal term recombination on their program terms. The two
resulting crossed-over chromosomes, embedded in a pop structure,
are returned.

```
Recombination[chromoPop_pop, opts___] :=
Module[{exprOne, exprTwo},

  exprOne =
    First[Last[Selection[chromoPop, opts]//First]];
  exprTwo =
    First[Last[Selection[chromoPop, opts]//First]];

  pop @@ Map[chromo[q[undef],p[#]]&,
    exprRecombination[{exprOne,exprTwo}]//First]
]
```

Program 7.7
Recombination of
GP chromosomes.

7.2.2 The problem with GP crossover

Let us take a closer look at the difference between terms and symbolic
expressions, which we have already discussed in Section 5.2. The fact
that GP terms, introduced in Section 7.1, are a proper subset of symbolic expressions, has critical consequences for GP recombination.
Term recombination, as defined in the previous section, can be transferred only to more general symbolic expressions (S expressions), with
a little effort—a consequence of the more restricted syntactic structures of terms.

   Therefore, we first show how symbolic expressions can be represented as term-structured trees. If the traditional genetic programming
approach (à la Koza 1992, Koza 1994) is used for evolving S expressions in general, then we have to take into consideration such structures as

*Terms vs. symbolic
expressions*

$$\texttt{Derivative[2][Sin][Plus[x, y]]}$$

where the function head can be a symbol as well as a term. There is an
easy way to map S expressions on tree structures. Obviously each
expression of the form

$$\texttt{s0[s1, . . . , sn],}$$

where all subexpressions $s_0, s_1, . . . , s_n$ can be terms as well,
$s_i \in$ GP-term$_{F \cup T}$, may be represented in one of the following ways:

$$\texttt{Expression[s0, s1, . . . , sn] or}$$
$$\texttt{expr[s0, s1, . . . , sn] or}$$
$$\texttt{List[s0, s1, . . . , sn].}$$

*Symbolic expressions as
trees*

The latter of these Mathematica representations corresponds to the syntax used in LISP:

$$(s_0 \; s_1 \ldots s_n).$$

Hence, each expression can also be represented as a tree structure (Figure 7.11). The newly introduced `Expression`, `expr`, or `List` constructors can be considered a new function of arbitrary arity extending the function set, $F' = F \cup \{\texttt{expr}\}$.

Typed GP

With these modifications in the term data structures, the GP operator can be used as a crossover operator even on general symbolic expressions—with a caveat. If GP crossover is the only operator used for structure modifications, apart from the initial generation of expressions, new structures can result only from an interchange of subterms. All terms are treated in the same way as recombinable structures, because tree nodes of subexpressions to be interchanged can be selected at random. However, if this is the case, then we can no longer guarantee the production of only syntactically correct terms. The example in Figure 7.12 illustrates this point. The symbol $f \in F$, resulting from this recombination, is not a constant. Therefore it may not appear without any argument subtree. We can compensate for this

Figure 7.11
Tree representation of symbolic expressions.

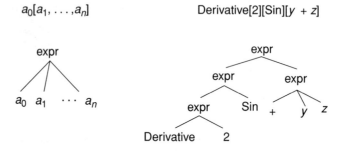

Figure 7.12
Problematic application of GP crossover on symbolic expressions, encoded as terms.

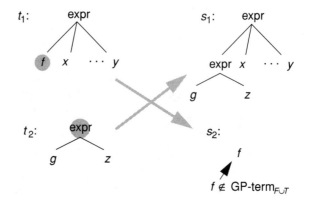

effect by restricting term recombinations to be performed only among subtrees with root symbols s = expr or $s \in F$.

We can eliminate these problems by extending the genetic operators, allowing structures that are actually in the scope of selection for recombination and modification. Based on these observations, selective GP recombination and mutation operators are used in the Evolvica system. Another, more restricted solution would be to introduce typed genetic programming systems as, for example, proposed in Haynes, Schoenefeld, et al. 1996; Jacob 1994; and Montana 1995.

7.3   GP mutation of program structures

In this section we introduce an operator on term structures, which is analogous to point mutation of genetic algorithms. Although in traditional genetic programming, crossover is said to be the only operator necessary (see, e.g., Koza 1992, pp. 105 ff.), we consider GP mutation a second essential operator for genetic programming. As we have seen, even among identical term structures GP recombinations are very likely to produce new expressions (see Figure 7.7), which in principle makes the evolved GP structures less prone to premature convergence effects. However, especially for small population sizes (with fewer than 100 individuals), which we will consider in later examples, the use of GP crossover as the only operator gradually increases the similarity of the evolved GP structures. In order to take full advantage of the "creative potential" of recombination, we enhance the GP operator set by mutation, which ensures a regular "refreshing" of the structure gene pool.

In genetic algorithms, (point) mutation replaces an allele with a new value from the allele alphabet. The mutative structures of genetic programming, however, are not just single bits or alleles but subtrees of program genomes. In a term tree, GP mutation substitutes a subterm (which might as well be the whole tree) with a newly generated term structure. In detail, it works as follows.

GP term mutation

A term $s \in$ GP-term$_{F \cup T}$ is given, the structure of which is recursively constructed from the set of functions F and terminals T. In this term s a node is selected at random, specifying the root of the subterm s' to be replaced. A new expression t', substituting this substructure s', is generated according to the term generation process described in Section 7.1.2, using building blocks from $F \cup T$. The mutated tree t results from s by substituting s' by t'.

Figure 7.13
Example of GP term
mutation.

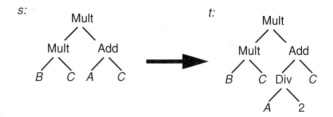

A typical example is depicted in Figure 7.13. A variable (A) is replaced by the newly generated term $Div[A, 2]$. The alphabet of symbols for these terms is defined as $\{Mult_2, Div_2, Add_2, Sub_2, A, B, C\}$.

Using the function randomExpr, defined in Section 7.1.2, GP mutation on term expressions can be easily implemented, as shown in Program 7.8. The function exprMutation takes the following inputs: the expression to be mutated (expr) and a list of patterns for the functions (patterns) and terminals (terminals).

Program 7.8
GP mutation on terms.

```
exprMutation[expr_, patterns_List, terminals_List]
:= Module[{randPos, newSubExpr},

   randPos =
     randomSelect[Position[expr, _, Heads → False]];

   newSubExpr =
     randomExpr[Depth[expr]- Length[randPos], _,
       patterns ~Join~ terminals, terminals];

   {ReplacePart[expr, newSubExpr, randPos], randPos}
 ]
```

GP mutation function on
terms

One node, corresponding to a subterm position (randPos), is selected at random from the node set of the expression. A new term newSubExpr is generated using the function randomExpr as defined in Program 7.1. At this point the exact definitions of the functional and terminal building blocks must be known. Here the argument structure of the mutation operator is different for GP crossover (compare exprRecombination in Program 7.5). For recombinations, it is irrelevant how the structures to be crossed over were composed, since the restructuring merely results from crosswise interchange of subterms. The mutation operator, however, must be able to generate new subterms, which must conform to the structural conditions of the term considered.

By `ReplacePart` the newly generated term is inserted into the expression `expr` at position `randPos`. Again the definition of the built-in Mathematica function `ReplacePart` must be extended according to Program 7.6 so that the special case of root selection is taken into account. In addition to the mutated term expression, `exprMutation` also returns the position at which the substitution was performed.

Starting from the following specifications of functions and terminals, we will consider a few term mutation examples.

```
In[1] := functions = {p[__], s[_,_], t[__], d[_,_]};
         terminals := {x, y, z, Random[Integer,{-3,3}]};
         functionsAndTerminals =
         functions ~Join~ terminals;
```

We generate a random expression of depth 3, which serves as the "parent" expression for subsequent mutations.

```
In[2] := expr =
         randomExpr[3, _,
         functionsAndTerminals, terminals]
```

```
Out[2] = t[p[z, y, y], z, s[3, x], -2]
```

In the following example, the first argument is substituted by a newly generated term (Figure 7.14[a]):

```
In[3] := {mutExpr, mutPos} =                              GP term mutation
         exprMutation[expr, functions, terminals]
```

```
Out[3] = {t[d[t[z, z, x], t[-2, x, x]], z, s[3, x], -2],
         {1}}
```

In Figure 7.14(b) the first argument of the third subterm (3) is replaced by the expression `s[-1, z]`:

```
In[4] := {mutExpr, mutPos} =
         exprMutation[expr, functions, terminals]
```

```
Out[4] = {t[p[z, y, y], z, s[s[-1, z], x], -2], {3, 1}}
```

If the root node is chosen as the mutation point, the whole expression is replaced by a new one (Figure 7.14[c]):

Figure 7.14
GP mutations on tree
structures.

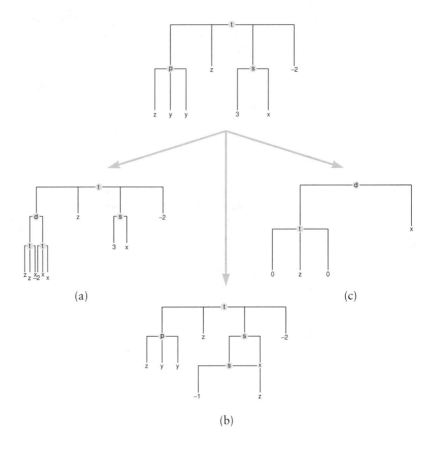

(a)   (c)

(b)

$In[5] :=$ **{mutExpr, mutPos} =**
         exprMutation[expr, functions, terminals]

$Out[5] =$ {d[t[0, z, 0], x], {}}

These examples show that the mutation operator is able to both
replace substructures and introduce totally new structures into the
gene pool of the program genomes.

As in GP recombination, exprMutation is used as a utility function by the populational GP mutation operator Mutation. This
Mutation function is defined for a population of GP chromosomes.
It combines the selection of a structure to be mutated with the actual
term mutation (Program 7.9). The result is a mutated GP chromosome embedded in a pop expression.

Finally, mutation of the GP chromosome structure is performed
by the Mutation function in Program 7.10, which modifies the program genome using exprMutation as demonstrated by the above
examples.

```
Mutation[chromoPop_pop, opts___] :=
pop[ Mutation[Selection[chromoPop, opts]//First,
   opts] ]
```

Program 7.9
Term mutation on a
population of GP
chromosomes.

```
Mutation[chromo[qual_q, prog_p], opts___] :=
Module[{},

  chromo[q[undef],
    p[exprMutation[prog//First,
        ExprPatterns /. {opts} /. Options[Mutation],
        ExprTerminals /. {opts} /. Options[Mutation]]
      //First]
  ]
]
```

Program 7.10
Mutation of a
GP chromosome.

The overloaded definition of the Mutation function might seem
too complicated in this situation. The choice to return both recombination and mutation operator results not as single GP chromosomes
but rather as GP population structures (pop[...]) is advantageous
for uniform implementations of GP evolution schemes (cf. Section 7.4
and Program 7.11). Applications of these GP operators are demonstrated by examples, in Section 7.5 in particular.

7.4 GP evolution scheme

Now that we know how to generate tree-structured chromosomes and
how to create new structures and substructures from a gene pool by
crossover and mutation, we will show in this section how the GP
operators, together with a suitable selection scheme, can be combined
into an evolution scheme.

Traditional genetic programming uses a variant of GA evolution
schemes, which we discussed in Section 3.5 (see Figure 3.45 in particular). Again we use the graphical notation introduced for evolution
strategies in Section 4.4. The following GP reproduction scheme is a
slightly modified version of the evolution scheme proposed in Koza
1992, p. 76. The scheme proposed here allows for a better comparison between GA and ES reproduction and selection methods.

The GP evolution scheme starts with the generation of an initial   *Initialization*
population of μ program genomes, the building blocks of which are
defined by the reservoir of problem-specific functions and terminals

(Figure 7.15). The program structures encoded in the GP chromosomes are evaluated by testing their phenotypes, the executable programs or data structures, and checking on their capability to provide an algorithmic solution for the problem-specific task. For each of the program genomes, their resulting fitness values determine the probability of reproduction into the next generation.

Copying, mutation, recombination

When reproducing the individuals from the current to the following generation, the GP system has three operators available: a mutation, a reproduction, and a copy operator. The latter operator, which we have added following Koza's evolution scheme, transfers a GP chromosome unchanged to the next generation. The reproduction scheme used in Koza 1992, p. 76, relies only on this copy operator in combination with GP crossover.

GP vs. GA scheme

The GP evolution scheme differs from the scheme used in genetic algorithms in terms of how the descendant individuals are generated. Instead of selecting individuals and applying (with specific probabilities) the set of operators (GA recombination, GA point mutation, etc.; see Figure 3.45) on each of them, in this GP scheme each program genome transferred from one generation to another is modified by only a single operator. The advantage of this approach is that the effects caused by the GP operators can be reconstructed by keeping a simple protocol of operator applications (this is much more difficult if several GA operators are applied one after the other).

Operator selection

Selection takes place on two levels. First, an operator has to be selected—copy, mutation, or crossover. Second, depending on the arity k of the operator to be applied, k individuals are selected from

Figure 7.15
Basic evolution scheme of genetic programming on term structures (comma-GP scheme).

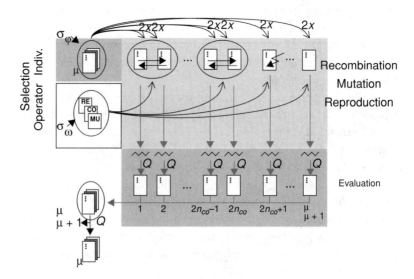

the current generation. This selection is usually performed in a fitness-proportionate fashion. In Figure 7.15 this bilevel selection is illustrated by the extended pool of individuals and operators in the upper-left corner.

Operator application

If the binary GP crossover is to be applied, two GP genomes are selected from the population. GP crossover results in two mutated structures, which are both available for inclusion into the next generation (whereas in GA crossover, only one of the recombination partners survives). For a unary operator from the operator pool, a single structure is selected from the population and either reproduced identically or by mutation. This loop of operator/individual selection and reproduction is performed until at least λ program individuals are generated. In the case that individual $\lambda - 1$ has been reproduced and the GP crossover operator is selected for the last program structure, a surplus individual is generated.

Finally, all newly generated program genomes are evaluated and the best μ structures are designated to be the parents of the following generation. As for the GA and ES schemes, we may also include the current parents into the selection pool from which the μ best-program genomes are filtered. This means that we extend the *comma-GP* scheme (Figure 7.15) into a *plus-GP* scheme as illustrated in Figure 7.16.

Evaluation and best selection

We use the formal notation (as already introduced for GA, ES, and EP) in order to specify GP evolution schemes and experiment settings. The "formula"

$$\lambda_1 \left(\mu_0 \genfrac{}{}{0pt}{}{+}{,} \lambda_0 \, \| \, \Omega_0 \right)^{\gamma_0} \text{GP}$$

Notation for a GP evolution scheme

characterizes a plus- or comma-GP strategy. In detail, it denotes λ_1 independent GP experiments, each performed over γ_0 generations. From μ_0 parent genomes, λ_0 individuals are generated by using the genetic operators, specified in the option vector Ω_0. From the resulting pool of program structures (including the parents in the case of a plus-GP strategy) the best μ_0 GP chromosomes are selected.

The available GP operators, their selection probabilities, and also necessary definitions to describe the experimental setup are specified by the option vector Ω_0. This vector might, for example, contain the following entries:

$$\Omega_0 = (\text{OpPool} \rightarrow \{ \text{Copy}_{0.25}, \text{Mutation}_{0.25}, \text{Crossover}_{0.5} \}).$$

Here the operator pool consists of three operators (copy, mutation, and crossover). The index denotes the selection probability for each operator.

Figure 7.16
Basic evolution scheme of
genetic programming
on term structures
(plus-GP scheme).

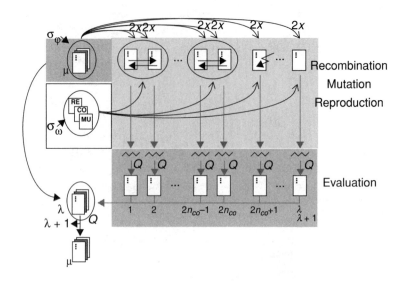

In Evolvica notation, plus-GP and comma-GP strategies can be written as follows:

Plus- and comma-GP strategies in Evolvica

$$\lambda_1 \; GP[\mu_0, \; PLUS, \; \lambda_0, \; \gamma_0, \; \Omega_0]$$

and

$$\lambda_1 \; GP[\mu_0, \; COMMA, \; \lambda_0, \; \gamma_0, \; \Omega_0].$$

As for the evolution algorithms already presented, we use this notational characterization for GP evolution experiments for the Evolvica function Evolution listed in Program 7.11, which implements the GP evolution scheme. A function call of the form

Starting GP evolution experiments ...

$$Evolution[\lambda_1 \; GP[\mu_0, \; PLUS, \; \lambda_0, \; \gamma_0, \; \Omega_0]]$$

generates λ_1 independent GP experiments, each over γ_0 generations. Each population consists of a set of μ_0 individuals, from which descendants are produced by using the operators specified in the option list Ω_0. After evaluation, the best μ_0 program genomes from the collection of the μ_0 parent and λ_0 newly generated structures are selected for the next generation.

GP evolution function

In Program 7.11 only those sections are listed that are immediately related to the GP reproduction scheme. The sections marked by ... correspond to the analogous commands of Programs 3.24 and 3.25 for GA evolution. Before entering the evolution loop, a function selectOperator is defined, which selects a GP operator by fitness-proportionate selection. The operator weights, which are interpreted as fitness values, are derived from the optional rules in Program 7.12. The actual reproduction is implemented by a While loop:

```
Evolution[
  GP[m_?IntegerQ,    (* parents            *)
     s_?AtomQ,       (* PLUS or COMMA      *)
     l_?IntegerQ,    (* children           *)
     g_?IntegerQ,    (* generations        *)
     opts___]        (* options            *)
  i_:1               (* independent runs *)
] :=
Module[{...},
  ...
  selectOperator := {Recombination, Mutation, Copy}[[
    selectFitProp[{recProb, mutProb, copProb}]]];
  ...
  (* Iterate for i independent runs *)
  Table[
    (* Iterate for g generations *)
    NestList[
    ( parents = #;
      children = pop[];

      While[Length[children] < l,
        children =
          children ~Join~ selectOperator[parents, opts]
      ];

      children =
        Map[Evaluation[#,opts]&, Take[children,l]];

      selPool = Switch[s,
        PLUS, Join[parents,children], COMMA, children];

      Selection[selPool,m,SelectionMode -> BEST]
    ) &,
      initialParents, g ], (* end nesting *)
    {i} (* independent runs *)
  ]
]
```

Program 7.11
Evolution scheme of genetic programming.

```
  While[Length[children] < l,
   children =
     Join[children,selectOperator[parents, opts]
  ];
```

The function `selectOperator` returns a single genetic operator. All GP operators (`Recombination` in Program 7.7, `Mutation` in Program 7.10, and `Reproduction`) have the same argument structure for their inputs. All of them operate on populations

GP operators

(pop[...]) of GP chromosomes and return a subpopulation of structures as well. This implies that after each application of an operator the current "child" population can be easily extended by additional individuals using the Join function.

Composition of the selection pool

The remaining code sections in Program 7.11 implement the composition of the selection pool, depending on the defined selection strategy (PLUS or COMMA) and the selection of parent structures for the following generation. Although genetic programming deals with more complex chromosome structures, this implementation of a GP evolution scheme seems to be less difficult compared to the ones used for genetic algorithms (cf. Program 3.24 and Program 3.25), which is mainly due to the separation of the GP operators.

Program 7.12
Options of the Evolution function.

```
Options[Evolution] =
{
    InitialPopulation → {}, SelectionMode → FITPROP,

    Operators → {{Mutation, 0.25},
                 {Recombination, 0.5},
                 {Copy, 0.25}},

    ExprMaxDepth → 2,
    ExprPatterns → {}, ExprTerminals → {}
};
```

Control options

Program 7.12 lists the most important options of the GP Evolution function. As for the ES and GA variants of this function, an initial population of GP chromosomes may be predefined (InitialPopulation). If the start population is specified by an empty list, initial GP terms are constructed at random, using the patterns for functions and terminals defined by ExprPatterns and ExprTerminals, respectively.

The option SelectionMode defines which selection method is used by the genetic operators. The default setting is fitness-proportionate selection (FITPROP). Rank-based (RANKBASED), best (BEST), and elitist (ELITE) selection may also be used. Of course, this list of selection schemes is easily extendable by user-defined functions.

Extendable set of GP operators

The Operators list defines the set of GP operators (here mutation, crossover, and copy) together with their relative selection weights. These weight values are interpreted as operator "fitnesses" on the basis of which fitness-proportionate operator selection is per-

formed. These values are treated as relative weights rather than probabilities in a strict sense, which means that their "selection
probabilities" do not necessarily have to sum up to a unit value of 1,
although it is recommended as a normalized representational form.

7.5 Genetic programming in action

In this section we present a simple application of genetic programming in Evolvica—the evolution of balanced mobiles. Each of us
knows the manifold shapes of mobiles. A collection of bars, with
weighted elements at their ends, hanging on threads, is arranged in
such a way that all bars are equally balanced (Figure 7.17). Mobiles   *Well-balanced mobiles*
are especially fascinating to watch when they are slowly moving,
when any slight breeze rearranges the mobile elements anew. The
most difficult part in designing a mobile is to find a well-balanced
arrangement of all the mobile arms.

Starting with rather simplistic, unbalanced mobile structures, we   *Section overview*
will use genetic programming to evolve more complex mobile designs.
For this purpose, we suggest a data structure for mobiles based on
symbolic expressions together with a transformation function for con-
verting these representational structures into GP terms (Section 7.5.1).
Graphical representations of mobiles in two and three dimensions are
presented in Section 7.5.2. Automatic generation of mobile structures
is discussed in Section 7.5.3. With these prerequisites we are able to
generate populations of mobiles and evaluate them with respect to
their number of balanced elements (Section 7.5.4). Subsequently,
genetic programming is used to breed more and more complex mobile
designs by evolution. An example of a GP evolution experiment is
illustrated in Section 7.5.5.

7.5.1 Encoding of mobiles

A mobile bar with weighted elements at its ends is characterized by a
symbolic expression of the form   *Mobile bars*

```
s[armLength1, armLength2][subMobile1, subMobile2].
```

This mobile consists of a top bar of length `armLength1 + arm-`
`Length2`, which is suspended at the point located at `armLength1`
units from the left end of the bar. At both ends of this bar, the mobiles
`subMobile1` and `subMobile2` are attached. The same data structure is used for the submobiles. We assume that the bars themselves

are weightless, so they can be neglected when calculating a mobile's overall balance. The diverse shapes of weighted elements are represented as simple terms, such that a symbolic expression of the form

```
s[a1, a2][x[w1], y[w2]]
```

describes a mobile bar with two elements of weights w1 and w2, respectively. The symbols x and y determine the concrete geometrical shape of such an element (circle, triangle, rectangle, etc.).

Figure 7.17 depicts a typical mobile together with the symbolic expression describing its structure. The symbols a, ..., f correspond to specific geometric shapes of the weighted elements. Neither the length of the strings connecting the bars nor the length of the strings attached to the elements is explicitly encoded into the mobile data structure. They do not have any influence on the overall balance of the mobile. In the graphical representations, the string lengths are either set at random (as in Figure 7.17) or can be explicitly defined.

7.5.2 Graphical representations of mobiles

Visualizations are quite helpful when evaluating the balance of mobile structures. For the computer it is an easy task to calculate the balance of each of the mobile substructures and hence evaluate the mobile. For us, however, it is much more convenient to evaluate a mobile on the basis of its graphical rather than its symbolic expression representation. Last but not least, GP evolution results in a number of artful structural mobile designs, which are fun to look at, especially in their three-dimensional representations, as we will demonstrate in this section.

Visualizing mobiles

We get a graphical representation of mobile structures by using the functions showMobile and showMobile3D, from the Evolvica notebooks for two- and three-dimensional mobile plots, respectively.

Figure 7.17

Graphical and symbolic representation of mobile structures.

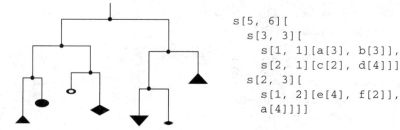

```
s[5, 6][
   s[3, 3][
      s[1, 1][a[3], b[3]],
      s[2, 1][c[2], d[4]]]
   s[2, 3][
      s[1, 2][e[4], f[2]],
      a[4]]]]
```

The notebooks are available on the *IEC* Web site (see Preface). The options for these two functions are listed in Program 7.13.

```
Options[showMobile] = Options[showMobile3D] =
{ StringLength → 2, StringLengthRange → {0,0},
  ColorFunction → GrayLevel, ColorRange → {0,0},
  TwistRange → {0,0}
};
```

Program 7.13
Options for showMobile and showMobile3D.

For the mobile in Figure 7.17, which we define as follows,

In[1] := **theMobile =**
    mobile[s[5,6][s[3,3][s[1,1][a[3],b[3]],
                        s[2,1][c[2],d[4]]],
                s[2,3][s[1,2][e[4],f[2]],
                    a[4]]]];

Mobile definition

we get the graphics in Figure 7.18(a) by the command

In[2] := **showMobile[theMobile];**

Mobile visualization

The elements are represented by geometric shapes, the sizes of which are directly proportionate to their weights. All strings are of the same length, set by the option StringLength. In Figure 7.18(b), the mobile strings have varying lengths, which can be determined by the StringLengthRange option:

In[3] := **showMobile[theMobile, StringLength → 5,**
            StringLengthRange → {-2, 2}]

The colors or gray levels of the weighted elements can be set by the ColorFunction option. ColorRange specifies the interval from which the color and gray values are randomly chosen. The following command results in the mobile plot in Figure 7.18(c):

In[4] := **showMobile[theMobile, StringLength → 5,**
            StringLengthRange → {-2, 2},
            ColorRange → {0,1}]

Determining the weights of each of the elements visually is much easier if all the elements are depicted by the same geometric shape. The parametrized substitution rule

Uniform graphical representation

Figure 7.18
A collection of graphical representations for mobile structures.

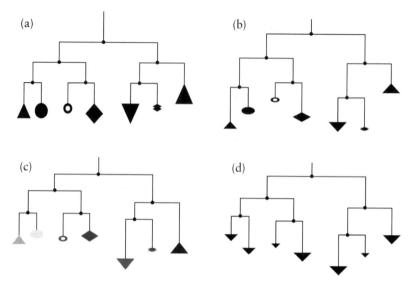

$In[5]$:= **commonElement[sym_] := Map[#** $\rightarrow$ **sym &,**
      {a,b,c,d,e,f}]

replaces all weight elements {a, ..., f} in the mobile expression by the symbol sym given as a parameter. Hence, a command of the form

$In[6]$:= **showMobile[theMobile /. commonElement[e],...]**

generates the mobile representation in Figure 7.18(d). From this graphic the relative weights of the elements can be estimated by simply comparing their sizes.

3D visualization   We now consider three-dimensional representations of mobiles, for which we use the function showMobile3D, which takes the same options as showMobile (Program 7.13). The ColorFunction and ColorRange rules do not have any effect, since the geometrical 3D elements are automatically colored and shaded. The TwistRange option, through which the horizontal twist of the mobile bars is controlled, may be used only for three-dimensional representations. Figure 7.19 gives a few examples. The two-dimensional mobile of Figure 7.18(a) is repeated in Figure 7.19(a). The corresponding 3D variant with uniform weight elements is depicted in Figure 7.19(b), whereas Figure 7.19(c) depicts the mobile with a variety of three-dimensional shapes.

A typical effect using the TwistRange option is shown in Figure 7.19(d). This mobile representation is generated by the command

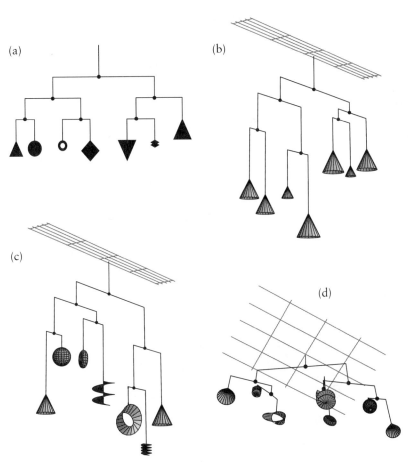

Figure 7.19
3D representations of mobile structures.

```
In[7] := showMobile3D[theMobile, StripLength → 3,
            StripLengthRange → {-2,2},
            TwistRange → {-30,30}];
```

Each mobile bar may be twisted by ±30 degrees. In order to get the impression of looking upward at the mobile hanging from the ceiling, the observer's viewpoint has been adjusted by using the View-Point option of the built-in Mathematica function Show.

Up to now we have only considered balanced mobile designs. To visually evaluate which mobile components are balanced or not, we present a few graphical illustrations. The functions showMobile and showMobile3D implicitly calculate for each bar whether it is balanced or not. The exact details are discussed in Section 7.5.3. Depending on which side of an arm is weighted more, the bar is tilted accordingly, as is illustrated in Figure 7.20. The figure shows the two- and three-dimensional variant for two mobiles. As can be seen from

Unbalanced mobiles

Figure 7.20
Two- and three-dimensional representations of unbalanced mobiles.

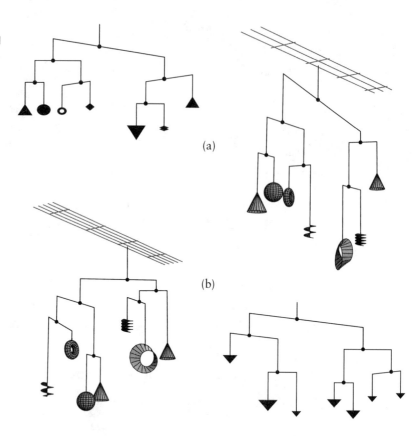

(a)

(b)

these examples, the perspective representation partially compounds the distinction between balanced and unbalanced bars.

7.5.3 Mobile evaluation by balance

In order to evolve complex mobile structures with as many balanced arms as possible, a suitable evaluation function for calculating the ratio of balanced bars is required. We need a function to recursively calculate the total weight attached to each node. Thus for each bar, the weights on its left and right end are known, and the two lever arms can be compared. We explain the functions for calculating mobile balance with the following example mobile structure (Figure 7.21[a]):

In[1] := **mobileOne = mobile[**
           s[5,7][s[2,3][s[1,1][a[3],b[3]],
                   s[2,1][c[2],d[2]]],

```
        s[2,3][s[1,2][e[4],f[2]],
            a[3]]]];
```

Using the function `mobileWeight` from Program 7.14, the weights of the submobiles on the left and right side are calculated. The function `mobileWeight` merely sums up all weight elements on both sides of the mobile.

In[2] := `{mobileWeight[mobileOne//First//First],`
`mobileWeight[mobileOne//First//Last]}`

Out[2] = `{10, 9}`

```
mobileWeight[s[_,_][s1_,s2_]] :=
  Plus @@ Flatten[Map[mobileWeight,{s1,s2}]]

mobileWeight[f_Symbol[x_Integer]] := x
```

Program 7.14
Calculating the weights of the left and right submobile.

Of course, the weights of these submobiles are important for calculating the balance of the bar. For a mobile structure of the form

```
s[w1, w2][s1, s2]
```

the function `balancedArms` in Program 7.15 determines the number of balanced arms. An arm is defined as being *balanced* if its lever arms are identical:

```
w1 mobileWeight[s1] == w2 mobileWeight[s2].
```

Identical lever arms

```
balancedArms[s[w1_,w2_][s1_,s2_]] :=
  If[w1 mobileWeight[s1] == w2 mobileWeight[s2],1,0]
+
  balancedArms[s1] + balancedArms[s2]

balancedArms[f_Symbol[x_Integer]] := 0
```

Program 7.15
Determining the number of balanced arms of a submobile.

Figure 7.21
Two examples of unbalanced mobiles.

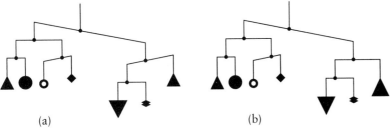

(a)   (b)

Checking a mobile for
balance

By simple traversing of the mobile structure, the function
`balancedArms` can identify and count all balanced arms. For our
example mobile, three of the total six arms are balanced:

In[3] := **balancedArms[mobileOne//First]**

Out[3] = 3

In[4] := **arms = Count[mobileOne,s[_,_][_,_],Infinity]**

Out[4] = 6

For comparison, let us consider a second mobile, which differs
from the first mobile only in its last weight element (Figure 7.21[b]):

In[5] := **mobileTwo = ReplacePart[mobileOne,a[4],{1,2,2}]**

Out[5] = mobile[s[5, 7][s[2, 3][s[1, 1][a[3], b[3]],
         s[2, 1][c[2], d[2]]], s[2, 3][s[1, 2][e[4],
         f[2]], a[4]]]]

The new weight results in a balanced right arm, so that now there are
four balanced arms:

In[6] := **balancedArms[mobileTwo//First]**

Out[6] = 4

Comparing mobiles

A reasonable fitness function should assign a higher score to the
second mobile than the first one. Program 7.16 implements such an
evaluation function using the fitness criterion

$$(1 + \text{arms})^{1 + \frac{\text{balArms}}{\text{arms}}} .$$

Program 7.16
Fitness function for mobiles,
evaluating their balance.

```
mobileFitness[mobile_] :=
Module[{arms, balArms},
    arms = Count[mobile,s[_,_][_,_],Infinity];
    balArms = balancedArms[mobile//First];

    N[(1 + arms) ^(1 + balArms/arms)]
]
```

Therefore, the `mobileFitness` function takes both the ratio of balanced arms (balArms/arms) and the total number of arms into account. The more complicated a mobile design is, the better its evaluation should be. With this definition, the following fitness values result for our two example mobiles:

In[7] := **Map[mobileFitness, {mobileOne,mobileTwo}]**

Mobile fitnesses

Out[7] = {14.6969, 19.8116}

Due to the additional balanced arm, the second mobile is evaluated better. Since both mobiles have the same structure, their fitnesses do not differ much. Further mobile evaluations are discussed in Section 7.5.5.

7.5.4 Generating mobile structures

We randomly compose mobile structures by using the function listed in Program 7.17, which defines the building block functions and terminals. Since the GP operators of mutation and recombination only work on terms, whereas the mobile structures are encoded as symbolic expressions, we have to convert these into a term representation.

```
mobileFunctions[x_,y_] :=
  Map[mobileTermForm[#][_,_]&,
    Outer[s,Range[x],Range[y]] // Flatten];

mobileTerminals[x_] :=
  Outer[#1[#2]&,{a,b,c,d,e,f},Range[x]] // Flatten;
```

Program 7.17
Parametrized functions and terminals as GP building blocks.

Instead of encoding the lengths of the mobile arms with a term of the form `s[i,k]`, we replace it with a corresponding symbol `sik`. Thus mobiles can be represented as pure term structures. If we allow mobiles with arm lengths of either 1 or 2, the functions look as follows:

In[1] := **mobileFunctions[2,2]**

Function building blocks for mobiles

Out[1] = {s11[_, _], s12[_, _], s21[_, _], s22[_, _]}

Analogously, we predefine the set of terminals available for specifying the weighted elements. An element term of the form g[k] is encoded by a symbol gk:

Terminal building blocks for mobiles

In[2] := **mobileTerminals[4]**

Out[2] ={a1, a2, a3, a4, b1, b2, b3, b4, c1, c2, c3, c4,
       d1, d2, d3, d4, e1, e2, e3, e4, f1, f2, f3, f4}

In this case the symbols a, . . . , f with weights in the range 1 to 4 are provided. With these preparations we can use the function create-Mobiles from the Evolvica notebook [available on the *IEC* Web site (see Preface)] to generate nine GP terms describing mobile structures with a maximum depth of 5:

In[3] := **mobiles = createMobiles[9,5,**
          Functions → mobileFunctions[3,3],
          Terminals → mobileTerminals[4]]

Out[3] ={mobile[s12[c2, f1]],
       mobile[s13[f3, s11[s32[s33[s33[e4, f3], f3],
         b3], b2]]],
       mobile[s22[e2, d4]], mobile[s23[a1, e2]],
       mobile[s31[s12[c3, b3], f3]],
       mobile[s31[s33[e4, e1], c2]],
       mobile[s32[b4, c2]], mobile[s32[c4, b2]],
       mobile[s33[c3, s12[s22[s21[c2, d2], f3], a2]]]}

The function createMobiles[n, d, ...] generates n mobile terms with a maximum depth of d, using the building blocks as specified by the Functions and Terminals options. For generating the GP terms the function randomExpr from Program 7.1 is used. The translation of these terms into the symbolic expression representation of mobile structures is provided by the function mobileExprForm. An example for the second mobile structure from the term set created above illustrates this term-expression mapping:

Mobiles in symbolic expression form

In[4] := **mobileExprForm[mobiles[[2]]]**

Out[4] = mobile[
       s[1, 3][f[3],
               s[1, 1][s[3, 2][s[3, 3][s[3, 3][e[4],
                                              f[3]],
                                      f[3]],

```
                                b[3]],
                    b[2]]]]
```

The retranslation into a GP term is performed by the "inverse" mapping `mobileTermForm`:

In[5] := **mobileTermForm[%]**   *Mobiles in term form*

Out[5] = mobile[s13[f3,
                    s11[s32[s33[s33[e4, f3], f3],
                    b3], b2]]]

We can visualize a population of mobile structures with the functions `showMobiles` and `showMobiles3D`, which are extensions of the `showMobile` function mapped onto a list of mobile structures displayed in matrix form. The following input generates the mobile graphics in Figure 7.22:

In[6] := **showMobiles[mobileExprForm /@ mobiles,**   *Visualizing a set of mobiles*
            StringLength → 3, StringLengthRange →
            {-2,2}, TableWidth → 3];

Above each mobile, its fitness value is displayed. The fitness function as defined in Section 7.5.3 is used. Comparison of the second and last mobiles (fitnesses 6 and 5) to the first mobile (fitness 4) shows that complex, unbalanced designs are occasionally evaluated better than simpler but well-balanced structures. On comparable levels of

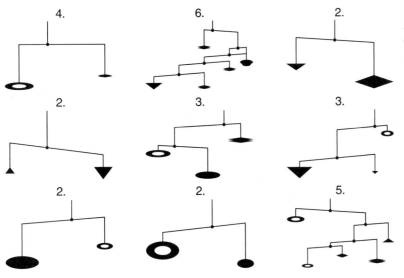

Figure 7.22
A collection of randomly generated and evaluated mobiles.

complexity, however, a well-balanced structure is always better evaluated, as a comparison of the first (fitness 4) with the fourth and fifth mobiles (fitnesses 2 and 3) illustrates.

With these preparations we know how to encode mobiles as GP terms, how to display and evaluate them, and how to generate populations of mobile structures. This provides the basis for the final experimental section, where we show how to use genetic programming to breed balanced mobile designs.

7.5.5 GP evolution of balanced mobiles

A critical aspect of actual experiments on the basis of evolutionary algorithms is the definition of the fitness function. In Section 7.5.3, we introduced an evaluation function (Program 7.16), where both the mobile balancing and the number of arms are taken into account. But this fitness function puts too much emphasis on the latter criterion, which only becomes obvious when the actual experiments are performed. The more bars a mobile structure has, the more its fitness increases (see Figure 7.22). As evolution experiments over just a few generations show, the developed mobiles are getting more and more complex but also highly unbalanced.

These observations demand a slightly modified version of a fitness function mobileFitness, which takes the imbalance of the arms into account instead of their balance (Program 7.18).

Program 7.18
Fitness function for GP evolution of balanced mobiles.

```
mobileFitness[mobile_] :=
Module[{arms, misBal},
   arms = Count[{mobile},s[_,_][_,_],Infinity];
   misBal = misBalance[mobile//First];

   N[(1 + arms)^(1/(1 + misBal))]
]

mobileFitness[p[_Symbol[_Integer]]] := 0
```

The function misBalance in Program 7.19 computes the difference of both lever arms for each mobile bar and sums them up over the whole mobile.

```
misBalance[s[w1_,w2_][s1_,s2_]] :=
  Abs[w1 mobileWeight[s1] - w2 mobileWeight[s2]] +
  misBalance[s1] + misBalance[s2]

misBalance[f_Symbol[x_Integer]] := 0
```

Program 7.19
Evaluating the imbalance of
mobiles.

Hence, for a mobile it is important not only how many arms are
unbalanced but also the degree of the unbalance:

$$(1 + \text{arms})^{\frac{1}{1+\text{misBal}}}$$

Mobile evaluation

The smaller the misBal value is, the larger the exponent becomes. This
new fitness definition has advantages for the genetic operators, too. It
is now easier to bring a mobile that is slightly out of balance into a
balanced (or more balanced) state by using recombinations and small
mutations. An extremely unbalanced mobile, however, can only gain a
better-balanced constellation through large-scale mutations.

In the following example, we perform a typical GP experiment for
evolving balanced mobiles. We call the Evolution function (Program 7.11), applying the notational convention introduced in Section
7.4. The following command initiates an evolution run over 20 generations according to a comma-GP strategy:

```
In[1] := GPmobiles =
    Evolution[
      GP[60, COMMA, 60, 20,
        ExprPatterns → mobileFunctions[3,3],
        ExprAtoms → mobileTerminals[4],
        ExprMaxDepth → 3,

        Operators v {{Mutation, 1},
                     {Recombination, 2}},

        KeepBest → 1,

        EvaluationFunction →
          (mobileFitness[mobileExprForm[#]]&),
        InitialPopulation → {}
      ]
    ];
```

*Initiating a GP mobile
evolution experiment*

From a population of 60 parent structures, 60 descendants are generated, using the GP operators of mutation and recombination. Among these the best 59 individuals are selected as parents for the next generation. The 60th individual is an identical copy of the best parent individual (KeepBest → 1) of the current generation. In an

Survival of the best with comma-GP strategy

extension of the general GP reproduction scheme, we can use the option KeepBest → k to carry the best *k* structures from generation to generation and generate the remaining λ – *k* genomes via GP operators as usual. By using a comma strategy, new mutants are steadily produced by the operators but successfully evolved individuals are not lost. Because of its strong tendency toward convergence, a plus strategy would be less suitable in this case.

Initial settings

As the InitialPopulation is set to an empty list, 60 mobile structures are randomly generated at the beginning of the evolution run. The building blocks are defined by mobileFunctions (Program 7.17) for the function set (ExprPatterns) and by mobile-Terminals for the terminal set (ExprAtoms). The maximum depth of the initial GP terms is restricted by ExprMaxDepth.

Recombination and mutation

GP mutation and crossover are used as operators, where the recombining operator ({Recombination, 2}) is on average applied twice as much as the mutation operator ({Mutation, 1}).

Evaluation

The mobile structures are evaluated (EvaluationFunction) according to the function mobileFitness as defined in Program 7.18. The GP term representation of the mobiles is mapped into symbolic expression form by the function mobileExprForm.

Results of a mobile evolution

Figure 7.23 shows the results of a typical GP evolution of more or less balanced mobiles. For each of the generations, the best 30 designs are displayed. The "champion" individual of each population is in the upper-left corner. The numbers above the mobiles denote their fitness and the total number of arms, respectively. In generation 0, only mobiles with a maximum depth of 3 appear, where only two of them are balanced (with only a single bar). All other structures are more or less unbalanced.

After 20 generations the situation is much changed. The creative potential of evolution is starting to come into play. A subpopulation of 11 well-balanced mobiles has evolved, the best of which are com-

Seven balanced arms

posed of seven bars. The first row consists of identical individuals; the second row displays a larger, though still small, variety of balanced designs. Even among the further along, less well evaluated designs, balanced substructures appear. Both these partly balanced structures and the completely balanced mobiles provide a reservoir of promising building blocks for evolutionary composition of even more complex constellations.

Gen. 0

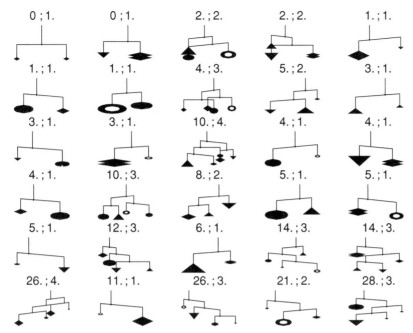

Figure 7.23
GP evolution of mobiles
(Part 1).

Gen. 20

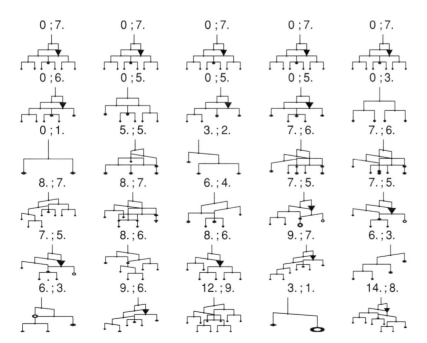

Continued evolution

Each experiment performed can be easily continued by defining the last generation of the finished evolution run as the subsequent initial population. Therefore, by replacing the `InitialPopulation` option in the command as described above by

$$\texttt{InitialPopulation} \rightarrow \texttt{(GPmobiles//First//Last)},$$

Eleven balanced arms

the GP evolution experiment will be continued for another 20 generations. Figure 7.24 displays the results. The dominating well-balanced mobiles now possess 11 or 10 arms. Furthermore, two variants of eight-bar mobiles are represented. In comparison to the populations in Figure 7.23, generation 40 contains designs of higher complexity and increased balance. Continuing the evolution for another 20 generations gives a renewed improvement of mobile constellations.

More fitness criteria . . .

In Figures 7.25 and 7.26, a collection of three-dimensional mobile plots of well-balanced mobiles are displayed, all of which were evolved by the genetic programming technique described so far. As these graphics suggest, many extensions are possible and many more criteria could be included in the fitness definition; for instance, How many different weighted elements does the mobile contain? Does the overall design appear aesthetic? (What does an "aesthetic" fitness function look like?) Can the bars move freely without interference and collisions with other arms?

7.6   Bibliographical notes

Genetic programming by John Koza and his group

GP I

The first volume of John Koza's books in the series on genetic programming, *Genetic Programming: On the Programming of Computers by Means of Natural Selection,* sparked the creation of the research field. His book describes the state of the art of genetic programming, ranging from the evolution of robot control programs, emergent behavior, coevolution, iteration, recursion, and constrained syntactic structures to demonstrations of parallelization and operational issues in genetic programming (Koza 1992).

GP II

The second volume, *Genetic Programming II: Automatic Discovery of Reusable Programs,* deals with the automatic reuse of building blocks, modular programming, automatically defined functional structures, and many more constructs and techniques of modern software programming—now all evolved by a genetic programming engine, almost without the need of manual input from a human programmer (Koza 1994).

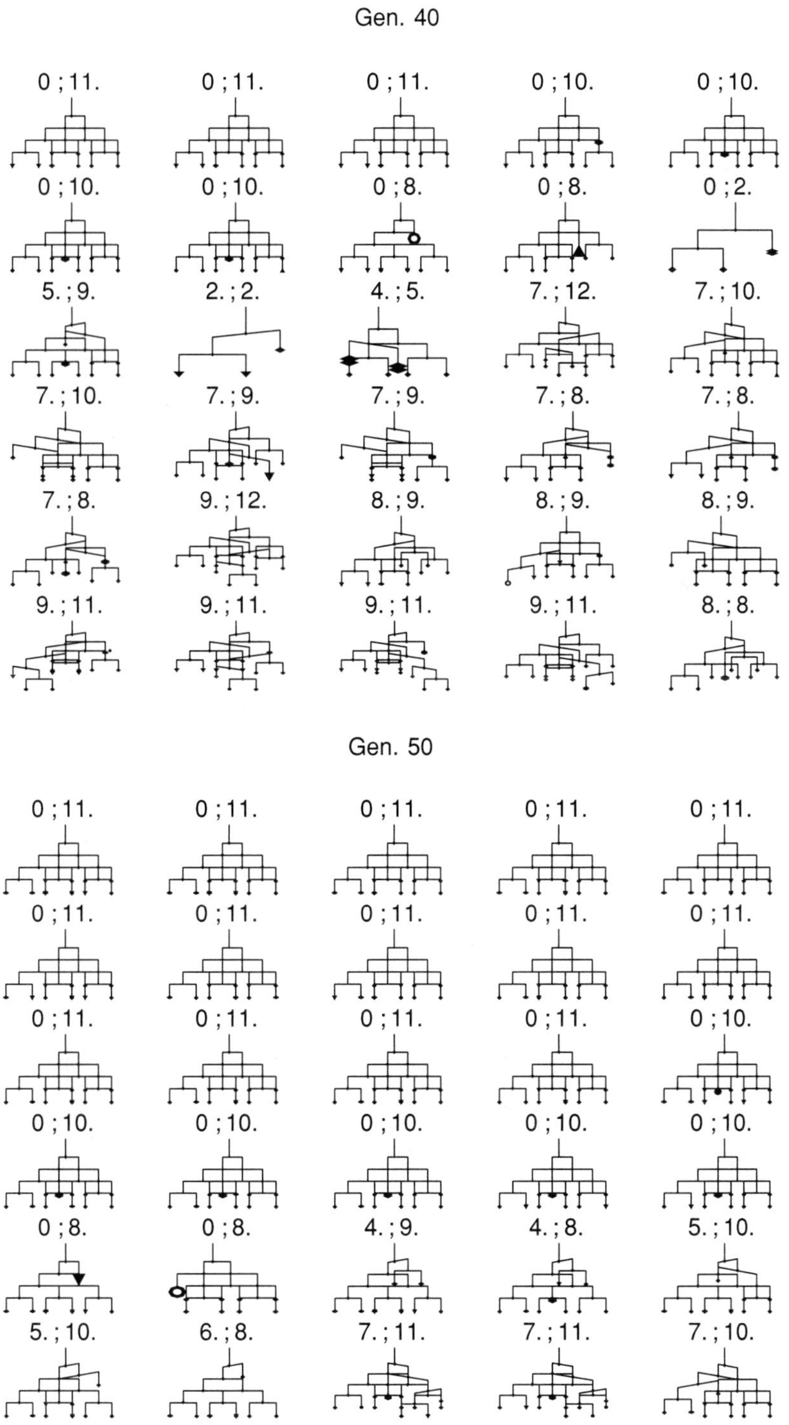

Gen. 40

Figure 7.24
GP evolution of mobiles
(Part 2).

Gen. 50

Figure 7.25
A selection of evolved, well-balanced mobile structures (Part 1).

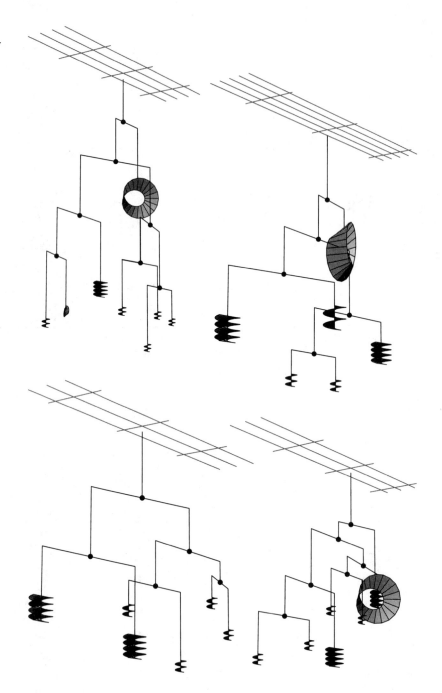

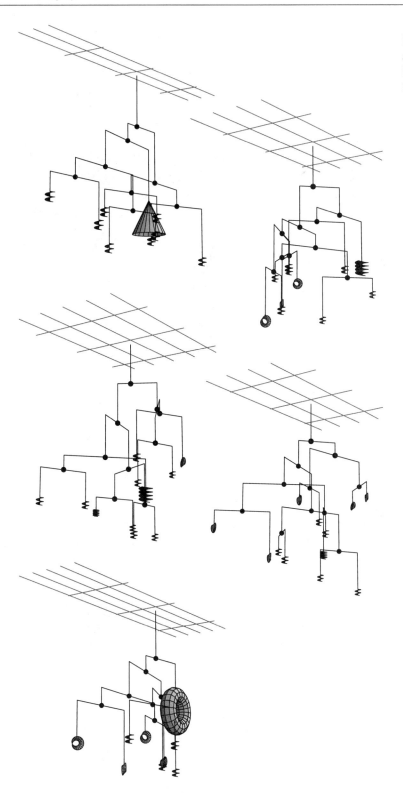

Figure 7.26
A selection of evolved, well-balanced mobile structures (Part 2).

GP III

The third volume, *Genetic Programming III: Darwinian Invention and Problem Solving,* gives a detailed overview of more recent extensions of the genetic programming technique, such as architecture-altering operations, automatically defined iterations, loops, recursion, storage, and self-organization of program architectures and hierarchies. An automatic programming system, the *Genetic Programming Problem Solver,* is introduced and demonstrated through examples of automated synthesis of a large variety of analog electrical circuits. The book also discusses the breeding of cellular automata rules, the discovery of motifs for molecular biology, and parallelization and implementation issues (Koza, Andre, et al. 1999).

Videos on genetic programming

GP videos

Each of the three GP volumes is accompanied by a videotape, surveying the key points of the corresponding book, with examples illustrating many of the discussed GP applications (Koza and Rice 1992; Koza and Rice 1994; Koza, Bennett III, et al. 1999).

Genetic programming textbooks

GP: an introduction

A general overview of genetic programming, including John Koza's GP approach to evolution on symbolic expressions, is provided in *Genetic Programming: An Introduction* (Banzhaf, Nordin, et al. 1997). This book describes genetic programming as a machine learning technique and discusses different variants of genetic programming using tree-structured, linear, and graph genomes, as well as other approaches to GP data structures. The book also provides a detailed analysis of genetic programming performance and operators, discusses implementation issues, and contains a large number of up-to-date GP applications.

GP + data structures = automatic programming!

In his book *Genetic Programming and Data Structures* (1998), William Langdon follows the phrasing of Zbigniew Michalewicz (1992), who said that evolution programs are simply a combination of genetic algorithms with appropriate data structures (*Genetic Algorithms + Data Structures = Evolution Programs*), derived from Niklaus Wirth's original "equation": *Algorithms + Data Structures = Programs* (Wirth 1975). Hence, under the motto *Genetic Programming + Data Structures = Automatic Programming!*, William Langdon gives an overview of advanced genetic programming techniques and how to evolve high-level data structures, such as stacks, queues, and lists. The book also draws some interesting connections between genetic programming and Price's selection and covariance theorem from population genetics and Fisher's theorem of natural selection.

Advances in genetic programming

The series *Advances in Genetic Programming* gives an up-to-date overview of current implementation and analysis issues in genetic programming. The main focus areas are how to increase the power of GP in combination with innovative applications or new GP environments (Kinnear 1994; Angeline and Kinnear 1996; Spector, Langdon, et al. 1999).

Advances in GP

Genetic programming conferences

The annual series of genetic programming (GP) conferences started in 1996. All of the proceedings give a state-of-the-art overview of GP research and applications (Koza, Goldberg, et al. 1996; Koza, Deb, et al. 1997; Koza, Banzhaf, et al. 1998).

GP conference

In 1999 the GP conference joined with ICGA, the International Conference on Genetic Algorithms, to form the annual Genetic and Evolutionary Computation Conference, GECCO (Banzhaf, Daida, et al. 1999; Whitley, Goldberg, et al. 2000).

GECCO

8 Advanced Genetic Programming at Work

Artificial Life is the study of man-made systems that exhibit behaviors characteristic of natural living systems. It complements the traditional biological sciences concerned with the analysis of living organisms by attempting to synthesize life-like behaviors within computers and other artificial media.

Langton 1989, p.1

8.1 Breeding of computer programs: the *AntTracker* example

In the context of artificial intelligence (AI), a multitude of disciplines has emerged during the past 15 years that deal with the modeled synthesis of living systems. Artificial neural networks imitate adaptive behaviors of nerve cell systems, with a particular focus on their capability to act as learning units. Cellular automata are used to investigate causes and effects of complex interacting systems in the context of self-organization. The manifold of evolutionary algorithms provides a first impression of the dynamics and potential of natural evolution principles, especially in regard to adaptations to specific environmental settings.

Neural networks

Cellular automata

Evolutionary algorithms

Christopher Langton is one of the key initiators and research pioneers of *artificial life* (AL). Following his definition of AL systems, we want to demonstrate in the following sections how specific search behaviors of simple organisms, acting in a relatively complex environment, can be evolved with genetic programming techniques. We refer to extensive simulation experiments on the basis of genetic algorithms performed by Jefferson et al., on simplistic imitations of ant foraging behaviors (Jefferson, Collins, et al. 1992). This modeling system can be considered a standard test environment in the area of

Simulated foraging behavior of ants

artificial life research and has already been investigated by many researchers, such as Angeline (1993), Collins (1992), and Koza (1992).

Since it is our intention to illuminate the basic principles of program evolution, we keep this example as simple as possible. We are not trying to model specific behaviors of natural ants, but the task of breeding foraging programs in a mazelike environment is sufficiently complicated to illustrate the essential dynamics resulting from the evolution of program structures.

Chapter overview

In this section, we present the "ant world" environment, the behavior repertory of the ants, and the structure of their control programs. We also deal with the generation of the program expressions, the evaluation function defined by the foraging task, and the genetic operators used for varying the program genomes. A careful analysis of a typical evolution experiment is presented in Section 8.2. An approach for automatic adaptation of operator weights is introduced in Section 8.3. Finally, in Section 8.4, more advanced GP operators are discussed.

This chapter differs from the previous ones because none of the algorithms used in the experiments described here are discussed. All the implementations and experiments are contained in the Evolvica notebooks for this chapter, available on the *IEC* Web site (see Preface). The evolution algorithms used here are based on the concepts presented in Section 7.4.

8.1.1 Hungry ants

Ants in their two-dimensional environment

An "ant" is modeled as a simple artificial organism, acting in a discrete, two-dimensional environment that consists of an 18×18 grid (Figure 8.1[a]). Forty-four food pieces (dark gray) and pheromones (light gray) are distributed along a path. Pheromones are used by ants to direct their species members to food sites. The trail we use is a sim-

John Muir Trail

plified version of Jefferson et al.'s John Muir Trail. This trail has the particular feature that food pieces are first densely packed together. Eventually the food trail is interrupted by one or two grid squares. At the end, the distances between the food pieces increase (Jefferson, Collins, et al. 1992). In addition, we constrain the mobility of the ants by obstacles, which completely surround and partition the grid world.

Walls

The black squares in Figure 8.1(a) represent walls through which the ants cannot walk. (In Jefferson et al.'s experimental setup, however, the ants may move everywhere; their environment is modeled as a double torus in the west-east and north-south directions.)

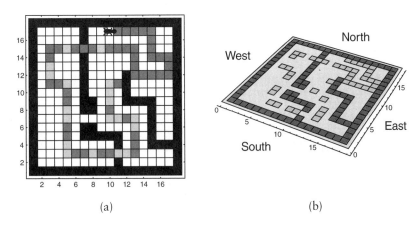

Figure 8.1
Grid environment of the ants
in a top (a) and perspective
(b) view.

Initially, the ant starts at position (10, 17), facing east, as indicated in Figure 8.1(a). The objective is to evolve control programs by genetic programming. With its program an ant should be able to visit all food squares within a limited number of action steps. The food-pheromone path, highlighted in gray, would be an optimal trail to follow.

Problem description

Why is this a difficult task? Control programs must be evolved so that the ants do not blindly bump against walls. Instead, the ants must search out passages between the wall-separated areas, and they must develop efficient strategies for discovering food pieces. Whether the pheromones between the food squares are used as "signposts" or whether the particular distribution of the food pieces along the path has any advantages depends on the ability of the program structures to adapt to this specific environment.

Difficulty of the ant foraging task

8.1.2   Ant actions and interpretation of control programs

The ants have the following repertoire of actions:

❏ `advance`: move one step forward,

❏ `turnLeft`: turn 90 degrees left,

❏ `turnRight`: turn 90 degrees right, and

❏ `nop`: no action.

Ant actions

An ant can also determine its actions depending on local environmental signals. Each ant is equipped with a *sensor*, which provides information about the state of the square directly in front of the ant. There are sensors for identifying food (dark gray), pheromones (light gray),

Sensors

dust (white), and walls (black) (Figure 8.1[a]). By using parametrized `ifSensor` commands, the ants can take environmental signals, `food`, `pheromone`, `dust`, and `wall`, into account:

Response to environmental signals

❑ `ifSensor[signal][A]`:
Action `A` is performed if the ant faces a *signal* square.

❑ `ifSensor[signal][A,B]`:
Command `A` is performed if a *signal* square is in front of the ant. Otherwise command `B` is performed.

Being able to localize food sites (`food`) is an essential precondition for solving this task in an "intelligent" manner. No ant can be successful without using any of the sensors for obstacle (`wall`) detection. Purely random exploration of the whole area does not result in any competitive behavior, especially since the ants' world is partitioned by insurmountable walls. The `pheromone` and `dust` sensors might make navigation easier because following a pheromone trail will eventually lead to another food site. However, successful foraging strategies do not necessarily rely on pheromones.

Time limit

During an evaluation run, an ant may perform a maximum of $ActionSteps_{max}$ action steps. Each of the commands, including sensor queries, counts as one action step. Each ant program is iterated until either all food squares are collected or $ActionSteps_{max}$ steps have been performed.

Figure 8.2 lists all the templates serving as building blocks for the ant control programs. The templates are to be interpreted as patterns, describing possible compositions of the building blocks (Jacob 1995, 1996a, 1996b). `AntTracker[_seq]` is the initial template. The maximum number of arguments for the `seq` terms, which specify command sequences, is set to three. All templates are attributed with the same weight.

Additional commands: stop and again

Introns

Besides the basic commands, `advance`, `turnLeft`, `turnRight`, and `nop`, the action sequence, encoded by the program genomes, and the decoding of the program genomes can be additionally controlled by the two commands `stop` and `again`. Any commands after a `stop` instruction are ignored, and the interpretation of the program genome starts from the beginning. `Stop` commands serve as an initial marker for so-called *intron regions,* which are also part of natural genomes (Gottschalk 1989, p. 57; Lewin 1983). Genome segments, which are not decoded and therefore do not take part in the expression of the phenotype (the program actions, in our case), are denoted as introns. In fact, introns can constitute up to 90%

```
AntTracker[_seq],

seq[advance], seq[turnLeft], seq[turnRight], seq[nop],
seq[stop],
seq[advance | turnLeft | turnRight, again],

seq[BlankSequence[
     Blank[ seq ] |
     Blank[ ifSensor[food] ] |
     Blank[ ifSensor[phero] ] |
     Blank[ ifSensor[dust] ]
]],

ifSensor[food][_seq,_seq],
ifSensor[phero][_seq,_seq]
ifSensor[dust][_seq,_seq]
ifSensor[wall][_seq,_seq]
```

Figure 8.2

Templates for the ant control programs.

of natural genome information. The stop command implicitly results in switching off all subsequent expressions.

Before an ifSensor command is interpreted, it is placed on top of a command stack, and after completion it is removed. If an again command occurs within an ifSensor[X] expression, the last command on the stack is repeated and the sensor conditions checked anew. The again interpretation does not imply any side effects; in particular, the contents of the stack are not changed. Thus the programs can implement implicit loops; for instance

Stack

```
ifSensor[food][seq[advance,again],seq[nop]],
```

Implicit loop

in order to follow any consecutive food path. The ifSensor expression would be executed as long as there are food squares in front of the ant's current position. Otherwise, the ant quits the loop and continues with any subsequent command. But as a single command, an again expression may turn out to be fatal for an ant. With the control program

```
ifSensor[food][seq[again],seq[advance]]
```

the ant stops in front of a food site and performs no further actions (except for looping until the maximum number of action steps is reached). Because of their inferior fitnesses, programs like this will be sorted out by the evolution and selection process if the number of visited food squares is taken into account by the fitness evaluation function. A closer look at the templates used for generating ant program expressions reveals that at least one other movement command must occur before any `again` expression (Figure 8.2).

8.1.3 Generating program genomes

Command sequences and sensor queries

We use the templates in Figure 8.2 to generate the ant control programs. The `seq` terms correspond to command sequences. Each of the single commands (`advance`, `turnLeft`, `turnRight`, `nop`, and `stop`) is embedded in a `seq` expression. An `again` command is always combined with a move instruction. With this encoding, the genetic operators can modify even single commands as atomic expressions and recombine them. This encoding scheme also results in a uniform representation for all instructions, since they are either `seq` or `ifSensor[X]` expressions.

Figure 8.3 lists a collection of expressions encoding ant control programs, generated by the building block templates in Figure 8.2. Many of the programs exhibit complex structures. A number of simplifications on the program expressions can be performed without changing their semantics. Simplifying the programs leads to reduced computation times for interpretation of the programs, and analysis of the programs is easier.

Simplification

Figure 8.4 summarizes the reduction rules, which are used as filters, applied before any interpretation of the program expressions is performed. The genetic operators (see Section 8.1.4), however, always work on the full program expressions. Most of the simplifications eliminate superfluous `seq` expressions or `nop` terms (Figure 8.4[a]). An `ifSensor` expression with the same program text in its `if` and `then` parts can be reduced accordingly. Also, nested `ifSensor` expressions with queries for the same signal can be reduced to a single `ifSensor` expression if no further commands are between the signal queries (Figure 8.4[b]).

After a `stop` command an instruction sequence is interrupted, and the interpretation continues at the beginning of the program. This is why after a `stop` command, all subsequent expressions can be eliminated (Figure 8.4[c]). An analogous reduction rule can be derived from the interpretation of the `again` expressions (Figure 8.4[d]). The simplification effects are illustrated in Figure 8.5 with an example of a program expression. If an encapsulation operator (see the Evolvica notebooks for this chapter and Section 8.3 for details on advanced GP operators) is among the genetic operators used, the program genome may also contain encapsulated substructures, which also must be decoded.

```
AntTracker[seq[advance]]

AntTracker[seq[nop]]

AntTracker[seq[seq[ifSensor[phero][seq[turnRight],
  seq[turnRight]]]]]

AntTracker[seq[ifSensor[food][seq[nop], seq[advance]]]]

AntTracker[seq[ifSensor[wall][seq[advance, again], seq[turnLeft]]]]

AntTracker[seq[advance, again]]

AntTracker[seq[seq[advance], ifSensor[dust][seq[turnLeft, again],
 seq[seq[advance]]]]]

AntTracker[seq[seq[nop], seq[turnRight]]]

AntTracker[seq[seq[nop], ifSensor[dust][seq[advance], seq[seq[stop],
  seq[stop], ifSensor[food][seq[turnRight], seq[turnLeft]]]]]]

AntTracker[seq[seq[seq[stop], seq[turnRight, again],
  ifSensor[food][seq[ifSensor[wall][seq[stop], seq[nop]]],
  seq[turnRight]]], seq[turnLeft]]]

AntTracker[seq[seq[seq[seq[turnLeft]], seq[seq[seq[advance],
  seq[turnRight, again], seq[turnRight]], seq[stop]],
  seq[turnRight]], ifSensor[wall][seq[advance], seq[nop]]]]

AntTracker[seq[seq[seq[ifSensor[dust][seq[nop], seq[advance]],
  seq[turnRight], ifSensor[dust][seq[advance],
  seq[ifSensor[wall][seq[nop], seq[seq[nop],
  ifSensor[dust][seq[turnLeft], seq[ifSensor[phero][seq[turnRight],
  seq[stop]], seq[advance], seq[nop]]]]],
  seq[ifSensor[wall][seq[turnRight], seq[turnLeft, again]]],
  seq[advance]]]], seq[turnRight], ifSensor[food][seq[turnLeft,
  again], seq[seq[turnLeft, again]]]],
  ifSensor[phero][seq[seq[turnLeft], seq[advance],
  seq[seq[turnLeft], ifSensor[food][seq[turnLeft],
  seq[ifSensor[food][seq[turnRight], seq[turnLeft]],
  seq[seq[turnRight], seq[turnRight, again]]],
  ifSensor[wall][seq[seq[turnRight], seq[advance]],
  seq[turnLeft]]]], seq[nop]], seq[seq[nop],
  ifSensor[dust][seq[turnRight], seq[nop]], seq[stop]]]]]

AntTracker[seq[seq[ifSensor[wall][seq[advance, again],
  seq[seq[turnLeft, again]]], seq[advance],
  ifSensor[dust][seq[turnRight, again], seq[turnLeft]]], seq[stop]]]
```

Figure 8.3
Examples of randomly generated ant control program genomes.

8.1.4 Evaluation and genetic operators

The control programs of each generation are evaluated one by one and independent of one another. Each ant cyclically performs its program until either all food sites have been visited or a maximum number of $\text{ActionSteps}_{\text{max}}$ action steps has been reached (400 steps in our example). Each command, including sensor queries, counts as one action step. The fitness $\mu(p_{\text{Ant}})$ of a control program p_{Ant} depends on

Figure 8.4
Reduction rules for
simplifications of the control
programs.

(a)   seq[advance] :> advance, seq[turnLeft] :> turnLeft,
        seq[turnRight] :> turnRight, seq[nop] :> nop,

        seq[x___,seq[y__],z___] :> seq[x,y,z],

        seq[x___,nop,y__] :> seq[x,y],
        seq[x__,nop,y___] :> seq[x,y],

(b)   ifSensor[i_][x_,x_] :> x,
        ifSensor[i_][ifSensor[i_][x_,y_],z_] :> ifSensor[i][x,z],
        ifSensor[i_][x_,ifSensor[i_][y_,z_]] :> ifSensor[i][x,z],

        ifSensor[i_][seq[ifSensor[i_][x_,y_],z___],r_] :>
          ifSensor[i][seq[x,z],r],
        ifSensor[i_][x_,seq[ifSensor[i_][y_,z_],r___]] :>
          ifSensor[i][x,seq[z,r]],

(c)   seq[x___,seq[stop],y___] :> seq[x,stop],
        seq[x___,stop,y___] :> seq[x,stop],

(d)   seq[x___,seq[again],y___] :> seq[x,again],
        seq[x___,again,y___] :> seq[x,again]

the number of visited food squares and on a complexity measure, which takes into account the nesting structure of the program:

Ant evaluation function

$$\mu(p_{Ant}) = \begin{cases} F+1 & \text{if } d_p \le d_{max}, \\ \dfrac{d_{max}}{d_p} \cdot F+1 & \text{if } d_p > d_{max}. \end{cases}$$

Evaluation: food sites and program depth

Here F denotes the number of collected food pieces or visited food sites, $d_p = d(p_{Ant})$ is the depth of the program expression p_{Ant}, and d_{max} is a predefined maximum depth. Thus, more compact programs have an advantage in the selection process. A program that is n times deeper than the maximum depth d_{max} must collect at least n times more food pieces than a comparable program with a depth less than d_{max}. Apart from that, the depth of the evolvable program structures is not constrained. (This is in contrast to Koza's approach to the Ant-Tracker task, where program terms larger than a certain depth are simply eliminated (Koza 1992, Section 7.2, pp. 147 ff.).

Taking the program depth into account compensates for the tendency of the recombining crossover operator to generate ever more complex program expressions. These result in longer interpretation times and are rather complicated to understand when the program semantics are analyzed. As previous experiments for our example problem have shown, programs with depths less than 10 can be successful. The maximum depth for the experiment discussed here is set to $d_{max} = 12$.

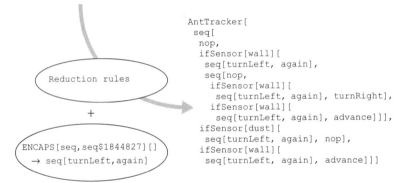

Figure 8.5
Application of reduction and decapsulation rules.

```
AntTracker[
 seq[
  nop,
  ifSensor[wall][
   seq[turnLeft, again],
   seq[nop,
    ifSensor[wall][
     ENCAPS[seq, seq$1844827][], seq[turnRight]],
     seq[seq[
      ifSensor[wall][
       seq[seq[turnLeft, again], seq[nop],
        ifSensor[wall][seq[again], seq[seq[nop]]]],
       seq[seq[advance]]]]]]],
   seq[
    ifSensor[dust][seq[turnLeft, again], seq[nop]],
    seq[
     ifSensor[wall][
      seq[
       ifSensor[wall][
        seq[seq[turnLeft, again],seq[nop],
         ifSensor[phero][seq[stop]]],
        seq[seq[seq[nop], seq[seq[advance]]]]]],
      seq[seq[advance]]]]
]]]]
```

```
AntTracker[
 seq[
  nop,
  ifSensor[wall][
   seq[turnLeft, again],
   seq[nop,
    ifSensor[wall][
     seq[turnLeft, again], turnRight],
     ifSensor[wall][
      seq[turnLeft, again], advance]]],
   ifSensor[dust][
    seq[turnLeft, again], nop],
   ifSensor[wall][
    seq[turnLeft, again], advance]]]
```

Reduction rules

+

ENCAPS[seq,seq$1844827][]
→ seq[turnLeft,again]

For variations on the program structures, the genetic operators listed in Figure 8.6 are used. Initially, recombination (GP crossover) and mutation are considered the main operators, which account for elementary construction from primitive to more complex program expressions. This is why relatively high initial weights are attributed to these two operators. In the course of the evolution process, these operator weights are adapted, depending on each operator's contribution to the fitness evolution of the whole population (see Section 8.2.2).

Genetic operators

Through the use of filtering templates, the selections of subexpressions to be modified focus on characteristic substructures. As _seq instances, all elementary commands are in the scope of the genetic operators. For deletions only, seq terms with at least two arguments are selectable. In particular the two templates

Selection templates

$$ifSensor[\_][\_\_]   \text{and } ifSensor[\_]$$

Figure 8.6

Genetic operators for
modification of the program
structures (see the Evolvica
notebooks for complete
descriptions of these
operators).

Operator	Weight	Selection template	Template weight

Mutation	4	`__, BlankSequence[]`
		`ifSensor[_][__]`
		`ifSensor[_]`
			1
			1
			0.5

Recombination	4	`__, BlankSequence[]`
		`ifSensor[_][__]`
		`ifSensor[_]`
			4
			1
			0.5

Deletion	1	`x__/;Length[{x}] > 1` `ifSensor[_][__]`	2 1
Duplication	2	`__, BlankSequence[]` `ifSensor[_][__]`	2 1
Permutation	2	`__, BlankSequence[]` `ifSensor[_][__]`	2 1
Encapsulation	1	`x__/;Length[{x}] > 1` `ifSensor[_][__]`	4 1
Decapsulation	1	`__, BlankSequence[]` `ifSensor[_][__]`	4 1

for selection of `ifSensor` expressions by mutation and crossover
demonstrate how the scope of the operators can be selectively constrained. Expressions selected by the first template are mutated or
recombined as complete `ifSensor` expressions, whereas by the second template only the expression head, that is, the sensor signal, can
be modified (cf. Jacob 1996a, 1996b, and the Evolvica notebooks on
the *IEC* Web site).

*Advantages of symbolic
expressions*

This example clearly shows one of the advantages of using symbolic expressions instead of simple term structures. If the programs
were encoded as terms, a unique function symbol for each of the
`ifSensor[signal]` expressions would be required. In addition,
new mutation and recombination operators would have to be defined,
which not only work on terms but also on a particular subset of the
function heads. This would mean that the advantageous universality
of the operators, gleaned from genetic algorithms, would be sacrificed
in favor of specific operator variants. If genetic operators are defined
on the basis of symbolic expressions, however, these problems do not
arise.

In the following sections we will take a detailed look at a few evolution experiments on the AntTracker task. The objective is to understand how and why evolutionary algorithms succeed in developing complex, functional ant control programs.

8.2 Analysis of an evolution experiment

In the following sections we discuss a typical evolution experiment for the AntTracker optimization problem. The development from initially primitive to "optimal" control programs is illustrated when we look at the phenotypical behavior of the ant programs and their genotypical encodings. We also take a closer look at a dynamic weight adaptation scheme for the genetic operators. The automatically adjusted operator ranks reflect the varying influence of the operators on the progress of the evolution processes.

8.2.1 Evolution of the best individuals

Starting from a population of 50 randomly generated control programs, derived from the templates in Figure 8.2, the objective is to evolve ant programs over at most 100 generations, which direct the ant to all food sites (within the given time limit of a maximum of 400 action steps). Figures 8.7 and 8.8 summarize the phenotypical interpretation of the best program genomes evolved over 59 generations. The sites entered by the ant are marked by small squares. The light gray, larger squares label food pieces, which have not been collected. The dark squares represent the walls.

In the course of evolution, the programs steadily increase their action radius. Initially, movements are restricted to a small subarea. In generation 16, however, a significant stride has been made by the ant's passing through a wall opening (Figure 8.7). For the first time, a passage through the wall is discovered and gone through. This behavior is only possible by integrating sensor queries in the control programs. All further, best-evolved programs will use this passage, too, through which the second large area of food sites is entered.

Extending the radius of action

Discovering walk-throughs

In order to make more progress, algorithms for localizing food squares must be developed, which indeed happens. Already in generation 22 an individual appears that is able to avoid hitting walls and almost perfectly follows a food trail (Figure 8.8). Since this ant always turns left in front of a wall, part of the food sites in the first (upper-right) area are not reached.

Localizing food sites

Following food paths

Figure 8.7
Evolution steps: behaviors of
the best-evolved programs,
generation 0 to 17.

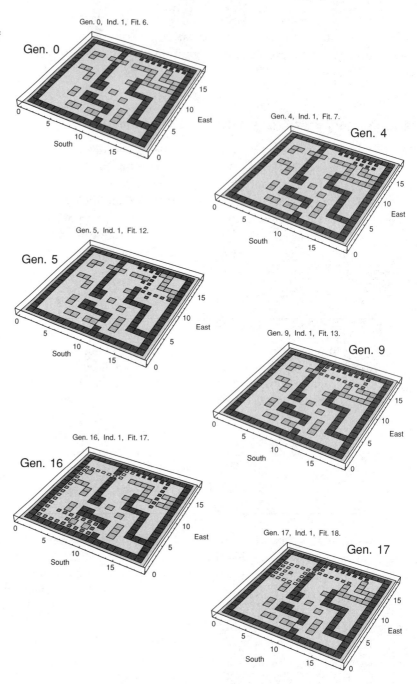

After another 16 generations, this control program has taken over
from a much more successful variant (generation 38), which is capable of performing a global search for food sites, although the evolved

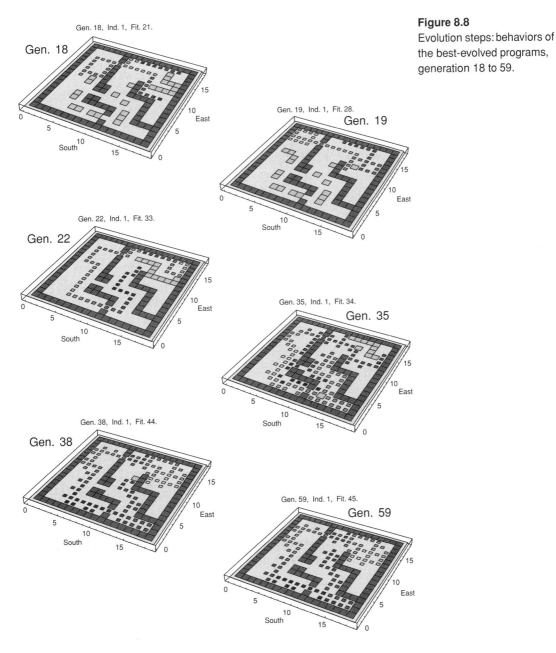

Figure 8.8
Evolution steps: behaviors of the best-evolved programs, generation 18 to 59.

control algorithm generates relatively "fuzzy" action sequences. After each two steps, this ant leaves a discovered food trail to the right but always navigates back on the trail. This results in a more or less rolling motion, which turns out to be an advantageous search behavior whenever the food sites are largely dispersed. Finally, the most successful program, which collects all the food pieces, is evolved in

Food search with digressions

generation 59. This control program is only a variant of the previously best individual of generation 38.

In order to better understand how the best-evolved program avoids walls, passes through wall openings, and discovers all food sites, it is revealing to analyze the programs in more detail with a few examples. The range of actions for the programs can be investigated more closely by answering the following questions:

Analysis of the best programs

❑ Are the food sites located in a sufficiently efficient way?

❑ How is the ant kept on or in the vicinity of a food trail? How do the ants cope with bends in the food path, and how do the ants react to interrupted food paths?

❑ How are walls evaded?

Figures 8.9–8.11 give a more detailed summary of the best-evolved program genomes together with graphics illustrating the encoded action sequences. In order to visualize time evolution of the ant movements, for each action step the ant position is depicted in vertical direction of the time axes (displaying action steps in 10 time units). The projection of these three-dimensional paths on the ground area correspond to the graphics in Figures 8.7 and 8.8.

Illustrating action steps

The best ant of the initial generation (Figure 8.9) moves from the start position at (10, 17) straight to the wall, collecting five food pieces, and bumps against the wall. This simple strategy is the most successful up to generation 4. In the long run, no program can be successful without using any sensor information, since the ability to turn from walls is an elementary precondition.

Straight ahead

In generation 5, the fitness of the best individual is doubled. This champion program implements three sensor commands. However, it is not able to usefully apply the wall sensor. When positioned directly in front of a wall, this program tries to advance the ant one step, which results in total stasis.

Applying sensors

A promising strategy for avoiding walls has evolved in generation 9 (Figure 8.9). This program differs from the best program of generation 5 only in its last instruction. This ant first moves one step forward, turns left in front of dust squares, and advances another step. In front of walls it always turns left. Otherwise, it takes another step forward (cf. the last ifSensor expression). This results in a cyclic movement within the first area, where the ant moves opposite to the actual direction of the food trail. The essential expression for avoiding walls,

Avoiding walls

Turning off from walls

```
ifSensor[wall][seq[turnLeft,again], advance]
```

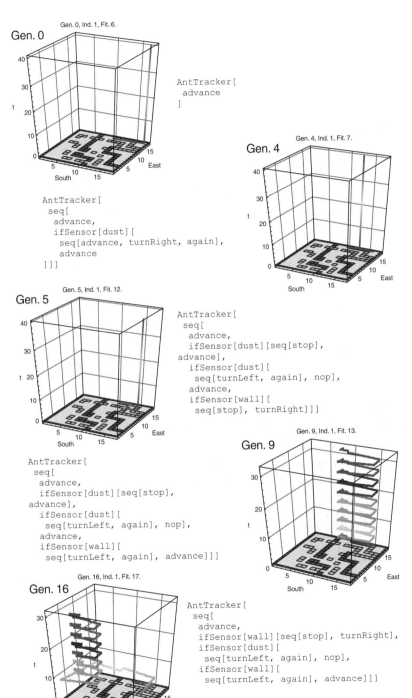

AntTracker[
  advance
]

AntTracker[
  seq[
   advance,
   ifSensor[dust][
    seq[advance, turnRight, again],
    advance
  ]]]

AntTracker[
  seq[
   advance,
   ifSensor[dust][seq[stop],
advance],
   ifSensor[dust][
    seq[turnLeft, again], nop],
   advance,
   ifSensor[wall][
    seq[stop], turnRight]]]

AntTracker[
  seq[
   advance,
   ifSensor[dust][seq[stop],
advance],
   ifSensor[dust][
    seq[turnLeft, again], nop],
   advance,
   ifSensor[wall][
    seq[turnLeft, again], advance]]]

AntTracker[
  seq[
   advance,
   ifSensor[wall][seq[stop], turnRight],
   ifSensor[dust][
    seq[turnLeft, again], nop],
   ifSensor[wall][
    seq[turnLeft, again], advance]]]

Figure 8.9

Evolution of the best-evolved programs and their encoded actions (Part 1).

Figure 8.10

Evolution of the best-evolved programs and their encoded actions (Part 2).

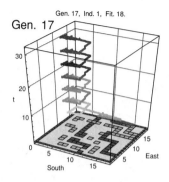

Gen. 17

```
AntTracker[
 seq[
  advance,
  ifSensor[dust][
   seq[
    ifSensor[dust][
     seq[turnLeft, again], nop, nop],
    advance,
    ifSensor[wall][seq[stop],advance]],
   advance],
  ifSensor[dust][
   seq[turnLeft, again], nop],
  advance,
  ifSensor[wall][
   seq[turnLeft, again], advance]]]
```

```
AntTracker[
 seq[
  advance,
  ifSensor[wall][seq[stop], turnRight],
  ifSensor[dust][
   seq[turnLeft, again], nop],
  ifSensor[wall][
   seq[turnLeft, again],
   seq[
    advance,
    ifSensor[dust][seq[stop], advance],
    ifSensor[dust][
     seq[turnLeft, again], nop],
    advance, advance]]]]
```

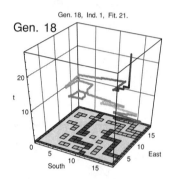

Gen. 18

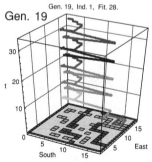

Gen. 19

```
AntTracker[
 seq[
  advance,
  ifSensor[dust][seq[stop], advance],
  ifSensor[dust][
   seq[turnLeft, again], nop],
  advance,
  ifSensor[wall][
   seq[turnLeft,
    ifSensor[phero][
     turnLeft, seq[stop]]],
   advance]]]
```

```
AntTracker[
 seq[
  ifSensor[wall][
   seq[turnLeft, again],
   seq[turnRight]],
  seq[ifSensor[dust][
   seq[turnLeft, again], seq[nop]],
   seq[
    ifSensor[wall][
     seq[seq[turnLeft, again],
     seq[nop],
     ifSensor[phero][seq[stop]]],
    seq[seq[advance]]], seq[nop]]]]
```

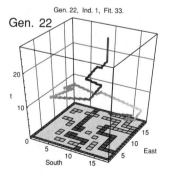

Gen. 22

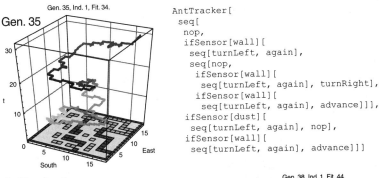

Gen. 35

Gen. 35, Ind. 1, Fit. 34.

```
AntTracker[
 seq[
  nop,
  ifSensor[wall][
   seq[turnLeft, again],
   seq[nop,
    ifSensor[wall][
     seq[turnLeft, again], turnRight],
    ifSensor[wall][
     seq[turnLeft, again], advance]]],
   ifSensor[dust][
    seq[turnLeft, again], nop],
   ifSensor[wall][
    seq[turnLeft, again], advance]]]
```

Figure 8.11
Evolution of the best-evolved programs and their encoded actions (Part 3).

```
AntTracker[
 seq[
  nop,
  ifSensor[wall][
   seq[turnLeft, again],
   seq[nop,
    ifSensor[wall][
     seq[turnLeft, again], turnRight],
    ifSensor[wall][
     seq[turnLeft, again], advance]]],
   ifSensor[dust][
    seq[turnLeft, again], nop],
   ifSensor[wall][
    seq[ifSensor[dust][advance]],
    advance]]]
```

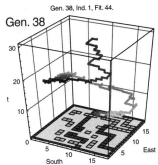

Gen. 38

Gen. 38, Ind. 1, Fit. 44.

Gen. 59

Gen. 59, Ind. 1, Fit. 45.

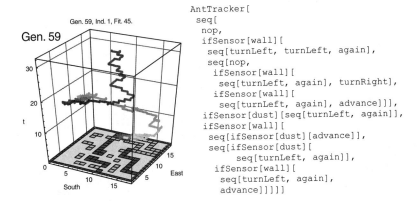

```
AntTracker[
 seq[
  nop,
  ifSensor[wall][
   seq[turnLeft, turnLeft, again],
   seq[nop,
    ifSensor[wall][
     seq[turnLeft, again], turnRight],
    ifSensor[wall][
     seq[turnLeft, again], advance]]],
   ifSensor[dust][seq[turnLeft, again]],
   ifSensor[wall][
    seq[ifSensor[dust][advance]],
    seq[ifSensor[dust][
       seq[turnLeft, again]],
     ifSensor[wall][
      seq[turnLeft, again],
      advance]]]]]
```

reappears in the subsequent best programs (cf. generations 16, 17, 22, 35, and 59). The ant turns left until it no longer faces a wall. Then it moves one step forward. Successful subprograms, encoding this strategy, are inherited over many generations, and in structures evolved later they are integrated in modified contexts.

Another key improvement in the course of this program evolution occurs in generation 16 (Figure 8.9). For the first time an opening in the wall is discovered, and the ant walks through. All subsequent best ants take this path into the second food site area. Apart from the first

Discovering walk-throughs

`ifSensor` expression, this generation 16 program is identical to the best program of generation 9. The new sensor instruction

`ifSensor[wall][seq[stop],turnRight]`

would have a fateful effect if the ant stood directly in front of a wall (it would stop). Fortunately, this situation does not occur in this specific environment with the given initial conditions. In combination with the second instruction

Walking along walls

`ifSensor[dust][seq[turnLeft,again],nop],`

this implies an action sequence for walking along walls. The third `ifSensor` expression takes care of turning away from walls.

After generation 17, the size of the program expressions increases noticeably (Figure 8.10). In generation 22, another important evolution step is taken. This relatively compact program enables an ant, after some initial irritations in the first area, to follow perfectly the food path up to the end. Here only the very last `advance` command is unconditional. All other actions are controlled by sensor queries. The first and last `ifSensor` expressions cause the ant to turn left from a wall and take a step along the wall:

Following the food path

`ifSensor[wall][seq[turnLeft,again],turnRight]`

· · ·

`ifSensor[wall][turnLeft,again], advance].`

Following paths, avoiding walls

In all other cases, the ant first turns to the right. If it faces a dust square, this last movement is corrected. This is an almost perfect strategy for staying on the food and pheromone sites and following them, since the last `advance` instruction always leads to a step forward. This program remains the best individual for another 13 generations.

Another essential increase in fitness is observable in generation 38 (Figure 8.11). The best individual misses only a single food square. Its control program contains several instructions for avoiding the wall or following along the wall. The ant periodically leaves the food trail, as described in the introduction, but it always returns to the food and pheromone sites. In the first area, the food path is followed in the opposite direction. The ant walks along the wall, walks through the passage, and finally follows the food and pheromone trail up to the end.

"Perfect" foraging

The champion individual, which visits all the food sites and is evolved only another 21 generations later (Figure 8.11, generation 59), differs from the program of generation 38 only in the very last instructions. Directly in front of a wall, the generation 59 program turns around. If there is no wall, the ant turns right and takes one step forward (Figure 8.12). If there is a wall, it is evaded by a left turn. Finally this action sequence is concluded by the ant's turning left from any dust square and stepping back in the original direction. Additional walls coming up are also avoided. With another iteration of its control program, after a right turn, the ant is again facing the direction from which it started—now, however, one step advanced.

Moving forward, glancing left and right

Figure 8.13 illustrates this particular sequence of movements. Here also the different behavior for left versus right turns is visible. For right turns on the food path, the corner square is never entered if the last bend lies at an odd number of steps behind—a situation that does not occur in the test environment. Figure 8.13 also illustrates that the evolved champion program is not specializing on the specific food path of the test environment. Even on a multibranched food-pheromone path (Figure 8.13[a]) all the food pieces are discovered by the ant's exploring the path forward and backward while visiting the branches on the right-hand side (Figure 8.13[b]).

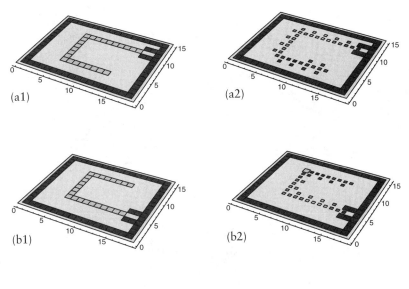

(a1) (a2)

(b1) (b2)

Figure 8.12
Actions of the champion ant control program (generation 59) on specific food-pheromone paths.

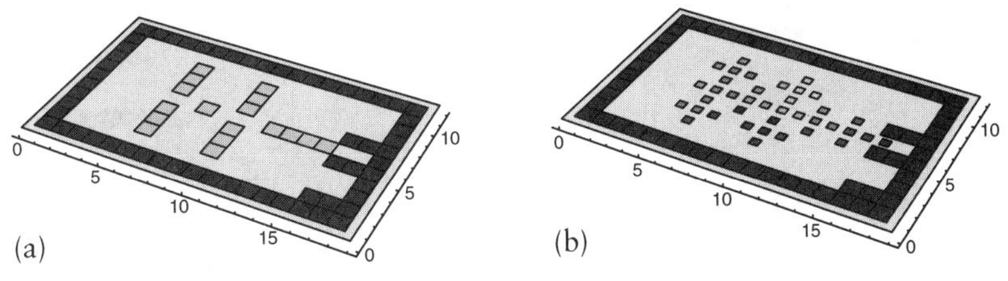

(a) (b)

Figure 8.13
Actions of the best ant program (generation 59) on a branching food-pheromone path.

8.2.2 Fitness evolution and genome complexity

Evolution of the gene pool

In the previous section we were interested in specific individuals and their evolutionary development on the level of their program genomes. Here we illuminate in more detail the evolution processes on the populational level of the gene pool. Using the example program evolution discussed previously, which has actually been run over 85 generations, we take a closer look at the fitness dynamics from generation to generation. We also investigate how the complexity of the program expressions changes in the course of the evolution process.

Figure 8.14 gives an overview of the evolution of the fitness values. In parts (a) and (b) the sorted fitnesses of the individuals for each generation are plotted. Part (c) depicts the fitnesses of the best and worst individual of each generation together with the mean fitness value per population.

Figure 8.14
Fitness evolution of the program genomes over 85 generations.

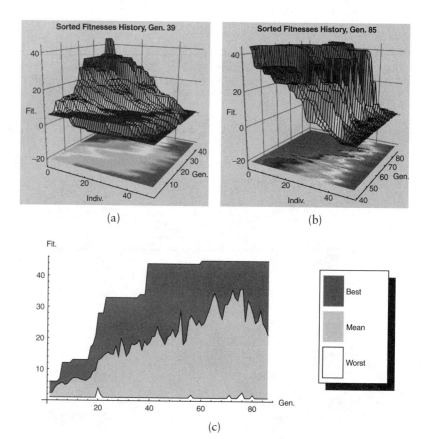

(a)   (b)

(c)

The fitness of the best individuals steadily increases in the course of the evolution process. The increase, however, is not continuous but occurs in relatively few jumps. Between these jumps are longer phases of stasis, with constant maximum fitness.

Fitness evolution of the champion programs

The stages on the evolutionary pathway to the champion individual, described in the previous section, are clearly visible (cf. Figures 8.9–8.11). It is striking that almost 20 generations are necessary for the very last fitness increase from 44 to 45 points, which is typical for the dynamics of the final stages of evolutions in the AntTracker problem. This is mainly due to the specific characteristics of the food path—the very last food sites are much more difficult to explore. The search task becomes more demanding; hence the evolutionary search effort increases.

The average fitness tends to grow up to about generation 70, which is mainly due to the combination of fitness-proportionate selection and fitness-improving structure adaptations by the genetic operators (Figure 8.14[c]). Since the fluctuations of the mean fitnesses are relatively small, it can be inferred that, in general, the genetic operators produce only a minor fraction of lethal mutants; that is, program structures with only low fitnesses are scarce. This is also because the complexity of the program expressions is increasing (Figure 8.15), so that modifications to the program structures have fewer detrimental effects on the phenotypical program behavior. In addition, many instructions are redundantly encoded, as demonstrated by the analyses of the program genomes in previous sections.

Increasing program complexity

As Figure 8.15 shows, structures of a maximum depth of 25 are created. The maximum program depth displays large fluctuations (Figure 8.16) and differs widely from the average depth values, which tend to increase up to generation 40 and finally level out at around $d_{\max} = 12$, since the fitness function prefers program expressions of

Evolution of program depths

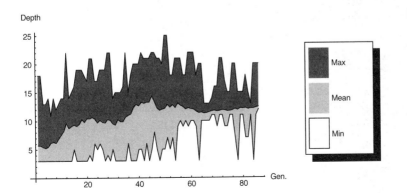

Figure 8.15
Evolution of program expression depth.

Figure 8.16
Depth of the best program
per generation versus
average program depth.

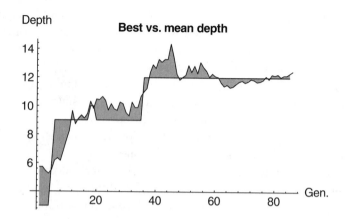

less depth (see Section 8.1.4). After an "optimal" program has been found in generation 59, the minimum program depth gradually approaches the average depth value.

8.2.3 Influence of operator adaptation

To adapt the operator ranks automatically during the evolution experiment, we use the weight adaptation scheme described in Section 8.3. Figure 8.17 summarizes the adapted weight settings for each of the genetic operators used in the AntTracker evolution experiment. The

Importance of recombinations

importance of the recombination or crossover operator as the primary creator of structures with ever increasing fitness is clearly visible. Up to generation 40, the crossover weights are kept at a relatively high level. Recombinations produce structures of steadily increasing complexity, and so the average depth of the programs also increases (cf. Figure 8.16).

At generation 40, the mean expression depth has reached the maximum value of d_{max}. Now most of the recombinations result in programs with even greater depths, mostly without any compensating improvements in fitness. Hence, the positive crossover effects diminish

Deletions and duplications

and the operator's rating decreases. Now fitness increases in the genomes result partly from duplications and partly from deletions on the program substructures.

Encapsulations

The weightings of macro extraction (encapsulation) and decapsulation fluctuate but only within a limited range (the scale for these two operator weights differs from that of the other plots). These two operators do not seem to make any large-scale contributions to the composition of fitness-increasing structures. Since only a few of the best-

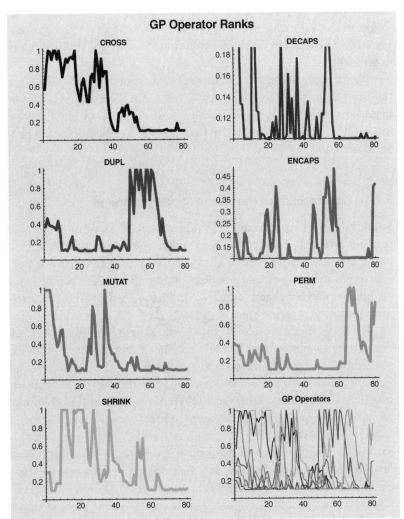

Figure 8.17

AntTracker: dynamics of the weights for the genetic operators of recombination (CROSS), duplication (DUPL), mutation (MUTAT), deletion (SHRINK), decapsulation (DECAPS), encapsulation (ENCAPS), and permutation (PERM).

evolved programs contain encapsulated structures (which we omitted in the example genomes in Figures 8.9–8.11), in the context of these AntTracker evolution experiments, encapsulation did not perform as successfully as we initially expected. For our example, however, this is basically due to the definition of the evaluation function. Any reduction in the depth of a structure by encapsulation leads to a fitness increase only if the corresponding program exceeds the maximum depth of d_{max}. Consequently, the encapsulation operator does not have the opportunity for fitness-increasing effects on the gene.

Permutations

Permutations do not seem to contribute much to the populations' fitness evolution, either. Only after a champion program has been discovered in generation 59 do permutations lead to improved program expressions.

Mutations

Positive effects of the mutation operator turn up only as long as the maximum program depth of d_{max} is not exceeded. Otherwise, mutations mostly have deleterious or neutral effects on the fitness of the modified structures, which in turn leads to a reduction of the operator's weight.

8.2.4 Comparison of the best-evolved programs

In addition to the program evolutions described up to now, 20 independent evolution runs for the AntTracker task were performed. In all of the evolution experiments, all over at most 100 generations, starting from different initial populations of 50 individuals, about 10 individuals were evolved that reached all 44 food sites within the given time limit of 400 action steps.

Variants of optimal path followers

We look more closely at three typical representatives of these champion programs, which are variants of optimal path follower algorithms, where the ant does not leave the food-pheromone trail. Figure 8.18 depicts the control programs of these three individuals, which need even fewer action steps than the less specialized champion program in Figure 8.12 ($d1$: 140 steps, $d2$: 230 steps, $d3$: 260 steps). It turns out that two of these programs ($d1$ and $d2$) have specialized to particular characteristics of the food-pheromone path. In the context of evolution, this can be considered an optimal adaptation to a specific environmental niche. One of the programs, however, $d3$, includes

The real champion

both features: it implements an efficient path follower algorithm, and even the branched path of Figure 8.12 does not pose any problem, as illustrated in Figure 8.18(c). This control program turns out to be the real champion of our evolution experiments. It exhibits the same flexibility as the generation 59 program in Figure 8.11 but takes fewer action steps to follow the food-pheromone trail.

Specialization vs. generalization

This example highlights the particular problem of developing a suitable definition for an evaluation function, especially if we expect to fulfill conflicting demands, as in our example: efficient control programs must be evolved, but any too specialized solution is not desirable. If for each program the number of action steps is included in the fitness function, program structures of the form ($d1$) or ($d2$) in Figure 8.18 would quickly evolve, specialized to cover specific paths.

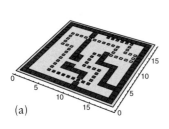

```
AntTracker[
 seq[
  ifSensor[dust][
   nop,
   seq[                          (d1)
    advance,
    ifSensor[dust][
     turnLeft,
     seq[
      advance,
      ifSensor[dust][
       turnLeft, advance]
     ]],
     ifSensor[food][
      advance, seq[turnRight, again]]
   ]],
   ifSensor[food][stop, nop]]]
```

Figure 8.18
AntTracker: Comparison of
optimal path followers.

(a)

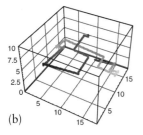

```
AntTracker[
 seq[                          (d2)
  advance,
  ifSensor[phero][
   seq[advance, again], stop],
  ifSensor[food][
   nop, seq[turnLeft, again]]]]
```

(b)

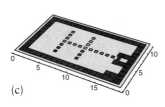

```
AntTracker[
 seq[
  ifSensor[dust][
   seq[turnLeft, again],
   seq[
    ifSensor[wall][                (d3)
     seq[
      ifSensor[food][
       stop,
       seq[
        ifSensor[phero][turnLeft,stop],
        turnRight
       ]],
      turnRight],
     advance],
    turnRight]]]]
```

(c)

8.2.5 Comparison of evolution runs

If we consider a set of evolution runs with populations of size N as a Bernoulli experiment, we can give an approximation of how many individuals must be generated on average in order to find an optimal individual for a given optimization task. Each evolution run is a stochastic event with success probability p_s, with the precondition that for each run the decision can be made whether it finished successfully or not (corresponding to either 0 or 1 as the result of a Bernoulli experiment). For optimization problems, for which a maximum fitness (the desired optimum) is known in advance (which is not always

Bernoulli experiment

the case, as we will see in Chapter 11), an evolution run is considered to be successful if within a given number of generations G_{max} at least one individual with maximum fitness is evolved. For the number K of evolution runs, the minimum number that must be performed in order to be successful, we can set up the equation

$$(1-p_s)^K = 1-z,$$

or, after a few transformations, we get a simple formula for K:

Number of necessary evolution experiments

$$K = \frac{\log(1-z)}{\log(1-p_s)} = \frac{\log \varepsilon}{\log(1-p_s)}.$$

Here $\varepsilon = 1-z$ denotes the probability that after K iterations of an evolution run (with different initial populations), no optimal individual is evolved. Conversely, z is the probability for a successful run. Figure 8.19 shows K as a function of the success probability p_s if an evolution experiment, as a set of evolution runs, were successful with a probability of 99% ($\varepsilon = 0.01$). Figure 8.19(b) depicts a zoomed plot for p_s in the interval between 0.5 and 0.8.

The number of individuals that have to be generated in order to finish an evolution experiment successfully can be calculated as follows:

How many individuals?

$$K \cdot G_{max} \cdot N < N_{total} \le (K+1) \cdot G_{max} \cdot N.$$

In each evolution run, at most $G_{max} \cdot N$ individuals are generated, and at least K runs are necessary in order to find an optimal individual in run $K+1$ with probability z.

In practical applications, we must take into account that individuals may occur in multiple copies, so that the number K of necessary runs increases accordingly.

We have performed 19 independent evolution runs for the Ant-Tracker task, each over at most $G_{max} = 100$ generations. Figure 8.20 shows a sorted bar chart plot of the number of generations until an optimal individual was found (light gray bars). The population size

Figure 8.19
Which number of evolution runs guarantees success with probability $z = 0.99$?

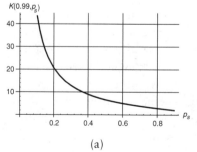

(a)

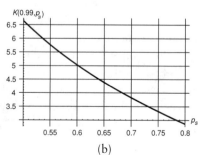

(b)

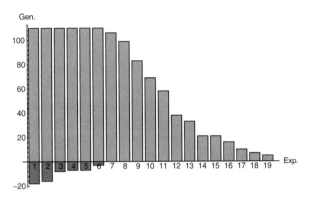

Maximum number of generations for 20 evolution runs

Figure 8.20
Comparison of required number of generations.

for each run is set to $N = 50$ individuals. Successful runs were stopped as soon as an optimal program (with a maximum fitness of 45) was found. In the unsuccessful runs (the first six bars in Figure 8.20), the differences between the current best fitness and the maximum fitness are plotted below the bars (dark gray). The difference from the optimum fitness is up to 20 points.

From this evolution experiment we can derive an empirical value of $p_s = 0.65$ for the success probability of a single evolution run. Consequently, after $K = 5$ independent runs, an optimal individual is evolved with probability $z = 0.99$ (cf. Figure 8.19[b]). This means that on average $25,000 = 5 \cdot 100 \cdot 50$ individuals have to be generated. When this result is compared to Koza's calculation for a similarly defined AntTracker problem (89 food sites on a 32×32 grid, no pheromones, no obstacles), for a population size of 1000 individuals evolved over 51 generations, a minimum of 408,000 individuals must be generated (Koza 1992, Section 7.2).

How many ant programs?

We have performed a few comparison evolution runs to assess whether the use of a larger set of genetic operators (recombination, mutation, permutation, deletion, duplication, encapsulation, and decapsulation) gives any advantage over relying solely on the two operators reproduction and crossover, as proposed by Koza (1992).

How is an extended set of genetic operators used?

We selected four of the successful evolutions (Figure 8.20), for which all of the operators mentioned above were used. Their weights were automatically adapted according to their contribution to an overall fitness increase of the gene pool (cf. Section 8.2.2). We denote these experiments as *multioperator* evolution (MO evolution). From each of these runs, the initial population was copied and used as the start population for another three evolution runs, for which, however,

MO evolution

RC evolution

reproduction and crossover were the only operators with constant selection weights ($p_{repro} = 0.1$ and $p_{cross} = 0.9$, respectively) according to the settings in Koza 1992. We refer to these experiments as *reproduction-crossover* (RC) evolution.

Figure 8.21(a) summarizes the results achieved. The bars depict the number of generations necessary to evolve an optimal individual or after which the evolution run is stopped. The maximum number of generations is set to 110. The first, dark bar is the result of an MO evolution run. Each group of three subsequent bars corresponds to RC runs, which are started with the same initial population as the corresponding MO run. For the stopped, unsuccessful RC evolutions, Figure 8.21(b) depicts the differences to the maximum fitness value of 45.

MO versus RC evolution

In the first set of evolution run comparisons (Figure 8.21[a], [1]), RC evolution, following a traditional genetic programming setup, seems clearly superior. Only one-fifth of the MO generations are necessary to generate optimal individuals. The remaining comparisons (Figure 8.21[a], [2, 3, 4]), however, favor MO evolution. In (2) none of the three RC runs evolves an individual with maximum fitness. In (3) two of the RC evolutions are unsuccessful; a third RC run is successfully completed. In the last experiment, MO evolution is clearly the winner.

This comparison shows that it might be reasonable to enhance the traditional set of GP operators—reproduction and crossover—by, for example, mutation, permutation, deletion, duplication, or encapsulation operators. The premier advantage of *multioperator* evolution is not only an acceleration in the creation of more and more fit individuals but the introduction of an adaptive weighting scheme for genetic operator selection. An evolution and selection mechanism on the level of individuals is now augmented by a corresponding selection scheme for the operators, analogous to meta-evolution, discussed in Section 4.5.

Multioperator GP

Figure 8.21
Comparison of MO and RC evolution experiments.

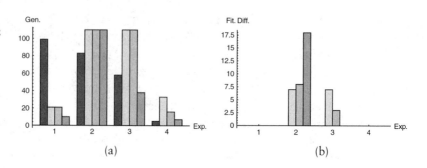

(a)   (b)

Hence, in combination with a suitable adaptation method for adjusting the operator rankings (e.g., as described in Section 8.3), an evolution system may more flexibly modify and adapt genotypical structures to a problem-specific context. In addition, careful analysis of the adapted operator weights allows us to draw conclusions on the evolutionary dynamics, as we have seen in Section 8.2.3.

8.3 Adaptive operator weights

In Section 8.1 we used a number of genetic operators in order to generate variations in program genomes. Additional GP operators are presented in Section 8.4. The range of operators available to a GP system in essence determines the creative potential of evolution. Therefore the question arises: Which genetic operators are the most suitable for a particular optimization problem? In addition, with a larger set of genetic operators it becomes more difficult to designate primary operators, which we consider to be the major composers of evolving building blocks and hence want to apply more often, and secondary operators, which from time to time enhance the variety of the structures in the gene pool.

Which operators "solve" the problem?

But designating genetic operators as primary or secondary constructors turns out to be a difficult task. An operator that has deleterious or neutral effects on the fitness distribution of the population during the initial phase of an evolution experiment may in later stages take over the role of a major constructor of highly fit individuals.

Thus it seems reasonable to assign weights to the operators, which are automatically adjusted during an evolution run. Operators that, on average, result in individuals with increased fitness should be applied more frequently. Conversely, structure mutations that lead to less-fit programs when observed over a certain time should have their weights reduced.

Weighted operators

8.3.1 Competition among genetic operators

The weight associated with an operator represents its current fitness measure with respect to the fitness evolution of the population. Initially, the operator weights, interpreted as relative fitnesses of the operators, are set by the user. Therefore, these settings depend very much on an experienced guess of how significant an operator's performance is going to be for the fitness evolution over the generations.

We define the probability $\wp(\omega)$ of selecting an operator $\omega \in \Omega$ from the operator set Ω. The operators are selected in a fitness-proportionate manner such that, depending on the operator weight $\gamma(\omega)$, the selection probability for an operator can be calculated as follows (cf. Section 3.5.1):

Operator selection

$$\wp(\omega) = \frac{\gamma(\omega)}{\displaystyle\sum_{\omega' \in \Omega} \gamma(\omega')}.$$

We compose a new generation t by applying genetic operators to individuals from the previous generation $t - 1$. For each program genome $s(t)$ of the current generation, we can keep track of which operator $\omega \in \Omega$ was used to generate $s(t)$ and from which structure or structures it was derived. Knowing the descent of each individual and the genetic operator involved allows us to determine whether the observed structure mutation resulted in a fitness increase or decrease. By investigating the fitness evolution for each individual of the population, we can determine the operators' average contributions to the fitness evolution of the population. If the application of an operator results on average in structures with increased or reduced fitnesses, this operator will be weighted higher or less, respectively.

An operator's contribution to fitness distribution

8.3.2 Adaptation of operator weights

We assume that for each individual $s_i(t) \in P(t)$ in generation t the function History informs us about the evolutionary descent of this particular individual in the following way:

Descent information for unary operators

❑ For unary genetic operators, History returns the parent structure and the operator through which individual $s_i(t)$ was created:

$$\text{History}(s_i(t)) = (s_k(t-1), \omega).$$

Descent information for recombination operators

❑ The descent of individuals that were generated by using a binary recombination operator, ω_{rec}, can be determined if History keeps track of the parent structures:

$$\text{History}(s_i(t)) = (s_{k_1}(t-1), s_{k_2}(t-1), s_j(t), \omega_{rec}).$$

A reference to the second structure, $s_j(t)$, that resulted from the recombination operation is also included.

This information about the origin of each program structure provides the basis for the automatic weight adaptation for the genetic operators. Let Ω be the set of operators. $\gamma(\Omega, t)$ denotes the list of operator weights for generation t. After composing a new generation of program structures, the weights, $\gamma(\omega, t)$, for each operator $\omega \in \Omega$ are recalculated. The adjusted fitness of each operator is determined as follows:

$$\gamma(\omega, t) = \gamma(\omega, t-1) \cdot \Delta\gamma(\omega, t) \cdot \gamma_{\text{decay}}(\omega).$$

Operator weight adaptation

The former weight $\gamma(\omega, t-1)$ is multiplied by the average fitness difference, $\Delta\gamma(\omega, t)$ (in percent), resulting from the applications of operator ω. The operator-specific value $\gamma_{\text{decay}}(\omega)$, where $0 \le \gamma_{\text{decay}}(\omega) \le 1$, is a decay constant that reduces the weight at minimum by the factor $\gamma_{\text{decay}}(\omega)$. Consequently, the weight of a neutral operator that mainly produces mutants with only minor changes in the offspring fitness will eventually be reduced to a minimum value of $\gamma_{\text{min}}(\omega)$.

Performance measure for unary genetic operators

For all unary genetic operators—that is, all mutations in particular—the weight change, $\Delta\gamma(\omega, t)$, is calculated as the mean of the relative fitness evolution of each individual generated by ω:

$$\Delta\gamma(\omega, t) = |P(\omega, t)|^{-1} \cdot \sum_{s \in P(\omega, t)} \frac{\tau(s)}{\tau(\text{History}(s)_1)}.$$

Delta function for the weights of unary operators

Here τ denotes the fitness of an individual structure. The notation $(\ldots)_i$ refers to the i-th component of a tuple. Furthermore,

$$P(\omega, t) = \{s \mid \text{History}(s)_2 == \omega\} \subseteq P(t)$$

defines the set of all structures within a population $P(t)$, which are generated as offspring from parents in population $P(t-1)$ using operator ω. The relative fitness of each ω mutant is determined in comparison to the fitness of its parent structure. The mean value of all these fitness ratios tells about the operator's overall performance.

Performance measure for recombination operators

For the GP crossover operator the fitness values of four individuals must be taken into account: the fitnesses of the two parents and their two offspring individuals. The application of recombination among two program structures does, rarely, result in two individuals of increased fitness. In most cases, only one of the recombined structures will have a higher fitness. To get a fair estimate of the performance of the recombination operator, only the "advantageous" descent is taken

Special case: recombinations

into account. In detail, the weight adaptation for a recombination operator, ω_{rec}, is calculated as follows:

*Delta function for the
weights of a recombination
operator*

$$\Delta\gamma(\omega, t) = \frac{1}{2} \cdot |P(\omega, t)|^{-1} \cdot \sum_{s \in P(\omega, t)} \tau^*(s).$$

Depending on which parent structure results in a fitness increase or fitness reduction of the mutant offspring, the relative fitness of the one or the other parent, respectively, is considered:

*Determining the
advantageous descent*

$$\tau^*(s) = \text{Max}\left(\frac{\tau(s)}{\tau(p_1(s))}, \frac{\tau(b(s))}{\tau(p_2(s))}\right),$$

where the parent individuals are determined by

$$p_i(s) = \text{History}(s)_i$$

and the corresponding offspring structure results from

$$b(s) = \text{History}(s)_3.$$

The factor $1/2$ in the formula for the weight adaptation adjusts for the fact that the two structures resulting from recombination are taken into account twice.

If the weights of the recombination operator were adapted in the same manner as for the other, unary operators, the weight of the recombination operator would generally remain unchanged. This is because a crosswise exchange of substructures usually results in an individual with a higher fitness than the parent structure and in a lethal individual with dramatically reduced fitness. Consequently, the fitnesses of the offspring structures tend to neutralize each other, and so we have adopted the opportunistic adaptation scheme described above.

8.4 Advanced GP operators and functionality

Diversity of GP applications

As genetic programming enters more and more application areas, where difficult optimization tasks must be solved, the representations for data structures and programs, genetic operators, and automatic programming schemes are becoming more diverse as well. This section can give only a brief overview of general GP mutation operators (Section 8.4.1) and techniques for automatically applying programming constructs, such as the definition of subroutines, iterations, loops, and recursion or automatic creation, clearance, and access of memory (Section 8.4.2).

8.4.1 Advanced GP mutation operators

The GP mutation operators come in many varieties, depending on the particular data structures that are used for a specific problem domain. Most of the more general GP mutations on symbolic expressions, however, basically substitute subterms or leaves of a tree structure with either newly generated or duplicated terms or terminals. Figure 8.22 gives a brief overview of mutation operators on tree-structured expressions.

GP mutation

The following list gives a brief description of the more advanced GP mutation operators on symbolic expressions applied to the tree structure in Figure 8.22(a):

Further GP mutation operators

Point mutation: A point mutation (b) exchanges a single node for a random node of the same signature or type. In the simplest case, this means that terminals are substituted by terminals and function symbols are substituted by function symbols with the same arity (and types, if applicable).

Point mutation

Permutation: A permutation (c) exchanges the sequence of arguments of a node.

Permutation

Hoist: The hoist operator (d) substitutes the whole tree by a randomly selected proper subtree. Terminals are not in the scope of selection for this operator.

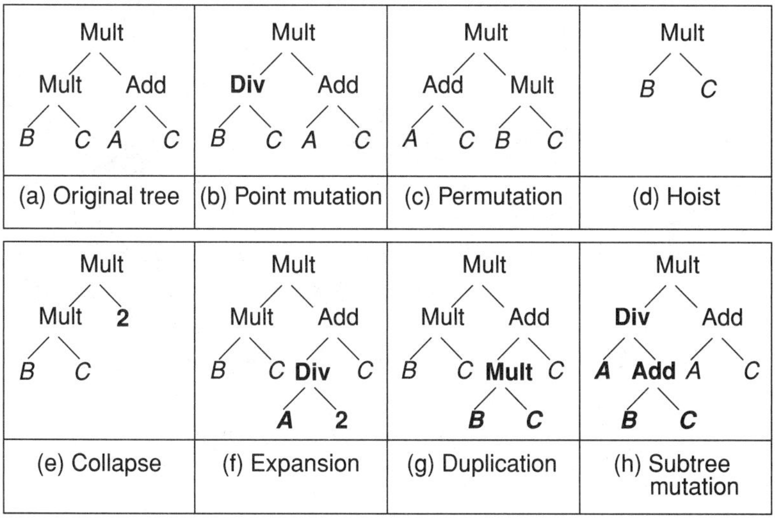

Hoist

Figure 8.22
GP mutations on symbolic expressions.

Collapse

Collapse subtree mutation: With the collapse subtree mutation (e), a subtree is replaced by a random terminal.

Expansion

Expansion mutation: The inverse operation to collapse subtree mutation is expansion mutation (f). A terminal is exchanged against a random, newly generated subtree, using, for example, the term generation method described in Section 7.1.2.

Duplication

Duplication: The duplication operator (g) replaces a terminal node with a copy of a proper subtree.

Subtree mutation

Subtree mutation: The most general mutation operator is defined by subtree mutation (h), where a subtree is substituted by a newly generated expression. This is the mutation operator presented in Section 7.3.

8.4.2   Architecture-altering operations

Modularization of programs

Subroutines are commonly used for structuring computer programs into smaller, reusable units. The resulting modularization and generality of programs and data structures is a widely used means to tackle complicated programming tasks. Therefore, automatic programming methods, such as the evolution-based GP approach, should also make use of hierarchical data structures and functionality. However, these hierarchies and the resulting modularization should evolve automatically. Therefore, we will outline some of the recent GP approaches to generating modular program architectures and data structures.

Automatically defined functions

To introduce subroutines into a program, the syntactic structure of the program expressions must be altered. Each program in the population now consists of two branches with a specific functionality: a function-defining branch and a result-producing branch (Figure 8.23). The function-defining branch defines a subroutine, identified by an automatically generated name (ADF0), a specific number of arguments, and the definition of the function body that performs the actual calculation for the value to be returned by the function. The result-producing branch basically contains the GP expressions, encoding the programs or data structures to be evolved, which we have been using up to now. The only difference is that these programs may contain

Function- and result-defining branches

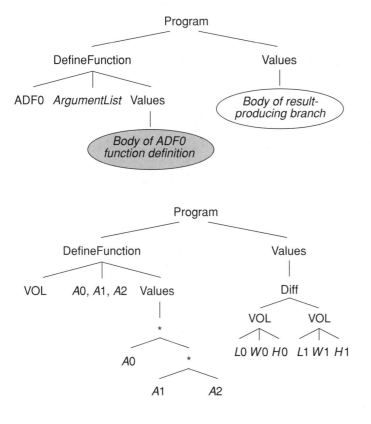

Figure 8.23
General program structure with an automatically defined function.

Figure 8.24
Example of a program expression with an automatically defined subroutine.

calls of the subroutine defined in the function-defining branch (see Koza 1994, p. 74).

Figure 8.24 gives an example of a program with an automatically defined function. The function computes the volume of a box of dimensions $A0$, $A1$, and $A2$ (see Koza 1994, p. 70). The program itself returns the difference of the volumes of two boxes.

In general, the number of automatically defined functions (ADFs) does not have to be limited to one. During the program evolution the ADF operator may create any number of new subroutines, which can then be used by the program in the result-producing branch. Since there is basically no difference between the body code within the function-defining and the result-producing branches, the subroutines can also be altered by GP operators during the evolution process. Therefore, the generation of subroutines in conjunction with code mutations of the automatically defined functions enhances the capability of genetic programming to build functional hierarchies and to breed modular program architectures.

Automatically defined iterations and loops

The idea of extending program structures by function-defining branches can be applied in a similar manner to automatically introduce iterations, loops, or recursion (see Koza, Andre, et al. 1999). Iterations, loops, or recursive definitions of functions have consistent structural properties, so that it is easy to map these structures, with specifically defined functionality, into tree-structured expressions. We explain the general idea with the example of automatically defined loops.

An automatically defined loop (ADL) is characterized by four distinct branches (Koza, Andre, et al. 1999, pp. 135 ff.): (1) a loop initialization branch, LIB; (2) a loop condition branch, LCB; (3) a loop body branch, LBB; and (4) a loop update branch, LUB.

Figure 8.25 shows the general structure of a program with an automatically defined loop. Introducing an automatically defined iteration (ADI) or recursion (ADR) can be achieved in a similar manner (for more details see Koza, Andre, et al. 1999).

We have to keep in mind, however, that program structures extended by branches with distinct functionalities, such as definitions of subroutines, loops, iterations, and result-producing branches, have a delicate syntactic structure; that is, general genetic operators can no longer be applied to *any* subexpression within the program genome, regardless of what the subexpression encodes. Instead, branch-specific and specialized GP operators must be applied in order to maintain the overall architecture and functionality of the different branches. For more details on how to define and apply these advanced architecture-altering GP operators, including automatic memory creation, deletion, and access to storage, consult Koza, Andre, et al. 1999.

Figure 8.25

General program structure with an automatically defined loop.

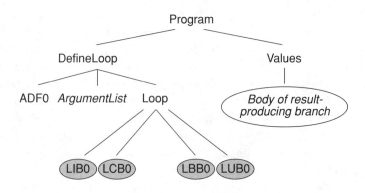

8.5   **Bibliographical notes**

The evolution of ant foraging behavior, including other, similar systems to evolve intelligent agents, is described in Steven Levy's excellent overview *Artificial Life* (Levy 1993a, pp. 257–263; 1993b).

Artificial Life

More advanced genetic programming concepts and techniques are described in *Genetic Programming II* (Koza 1994) and *Genetic Programming III* (Koza, Andre, et al. 1999). For more details on these two volumes and on the evolution of modular programs and high-level data structures (Langdon 1998), see Section 7.6.

GP II and III

The textbook *Genetic Programming: An Introduction* contains several chapters on advanced GP techniques and data structures, such as graph genomes, linear genomes, and rule-based genomes (Banzhaf, Nordin, et al. 1997).

GP: an introduction

Early versions of advanced operators for genetic programming applications are described in Angeline's *Evolutionary Algorithms and Emergent Intelligence* (Angeline 1993).

EAs and emergent intelligence

Detailed descriptions of the advanced GP operators built into the Evolvica system can be found on the *IEC* Web site (see Preface).

Evolvica

Evolution of Developmental Programs   Part III

9 Computer Models of Developmental Programs

*The development of an organism may . . . be considered as the
execution of a "developmental program" present in the fertilized egg.
The cellularity of higher organisms and their common DNA components
force us to consider developing organisms as dynamic collections
of appropriately programmed finite automata. A central task of
developmental biology is to discover the underlying algorithm for
the course of development.*

Lindenmayer and Rozenberg 1975

Morphogenesis, or structure formation, in nature is determined by
complex growth processes (see, e.g., Deutsch 1994 and Paton 1994).
By multiple divisions a cell develops into a cluster of cells, which
evolve into three-dimensional arrangements by morphogenetic movements. Cells differentiate according to their spatial contexts in order
to take over more and more specialized tasks. Eventually, these evolution processes result in the formation of a complex organism with a
great variety of interacting units—proteins, organelles, cells, and
organs. In essence, the complexity of these morphogenetic processes
results from interactions of smaller components (*agents*) resulting in
the emergent behavior of the organisms as a whole.

Morphogenesis

Differentiation

Agents

In this chapter we introduce two variants of modeling "developmental programs"—cellular automata and Lindenmayer systems. All
these models are based on the principle of substituting elementary
building blocks (comparable to cells) with additional, possibly more
complex elements (e.g., a cell cluster). In Section 9.1 we introduce cellular automata as context-sensitive developmental programs, and we
discuss their relation to Lindenmayer systems. These parallel rewriting
systems, also known as L-systems, work on strings or symbolic

*Cellular automata and
Lindenmayer systems*

expressions. They provide a flexible tool for the simulation of structure formation processes, as we will show with several examples on growth of cell layers and tree structures.

9.1   Cellular automata and cellular programming

Cellular automata as models of complexity

Stephen Wolfram is not only the chief developer of Mathematica but also a strong supporter of the thesis that cellular automata can be considered as *the* model of complexity per se. In the early 1980s, Wolfram proposed modeling nature's complex systems with local interactions of relatively simple computer programs rather than with mathematical equations. These ideas finally inspired his research on cellular automata (Wolfram 1984a; Wolfram 1984b; Wolfram 1986; Wolfram 1994).

> In some cases . . . complex behavior may be simulated numerically with just a few components. But in most cases the simulation requires too many components, and this direct approach fails. One must instead attempt to distill the mathematical essence of the process by which complex behavior is generated. The hope in such an approach is to identify fundamental mathematical mechanisms that are common to many different natural systems. Such commonalities would correspond to universal features in the behavior of very different complex natural systems.
>
> Wolfram 1994, p. 411

Cells in discrete space

Cellular automata (CA) represent a simple mathematical idealization of natural, self-organizing systems. Usually, they consist of a one- or two-dimensional grid of cells, which can take on a finite number of states (Ulam 1962; Ulam 1966; Baer and Martinez 1974; Preston and Duff 1984; Gaylord and Wellin 1995; Gaylord and Nishidate 1996). The parallel, discrete state transitions are determined by local, deterministic rules, where the previous cell state and the states of respective neighboring cells are taken into account. Figure 9.1 illustrates typical neighborhood definitions for one- and two-dimensional cellular automata. The state of the cell in the center changes, depending on the states of its neighbor cells. For a single-layer cell arrangement, the neighborhood is defined by the n left and right adjacent cells, respectively (Figure 9.1[a]).

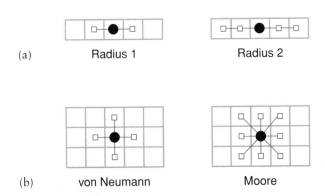

For two-dimensional grids the *von Neumann* neighborhood is often used, where the states of the northern, southern, western, and eastern neighbors determine the cell update. In a *Moore* neighborhood, the diagonal cells are taken into account, too (Figure 9.1[b]).

9.1.1 Pattern formation in one dimension

Even on the basis of extremely simple update rules, a remarkable dynamic of cell evolution patterns can be achieved with cellular automata. The small collection of patterns in Figure 9.2, produced from one-dimensional cellular automata, gives an impression of the resulting variety. All of these binary automata start with a chain of 101 cells, where the center cell is in state 1 (on) and all other cells in state 0 (off). From the top row to the bottom, each cell matrix shows the CA evolution over 50 update steps. In each of these update steps, the states of all cells are transformed into their new states, taking the left and right neighbor cell into account. The update rules are written in compact notation on top of the diagrams.

Pattern formation in one-dimensional cell layers

The abbreviating notation encoding the update rules is explained as follows. In a one-dimensional, deterministic automaton with two update neighbors, the following eight configurations must be taken into account in order to define a complete set of cell update rules:

1: $\{1, 1, 1\} \rightarrow 0$ 5: $\{0, 1, 1\} \rightarrow 1$
2: $\{1, 1, 0\} \rightarrow 0$ 6: $\{0, 1, 0\} \rightarrow 1$
3: $\{1, 0, 1\} \rightarrow 0$ 7: $\{0, 0, 1\} \rightarrow 1$
4: $\{1, 0, 0\} \rightarrow 1$ 8: $\{0, 0, 0\} \rightarrow 0$

Example of a complete rule set for 1D CAs with two neighbors

The first and last element of each tuple represents the left and right neighbor, respectively. The middle element denotes the current state of the cell to be transformed. If the sequence of the left-hand sides of the

Figure 9.2

One-dimensional cellular automata encode developmental programs.

Abbreviating notation

rules is kept fixed, a list of the eight new states $\{0, 0, 0, 1, 1, 1, 1, 0\}$ would suffice to completely describe the CA update rules. If these list entries are interpreted as binary digits encoding an integer number, each automaton is uniquely characterized by a single number, 30 in our example. In Figure 9.2, both the numbers and the list encodings for the rules are given.

For the CA implementation and the generation of the graphics in Figure 9.2, we have used the definitions in Wolfram 1996, p. 18. The necessary functions as well as a collection of the evolutions of all one-dimensional binary, one-neighbor CAs are in the Evolvica notebook, available on the *IEC* Web site (see Preface).

9.1.2 Structure formation and self-reproduction

Even more interesting possibilities for modeling morphogenetic pro-cesses are provided by two-dimensional cellular automata, which were intensively studied in the 1950s by John von Neumann. He con-sidered CAs an ideal platform for modeling "self-reproducing machines." Von Neumann was finally able to define a *universal con-structor* Turing machine working on a two-dimensional cell grid (Neumann and Burks 1966; Burks 1968). This cellular machine with 29(!) states per cell is able to construct any (cellular) machine described on its input tape, copy the input tape, and pass it to the newly constructed machine. This machine performs self-reproduction if the constructor itself is described on the input tape.

Self-reproducing machines

A variant of a universal constructor with substantially reduced complexity was defined by E. F. Codd, who succeeded in reducing the number of states per cell to eight. Self-reproduction is treated as a spe-cial case of universal construction (Codd 1968). The automaton struc-tures defined by Codd are derived from the physiology of nervous systems. Signals, encoding instructions for structure formation of the automaton, travel along "data paths," analogous to electrical impulses directed through axons and dendrites in nerve cells. Codd models data paths as a triple row of cells, as depicted in Figure 9.3.

Codd's universal constructors

Paradigm: nervous systems

Each data path is considered as a signal duct, consisting of kernel cells in state 1, surrounded by cover cells in state 2. By according transformation rules, signals (e.g., 0 or 7) are moved by one cell in each iteration (Figure 9.3[b, c]). If a sequence of signals meets a T crossing, the incoming signals are copied to the top and to the right (Figure 9.4). The signal is duplicated.

Data paths conduct signals

Signal copy at T crossings

```
2 2 2 2 2 2 2 2        2 2 2 2 2 2 2 2        2 2 2 2 2 2 2 2
1 1 1 0 7 1 1 1 1      1 1 1 1 0 7 1 1 1      1 1 1 1 1 0 7 1 1
2 2 2 2 2 2 2 2        2 2 2 2 2 2 2 2        2 2 2 2 2 2 2 2

        (a)                    (b)                    (c)
```

Figure 9.3
Data paths.
(a) $i = 0$. (b) $i = 1$. (c) $i = 2$.

Loops as storage elements

If a data path is arranged as a loop (Figure 9.5), a perfect storage element results. All signals copied at the T crossing are reentering the loop but can also be used for initiating constructions at the rightmost end of the data path.

Self-reproducing loops

This specific feature of Codd's loop automata was rediscovered by Christopher Langton and used for the modeling of a self-reproducing system (Langton 1984). This model does not have the characteristics of a universal constructor à la Codd or von Neumann, but it shows all the essentials of a self-reproducing system. Langton's cellular automaton is defined by 877 rules, with 219 base rules, each in four variants (rotated by 90 degrees) for the von Neumann neighborhood and an additional neutral rule.

Figure 9.6 depicts some steps on the way toward iterated self-reproduction (see also Color Plate 4). Starting from the loop configuration of Figure 9.5, the arm is first elongated ($i = 40$) and constructs a turn to the left ($i = 80$). The instructions for the arm construction are encoded in the signal sequence stored in the loop. Iterating this growth process initiates the construction of a second loop ($i = 120$), which finally separates from the "mother loop" ($i = 130$). The offspring loop has a complete copy of the original signal sequence.

Coral-like growth

Now the two structures act independently from each other ($i = 150$). Again each loop starts its reproduction cycle ($i = 200$, $i = 250$). Continuing the evolution results in a coral-like growth process, where loops completely surrounded by other structures stop their

Figure 9.4

Duplication of signals at a T crossing. (a) $i = 0$. (b) $i = 1$. (c) $i = 2$.

```
      2 1 2                    2 1 2                  2 1 2
      2 1 2                    2 1 2                  2 7 2
  2 2 2 2 1 2 2 2 2      2 2 2 2 7 2 2 2 2      2 2 2 2 0 2 2 2 2
  1 1 1 0 7 1 1 1 1      1 1 1 1 0 7 1 1 1      1 1 1 1 1 0 7 1 1
  2 2 2 2 2 2 2 2 2      2 2 2 2 2 2 2 2 2      2 2 2 2 2 2 2 2 2

        (a)                      (b)                    (c)
```

Figure 9.5

Configuration of a self-reproducing loop.

```
            2 2 2 2 2 2 2 2
          2 1 7 0 1 4 0 1 4 2
          2 0 2 2 2 2 2 2 0 2
          2 7 2            2 1 2
          2 1 2            2 1 2
          2 0 2            2 1 2
          2 7 2            2 1 2
          2 1 2 2 2 2 2 2 1 2 2 2 2 2
          2 0 7 1 0 7 1 0 7 1 1 1 1 1 2
            2 2 2 2 2 2 2 2 2 2 2 2 2
```

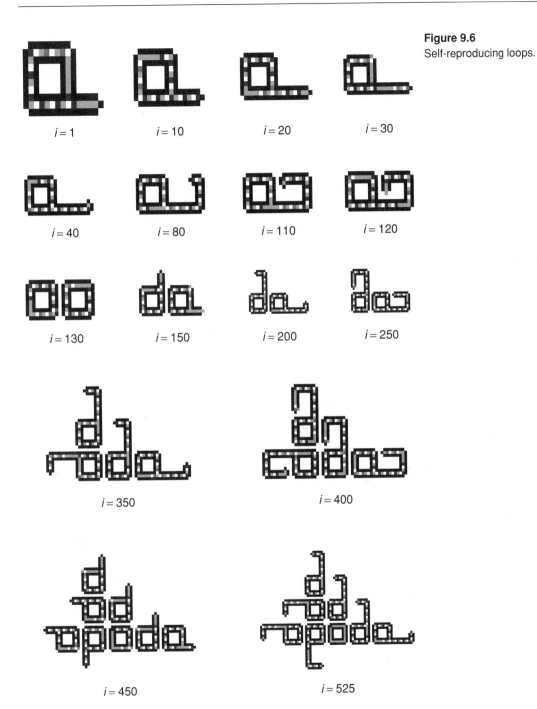

Figure 9.6
Self-reproducing loops.

$i = 1$ $i = 10$ $i = 20$ $i = 30$

$i = 40$ $i = 80$ $i = 110$ $i = 120$

$i = 130$ $i = 150$ $i = 200$ $i = 250$

$i = 350$ $i = 400$

$i = 450$ $i = 525$

reproduction activities. Their signal sequence is dissolved ($i = 525$), while the whole colony of loops continues growing at the margins.

Life cycle of a loop

Interestingly, each loop performs a kind of "life cycle." In its fetal phase, the arm of the mother loop is elongated and closed into another loop. The "umbilical cord" serves as an information channel for transmitting the growth signals. After the separation of the offspring loop, a ripening process is started in which a new construction arm is developed. Finally, the loop enters an "adult stage," in which as many offspring as the environment can accommodate are produced.

Instructions and data

In analogy to cells, which are nature's self-reproducing systems, the signal sequence can be looked at in two ways. First, the signals represent *instructions*, which are interpreted and lead to the structure formation of the automaton. Second, the signals are considered as passive, noninterpreted *data*, which are merely copied to the offspring loop. This is comparable to the *transcription* phase of natural cells,

Transcription and translation

where (negative) duplicates of DNA segments are generated. The signal interpretation, however, corresponds to *translation*, where triplet sequences are transformed into proteins.

Mutated "loops"

Figures 9.7 and 9.8 give a few examples of mutants of loop automata. All rules have the form {C, {N, E, S, W}} → I, where the parameters can take values from the interval {0, . . . , 7}. The state of the cell in the center of the von Neumann neighborhood is denoted by C. N, E, S, and W refer to the cells in the north, east, south, and west. The new state of the cell is represented by I.

Point mutations on automata rules

Mutations on these rules are performed for each parameter with a probability of μ_{mut}. A point mutation substitutes the value x of a parameter with a number from the set $\{x - \rho, . . . , x + \rho\}$, where ρ denotes the mutation radius (cf. the string mutations in Section 1.3). In Figures 9.7 and 9.8 the mutation probability μ_{mut} is given as a percent value and the radius as $\pm\rho$. The mutations are applied to the 219 base rules (see Color Plate 5).

Mutation effects

The examples show that after mutation, most of the automata lose their capability to self-reproduce. This is not a surprise, since the intricate set of CA rules is specifically designed for this self-reproduction task. Any minor variation can disturb the precisely coordinated interactions. Most of the automata, however, maintain their ability to propagate signals using the data paths. Sometimes these paths are interrupted or completely destroyed, but many automata are still capable of reproducing at least part of their structure. Growing and developing patterns are fundamental to the whole system of rules; hence, this feature may not be easily eliminated. The examples illustrated should be considered only as a first, simple attempt to combine self-reproduction and evolutionary variation, although the variety of

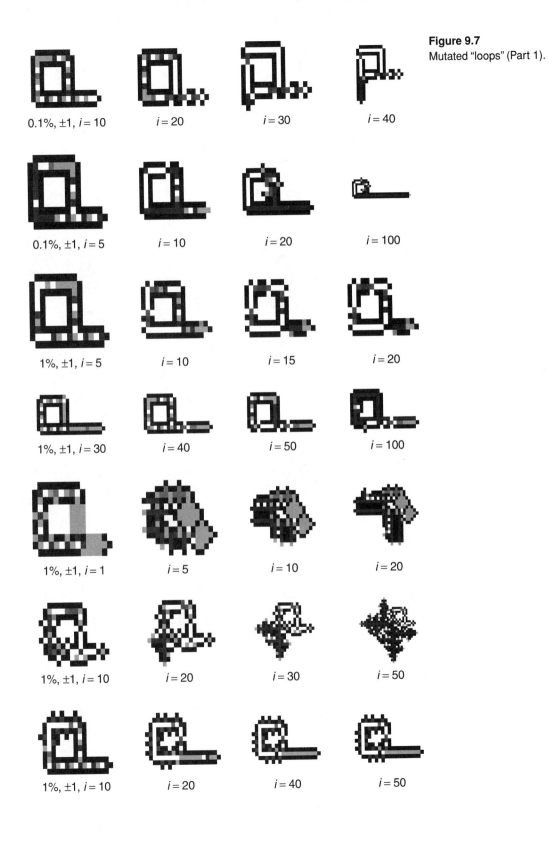

Figure 9.7
Mutated "loops" (Part 1).

0.1%, ±1, $i = 10$ $i = 20$ $i = 30$ $i = 40$

0.1%, ±1, $i = 5$ $i = 10$ $i = 20$ $i = 100$

1%, ±1, $i = 5$ $i = 10$ $i = 15$ $i = 20$

1%, ±1, $i = 30$ $i = 40$ $i = 50$ $i = 100$

1%, ±1, $i = 1$ $i = 5$ $i = 10$ $i = 20$

1%, ±1, $i = 10$ $i = 20$ $i = 30$ $i = 50$

1%, ±1, $i = 10$ $i = 20$ $i = 40$ $i = 50$

Figure 9.8
Mutated "loops" (Part 2).

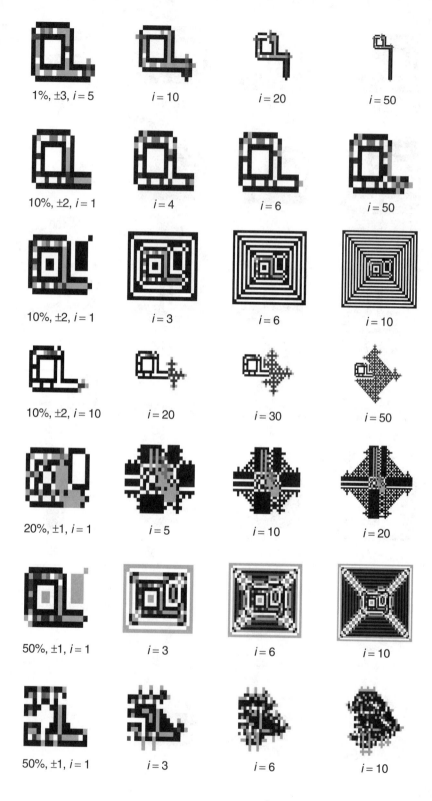

1%, ±3, $i = 5$ $i = 10$ $i = 20$ $i = 50$

10%, ±2, $i = 1$ $i = 4$ $i = 6$ $i = 50$

10%, ±2, $i = 1$ $i = 3$ $i = 6$ $i = 10$

10%, ±2, $i = 10$ $i = 20$ $i = 30$ $i = 50$

20%, ±1, $i = 1$ $i = 5$ $i = 10$ $i = 20$

50%, ±1, $i = 1$ $i = 3$ $i = 6$ $i = 10$

50%, ±1, $i = 1$ $i = 3$ $i = 6$ $i = 10$

resulting patterns and structures is already stunning. Evolution of cellular automata is a fascinating topic, but we do not have the space here to explore it further. The interested reader is referred to Sipper 1997; Sipper 1998; Mange and Sipper 1998; Reggia, Lohn, et al. 1998; and Tempesti, Mange, et al. 1998.

Langton's "self-reproducing loops" have created quite a stir in the field of modeling artificial life systems, which is why numerous authors have already pursued research on the subject; for example, Levy 1993b, pp. 124 ff., and Gerhardt and Schuster 1995, pp. 167–173. Similar automata for modeling neural network signal processing and learning are described in de Garis's Brain Builder Project (de Garis 1991; de Garis 1992; de Garis 1996).

Cellular automata represent a specific class of agent systems, the dynamics of which are based on local, context-sensitive substitution of subunits (cells, elements, objects, states) by possibly modified units. Another variant of parallel "rewriting" is Lindenmayer systems (L-systems), an extension of Chomsky grammars (Chomsky 1956). In the following sections, we will use L-systems for encoding developmental programs. Unlike cellular automata, where the number of cells remains fixed in a predefined lattice configuration, Lindenmayer systems can model dynamically growing structures such that, for instance, a cell can evolve into two cells by "subdivision."

Parallel rewriting

9.2 Lindenmayer systems

At the end of the 1960s, Aristid Lindenmayer introduced parallel rewrite systems to theoretical biology in order to describe and simulate natural morphogenetic processes (Lindenmayer 1968). In their simplest form, these formal rule systems, known today as L-systems, manipulate strings of characters. At each derivation step, all symbols of a given word are substituted by new symbols in parallel, analogous to state transformations of cellular automata. This simultaneous rewriting strategy predestines L-systems for the description of manifold natural developmental processes; for example, cell division of multicellular organisms or the modeling of growth and inflorescence of plants (Prusinkiewicz and Hanan 1989; Prusinkiewicz and Lindenmayer 1990).

Parallel rewriting of strings

In the following sections, we first give a formal description of L-systems in their simplest, context-free form (Section 9.2.1). In Section 9.2.2 we deal with extensions to context-sensitive L-systems and their relation to cellular automata. A combination of (bracketed) Lindenmayer systems and so-called turtle interpretations allow for a detailed

Section overview

modeling of morphogenesis in two- and three-dimensional space. In
this scope, the basics of turtle interpretation are presented in Section
9.2.3. Finally, a brief introduction to the modeling of branching structures is given in Section 9.2.4.

9.2.1 Context-free, parametrized L-systems

L-systems without any context are the simplest class of Lindenmayer
systems and are denoted as 0L-systems. We first look at deterministic
0L-systems, known as D0L-systems. Formally, a D0L-system $G_{D0L} =
(\Sigma, \pi, \alpha)$ is specified by

DOL-system

- ❏ An alphabet $\Sigma = \{s_1, s_2, \ldots, s_n\}$,

- ❏ A structure-preserving mapping $\pi\colon \Sigma^+ \to \Sigma^*$, and

- ❏ An axiom $\alpha \in \Sigma^+$ (cf. Rozenberg and Salomaa 1980, pp. 43
  ff.).

Productions

The mapping π is defined by a finite set of *productions* or *rules* $\pi\colon \Sigma \to
\Sigma^*$ with $s \to \pi(s)$ for each symbol $s \in \Sigma$. If no explicit mapping for a
symbol is given, the identity production is assumed; that is, $\pi(s) = s$. In
a deterministic L-system, there is at most one production rule for each
symbol $s \in \Sigma$. The *word sequence* $E(G_{D0L})$ defined by a D0L-system
$G_{D0L} = (\Sigma, \pi, \alpha)$ is defined as the series of iterated applications of π
starting from the axiom α:

Word sequence

$$\alpha^{(0)} = \pi^0(\alpha),\ \alpha^{(1)} = \pi^1(\alpha),\ \alpha^{(2)} = \pi^2(\alpha) = \pi(\pi(\alpha)), \ldots$$

Each string $\alpha^{(i+1)}$ results from the previous word

$$\alpha^{(i)} = \alpha_1^{(i)} \alpha_2^{(i)} \ldots \alpha_m^{(i)}$$

by simultaneously applying the production rules π to all m symbols in
$\alpha^{(i)}$:

*Parallel application of
production rules*

$$\alpha^{(i+1)} = \pi\!\left(\alpha_1^{(i)}\right)\pi\!\left(\alpha_2^{(i)}\right) \ldots \pi\!\left(\alpha_m^{(i)}\right).$$

The *language* $L(G_{D0L}) = L^\infty(G_{D0L}, \alpha)$ generated by G_{D0L} is specified by the following definition:

Language of a D0L-system

$$L^i(G_{D0L}, x) = \{y \in \Sigma^* \,|\, y \in \pi^i(x)\}.$$

A *derivation* or a *derivation sequence* for $x, y \in \Sigma^*$ is characterized as
follows. A word y is derivable from x in n steps in G_{D0L},

$$x \underset{G_{D0L}}{\overset{n}{\Rightarrow}} y,$$

if the following is true:

$$y \in L^n(G_{\text{D0L}}, x).$$

Derivability

Simulating *Anabaena catenula* growth

We now demonstrate a simple application of D0L-systems with an example of simulated evolution of multicellular filaments, also described by Prusinkiewicz and Hanan (1989, p. 9). The growth process modeled by the following D0L-system is observable in diverse algae species and in particular in the blue-green bacterium *Anabaena catenula*.

We assume that a cell can take on either of two cytological states *A* or *B*. Additional indices *l* (left) and *r* (right) denote cell polarity; that is, the directions in which the daughter cells evolve after cell division. The development of a filament of cells can be characterized by a D0L-system $G_{\text{D0L}} = (\{A_l, A_r, B_l, B_r\}, \{p_1, p_2, p_3, p_4\}, A_r)$ with the following productions:

Cell layer growth

$p_1:\quad A_r \rightarrow A_l\, B_r$ $\qquad\qquad$ $p_3:\quad B_r \rightarrow A_r$

$p_2:\quad A_l \rightarrow B_l\, A_r$ $\qquad\qquad$ $p_4:\quad B_l \rightarrow A_l$

Rules for Anabaena catenula

An *A* cell with right polarity (A_r) divides into an *A* cell with opposite orientation and a right-polarized *B* cell (production p_1). The second production can be interpreted in an analogous manner. Productions p_3 and p_4 turn a *B* cell into an *A* cell with equal orientation. Starting from axiom A_r, a word sequence results from iterated applications of these rules, which can be interpreted as a simulation of parallel growth processes within a cell layer:

```
Ar
Al Br
Bl Ar Ar
Al Al Br Al Br
Bl Ar Bl Ar Ar Bl Ar Ar
Al Al Br Al Al Br Al Br Al Al Br Al Br
. . .
```

Growth of a cell layer modeled by string rewriting

The Evolvica notebooks, available on the *IEC* Web site (see Preface), contain all definitions necessary for implementing (context-sensitive) L-systems as discussed in the following examples. An L-system production has the general form $p \rightarrow s$, where the left side, *p*, is denoted as the *predecessor* and the right side, *s*, as the *successor*. In

Evolvica we implement such an L-system rule (L-rule) with an expression of the form

L-rule

```
LRule[ PRED[ p ], SUCC[ s ] ].
```

A list of productions is described by an expression of the form

Productions

```
LRULES[ __LRule ].
```

Finally, a Lindenmayer system is characterized by the pattern

L-system

```
LSystem[ _AXIOM, _LRULES ].
```

Hence the D0L-system of the example above is specified as follows:

```
In[1] := axiom = AXIOM[ A_r ];
         lrules =
         LRULES[
           LRule[PRED[ A_r ], SUCC[ A_1,B_r ]],
           LRule[PRED[ A_1 ], SUCC[ B_1,A_r ]],
           LRule[PRED[ B_r ], SUCC[ A_r ]],
           LRule[PRED[ B_1 ], SUCC[ A_1 ]]
         ];
         lsystem = LSystem[axiom,lrules];
```

With `Format` definitions, the L-system can be displayed in a compact form that is also used in the literature (see, e.g., Prusinkiewicz and Lindenmayer 1990):

```
In[2] := lsystem
```

```
Out[2] = Axiom: A_r
         Rules:  < A_r >   → A_1 B_r
                 < A_1 >   → B_1 A_r
                 < B_r >   → A_r
                 < B_1 >   → A_1
```

The < and > symbols on the left side of the rules are used in context-sensitive L-systems (Section 9.2.2) in order to distinguish between the left and right contexts and the predecessor, respectively. In this example the contexts are empty, because we use only context-free productions. The Evolvica function `runKLSystem[`*lsystem_,* *n_*`]` performs n derivation steps of the L-system *lsystem* and returns the resulting word sequence as a list:

Iterated rewriting

```
In[3] := anabaenaGrowth = runKLSystem[lsystem, 6]
```

$Out[3]$ = {A_r , A_1 B_r , B_1 A_r A_r , A_1 A_1 B_r A_1 B_r ,

   B_1 A_r B_1 A_r A_r B_1 A_r A_r ,

   A_1 A_1 B_r A_1 A_1 B_r A_1 B_r A_1 A_1 B_r A_1 B_r ,

   B_1 A_r B_1 A_r A_r B_1 A_r B_1 A_r A_r B_1 A_r A_r B_1 A_r B_1 A_r

   A_r B_1 A_r A_r }

Formatting the output in centered column form more clearly reveals the analogy to a developing layer of cells:

$In[4]$:= **ColumnForm[%, Center]**

$Out[4]$ =

$$A_r$$
$$A_1B_r$$
$$B_1A_rA_r$$
$$A_1A_1B_rA_1B_r$$
$$B_1A_rB_1A_rA_rB_1A_rA_r$$
$$A_1A_vB_rA_1A_1B_rA_1B_rA_1A_1B_rA_1B_r$$
$$B_1A_rB_1A_rA_rB_1A_rB_1A_rA_rB_1A_rA_rB_1A_rB_1A_rA_rB_1A_rA_r$$

Growth of a cell layer

Figure 9.9 displays the development of a cell layer, described by the following parametrized L-system:

$In[5]$:= **cellLayerAxiom = AXIOM[A₁[1]];**

   cellLayerRules =

   LRULES[

      LRule[PRED[A₁[a]], SUCC[A₁[1],Bᵣ[1]]],

      LRule[PRED[Aᵣ[a]], SUCC[B₁[1],Aᵣ[1]]],

      LRule[PRED[B₁[b]], SUCC[A₁[1],Bᵣ[1]]],

      LRule[PRED[Bᵣ[b]], SUCC[B₁[1],Aᵣ[1]]],

      LRule[PRED[A₁[i_ /; i < a]], SUCC[A₁[i + 1]]],

      LRule[PRED[Aᵣ[i_ /; i < a]], SUCC[Aᵣ[i + 1]]],

      LRule[PRED[B₁[i_ /; i < b]], SUCC[B₁[i + 1]]],

      LRule[PRED[Bᵣ[i_ /; i < b]], SUCC[Bᵣ[i + 1]]]

   ];

Parametrized D0L-system describing cell layer growth

$In[6]$:= **cellLayerLSystem =**
   LSystem[cellLayerAxiom,cellLayerRules];

The parameters a and b denote the time steps, after which an A or a B cell divides. For a = 2 and b = 5, the following L-system results.

Figure 9.9
Growth simulation of a
cellular layer, modeled by a
D0L-system.

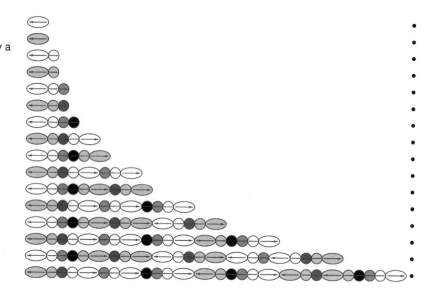

$In[7] := \mathtt{a = 2; \ b = 5;}$

$\mathtt{cellLayerLSystem}$

$Out[7] = \mathtt{Axiom: \ A_1[1]}$

$Out[7] = \mathtt{Rules:} \quad \begin{aligned} &\mathtt{< \ A_1[2] \ >} \quad \to \quad \mathtt{A_1[1]B_r[1]} \\ &\mathtt{< \ A_r[2] \ >} \quad \to \quad \mathtt{B_1[1]A_r[1]} \\ &\mathtt{< \ B_1[5] \ >} \quad \to \quad \mathtt{A_1[1]B_r[1]} \\ &\mathtt{< \ B_r[5] \ >} \quad \to \quad \mathtt{B_1[1]A_r[1]} \end{aligned}$

$\begin{aligned} &\mathtt{< \ A_1[i\_ \ /; \ i < 2] \ >} \quad \to \quad \mathtt{A_1[1 + i]} \\ &\mathtt{< \ A_r[i\_ \ /; \ i < 2] \ >} \quad \to \quad \mathtt{A_r[1 + i]} \\ &\mathtt{< \ B_1[i\_ \ /; \ i < 5] \ >} \quad \to \quad \mathtt{B_1[1 + i]} \\ &\mathtt{< \ B_r[i\_ \ /; \ i < 5] \ >} \quad \to \quad \mathtt{B_r[1 + i]} \end{aligned}$

Cell layer growth

The first four rules describe the division of *A* and *B* cells after they have reached their maturity states of 2 and 5, respectively. The specific nature of these division processes for the A_l, A_r and B_l, B_r cells is defined by the right sides of the productions. The additional rules allow the grown-up cells to "mature" by increasing the cell parameter with every derivation step.

The following command computes 16 iteration steps for the simulated development of the cell layer described by the `cellLayerL-System` L-system:

In[8] := **parametrizedCells =**   *Cell layer growth*
        runKLSystem[cellLayerLSystem, 16];   *in 16 steps*

In Figure 9.9, this developmental process is illustrated graphically.
Each *A* term is represented by a large, oval cell; each *B* term is
depicted by a smaller, circular cell. The orientation of each cell is   *Cell ripening and division*
marked by a corresponding arrow pointing in the growth direction.
The gray values (light to dark) represent cell states of increasing maturity. The large *A* cells divide after every second step, whereas the
smaller *B* cells require four ripening steps before they subdivide.

L-systems versus cellular automata

Comparing these very simple forms of Lindenmayer systems to cellu-   *L-systems vs. cellular*
lar automata already reveals the major differences between these two   *automata*
modeling approaches. L-systems work as true rewriting systems. A
single unit (symbol) within a string can be substituted by any number
of symbols. Hence, the length of the generated strings is, in principle,
not limited, unlike the fixed lattices usually used for cellular automata. This argument also holds for deletions of subunits. Any symbol
within an L-system generated string can be erased by using a rule with
an empty right side. L-systems incorporate the dynamics of grammars,   *Dynamic strings*
which are also used for describing programming languages (Chomsky
1956; Backus 1959). In principle, universal programming languages
are not restricted in length or in the complexity of their hierarchical
structure (cf. nested loops, conditionals, etc.).

   At first it seems restrictive that L-systems work only with strings
or, in a more general form, with symbolic expressions, while cellular
automata perform their operations on lattices in two, three, and more
dimensions. However, the expressions generated by an L-system can   *Two and three dimensions*
be interpreted as developmental programs, which implicitly describe
the composition of a two- or three-dimensional structure (cf. turtle
interpretation, Section 9.2.3). In this way, Lindenmayer systems provide an adequate computational model for the simulation of developmental processes in two- and three-dimensional space. The stunning
results of using L-systems for simulating the growth of plants, their
visualization and animation, clearly show the potential of this form of
parallel rewriting systems (Prusinkiewicz and Lindenmayer 1990; Prusinkiewicz, Hammel, et al. 1997; Deussen, Hanrahan, et al. 1998).

   However, the D0L-systems discussed thus far are missing an
essential feature of cellular automata rules; namely, contextual depen-
dency. The extension to so-called context-sensitive IL-systems will   *Context*

show that these L-systems are capable of simulating one-dimensional cellular automata, as illustrated by examples in Figure 9.2.

9.2.2 Context-sensitive L-systems

In the 0L-systems used up to now, the substitution of each symbol in a string is carried out independently of the context in which the symbol appears. Simulations of morphogenetic processes, however, should also allow for interactions between subunits or agents, represented by symbols or expressions. These features can be implemented by context-sensitive IL-systems.

IL-systems

The most general definition of context-sensitive *IL-systems* is given by (m, n) L-systems, $m, n \in \mathrm{IN}_0 = \{0, 1, 2, \ldots\}$, where the rewriting of a symbol within a string depends on the m left and n right neighboring context symbols, respectively. IL-systems are very similar to context-sensitive Chomsky grammars (Chomsky 1956). The essential difference lies in the parallel rewriting of all symbols within a string. The substitutions are performed in parallel, even though the symbols' contexts may overlap. This is why the rewriting process is analogous to the state transformations of (one-dimensional) cellular automata.

The productions of an (m, n) L-system $G_{(m, n)L} = (\Sigma, \pi, \alpha)$ can be specified as follows:

Productions of an
(m, n) L-system

$$l < p > r \rightarrow s$$

$$p \in \Sigma, s \in \Sigma^*, l \in \bigcup_{0 \leq i \leq m} \Sigma^i, r \in \bigcup_{0 \leq i \leq n} \Sigma^i.$$

The symbols p and s are denoted as the *predecessor* and the *successor*, respectively. The *left* and *right contexts* are represented by the symbols l and r. In an (m, n) L-system, the left contexts consist of words with a length of at most m, and the right contexts are at most n characters long. $(1, 0)$ and $(0, 1)$ L-systems are abbreviated as 1L-systems; that is, they contain productions with at most one symbol in their left or right contexts. $(1, 1)$ L-systems with one-symbol contexts on both sides are also known as 2L-systems.

1L- and 2L-systems

A 2L-system example

Let us look at a context-sensitive L-system example. The following 2L-system simulates simple signal propagation in a cell filament, the cells of which can take on four different states: a, b, c, or d (Figure 9.10). The symbol T serves as a separator from any other filament. The L-system consists of 14 productions with at most two-sided, one-symbol contexts, which are analogous to the one-dimensional cellular automaton rules. Unlike cellular automata, the productions may also have empty left and/or right contexts.

```
TaaaaaaaaabaaaaaabaaaaabaaaT
TaaaaaaadacaaaadacaaadacaaT
TaaaaaadaaacaadaaacadaaacaT
TaaaaadaaaaacdaaaaabaaaaacT
TaaaadaaaaaadcaaaadacaaaadT
TaaadaaaaaadaacaadaaacaadaT
TaadaaaaaadaaaacdaaaaacdaaT
TadaaaaadaaaaadcaaaaadcaaT
TdaaaaadaaaaadaacaaadaacaT
TcaaaaadaaaaadaaaacadaaaacT
TacaaadaaaaadaaaaaabaaaaadT
TaacadaaaaadaaaaaadacaaadaT
TaaabaaaaadaaaaaadaaacadaaT
TaadacaaadaaaaaadaaaaabaaaT
TadaaacadaaaaadaaaaadacaaT
TdaaaaabaaaaadaaaaadaaacaT
TcaaaadacaaaadaaaaadaaaaacT
TacaadaaacaadaaaaadaaaaaadT
TaacdaaaaacdaaaaadaaaaaadaT
TaadcaaaaadcaaaadaaaaaadaaT
TadaacaaadaacaadaaaaaadaaaT
```

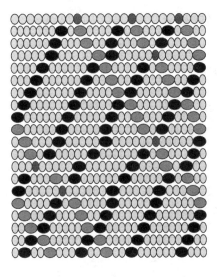

Figure 9.10
Simulated propagation of
signals, modeled by
a 2L-system.

(a)   (b)

$$G_{2L} = (\{a, b, c, d, T\}, P, \alpha)$$

*Signal propagation in a
cell layer, modeled with a
2L-system*

α: $TaaaaaaaaabaaaaaabaaaaabaaaT$

P: p_1: $c < a > \quad \to c$ p_8: $a < b > a \to a$

      p_2: $< c > a \to a$ p_9: $< c > d \to d$

      p_3: $< a > d \to d$ p_{10}: $c < d > \quad \to c$

      p_4: $a < d > \quad \to a$ p_{11}: $T < d > \quad \to c$

      p_5: $c < a > d \to b$ p_{12}: $< c > T \to d$

      p_6: $< a > b \to d$ p_{13}: $c < T > c \to a$

      p_7: $b < a > \quad \to c$ p_{14}: $d < T > d \to a$

Each cell in state b sends a d signal to its left and a c signal to its right neighbor cell (p_6, p_7, p_8). The d signals (c signals) are successively propagated to the left (right) (p_3, p_4 and p_1, p_2). Whenever a c and a d signal meet, a b cell is created (p_5) or the signals coincide (p_9, p_{10}). At the boundaries of the filament, the signals are converted (p_{11}, p_{12}). A filament boundary is converted into an a cell if equal signals approach from left and right (p_{13}, p_{14}).

Interaction of signals

Figure 9.10(a) shows the derivation sequence over 20 iteration steps. Substituting the symbols for cells and signals with corresponding graphical elements (circles and ovals) results in the graphical representation in Figure 9.10(b), which illustrates the interactions between the cells.

In the Evolvica notebooks, available on the *IEC* Web site (see Preface), the context-sensitive productions are extended by `LEFT[...]` and `RIGHT[...]` terms, describing the left and right contexts, respectively. Hence, an IL-rule has the general form

IL-rule representation

```
LRule[ LEFT[ l ], PRED[ p ], RIGHT[ r ], SUCC[ s ] ].
```

The ordering of the `LEFT`, `RIGHT`, `PRED`, and `SUCC` terms is irrelevant. If any of the contexts remains empty, the corresponding `LEFT[]` and `RIGHT[]` expressions can be omitted.

9.2.3 Implicit description of spatial structures

In the L-system examples discussed so far, each symbol of a one-dimensional string was interpreted as a graphical object and mapped into a corresponding one-dimensional graphical representation (cf. the cell layers in Section 9.2.2). In order to model nature's morphogenetic processes—as observed in natural plants, for example—mappings from one-dimensional strings to two- or three-dimensional structures are needed.

From strings to spatial structures

A simple realization of 1D to 3D transformations, mimicking nature's genotype-phenotype mapping, can be implemented with L-systems encoding control signals with which a virtual "drawing tool," known as a *turtle*, can be navigated in three-dimensional space. This *turtle interpretation* provides a flexible technique to graphically compose two- and three-dimensional structures.

Turtle interpretation

Using turtles as virtual drawing devices became popular through Simon Papert's programming language *LOGO* (Papert 1980; Papert 1993). Szilard and Quinton were the first to introduce turtle interpretations with D0L-systems (Szilard and Quinton 1979). Prusinkiewicz and Hanan extended turtle interpretations to more general L-systems and developed them further for realistic visualization of plant structures (Prusinkiewicz 1986; Prusinkiewicz 1987; Hanan 1988; Hanan 1992).

The state T of a turtle

$$T = (\vec{P}, \Psi) = \left(\begin{pmatrix} x_p \\ y_p \\ z_p \end{pmatrix}, (\vec{H}, \vec{L}, \vec{U}) \right)$$

is characterized by its space or position vector $\vec{P}$ and a matrix Ψ with orthonormal column vectors $\vec{H}$, $\vec{L}$, and $\vec{U}$, which describe the 3D

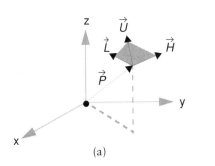
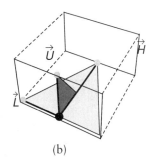

Figure 9.11
Description of turtle position
and orientation in three-
dimensional space.

(a) (b)

orientation of the turtle (Figure 9.11[a]). Vector $\vec{H}$ describes the turtle's *heading*; $\vec{L}$ and $\vec{U}$ denote the *left* and *up* directions, respectively. The turtle is positioned in the plane spanned by the vectors $\vec{H}$ and $\vec{L}$; $\vec{U}$ corresponds to the normal vector of this plane.

Position and orientation of the turtle

In Figure 9.11(b), a turtle is depicted schematically as a polygon shape, which we will use in the following examples to illustrate turtle navigation. The dots at the corners of the two triangles mark the corresponding heading, left, and up direction vectors. The current turtle position is denoted by the dark dot at the rear end of the turtle.

The Evolvica notebook, available on the *IEC* Web site (see Preface), provides a number of commands to navigate the turtle in three-dimensional space, to change the turtle's position and orientation, to draw graphical elements at the current turtle position, or to change attributes of the "drawing tool"; for example, the color or line thickness of a pen. The following summary gives an overview of the most common turtle commands, implemented by the Evolvica function `turtleInterpretation`.

Changing the position of the turtle

Changes to the turtle position $\vec{P}$ are accomplished by vector addition. One of two sets of move operations is used, depending on whether a line from the initial to the new position is drawn or whether the turtle "jumps" to the new position without drawing a line.

FO[*s*]: *Forward*

Advances the turtle by a step size of *s* in the direction of vector $\vec{H}$ and draws a line depending on the current color and line thickness settings. The new turtle position is $\vec{P} := \vec{P} + s \cdot \vec{H}$.

BA[s]: *Back*

> Moves the turtle backward by a step size of s in the direction of vector $-\vec{H}$ and draws a line according to the current color and line thickness settings. The new turtle position is $\vec{P} := \vec{P} - s \cdot \vec{H}$.

JF[s]: *Jump Forward*

> Moves the turtle by a step size of s in direction $\vec{H}$. The new turtle position is $\vec{P} := \vec{P} + s \cdot \vec{H}$. Within a *POLYGON* command, each JF marks a polygon node.

JB[s]: *Jump Back*

> Moves the turtle back by a step size of s in direction $-\vec{H}$. The new turtle position is $\vec{P} := \vec{P} - s \cdot \vec{H}$.

JU[s]: *Jump Up*

> Moves the turtle upward by a step size of s in direction $\vec{U}$. This movement is implemented as a 90-degree up rotation around the transverse axis and a subsequent forward movement (cf. Figure 9.12):

$$\Psi := \Psi \cdot P(-90°); \quad \vec{P} := \vec{P} + s \cdot \vec{H}; \quad \Psi := \Psi \cdot P(90°).$$

> The original direction is accomplished by an inverse rotation.

JD[s]: *Jump Down*

> Moves the turtle down by a step size of s in the direction $-\vec{U}$. The sequence of movements is analogous to the *Jump Up* command:

$$\Psi := \Psi \cdot P(90°); \quad \vec{P} := \vec{P} - s \cdot \vec{H}; \quad \Psi := \Psi \cdot P(-90°).$$

Changing turtle orientation

The turtle orientation, described by the matrix $\Psi = (\vec{H}, \vec{L}, \vec{U})$, is changed using the parametrized rotation matrices as depicted in Figure 9.12.

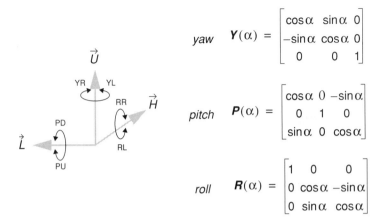

$$yaw \quad \mathbf{Y}(\alpha) = \begin{bmatrix} \cos\alpha & \sin\alpha & 0 \\ -\sin\alpha & \cos\alpha & 0 \\ 0 & 0 & 1 \end{bmatrix}$$

$$pitch \quad \mathbf{P}(\alpha) = \begin{bmatrix} \cos\alpha & 0 & -\sin\alpha \\ 0 & 1 & 0 \\ \sin\alpha & 0 & \cos\alpha \end{bmatrix}$$

$$roll \quad \mathbf{R}(\alpha) = \begin{bmatrix} 1 & 0 & 0 \\ 0 & \cos\alpha & -\sin\alpha \\ 0 & \sin\alpha & \cos\alpha \end{bmatrix}$$

Figure 9.12
Changing turtle orientation by rotation around the three main axes.

YL[α]: *Yaw Left*

The turtle is rotated left (counterclockwise) around its vertical axis $\vec{U}$ by an angle of α degrees. The new turtle orientation is $\Psi := \Psi \cdot Y(\alpha)$.

YR[α]: *Yaw Right*

The turtle is rotated right (clockwise) around its vertical axis $\vec{U}$ by an angle of α degrees. The new turtle orientation is $\Psi := \Psi \cdot Y(-\alpha)$.

PD[α]: *Pitch Down*

The turtle is tilted down around its transverse axis $\vec{L}$ by an angle of α degrees. The new turtle orientation is $\Psi := \Psi \cdot P(\alpha)$.

PU[α]: *Pitch Up*

The turtle is tilted up around its transverse axis $\vec{L}$ by an angle of α degrees. The new turtle orientation is $\Psi := \Psi \cdot P(-\alpha)$.

RL[α]: *Roll Left*

The turtle is rotated left (counterclockwise) around its longitudinal axis by an angle of α degrees. The new turtle orientation is $\Psi := \Psi \cdot R(\alpha)$.

RR[α]: *Roll Right*

The turtle is rotated right (clockwise) around its longitudinal axis by an angle of α degrees. The new turtle orientation is $\Psi := \Psi \cdot R(-\alpha)$.

TN: *Turn*

The turtle is oriented backward; that is, it is rotated around its vertical axis $\vec{U}$ by 180 degrees. The new turtle orientation is $\Psi := \Psi \cdot Y(180°)$.

Drawing graphical elements

Whenever the turtle changes position through one of the commands described above, lines only are drawn. To insert more complex graphical elements, the following commands can be used. Any `Graphics3D` object can be inserted at the current turtle position. Polygons can be defined in two ways. The nodes of a polygon are either specified by an explicit list of coordinates (*Draw Polygon*) or implicitly by using turtle commands (*Implicit Polygon*).

Graphic objects and polygons

Explicit polygon

DP[*s, c*]: *Draw Point*

Draws a point with scaling *s* and color *c* at the current turtle position.

DPLY[*s, c,* {*coords*}]: *Draw Polygon*

Draws the polygon, described by the (relative) coordinates *coords*, with scaling *s* and line color *c*. The polygon drawing starts at the current turtle position.

Implicit turtle polygon

POLYGON[*turtleCommands*]: *Implicit Polygon*

The nodes of the polygon are implicitly defined by a sequence of turtle commands. Each JF[*s*] command defines the resulting turtle position as a polygon node. The polygon is drawn immediately after all instructions in `turtleCommands` have been executed.

Graphics3D objects

GRAPHICS[*g, s*]: *Graphics3D*

An arbitrary `Graphics3D` object with scaling *s* is drawn at the current turtle position.

Variation of drawing tool attributes

The variable settings of the drawing device are line thickness and color.

Color

CO[*c*]: *Set Color*

Sets the color of the drawing pen to color value `Hue[c]`.

CI[i]: *Color Increment*
The current pen color is increased by *i*. The color values are calculated *modulo 1*; that is, they are constrained to the interval [0, 1].

CD[d]: *Color Decrement*
The current pen color is decreased by *d*. The color values are calculated modulo 1.

TH[t]: *Thickness*   *Line width*
The line thickness is set to a (relative) value of *t*.

TI[i]: *Thickness Increment*
The current line thickness is increased by *i*.

TD[d]: *Thickness Decrement*
The current line thickness is decreased by *d*.

TS[s]: *Thickness Scale*
The line width is scaled by *s*.

The following example shows how the structure of a three-   *Hilbert curve demo*
dimensional *Hilbert curve* is described by a simple sequence of navigation commands for a turtle (Prusinkiewicz and Lindenmayer 1990, p. 20). The four basic building blocks (*A*, *B*, *C*, and *D*) of the 3D Hilbert curve are implemented by parametrized L-system rules.

```
In[1] := hilbertRules[s_,a_] :=                    Parametrized
    LRULES[                                        L-rules of "Hilbert building
      LRule[LEFT[], PRED[ s ], RIGHT[],            blocks"
        SUCC[CO[.1],B,YR[a],FO[s],YL[a],C,FO[s],C,YL[a],
          FO[s],YR[a],D,PD[a],FO[s],PU[a],D,YR[a],FO[s],
          YL[a],PD[a],PD[a],C,FO[s],C,YL[a],FO[s],YL[a],
          B,RR[a],RR[a]
        ]],...
    ]
```

Here the turtle's description is given only for the first basic building block. The parameters *s* and *a* define the turtle's step size and rotation angle, respectively. For *s* = 1 and *a* = 90, the structure depicted in Figure 9.13 (Iteration 1) results. The building blocks represented by *B*, *C*, and *D* are merely rotated versions of structure *A*. An L-system for a three-dimensional Hilbert curve starting from building block *A* is defined as follows:

Figure 9.13

Three-dimensional version
of the Hilbert curve.

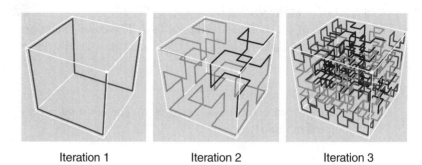

Iteration 1   Iteration 2   Iteration 3

L-system for a 3D Hilbert
curve

```
In[2] := hilbertLSystem[s_,a_] :=
            LSystem[AXIOM[ A ], hilbertRules[s,a]];
```

Performing one iteration of this L-system results in a sequence of commands for moving the turtle and varying its orientation, separated by building block symbols:

```
In[3] := hilbertCurve =
            runKLSystem[hilbertLSystem[1,90], 1] // Last
```

Turtle command sequence
for the initial Hilbert building
block

```
Out[3]= AXIOM[CO[0.1], B, YR[90], FO[1], YL[90], C,
            FO[1], C, YL[90], FO[1], YR[90], D, PD[90],
            FO[1], PU[90], D, YR[90], FO[1], YL[90],
            PD[90], PD[90], C, FO[1], C, YL[90], FO[1],
            YL[90], B, RR[90], RR[90]]
```

The following Evolvica command interprets the turtle instructions and translates them into a graphical object. The option Show-Turtle → True generates an animation sequence for visualizing each turtle action step.

Animated, step-by-step
turtle interpretation

```
In[4] := turtleInterpretation[hilbertCurve,
            ShowTurtle → True];
```

Figure 9.14 illustrates the resulting animation sequence. Each single image displays the turtle state after step-by-step interpretation of the expressions contained in the AXIOM term. The interpretation of one of the symbols *B*, *C*, or *D* does not change the turtle state; therefore no new image is drawn. Each FO command draws a line, and the YL, YR, and RR commands result in changes to the turtle's orientation.

The evolution of this three-dimensional Hilbert structure for further iterations is depicted in Figure 9.13. Accordingly, a complete animation sequence of these turtle commands would be much larger.

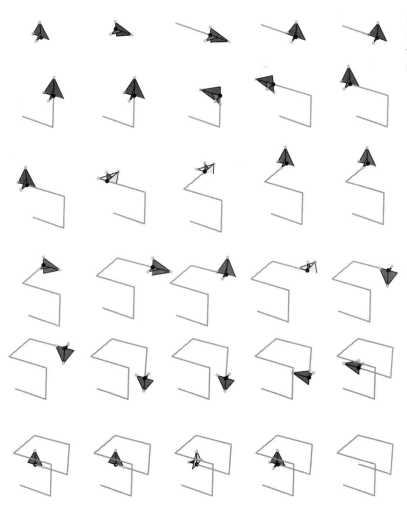

Figure 9.14
Illustration of step-by-step turtle interpretation: action sequence of a 3D turtle.

Given the navigation commands introduced thus far, an instruction set is interpreted as a sequence of line segments. Lines generated in this manner can describe complex shapes. Even if *Jump* commands are used, basically only a single path is drawn. But branching structures, more common in natural plants, are too tedious to model with this approach. An extension of turtle interpretations by a simple stack mechanism provides an easy, flexible technique for modeling these branching structures.

9.2.4 Modeling of branching structures

In order to describe branching structures by L-systems, turtle interpretation is extended by a *stack* mechanism. A *Push* instruction stores the

Stack commands

current turtle state on a push-down stack, following a LIFO strategy (last in, first out). With a *Pop* command the turtle state placed last on the stack is restored and deleted from the stack. Following our example of branching plant structures, the turtle is now able to save its current state before drawing a (side) branch. After finishing the construction of this branch, the turtle can restore its former state and continue drawing further (plant) structures.

Bracketed L-systems

L-systems extended by such a push-pop mechanism are denoted as *bracketed* L-systems (Prusinkiewicz and Lindenmayer 1990, p. 24). Usually the *Push* and *Pop* commands are represented by the bracket symbols "[" and "]," respectively. This is where we get the name bracketed L-systems. Square brackets have a different meaning in Mathematica. Therefore, a Stack term is used to denote bracketed segments. Consequently, our set of turtle commands is extended as follows:

Stack[...]: *Push . . . Pop*

Before the expressions enclosed by the *Stack* term are interpreted, the current turtle state is saved on the stack. In addition to the position and orientation of the turtle, other attributes such as line color and width can be stored. After the interpretation of all expressions, the former turtle state is restored.

Push and Pop

We could also have used the single symbols *Push* and *Pop* to represent the brackets. But because we intend to use L-systems in combination with genetic programming in the following chapters, a term representation ensuring proper bracket structures turns out to be more advantageous. Using the single symbols *Push* and *Pop,* genetic operators, such as mutations, duplications, and deletions, would easily lead to inconsistently bracketed expression structures.

Modeling growth patterns of plant structures is a typical application of bracketed L-systems with turtle interpretation. We demonstrate how easily branching structures can be described and constructed with a few examples of schematic tree structures, specified by parametrized, bracketed L-systems. The "trees" depicted in Figure 9.15 result from the turtle interpretation of the following set of L-system productions:

Bracketed L-system for a tree structure

```
In[1] := treeAxiom[] := AXIOM[ A[1,0.02] ];
         treeRules[r1_,r2_,a0_,a2_,d_,wr_] :=
         LRULES[
           LRule[PRED[ A[l_,w_] ],
             SUCC[ TH[w], FO[l],
```

```
        STACK[ PD[a0], B[l*r2,w*wr] ],
        RR[d], A[l*r1,w*wr]]],
    LRule[PRED[ B[l_,w_] ],
      SUCC[ TH[w], FO[l],
        STACK[ YR[a2], C[l*r2,w*wr] ],
        C[l*r1,w*wr]]],
    LRule[PRED[ C[l_,w_] ],
      SUCC[ TH[w], FO[l],
        STACK[ YL[a2], B[l*r2,w*wr] ],
        B[l*r1,w*wr]]]
  ];
```

The expressions of the form A[l,w], B[l,w], and C[l,w] represent trunk and branch segments, where the parameters l and w denote their length and thickness, respectively. Tree structures of a large variety are characterized by the following parametrized L-system:

```
In[2] := treeLSystem[r1_,r2_,a0_,a2_,d_,wr_] :=
    LSystem[treeAxiom[],
    treeRules[r1,r2,a0,a2,d,wr]];
```

Parametrized tree L-system

The six parameters with which the shape of the trees is in essence determined are the contraction rates of the length of the trunk (r1) and the branches (r2); the branching angle of the branches toward the trunk (a0) or of the lateral, secondary branches (a2); the divergence angle (d), by which the main branches are rotated around the main trunk; and the scaling for reducing the trunk and branch radius (wr) in the direction of the branch tips.

The tree groups depicted in Figure 9.15 represent only a small set of possible variants. Prusinkiewicz and Lindenmayer give an extensive overview of structures that can be generated from this and similar parametrized L-systems (Prusinkiewicz and Lindenmayer 1990, pp. 56 ff.). The Evolvica notebook, available on the *IEC* Web site (see Preface), contains a number of further examples and may serve as a starting point for your own tree growth experiments.

9.3 Bibliographical notes

Cellular automata

One of the classic texts on cellular automata is Stephen Wolfram's *Cellular Automata and Complexity* (Wolfram 1994), which is a

CAs and complexity

Figure 9.15

Modeling of tree structures with bracketed L-systems.

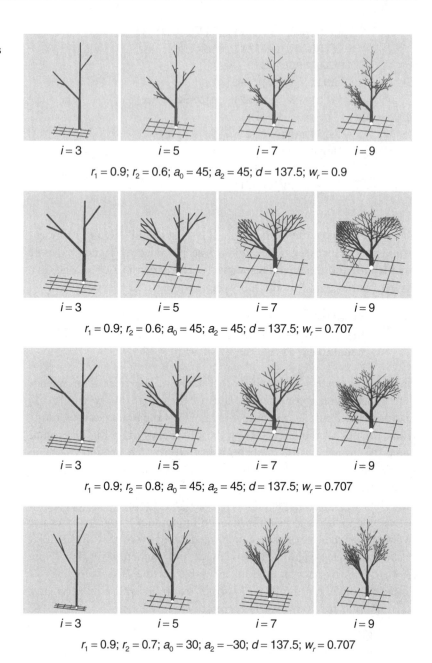

$i = 3$ $i = 5$ $i = 7$ $i = 9$

$r_1 = 0.9; r_2 = 0.6; a_0 = 45; a_2 = 45; d = 137.5; w_r = 0.9$

$i = 3$ $i = 5$ $i = 7$ $i = 9$

$r_1 = 0.9; r_2 = 0.6; a_0 = 45; a_2 = 45; d = 137.5; w_r = 0.707$

$i = 3$ $i = 5$ $i = 7$ $i = 9$

$r_1 = 0.9; r_2 = 0.8; a_0 = 45; a_2 = 45; d = 137.5; w_r = 0.707$

$i = 3$ $i = 5$ $i = 7$ $i = 9$

$r_1 = 0.9; r_2 = 0.7; a_0 = 30; a_2 = -30; d = 137.5; w_r = 0.707$

collection of his major contributions to the field from 1982 to 1986. Since 1986, Wolfram has concentrated on the development of Mathematica (Wolfram 1996).

Modern CAs

Two other textbooks on cellular automata are *Modern Cellular Automata: Theory and Applications* (Preston and Duff 1984) and

Cellular Automata Machines: A New Environment for Modeling (Toffoli and Margolus 1987).

Richard Gaylord and Paul Wellin's book *Computer Simulations with Mathematica* explores complex physical and biological systems on the basis of cellular automata and probabilistic systems (Gaylord and Wellin 1995). In *Modeling Nature* (Gaylord and Nishidate 1996) and *Simulating Society* (Gaylord and D'Andria 1999), Gaylord and his coworkers provide CA-based models for simulating natural developmental and evolutionary processes and socioeconomic behavior.

StarLogo is a system developed for simulating massively parallel and decentralized systems. It combines cellular automata with turtles, moving on a 2D grid (Resnick 1997).

Computer Simulations with Mathematica

Modeling Nature; Simulating Society

StarLogo

Evolution of cellular automata

An approach to the evolution and coevolution of cellular automata rules is described in Moshe Sipper's *Evolution of Parallel Cellular Machines* (1997).

Evolution of Parallel Cellular Machines

Artificial life and self-reproduction

In *Artificial Life: A Report from the Frontier Where Computers Meet Biology*, Steven Levy gives an excellent introduction to the wide field of "biocomputing," with an impressive amount of background information on the researchers and their work (Levy 1993a; 1993b).

Artificial Life

An overview of research in the area of artificial life is provided in *Artificial Life* (Langton 1994).

Christoph Adami's *Introduction to Artificial Life* discusses self-organizing and self-replicating systems in the context of thermodynamics, complexity, criticality, and percolation. The book also contains example experiments based on Adami's *avida* system (Adami 1998).

Introduction to Artificial Life

The special issue of the *Artificial Life* journal (Volume 4, Number 3, 1998), *Self-Reproduction*, contains a number of articles on John von Neumann's original work, an overview of research on self-reproduction over the last 50 years, and examples of self-replicating structures and multicellular automata (Mange and Sipper 1998; Marchal 1998; Sipper 1998; Tempesti, Mange, et al. 1998; Reggia, Lohn, et al. 1998).

Artificial Life *journal: special issue*

Artificial Life journal

The journal *Artificial Life* is published quarterly by MIT Press. The first issue came out in fall 1993.

Artificial life conferences

Artificial life conferences

In 1987 Christopher Langton organized the first Artificial Life Conference in Los Alamos, New Mexico (Langton 1989). From this event, a series of conferences evolved, with ever growing interest and an ever growing range of research areas related to artificial life (Langton, Taylor, et al. 1992; Langton 1994; Brooks and Maes 1995; Langton and Shimohara 1997; Adami, Belew, et al. 1998; Bedau, McCaskill, et al. 2000).

Lindenmayer systems

For references on Lindenmayer systems see Chapter 10.

10 Evolutionary Inference of Lindenmayer Systems

Random modification of productions gives little insight into the relationship between L-systems and the figures they generate. However, we often wish to construct an L-system which captures a given structure or sequence of structures representing a developmental process.

Prusinkiewicz and Lindenmayer 1990, p. 11

Solving the *inference problem* for L-systems means finding a suitable axiom and a set of productions that model a given structure or a particular growth process. Generally, in order to build an L-system model for a natural morphogenetic process, the following steps are necessary (Peitgen, Jürgens, et al. 1992):

1. Analysis of the biological object,
2. Informal definition of the structure formation rules,
3. Definition of an L-system with axiom and productions,
4. Interpretation of the derivation sequence in a computer simulation,
5. Visualization of the generated structures,
6. Comparison of the virtual objects to the behavior of the real objects simulated, and
7. Probable modification of the L-system and repetition of respective steps.

This brief outline shows that the synthesis of L-systems may involve difficult, time-consuming procedures. Thus it would be helpful to have a procedure that in part automates inference tasks. Prusinkiewicz also points out that purely random modifications of production rules are generally not suitable for determining relations between L-systems and their corresponding graphical structures encoded therein (Prusinkiewicz and Lindenmayer 1990, pp. 11 ff.) unless the L-systems feature a relatively simple encoding structure (Hamilton

L-system inference

Building L-system models of natural growth processes

1994). Furthermore, the inference algorithms discussed in the literature are still too constrained to be applied to infer developmental programs for complex pattern formation processes; for example, the growth of plant structures (Prusinkiewicz and Lindenmayer 1990, pp. 39, 62).

L-system inference by evolution

This and the following chapter present a few approaches to applying *evolutionary algorithms* to infer L-systems. Evolution-based techniques and genetic programming in particular can be applied to the steps of mathematical and algorithmic definitions of models (step 3), the comparison of artificially generated to actual objects (step 6), and the iterated adaptation of the model (step 7). Hence, in the context of L-systems, the following functions must be provided:

Functions required for L-system inference

❑ *Generation functions* that encode L-systems,

❑ *Modification functions* that generate new L-system variants,

❑ *Evaluation functions* that provide a fitness value for each phenotypical L-system interpretation, and

❑ *Selection functions* for interactive or fitness-dependent automatic selection for the composition of a new L-system gene pool.

Section overview

In Section 10.1, we discuss the encoding of L-systems using symbolic expressions. We compare these with bit string encodings for L-systems, illustrating the advantages of a hierarchical encoding based on symbolic expressions, which we will use in our genetic programming approach to L-system inference. Section 10.2 demonstrates a simple example of evolution-based inference of L-systems generating fractal, two-dimensional structures.

10.1 Encoding of IL-systems

In order to apply evolutionary optimization methods to Lindenmayer systems, a suitable representation of the evolvable structures must be determined. Again we propagate the idea of encoding L-systems with symbolic expressions, but first we will introduce a binary string-based form of representing L-systems (Figure 10.1).

Bit strings encode for L-systems

Boers and Kuiper generate descriptions of parallel rewrite systems based on genetic algorithms (Boers and Kuiper 1992). Initially random bit strings, up to a maximum length, are generated. Bit sequences are then mapped to characters over an L-system alphabet. Six bits each encode a single character from the alphabet {A, B, C, D, E, F, G,

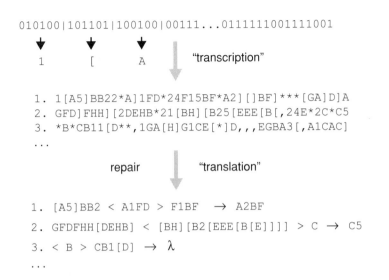

Figure 10.1
From bit strings to
L-systems.

H, 1, 2, 3, 4, 5, *, [,], ´, ˝}. Consequently, the syntactical structure of these randomly generated strings must be adjusted by a repair mechanism, finally resulting in correct L-system rule descriptions. Since the genetic operators do not work on the rules themselves but on the bit sequences unrelated to the hierarchical structure of the L-system rules, the transcription, repair, and translation routines have to be invoked after each operator application or, at the latest, before any decoding of the rules is initiated.

"Repair" and translation

The situation is much simpler if we rely on symbolic expressions as the form of representing L-systems. A production for a context-sensitive L-system has the general form

Context-sensitive L-systems

$$l < p > r \rightarrow s,$$

which can be encoded by a symbolic expression of the form (see Section 9.2 and Section 11.1 for details)

`LRule[ Left[ l ], Pred[ p ], Right[ r ], Succ[ s ] ].`

IL-rule

A finite set of L-rules is comprised in a term expression,

`LRules[ LRule[...], ..., LRule[...] ],`

Productions

which, together with an axiom, encodes an IL-system:

`LSystem[Axiom[...], LRules[...] ].`

L-system

This representation provides a simple, problem-specific data structure for context-sensitive L-systems. The head symbols of the expressions serve as type descriptors, whereas the L-system expressions have a

Figure 10.2
Templates for generating
IL-system encodings.

```
LSystem[_AXIOM,_LRULES],

  AXIOM[...],

  LRULES[__LRule],

  LRule[_LEFT,
        _PRED,
        _RIGHT,
        _SUCC,
        BlankSequence[_LEFT|_PRED|_RIGHT|_SUCC]
  ],

  LEFT[...], PRED[...], RIGHT[...], SUCC[...], ...
```

fixed syntactical structure. The actual order of the subexpressions is irrelevant as long as certain restrictions are met:

Constraints for L-system building blocks

❑ An LSystem expression must contain (at least) an Axiom and (at least) an LRules expression.

❑ In each LRule expression, (at least) one Left, Pred, Right, and Succ term must be present as arguments.

These IL-system encodings are generated using the templates listed in Figure 10.2. The templates ensure that each generated L-system description is uniquely decodeable. In the case of multiple occurrences of Left, Pred, Right, or Succ terms within any LRule expression, this is true at least when the first term from the left is selected for decoding.

Stochastic and table L-systems

Further L-system variants, for example, *stochastic* L-systems or *table* L-systems (cf. Prusinkiewicz and Lindenmayer 1990, pp. 28 ff. and p. 66), can be similarly encoded (Figure 10.3). These variants, however, will not be used in the experiments discussed in the following sections.

In the next section, we present a simple method of evolutionary inference of Lindenmayer systems, which describes two-dimensional fractal curves.

10.2 Evolution of fractal structures

Fractal structures play a prominent role in the modeling and simulation of natural growth and structure formation processes (Peitgen and Richter 1986; Peitgen, Jürgens, et al. 1992). Parallel rewrite systems,

```
StochasticLSystem[_AXIOM,_LRULES],

...

LRULES[__LRule],

LRule[_Prob,_LEFT,...,_SUCC], ...
```

Figure 10.3
Encodings for stochastic (a)
and table L-systems (b).

(a)

```
TableLSystem[__Table]

Table[__LSystem | __StochasticLSystem]
```

(b)

such as Lindenmayer systems, provide a compact way to describe recursive and fractal structures in particular. We demonstrate this with an example from classical fractal constructions such as the Cantor set, the Koch curve, the Sierpinski triangle, and the Peano curve.

In this example we refer to a variant of the *Koch* construction. For an iterative description of the so-called *quadratic Koch island* we use the D0L-system $G_{Koch} = (\{F, L, R\}, \{p_1\}, \alpha)$:

α: FLFLFLF

L-system for the quadratic Koch island

p_1:   F $\rightarrow$ FLFRFRFFLFLFRF.

The strings generated by this L-system are interpreted as turtle commands in two-dimensional space. The commands L or R denote a 90-degree turn to the left or right, respectively: L = YL[90] and R = YR[90] (cf. Section 9.2.3). The F command moves the turtle one unit step ahead: F = FO[1]. Figure 10.4 shows the graphical interpretation of the axiom and the rewrite rule for the quadratic Koch island, as well as the fractal structures resulting from the first and second L-system iteration.

L, R, and F

Imagine showing the structure in Figure 10.4(b) to a person who is familiar with parallel rewrite systems and asking for the corresponding L-system. If we discover the inherent recursion of the structure, this task is relatively easy to solve. We will now approach this exact problem of L-system inference by using an evolutionary algorithm.

To evolve these "fractal programs," we again rely on genetic programming of symbolic expressions, introduced in Chapter 7 and demonstrated with the example of breeding ant control programs in

GP evolution of fractals

Figure 10.4

Turtle interpretation of the
D0L system for the quadratic
Koch island. (a) Axiom. (b)
Iteration 1. (c) Interation 2.

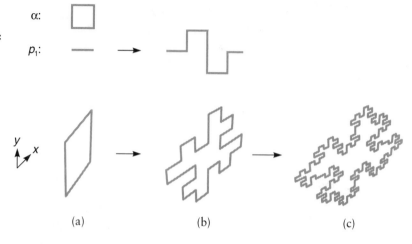

(a)   (b)   (c)

Figure 10.5

L-system templates for Koch
fractals.

```
LSystem[_AXIOM,_LRULES],

AXIOM[SEQ[_FO,_YL,_FO,_YL,_FO,_YL,_FO]],

LRULES[LRule[LEFT[], _PRED, RIGHT[], _SUCC]],

LRule[LEFT[],_PRED,RIGHT[],_SUCC],

PRED[_FO ],
SUCC[_SEQ ],

SEQ[_FO, _YL],
SEQ[_FO, _YR],
SEQ[BlankSequence[_FO | _SEQ ]],

STACK[BlankSequence[_FO | _YL | _YR ]],
STACK[BlankSequence[_FO | _YL | _YR | _SEQ | _STACK ]],

FO[stepSize],
YL[yawAngle],
YR[yawAngle]
```

Chapter 8. The building blocks necessary to generate the fractal L-
systems are listed in Figure 10.5. These templates allow for the generation of bracketed L-systems. We know that the Koch construction
does not need stack mechanisms, but we expect the evolution system
to discover this by itself. The only parameters that are predefined are
the step size, stepSize = 1, and the rotation angle, yawAngle = 90.

In addition, we include the correct axiom into the L-system templates. Hence, only suitable sequences of FO, YL, and YR commands must be evolved.

The genetic operators, modifying the L-system expressions, and their weights and selection templates are summarized in Figure 10.6. Structure modifications are performed only on subterms of SUCC expressions; that is, they are restricted to the right sides of L-rules. In particular, the axiom is protected by the selection templates from being modified by the genetic operators. The selection template {_SUCC, $ _SEQ} means that mutations and recombinations are performed on SEQ expressions that appear within SUCC expressions. The duplication and permutation operators work on SUCC expressions that contain SEQ subexpressions (cf. Jacob 1996a, 1996b, and the Evolvica notebooks on the *IEC* Web site for details). The operator weights remain unchanged during the evolution runs—they are not being adapted in this experiment. Mutation and recombination are rated as the main operators (weight = 2), whereas deletion, duplication, and permutation serve as secondary operators.

Genetic operators

The fitness of each L-system genome is calculated by decoding the corresponding L-system and interpreting it for a fixed number N of iterations. For our examples, we have set $N = 1$. The character string generated from the L-system iteration is interpreted as a sequence of turtle commands. This results in a symbolic representation of a structure, consisting of unit-length line segments in an equidistant grid (Figure 10.7). The set of line segments in each generated structure is compared to the corresponding lines of the reference fractal of iteration N. Overlapping as well as disjunct line segments must be taken

Evaluation

Similarity to a reference graphic

Operator	Weight	Selection template	Template weight
Mutation	2	{_SUCC, $ _SEQ}	1
Recombination	2	{_SUCC, $ _SEQ}	1
Deletion	1	{_SUCC, $ x_SEQ /;Length[{x}] > 1}	1
Duplication	1	{$ _SUCC, _SEQ}	1
Permutation	1	{$ _SUCC, _SEQ}	1

Figure 10.6
L-system inference of Koch curves: genetic operators.

Figure 10.7
Calculating the similarity
between generated line sets
and a reference structure.

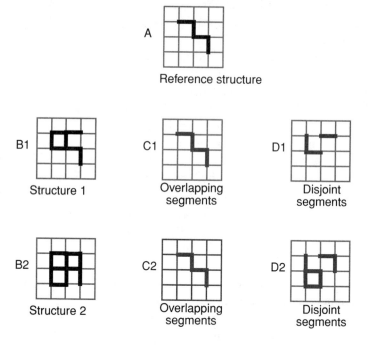

L-system fitnesses

into account in order to define a similarity measure (i.e., a fitness value) for the line structures (Figure 10.7, B, C, and D).

The fitness value $\mu(g_{LSys})$ of an L-system genome g_{LSys} is calculated from the similarity between the encoded fractal figure B = $Fig(g_{LSys}, N)$, after N iterations, and the corresponding reference structure A = $Fig_{Koch}(N)$. In detail, the fitness is calculated as follows:

$$\mu(g_{LSys}) = w_1|\text{Lines}(B) \cap \text{Lines}(A)| - w_2|\text{Lines}(B) - \text{Lines}(A)|.$$

The number of overlapping line segments of structures A and B is determined (Figure 10.7, C1 and C2) and scaled by w_1. From this value we subtract the number of lines appearing in structure B but not in reference structure A (Figure 10.7, D1 and D2), which is scaled by w_2. From our evolution experiments, we concluded that a weighting of $w_1 = 9$ and $w_2 = 1$ yields good results, because any overlap of line segments is emphasized. Too many lines disjoint from the reference structure results in considerable fitness reduction. Hence, the larger the number of overlapping and the smaller the number of exclusive line segments, the better a structure matches a reference graphic. For the two structures B1 and B2 in Figure 10.7, we get the following evaluations:

$$\mu(B1) = 9 \cdot 4 - 3 = 33 \text{ and } \mu(B2) = 9 \cdot 4 - 7 = 29.$$

The line configuration in B1 resembles reference A more than the lines in structure B2, because $\mu(B1) > \mu(B2)$. For a structure consisting of 32 line segments, perfectly matching the quadratic Koch island (after one iteration), the fitness value is $288 = 9 \cdot 32 - 0$.

We illustrate an inference example by looking at a typical evolution experiment over 80 generations, starting from an initial population of 35 individuals, as shown in Figure 10.8. We intend to evolve an L-system that perfectly encodes the single-iterated quadratic Koch island. Due to the definition of the similarity measure μ, structures such as individuals 6 or 35 in generation 0 are quickly sorted out. The number of structures that have few or no lines in common with the reference structure decreases over the generations, such that the proportion of more overlapping structures is gradually increased (Figure 10.8). An optimal individual appears for the first time in generation 76, which is why in generation 80 the Koch island already has four representatives (Figure 10.9).

Evolution of fractal L-systems

Although only a relatively small number of building blocks for encoding the L-systems is used, the excerpts of the evolution stages in Figures 10.8 and 10.9 illustrate a remarkable phenotypical diversity in the generated structures. To some extent this is due to the fact that there are no restrictions on how the genotypical building blocks are combined—apart from the syntactical constraints. A wide spectrum of mutations results from the genetic operators.

Figure 10.10 shows more detailed pictures of the evolution of fitness values over consecutive sequences of 20 generations. The fitness values are sorted for each generation. Note that the fitness of the best individuals remains constant over long phases and does not change continuously but rather in large steps. A first saltation occurs only after three generations. The fitness rises from an initial value of 16 to 60. Another fitness doubling is observed in generation 33. Finally, in generation 76, the fitness jumps to the maximum value of 288 (Figure 10.11).

Fitness evolution

The dispersion of the fitness values within each generation is noticeably large. However, this is an essential ingredient for the evolutionary dynamics, since new individuals are less often previously well-fit individuals but are derived from partly modified genotypical structures of below-average-fitness individuals (cf. Figure 10.13).

The projection of the contour lines below the fitness graphics in Figure 10.10 illustrates the dynamics of the fitness dispersions. We can clearly see three regions. The darker region on the left maps the above-average individuals. The middle, brighter regions represent the approximate share of individuals with average fitness. The right,

Dynamics of the fitness evolution

Figure 10.8

Evolution of fractal
L-systems: generations 0,
20, and 40.

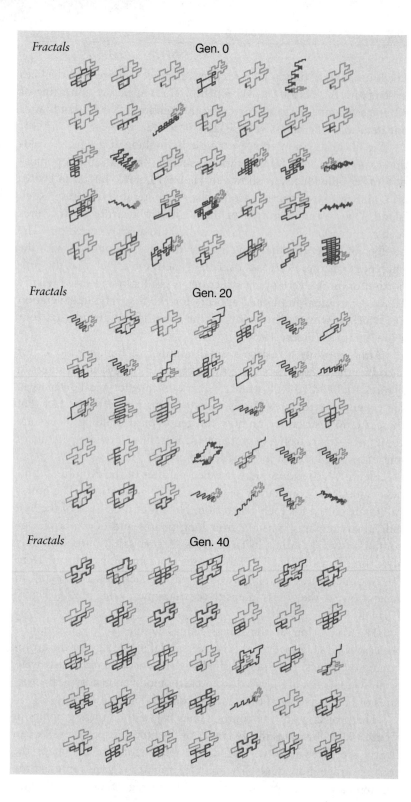

Fractals   Gen. 0

Fractals   Gen. 20

Fractals   Gen. 40

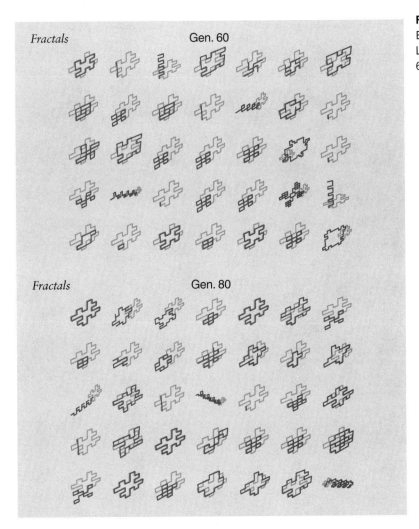

Figure 10.9
Evolution of fractal
L-systems: generations
60 and 80.

darker region reflects the portion of the population that received low fitness. The hues are relative within each of the graphics. The ratio of above-average individuals is about 10 to 20% and of average-fit individuals is between 20 and 40%. Figure 10.11 summarizes the evolution of the best and mean fitness values.

Figure 10.12 shows a selection of best individuals from generation 1 to generation 76, in both their phenotypical turtle interpretation and their encoding L-system genotypes. Basically the evolution toward the optimum structure involves only a few individuals, the fitnesses of which increase exponentially. A gradual fitness increase in small steps is not to be expected for this type of problem with a complex genotype-phenotype mapping. The transformation from an

*Evolution of the genotypes
and phenotypes*

Figure 10.10
Evolution of the fitness
values.

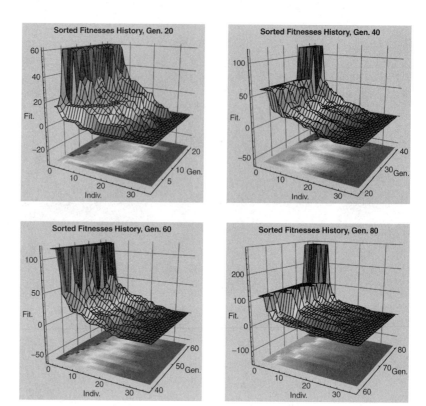

Figure 10.11
Best and mean fitnesses.

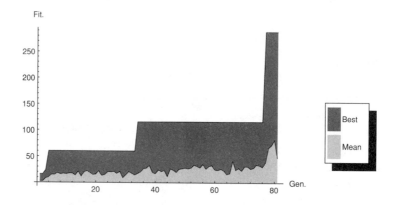

L-system encoding, over iterated applications of the encoded rule systems and their interpretation by turtle commands, is a highly nonlinear mapping process. Small changes of the genotype might result in totally new derivation sequences for the encoding L-system.

Effects of the genetic operators

The nonlinear effects are especially noticeable when we take a closer look at how the best individuals were generated by the genetic

```
LSystem[
  AXIOM[...],
  LRULES[LRule[
  LEFT[],PRED[FO[1]],Right[],
  SUCC[SEQ[FO[1], YR[90]]]]]]]
```

Figure 10.12
The best fractal L-systems.

Gen. 1   Fit. 16

```
LSystem[
  AXIOM[...],
  LRULES[LRule[
  LEFT[],PRED[FO[1]],RIGHT[],
  SUCC[SEQ[
    SEQ[FO[1],YR[90]],
    SEQ[FO[1],YL[90]]],
    SEQ[FO[1],YR[90]],
    SEQ[FO[1], YL[90]]]]]]]
```

Gen. 2   Fit. 24

```
LSystem[
  AXIOM[...],
  LRULES[LRule[
  LEFT[],PRED[FO[1]],RIGHT[],
  SUCC[SEQ[
    SEQ[FO[1],YL[90]],
    SEQ[FO[1],YR[90]],
    SEQ[FO[1],YR[90]],
    SEQ[FO[1], FO[1]]]]]]]
```

Gen. 3   Fit. 60

```
LSystem[
  AXIOM[...],
  LRULES[LRule[
  LEFT[],PRED[FO[1]],RIGHT[],
  SUCC[SEQ[
    SEQ[FO[1],YL[90]],
    SEQ[FO[1],YR[90]],
    SEQ[FO[1],YR[90]],
    SEQ[FO[1],YL[90], FO[1]],
    FO[1]]]]]]
```

Gen. 33   Fit. 116

```
LSystem[
  AXIOM[...],
  LRULES[LRule[
  LEFT[],PRED[FO[1]],RIGHT[],
  SUCC[SEQ[
    SEQ[FO[1],YL[90]],
    SEQ[FO[1],YR[90]],
    SEQ[FO[1],YR[90]],
    SEQ[FO[1],
    SEQ[FO[1],YL[90]],
    SEQ[FO[1], YL[90]],
    SEQ[FO[1], YR[90]]],
    FO[1]]]]]]
```

Gen. 76   Fit. 288

operators. Figures 10.13 and 10.14 illustrate with which recombination and mutation operations the best individuals emerged from individuals of the respective previous generations. Better individuals do not evolve from the current best individuals. Rather, it is often the case that only average-fit or below-average individuals provide the basis for mutations or recombinations to above-average individuals.

Figure 10.13
The path toward a perfect overlapping.

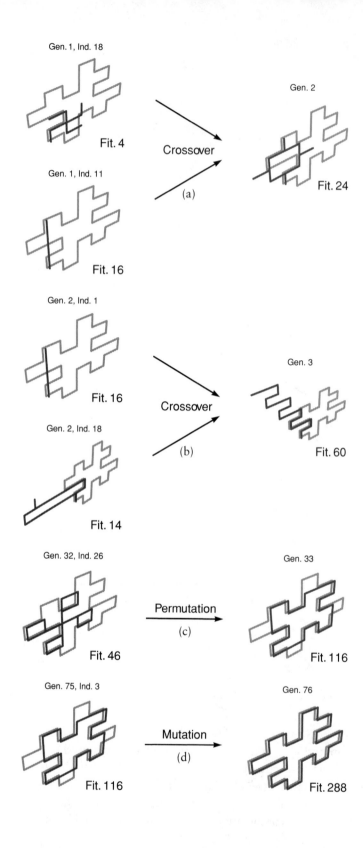

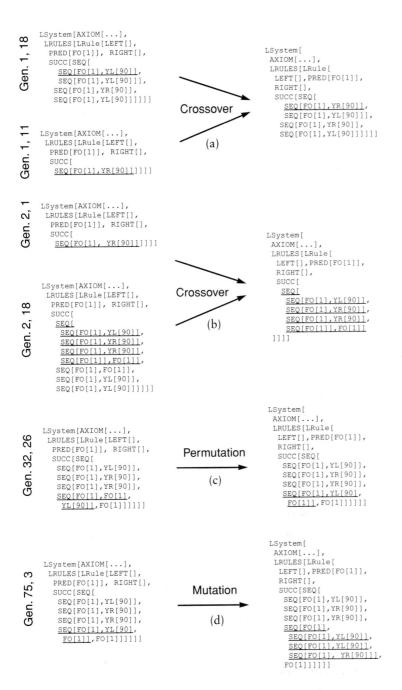

Figure 10.14
The (genotypical) path
toward a perfect L-system.

Especially the recombination operator seems to contribute much to the composition of more complex structures in the genotypes. This operator also provides sufficient "genetic material" for the other structure modifiers to arrive at improved genotypical structures.

The evolutionary path toward an "optimal" L-system

In generation 1 (Figure 10.13[a]), the effect of the crossover operator corresponds to that of a simple mutation, while in generation 2 the recombination has a deletion effect (b). Changing the order of a subsection of the turtle commands by a permutation operator in generation 32 leads to a first suboptimal overlap with the reference structure (c). The genotype resulting from this operation provides the starting point for the last, decisive mutation step to the optimum (d). More examples of L-system inference are discussed in the Evolvica notebooks on the *IEC* Web site (see Preface).

10.3   Bibliographical notes

Lindenmayer systems

Cellular interaction in development

The classic article on how to use rewrite systems to model cellular development is Aristid Lindenmayer's "Mathematical Models for Cellular Interaction in Development" (1968).

Automata, Languages, Development

In *Automata, Languages, Development*, Lindenmayer and Rozenberg give an overview of rewrite systems, including graph grammars and L-systems, and their applicability to model developmental processes (Lindenmayer and Rozenberg 1975).

Structure, languages, and growth functions

P. Vitányi studies L-systems and their relation to growth functions in *Lindenmayer Systems: Structure, Languages, and Growth Functions* (Vitányi 1980).

Dendritic growth

P. Hamilton describes his methodology and implementation of how to use L-systems for computing dendritic growth in neural networks (Hamilton 1994).

L-systems, fractals, and plants

In *Lindenmayer Systems, Fractals, and Plants*, Jim Hanan and Przemyslaw Prusinkiewicz present an L-system programming environment for simulating growth patterns of fractal and branching structures (Prusinkiewicz and Hanan 1989).

Evolution of Lindenmayer systems

GP inference of CA and L-system rules

John Koza describes his genetic programming approach of evolving L-system rules for fractal structures in Koza 1993.

A meta-evolution strategy for evolving L-systems on the basis of genetic algorithms and evolution strategies is described in Kókai, Ványi, et al. 1998. A promising application of L-systems to model blood vessels and their development is proposed in Kókai, Tóth, et al. 1999.

Evolution of L-systems

Gabriela Ochoa gives an overview of genetic algorithm evolution of Lindenmayer systems in Ochoa 1998.

GAs and L-systems

Using a GP approach to breed and coevolve L-systems for three-dimensional designs is described and nicely illustrated in *Exploring Three-Dimensional Design Worlds Using Lindenmayer Systems and Genetic Programming* (Coates, Broughton, et al. 1999).

3D design worlds

11 Artificial Plant Evolution

*We explore the world
with imperfect, lopsided
and incomplete models—
as if we were blind
and had to invent our
own methods of seeing.*

Rudi Gerharz
(author's translation)

Imagine watching a time-lapse animation of a sprout developing into an adult plant. Stalks are formed; they become longer and stronger; leaves emerge and grow in size. Finally, magnificent blooms unfold. How can we model structure formation processes like these? Can we design Lindenmayer systems that describe and model such morphogenetic processes?

Evolution of plant structures

This chapter provides a glimpse of the evolution of plantlike structures when L-systems are used in combination with genetic programming techniques. We specifically focus on simple inflorescent plants, demonstrating how realistic-looking growth simulations and their evolution can be modeled with genetically bred L-systems. Turtle interpretations implement the mapping from the developmental programs to sequences of three-dimensional graphics, which can be easily animated in Evolvica. For further details on the experiments and implementation concepts presented in this chapter, visit the *IEC* Web site (see Preface).

L-systems

The encoding of the growth programs is accomplished by using parallel rule systems in the form of Lindenmayer systems, introduced in Sections 9.2 and 10.1. The L-system genomes are represented by symbolic expressions. In the course of each evolution experiment, the

Genetic L-system
programming

genotypical structures are subject to variations and selections. Even
for extremely simple L-systems, this *genetic L-system programming*
(GLP) approach leads to an amazing diversity of evolvable structures,
as we have already illustrated with the L-system inference of fractal
structures in Chapter 10. Again we intend to make use of this inherent
"creativity" of evolutionary systems, which results from the synthesis
of encoded rule systems, genome variations, and selections. Here the
objective is to infer more complex and, to a certain degree, optimized
L-systems for inflorescent plants.

Objective of the evolution?

Unlike the setup in the previous chapter, where we wanted to
evolve a structure that matches perfectly with a reference fractal, in
the following sections the objective of the evolution is not predefined.
In complex pattern formation processes, it is often impossible to give
a precise definition of an evaluation function. Rather, we have to con-
tent ourselves with the fact that only certain features of the evolved
structures can be determined with a fitness function. Additional traits,
which cannot be immediately covered by the evaluation function, may
then be selected by interactive breeding techniques.

Section overview

In the following sections, we first describe a typical example of an
L-system for modeling the morphogenesis of plantlike structures (Section 11.1). The breeding of artificial flowers, exhibiting particular
characteristics in regard to structure compositions and growth patterns, will be demonstrated in Section 11.2 and Section 11.3. In Section 11.4, we outline extensions of L-systems for the modeling of
plants. Finally, Section 11.5 describes coevolutionary effects in a plant
ecosystem.

11.1 The ArtFlower garden

We use symbolic expressions to encode the genomes, representing Lindenmayer systems that simulate growth processes of artificial plants.

L-system of a flowering plant

A parallel rewrite system G_{Lychnis} is shown in Figure 11.1. This L-
system models the pattern formation of an angiosperm, a flowering
plant, from the formation of a sprout to its full inflorescence. The system simulates the formation of branching structures, the growth of
stalk segments and leaves, and the expression of blooms and their
decay. G_{Lychnis} is an extended variant of the L-system for the rose

Lychnis coronaria

Lychnis coronaria described in Prusinkiewicz and Lindenmayer 1990,
pp. 83 ff.

Macro turtle commands

The strings encoded by the rule system G_{Lychnis} are interpreted as
turtle commands, as described in Section 9.2.3 and Section 9.2.4. In
addition to the standard turtle commands, we use macros for scaled

$G_{\text{Lychnis}} = (\Sigma, \pi = \{p_1, \ldots, p_9\}, \alpha)$

$\Sigma = \{\text{f}, \text{pd}, \text{pu}, \textit{sprout}, \textit{stalk}, \textit{leaf}, \textit{Leaf}, \textit{bloom}\}$

Figure 11.1
L-system for modeling
structure formations of a
flowering plant.

α: $\textit{sprout}(4)$

π: **A sprout initiating two leaves and a bloom:**

p_1: $\textit{sprout}(4) \quad \rightarrow \quad$ f $\textit{stalk}(2)$ [pd(60) $\textit{leaf}(0)$]
pu(20) [pu(25) $\textit{sprout}(0)$]
[pd(60) $\textit{leaf}(0)$] pd(20)
[pu(25) $\textit{sprout}(2)$]
f stalk(1) $\textit{bloom}(0)$

Ripening of sprouts:

p_2: $\textit{sprout}(t < 4) \rightarrow \quad \textit{sprout}(t + 1)$

Elongation of stalks:

p_3: $\textit{stalk}(t > 0) \quad \rightarrow \quad$ f f $\textit{stalk}(t - 1)$

Variation of leaf sizes:

p_4: $\textit{leaf}(t) \qquad \rightarrow \quad \textit{leaf}(t + 1.5)$
p_5: $\textit{leaf}(t > 7) \quad \rightarrow \quad \textit{Leaf}(7)$
p_6: $\textit{Leaf}(t) \qquad \rightarrow \quad \textit{Leaf}(t - 1.5)$
p_7: $\textit{Leaf}(t < 2) \quad \rightarrow \quad \textit{leaf}(0)$

Bloom growth and "decay":

p_8: $\textit{bloom}(t) \qquad \rightarrow \quad \textit{bloom}(t + 1)$
p_9: $\textit{bloom}(7) \qquad \rightarrow \quad \textit{bloom}(1)$

representations of blooms (*bloom*) and leaves (*leaf*, *Leaf*). The symbols *sprout* and *stalk* are ignored by the turtle interpretation. The f command, which normally advances the turtle forward, is a macro command, too, and is interpreted as follows:

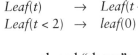

The forward moves (FO) are accompanied by a small rotation (YR) around the vertical axis of the turtle. Hence, an f command results in a short, slightly bent stalk segment. In combination with the other turtle commands, this results in an overall more natural appearance of the plant structure.

Structure formation
and growth

The growth modeling in Figure 11.1 commences with a ripe sprout, axiom *sprout(4)*, which has no graphical representation. The first production, p_1, replaces the sprout with two stalk segments, f *stalk(2)* and f *stalk(1)*, at the branch node of which two leaves, *leaf(0)*, are expressed. Between the leaves, sprouts for additional shoots (*sprout*) appear, which differ only in the time needed for ripening: *sprout(0)* and *sprout(2)*. At the very top of the stalk, *bloom(0)* initiates the expression of a flower. However, a bloom, *bloom(t)*, is only visible for $t > 0$ (Figure 11.2, iterations 1 and 2).

Growth and recursive
branching

Although production p_1 describes the basic plant structure and its branching dynamics, additional rules control the growth of the subcomponents. Production p_2 advances the ripening status of a sprout. Whenever level 4 is reached, new recursively branching structures are generated. Besides the growth rules for leaves and blooms (p_4, p_5), some productions make leaves "shrink" (p_6, p_7) after they have

Figure 11.2
Growth simulation by turtle interpretation of the L-system of Figure 11.1: iterations 1–4.

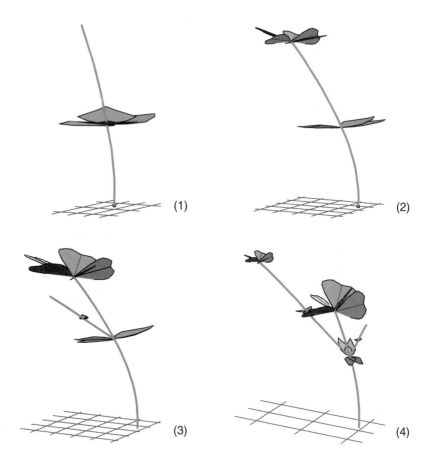

(1)

(2)

(3)

(4)

reached a maximum size, *leaf(7)*. An analogous mechanism is used for the blooms, which, however, decay in only a single step (*p*₉).

In Figure 11.2 and Figure 11.3 the growth process of a plant structure modeled with this L-system is visualized. The plant exhibits a multiple-branched growth pattern, with blooms and leaves in different stages of development. In order to make the generated plant structures appear more natural, small variations are inserted. The growth steps (forward turtle movements) vary by 20%, the angles for the turtle rotations by 10%.

Whereas in Figures 11.2 and 11.3 the plants are scaled to show most details, Figure 11.4 allows for a direct comparison of the unscaled plant sizes in different stages of their development.

The described L-system, the extended turtle interpretations, and the additional options for controlling the growth processes are summarized in the Evolvica notebooks, available on the *IEC* Web site (see Preface). These notebooks also contain an animated version of the growth process depicted in Figure 11.2 and Figure 11.3, which gives a more lively impression of the pattern formation processes involved.

On the basis of this *Lychnis coronaria* L-system variant, the following sections will demonstrate how additional variants of this plant species can be evolved by genetic programming and interactive breeding. We will show what effects, caused by mutations and recombinations in the L-system genomes, occur in the morphogenetic patterns of the encoded structures. Finally, we demonstrate how the evolutionary process can be directed toward specific traits by including interactive breeding.

11.2 Breeding artificial flowers

Starting from the "wild type" specified by the L-system G_{Lychnis}, we will evolve or breed a number of *Lychnis coronaria* mutants. These mutated plant structures should exhibit specific phenotypical features, such as fast growth or increased inflorescence. Genetic programming will help us to achieve this goal. Structural mutations on the L-system descriptions lead to new developmental programs and consequently to newly expressed traits of the encoded plant. The automatic selection of plants with specific growth and form characteristics is controlled by fitness functions. The evolved plant individuals then form the basis for further iterated breedings.

Evolution of the Lychnis *wild type*

In Section 11.2.1, we introduce the building blocks that we use for generating plant-encoding L-systems. All building blocks are specified by templates. We next give an overview of the genetic operators

Section overview

Figure 11.3
Growth simulation by turtle
interpretation of the
L-system of Figure 11.1:
iterations 5–10.

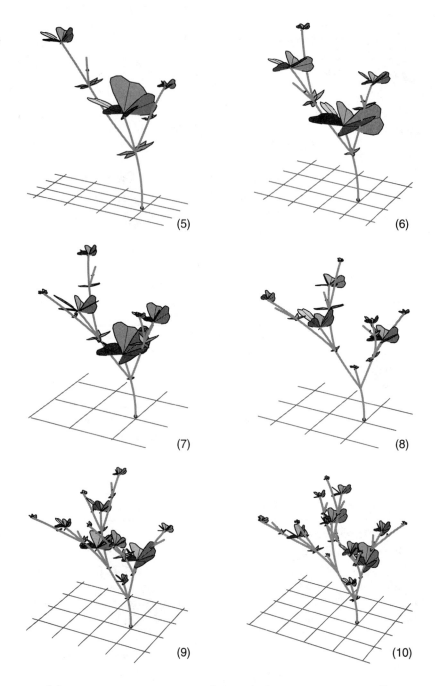

used for structure mutations on the symbolic expressions. Finally, we
define a fitness function that favors wide-spreading plants with a large
number of flowers. Section 11.2.2 illustrates a simple breeding experiment that results in a first set of mutants of the *Lychnis* wild type. In

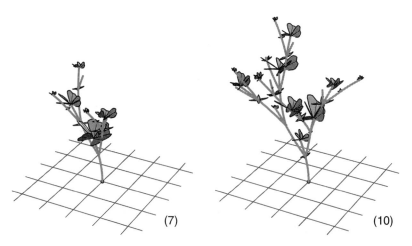

Figure 11.4
Comparing the sizes of the
generated "plants."

(7)   (10)

Sections 11.2.3 and 11.2.4, we discuss in detail how specific features of the phenotypes result from mutations and recombinations in the genotypical structures. In Section 11.3 we conclude with the description of another breeding experiment where we try to evolve lushly blooming, bushy flower arrangements.

11.2.1 Preparations for the breeding experiments

In order to generate an initial population of L-systems, with which we can start our breeding experiments, we have to describe the expression syntax and basic building blocks for composing the L-system representations. In Figure 11.5 these building blocks are specified as a list of weighted templates, which we use both for newly generating complete L-systems and for regenerating substructures, such as rules or command sequences.

The bracketed numbers to the right of each template in Figure 11.5 denote their weights. The first template describes the term representation of an L-system, consisting of an axiom (_AXIOM) and a list of L-rules (_LRULES). The second template determines the axiom. The third template, specifying the set of productions (LRULES [...]), contains a complete description of the $G_{Lychnis}$ L-system (cf. Figure 11.1). The first LRule term corresponds to production p_1 in Figure 11.1, the second term specifies production p_2, and so on. In addition, the first LRule template contains the pattern ___SEQ. This enables the base rule (production p_1) to be extended by new command sequences, which allows for generating slight variations of the *Lychnis* L-system. The final argument of the LRULES template, the pattern

Description of the templates

Predefined and new rules

Figure 11.5
Weighted templates as
building blocks for the
representation of ArtFlower
L-systems.

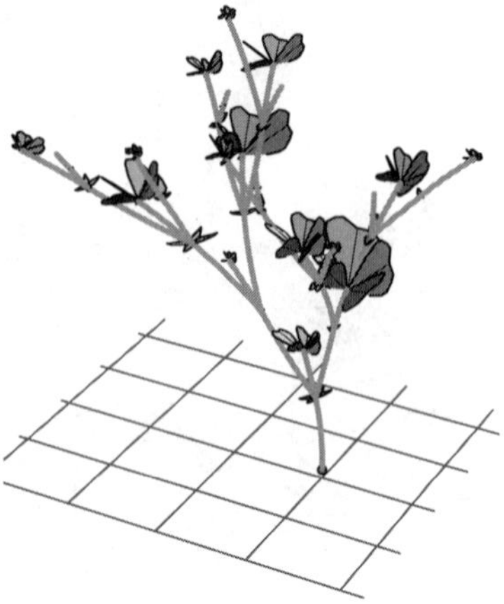

```
LSystem[_AXIOM,_LRULES],              (1)

AXIOM[sprout[4]],                     (1)

LRULES[
  LRule[LEFT[], PRED[ sprout[4] ],
          RIGHT[],
          SUCC[
            SEQ[
              SEQ[f],SEQ[stalk[2]],
              STACK[pu[60],leaf[0]],
              SEQ[rr[90]],
              STACK[pu[20],sprout[3]],
              SEQ[rr[90]],
              ___SEQ,
              STACK[pu[60],leaf[0]],
              SEQ[rr[90]],
              STACK[pu[20],sprout[2]],
               SEQ[f],SEQ[stalk[1]],
              bloom[0]
            ]
          ]
  ],    (1)
  LRule[LEFT[], PRED[ sprout["t_/;t < 4"] ], RIGHT[], SUCC[sprout[t + 1]]
  LRule[LEFT[], PRED[ stalk["t_/;t > 0"] ], RIGHT[],
        SUCC[SEQ[f,f,stalk[t - 1]]]],
  LRule[LEFT[], PRED[ leaf["t_"] ], RIGHT[], SUCC[ leaf[t + 1.5]]],
  LRule[LEFT[], PRED[ leaf["t_/;t > 4"] ], RIGHT[], SUCC[ Leaf[4]]],
  LRule[LEFT[], PRED[ Leaf["t_"] ], RIGHT[],SUCC[ Leaf[t - 1.5]]],
  LRule[LEFT[], PRED[ Leaf["t_/;t < 2"] ], RIGHT[], SUCC[ leaf[0]]],
  LRule[LEFT[], PRED[ bloom["t_"] ], RIGHT[], SUCC[ bloom[t + 1]]],
  LRule[LEFT[], PRED[ bloom[6] ], RIGHT[], SUCC[ bloom[1]]],
  ___LRule
],                                                              (1)

LRule[LEFT[],_PRED,RIGHT[],_SUCC],                              (1)

PRED[sprout[aIndex]],                                           (1)
SUCC[_SEQ | _STACK],                                           (1)

SEQ[BlankSequence[_sprout | _stalk | _leaf | _bloom | _f |
                  _YL | _YR | _PU | _PD | _RL | _RR | _SEQ]],   (1)
SEQ[BlankSequence[_sprout | _stalk | _leaf | _bloom | _f |
                  _YL | _YR | _PU | _PD | _RL | _RR ]],         (4)
STACK[BlankSequence[_sprout | _stalk | _leaf | _bloom | _f |
                  _YL | _YR | _PU | _PD | _RL | _RR | _STACK]], (1)
STACK[BlankSequence[_sprout | _stalk | _leaf | _bloom | _f |
                  _YL | _YR |_PU | _PD | _RL | _RR ]],          (4)

FO[stepSize],
YL[yawAngle], YR[yawAngle],                          (1),    (1)
PU[pitchAngle], PD[pitchAngle],                      (1),    (1)
RL[rollAngle], RR[rollAngle],                        (1),    (1)

sprout[sproutIndex], stalk[stalkIndex],              (1),    (1)
leaf[leafIndex], bloom[bloomIndex]                   (2),    (2)
```

L-rules

___LRule, allows for another modification of the rule set, where totally new rules may be inserted.

The basic structure of the L-system rules is described by the fourth template, LRule[LEFT[], _PRED, RIGHT[], _SUCC]. The empty LEFT and RIGHT terms account for context-free productions. For the left side of a rule, the predecessor, only sprout terms with an arbitrary index from the set $\{0, 1, \ldots, 4\}$ are allowed. The right side of a rule, the successor, can be composed of a nested sequence of SEQ and STACK expressions, where both recursive and nonrecursive templates are provided. The nonrecursive templates receive a higher weight (4:1), which, on average, leads to an implicit limitation for the depth of the generated rule expressions.

The remaining templates specify parametrized expressions, where *Parametrized expressions* each symbol stepSize, yawAngle, pitchAngle, rollAngle, and all symbols of the form xIndex denote a random number from a respectively defined interval. These templates appear to be relatively complex compared to the ones in Section 8.1.3 or 10.2. However, for the composition of new L-system rules, we want to allow for all the essential turtle commands and the use of macros (sprout, stalk, leaf, bloom) to be built into the L-systems in any order (SEQ) and any bracketing (STACK).

By integrating a fully functional L-system into the templates set, we can make sure that each symbolic expression genome, generated from these templates, results in an inflorescent, growing plant structure after turtle interpretation. This is true at least before any mutation starts to modify the overall structure of any L-system genome. Inserting the growth rules among the building blocks is also an essen- *The "critical mass" of preset* tial precondition for this kind of L-system evolution to be successful *structures* and to be manageable within acceptable computing time constraints. We cannot expect that from a randomly generated set of L-systems, growing plantlike structure encodings could be evolved. Consequently, we start our evolution experiments with a certain "critical mass," like a breeder who starts from a wild type and its complete genome structure. A successful breeding experiment would then elaborate on specific features of the wild type or on characteristics that emerge during this controlled evolution process.

However, these presettings only help the evolution system at the very beginning of an experiment; that is, whenever new L-systems are composed or new substructures are generated by mutations. The operators used for modifying the expression structures, which are *Genetic operators* listed in Figure 11.6, may alter any of the expressions. All operators may choose SEQ or STACK terms and modify these accordingly. Mutations are also applicable to LRule expressions, which enables the evolution system to recompose any of the L-system rules. Recombinations may exchange SEQ, STACK, and LRule terms among different L-system genomes.

The unary genetic operators of deletion, duplication, and permutation work both on complete rules (LRULES) and on command sequences (SEQ) or bracketed modules (STACK) of the successors.

Figure 11.6
ArtFlowers:
genetic operators.

Operator	Weight	Selection template	Template weight
Mutation	2	_LRule _SEQ _STACK	1 2 2
Recombination	2	_LRule _SEQ _STACK	1 2 2
Deletion	1	{LRULES, x__ /;Length[{x}] > 1} {SEQ, x__ /;Length[{x}] > 1} {STACK, x__ /;Length[{x}] > 1}	1 2 2
Duplication	1	{LRULES, x__ /;Length[{x}] > 1} {SEQ, x__ /;Length[{x}] > 1} {STACK, x__ /;Length[{x}] > 1}	1 2 2
Permutation	1	{LRULES, x__ /;Length[{x}] > 1} {SEQ, x__ /;Length[{x}] > 1} {STACK, x__ /;Length[{x}] > 1}	1 2 2

They delete, duplicate, or change the ordering of any of these specified substructures. The templates ensure that only those expressions are selected for which these operations make sense; the expressions must contain at least two arguments.

Selection templates

We briefly explain our notation for templates with the following example of a selection pattern (see the Evolvica notebooks or Jacob 1995, Jacob 1996a, and Jacob 1996b for details):

{LRULES, x__ /; Length[{x}] > 1]}.

The instance set of this template contains all expressions with head symbol LRULES, which have at least two (LRule) terms as their arguments. Analogous descriptions hold for the {SEQ,...} and {STACK,...} templates.

All the selection templates are attributed by weights such that, for example, SEQ or STACK expressions, which compete with LRule or

LRULES terms for being part of the composition, are selected at a ratio of 4 to 1. Consequently, the right-hand sides of rules are modified more frequently. However, modifications of L-rules (LRule) or production sets (LRULES) are not completely excluded. For further details on selection templates of genetic operators, see the Evolvica notebooks on the *IEC* Web site and Jacob 1996a, 1996b.

The following sections describe a few evolution experiments on artificial plant structures for which some typical breeding effects appear, such as the evolution of specific structural traits.

11.2.2 First variants of the *Lychnis* wild type

Starting from the *Lychnis* L-system in Figure 11.1, we want to evolve its plant structures into variants of increased width and height that also carry more flowers than the wild type. A suitable evaluation function for the L-system genomes and their corresponding phenotypes can be formulated as follows. Each L-system G is applied for a fixed number N of iterations. By using the turtle interpretation function τ, the resulting strings are mapped into graphical, three-dimensional representations. The fitness criterion $\mu(G)$ of an L-system G is then defined as the product of the number of blooms and a measure for the overall extension of the encoded plant:

$$\mu(G) = B(G_N) \cdot (\Delta x(\tau(G_N)) + \Delta y(\tau(G_N)) + \Delta z(\tau(G_N))).$$ *Plant evaluation*

Here G_N denotes the string resulting from N L-system iterations and $\tau(G_N)$ is the phenotype; that is, the graphics generated by the turtle interpretation of the N-th iteration of L-system G.

Since the turtle command sequence G_N, generated by the L-system, provides us with an implicit description of the plant structure in the form of a symbolic expression, we only have to count the *bloom* expressions in G_N if we want to calculate the number of expressed blooms, $B(G_N)$. In the symbolic representation of the plant graphics, however, this information would not be immediately accessible, because each bloom is composed of several polygons, such that the graphical elements corresponding to a single bloom would be much harder to identify.

Counting the blooms

In order to measure the plant's dimensions along the three main axes, we must refer to its graphical representation. Each plant is described by a Graphics3D expression, as is true for all 3D graphics generated in Mathematica. This symbolic expression contains all the graphical elements (lines, polygons, etc.), together with their coordinates, of which the graphical scene is composed. In this expression we

Measuring the plant

Wide, high plants with many blooms

have to find the minimum and maximum x, y, and z coordinates, from which we calculate the width Δx, depth Δx, and height Δz of the graphical structure $\tau(G_N)$.

This fitness function does favor wide, high plants with many blooms. Let us look at a typical breeding experiment for this fitness evaluation. To make the display of the whole population easier and because some essential evolutionary effects are observable even within small populations, we use only six individuals per generation. Also, since most of the computing time for these example experiments is used for producing the graphics and their display on the screen, smaller populations make the simulated breeding process more manageable.

Initial population

We start from the six L-system genomes depicted in Figure 11.7 as generation 2. All these L-systems are randomly generated using the templates in Figure 11.5. The plant structures represent the sixth iteration of each L-system. Although these L-systems share the base rules integrated in the templates, obviously different phenotypes result from the stochastic generation process. They range from nongrowing structures (individual 4) or structures with only two leaves (individual 5) to plants that exhibit the essential characteristics of the *Lychnis* wild type (cf. individual 1 of iteration 6 from Figure 11.3).

Further generations

Figures 11.7 through 11.9 show an example evolution experiment over another six generations. The number of iterations N is constant (here $N = 6$) for each L-system. The individuals are selected in a fitness-proportionate manner (cf. Section 3.5.1). In the graphics, the fitness values are given on the left side below each plant structure.

Formation of complex structures

This brief example illustrates that this evolutionary system is capable of generating surprisingly complex structures after only a few generations. This effect is also visible in a rapid increase of the fitness values (Figure 11.10). The maximum fitness in the initial generation is 36.0, whereas the fitness in generation 8 has risen to 2500.

Ramification with long branches

Most of the individuals evolved reflect the characteristic branching pattern of the wild type plant from which we started. This is mostly due to the fact that the fitness criterion can be better fulfilled by bloom-carrying, wide ramifications. From generation to generation, plants with these traits prevail more and more. In generation 4, long branches are established within the population. An essential evolution step occurs in generation 5 for individuals 2 and 3. Blooms are distributed on the branching segments. The fitness is increased by another order of magnitude to values between 500 and 700. Further increases in fitness result from elongations of the stalks (generation 6, individual 5) or by reducing the time for ripening (generation 7, individual 4, and generation 8, individual 3).

Increase of the number of blooms

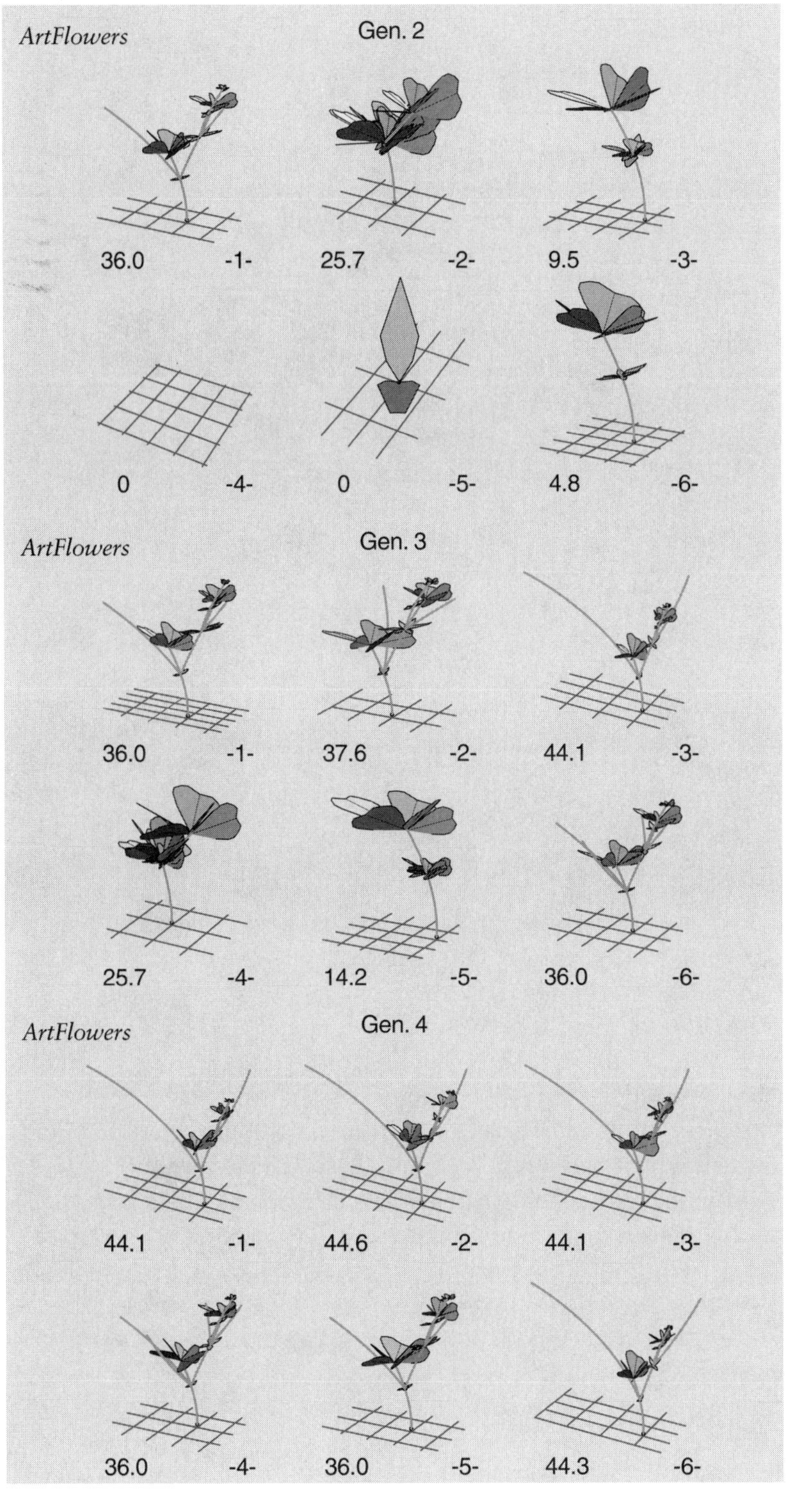

Figure 11.7
Evolution of flowering plants: generations 2–4.

Figure 11.8
Evolution of flowering plants:
generations 5–7.

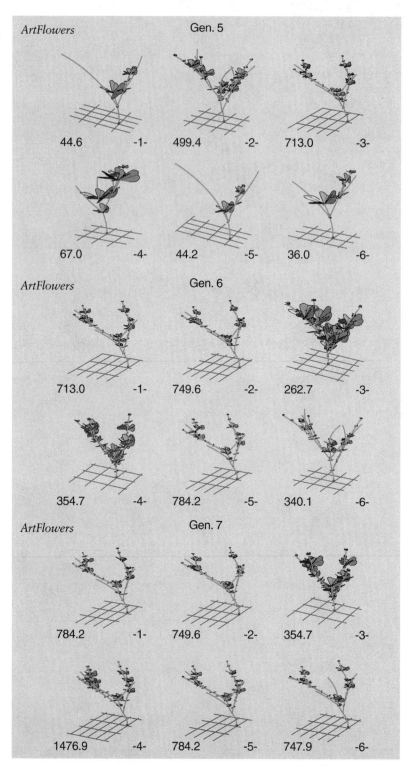

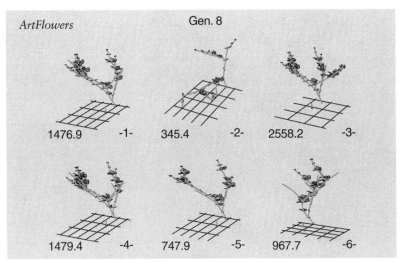

Figure 11.9
Evolution of flowering plants: generation 8.

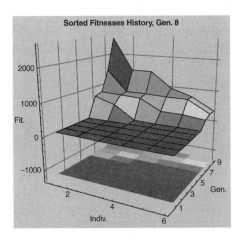

Figure 11.10
Fitness values for the *Lychnis* evolution experiment.

Figure 11.10 illustrates the evolution of the fitness values. The fitness curves are not continuously ascending but increase in rather large steps, which is especially true for the maximum fitness per generation. The transformation from expressions generated from an L-system to three-dimensional structures is a highly nonlinear process. Here we 0might draw the parallel to transcription processes as they occur in natural cells. Small modifications of the L-systems may result in dramatic effects on the corresponding phenotype.

Although the individuals of the first generations do not differ greatly in their evaluations, two individuals in generation 5 appear to be clearly superior to their competitors (Figure 11.8). Consequently, the average fitness is increased in the next generation. Now even three

Evolution of the fitness values

individuals are attributed with a high fitness value. A similar picture can be drawn for the two following generations. Again, a plant with superior fitness enters the stage and initiates an extreme saltation for the next generation (generation 8, individual 3).

11.2.3 Mutation effects

Genealogical tree of a Lychnis mutant

The phenotypical evolution just described, which leads to the best individual of generation 8 (Figure 11.9, individual 3), is depicted as a "genealogical tree" in Figure 11.11. This plant structure is created by iterated mutations and duplications only. In particular, no recombination operator is involved. Therefore, this plant's path of evolution from the first individual in the initial population (generation 2) can be followed step by step. Figure 11.11 reenacts this evolution for the phenotypes. The analogous evolutionary path for the program genomes is illustrated in Figures 11.12 through 11.14.

Step-by-step evolution of structural traits

Bloom-carrying branches

Elongation of stalks

The essential evolution steps described can be clearly identified by looking at the expressed characteristics of the plants (Figure 11.11). First of all, the branching stalk segments increase in length (generations 2, 3, and 4), as can be seen from the superimposed scales. When we keep in mind that increased florescence raises a plant's fitness, the decisive evolution jump results from the introduction of recursive, bloom-carrying branching structures (generation 5). Basically, the plants can generate a large number of blooms in two ways: they either produce extremely long stalks, along which blooms can be aligned, or the plant exploits its inherently parallel structure given by a multitude of ramifications.

Looking at the evolution over the next generations, we observe that exactly these characteristics are expressed by the plant structures (generations 6, 7, and 8). The dimensions of the plants are increasing, while more and more smaller branches are formed, which are densely occupied by flowers. This seems only a continuation and extension of the modules created in the fifth generation.

Evolution of the genome expressions

When we follow this evolution sequence on the level of genotypes, a closer inspection of the L-system encoding expressions unveils that no recombination operators are taking part in these structure modifications (Figures 11.12 through 11.14). The figures show the L-system genomes corresponding to the phenotypes in Figure 11.11. For each of these L-system encodings, only those sections are printed that are necessary to understand the mutation effects. The omitted expressions

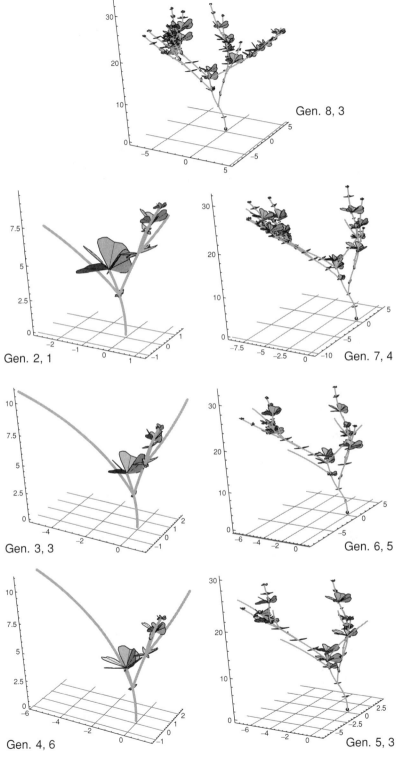

Figure 11.11
Genealogical tree of a *Lychnis* mutant.

Gen. 8, 3

Gen. 2, 1

Gen. 7, 4

Gen. 3, 3

Gen. 6, 5

Gen. 4, 6

Gen. 5, 3

Figure 11.12

Evolution of the best
genome from generation 8,
individual 3 (Figure 11.11).

```
Gen. 2, Indiv. 1:

LSystem[AXIOM[a[4]],
 LRULES[
  LRule[LEFT[], PRED[a[4]], RIGHT[],
   SUCC[SEQ[SEQ[f], SEQ[ii[2]],
    STACK[pd[60], l[0]], SEQ[rr[90]],
    STACK[pd[20], a[3]], SEQ[rr[90]],
    SEQ[ii[0], RR[17], l[2]],
    STACK[pd[60], l[0]], SEQ[rr[90]],
    STACK[pd[20], a[2]], SEQ[f],
    SEQ[ii[1]], m[0]]]],
  LRule[LEFT[], PRED[a[t_/;t < 4]], RIGHT[], SUCC[a[1 + t]]],
  ...
  LRule[LEFT[], PRED[m[6]], RIGHT[], SUCC[m[1]]],
  LRule[LEFT[], PRED[a[2]], RIGHT[], SUCC[STACK[ii[4], YR[34]]]],
  LRule[LEFT[], PRED[a[0]], RIGHT[], SUCC[STACK[YR[18], YR[18]]]]]]
```

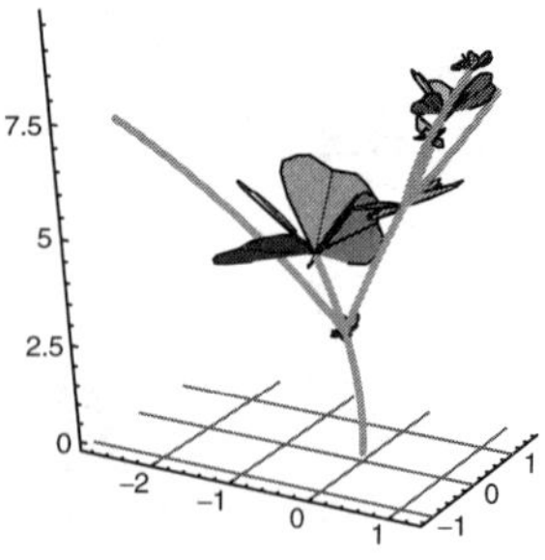

```
Gen. 3, Indiv. 3: (Duplication)

LSystem[AXIOM[a[4]],
 LRULES[
  LRule[LEFT[], PRED[a[4]], RIGHT[],
   SUCC[SEQ[SEQ[f], SEQ[ii[2]],
    STACK[pd[60], l[0]], SEQ[rr[90]],
    STACK[pd[20], a[3]], SEQ[rr[90]],
    SEQ[ii[0], RR[17], l[2]],
    STACK[pd[60], l[0]], SEQ[rr[90]],
    STACK[pd[20], a[2]], SEQ[f],
    SEQ[ii[1]], m[0]]]],
  LRule[LEFT[], PRED[a[t_/;t < 4]], RIGHT[], SUCC[a[1 + t]]],
  ...
  LRule[LEFT[], PRED[m[6]], RIGHT[], SUCC[m[1]]],
  LRule[LEFT[], PRED[a[2]], RIGHT[], SUCC[STACK[ii[4], ii[4], YR[34]]]]
  LRule[LEFT[], PRED[a[0]], RIGHT[], SUCC[STACK[YR[18], YR[18]]]]]]
```

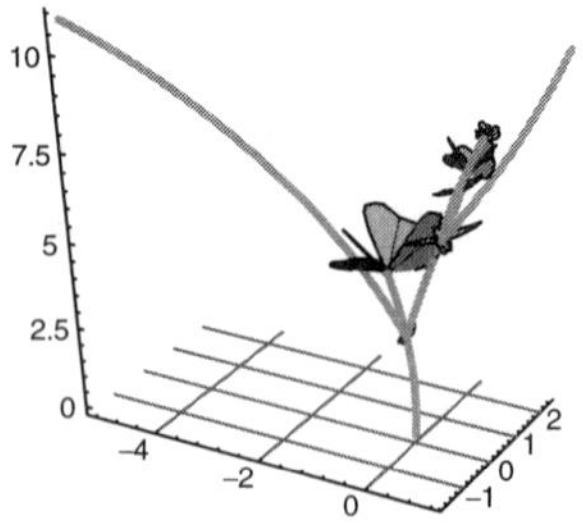

```
Gen. 4, Indiv. 6: (Duplication)

LSystem[AXIOM[a[4]],
 LRULES[
  LRule[LEFT[], PRED[a[4]], RIGHT[],
   SUCC[SEQ[SEQ[f], SEQ[ii[2]],
    STACK[pd[60], l[0]], SEQ[rr[90]],
    STACK[pd[20], a[3]], SEQ[rr[90]],
    SEQ[ii[0], RR[17], RR[17], l[2]],
    STACK[pd[60], l[0]], SEQ[rr[90]],
    STACK[pd[20], a[2]], SEQ[f],
    SEQ[ii[1]], m[0]]]],
  LRule[LEFT[], PRED[a[t_/;t < 4]], RIGHT[], SUCC[a[1 + t]]],
  ...
  LRule[LEFT[], PRED[m[6]], RIGHT[], SUCC[m[1]]],
  LRule[LEFT[], PRED[a[2]], RIGHT[], SUCC[STACK[ii[4], ii[4], YR[34]]]],
  LRule[LEFT[], PRED[a[0]], RIGHT[], SUCC[STACK[YR[18], YR[18]]]]]]
```

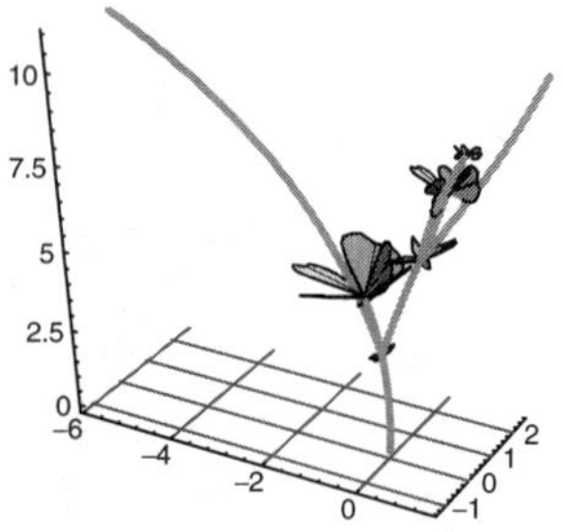

Gen. 5, Indiv. 3: (Mutation)

```
LSystem[AXIOM[a[4]],
 LRULES[
  LRule[LEFT[], PRED[a[4]], RIGHT[],
   SUCC[SEQ[SEQ[f], SEQ[ii[2]],
    STACK[pd[60], l[0]],
    SEQ[SEQ[f], SEQ[ii[2]]],
     STACK[pd[60], l[0]], SEQ[rr[90]],
     STACK[pd[20], a[3]], SEQ[rr[90]],
     SEQ[ii[3], m[4], RL[30]],
     STACK[pd[60], l[0]], SEQ[rr[90]],
     STACK[pd[20], a[2]], SEQ[f],
     SEQ[ii[1]], m[0]],
    STACK[pd[20], a[3]], SEQ[rr[90]],
    SEQ[ii[0], RR[17], RR[17], l[2]],
    STACK[pd[60], l[0]],
    SEQ[rr[90]], STACK[pd[20], a[2]],
    SEQ[f], SEQ[ii[1]], m[0]]]],
  LRule[LEFT[], PRED[a[t_/;t < 4]], RIGHT[], SUCC[a[1 + t]]],
  ...
  LRule[LEFT[], PRED[m[6]], RIGHT[], SUCC[m[1]]],
  LRule[LEFT[], PRED[a[2]], RIGHT[], SUCC[STACK[ii[4], ii[4], YR[34]]]],
  LRule[LEFT[], PRED[a[0]], RIGHT[], SUCC[STACK[YR[18], YR[18]]]]]]
```

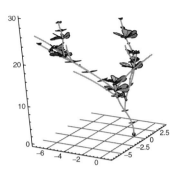

Figure 11.13
Evolution of the best genome from generation 8, individual 3 (Figure 11.11) *(continued).*

Gen. 6, Indiv. 5: (Duplication)

```
LSystem[AXIOM[a[4]],
 LRULES[
  LRule[LEFT[], PRED[a[4]], RIGHT[],
   SUCC[SEQ[SEQ[f], SEQ[ii[2]],
    STACK[pd[60], l[0]],
    SEQ[SEQ[f], SEQ[ii[2]]],
    STACK[pd[60], l[0]], SEQ[rr[90]],
    STACK[pd[20], a[3]], SEQ[rr[90]],
    SEQ[ii[3], m[4], RL[30]],
    STACK[pd[60], l[0]], SEQ[rr[90]],
    STACK[pd[20], a[2]], SEQ[f],
    SEQ[ii[1], ii[1]], m[0]],
    STACK[pd[20], a[3]], SEQ[rr[90]],
    SEQ[ii[0], RR[17], RR[17], l[2]],
    STACK[pd[60], l[0]], SEQ[rr[90]],
    STACK[pd[20], a[2]], SEQ[f],
    SEQ[ii[1]], m[0]]]],
  LRule[LEFT[], PRED[a[t_/;t < 4]], RIGHT[], SUCC[a[1 + t]]],
  ...
  LRule[LEFT[], PRED[m[6]], RIGHT[], SUCC[m[1]]],
  LRule[LEFT[], PRED[a[2]], RIGHT[], SUCC[STACK[ii[4], ii[4], YR[34]]]],
  LRule[LEFT[], PRED[a[0]], RIGHT[], SUCC[STACK[YR[18], YR[18]]]]]]
```

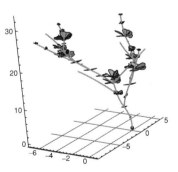

Figure 11.14
Evolution of the best
genome from generation 8,
individual 3 *(continued)*.

```
Gen. 7, Indiv. 4: (Mutation)

LSystem[AXIOM[a[4]],
 LRULES[
  LRule[LEFT[], PRED[a[4]], RIGHT[],
   SUCC[SEQ[SEQ[f], SEQ[ii[2]],
    STACK[pd[60], l[0]],
    SEQ[SEQ[f], SEQ[ii[2]],
    STACK[pd[60], l[0]], SEQ[rr[90]],
    STACK[pd[20], a[3]], SEQ[rr[90]],
    SEQ[ii[3], m[4], RL[30]],
    STACK[pd[60], l[0]], SEQ[rr[90]],
    STACK[pd[20], a[3]], SEQ[f],
    SEQ[ii[1], ii[1]], m[0]],
    STACK[pd[20], a[3]], SEQ[rr[90]],
    SEQ[ii[0], RR[17], RR[17], l[2]],
    STACK[pd[60], l[0]],
    SEQ[rr[90]], STACK[pd[20], a[2]],
    SEQ[f], SEQ[ii[1]], m[0]]]],
   LRule[LEFT[], PRED[a[t_/;t < 4]], RIGHT[], SUCC[a[1 + t]]],
   ...
   LRule[LEFT[], PRED[m[6]], RIGHT[], SUCC[m[1]]],
   LRule[LEFT[], PRED[a[2]], RIGHT[], SUCC[STACK[ii[4], ii[4], YR[34]]]],
   LRule[LEFT[], PRED[a[0]], RIGHT[], SUCC[STACK[YR[18], YR[18]]]]]]
```

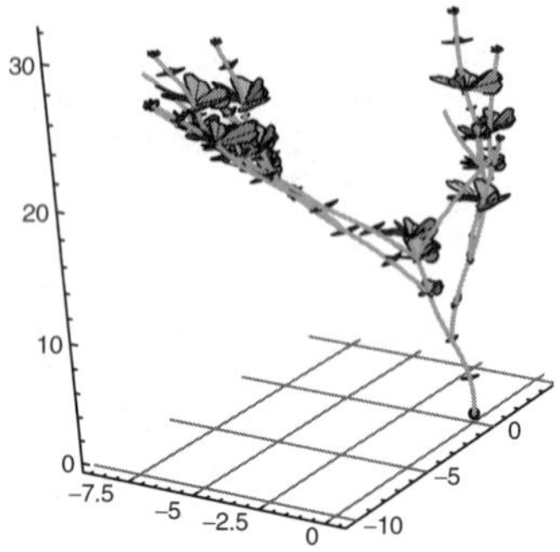

```
Gen. 8, Indiv. 3: (Mutation)

LSystem[AXIOM[a[4]],
 LRULES[
  LRule[LEFT[], PRED[a[4]], RIGHT[],
   SUCC[SEQ[SEQ[f], SEQ[ii[2]],
    STACK[pd[60], l[0]],
    SEQ[SEQ[f], SEQ[ii[2]],
    STACK[pd[60], l[0]], SEQ[rr[90]],
    STACK[pd[20], a[3]], SEQ[rr[90]],
    SEQ[ii[3], m[4], RL[30]],
    STACK[pd[60], l[0]], SEQ[rr[90]],
    STACK[pd[20], a[3]], SEQ[f],
    SEQ[ii[1], ii[1]], m[0]],
    STACK[pd[20], a[3]], SEQ[rr[90]],
    SEQ[ii[0], RR[17], RR[17], l[2]],
    STACK[pd[60], l[0]], SEQ[rr[90]],
    STACK[pd[20], a[2]],
    SEQ[f], SEQ[ii[1]], m[0]]]],
   LRule[LEFT[], PRED[a[t_/;t < 4]], RIGHT[], SUCC[a[1 + t]]],
   ...
   LRule[LEFT[], PRED[m[6]], RIGHT[], SUCC[m[1]]],
   LRule[LEFT[], PRED[a[2]], RIGHT[], SUCC[STACK[pd[20], a[3]]]],
   LRule[LEFT[], PRED[a[0]], RIGHT[], SUCC[STACK[YR[18], YR[18]]]]]]
```

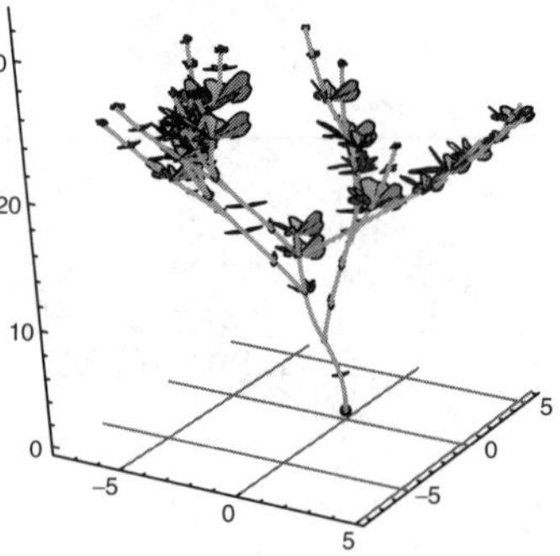

have been left unchanged by the genetic operators. To make the program genomes more readable, the following abbreviations are used:

      a = sprout, ii = stalk, l = leaf, m = bloom.

In all growth programs those subexpressions that are modified by mutation operators appear in boldface. For the first mutant (generation 3, individual 3) the `ii[4]` term within `STACK[ii[4]`, `YR[34]]` of the first individual in generation 2 is duplicated, which initiates another stalk segment.

Duplication

The double rotation (`RR[17]`) before the leaf expression in generation 4 does not cause any clearly visible phenotypical effect. The evolutionary jump in generation 5, however, is due to a major mutation, through which the genome is enhanced by commands for further ramification (increased number of `STACK` terms) and blooms (`m[4]`). All further evolutionary improvements rely on these newly created genetic building blocks.

Mutation

In generation 6, the length of some stalk segments has doubled (`SEQ[ii[1],ii[1],...]`). Another branch with an adjoining sprout (`STACK[pd[20,a[3]]`) is added in generation 7. Finally, in generation 8, one of the additional sprout rules (`...PRED[a[2]] ...`) is mutated in such a way that two stalk segments are substituted by another sprout initiator (`...SUCC[STACK[pd[20], a[3]]]...`).

Duplication

Mutation

Furthermore, the initial genome contains an increased set of L-rules. Two rules have been added, which would take care of expression sprouts (`PRED[a[2]]` and `PRED[a[0]]`) if the default rule for `PRED[a[t_/; t < 4]]` did not overrule them. However, the two additional rules would have a lethal effect on the whole plant structure, since it would not be able to recursively compose sprout elements. No a terms would appear on the right side of the rules. This observation reinforces our argument to include well-defined growth rules in the basic template set, because a random composition of rules would hardly lead to any of the desired morphogenetic effects.

Enhanced L-rule set

Unary mutation operators play a major role in our L-system evolution experiments. The importance of nonrecombining operators should therefore not be underestimated, as we have already demonstrated with the breeding of ant control programs in Chapter 9. On the other hand, recombination effects are the ones preferably utilized in breeder experiments. One plant has particularly lush flowers; another plant impresses through specific ramifications. Here recombinations would offer an opportunity to combine the two traits in a single plant. The following section will demonstrate such recombination effects with a few simple examples.

Mutations vs. recombinations

11.2.4 Recombination effects

Another example of an evolution sequence, which is partly illustrated in Figure 11.15, demonstrates how recombinations result in the expression of fitness-increasing characteristics. As in the previous experiment, we start from the *Lychnis* L-system wild type (cf. Section 11.1). Compare the plant population in Figure 11.15 with the plants evolved in Figure 11.9. The plants shown in Figure 11.15, which are evolved using recombination operators, accomplish more balanced branching structures, resulting in a more natural appearance of the plants (see e.g., generation 9, individual 2). The essential achievement of this evolution experiment is the expression of a third main sprout, following the growth direction of the central stalk (generation 5, individuals 1 and 3). This trait becomes more and more developed during the following four generations, where recombinations initiate the composition of further genome sections, which eventually result in these fitness-increasing features.

Equal branching

Let us look at two specific individuals that were evolved by crossing over (Figure 11.16). A phenotype with an additional large sprout results from the recombination of two individuals of the third generation. In their genotypes (Figure 11.17), the instruction for forming a leaf, STACK[pd[60], l[0]], is substituted by a command sequence to grow a sprout, STACK[pd[20], a[2]], which originally initiates the expression of one of the two main branches in the phenotype of the recombination partner. The resulting plant in generation 4 is identical to the two best individuals of generation 5 (individuals 1 and 3). An analogous effect is achieved from crossing over two identical genomes of generation 8. Once more a leaf, STACK[pd[60], l[0]], is replaced by a new sprout segment, STACK[pd[20], a[3]]. In the following, ninth generation, a plant with a multiple bifurcation pattern and an increased number of flowers originates. With the additional middle branch, the overall plant structure also appears more harmonic. The fitness of this plant, however, does not differ much from that of any other nonsymmetric structure (Figure 11.15, generation 9, individual 5). This situation exemplifies the difficulty of integrating criteria such as "esthetic and harmonic appearance" or "symmetry" into a fitness evaluation function. In a case like this, however, the evolutionary algorithm must rely on interactive selection. By determining that only mutants from the second individual should be part of the selection pool for the following generation, the evolutionary process becomes focused on the gradual improvement of specific traits.

An additional main sprout

Crossover of identical genomes

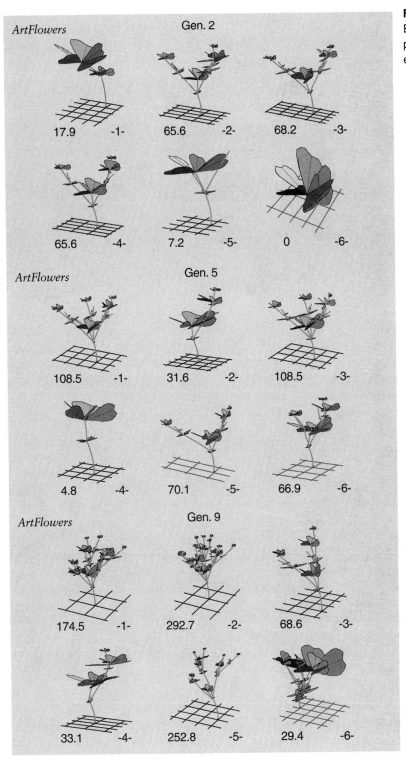

Figure 11.15
Evolution of inflorescent plants using recombination effects: generations 2–9.

Figure 11.16
Effects of recombination, shown with two phenotypes.

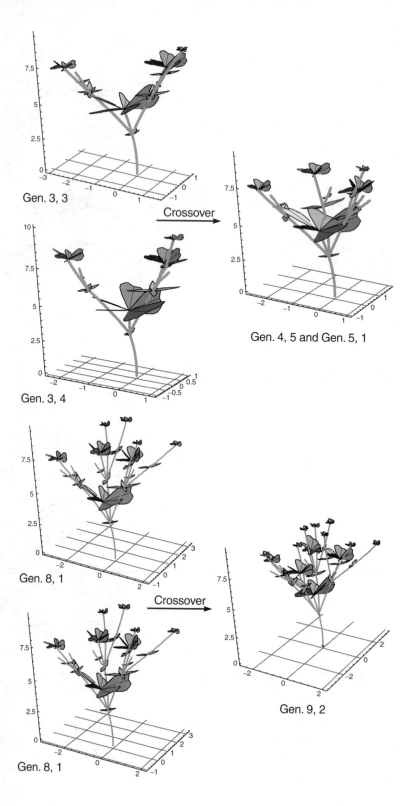

Gen. 3, 3

Crossover

Gen. 4, 5 and Gen. 5, 1

Gen. 3, 4

Gen. 8, 1

Crossover

Gen. 9, 2

Gen. 8, 1

```
LSystem[AXIOM[a[4]],
 LRULES[
  LRule[LEFT[], PRED[a[4]],    RIGHT[],
   SUCC[SEQ[SEQ[f], SEQ[ii[2]],
    STACK[pd[60], l[0]],
    SEQ[rr[90]],
    STACK[pd[20], a[3]],
    SEQ[rr[90]], SEQ[l[2]],
    STACK[pd[60], l[0]],
    SEQ[rr[90]], STACK[pd[20],
    a[2]], SEQ[f], SEQ[ii[1]],
    m[0]]]],
...]
```

Crossover →

```
LSystem[AXIOM[a[4]],
 LRULES[
  LRule[LEFT[], PRED[a[4]],
   RIGHT[],
   SUCC[SEQ[SEQ[f], SEQ[ii[2]],
    STACK[pd[20], a[2]],
    SEQ[rr[90]],
    STACK[pd[20], a[3]],
    SEQ[rr[90]], SEQ[l[2]],
    STACK[pd[60], l[0]],
    SEQ[rr[90]], STACK[pd[20],
    a[2]], SEQ[f], SEQ[ii[1]],
    m[0]]]],
...]
```

```
LSystem[AXIOM[a[4]],
 LRULES[
  LRule[LEFT[], PRED[a[4]],
   RIGHT[],
   SUCC[SEQ[SEQ[f], SEQ[ii[2]],
    STACK[pd[60], l[0]],
    SEQ[rr[90]],
    STACK[pd[20], a[3]],
    SEQ[rr[90]], SEQ[YR[10]],
    STACK[pd[60], l[0]],
    SEQ[rr[90]], STACK[pd[20],
    a[2]], SEQ[f], SEQ[ii[1]],
    m[0]]]],
...]
```

Figure 11.17
Effects of recombination,
shown with two genotypes.

```
LSystem[AXIOM[a[4]],
 LRULES[
  LRule[LEFT[], PRED[a[4]],
   RIGHT[],
   SUCC[SEQ[SEQ[f], SEQ[ii[2]],
    STACK[pd[20], a[3]],
    SEQ[rr[90]],
    STACK[pd[20], a[3]],
    SEQ[rr[90]], SEQ[l[2]],
    STACK[pd[60], l[0]],
    SEQ[rr[90]], STACK[pd[20],
    a[2]], SEQ[f], SEQ[ii[1]],
    m[0]]]],
...]
```

Crossover →

```
LSystem[AXIOM[a[4]],
 LRULES[
  LRule[LEFT[], PRED[a[4]],
   RIGHT[],
   SUCC[SEQ[SEQ[f], SEQ[ii[2]],
    STACK[pd[20], a[3]],
    SEQ[rr[90]],
    STACK[pd[20], a[3]],
    SEQ[rr[90]], SEQ[l[2]],
    STACK[pd[20], a[3]],
    SEQ[rr[90]], STACK[pd[20],
    a[2]], SEQ[f], SEQ[ii[1]],
    m[0]]]],
...]
```

```
LSystem[AXIOM[a[4]],
 LRULES[
  LRule[LEFT[], PRED[a[4]],
   RIGHT[],
   SUCC[SEQ[SEQ[f], SEQ[ii[2]],
    STACK[pd[20], a[3]],
    SEQ[rr[90]],
    STACK[pd[20], a[3]],
    SEQ[rr[90]], SEQ[l[2]],
    STACK[pd[60], l[0]],
    SEQ[rr[90]], STACK[pd[20],
    a[2]], SEQ[f], SEQ[ii[1]],
    m[0]]]],
...]
```

11.3 The ArtFlower garden in full bloom

In the previous examples of breeding plant-modeling L-systems, the generated structures are considered static. The fitness for each individual is calculated for the strings generated after a fixed number of L-system iterations and their resulting graphical interpretation. The

Taking the structure formation dynamics into account

growth processes per se were included in the fitness evaluation. Thus we demonstrate with a final example in this section how the dynamics of the structure formation can be included into the fitness function.

To compare the results achieved so far, we define a similar fitness function, now extended by a dynamic component. The fitness $\mu(G)$ of an L-system genome G is calculated as follows:

L-system evaluation

$$\mu(G) = \sum_{i=0}^{m} \Delta(\tau(G_i)) + 2 \cdot B(G_i) + L(G_i).$$

Here $\tau(G_i)$ denotes the turtle graphics generated from the string associated with the i-th iteration of L-system G. The extension, $\Delta(\tau(G_i))$, of this graphical structure in the x, y, and z directions is defined as

$$\Delta(\tau(G_i)) = \Delta x(\tau(G_i)) \cdot \Delta y(\tau(G_i)) \cdot \Delta z(\tau(G_i)).$$

The number of flowers (`bloom` terms) is denoted by $B(G_i)$, whereas $L(G_i)$ describes the number of leaves (`leaf` or `Leaf` terms) in the expression G_i. The parameter m stands for the maximum number of iterations for which the growth process is evaluated.

ArtFlower L-system breeding

Therefore, the total fitness of a plant is composed of the sum of its volume and the number of expressed flowers and leaves, where the partial sums are calculated for each iteration step. To fulfill these fitness criteria, a plant not only has to grow large and express many blooms and leaves at a certain developmental stage, but these criteria must be met as much as possible for each iteration step. This way, the dynamics of the growth process are also taken into account. The following breeding experiment starts with six randomly generated L-system genomes, where templates similar to the ones introduced in the previous examples are used. The Evolvica notebooks, available on the *IEC* Web site (see Preface), contain the program code, experimental results, and animations of the evolved plants.

Evolution's creativity

Figure 11.18 and Figure 11.19 illustrate certain stages of a breeding experiment over 13 generations (see also Color Plate 6). The initial L-systems encode relatively simple phenotypical structures. The creativity of evolution is shown in generation 4. Here a plant emerges, the structure of which is much more complex than its competitors' growth patterns. The individuals of the next generation reflect this increased complexity in growth and structure. The plants with simpler configurations disappear from the population.

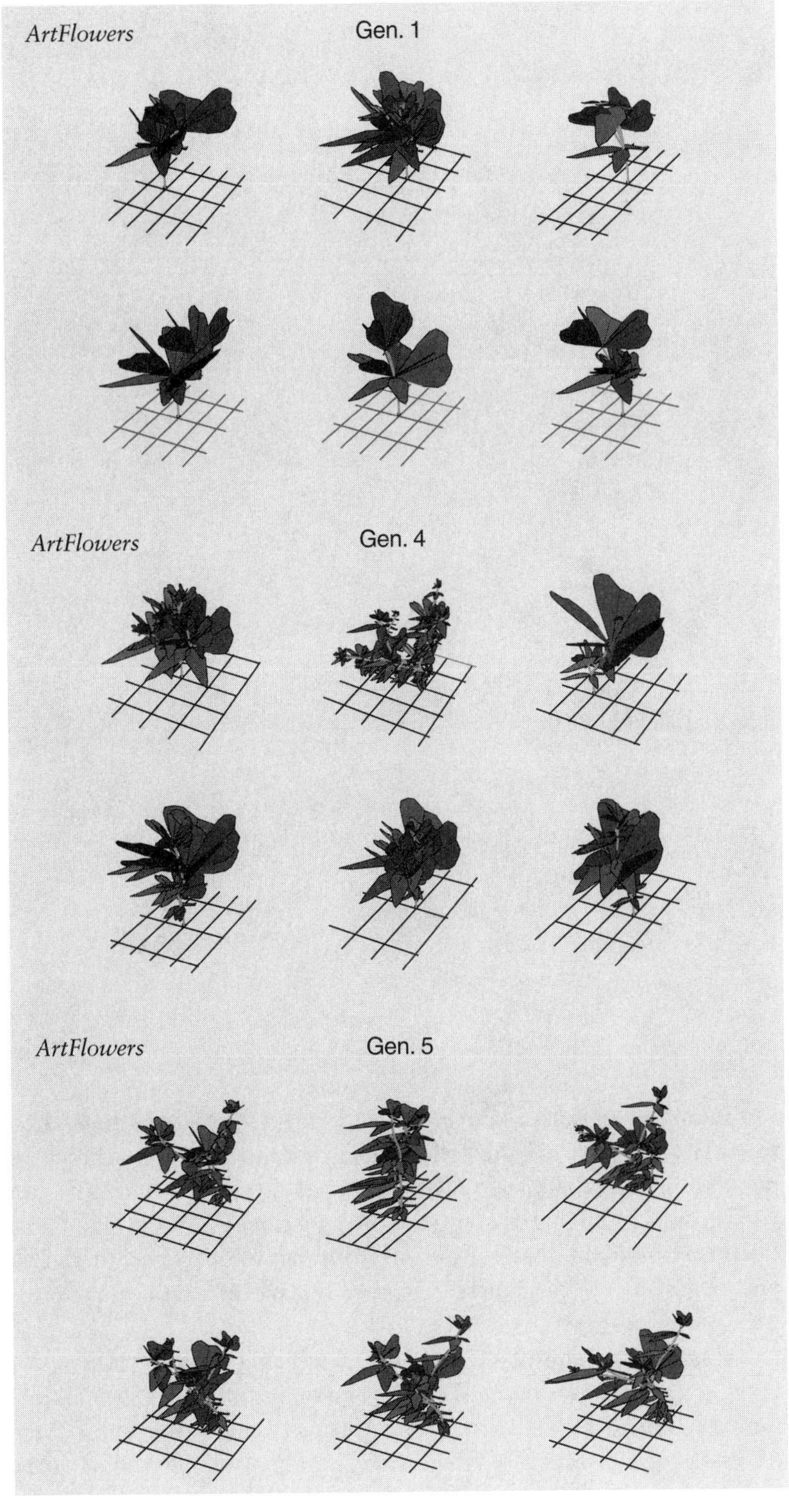

Figure 11.18
Inflorescent plants: generations 1, 4, and 5.

ArtFlowers   Gen. 1

ArtFlowers   Gen. 4

ArtFlowers   Gen. 5

Figure 11.19
Inflorescent plants:
generations 12 and 13.

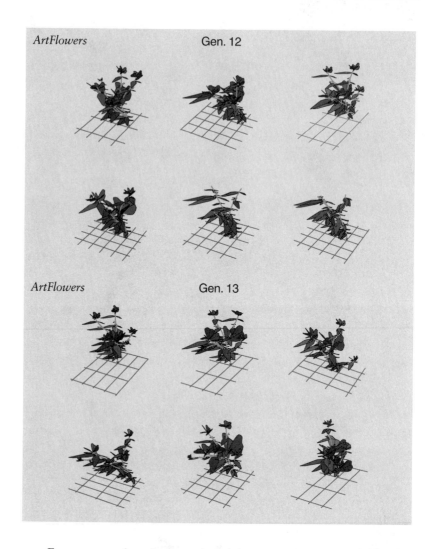

From generation 5 on, more elaborate structures unfold. This trend is continued for the following generations. Despite the small population size, the variety of the evolved structures is striking. In generation 12, there are even two plants without any flowers. Since the fitness function does not punish the absence of blooms, these two phenotypes meet the fitness criterion by an increased number of leaves.

Finally, in generation 13, the inflorescent plants have completely taken over. All the individuals differ from one another, yet they all feature the desired characteristics. The plants are growing in all three directions and display a relatively large number of flowers and leaves.

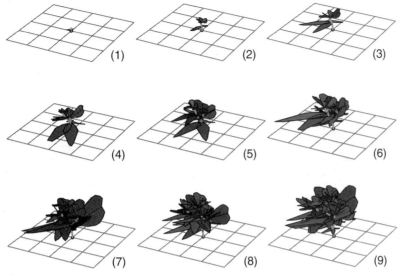

Figure 11.20
Growth of the best plant of generation 1.

The following considerations show that the plants did indeed improve their growth characteristics over the 13 generations. To illustrate how the structure formation processes are changing during evolution, we compare the best individual of the initial population (individual 1) with the best-evaluated plant of the last generation (individual 1). Figure 11.20 shows the first nine growth stages of the best plant in generation 1. The plant's dimensions do increase, and the leaves and blooms are growing. However, this growth sequence does not appear to be very realistic. Since this generation consists of only randomly generated phenotypes, this result is not surprising.

Comparing the growth dynamics

What kind of progress has our genetic L-system programming approach achieved? Let us look at the growth stages of the best-evaluated plant structure in generation 13 (Figure 11.21 and Color Plate 7). Obviously, this plant grows in a much more natural fashion. The number of flowers and leaves, expressed during the whole developmental period, has largely increased. In the end, the "creative potential of evolution" has provided us with a splendid flower bouquet (Jacob 1996b).

Genetic L-system programming

Evolutionary bloom . . .

11.4 Extensions for more realistic plant modeling

With the examples of plant evolution presented, we have shown that the combination of L-systems and evolution-based selection and mutation techniques provides a flexible approach both for L-system inference and for a detailed analysis of morphogenetic processes,

Figure 11.21
Growth of the best plant of
generation 13.

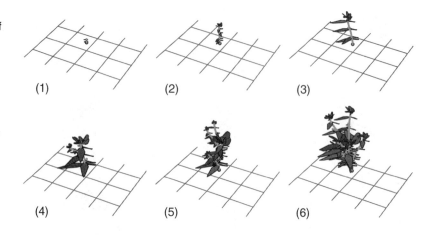

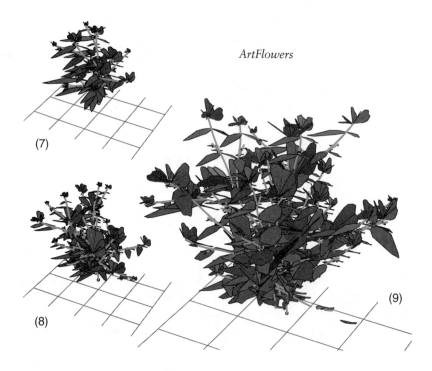

ArtFlowers

particularly in plants. Since we are using templates to generate the
genomes (plant growth programs) and to restrict the domain of the
genetic operators, the evolution system can, on the one hand, rely on a
multitude of diverse and composable structural building blocks. On
the other hand, the templates ensure that the majority of mutations do
not result in lethal effects but produce "reasonable" new phenotypic
variants, as is especially demonstrated by the examples in Section

11.3. However, we have not yet taken into account a few more aspects of our genetic L-system programming approach. Here is a brief outline of these ideas.

The evaluation function, which we have used to calculate a fitness value for each plant individual, considers only the number of flowers, the number of leaves, and the extension of the plant. Of course, the plant anatomy, the sizes of the flowers and leaves, and their position and orientation also play a major role in a plant's survival capability. These factors—and many more—should inspire researchers to develop extended, more sophisticated evaluation functions.

Extended evaluation functions

The growth dynamics of the plant structures are integrated in the evaluation only to a certain extent. In particular, whether the speeds of growth of the diverse submodules are within the ranges observed in natural plants must be taken into account.

Growth dynamics

To bring the simulations even closer to natural growth processes, the L-systems and their turtle interpretation functions could be extended as follows. Imagine an environmentally sensitive turtle that, for example, tends to point in the direction of a light source or the step size of which depends on the local amount of light that the turtle receives. A similar approach was proposed and tested by Mech and Prusinkiewicz (1996). Furthermore, imagine that each turtle action consumes a certain amount of energy, which is taken from a limited energy reservoir. This would implicitly constrain the possible growth processes, thus avoiding "superplants" that would grow without any bounds.

Environmentally sensitive turtle interpretation

Energetic turtle

The interaction of plants in an ecosystem is an additional aspect that will make simulations more realistic, with many possibilities for prediction and modeling. Coevolution within plant ecosystems is discussed in the following section.

11.5   Evolution of plant ecosystems

Another aspect of our plant evolution experiments that we have not yet considered is the *interaction* of phenotypes within a population. In the examples in Section 11.3, each plant individual exists in a self-sufficient environment and is evaluated independently of all the other plants in the population. If groups of L-systems are interpreted within their phenotypical environment in spatial relationship, the forming plant structures will enter a coevolutionary scenario with competition for necessary nutrients or sunlight. In this section, we discuss first steps toward the simulation of (plant) ecosystems and demonstrate our preliminary results with a few examples.

Plant interactions

Coevolution

What would a coevolutionary scenario look like that could be used to simulate and investigate interactions among phenotypical agents (e.g., plants) with modifiable developmental programs and selection criteria specified by their environment? Such an evolution model would have to incorporate features of self-organization and coevolution; that is, evolution in competition. For the modeling of plant ecosystems, we envisage the following scenario:

A plant ecosystem scenario

❑ Plant seeds, the genomes of which contain the developmental programs, are randomly distributed on a clearly defined, two-dimensional area.

❑ The seeds gradually develop into grown-up plants, which compete for nutrients and sunlight.

❑ Depending on the number of flowers, each plant generates seeds, which are dispersed in the neighborhood of the plant. Some of the seeds slightly change their genome programs by mutations (including crossover effects resulting from pollination).

❑ If a plant has reached a certain age, it dies, and its remains are added to the nutrient reservoir.

Compared to the evolution algorithms discussed so far, a model scenario like this would be much more difficult to analyze. However, such a simulation environment would allow us to gain more insight into the fascinating interplay between morphogenetic processes on the level of individual organisms and evolutionary processes on the level of populations. Evolution scenarios with more restricted settings as described above have been investigated by Cannas et al. (1998), using cellular automata, and Niklas (1986; 1992; 1997a; 1997b), using parametrized L-systems. Another cellular automaton model for modeling plants in landscapes is reported by Green (1997).

11.5.1 A simple model for plant ecosystems

To simulate plant ecosystems, in which different species compete with one another or coevolve in symbiotic or parasitic relationships, a large number of influential factors—affecting, for example, growth rates or reproduction capability—must be taken into account. For investigating the principal influence of different plant and environmental parameters on structure formation and reproduction, we have extended our Evolvica system (see the *IEC* Web site) to incorporate coevolution in a plant ecosystem with respect to the following parameters of a plant:

❑ The plant species,

Parametrized plants

❑ The coordinates of its location,

❑ The height and its growth rate,

❑ The canopy radius and its growth rate,

❑ The root radius and its growth rate,

❑ The plant age and its maximum age,

❑ The number and the weight of the seeds to be produced,

❑ The reproduction interval, and

❑ The plant's sensitivity to light or to being shaded.

Based on this simplified plant model, we can perform simulations of primary succession evolution. Primary succession describes the colonization or recolonization of habitats through the establishment of an interplay and sequence of plant communities. A typical example is the step-by-step invasion of different plant species of abandoned agricultural fields or the reestablishment of plant populations after forest fires. In these particular cases, succession seems to follow a specific scheme. At the beginning, a variety of annual plants invades the fallow habitat. Within a few years, though, most of these annuals are replaced by herbaceous perennials and shrubs, which are eventually competing against pines. However, pines are still not the last stage of the successional sequence—in the end, hardwood species take over (Ricklefs 1996, p. 523).

Primary succession

We can simulate evolutionary effects of succession through a simple simulation. Let us suppose we have two plant species, A and B. Species A individuals are typical representatives of plants that appear in the early phases of succession. Plants of species A are characterized by lightweight seeds, so that their seeds can distribute over a large area. Furthermore, A plants can grow fast. But the rapid growth of an A plant very much depends on how much sunlight it receives.

Succession simulation

Compared to their A-species competitors, B plants produce heavier seeds, which restricts their radius of distribution. B plants also grow much slower. However, they are less sensitive to receiving a reduced amount of sunlight—less sunlight does not affect their growth as much as it does for the species A plants. Figure 11.22 lists the concrete parameter settings that we use in the following coevolution experiment. Each plant species has a range for the growth rates of the height and the canopy radius; that is, each plant of a particular species can pick any value within the specified range. This gives the

Two species in competition

Growth rate

Figure 11.22

Plant-specific parameters for the succession model.

Parameter	Species *A*	Species *B*
Growth rate range: height	1.2–1.3	1.0–1.1
Growth rate range: canopy	1.0–1.1	1.1–1.2
Shade tolerance	0.1	0.9
Seed weight	0.4	0.8
Number of seeds	10	10
Reproduction interval	1	2
Maximum age	10	20

Reproduction interval

simulation a more natural setting, where even different plants of the same species exhibit slightly different growth behaviors. The most important parameter, however, is the shade tolerance, which is explained in more detail in the following section. *B*-species plants produce seeds twice as heavy and reproduce only every other "season" compared to plants from species *A*. The number of seeds is the same for both species, because this shows more clearly that the succession effect does not depend on the number of seeds but mostly on the demand for light- versus shade-tolerant behavior. The maximum age of the plants also plays only a minor role in this succession scenario, as the examples in the following section show.

11.5.2 Coevolution of plant species

Figure 11.23 shows the initial configuration of a plant ecosystem with *A* and *B* species, as characterized in Figure 11.22. Each plant is depicted as an abstract shape, a rosette on a stalk. The rosette radius corresponds to the canopy radius of the plant. Its height is visualized by the length of the stalk. The gray area at the stalk bottom represents the root area, which in this example is not growing in size. Plants of species *A* have a gray rosette center, whereas the *B*-species plants are marked by a black "umbel." The seedlings corresponding to a particular species, *A* or *B*, are depicted as white disks with either gray or black rims, respectively.

All plants are restricted to grow within the specified area ($[0, 20] \times [0, 20]$). For each species, 10 plants are placed along the rim of this area. In the center area, the first seedlings of *A*-species plants are visible, which have already covered this region quite well.

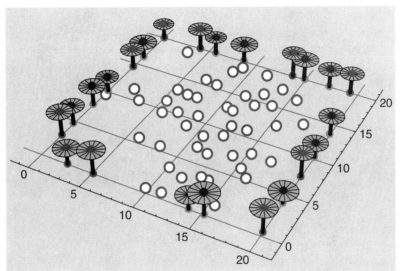

Figure 11.23
Initial ecosystem
configuration for testing the
succession model: *A* and *B*
plants are distributed along
the margins. The central
area already shows
seedlings of the *A*-species
plants.

For the succession simulation, we assume that light shines directly on the scene from the top; that is, light rays flow vertically onto the two-dimensional growth area. The plants react to whether they are shaded by larger plants in the following manner. For each plant we calculate what portion of its current rosette intersects with the rosette of another, higher-grown plant. If this portion is greater than the plant's shade tolerance, the plant will stop growing or reduce its rate of growth.

Competition for light

The height of a plant not only has an influence on whether it casts shade on other plants but also determines how far its seeds can be dispersed, depending on the seed weights as well. Consequently, the best survival and reproduction strategy for light-sensitive plants is to grow faster than any competitors and so not get in the shadow of another plant.

Figures 11.24 and 11.25 show an example succession starting from the plant configuration in Figure 11.23. It is the *A* plants that take over most of the territory very quickly. This is because these plants reproduce twice as often as their competitors of species *B*. Eventually the *B* plants also succeed in establishing their seedlings. These are much more shade tolerant than their *A*-species coinhabitants. Although the plants of species *B* grow slower, finally more and more of them exceed their *A* plant competitors in size and so cast shadows on them. Consequently, the light-sensitive plants tend to reduce their growth rates, which puts them in an even less competitive position. In the end, the gradually developing dense canopy of the *B*

Example succession

Figure 11.24

Succession example: competition between A-species (gray rosette) and B-species (black rosette) plants.

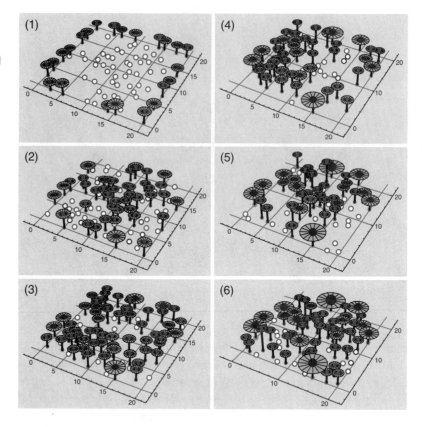

plants leaves the A-species plants with almost no chance to establish their seedlings. The B plants have taken over and form the final stage of this successional sequence (Color Plate 8).

A previous version of this ecosystem modeling approach was reported in Jacob 1998 and Jacob 1999a. Deussen et al.'s work (1998) toward realistic modeling and rendering of plant ecosystems was inspired by this approach.

11.6 Bibliographical notes

Lindenmayer systems and plant modeling

The Algorithmic Beauty of Plants

The Algorithmic Beauty of Plants, by Przemyslaw Prusinkiewicz and Aristid Lindenmayer (1990), provides the best and most illustrative overview of L-system-based models and computer-generated visualization techniques for simulating plant growth and structure formation processes in biological systems.

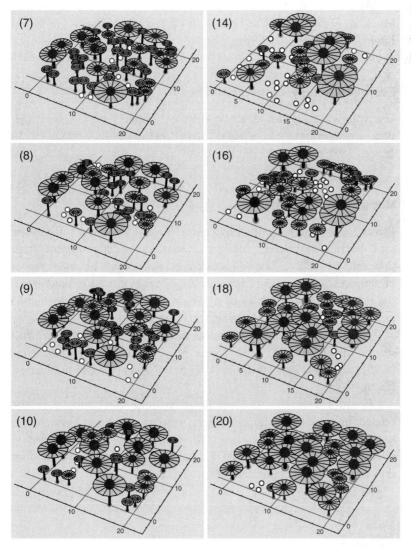

Figure 11.25
Succession example:
takeover of the *B*-species
plants.

In *Visual Models of Plants Interacting with Their Environment*, Radomir Mech and Przemyslaw Prusinkiewicz present a modeling scenario for plants interacting with environmental signals, using context-sensitive L-systems (Mech and Prusinkiewicz 1996).

Karl Niklas provides an in-depth investigation in *The Evolutionary Biology of Plants*, based on fossil records, biomechanics, and computer models using iterated adaptations of parametrized L-systems (Niklas 1997a).

Plants interacting with their environment

The Evolutionary Biology of Plants

Wildwood

An evolutionary system for simple plants is reported by Kenrick Mock in *Wildwood: The Evolution of L-System Plants for Virtual Environments* (Mock 1998).

Evolution of L-systems for plants

Genetic L-system programming

The following articles describe different aspects of the genetic L-system programming approach: Jacob 1994a, 1994b, 1995a, 1995b, 1996a, 1996b, 1998, 1999a.

Modeling of ecosystems

Plants to Ecosystems

Plants to Ecosystems, edited by Marek Michalewicz, is a state-of-the-art collection of different approaches to plant modeling in ecosystems (Michalewicz 1997). The issues discussed range from practical aspects of plant research, quantification, and modeling of tree architectures to the measuring and analysis of plants, their integration in agronomic processes, and models of marine ecosystems.

A first report of the succession model described in the previous section appeared in the special issue *Modeling Collective Phenomena in the Sciences,* published by Computer Physics Communications (Jacob 1999a).

The plant ecosystems

Bernd Lintermann, Oliver Deussen, and their colleagues succeeded in visualizing large-scale ecosystems of plants, which they describe in *Realistic Modeling and Rendering of Plant Ecosystems* (Deussen, Hanrahan, et al. 1998). For simulating plant interactions, they use a simple competitive 2D model.

References

Adami, C. (1998). *Introduction to Artificial Life*. New York: TELOS/ Springer-Verlag.

Adami, C., R. K. Belew, et al., eds. (1998). *Artificial Life VI: Complex Adaptive Systems*. Cambridge, MA: MIT Press.

Altenberg, L. (1995). The schema theorem and Price's theorem. In *Foundations of Genetic Algorithms*. Vol. 3. L. D. Whitley and M. D. Vose, eds. San Francisco: Morgan Kaufmann, 23–49.

Angeline, P. J. (1993). Evolutionary algorithms and emergent intelligence. Dissertation. Columbus, Ohio: Ohio State University.

Angeline, P. J., and K. E. Kinnear, Jr., eds. (1996). *Advances in Genetic Programming*. Vol. 2. Cambridge, MA: MIT Press.

Angeline, P. J., Z. Michalewicz, et al., eds. (1999). *CEC99: Proceedings of the 1999 Congress on Evolutionary Computation*. Washington, DC: IEEE Press.

Angeline, P. J., R. G. Reynolds, et al., eds. (1997). *Evolutionary Programming VI: Proceedings of the Sixth Annual Conference on Evolutionary Programming*. LNCS 1213. Berlin: Springer-Verlag.

Axelrod, R. (1997). *The Complexity of Cooperation: Agent-Based Models of Competition and Collaboration*. Princeton, NJ: Princeton University Press.

Bäck, T. (1996). *Evolutionary Algorithms in Theory and Practice*. Oxford: Oxford University Press.

Bäck, T., ed. (1997). *Proceedings of the Seventh International Conference on Genetic Algorithms*. San Francisco: Morgan Kaufmann.

Bäck, T., D. B. Fogel, et al. (1997). *Handbook of Evolutionary Computation*. New York: Oxford University Press.

Bäck, T., U. Hammel, et al. (1997). Evolutionary computation: Comments on the history and current state. *IEEE Transactions on Evolutionary Computation* 1(1):3–17.

Backus, J. W. (1959). The syntax and semantics of the proposed international algebraic language of the Zurich ACM-GAMM conference. In *International Conference on Information Processing*. Paris: UNESCO.

Baer, R. M., and H. M. Martinez (1974). Automata and biology. *Annual Review of Biophysics and Bioengineering* 3:255–291.

Bak, P. (1996). *How Nature Works—The Science of Self-Organized Criticality*. New York: Copernicus, Springer-Verlag.

Banzhaf, W. (1993). Genetic programming for pedestrians. In *ICGA-93, International Conference on Genetic Algorithms*. San Francisco: Morgan Kaufmann.

Banzhaf, W., J. Daida, et al., eds. (1999). *Proceedings of the Genetic and Evolutionary Computation Conference (GECCO 1999)*. San Francisco: Morgan Kaufmann.

Banzhaf, W., P. Nordin, et al. (1997). *Genetic Programming: An Introduction on the Automatic Evolution of Computer Programs and Its Applications*. San Francisco: Morgan Kaufmann.

Banzhaf, W., and C. Reeves, eds. (1999). *Foundations of Genetic Algorithms (FOGA-5)*. San Francisco: Morgan Kaufmann.

Bappert, R., S. Benner, et al. (1996). *Bionik: Zukunfts-Technik lernt von der Natur*. Mannheim, Germany: Landesmuseum für Technik und Arbeit.

Bedau, M. A., J. S. McCaskill, et al., eds. (2000). *Artificial Life VII: Proceedings of the Seventh International Conference*. Cambridge, MA: MIT Press.

Belew, R. K., and L. B. Booker, eds. (1991). *Proceedings of the 4th International Conference on Genetic Algorithms*. San Francisco: Morgan Kaufmann.

Belew, R. K., and M. Vose, eds. (1997). *Foundations of Genetic Algorithms (FOGA-4)*. San Francisco: Morgan Kaufmann.

Bentley, P. J., ed. (1999). *Evolutionary Design by Computers*. San Francisco: Morgan Kaufmann.

Benyus, J. M. (1997). *Biomimicry—Innovation Inspired by Nature*. New York: William Morrow.

Bickel, A. S., and R. W. Bickel (1987). Tree structured rules in genetic algorithms. In *Genetic Algorithms and Simulated Annealing*. L. Davis, ed. London: Pittman.

Blickle, T., and L. Thiele (1995). A comparison of selection schemes used in genetic algorithms. Technical Report TIK-Report 11. Zurich: ETH Technical University of Zurich.

Boers, E., and H. Kuiper (1992). Biological metaphors and the design of modular artificial neural networks. Master thesis. Leiden, Nederlands: University of Leiden.

Bonner, J. T. (1988). *The Evolution of Complexity by Means of Natural Selection*. Princeton, NJ: Princeton University Press.

Booker, L. B., D. E. Goldberg, et al. (1989). Classifier systems and genetic algorithms. In *Machine Learning: Paradigms and Methods*. J. G. Carbonell, ed. Cambridge, MA: MIT Press / Elsevier, 235–282.

Bremermann, H. J. (1962). Optimization through evolution and recombination. *Self-Organizing Systems*. M. C. Yovits, G. T. Jacobi, and D. G. Goldstein, eds. Washington, DC: Spartan Books, 93–106.

Bremermann, H. J., M. Rogson, et al. (1965). Search by evolution. In *Biophysics and Cybernetic Systems: Proceedings of the 2nd Cybernetic Sciences Symposium*. Washington, DC: Spartan Books.

Brindle, A. (1981). Genetic algorithms for function optimization. Dissertation. Edmonton: University of Alberta.

Britten, R. J., and E. H. Davidson (1969). Gene regulation for higher cells: A theory. *Science* 165:349–357.

Brooks, R. A., and P. Maes, eds. (1995). *Artificial Life IV*. Cambridge, MA: MIT Press.

Burks, A. W. (1968). *Essays on Cellular Automata*. Champaign, IL: University of Illinois Press.

Cannas, S. A., S. A. Páez, et al. (1998). Modelling plant spread in forest ecology using cellular automata. In *CCP 1998, International Conference on Computational Physics*. Granada, Spain: European Physical Society.

Cannas, S. A., S. A. Páez, et al. (1999). Modelling plant spread in forest ecology using cellular automata. *Computer Physics Communications*. Special Issue, Vol. 121–122 (Modeling Collective Phenomena in the Sciences).

Chernoff, H. (1973). The use of faces to represent points in k-dimensional space graphically. *Journal of the American Statistical Association* 68(342):361–368.

Chomsky, N. (1956). Three models for the description of language. *IRE Transactions on Information Theory* 2(3):113–124.

Coates, P., T. Broughton, et al. (1999). Exploring three-dimensional design worlds using Lindenmayer systems and genetic programming. In *Evolutionary Design by Computers*. P. J. Bentley, ed. San Francisco: Morgan Kaufmann, 323–341.

Codd, E. F. (1968). *Cellular Automata*. New York: Academic Press.

Collins, R. J. (1992). Studies in artificial evolution. Dissertation. Los Angeles: University of California.

Cramer, M. L. (1985). A representation for the adaptive generation of simple sequential programs. In *1st International Conference on Genetic Algorithms and Their Applications*. Hillsdale, NJ: Lawrence Erlbaum Associates.

Darwin, C. (1859). *On the Origin of Species*. London: Murray.

Darwin, C. (1996). *On the Origin of Species*. Oxford: Oxford University Press.

Davidor, Y., H.-P. Schwefel, et al., eds. (1994). *Parallel Problem Solving from Nature—PPSN III*. LNCS 866. Berlin: Springer-Verlag.

Davis, L., ed. (1991). *Handbook of Genetic Algorithms*. New York: Van Nostrand Reinhold.

Dawkins, R. (1976). *The Selfish Gene*. Oxford: Oxford University Press.

Dawkins, R. (1986). *The Blind Watchmaker*. Oxford: Longman.

Dawkins, R. (1989). The evolution of evolvability. In *Artificial Life*. C. G. Langton, ed. Redwood City, CA: Addison-Wesley, 201–220.

Dawkins, R. (1990). *Der Blinde Uhrmacher*. Munich: Deutscher Taschenbuchverlag.

Dawkins, R. (1996). *Climbing Mount Improbable*. New York: W W Norton & Company.

Dawkins, R. (1998). *Unweaving the Rainbow: Science, Delusion and the Appetite for Wonder*. Boston: Houghton Mifflin.

Dearholt, W. (1976). Some experiments on generalization using evolving automata. In *9th International Conference on System Sciences*. Honolulu: IEEE Computer Society Press.

Deb, K., and D. E. Goldberg (1993). Analyzing deception in trap functions. In *Foundations of Genetic Algorithms 2*. D. Whitley, ed. San Francisco: Morgan Kaufmann, 93–108.

de Garis, H. (1991). Genetic programming: Building artificial nervous systems with genetically programmed neural network modules. In *Neural and Intelligent Systems Integration*. B. Soucek and the IRIS Group, eds. New York: John Wiley & Sons, 207–234.

de Garis, H. (1992). Artificial embryology: The genetic programming of an artificial embryo. In *Dynamic, Genetic, and Chaotic Programming*. B. Soucek and the IRIS Group, eds. New York: John Wiley & Sons.

de Garis, H. (1996). CAM-BRAIN: The evolutionary engineering of a billion neuron artificial brain by 2001 which grows/evolves at electronic speeds inside a cellular automata machine (CAM). In *Towards Evolvable Hardware: The Evolutionary Engineering Approach*. E. Sanchesz and M. Tomassini, eds. LNCS 1062. Berlin: Springer-Verlag.

De Jong, K. (1975). An analysis of the behavior of a class of genetic adaptive systems. Dissertation. Ann Arbor: University of Michigan.

De Jong, K. (1987). On using genetic algorithms to search program spaces. In *2nd International Conference on Genetic Algorithms*. Hillsdale, NJ: Lawrence Erlbaum Associates.

Deussen, O., P. Hanrahan, et al. (1998). Realistic modeling and rendering of plant ecosystems. In *SIGGRAPH 98, Computer Graphics, Annual Conference Series*. New York: ACM.

Deutsch, A., ed. (1994). *Muster des Lebendigen: Faszination ihrer Entstehung und Simulation*. Braunschweig, Germany: Vieweg.

Dickson, S. (1995). Faces.ma. *http://www.mathsource.com*.

Eiben, A. E., T. Bäck, et al., eds. (1998). *Parallel Problem Solving from Nature—PPSN V*. LNCS 1498. Berlin: Springer-Verlag.

Eldredge, N. (1998). *The Pattern of Evolution*. New York: W. H. Freeman.

Eshelman, L. J., ed. (1995). *Proceedings of the Sixth International Conference on Genetic Algorithms*. San Francisco: Morgan Kaufmann.

Fabian, A. C., ed. (1998). *Evolution—Society, Science and the Universe*. Cambridge: Cambridge University Press.

Fogel, D. B. (1988). An evolutionary approach to the traveling salesman problem. *Biological Cybernetics* 60(2):139–144.

Fogel, D. B. (1992). Evolving artificial intelligence. San Diego: University of California.

Fogel, D. B. (1995). *Evolutionary Computation: Towards a New Philosophy of Machine Intelligence*. New York: IEEE Press.

Fogel, D. B., ed. (1998). *Evolutionary Computation: The Fossil Record*. New York: IEEE Press.

Fogel, D. B., and W. Atmar, eds. (1992). *Proceedings of the First Annual Conference on Evolutionary Programming*. La Jolla, CA: Evolutionary Programming Society.

Fogel, D. B., and W. Atmar, eds. (1993). *Proceedings of the Second Annual Conference on Evolutionary Programming*. La Jolla, CA: Evolutionary Programming Society.

Fogel, L. J. (1986). Artificial intelligence through evolutionary programming. Technical Report. San Diego: Titan Systems, Inc.

Fogel, L. J. (1994). Evolutionary programming in perspective: The top-down view. In *Computational Intelligence Imitating Life*. J. M. Zurada, R. J. Marks II, and C. J. Robinson, eds. New York: IEEE Press, 135–146.

Fogel, L. J. (1999). *Intelligence Through Simulated Evolution, Forty Years of Evolutionary Programming.* New York: John Wiley & Sons.

Fogel, L. J., P. J. Angeline, et al., eds. (1996). *Evolutionary Programming V.* Cambridge, MA: MIT Press.

Fogel, L. J., A. J. Owens, et al. (1965). Artificial intelligence through a simulation of evolution. In *Biophysics and Cybernetics: Proceedings of the 2nd Cybernetic Sciences Symposium.* Washington, DC: Spartan Books.

Fogel, L. J., A. J. Owens, et al. (1966). *Artificial Intelligence Through Simulated Evolution.* New York: John Wiley and Sons.

Forrest, S., ed. (1993). *Proceedings of the Fifth International Conference on Genetic Algorithms.* San Francisco: Morgan Kaufmann.

Forrest, S., and M. Mitchell (1993). Relative building-block fitness and the building block hypothesis. In *Foundations of Genetic Algorithms 2.* D. Whitley, ed. San Francisco: Morgan Kaufmann, 109–126.

Friedberg, R. M. (1958). A learning machine: Part I. *IBM Journal of Research and Development* 2(1):2–13.

Friedberg, R. M., B. Dunham, et al. (1959). A learning machine: Part II. *IBM Journal of Research and Development* 3(3):282–287.

Fujiki, C. (1986). An evaluation of Holland's genetic algorithm applied to a program generator. M.S. thesis. Moscow, ID: Department of Computer Science, University of Idaho.

Fujiki, C., and J. Dickinson (1987). Using the genetic algorithm to generate LISP source code to solve the prisoner's dilemma. In *2nd International Conference on Genetic Algorithms.* Hillsdale, NJ: Lawrence Erlbaum Associates.

Gaarder, J. (1996). *Sophie's World: A Novel About the History of Philosophy.* New York: Berkley Books.

Gaylord, R. J. and L. J. D'Andria (1999). *Simulating Society: A Mathematica Toolkit for Modeling Socioeconomic Behavior.* New York: TELOS/Springer-Verlag.

Gaylord, R. J., and K. Nishidate (1996). *Modeling Nature: Cellular Automata Simulations with Mathematica.* New York: TELOS/Springer-Verlag.

Gaylord, R. J., and P. R. Wellin (1995). *Computer Simulations with Mathematica: Explorations in Complex Physical and Biological Systems.* New York: Springer-Verlag.

Gerhardt, M., and H. Schuster (1995). *Das Digitale Universum: Zelluläre Automaten als Modelle der Natur.* Braunschweig, Germany: Vieweg.

Goldberg, D. (1989). *Genetic Algorithms in Search, Optimization, and Machine Learning.* Reading, MA: Addison-Wesley.

Goldberg, D. E. (1986). The genetic algorithm approach: Why, how, and what next? In *Adaptive and Learning Systems.* K. S. Narenda, ed. New York.

Goldberg, D. E., K. Deb, et al. (1992). Massive multimodality, deception, and genetic algorithms. In *PPSN II—Parallel Problem Solving from Nature.* R. Männer and B. Manderick, eds. Amsterdam: Elsevier Science Publishers.

Goodwin, B. (1994). *How the Leopard Changed Its Spots: The Evolution of Complexity.* New York: Touchstone Books, Simon & Schuster.

Gottschalk, W. (1989). *Allgemeine Genetik.* Stuttgart, Germany: Thieme.

Green, D. G. (1997). Modelling plants in landscapes. In *Plants to Ecosystems.* M. T. Michalewicz, ed. Collingwood, Australia: CSIRO Publishing, 85–96.

Grefenstette, J. J., ed. (1985). *Proceedings of the 1st International Conference on Genetic Algorithms and Their Applications.* Hillsdale, NJ: Lawrence Erlbaum Associates.

Grefenstette, J. J., ed. (1987). *Proceedings of the 2nd International Conference on Genetic Algorithms.* Hillsdale, NJ: Lawrence Erlbaum Associates.

Grefenstette, J. J. (1993). Deception considered harmful. In *Foundations of Genetic Algorithms 2.* D. Whitley, ed. San Francisco: Morgan Kaufmann, 75–92.

Hamilton, P. (1994). Computing dendritic growth. In *Computing with Biological Metaphors.* R. Paton, ed. London: Chapman & Hall, 86–102.

Hanan, J. S. (1988). PLANTWORKS: A software system for realistic plant modelling. Master thesis. Regina, Canada: University of Regina.

Hanan, J. S. (1992). Parametric L-systems and their application to the modelling and visualization of plants. Ph.D. thesis. Regina, Canada: University of Regina.

Haynes, T. D., D. A. Schoenefeld, et al. (1996). Type inheritance in strongly typed genetic programming. In *Advances in Genetic Programming*. P. J. Angeline and K. E. Kinnear, Jr., eds. Cambridge, MA: MIT Press, 359–375.

Hertz, J., A. Krogh, et al. (1991). *Introduction to the Theory of Neural Computation*. Redwood City, CA: Addison-Wesley.

Hicklin, J. F. (1986). Application of the genetic algorithm to automatic program generation. M.S. thesis. Moscow, ID: Department of Computer Science, University of Idaho.

Hoffmeister, F., and T. Bäck (1992). Genetic algorithms and evolution strategies: Similarities and differences. Dortmund, Germany: University of Dortmund, SYS-1/92.

Holland, J. H. (1962). Outline of a logical theory of adaptive systems. *Journal of the Association for Computing Machinery* 3:297–314.

Holland, J. H. (1975). *Adaptation in Natural and Artificial Systems*. Ann Arbor, MI: University of Michigan Press.

Holland, J. H. (1992a). *Adaptation in Natural and Artificial Systems*. Cambridge, MA: MIT Press.

Holland, J. H. (1992b). Genetic algorithms. *Scientific American* 267(1):66–72.

Holland, J. H. (1995). *Hidden Order: How Adaptation Builds Complexity*. Reading, MA: Helix Books, Addison-Wesley.

Holland, J. H. (1998). *Emergence: From Chaos to Order*. Reading, MA: Helix Books, Addison-Wesley.

Jacob, C. (1994a). Genetic L-system programming. In *Parallel Problem Solving from Nature—PPSN III*. Jerusalem: Springer-Verlag.

Jacob, C. (1994b). Typed expressions evolution of artificial nervous systems. In *First IEEE Conference on Evolutionary*

Computation. Orlando, FL. Los Alamitos, CA: IEEE Computer Society Press.

Jacob, C. (1995a). Genetic L-system programming: Breeding and evolving artificial flowers with Mathematica. In *Mathematics with Vision: IMS '95, First International Mathematica Symposium.* Southampton, UK: Computational Mechanics Publications.

Jacob, C. (1995b). Modeling growth with L-systems and Mathematica. *Mathematica in Education and Research* 4(3):12–19.

Jacob, C. (1996a). Evolution programs evolved. In *Parallel Problem Solving from Nature—PPSN-IV.* Berlin: Springer-Verlag.

Jacob, C. (1996b). Evolving evolution programs: Genetic programming and L-systems. In *Genetic Programming 1996: First Annual Conference.* Cambridge, MA: MIT Press.

Jacob, C. (1997). Simulating evolution with Mathematica. In *IMS '97, Second International Mathematica Symposium.* Rovaniemi, Finland. Southampton, UK: Computational Mechanics Publications.

Jacob, C. (1998). Evolving developmental programs. In *Second Workshop on Frontiers of Evolutionary Algorithms (FEA), Joint Conference on Information Sciences (JCIS).* Research Triangle Park, NC: AIM.

Jacob, C. (1999a). Evolution and co-evolution of developmental programs. *Computer Physics Communications.* Special Issue, Vol. 121–122, pp. 46–50. (Modeling Collective Phenomena in the Sciences).

Jacob, C. (1999b). Stochastic search methods. In *Intelligent Data Analysis.* M. Berthold and D. J. Hand, eds. Berlin: Springer-Verlag, 303–356.

Jefferson, D., R. Collins, et al. (1992). Evolution as a theme in artificial life: The genesys/tracker system. In *Artificial Life II.* C. G. Langton, C. Taylor, J. D. Farmer, and S. Rasmussen, eds. Redwood City, CA: Addison-Wesley, 549–578.

Keller, R. E., and W. Banzhaf (1996). Genetic programming using mutation, reproduction and genotype-phenotype mapping from linear binary Genomes into linear LALR(1) phenotypes.

Technical report. Dortmund, Germany: University of Dortmund.

Kinnear, K., ed. (1994). *Advances in Genetic Programming.* Cambridge, MA: MIT Press.

Kókai, G., Z. Tóth, et al. (1999). Modelling blood vessels of the eye with parametric L-systems using evolutionary algorithms. In *Joint European Conference on Artificial Intelligence in Medicine and Medical Decision Making, AIMDM '99.* Aalborg, Denmark. LNCS 1620. Berlin: Springer-Verlag.

Kókai, G., R. Ványi, et al. (1998). Application of genetic algorithms with more populations for Lindenmayer systems. In *International Symposium on Engineering of Intelligent Systems.* Tenerife, Spain: University of Laguna.

Koza, J. R. (1989). Hierarchical genetic algorithms operating on populations of computer programs. In *11th International Joint Conference on Artificial Intelligence.* San Francisco: Morgan Kaufmann.

Koza, J. R. (1990). Genetic programming: A paradigm for genetically breeding populations of computer programs to solve problems. Technical report. Stanford, CA: Department of Computer Science, Stanford University.

Koza, J. R. (1992). *Genetic Programming: On the Programming of Computers by Means of Natural Selection.* Cambridge, MA: MIT Press.

Koza, J. R. (1993). Discovery of rewrite rules in Lindenmayer systems and state transition rules in cellular automata via genetic programming. In *SPF-93, Symposium on Pattern Formation.* Stanford, CA: Department of Computer Science, Stanford University.

Koza, J. R. (1994). *Genetic Programming II: Automatic Discovery of Reusable Programs.* Cambridge, MA: MIT Press.

Koza, J. R., D. Andre, et al. (1999). *Genetic Programming III: Darwinian Invention and Problem Solving.* San Francisco: Morgan Kaufmann.

Koza, J. R., W. Banzhaf, et al., eds. (1998). *Genetic Programming 1998: Proceedings of the Third Annual Conference.* San Francisco: Morgan Kaufmann.

Koza, J. R., F. H. Bennett III, et al. (1999). Genetic programming III: Darwinian invention and problem solving (video). San Francisco: Morgan Kaufmann.

Koza, J. R., K. Deb, et al., eds. (1997). *Genetic Programming 1997: Proceedings of the Second Annual Conference*. San Francisco: Morgan Kaufmann.

Koza, J. R., D. E. Goldberg, et al., eds. (1996). *Genetic Programming 1996: Proceedings of the First Annual Conference*. Cambridge, MA: MIT Press.

Koza, J. R., and J. P. Rice (1992). Genetic programming: The movie. Cambridge, MA: MIT Press.

Koza, J. R., and J. P. Rice (1994). Genetic programming II: The next generation (video). Cambridge, MA: MIT Press.

Küppers, B.-O. (1990). *Der Ursprung Biologischer Information*. Munich: Piper.

Langdon, W. (1998). *Genetic Programming and Data Structures*. Boston: Kluwer Academic Publishers.

Langton, C. G. (1984). Self-reproduction in cellular automata. *Physica 10D, Nonlinear Phenomena* 10 D:135–144.

Langton, C. G., ed. (1989). *Artificial Life*. Redwood City, CA: Addison-Wesley.

Langton, C. G., ed. (1994). *Artificial Life III*. Reading, MA: Addison-Wesley.

Langton, C. G., and T. Shimohara, eds. (1997). *Artificial Life V*. Cambridge, MA: MIT Press.

Langton, C. G., C. Taylor, et al., eds. (1992). *Artificial Life II*. Redwood City, CA: Addison-Wesley.

Levy, A. (1991). Automata.m software package. Champaign, IL: MathSource, Wolfram Research. *http://www.mathsource.com*.

Levy, S. (1993a). *Artificial Life—A Report from the Frontier Where Computers Meet Biology*. New York: Vintage Books.

Levy, S. (1993b). *KL—Künstliches Leben aus dem Computer*. Munich: Droemer Knaur.

Lewin, B. (1983). *Genes*. New York: John Wiley & Sons.

Lewontin, R. C. (1970). The units of selection. *Annual Review in Ecological Systems* 1:1–18.

Liepins, G. E., and M. D. Vose (1991). Deceptiveness and genetic algorithm dynamics. In *Foundations of Genetic Algorithms*. G. Rawlins, ed. San Francisco: Morgan Kaufmann, 36–52.

Lindenmayer, A. (1968). Mathematical models for cellular interaction in development, Parts I and II. *Journal of Theoretical Biology* 18:280–315.

Lindenmayer, A., and G. Rozenberg, eds. (1975). *Automata, Languages, Development*. Amsterdam: North-Holland.

Liu, B. (1999). *Uncertain Programming*. New York: John Wiley & Sons.

Macready, W. G., and D. H. Wolpert (1998). Bandit problems and the exploration/exploitation tradeoff. *IEEE Transactions on Evolutionary Computation* 2(1):2–22.

Mange, D., and M. Sipper (1998). Von Neumann's quintessential message: Genotype + ribotype = phenotype. *Artificial Life* 4(3):225–227.

Männer, R., and B. Manderick, eds. (1992). *Parallel Problem Solving from Nature—PPSN II*. Amsterdam: Elsevier Science Publishers.

Marchal, P. (1998). John von Neumann: The founding father of artificial life. *Artificial Life* 4(3):229–235.

Mayr, E. (1997). *This is Biology: The Science of the Living World*. Cambridge, MA: Harvard Press.

McDonnell, J. R., R. G. Reynolds, et al., eds. (1995). *Evolutionary Programming IV*. Cambridge, MA: MIT Press.

Mech, R., and P. Prusinkiewicz (1996). Visual models of plants interacting with their environment. *SIGGRAPH '96*. New Orleans, Louisiana. New York: ACM.

Michalewicz, M. T., ed. (1997). *Plants to Ecosystems: Advances in Computational Life Sciences*. Collingwood, Australia: CSIRO Publishing.

Michalewicz, Z. (1992). *Genetic Algorithms + Data Structures = Evolution Programs*. New York: Springer-Verlag.

Mitchell, M. (1996). *An Introduction to Genetic Algorithms.* Cambridge, MA: MIT Press.

Mock, K. J. (1998). Wildwood: The evolution of L-system plants for virtual environments. In *IEEE Conference on Evolutionary Computation.* Anchorage, AL. New York: IEEE Press.

Montana, D. J. (1995). Strongly typed genetic programming. *Evolutionary Computation* 3(2):199–230.

Mühlenbein, H., and D. Schlierkamp-Voosen (1993). The science of breeding and its application to the breeder genetic algorithm (BGA). *Evolutionary Computation* 1(4):335–360.

Mühlenbein, H., and D. Schlierkamp-Voosen (1994). Theory and application of the breeder genetic algorithm. In *Computational Intelligence Imitating Life*, Orlando, FL. New York: IEEE Press.

Nachtigall, W. (1992). *BIONA Report VIII: Technische Biologie und Bionik I.* Stuttgart, Germany: Gustav Fischer.

Nachtigall, W. (1994). *Technische Biologie und Bionik II.* Stuttgart, Germany: Gustav Fischer.

Nachtigall, W. (1997). *Vorbild Natur: Bionik-Design für funktionelles Gestalten.* Berlin: Springer-Verlag.

Nachtigall, W. (1998). *Bionik: Grundlagen und Beispiele für Ingenieure und Naturwissenschaftler.* Berlin: Springer-Verlag.

Nachtigall, W., and C. Schönbeck (1994). *Technik und Natur.* Heidelberg, Germany: Springer-Verlag.

Nachtigall, W., and A. Wisser (1996). *Technische Biologie und Bionik III.* Stuttgart, Germany: Gustav Fischer.

Niklas, K. J. (1986). Computer-simulated plant evolution. *Scientific American* 254(3):68–75.

Niklas, K. J. (1992). *Plant Biomechanics: An Engineering Approach to Plant Form and Function.* Chicago: University of Chicago Press.

Niklas, K. J. (1997a). *The Evolutionary Biology of Plants.* Chicago: University of Chicago Press.

Niklas, K. J. (1997b). Adaptive walks through fitness landscapes for early vascular land plants. *American Journal of Botany* 84(1):16–25.

Nordin, P. (1995). Comparison of a compiling genetic programming system versus a connectionist approach. In *Handbook of Evolutionary Computation*. Oxford: Oxford University Press.

Ochoa, G. (1998). On genetic algorithms and Lindenmayer systems. In *Parallel Problem Solving from Nature—PPSN V*. Berlin: Springer-Verlag.

Osche, G. (1972). *Evolution: Grundlagen—Erkenntnisse— Entwicklungen der Abstammungslehre*. Freiburg, Germany: Herder.

Papert, S. (1980). *Mindstorms: Children, Computers, and Powerful Ideas*. New York: Basic Books.

Papert, S. (1993). *Mindstorms: Children, Computers, and Powerful Ideas*. New York: Harvester Wheatsheaf.

Paton, R., ed. (1994). *Computing with Biological Metaphors*. London: Chapman & Hall.

Peitgen, H.-O., H. Jürgens, et al. (1992). *Chaos and Fractals: New Frontiers of Science*. New York: Springer-Verlag.

Peitgen, H.-O., and P. H. Richter (1986). *The Beauty of Fractals: Images of Complex Dynamical Systems*. Berlin: Springer-Verlag.

Porto, V. W., N. Saravanan, et al., eds. (1998). *Evolutionary Programming VII: Proceedings of the Seventh Annual Conference on Evolutionary Programming*. LNCS 1447. Berlin: Springer-Verlag.

Preston, K., Jr., and M. J. B. Duff (1984). *Modern Cellular Automata: Theory and Applications*. New York: Plenum Press.

Principe, J. C., N. R. Euliano, et al. (2000). *Neural and Adaptive Systems—Fundamentals Through Simulations*. New York: John Wiley & Sons.

Prusinkiewicz, P. (1986). Graphical applications of L-systems. In *Graphics Interface '86—Vision Interface '86*. Toronto: CIPS.

Prusinkiewicz, P. (1987). Applications of L-systems to computer imagery. In *Graph Grammars and Their Application to Computer Science, Third International Workshop*. Berlin: Springer-Verlag.

Prusinkiewicz, P., M. Hammel, et al. (1997). Visual models of plant development. In *Handbook of Formal Languages*. G. Rozenberg and A. Salomaa, eds. New York: Springer-Verlag.

Prusinkiewicz, P., and J. Hanan (1989). *Lindenmayer Systems, Fractals, and Plants*. New York: Springer-Verlag.

Prusinkiewicz, P., and A. Lindenmayer (1990). *The Algorithmic Beauty of Plants*. New York: Springer-Verlag.

Rahmat-Samii, Y., and E. Michielssen, eds. (1999). *Electromagnetic Optimization by Genetic Algorithms*. New York: John Wiley & Sons.

Rawlins, G. J. E., ed. (1991). *Foundations of Genetic Algorithms (FOGA)*. San Francisco: Morgan Kaufmann.

Ray, T. S. (1991). Is it alive or is it GA? *4th International Conference on Genetic Algorithms*. San Francisco: Morgan Kaufmann.

Rechenberg, I. (1965). Cybernetic solution path of an experimental problem. Royal Aircraft Establishment, Library Translation 1122. Also in Fogel 1998, pp. 301–313.

Rechenberg, I. (1973). *Evolutionsstrategie: Optimierung Technischer Systeme nach Prinzipien der Biologischen Evolution*. Stuttgart, Germany: Frommann-Holzboog.

Rechenberg, I. (1978). Evolutionsstrategien. In *Simulationsmethoden in der Medizin und Biologie*. B. Schneider and U. Ranft, eds. Berlin: Springer-Verlag.

Rechenberg, I. (1989). Evolution strategy: Nature's way of optimization. In *Optimization: Methods and Applications, Possibilities and Limitations*. Lecture Notes in Engineering 47. Berlin: Springer-Verlag.

Rechenberg, I. (1994a). Evolution strategy. In *Computational Intelligence Imitating Life*. J. M. Zurada, R. J. Marks II, and C. J. Robinson, eds. New York: IEEE Press, 147–159.

Rechenberg, I. (1994b). *Evolutionsstrategie '94*. Stuttgart, Germany: Frommann-Holzboog.

Reggia, J. A., J. D. Lohn, et al. (1998). Self-replicating structures: Evolution, emergence, and computation. *Artificial Life* 4(3):283–302.

Resnick, M. (1997). *Turtles, Termites, and Traffic Jams: Explorations in Massively Parallel Microworlds*. Cambridge, MA: MIT Press.

Ricklefs, R. E. (1996). *The Economy of Nature: A Textbook in Basic Ecology*. New York: W. H. Freeman.

Ridley, M. (1996). *Evolution*. Cambridge, MA: Blackwell Science.

Ridley, M., ed. (1997). *Evolution*. Oxford: Oxford University Press.

Rojas, R. (1996). *Neural Networks—A Systematic Introduction*. Berlin: Springer-Verlag.

Rozenberg, G., and A. Salomaa, eds. (1980). *The Mathematical Theory of L-Systems*. New York: Academic Press.

Schaffer, J. D., ed. (1989). *Proceedings of the 3rd International Conference on Genetic Algorithms and Their Applications*. San Francisco: Morgan Kaufmann.

Schoenauer, M., K. Deb, et al., eds. (2000). *Parallel Problem Solving from Nature—PPSN VI*. LNCS 1917. Berlin: Springer-Verlag.

Schwefel, H.-P. (1977). *Numerische Optimierung von Computer-Modellen mittels der Evolutionsstrategie*. Basel, Switzerland: Birkhäuser.

Schwefel, H.-P. (1981). *Numerical Optimization of Computer Models*. Chichester: John Wiley & Sons.

Schwefel, H.-P. (1994). On the evolution of evolutionary computation. In *Computational Intelligence Imitating Life*. J. M. Zurada, R. J. Marks II, and C. J. Robinson, eds. New York: IEEE Press, 116–124.

Schwefel, H.-P. (1995). *Evolution and Optimum Seeking*. New York: John Wiley & Sons.

Schwefel, H.-P., and R. Männer, eds. (1991). *Parallel Problem Solving from Nature*. LNCS 496. Berlin: Springer-Verlag.

Sebald, A. V., and L. J. Fogel, eds. (1994). *Proceedings of the Third Annual Conference on Evolutionary Programming*. Singapore: World Scientific.

Sipper, M. (1997). *Evolution of Parallel Cellular Machines: The Cellular Programming Approach*. Berlin: Springer-Verlag.

Sipper, M. (1998). Fifty years of research on self-replication: An overview. *Artificial Life* 4(3):237–257.

Smith, J. M. (1993). *The Theory of Evolution*. Cambridge, UK: Cambridge University Press.

Spector, L., W. B. Langdon, et al., eds. (1999). *Advances in Genetic Programming, Vol. 3*. Cambridge, MA: MIT Press.

Starr, C., and R. Taggart (1998). *Evolution of Life*. Belmont, CA: Wadsworth.

Steel, G. L., and G. J. Sussman (1975). Scheme: An interpreter for the extended lambda calculus. Technical Report Memo 394. Cambridge, MA: MIT Artificial Intelligence Laboratory.

Storch, V., and U. Welsch (1973). *Evolution: Tatsachen und Probleme der Abstammungslehre*. Munich: Deutscher Taschenbuch Verlag.

Syswerda, G. (1991). A study of reproduction in generational and steady-state genetic algorithms. In *Foundations of Genetic Algorithms*. G. Rawlins, ed. San Francisco: Morgan Kaufmann, 94–101.

Szilard, A. L., and R. E. Quinton (1979). An interpretation for D0L systems by computer graphics. *The Science Terrapin* 4:8–13.

Tempesti, G., D. Mange, et al. (1998). Self-replicating and self-repairing multicellular automata. *Artificial Life* 4(3):259–282.

Todd, S., and W. Latham (1992). *Evolutionary Art and Computers*. London: Academic Press.

Toffoli, T., and N. Margolus (1987). *Cellular Automata Machines: A New Environment for Modeling*. Cambridge, MA: MIT Press.

Ulam, S. (1962). On some mathematical problems connected with patterns of growth of figures. In *Symposia in Applied Mathematics*. Providence, RI: American Mathematical Society.

Ulam, S. (1966). Patterns of growth of figures: Mathematical aspects. In *Module, Proportion, Symmetry, Rhythm*. G. Kepes, ed. New York: Braziller, 64–74.

Vitányi, P. M. B. (1980). Lindenmayer systems: Structure, languages, and growth functions. Technical Report. Amsterdam: Mathematisch Centrum.

Vogel, S. (1992). *Lexikon Gentechnik*. Reinbek, Germany: Rowolth Taschenbuch Verlag.

Voigt, H.-M., W. Ebeling, et al., eds. (1996). *Parallel Problem Solving from Nature—PPSN IV*. LNCS 1141. Berlin: Springer-Verlag.

von Neumann, J., and W. Burks (1966). *Theory of Self-Reproducing Automata*. Urbana, IL.: University of Illinois Press.

Vose, M. D. (1999). *The Simple Genetic Algorithm: Foundations and Theory*. Cambridge, MA: MIT Press.

Whitley, D., ed. (1993). *Foundations of Genetic Algorithms (FOGA-2)*. San Francisco: Morgan Kaufmann.

Whitley, D., D. Goldberg, et al., eds (2000). *Proceedings of the Genetic and Evolutionary Computation Conference (GECCO '00)*. San Francisco: Morgan Kaufmann.

Whitley, D., and M. D. Vose, eds. (1995). *Foundations of Genetic Algorithms (FOGA-3)*. San Francisco: Morgan Kaufmann.

Whitley, L. D. (1991). Fundamental principles of deception in genetic search. In *Foundations of Genetic Algorithms*. G. Rawlins, ed. San Francisco: Morgan Kaufmann, 221–241.

Wieser, W. (1994). Gentheorien und systemtheorien: wege und wandlungen der evolutionstheorie im 20. Jahrhundert. In *Die Evolution der Evolutionstheorie: Von Darwin zur DNA*. W. Wieser, ed. Heidelberg, Germany: Spektrum Akademischer Verlag, 15–48.

Wilson, S. (1987a). Classifier systems and the animat problem. *Machine Learning* 3(2):199–228.

Wilson, S. (1987b). Hierarchical credit allocation in a classifier system. In *Tenth International Joint Conference on Artificial Intelligence*. San Francisco: Morgan Kaufmann.

Wineberg, M., and F. Oppacher (1994). A representation scheme to perform program induction in a canonical genetic algorithm. In *Parallel Problem Solving from Nature—PPSN III*. Jerusalem: Springer-Verlag.

Wirth, N. (1975). *Algorithms + Data Structures = Programs*. London: Prentice Hall International.

Wolfram, S. (1984a). Cellular automata as models of complexity. *Nature* 311:421–424.

Wolfram, S. (1984b). Universality and complexity in cellular automata. *Physica 10D, Nonlinear Phenomena* 10D:1–35.

Wolfram, S. (1986). *Theory and Applications of Cellular Automata.* Singapore: World Scientific.

Wolfram, S. (1994). *Cellular Automata and Complexity.* Reading, MA: Addison-Wesley.

Wolfram, S. (1996). *The Mathematica Book.* Cambridge, MA: Cambridge University Press.

Young, D. (1992). *The Discovery of Evolution.* Cambridge, UK: Cambridge University Press.

Young, D. (1994). *Die Entdeckung der Evolution.* Basel, Switzerland: Birkhäuser.

Zalzala, A., et al., eds. *Proceedings of the 2000 Congress on Evolutionary Computation.* La Jolla, CA. Piscataway, NJ: IEEE Press.

Zurada, J. M., R. J. Marks II, et al., eds. (1994). *Computational Intelligence Imitating Life.* New York: IEEE Press.

Index